Sunset Over
Bootham Crescent

DAVE FLETT

York City Football Club Limited

ISBN 978-1-3999-2339-2

Published in 2022 by:
York City Football Club Limited
LNER Community Stadium
Kathryn Avenue
Monks Cross Dr
Huntington
York
YO32 9AF

www.yorkcityfootballclub.co.uk

Design & typeset by Julie Skelton - appletreedesigns.co.uk
Printed by Hardings Print Solutions Ltd, Feltham, Middlesex TW14 0RB

CONTENTS

PREFACE

My earliest memories of Bootham Crescent will, I imagine, be very different to almost every reader of this book, forged as they were as a visiting fan, watching on from the Grosvenor Road away end. They date back to the mid-1980s when, having grown up as a supporter of my home-town club Doncaster Rovers and been taken to the also dearly-departed Belle Vue by my dad from an age I am too young to recall, York City became our nemesis.

It was the era of the Snodin brothers - Ian and Glynn - at Doncaster, under the exciting reign of football legend Billy Bremner but, frustratingly, York were always that bit better. Those derby clashes in North Yorkshire, nevertheless, have endured long in the memory and cemented my passion for a game that would eventually provide me with a living - even if the good times at Bootham Crescent were fleeting for Rovers back then.

I remember seeing Dennis Peacock save a John Byrne penalty and the adrenalin rush of the subsequent surge in a packed visitors enclosure. Indeed, everything about those fixtures was intoxicating for me as a pre-secondary school innocent and I can still see myself staring up at the bearded giant John MacPhail in awe as he lined up to defend a corner and wondering how on earth one of our strikers was ever going to get the better of him.

There was also the pain of a 5-0 League Cup defeat and the fear when a miner, during the strike, turned up in his works' donkey jacket and was set upon by his fellow Donny fans close to the refreshment kiosk, because the threat of violence was never far away for any youngster who started following the sport during an era of hooliganism.

In general, though, games at Bootham Crescent were never as hostile as Doncaster's tussles with Rotherham and the car journey up the A19 would be made in hopeful anticipation, rather than trepidation. Had somebody told me back then that, in adulthood, I would watch York City every weekend for 16 years while willing the club to succeed, I just couldn't have believed it possible. But the club and its ground, because one defined the other for more than 88

John Byrne's penalty is saved by Doncaster's Dennis Peacock in the derby match between Division Four's top two in April 1984

years, had a charm that consumed visitors in a way that never quite felt the same when I reported on Luton Town for seven years, before moving back up north in 2003. Watching City and Luton subsequently become bitter rivals was another surprise I would have never envisaged.

On my visits as an opposition journalist with Luton, aside from finding the ground very difficult to locate in the absence of any signposts pre-satellite navigation and Google Maps, I remember daft things like being able to get mushy peas with my pie - a virtually unheard of delicacy during my decade-long exile in the south. I also loved the feeling of sentimentality at the ground, where a former club favourite - normally somebody who had represented both teams - was invited onto the pitch at half-time to make the 50-50 draw. That link with the past was something I felt was charmingly unique having made trips to grounds all over the country and, hopefully, is a feature that can be resurrected at Monks Cross.

Once I was bestowed with the privilege of succeeding Dave Stanford as City's full-time reporter for what was the Evening Press, and is now The Press, just before my 30th birthday in November 2003, I then had to grow accustomed to the challenges of making Bootham Crescent my work-base every other Saturday afternoon, as well as on frequent Tuesday nights. The press box had a quirkiness that it's fair to say won't be missed by many scribes from opposition teams. Seated in rows of two in the Main Stand, to the right of the directors' box and behind the home dugout, it's small, slanted accompanying ledges were designed for notepads and pens rather than laptops, which had a habit of sliding off at regular intervals during games.

The view of the David Longhurst End penalty box was also obstructed by girders supporting the Main Stand roof, making the accurate reporting of set-pieces particularly problematic and often requiring rapid neck craning from left to right - something my long-time and much-missed media companion Malcolm Huntington probably coped with better than myself as a former Wimbledon umpire. Sitting next to Malcom, in itself, was quite troublesome, with two 6ft-plus blokes jammed in close together. His big coat would constantly get stuck under my flip-forward seat and you almost required the skills of a contortionist to find the electricity plug points down near our feet. The fluorescent bulbs, meanwhile, would flash on and off during night games - a problem that could normally be remedied with a swift tap in the right area, but applying a little too much force would often result in it flying out of its casing. One visiting hack was even given a nasty electrical shock once, as he tried to get his light back on but, thankfully, he wasn't seriously injured.

Complimentary half-time refreshments, when I first started the job, still came in the form of a big urn of weak tea, delivered by a youth-team player and which, former City writer Tony Kelly informed me, most people left well alone during the Douglas Craig era due to suspicions of tampering and contamination of the most unpleasant kind given the unpopular owner's distaste for the media. Later, the lovely Carol Beck, wife of late former chairman Steve, would bring out any soup left over from the boardroom for us on a cold afternoon and, before they stepped down from their roles as club directors, Sophie or Rob McGill would always carry up a welcome cup of coffee, sugared and milked to your taste - a gesture unheard of from any of their counterparts in the country. Sandwiches, brought out in a box by then press officer Niall Cope, also became a feature for a spell, but were quickly off the menu following the club's relegation from the Football League in 2016.

Countless memorable goals have been recorded from the obscured vantage point, with assists wrongly credited, as former right-back and future PFA chairman Ben Purkiss would - and regularly did - testify. It is not the correct etiquette, meanwhile, to celebrate City goals over-zealously in the press box - for practical reasons in the modern age as you have to ensure the score update is posted on social media platforms as soon as possible - but the one occasion I did jump out of my seat and punch the air was when Richard Brodie fired in his late winner during the 2010 play-off, semi-final, first-leg victory over Luton.

The location of post-match interviews, meanwhile, varied from manager to manager, with some preferring the sanctuary of the family room, garishly decorated in Smarties wallpaper for years when it was sponsored by Nestle and even for quite a few more after that deal had expired. Others offered their views at the back of the Main Stand where Radio York's commentary point was positioned.

In my privileged role, I spent many cold afternoons and evenings waiting in the players' tunnel for interviews, as apprentices - the possible future stars of tomorrow - swept around my feet. Managerial changes and certain new signings would also see the boardroom door swung open to the media, with its grand table and chairs always an evocative reminder of bygone eras. Other times, the revered chamber was used for long meetings during periods when, as is virtually inevitable and unavoidable in my profession, relations between myself and the club might have become strained with heated arguments often taking place and fingers pointed between the all-knowing four walls.

Some managers, not all, would conduct pre-match press conferences in their office, just behind the main ticket office, with each appointment adding their own personal touches to the room. Doting granddad Billy McEwan had pictures of his family, belying his gruff Scottish persona, and also had a sofa delivered to give the place a more welcoming feel. His successor Colin Walker, meanwhile, displayed a signed Aldair Brazil shirt on the wall, reminding visitors of his international playing past with New Zealand.

Undoubtedly, my fondest memory of Bootham Crescent, though, will be the Sunday afternoon I was invited to run out on the hallowed turf having got stripped in the cherished home dressing room, where the likes of Denis Smith, Sam Bartram, Tom Johnston and Tom Lockie had all delivered vital team talks. Sadly, I could not prevent the York City veterans' team from suffering one of the most embarrassing defeats to be witnessed at a stadium where London giants Tottenham and Arsenal had both been vanquished. We were defeated 3-1 by an *Emmerdale* XI - but patrolling the same left wing that Billy Fenton, Andy Provan, Brian Pollard, Tony Canham and Martyn Woolford had graced in the past and benefitting from the immaculate service of an evergreen 61-year-old Chris Topping behind me was an unforgettable experience - even against a side of TV soap stars, extras and crew members!

Writing this book has also been a terrific pleasure, reliving the great and not-so-great times at Bootham Crescent with so many club legends, who were all happy to reminisce and spare me their considerable time, as were the gracious Sir Alex Ferguson and Charlie Nicholas despite being on the receiving end of two of the biggest shocks the old ground witnessed.

Delving into every era of the past only serves as a reminder of the countless happy, tense and, sadly, tragic occasions that were played out at Bootham Crescent. As every proud City fan can attest, the two biggest names in English football - Sir Alf Ramsey and Bobby Moore - both ended games in the losers' dressing room, as did the likes of Gordon Banks, David Beckham and Sir Alex, albeit the last two were beaten on aggregate admittedly. The great Dixie Dean also represented City during the war years when the stadium was damaged by a bomb, while another prolific marksman Michael Owen first announced his striking talents to the footballing public with a four-goal blast for England under-18s at the ground. Chelsea, Manchester United and Manchester City played there too as City's Football League equals in my lifetime, however unbelievable that now seems.

Off the pitch, there were many famous visitors through the ages, none more so perhaps than a certain Elton John, who arrived unannounced and unexpectedly to sign a fans' favourite in the late 1970s, as chronicled later in these pages.

Bootham Crescent will also forever hold a place in the Football League's record books as the first ground that any professional team reached 100 points on during a campaign.

These memories and many more are detailed in the following pages and I hope you enjoy reading them as much as I did collating them, as we all bid an emotional and fond farewell to Bootham Crescent.

CHAPTER 1

Field View, Fulfordgate and the Football League

"My granddad used to have pig sties next to the pitch and I was farrowing them from the age of six."

In many respects, bidding goodbye to Bootham Crescent can be likened to the loss of a dear-old relative. Few would dispute, after all, that reaching 88 years of age as a football stadium represents a "good innings". Indeed, such an analogy couldn't be more appropriate, given cricket was the first sport to be played at the ground. Primarily, though, it will forever be remembered as the home of York City Football Club.

Over the years, so much of the ground was paid for by the club's supporters, who also helped in the team's previous relocation project, carrying all kinds of heavy equipment by hand from the old Fulfordgate stadium, as the move across the city was inconceivably completed in a matter of months. During one close season - a period of the year which is now reserved for a few weeks of transfer business, staff holidays and pre-season friendlies - the York public amazingly helped to construct a whole new arena to watch their side play in.

It has, since, been used for other purposes too. For one summer in the 1930s, it was shared with the short-lived York City Maroons baseball team. A Rock 'n' Roll Revival concert, featuring number-one artist Alvin Stardust, was staged there in September 1979, while the stadium also hosted an American football game in 1988 and, at the start of the following year, a crowd of 11,347 witnessed the ground's first ever rugby-league fixture as York entertained Leeds in the first round of the Challenge Cup and lost 28-9.

York's rugby league team also shared the ground, as they now do at the new community stadium, during Bootham Crescent's final years but it is the football memories that will endure the longest, with some of the best conjured up by the English game's oldest competition. Indeed, FA Cup ties accounted for the ground's four biggest attendances and six of its top-eight crowds.

Just as there will be life for York City after Bootham Crescent, though, there was also an existence for the club prior to the move to YO30 7AQ. Twenty-four years before Bootham Crescent became home, the first York City Football Club played in Holgate Road at the end of Lindley Street and Murray Street from 1908. The ground boasted a couple of open stands from York Racecourse, with one having a canvas roof, allowing 300 people to be accommodated. That City team beat South Bank 2-1 in their first Northern League home game but, by 1912, a plot of land was obtained in Burton Stone Lane, known as Field View, situated not far behind what would become the Shipton Street End at Bootham Crescent. It was rented from the feoffees of All Saints' Church in the city and a local firm turfed a playing area 120 yards by 100 yards for £36.

The first game at the new ground was against Rotherham Town in the Midland League and attracted 5,000 fans, including dignitaries such as MP Sir John Butcher, the Lord Mayor, General Plumer and General Reade. The occasion was also filmed and later shown at the Empire and Victoria Hall picture houses in Goodramgate. Admission for the fixture was sixpence for men, threepence for boys and ladies were admitted free of charge, with season tickets costing 7s 6d (37.5p).

The FA, meanwhile, staged a North v South match there, but the receipts, in a city that was then an established rugby-league stronghold, only amounted to £36, prompting FA Secretary Frederick Wall to declare: "Never again," when learning of the gate.

That incarnation of the club folded in 1917, going into liquidation through the bankruptcy court. The stand and equipment were subsequently disposed of and Field View was eventually turned into allotments and later a housing estate. It emerged that the stand had not been paid for and one creditor was pressing for payment.

Football was still played there, however, when lifelong City fan Graham Munday, who went to the first game at Bootham Crescent and so many more until he was prevented from doing so when the Covid-19 pandemic struck in 2020 and he passed away during the country's lockdown period.

"We lived just behind Field View in one of the three railway houses that were there at the time," Munday explained. "It's became Tennyson Avenue and our gardens went right down to where Rowntree's kept their horse and carts. My granddad used to have pig sties next to the pitch and I was farrowing them from the age of six. We would walk out of our back door and, through a gap in the hedge, to where the pitch was. That's how my aunt had first gone to City games when they were playing there - without paying through the gates. It was a thorn hedge that we used to go through. I know because I fell in it a few times. I was a bairn in long clothes for the first game I saw there and was only months' old. We would all go. Me, my aunt, my mother and my granddad."

Supporters then bought shares in weekly instalments in 1922 to help fund the purchase of a new ground at Heslington Lane, Fulfordgate and eight acres of land were secured for £2,000, not far from where the University of York is now situated. At the new site, hawthorn hedges formed the boundaries. There were also no turnstiles, only gates. Initially, there were no covered stands either and the dressing rooms were housed in an old army hut, with one corner partitioned off for the use of the directors and the secretary. Open stands were subsequently bought from the York Race Committee. But the ground was not ready for the club's first two Midland League home games in its new guise, so they played the matches at Mille Crux in Haxby Road - the ground of Messrs Rowntree & Company Ltd, where attendances were reportedly good. The first Mille Crux match took gate receipts of £122 when Lincoln City reserves were beaten 3-2 and, offering his views on the original decision to move out to Fulfordgate, as rumours first circulated about possible relocation to Bootham Crescent, *Yorkshire Evening Press* journalist "Citizen" reported in March 1932 that: "It had been well-nigh impossible to get what might be termed a central piece of land. Prices were prohibitive because those with land to sell knew that the club had to have a home and, in the circumstances, were considered fair game for the making of substantial profits. The move to Fulfordgate was not made so much from choice as from necessity and, probably, those responsible did not consider the locality ideal."

The first game at Fulfordgate was on Wednesday, September 20, 1922 when City beat Mansfield 4-1. It was a fixture that only went ahead after club director John Fisher had paid the £180 deposit required to play the match a matter of hours before kick-off.

The start of decades of assistance for the club from the Supporters' Club to help fund ground improvements also began at Fulfordgate. By 1927, new turnstiles were being fitted and stronger fencing was built around the pitch, aimed at reducing the prospect of pitch invasions. Behind one of the goals, nine-tier terracing also replaced the old banking. The covered Popular Stand, meanwhile, was extended to house 1,000 spectators and a small, seated stand was incorporated.

Before City were elected into the Football League, though, the biggest crowd recorded at the ground was the 8,318 that witnessed the English Schools

Trophy semi-final between York Boys and Brighton Boys on May 12, 1928, with gate receipts of £366. Reg Stockill and Dave Halford, who would go on to have distinguished careers in the game at the likes of Arsenal and Derby respectively, both played for a defeated York team that day.

By the time the club were elected into the Football League, meanwhile, it was estimated that Fulfordgate could accommodate 17,000 supporters. Indeed, included in the letter of application to the Football League, the club announced that the ground was: "splendidly drained, well-equipped, spacious and capable of being extended to hold up to 40,000 spectators".

Fred Hemenway, who was still a regular at Bootham Crescent in his 90s, had clear memories of his early visits to Fulfordgate as a child when interviewed for this book two years before passing away in October 2017. "My dad was there from the beginning," he said. "He paid half-a-crown-a-week for eight weeks to get a £1 share in the club and I started watching the club at Fulfordgate. I remember the ground having a good, drying pitch. Before the games, we used to have a kickaround in the backyard, then we would have our dinner before going to the match. Fred Barnes used to be on the turnstile there and my dad knew him because he lived just down the road from us. He used to shove me under the turnstile because I was so small, so I owed the club a bob or two, but I like to think I made up for that over the years. We used to stand in line with the penalty area and I started going when I was about five. We usually went by tram or, sometimes, my dad would put me in his sidecar and we'd go by motorbike. There were loads of trams and they would drop you off at Heslington Lane. Going back, there would be a great long line of them down Fulford, as far as you could see. I think it was a penny each way or tuppence for a return and all the trams were always full."

The Munday family, meanwhile, would make the four-mile round trip to Fulfordgate by foot, having moved to Layerthorpe by that time.

"I used to walk or be carried a lot of the way to Fulfordgate with my aunt because it was quicker than the trams," Graham Munday explained. "On the way home, I would get tired and we'd often call in at one of my aunt's pals for a cup of tea. There was only one route and a loop near Imphal Barracks because the tram sheds were on the other side of the road where the Aldi and Iceland supermarkets were built. The trams used to line up at Heslington Lane. Then, they used to come down but, if there was one coming up, you would have to wait on the loop."

Munday's aunt Caroline Pearce was a well-recognised City supporter from the club's early days at Fulfordgate until her death in 1993. She was among a loyal group of female fans during that pre-War period and the Supporters Club, who were formed in 1922, introduced a ladies' section just one year later. "She was an avid City fan who still went when she was 100," her devoted nephew recalled. "The last football game she went to was an England friendly against Brazil seven months before she passed away. She knew York City inside and out and she was a big England fan too right to the end. I remember her doing her nut when Graham Taylor took Gary Lineker off in the 1992 European Championships. She wasn't frightened to let people know her opinion and she used to go to matches with Blanche Granger, who was a cousin of Mick's - the City goalkeeper in the 1950s. My aunt was a Methodist and Blanche was a Catholic but they were always together. They would go rugby one weekend and City the next because, in those days, the clubs would play at home on alternate weekends. Not as many women went to football in those days but I think my aunt started going and became smitten with City because of Jock Collier. He married one of the Barnes girls who lived next door to us and he played for City before later becoming manager."

In 1929, City gained admission into the Football League's third division north at the expense of Ashington and the first home match at the new rarefied level was a 0-0 draw against Wrexham in front of a crowd of 8,726. Midway through that first Football League campaign, Billy Sherrington - who would later earn the nickname "Mr York City" after filling almost every role at the club during his life - had given up his day job as a civil servant to look after Minstermen affairs as the full-time secretary. Taking up the story, his daughter Terry Fowler said: "My father was a civil servant from Newcastle who moved to York with his job. He was born in Gateshead and was a Newcastle United supporter. Like most Geordies, he was keen on football and, when he came to York, they were a Midland League side but he got involved and became honorary secretary. Then, when the club got Football League status, he gave up his civil service job to run the club."

That first League season also came with the added bonus of a plum FA Cup third round tie against first division giants Newcastle who, after a 1-1 replay at St James' Park, were brought back to North Yorkshire with 12,583 packing in to Fulfordgate. Sam Evans drew first blood for the home side, scoring after 23 minutes, but legendary Scottish international centre-forward Hughie Gallacher, who had a spot kick saved by City keeper Jack Farmery during the game, equalised before the interval and the Magpies' Duncan "Hurricane" Hutchinson went on to get the winning goal midway through the second half. The place was heaving that day with the little wooden box, housing the

11

steward, swaying due to the force of those surging forward in the queue for admission. Remembering the occasion two decades later, Gallacher said: "We rolled our sleeves up for the replay and, although we won by the odd goal of three, if that match had been decided on guts, determination and teamwork, York undoubtedly would have been awarded the tie."

Hemenway and Munday, who would travel to games at Bootham Crescent together in the same car more than 80 years later, were both in the crowd for that match and, remembering the thrill of seeing one of the game's greats at close quarters, the former said: "I can still see in my mind a stoppage in play and, right in front of us, on the corner of the penalty area, a bloke was sat on the ball. My dad turned to me and said 'That's Hughie Gallacher, the Scottish international'. I was only five, but I remember that very clearly." Munday also recalled Gallacher being the main attraction that afternoon. "When Newcastle came, all the kids were lifted onto the side of the pitch," he added. "That was a great game. I can remember seeing Hughie take his penalty that Farmery saved. He was a terrific player and everybody wanted to see him. We always stood behind the goal to the left or right and never down the sides."

Munday also remembered his pre-match ritual involving a trip to the nearby pub - believed to be the Bay Horse - that he claimed was owned at the time by City player Tommy Fenoughty's family. "Tommy played at Fulfordgate and Bootham Crescent and he was a ball-playing wing-half," Munday explained. "We got to know him through Billy Nicklin, who was Tommy's friend from Rotherham and married Gladys Holmes - a pal of my mother's. Tommy played in the Midland League and Football League days and his relations used to have the pub just outside the ground. All our lot, including Gladys Holmes, all went into the pub before the games and I was shoved upstairs. We never saw Tommy until he ran out onto the pitch, but his parents were always there before the game."

Like many impressionable schoolboy supporters after him, Munday admitted, though, that the players who put the ball in the net were his biggest early heroes, none more so than Jimmy Cowie, who once plundered six goals at Fulfordgate during an 8-2 Midland League triumph over Worksop Town reserves in 1929. "All you used to hear back then was 'give the ball to Cowie'," he said. "I used to look around and think 'who's Cowie' as a young boy, but he was a centre forward and a sniffer who could pinch goals. He was Scottish because the manager Jock Collier had played for City following the First World War and, after going back to Scotland, he brought a lot of players down with him and chaps coming out of the army. That's what York City were made up of back then."

Another crowd of 10,120 would go on to witness a 2-0 Easter Monday defeat against visiting, champions-elect Port Vale, but there was no players' tunnel or dressing rooms in the stand during that first season of League football with Munday having clear memories of how the team would make their way to the pitch. "There was a house and bungalow there owned by the club," he said. "The players used to come out of the army hut changing rooms and come through the crowd to get to the pitch too. Everybody parted to let them on the pitch. There was no nastiness back then. It was just a football game. There were also mud heaps and timber sleepers around the pitch and there was no concrete then."

Fowler went on to reveal that one of the properties on site was also used by the club secretary at the time. "The bungalow on the Fulfordgate estate was my father's office," she explained. "It was made into a house for people to live in when the club moved and is still there as far as I know. There were also tennis courts down there. They were not owned by the club, but it was a sporting place."

The following campaign - 1930/31 - would see the Newcastle attendance eclipsed when City entertained Sheffield United in the Cup with a record Fulfordgate crowd of 12,721 watching a 2-0 win for the Blades, which also attracted £1,058 in gate receipts. Another notable game saw England take on Ireland in an amateur international at the ground in November 1931, before the final Fulfordgate fixture was played five months later. Halifax were seen off 7-2 on April 23, 1932 with a poor crowd of 1,618 blamed on that day's broadcasting of the FA Cup final. It was the first occasion the club had scored so many times in a Football League contest and nobody knew at the time the match would be the last competitive first-team fixture the ground would host. Indeed, season tickets were being sold by mid-May on the understanding that the new season would kick off at Fulfordgate. The cost for reserved seats was £2 for men and £1.10 for women, whilst admittance to the ground only was £1 for men, 10s for women and 7s 6d for boys (there was no advertised price for girls). Life-member tickets, meanwhile, were still available for 10 guineas (the equivalent of £10.50 in modern money), guaranteeing a reserved seat until death. Women life-member tickets were also introduced prior to the move to Bootham Crescent for five guineas.

An average crowd of 4,330 in 1931/32 - a figure that would be last bettered at Bootham Crescent in 1993/94 - was influential in the decision to move, after it had resulted in a deficit of £1,539 over the season. Fulfordgate was also considered to be somewhat inaccessible because of its distance from the railway station and the tram service that only had a single track, with its loop system for passing restricting the service's efficiency even further. Bus routes, at the time, had not been fully developed either and car ownership was still a long way in the future for most families.

Club secretary Sherrington was a big advocate for the move to Bootham Crescent due to those transport concerns, with his daughter Fowler pointing out: "My father had a house built on Heslington Lane when the club were at Fulfordgate to be close by, but he thought the move to Bootham Crescent was a good thing. It was not as easy getting on a tram from the centre of the city to Fulford as it would become later on buses. It was also a fairly long distance for people to walk from the city centre - about a mile-and-a-half or two miles. He thought it was better being near the centre. More people obviously have cars now than was the case then and, in the war-time, even if people did have cars, they didn't have petrol. Most people always walked to Bootham Crescent, though, because the car park was never any bigger. With the move from Bootham Crescent, my father might not like the idea of moving out of town because he always thought that was important. He would see the need for progress, though, if he thought it was progress and so many clubs have moved out of town and made the move successful. There was always a friendly atmosphere at Bootham Crescent too and, historically, it has been considered a well-run club that visitors liked coming to. I hope that's still the case at the new stadium."

Former club secretary Billy Sherrington was a key figure in the move from Fulfordgate to Bootham Crescent and was known as Mr York City for decades

Graham Munday, pictured at his home in 2015, watched York City play at Fulfordgate and was in the crowd for the first match at Bootham Crescent against Stockport on Wednesday, August 31, 1932. He passed away in September 2020 at the age of 100 but had remained a regular at the ground until the start of the Covid-19 pandemic

CHAPTER 2

Moving into the cricket ground

"Ask yourselves if you are satisfied with York City going on for years with an average 4,000 attendance?"

When the idea of relocating to a more central position in the city was first mooted in March 1932, *Yorkshire Evening Press* columnist Citizen, while making reference to the Fulfordgate pitch's excellent drainage, added: "It is difficult to make out a case repudiating that increased attendances would occur if a move was made." He warned, however, that any move would probably need to be overseen during a two or three-year period due to the big capital outlay and the transportation of equipment from one site to the other. But an idea to initially operate a third team of amateurs from the ground to "break it in" and discover whether the turf was heavy, like the adjoining Lumley Barracks' ground, was shelved as, one week later, Citizen was reporting that "gossip associating York City's future home with Bootham Crescent...had caught the imagination of a large number of the club's supporters".

York Corporation had also expressed an interest in acquiring the Bootham Crescent land with the intention of providing a children's playground on the site that had become vacant early in 1932 after housing the city's senior cricket club for 51 years.

Previous publications have suggested that, in June 1890, the ground hosted the only County Championship match ever to be played at York when Yorkshire beat Kent by eight wickets. But that game was, in fact, played at the Wigginton Road

A team photograph of York Cricket Club at their Bootham Crescent home in 1925 with Shipton Street School in the background

ground where York Cricket Club were relocating. At the time of the county game, that pitch was the home of the Yorkshire Gentlemen, who moved to Escrick Park prior to York taking up residency. Yorkshire's cricketers, including legendary opening England batsman Herbert Sutcliffe, did visit Bootham Crescent in 1930, though, playing a match against a York & District 16 to mark the opening of that year's York & County League season.

Legendary Yorkshire and England batsman Herbert Sutcliffe signs autographs during the county team's 1930 match against a York & District 16 at Bootham Crescent

Back in 1881, Sir Joseph Terry, the head of the famous local confectioners and York Cricket Club president, had funded the club's move from the Knavesmire to Bootham Crescent. As well as York's fixtures, the ground also hosted evening cricket in the form of the popular Myers & Burnell Cup competition, which was founded in 1919. The first final that year was won by Heworth Parish Church, with subsequent victors at Bootham Crescent including York Ramblers, Dringhouses, Escrick Park, Rowntree's, York Amateurs, North Riding Mental Hospital, Bootham Park Hospital, Acomb and York Reserves. Among those that played in the Myers & Burnell Cup competition at Bootham Crescent was Reg Baines who, in between two spells as a popular striker with City, scored 111 not out as Clarence Club & Institute beat York Amateurs in June 1929. Indeed, some of the formative childhood memories of Graham Munday and Fred Hemenway included seeing the summer sport played in what was, at that time, a cosy ground with brick walls on the east and northern sides - the respective future locations of the Main Stand and the Shipton Street End.

"I watched the cricket at Bootham Crescent from when I was about four," Munday recalled. "One of my earliest memories is running along the railway sleepers they put down around the pitch. There were trees along three of the sides then, but the front gates were always in the same place. Tony Hobson was captain. My mother and aunt were friendly with the Allenbys and he was courting the Allenbys' daughter."

Hemenway, meanwhile, remembered: "We used to sit on the same wall around the car park of the football stadium because that was close to the boundary at the cricket ground."

Club legend Alf Patrick also had connections with the ground's past as the city's home of cricket. "My father-in-law won the York & District League Cricket Cup there in 1923," he pointed out prior to his death at the age of 100 in 2021. Patrick, himself, went on to play for Dringhouses in the Wigginton Road-hosted 1948 Myers & Burnell Cup final, going in at number eight and scoring eight, having missed the first part of his team's 151-9 innings against Acomb, whilst he was scoring two goals in the first half of a City practice match at Bootham Crescent. He subsequently made the short dash over the railway bridge to join his cricket team-mates, having been given permission to leave the football game at half-time. The City player also claimed a superb run-out from cover point in the final, but Acomb went on to win at the ground where the York & District Hospital is now situated.

By then, the football club had been in situ at Bootham Crescent for 16 years with a special meeting of its shareholders having been called at St George's Hall in Castlegate on Tuesday, April 26, 1932. There, the board of directors urged those present to consider the "greater good to the greater number" when considering a move from Fulfordgate to the more central site. Prior to the meeting, Citizen also deplored shareholders to: "ask yourselves if you are satisfied with York City going on for years with an average 4,000 attendance?" and "whether after being in the leading six more than half the season, you are content for the club to lose hundreds of pounds in spite of it?" Others made forceful arguments at the meeting, including director Mr GW Halliday, who pointed out that the population within a one-mile radius of Bootham Crescent was 30,000, compared to a respective figure of 3,000 surrounding Fulfordgate. The belief was that the venue would make football matches more accessible for men, who were often working a five-and-a-half-day week and didn't finish their Saturday shift until 1pm during a pre-floodlit era when games would kick off before today's traditional 3pm start. Chairman Arthur Brown also stated that Fulfordgate was mortgaged as far as possible and that the mortgage, bank interest and overdraft would exceed the rent and rates at Bootham Crescent by £40 per year.

While the site of York's new home was an irregular shape and was hemmed in from four sides with a narrow track to the south, barracks to the west, a school and almshouses to the north and terraced houses to the east, there were no prohibitive restrictions in terms of banking, terracing and the erection of stands. The dressing rooms and oldest stand at Fulfordgate were, by then, in need of replacing, but the suggestion was also made that a structure three times the size could be built at Bootham Crescent and another advantage would be that the football, cricket and rugby-league clubs would all be situated within a few hundred yards of each other. Former director John Fisher was opposed to the move, however, condemning the proposal of renting a ground from the Ecclesiastical Commissioners instead of owning it. Another concern expressed was how long the effects of marl preparation on the cricket pitch, which discouraged the quick drying of turf, would take to correct. The Fulfordgate playing surface had an excellent reputation for drainage, while the new ground was on land subject to severe flooding.

Munday remembered the pitch at Fulfordgate having remarkable powers of recovery in the face of adverse weather conditions - something that, he felt, was never quite replicated at Bootham Crescent. "The land at Fulfordgate was owned by H Douglas & Sons," he pointed out. "They were builders who also built half of Selby and Tadcaster and we lived opposite his grandson Ken Douglas later in life. It could chuck it down with rain for a week or snow at Fulfordgate but, if that was then cleared off and provided they didn't play on it for about two hours, it was drained because they built the houses and the roads with the sand and gravel that they dug out. Ken was always playing hell about Bootham Crescent. He said it should have been dug out and tapered like a lot of clubs did, so it could drain better. He used to maintain that the water table at Bootham wasn't right because you only have to think where the river is, and it needed to be brought across to a level plain."

There was also a danger of Bootham Crescent becoming more heavily rated once more valuable equipment was on it and another former director, Councillor WH Shaw, opposed the scheme due to his doubts over the approaches to the ground and, with one eye on the future, its limitations in terms of car-parking space. A vote of shareholders, however, saw a 115-37 decision in favour of taking on an initial 21-year lease at Bootham Crescent with Billy Sherrington staking his family home on the move being successful. "We had a mortgage on the house in Heslington Lane and National Provincial wanted a guarantee when the club moved from Fulfordgate to Bootham Crescent, so my father put the deeds of the house up as a guarantee for the bank," the then club secretary's daughter Terry Fowler explained. "My mother must have been very tolerant, and I think she just accepted that he knew what he was doing."

The Sherringtons' neighbours in Heslington Lane would have included fellow York City-mad family the Masons, whose father Bill was also a director, while daughter Irene became a keen fan. Moving to Bootham Crescent for them would be an inconvenience and financial risk for the family too as Irene

Hagyard (her married name) recalled when interviewed for this book at the age of 97 in September 2018. "My father was one of the original people who started York City Football Club in 1922," she said. "He was a Yorkshire League referee and I remember a match at Fulfordgate when everybody was shouting at him and I got quite upset. We lived on Heslington Lane and there were three directors who lived near Fulfordgate, while John Fisher owned most of the land there. We had players and the trainer Hughie Murphy living with us because our house was so close to the ground and it always smelled of liniment. My mother made the cups of tea at half-time and washed the shirts as well, because the club couldn't afford to send them to the laundry. All the supporters also did a lot of hard voluntary work to help out. My father (Bill Mason) was a factory worker for Cooke, Troughton and Simms, which later became Vickers, all his life, but he mortgaged his house to help York City and, if the club lost money, we could have lost everything. He put our deeds up as security and everything on the line, because that's what the directors had to do. I remember asking my father why the club was being moved so far from Fulfordgate and he said they were looking to the future because, if they wanted more people to come, they needed a ground that people could walk to. If the stadium was more central, more people would be able to do that, because Fulfordgate was hard to get to and he was very much in favour of the move. He thought the club could grow with more people, because Fulford was just a little village on its own really. It didn't even belong to York. It was part of the East Riding and Beverley was the headquarters back then. You couldn't do much to expand at Fulfordgate either. Much of the land surrounding it was owned by farmers or lords, who would have wanted a lot of money, even if they were prepared to sell. My father was very progressive, and he would have also been in favour of the move to Monks Cross if he thought it was the right thing to do and it would attract more people to games. He wouldn't have liked it when the ground was called KitKat Crescent though - that was awful."

With the decision made, rumours began to circulate in May that the club could be playing in the new stadium by November. On May 21, it was then announced that the club were contemplating kicking off the new campaign at Bootham Crescent. This was publicised as a definite target on June 3 with the first Football League fixtures due to take place on August 27.

A debenture share scheme was quickly set up to help fund the move at a cost of £50 per share and, from Monday, June 6, the ground was open from 9am to 5pm for the receipt of hard material for banking. Local builders were encouraged to deposit any spare materials too, as the grass was cut to prepare the ground for an effective drainage system, which was in place by June 21. From one end to the other, meanwhile, an architect's survey revealed there was only a four-inch drop in pitch height, which didn't necessitate any work. After the area was drained, the ground was then built to the design of York architects Messrs Ward & Leckenby. It was decided that two stands would be erected. The Members' (Main) Stand accommodated members and season-ticket holders, whilst also housing changing facilities, a directors' room, a tea room, press room, store room and offices in centrally-heated brick buildings, which were constructed first before the seats were put in. It was a much higher structure than the Members' Stand at Fulfordgate, although it was not as long with plans for it to stretch along the whole of that side of the pitch revised. A thousand fans would be accommodated in the seating area, which was a similar number to Fulfordgate. On the west side, the Popular Stand would, like the Members' Stand opposite, measure 100 feet in length.

Fans helped with the move night after night by carrying railway sleepers for more than three miles from Fulfordgate to Bootham Crescent to enable the building of the Popular Stand and there was feverish activity as the new ground was equipped. A great deal of the waste material needed to form the Popular Stand banking was also transported from the old ground to the new stadium thanks to Supporters' Club members taking on the responsibility of loading and unloading lorries full of rubble. Fans dedicated many weeks of voluntary work and even gave up holiday time to ensure the move was completed on schedule. Transport, meanwhile, was provided for no charge by City director Mr Knowles on the understanding that the Supporters' Club paid the drivers. The Supporters' Club also committed to covering the £1,500 cost of building the Popular Stand, as a signal of their intention to provide an area for the ordinary shilling supporter that was paid for by the fans, rather than at the expense of the football club. But, with the builders insisting on receiving £500 to start the work, that money was raised by the means of a bank loan after another club director Bill Leckenby offered the deeds of his home as security. The Supporters' Club's barrowing of rubbish to form the new structure's raised base and placing down of terracing was a process which they managed to complete within a month, starting a pattern of dedicated assistance that would see the fans' body continue to play their part in maintaining and improving the ground for many decades afterwards. Gallons of paint, for example, would regularly be used to keep the perimeter railings and tea bars looking smart, while sections of the Popular Stand's corrugated iron roof would be replaced when necessary using voluntary labour in years to come. Members also manned the turnstiles and provided match balls and future manager Tom Lockie would even get players to help the supporters with such work during the 1960s for extra pay in the summer and fans were often rewarded with a season ticket for their efforts.

The cricket pavilion, meanwhile, remained at the ground and was used for Supporters' Club meetings. It later became the ground's main tea bar, but the committee room was still used above it by several local football bodies for meetings - free of charge on the insistence of Sherrington.

On the Popular Stand side, the West Riding Territorial Association initially deliberated as approval was sought by the club to acquire a portion of the drill field at Lumley Barracks. A £225 price for the 252 square-yard plot was agreed by the Association, who owned the land, on condition that a brick wall was erected to an architect's satisfaction and maintained by the club.

Messrs W Birch & Sons, of York, who were also responsible for the drainage, were given the contract to assemble the two steel-structure stands and, within an incredible four-month period, the ground had been completed in readiness for the 1932/33 season. Commenting on the remarkable speed and ease of relocation, Fowler reasoned: "People helped with the move. Nowadays, you wouldn't have supporters doing things like that and I think it also helped that two of the directors at the time - my father's next-door neighbour George Douglas and Mr Fisher - were both builders. They both owned some of the land there. There didn't seem to be any problems with the move but there were not as many planning restrictions those days either." With a need for all hands to the pump, club officials also pulled their weight, with Hagyard adding: "When the move was happening, my father was on short-time working at the factory, so he spent his time helping out, and doing whatever he could."

The players returned for pre-season training at Fulfordgate while the ground was being built, but that site would eventually be sold and developed for housing and there is nothing now to identify it as the football club's former home. Plans had been submitted to turn it into a £35,000 greyhound racing stadium - a sport that had become highly fashionable during 1927 - but the proposal was rejected by the York Corporation Streets and Buildings Committee in November 1932 because it did not conform with the regulations laid down concerning the scheme of town planning.

At the football club's AGM in the summer of 1932, the directors were commended by the shareholders for the bold policy they had pursued in moving to the new ground - which was considered well-equipped and with

21

strong development potential - in such a short time. The directors had also contributed £2,000 towards the cost of relocation and, to mark the new start, the team changed colours from maroon and white to chocolate shirts with cream cuffs in recognition of the city's confectionary industry. The strip was later changed to stripes using the same colours but, following complaints that the team looked too dull and sombre in chocolate, the kit was changed to red jerseys with white collars, white shorts and white socks for the 1936/37 season. Stripes had also been dispensed with, as several other clubs had the same style.

Charles Sutcliffe, the vice-president of the Football League, inspected the new ground a couple of weeks before the opening fixture. The first football game to be played at Bootham Crescent was then the annual practice match, which pitched the Blues against the Maroons on Saturday, August 20, 1932. In the Blues team

A view of the first game of any kind to be played at Bootham Crescent – an in-house club practice match between Blues and Maroons teams on August 20, 1932

were: Joe Duckworth; David Archibald, Sam Johnson; Joe Harris, Stephen Spargo, James Bolton; Bert Williams, Tommy Fenoughty, Reg Baines, Tommy McDonald, Peter Spooner. Playing for the Maroons were: Cant; Jack Pinder, Ted Wass; George Maskill, Dai Jones, Walter Bolton; Jackburn, John Turnbull, Stan Fox, Willie Moore, Tom Mitchell.

The fixture kicked off at 3.15pm with admission 6d for men and 3d for ladies and boys, with all proceeds going towards charity, principally the County Hospital. An estimated crowd of 3,000 turned up, which was reported to be double the number that could have been expected at Fulfordgate, with £70 raised and the game ending in a 3-3 draw. Such fixtures would take place every pre-season for a number of decades until they were fazed out in the late 1960s and became more commonly known as Reds v Blues contests. Sometimes, the first-choice attack would be pitted against the first-choice defence. Other times, it would be a straight First Team v Reserves, or Probables v Possibles clash with trialists also involved. Local players were given their chance to impress in the contests too when numbers were needed to provide a competitive match.

A Midland League reserve match against Bradford City, which also kicked off at 3.15pm, was subsequently the first competitive match to be played at the ground on Saturday, August 27. Bradford won 4-2 with admission the same cost as for the practice match. Reserve fixtures were, at the time and as they would be up until the late 1960s, staged at the ground on Saturday afternoons when the first team were playing away. First-team midweek games in 1932, meanwhile, would be played at a variety of times including 2.15pm on half-day holiday Wednesdays or from any time between 5.20pm to 6.30pm during late summer and early spring months.

The night before the Bradford game, during the Supporters' Club's monthly meeting at the Windmill Hotel, a £500 cheque was presented to the City directors as the first donation towards the cost of building the new Popular Stand. Organised dances at the Rialto Ballroom had gone a long way towards funding that first instalment.

Four days later, on Wednesday, August 31, the first Football League fixture against Stockport was staged, kicking off at 6.30pm. The club president Sir John Hunt formally opened the ground, which had cost just £6,000 to construct, by cutting a chocolate-and-cream-coloured ribbon and speeches were relayed via loudspeakers around the new stadium. High tribute was paid to the Supporters' Club's band of voluntary workers by Hunt, who had been a brewer in the late 19th century. Chairman Brown, meanwhile, presented a silver salver to Sir John that recorded the opening of the ground and The Sheriff of York Arnold Rowntree added that he was sure good sportsmanship would be displayed by the teams and spectators. Roger Lumley MP went on to express his hope that the club would meet with the success the enterprise of the management deserved and, during the interval, Arnold Kingscott, the FA's treasurer, also proposed a toast to Sir John's health. Sadly, the latter would die the following year, having left funds and instructions in his will for the creation of almshouses to help the less fortunate.

A souvenir programme, meanwhile, was on sale at the match for 3d, featuring numerous photographs of club personalities, teams and the ground. Programmes during that opening season would normally cost a penny, while seats in the Main Stand were priced at two shillings, with an extra charge of a penny for a cushion.

On the pitch, a crowd of 8,106 witnessed a 2-2 division three north draw with receipts of nearly £400. The attendance was less than the 9,000 that had watched the first Football League game against Wrexham at Fulfordgate in 1929. Bootham Crescent had also not yet achieved its intended capacity, following a temporary cessation in the carting of material for banking to bring some order and tidiness to the new surroundings. The home team for the historic fixture was: Joe Duckworth, David Archibald, Sam Johnson, George Maskill, Joe Harris, James Bolton, Bert Williams, Tommy Fenoughty, Reg Baines, Tommy McDonald, Tom Mitchell.

Former Hull City and Blackpool midfielder Percy Downes scored the first Football League goal at the ground on 16 minutes. Downes was reported to have "glided" the ball into the net after City keeper Duckworth could only parry a hard cross by Jabez Foulkes. City left-back Johnson went on to strain a thigh muscle on the half-hour mark, leading to a reshuffle that saw him asked to operate at outside-left. Soon afterwards, centre-forward Albert Lambourne doubled the visitors' lead, heading in after Duckworth had missed the ball from a corner. But the first goal to be scored in a first-team game by a City player came two minutes later when 32-year-old winger Mitchell, who had been moved from outside to inside left, received the ball from a Bolton free kick and shot for goal. County defender Eddie Lloyd chased the ball and got his foot to it but could only help it into the net. On 60 minutes, Fenoughty was then described as having been "somersaulted" by Stockport midfielder Jacob Taylor as the City striker looked to collect a ball into the box. The referee subsequently gave a penalty that saw away keeper Thomas Gale jump the wrong way as Baines successfully converted from the spot. Bolton, meanwhile, was reported to be a "hero" in the home defence after dropping back from midfield to cover for Johnson's injury, while Maskill made a goal-saving tackle late on to prevent City from losing their first senior Bootham Crescent contest.

Mitchell, City's first-ever Football League scorer at Bootham Crescent, was born in Spennymoor and only played 24 games for the club, scoring five goals, of which his historic strike represented a second in the club's colours. He had hardly played any football at school but impressed after being persuaded to join Parkside United juniors. Going on to make quick progress as an amateur, Mitchell then left Blyth Spartans in a £100 deal to join Newcastle United, where he played for six seasons and was selected for an FA XI representative side in 1924. He went on to sign for Leeds, costing £785 and became an ever-present in their 1927/28 division two promotion-winning side. Mitchell would later become City manager in 1937, taking over from the retired Jock Collier and guiding the club to the FA Cup quarter-finals during his first full season in charge. He went on to hold the job for 13 years before resigning in 1950 and opened a sports shop in York at the top of Bootham Crescent, having run a similar business in Whitley Bay. Later, he became a director of the club and ran a pub in Leeds.

Munday, meanwhile, could not have got much closer to the action for that historic fixture, recalling: "I was 12 in 1932 and I enjoyed going to that first game. It was the first time I had ever seen a ground covered with straw to protect the pitch. They used to rake it back and there was no need to ask for people to do that. They used to just turn up with their rakes and, then, if there were too many in the crowd, they used to drag us kids over and we would sit in the straw, like we would have done for that first game. They hadn't needed to do that at Fulfordgate because the drainage was terrific although I did see some games kick off there in inches of snow and the lines dug out with shovels."

Munday also remembered being impressed by the improved facilities at the new stadium, however modest, disturbing and amusing his description might seem by modern standards. He said: "Bootham Crescent was much better than Fulfordgate. It was built as a proper ground and had all the facilities that were required. There were more places to pee for starters, although the quickest way to the loos in the Shipton Street End was over a big mound of muck, which led down to a wall. We young 'uns used to scramble down to get to it and some of the dirty buggers, who had been in the pub before the game, used to stand at the top of the mound and pee down so you could hear it rattling on the roof of the toilets. There were also old bikes, tins and all sorts of other things that had been dumped there at the bottom of the mound."

Munday recalled, though, how the stadium improved season by season and also remembered many of the people who were responsible for its development. "In the close season, they would move the sleepers further up and put concrete down," he explained. "That went on for a few years. I also know that the first crash barriers were made in J Shouksmith & Sons' workshop by a bloke called Scotty. I don't know if the Shouksmiths knew about it or not, but I found out because I used to work as a plumber there. He bent a two-inch iron pipe and a piece went in the railway track at the ground. They used to bore it and those were the first crash barriers in the Popular Stand. (Future 1990s City striker) Glenn Naylor's granddad George, who was the same age as me, also did all the electrical work in the tunnel."

Like Munday, Hemenway was at that first Bootham Crescent match but remembered nothing about it in later life. He had vivid memories, however, of his formative years watching the club at their new home. "I used to play for the Young People's Fellowship Youth Club and York & District Boys," he explained. "We had 2.30pm kick-offs, so we would finish just after 4pm and race down to Bootham Crescent on our bikes because they used to open the gates at half-time and we could get to see nearly half the game. There was a group of us who did that, including Charlie Ware, who played for our youth club and went on to play for City and Scarborough. (Ware played nine games for City during the 1953/54 season before turning out for the Seadogs against his home-town club in the first round of the Happy Wanderers' famous FA Cup run). He was a good player, Charlie, who rarely got tackled."

Hemenway and his pals also used to recreate passages of play they had witnessed at Bootham Crescent with the then nonagenarian recalling: "I remember one match when the opposition got a penalty and their player hit the old leather ball right over the crossbar. I don't know how he managed that and, the next time we had a kickabout, I had 22 goes at doing it and couldn't get any over the bar because the balls were so heavy in those days. I've watched games in all areas of the ground and I remember watching the Coventry and Middlesbrough Cup ties before the War in the Popular Stand. I sat in the Main Stand during later years and I've also watched them at both ends of the pitch. We used to pass the other team's fans in the tunnel and there were no problems at all. The most trouble I ever got into was for chucking some orange peel at a linesman!"

Like Hemenway and many adolescents after them, Munday's matchday-routine would also soon change at Bootham Crescent. "I still used to go with my aunt at first and, then, when I got older, I used to go with the lads - Jack and Walt Billington and Ted Fogg," he recalled. "We would stand behind whichever goal City were kicking towards, cheering them on and hoping they would score past their keeper. I think people would still swap ends if they had the chance."

Hagyard was also at that first game, but admitted she was more taken with the new surroundings than the action on the pitch. "I was 11 and, whilst I can't remember the actual game, I can remember being in the directors' box with my mum and Bootham Crescent just felt massive and more sophisticated than Fulfordgate, because it had two good stands, although there was also so much soil piled up at both ends," she said. "The baths at Fulfordgate had been just funny, little, ordinary things, but the Bootham Crescent baths were a lot better too. The facilities were a big improvement and you would have had to knock Fulfordgate down and start again to make it as good. I remember going into the boardroom afterwards as well. Everybody was milling about, but there was a little passageway that went through to the secretary's office and that was known as the inner sanctum. My father and all the other directors went into there, if they ever needed to discuss anything. I also remember the ball used to go over into Shipton Street School's playground when games were being played. But Bootham Crescent was a lot better than most grounds back then - it was quite good and modern. We went to Rotherham once and I asked my father if he could ask the gentleman where the toilet was, and he said: 'Aye lass. Just go over there to Mrs So and So's and knock on the door', and I had to go into their house!"

As a young girl, Hagyard would quickly grow to enjoy a matchday routine at Bootham Crescent that would take her right the way through adolescence and into motherhood, adding: "Hartas Foxton - who had the Pullman Bus Company - used to sit behind me and my mother and Mrs Foxton would sit beside me, while my father sat in front with Taffy Shaw. I always remember when I was expecting with my daughter Patricia, Mrs Sessions - the chairman's wife who was also sat behind me and was a lovely lady - used to say: 'Don't get too excited, Irene', and Mrs Sessions didn't shout as much as me and Mrs Foxton. I also used to sit next to the partition for the directors' box and I knew people on the other side as well and they used to put their heads up and tell me to sit down and not get excited when I was pregnant, but I couldn't help it if we were winning 1-0 or it was a close game. When it was cold, Mrs Foxton used to put her fur coat over my legs as well to cover my knees."

Hagyard's memories of those formative years at Bootham Crescent as an impressionable youngster, meanwhile, are dominated by her observations of what was happening off the pitch. "The Evening Press' Wilf Meek used to write his match reports in shorthand in the press box and, then, pass it to a little lad, who I would see go down the stairs of the directors' box and then down the corridor, where he'd turn right and there was a phone box that he used to send the game through from up to that point during the match," she recalled. "At 5.10pm, the Green Press would then be out with a picture and a full report. At Fulfordgate, there also used to be a man outside, shouting: 'Don't forget your Wrigley's' and he'd be selling Wrigley's chewing gum. There was then another man who must have got injured in the first World War who played gramophone records. He was always outside Fulfordgate and Bootham Crescent and people put money into his bag. I think he had lost his legs, because he was in a kind of pram that he steered himself, but he used to be outside York railway station and the football ground. I also remember Billy Leckenby had an ice-cream business and his brother Alf used to go around the pitch before games at Bootham Crescent selling them and he carried tubs in a tray that was held around his neck, like they used to do in the cinema."

For Fowler, meanwhile, the new ground was to become almost a second home. "I was pretty much brought up at Bootham Crescent as a school child," she remembered. "Later, my husband Clifford Fowler did the hospital radio and used to look after the hospitality room, including running the bar. I got to know Don Revie quite well because he used to come and watch players and Lawrie McMenemy was there a lot too when he was Grimsby and Doncaster manager. He was a nice bloke and a Geordie like my dad."

Tradesmen and volunteers help build the Main Stand during a frenzied summer of work to get the stadium ready for the start of the 1932/33 season

Irene Hagyard (left) as a child with her father, the then York City director Bill Mason, and her mother

Jack Pinder was a 1930s and 40s stalwart at Bootham Crescent, who often entertained fans in the Social Club with his mouth-organ talents

CHAPTER 3

Settling into Bootham Crescent and hosting baseball

"Nobody could believe it - losing to Scarborough! It was an awful feeling and you felt so down."

With everybody committed to ensuring the stadium move proved successful, a pro-active York City made immediate attempts to attract the next generation of supporters to their new home by distributing free tickets in schools for Saturday Midland League reserve games with the Women's Supporters' Club anxious for teachers to hand them over to girls as well as boys. Football League rules at the time, however, prevented the club from extending the gesture to third division matches. Admission for supporters aged 14 and under was, though, changed from 6d to 3d by mid-September, with youngsters admitted through the entrance in the Lumley Barracks corner. The Supporters' Club, meanwhile, continued to smarten the new ground up, working on the terracing in the Popular Stand, as well as coating the Enclosure in front of the Main Stand, and the car park with ashes.

Reg Baines would go on to score Bootham Crescent's first hat-trick in the third Football League fixture to be staged at the ground - a 4-3 triumph over Mansfield, which also represented the club's maiden victory at their new home. The first goal of Baines' treble opened the scoring on five minutes after he was picked out from a corner. His second was controversial when, after chasing a long ball forward by Sam Johnson, he let fly with a tremendous drive that Jack Clough got a hand to, before the ball spun behind him. Mansfield defender Ernie England raced back to kick the ball away but, despite strong and prolonged protests from the visitors, Baines' shot was adjudged to have crossed the line to level the scores at 2-2. Baines' hat-trick goal came from the penalty spot and was another equaliser after Peter Spooner was tripped by England on 67 minutes. The winner was then scored by Tommy Fenoughty with five minutes to play, as he called for Baines to leave the ball and beat Clough with a well-struck shot.

By mid-October, the Popular Stand terracing had been completed with 32 tiers, meaning 6,000 people could now enjoy covered accommodation on that side of the stadium, with 2,000 capable of being sheltered in the Main Members' Stand and the Enclosure. Floodlighting apparatus was also installed on the Main Stand to facilitate training during the dark nights. The York Excelsior Silver Band, meanwhile, began to perform on match days, as they had at Fulfordgate.

In November, the patch of grass just in front of the players' entrance onto the pitch was relaid, having been left heavy and greasy after rainfall, as fears that the drainage would not match Fulfordgate's standards began to be realised. Irene Hagyard also remembered problems with the playing surface during the early years at Bootham Crescent, declaring: "My father said the ground was poor. At Fulfordgate, the water just went away, but it didn't at Bootham Crescent and I can remember certain parts being mud heaps. The centre spot was always a problem and I expect the club spent thousands of pounds over the years trying to get that area and the grass in front of both goals right, because those bits were so bad.

"But, each summer, as the years went on and the Agricultural College was opened at Askham Bryan after the War, people started to look at the grass scientifically and they tapped into their knowledge, but it was very difficult at the start."

Her own concerns about the pitch's condition, though, would play a part in meeting her future husband Eric who, unbeknown to Irene, was watching her from afar at games as she performed one of her pre-match rituals. On one of several romances that will have, no doubt, blossomed at Bootham Crescent through the decades, Hagyard smiled: "Bootham Crescent was how I met my husband. When I first met him, he said: 'I know you' and I said: 'Do You?' He said: 'Yes, don't you go to Bootham Crescent?' "I said: 'Yes', and he said: 'You go and check the pitch every time there's a match, don't you?' He then asked me if I liked football and that was that. He was right - I did used to walk to the gate and check the pitch to see what it was looking like and whether it was going to be kicking up or if there was water on it and it was going to be a mud bath. I always wanted to see how many people were arriving at the game as well, because I once said to my mother: 'Why do we worry so much about why the team wins or not?' She said: 'Because we could lose our home if the club closed down', due to the deeds my father had put up as security. I always remembered that as a child so I knew how important it was for the fans to come, but the whole family was football mad and my father would have been over the moon if he had lived to see when they got into the second division, because that's all he ever wanted."

Turnstile operators were also instructed not to admit fans into the ground posing as boys to benefit from the reduced junior rate or unemployed supporters looking for sympathy with no money, as both had been a feature of the early matches at Bootham Crescent.

Midland League Scarborough, meanwhile, caused an FA Cup shock in City's first campaign at their new home with York-born, former England schoolboy international Dave Halford and ex-City outside-right Matt Jenkinson on target in a 3-1 victory for the visitors.

The home side had taken the lead when Spooner headed in a Stephen Spargo free kick on 14 minutes. Scarborough levelled six minutes later, though, in unusual fashion. Many of the home side's players stopped when the ball was played to Jenkinson in anticipation of an offside decision, but the referee allowed play to continue and the former Fulfordgate campaigner went on to beat City keeper Des Fawcett. Billy Clayson gave the visitors a 56th-minute lead after more good play by Jenkinson on the right. Victory was then wrapped up on 73 minutes through Halford from a tight angle after Fawcett had been unable to hold on to a shot by Scarborough's Wraith.

The horror of such a defeat is something that stayed with Hagyard countless decades later, as she admitted: "One game that I remember very much was playing Scarborough and they beat us at Bootham Crescent. Nobody could believe it - losing to Scarborough! It was an awful feeling and you felt so down."

In January 1933, meanwhile, the Supporters' Club launched a new penny ticket scheme, in aid of the special Popular Stand fund aimed at repaying the costs of its construction, which gave the 1,000 members a chance to win the match ball with the nearest estimate for that game's attendance.

Unfortunate weather conditions didn't help matters during the club's first campaign at Bootham Crescent with two home matches postponed in quick succession - first on Boxing Day against Barrow due to fog, before frost meant a clash with Southport was also unplayable, depriving the club of a full month's gate income, estimated to be around £600. A subsequent packed schedule in April meant plans to revive the Inter-Works Cup competition were shelved with Bootham Crescent unavailable, but games in the tournament - not just the final - would be played at the stadium in future years.

Re-election, meanwhile, was only avoided following a final-day 6-1 home victory over Darlington. The club finished third-bottom and, whilst in three Football League campaigns at Fulfordgate the club had only lost nine home games, they were beaten seven times during their opening season in their new surroundings, along with the Cup shock against Scarborough.

The final of the Half-Holiday Trophy between Co-operative Employers and North Riding Mental Hospital did go ahead at the ground. Fishergate also beat Poppleton Road in the final of the York Schools Junior Cup at the stadium before defeating St Deny's too in the League Cup final. In addition, Manor High Grade overcame Priory Street in the final of the All Schools Cup, while York Boys took on their Sheffield counterparts in the final of the Yorkshire County Shield, with a 4-2 replay defeat being watched by a healthy 6,204 supporters. Aggregate gate receipts for the two games held at Bootham Crescent, with admission set at 6d for adults and 3d for boys, amounted to £250.

After the cup finals, work started on laying a cinder track in front of the Main Stand to facilitate training and the banking at the Shipton Street and Bootham Crescent ends was also straightened and finished off, with the new capacity of the ground now estimated at 20,000.

The ticket office, meanwhile, was open from 7.30pm to 9pm on weekdays and 3pm to 5pm on Saturday during the first week that season tickets went on sale. Some areas of the pitch were also dug up for re-drainage and re-turfing.

The club's average gate during that first season at Bootham Crescent was a disappointing 4,370 - almost identical to the last campaign at Fulfordgate, leading to a deficit of £624, which rose to £3,388 when the expense of moving to the new ground was factored in. A start to the league campaign that was the club's poorest ever played a significant part in the apparent lack of enthusiasm for the new stadium. With all money being funnelled towards relocation, a lack of investment in the team had not helped matters either and the club responded by making several new signings within the first six weeks of the season. Only a small portion of the old equipment at Fulfordgate had ultimately proved usable, meanwhile, at Bootham Crescent and the total value of the stands and equipment at the new ground was £6,165 15s 11d.

The directors had predicted that attendances would rise by 1,000 for the first team and 600 for the reserves, which would have led to £50 and £15 rises in receipts respectively. Sherrington's confidence that gates would eventually improve, though, remained unshakable. "He was a very calm man and was never worried when the crowds didn't come at first," Fowler pointed out.

Reserve games were also still attracting decent crowds when compared to modern figures, with Hagyard confessing: "I enjoyed going to reserve games. We played Altofts Colliery once and the bus driver had to go in goal, because they had come with one man short and I think we beat them 12-1."

Fans, meanwhile, were invited to inspect the new ground, ahead of the start to a second season there, which would include a look inside the "dressing rooms, modern baths, tea rooms and club offices". It was opened up for public viewing during the third Sunday in August between the hours of 3pm to 5pm and 6.30pm to 8.30pm and more than 2,000 people took up the offer with directors and Supporters' Club members acting as stewards. By September 1933, meanwhile, a large games room had been opened under the Main Stand, acting as a rest area for the players, with a billiards table later added, whilst a writing room was also provided for journalists.

Future club favourite Alf Patrick was among those who got an early taste of playing in the brand-new arena. "The first games I played on the pitch were for City boys," he recalled. "Charlie Bradley, who later played for City at inside left, was also in that team with me. They used to put another crossbar under the existing one for us little ones. It was great. Later, when I was playing for the first team, some of the grounds we used to go to were pretty ropey and rubbish, but Bootham Crescent was always a good ground at second and third division level. It was a nice, little stadium, whereas places like Rochdale and Hartlepool were right dumps."

Concerns over finances at Bootham Crescent, meanwhile, were still being expressed at the AGM in 1934, but the board of directors continued to maintain that the move from Fulfordgate would prove beneficial during the years ahead. The road approaching the ground at the Bootham Crescent end was also widened and laid with Tarmac to greater facilitate the arrival and departure of supporters and the improvement was made at no extra expense to the club. Previously, the approach had been a narrow cinder track, which was frequently in a bad condition during wet weather. The entrances to the ground were also moved back several yards.

In March 1934, the North Riding Cup final was staged in York for the first time as City met Middlesbrough reserves, having reached the final for only a second occasion in the club's history. The game finished 2-2, meaning a replay was staged at Boro's old Ayresome Park ground.

Muddy conditions, though, remained difficult at Bootham Crescent with one player telling The *Yorkshire Evening Press'* Citizen for some games the pitch became a "treacle trap".

An incident also saw a referee and his linesman discovered unconscious in their dressing room with their conditions thought to have been caused by fumes from a faulty heater before a game that month.

The efforts to help meet the costs of building the Popular Stand, meanwhile, were ongoing and, in April 1934, the Women's Supporters' Club donated £45 from their annual supper and smoking concert at the Windmill Hotel. A match between a York & District XI side, managed by City boss Jock Collier, and a York City Police team was also staged the same month with the proceeds going towards the Building Fund of the York County Hospital. The two teams played for the Sir John J Hunt Hospital Cup and the match was established as an annual event to be played at the ground. Collier's team would include guests like rugby-league player Melville Rosser, with the trophy presented by the Lord Mayor or Sheriff of York. Sir John had donated the cup for the purpose of the challenge match before his death.

At the end of the 1933/34 campaign, club stalwart Fenoughty was awarded a benefit match against Leeds, which the visitors won 7-1 in front of 4,000 spectators. Fenoughty had a penalty saved in the game and Tom Lockie also scored an own goal.

Baseball, meanwhile, was staged at the ground on Whit Monday with two of the best teams in the country - the Merseyside-based pair British Enka and Crystal - doing battle in an exhibition match. Both sides boasted English and Welsh international players with the American sport gaining in popularity this side of the Atlantic at the time. Scorecards were sold so the public could keep a record of the game as it progressed and football, rugby and cricket enthusiasts were all reported to be among a "good" crowd, as Crystal claimed victory.

In June, as part of York Civic Week's Children's Festival, a mass gymnastic display was staged at the ground, with other events taking place all across the city, as the stadium started to embrace its potential as a hub for all of the community. But football remained the main attraction and, in January 1935, Bootham Crescent staged its first big City game when top-flight Derby County travelled to North Yorkshire for an FA Cup tie that attracted a then record crowd of 13,612, leading to gate receipts of £1,040. Interest in the tie was huge with fans turning up and queuing at the club's offices two hours before the advertised time for ticket sales. It was the first occasion a team from the top division had visited the city for a Saturday cup tie, with the Fulfordgate games against Sheffield United and Newcastle both replays that were played on a Wednesday. Crush barriers were erected for the game at both ends of the pitch and turnstiles were placed at the Shipton Street End, while two were borrowed from York Rugby League Club for the Main Stand side. Five special trains were put on for Derby supporters too and a 20-page souvenir programme was produced, costing 2p, while Main Stand ticket supporters were asked to be seated by 2.20pm. Lumley Barracks was also opened up as a car park for the game with a small charge applicable and the York Excelsior Band played from 1.30pm with City fans having begun to file in for the game at noon. Hughie Gallacher, who had played for Newcastle at Fulfordgate, was now a Derby player, but he was well shackled by City's Bill Routledge on the day and the hosts looked like they were going to force a replay until England international winger Sammy Crooks grabbed the only goal of the game on 87 minutes. The public's reaction to the big match was a major boost for the club and it soon emerged that discussions had taken place regarding the establishment of a trust fund with the aim of buying the ground before the lease ran out in 1953.

As the 1934/35 season drew to a close, the club's close relationship with local grassroots football at the new stadium was emphasised as a host of tournaments were staged and decided on the turf. It was now not unusual, come April, for the ground to be used every night of certain weeks. Representative teams from the York and Scarborough Minor Leagues for 14 to 16-year-olds would play each other at Bootham Crescent and the York Half-Holiday Trophy final would also be contested at the ground. The York City Supporters' Club Inter-Works Cup's fixtures would be staged at the ground over numerous nights too and proved popular with the Lord Mayor, who was often in attendance. A whole host of junior finals, meanwhile, would be decided on the ground and many of the local contests back then would be played during weeks when the first team were still completing their fixtures. Other games to be played in those early years pitched the York & District Referees against their Bishop Auckland counterparts, whilst another hospital charity match saw York Boys meet Hull Boys in front of 1,500 spectators with Alf Patrick in the hosts' team.

The football club made a difficult start to the 1935/36 campaign, however, with no respite in the FA Cup either as first-round Midland League visitors Burton Town won 5-1 at a dumbfounded and bewildered Bootham Crescent. Just a fortnight earlier, visitors Mansfield had also managed to net five times in a league contest, but with James Hughes (2), Peter Spooner (2), Albert Banfield, Duncan Lindsay and Harold Green on target for the hosts a record aggregate score of 7-5 for an official fixture was played out at Bootham Crescent.

The club's poor form, meanwhile, was struggling to attract the 5,000-sized crowds that were expected following the move to Bootham Crescent and then deemed necessary to make the team competitive in the northern section. February also saw the club ballot supporters in the matchday programme with a "yes" or "no" sought to the question: "Are you in favour of football pool coupon betting as at present in operation?" In one of the most controversial proposals introduced by the Football League, who wanted the pools promoters to pay for the use of fixture lists, the existing programme of games was scrapped, with football clubs and the public not being made aware of who their opponents would be until late on a Friday before a Saturday game. That led to Rotherham being replaced by Oldham as the visitors to Bootham Crescent with less than 24 hours' notice on the last Saturday in February. Unsurprisingly, the policy caused chaos up and down the country for clubs' travelling plans and the Bootham Crescent ballot saw 390 vote in favour of the existing football coupon system and 40 against. City's unpromoted clash with Rotherham went on to comfortably attract the lowest Bootham Crescent gate of the season with just 1,811 turning up for a 2-1 victory and that dip in attendance was mirrored at other grounds in the country with the controversial initiative dropped after just two weekends. Following the return to the original fixture list, City hosted Oldham on the day they had been due to entertain Rotherham.

In the 1936/37 season, a good start by City saw crowds in excess of 7,000 flock to the first two home fixtures and 10,619 turn up for the third against Chester, although indifferent results meant attendances had dipped to under 4,000 by mid-October. The club did beat higher-division opponents at Bootham Crescent for the first time, though, with second division Bradford City seen off thanks to an 87th-minute James Nicol goal in a third-round FA Cup replay.

Illustrating how the new ground was helping players and fans mix together away from football, meanwhile, the Social Club and Supporters' Club's committee members entertained the City team on the Thursday night before an FA Cup trip to Swansea City. Taking part in a "sing-song" was goalkeeper Norman Wharton and his fellow members of the Burton Lane Male Voice Choir, while Jack

York City on the way to a 3-1 defeat against Swansea on a quagmire of a pitch at Bootham Crescent during an FA Cup fourth-round replay in 1937. At the time it was the furthest stage of the competition that had seen a tie hosted in the city

Pinder did a mouth-organ turn. When the game was drawn and the match was to be replayed at Bootham Crescent, ten pubs on the route to the ground from the city centre enjoyed successful applications to extend their opening hours, enabling them to serve between 4pm and 5.30pm after the 2.15pm Wednesday afternoon kick-off. The fourth-round tie represented the furthest point in the competition that a match had been staged in the city at that point and interest in the game was again high. City went on to lose 3-1 in front of 11,545 on a quagmire of a pitch with water lying on the surface despite considerable amounts of sand being thrown on to it.

In March, meanwhile, trainer Collier's resignation saw him entertained in the Social Hut after his final match. There, directors, officials and players presented him with gifts, including a silver fountain pen, silver pencil and a silver cigarette case.

The club were also being forced to turn away supporters at this time with appeals from unemployed and pension-aged fans for half-price admission unable to be acted upon, as Football League rules insisted that the minimum charge for any adult must remain at one shilling. "It may seem hard, but it is simply the rule of the League and must be adhered to," reported Citizen. The playing surface remained problematic as well, with the Lincolnshire Echo reporting in April 1937 that the pitch was "almost a morass, with extensive pools of water in front of the goals" during a 0-0 draw with Lincoln.

Nevertheless, plans to run a professional York City Baseball Club from Bootham Crescent, which would include a small band of overseas signings from Canada who arrived on the Duchess of York liner from Montreal, also emerged in January 1937 with fixtures to take place during the close-season months. They were to compete in the Yorkshire League against teams from Sheffield, Hull, Leeds, Barnsley, Harrogate, Scarborough, Dewsbury and Wakefield and would be known as the Maroons. Crowds of 3,000 were anticipated and there were also proposals to establish a York & District Baseball League, with York Nomads, LNER Builders,

The York City Maroons team that beat Scarborough Seagulls 9-3 in their first fixture at Bootham Crescent

Terry's and Rowntree's all setting up sides. New City manager Tom Mitchell was described as an expert baseball player too, having assisted the Leeds team in the past and the York club initially signalled their intention to call on his playing services, as well as those of one or two members of the football team. That never materialised but the opening game for the new Maroons team

D Rollo in baseball action for York City Maroons during a game against Scarborough Seagulls

did take place at 6.45pm on the first Wednesday in May against Scarborough Seagulls, as the club forged ahead despite concerns that it might draw interest away from the city's cricket team. The Sheriff of York Cllr RJ Pulleyn pitched the first ball, whilst AT Grogan, who was secretary of the Yorkshire Baseball League, acted as a commentator with loud speaking apparatus installed. Admission was 6d and 1/2 for adults and 2d for boys and York won 9-3 in seven innings. A crowd of 2,000 watched the game on a cold night, although it was reported by Citizen that "the batsmen seldom connected bat with ball, particularly on the Scarborough side". Mitchell might not have played, despite plans for him to do so during the week building up to the match, but the four Canadian overseas signings did.

One letter sent to the *Yorkshire Evening Press* by "Old Sportsman" made it clear that he enjoyed the occasion, as he wrote: "The many charming and smartly attired bright young things who attended were obviously thrilled to bits by the slick, gum-chewing, good-looking, stolid and humorous York Maroons, who instantly won pride and popularity in the hearts of the spectators, who must have longed to have been able to have joined in that glorified version of 'cricket-with-a-kick-in-it, cum-he-man rounders'. Citizens should give every support to the promoters who have made it possible for us to enjoy such inexpensive, fascinating outdoor enjoyment."

Hagyard - the daughter of City director Bill Mason - was also a big fan too, enthusing: "I loved it when Pulleyn put that baseball team together and brought some players over from Canada. I got hooked on the game, because it was similar to rounders and I was captain of the rounders team at school. I remember them playing Hull Zingari, Leeds and Barnsley and, whilst it was a strange sort of game, the people who went that understood it really enjoyed it, because it was very interesting if you knew how to score. But not many people I socialised with went and not many did from the football club either. They were all a little bit older than me and I don't think they were interested in baseball. I worked with a girl who got very friendly with the team and she used to say they were all really nice guys that had come over and were very easy to speak to. I was very into anything Canadian or American back then just before the War and, at Fulfordgate, nothing else had ever happened in the summer. They used to just put sheep on it to keep the grass short, so it was great to have another sport to watch at the ground when there was no football. But, when the War started, it all ended and I wouldn't have thought it would have taken off to make it a paying concern. There wasn't a lot of people at games."

In an attempt to try and heighten the sport's popularity, local sides York Nomads and Railway Tigers also played a game at Bootham Crescent, while touring sides from West Ham and Romford met the Maroons during a busy summer of fixtures and a ladies' night saw female supporters admitted free of charge for a victory over a Rest of the Yorkshire League team. Another game against the previous year's Yorkshire double winners Greenfield Giants was nominated Children's Day with youngsters admitted for a half-price 1d. The Maroons also played against a York Amateur League representative team at Bootham Crescent, although there were no players from Rowntree's or Terry's, as it was the factories' holiday week.

York Nomads, meanwhile, went on to beat Terry's Spartans 24-2 at the ground in the York City Maroon Cup final. Baseball at Bootham Crescent proved short-lived, however, with the team playing their games at the rugby club's Clarence Street stadium the following summer and, then, as interest began to wane, going on to set up base at the Knavesmire.

Work was completed, meanwhile, at Bootham Crescent on a new 84ft x 26ft Supporters' and Social Club building, which was described in the *Yorkshire Evening Press* as "the most elaborate to be found on any Northern Section ground". It had admittance from the Main Stand Enclosure and would remain in the same location until the closure of the ground. The new facility was the brainchild of club director Sam Gawthorne but, due to financial difficulties, City asked for a loan to fund the brick building with only the Yorkshire Clubs Brewery agreeing to offer financial assistance. The brewery bought, dismantled and reassembled in their own yard the old cricket club wooden hut that had served as the ground's social club since 1934 and also housed second-hand cinema seats. Work on the new building took two years to complete and the facility had a folding partition, primitive heating, bare walls and floor and a 42ft-long bar. But it was a massive improvement. There was also accommodation for 80 whist tables and a floor suitable for dancing, with as many as 400 people able to be accommodated. The partition separated stand patrons from ground patrons, with modern seating and decorations other welcome embellishments. A smoking concert was staged on the opening night and, by the end of the season, a cheque for £250 had been handed over to the football club from the new venue's proceeds.

Bootham Crescent's Popular Stand was also completed at its projected cost of £1,500. The Supporters' Club, who by then boasted 1,489 members, had covered the majority of the expense with the running of the Shilling Fund proving of major assistance. A plaque noting the efforts of the fans in the Popular Stand's building and maintenance went on to become part of the structure and remained in place until falling into disrepair during the 1970s.

In November 1937, meanwhile, ten loud speakers were installed at the ground, linked up to a portable microphone with the intention to use the new equipment for coaching and training purposes, as well as for entertainment and announcements at games. The Norwegian international team that were due to take part in the following summer's World Cup also stopped off in York en-route to a match in Ireland and were shown around Bootham Crescent by manager Mitchell, who used to coach in the Scandinavian country.

By Christmas 1937, Bootham Crescent's position at the heart of the community was firmly cemented - a feeling that was probably best illustrated by the City players' decision to organise and host a party for 120 children from unemployed families in the Social Club, where entertainment was laid on by artists, while keeper Wharton dished out presents dressed up as Santa. The gesture was repeated the following Christmas, which proved the last before War broke out.

Reg Baines scored the first-ever hat-trick at Bootham Crescent during a 4-3 victory against Mansfield in only the third league fixture to be played at the ground. He is pictured winning a header

CHAPTER 4

Record attendances and a run to the FA Cup quarter-finals

"Against West Brom, a couple of their supporters got hold of my scarf and started strangling me."

The 1937/38 campaign was to be the first that put York City firmly on the football map and captured the imagination of the locals, who flocked to Bootham Crescent during a run to the FA Cup quarter-finals. The all-time record attendance was set in four successive rounds, rising dramatically from 13,917 to 28,123 and justifying the belief officials like Billy Sherrington had always held about the crowd potential at the fledgling ground.

Second division Coventry arrived at Bootham Crescent in the third round having only lost two of their previous 22 fixtures, with special preparations in the build-up to the match seeing City players drink sherry flips, which was then regarded as a fortifying beverage for cold weather. Sun-ray treatment was also administered and salt baths enjoyed. Fans, meanwhile, arrived early in the morning for the queue to get in the ground, with many eating fish and chips for their lunch. But Coventry's away following was reduced with armament and motor works so busy in the city that many men were not excused work on the morning of the match, leading to the cancellation of one of the special trains that had been organised for the contest.

City prevailed with Reg Baines dragging commanding centre-back George Mason out onto the flanks and creating space for his team-mates, as Peter Spooner, Jimmy Hughes and Sam Earl got on the scoresheet in a 3-2 win. A dramatic ending also saw the final minutes played out with Earl unconscious in the dressing room and blood streaming from the head of Ted Wass, who refused to go off to have it plastered, as the home crowd willed and roared their team on.

West Brom were then seen off by the same scoreline in the fourth round thanks to a Baines hat-trick. The interest in that match was huge with Main

Stand tickets all snapped up pretty much before the advertised on-sale time of 7.30pm. Fans had flocked to the ground and the club decided to open the office earlier, rather than let them get wet in the rain, reasoning that anybody arriving at the correct time would have had to join the back of the queue anyway. With a quarter of the seats allocated to West Brom fans and a further quarter reserved for season-ticket holders, there were many disappointed fans with only 450 stand tickets up for grabs.

Preparation for the tie, meanwhile, was meticulous with manager Tom Mitchell running through his tactics at Bootham Crescent the night before the game after taking the players to Scarborough for the day. He based his game plan on watching the previous season's beaten Cup semi-finalists play at Chelsea. Most local amateur games were postponed due to the heightened interest in the tie and a crowd of 18,795 turned up on the day.

But, when the action got underway, City did not get off to the best start, falling behind to an unfortunate Jack Pinder own goal on 23 minutes. After penalty appeals were waved away when Baines appeared to be brought down, the visitors also hit the post. But, when Baines was felled in the area again on 55 minutes, the referee pointed to the spot and the local centre-forward made no mistake from 12 yards. Pinder was then injured midway through the half and, whilst he was off the pitch receiving treatment from ambulance staff, West Brom regained the lead through Ginger Richardson. Pinder returned to the fray but, with six minutes left, hundreds of home fans had started streaming out of the ground and onto Bootham Crescent to make an early getaway. They were halted when a terrific roar reverberated around the ground and raced back for the terraces to be told that Hughes had been fouled on the halfway line, close to the Popular Stand, allowing Pinder to send in a free kick that Baines, after making a "flying leap", headed to the left of the keeper to level the scores.

It was reported that bells and rattles would go on to create a "real din" around the ground for the rest of the contest and Citizen, recalling that moment years later, said: "You could feel the tenseness in the press box. Often a sports journalist has a hunch that something is going to happen. I felt it that day. Something seemed bound to crack. It did - and it was the Albion defence."

Sure enough, on 87 minutes, Baines forced the ball home from a yard after Earl's right-wing cross with the goal standing despite West Brom players protesting that their keeper James Adams had been fouled. The final whistle then saw supporters spill onto the pitch to mob their team in what is believed to be Bootham Crescent's first pitch invasion. Fans also hoisted the players on to their shoulders and carried them back to the changing room. "My father wouldn't have liked the pitch invasion because he would have thought they were tearing up the pitch," Terry Fowler said.

For Graham Munday, meanwhile, Baines' winning goal would remain his most exhilarating moment in 88 years of watching the club at Bootham Crescent and he also remembered nearly being lynched by angry Baggies fans in the ensuing celebrations. "The first time I saw any trouble was when West Brom came to Bootham Crescent and we beat them in the last minute," he grinned. "In the old days, all the older men wore flat caps and they were good lads. They made sure that if anybody stepped out of line they were out of the ground. You didn't need stewards. But, against West Brom, a couple of their supporters got hold of my scarf and started strangling me because we were cheering, so my mate Ronnie Elliott hit one and a bloke behind me - I don't know who he was - grabbed the other one and smacked him. I never wore a scarf again! Other than that, there was never any real nastiness. We had the tunnel, so fans could swap ends at half-time and you would be going one way and the opposing supporters were going the other."

For Munday, Baines' equaliser stood out in particular. He added: "It was the best game I ever saw at Bootham Crescent and I will never forget it because of the crowd and the way we won it in the dying seconds. But the equaliser was special too. Jack Pinder, who I got to know later in life when he worked on the railway signals and I was at Shouksmith's, took the best free kick I'd ever seen him take. He was about five or six yards in from the Main Stand side corner at the Shipton Street End when he got clattered and went down like a sack of spuds. Jack was a big lad too, so he just got up, put the ball in and, bang, Reg Baines was in there with his head and his fist. A lot of people said he put it in with his hand, but the goal stood. Then, he made it 3-2 and the uproar was terrific. It really sticks in my mind because of the drama attached to the game."

Next, 23,860 fans packed into the ground to see Middlesbrough - another first division outfit - defeated thanks to a Spooner goal. Fowler remembered the Boro game for throwing up one of those dilemmas every supporter faces from time to time when a friend or relative's special occasion clashes with an important game for your team. "I was nine during the 1938 Cup run and I remember I was supposed to be going to a school friend's party when the club were going to play against Middlesbrough," she explained. "They were one of the teams near us and I didn't want to go to the party so my family made excuses and I went to the game."

43

Middlesbrough, clearly perturbed by a trip to Bootham Crescent after events of the previous two rounds, tried to persuade City directors to switch the tie to their Ayresome Park home with an application to the FA, arguing they could cater for the high demand for tickets, but the suggestion was given short shrift. A proposal by the north-east club to double the price of tickets was also rejected with City refusing to place that burden on their regular supporters. Local contractors, meanwhile, were consulted on plans to erect temporary stands for the game to swell the ground's capacity to 30,000, but it was eventually decided that the cost would not justify the return. Banking at the St Olave's Road End, however, was extended right to the hoardings and further banking was added to the opposite end of the ground to cater for several more thousand people, with that process requiring the delivery of 1,000 tons of material, along with a supply of sleepers. Two rows of seats were also lined up around the pitch and inside the fence on the Enclosure and Popular sides to create room for another thousand supporters. There were no seats behind the goalmouth, though, to prevent excited spectators interfering with play, rather than for health-and-safety concerns.

Home tickets were sold out within an hour-and-a-half of going on sale in unprecedented scenes at the club and, despite the office being advertised as open for business at 6.30pm, the first fan arrived at 1pm. A big queue of people was left disappointed when the "sold-out" notices went up at 8pm, with estimates that demand was double the supply. Away tickets were just as sought-after, with Boro's club secretary so harassed that he left his home phone off the hook, only for fans to call his neighbours instead. Ten special trains were put on for the visitors, with most businesses closing down for the day to enable their employees to get to the game.

With the two clubs' colours both being red, rules at the time required each side to change and, after winning a toss to get first choice, Boro elected to play the game in white while City decided on tangerine shirts, supplied by Bert Wilkins, of Clifton, with black shorts. Before the game, meanwhile, one fan wrote into the *Yorkshire Evening Press* asking for fellow supporters to refrain from wearing bowler or trilby hats, as they obscured people's views. He was happy for caps to be worn though! Gates were opened at 12noon with the York Excelsior Band leading the pre-match entertainment. A police transport plan, meanwhile, was put in place to direct motorists to and from the game in an efficient manner with a record number of visitors, even greater than for race meetings, descending upon the city. Alongside a movie camera operator, police were also stationed on top of the Social Club to prevent people climbing on the roof, as had happened against West Brom. Elsewhere, fans who climbed to the top of the scoreboard were ordered down, but some did manage to catch a view of the action from the walls of Lumley Barracks - a good 100 yards away from the playing surface. Adding to the carnival atmosphere at the game, Middlesbrough fans even recreated Dick Turpin's famous ride to York, complete with fancy dress costumes and hobby horses. Hundreds of away fans also cycled the 52-mile trip, with a group of tandem riders arriving singing the popular "Ol' Faithful" chorus. Two female fans were the first City supporters to arrive at the ground at 8.30am, along with camp stools as al fresco dining was the order of the day as the wait for the gates to open began. Untrue rumours that Baines wasn't fit to play also circulated, as outside vendors did a roaring trade selling their wares in both sides' club colours - tangerine and black on this occasion for the hosts. By 1pm, the ground was practically packed with wildly-excited fans engaging in community singing, while rattles, bells and whistles added to the occasion. The *Yorkshire Evening Press* also reported that Middlesbrough's "black-faced mascots marched round with the band and amused the crowd with their antics", including dancing to the music. Before kick-off, City's club mascot, dressed in black trousers, tangerine jacket and black top hat, also marched around the ground with a little Middlesbrough supporter, dressed in his club's normal blue-and-white colours. Keeper Norman Wharton revealed on arrival, meanwhile, that City's players, who were being dubbed the "£50 team", had been instructed to get to the ground early to avoid getting caught up in the chaos.

The Minstermen went on to prevail thanks to Spooner, who ripped in an unstoppable shot, which saw the "crowd on the banks surge forward rather alarmingly, swaying this way and that", according to Citizen who, describing the scenes at the final whistle, wrote: "The pitch was covered with spectators as they carried in the York players; stand cushions whizzed in all directions, and accompanying it was the Yorkshire roar."

Wharton also made two fine first-half saves in the game, while Pinder and bricklayer Claude Barrett were said to have "blotted out" wingers Ralph Birkett and Jackie Milne, who were England and Scotland internationals respectively. Dick Duckworth, Wass and Ted Hathway's quick tackling, meanwhile, subdued England international trio Micky Fenton, Wilf Mannion and George Camsell - the latter being limited to only one good shot all game, despite a record of 18 goals in nine appearances for his country. Perhaps the biggest illustration of the game's significance came when referee JE Williams, of Bolton, deemed the contest so memorable that he asked to keep the match ball - a request that was granted.

Among the messages of congratulations that flooded in at Bootham Crescent afterwards was one from the crew of HMS York, who sent a cablegram from the West Indies, reading: "Heartiest congratulations on your win on Saturday. Keep it up." A few years earlier, City had provided the ship's team with a kit to play in, boasting the club colours. The Social Club, meanwhile, hosted a dance a few days after the victory, attended by supporters, players and their wives with everybody described as being in the "jolliest of spirits".

Views at the ground were not pleasing everybody, though, with Mr W Turner, of Herbert Street, York, writing in to the *Yorkshire Evening Press* to complain: "Would it be too much to ask the directors to see that the banks at both ends of the ground are made so that we can see the game? I think that everybody is entitled to that privilege when they pay for it, but how many get it? The bankings are not uniform. There are big drops and holes all over them. I am surprised that the levels were not taken from two feet below the playing-pitch level. This would have done away with the expense of the wooden rails round the ground and given everybody a chance to see the game."

The quarter-finals brought an all-Yorkshire clash at Bootham Crescent against Huddersfield on March 5, 1938. It was the tie that manager Mitchell was relishing, as he reasoned: "I do not think we could have had a better draw, because it gives us a great chance of going into the semi-final. After beating West Bromwich and Middlesbrough, we are not afraid of Huddersfield, however good their cup reputation maybe."

For the first time during the run, ticket prices were increased for the last-eight contest, although it was estimated that there would still be room for 10,000 "shilling" spectators on the Shipton Street bank in "an effort to cater for all classes", according to Citizen. In the following days, a decision was subsequently made to drop the price at the St Olave's Road end of the ground to one shilling too. Prices for the Main Stand, Popular Stand and Enclosure remained at the higher prices. Licencing hours in the city, meanwhile, were extended until 5.30pm on the day of the game, although an application to open an hour earlier than 11am was rejected. The players spent four days at Scarborough in preparation for the game and paid a visit to the Regal Cinema the Thursday evening before the tie when organist Mr Edward Farley played his latest City theme song that subsequently rang out at the match. A special 20-page souvenir programme was also published for the club at the Herald Printing Works and sold for two pence.

Fans pack into Bootham Crescent for the FA Cup quarter-final against Huddersfield Town in 1938, which attracted the ground's record attendance of 28,123

Turnstiles, which opened at noon, were closed shortly before kick-off and an all-time record crowd of 28,123, reaping receipts of £2,736, witnessed a 0-0 draw. Such was the clamour to see the tie that one house owner close to Bootham Crescent had nine people ask him on the day of the game if they could watch the action from one of his bedroom windows. From a more conventional viewing point, Viscount Halifax, the foreign secretary, watched the game with his wife and was accompanied by the Hon Charles Wood MP for York and his partner at the front of the directors' box, attracting 20 photographers poised to take his picture. Five days later, Viscount Halifax would meet German foreign minister Herr von Ribbentrop with the prospect of World War Two looming on the horizon. Five newsreel cameras were also erected on top of the Popular Stand and others were on the field waiting for the appearance of the teams. Bells, rattles, whistles and accordions all added to the pre-match atmosphere, meanwhile, as did the performance of the York Excelsior Band, whose drum major received the biggest cheer during their march around the ground when he threw his staff in the air. Some spectators spilled over the barriers and lined the touchlines, whilst others were perched on top of the Popular Stand or the Social Club, with Munday recalling: "We were all crammed in against

47

Supporters cram in for Bootham Crescent's record crowd of 28,123 for the 1938 FA Cup quarter-final against Huddersfield

Huddersfield and, while there were 28,000 there who paid, those that came over the school wall was nobody's business. That's why it was so packed behind the goal."

When the game kicked off, City controlled long periods of the first half with the first division visitors unsettled by their hosts' pace and strong tackling. But, after half-time, the game was a more even affair with the Terriers hitting the bar and Spooner seeing his header cleared off the line. Both defences ultimately came out on top with Pinder outstanding for Mitchell's team. The big crowd also meant a bumper pay day for a teenaged Hemenway. "I was selling programmes that day," he explained. "They cost a penny

York City captain Dick Duckworth (left) and Huddersfield Town's skipper Alf Young toss-up ahead of kick-off for the 1938 FA Cup quarter-final against Huddersfield Town

back then and, for every dozen we sold, we were paid a penny. That was a good day because, if you sold four-dozen, that meant you were well-off back then. In those days, you could sell programmes outside the ground, so I used to dash straight up Bootham Crescent, where there was a chemist's on the corner because they had got cover there if it rained. I was a bit quicker on my feet than the other lads and could get there before them. As soon as the fans stopped walking towards the ground, we could go to the match and, after I had handed my money in, I forced my way right down to the front. I used my elbows to get there because I was 14 and not that small anymore."

Billy Sherrington's post-match taxi to NatWest Bank might have also strained under the weight of the proceeds with his daughter saying: "My father used to go off to the ground at 9am for match days and he would not leave until all the gate money had been counted. The stewards manned the gates and took the money in during those early years at Bootham Crescent and a chap called Harry Ward from the Supporters' Club used to count it - all in coppers and silvers. Then, my father had a taxi booked for a certain time after the match. He would take all the money to NatWest Bank in Coney Street and they would put it all in the night safe. The taxi would wait while he did it. People wouldn't dare do that now because they would be attacked. My father never had a car - he used to cycle everywhere. I went to games with my mother initially and then my mother and my husband so, later, when we drove, we had his parking space and we watched games in the directors' box." That routine was still being followed in 1963, when City fan John Chaplin, then a teenager in his first job, was asked to help with the money counting. "I worked for National Provincial and a friend of mine worked in the little bank in York," Chaplin recalled. "He knew I supported the club so he said, if I wanted, I could come down at half-time and get a cup of tea while counting the money. It was in 1963 and there wasn't that much to count. There would also be a couple of us doing it, so I got to see most of the second half. It would then get bagged up and somebody else took it to the night safe in Coney Street."

Hemenway, meanwhile, remembered that Cup side's ability to punch their own weight. "Dick Duckworth was a dirty devil, Ted Wass was as hard as nails, Ted Hathway was another rough one and they didn't get past Jack Pinder too often," he laughed. Along with the intimidation, there was some flair, however, with Hemenway adding: "Peter Spooner was a good player." City were knocked out 2-1 in the replay at Leeds Road in front of 58,066 fans, with Sunderland awaiting the winners in the semi-finals.

York City's team for the 1938/39 season pose for a photograph at Bootham Crescent

A few years later, meanwhile, Hemenway was even using the ground for courting purposes. "I used to take my future wife there," he laughed. "We would go there with my dad but split when we got through the turnstiles. Once, she said to me: 'Why don't we watch the games with your dad?' But I told her: 'He's too embarrassing.'"

The end of the season, meanwhile, saw Pinder awarded a benefit match at Bootham Crescent against Grimsby and he also received a share of the proceeds from a series of whist drives held in the social club. He was the first York-born player to be bestowed with such an honour and Hughie Gallacher played for the visitors with a crowd of almost 5,000 turning up. Both teams then toasted Pinder's loyalty at the Royal Station Hotel afterwards. The final league game went on to double up as a benefit match for another loyal servant Stan Fox, with the pair receiving a total of £300 to split between each other.

At the annual shareholders' meeting, meanwhile, it was revealed that a profit of £3,518 had been made by the club over the season and, following the big Cup-tie attendances, chairman Arthur Brown declared: "I am satisfied that there is a public to cater for and the board is determined to do its utmost to meet the demand for good class football."

Improvements to the stadium also continued to be made with tarmac laid on the Main Stand's Enclosure terracing during the off-season. In October, meanwhile, the old recreation and games room at the Shipton Street End of the Social Club was transformed into a newly-furbished lounge, with the entrance from the car park, allowing stand patrons to enjoy their refreshments in "good surroundings". Former player Malcolm Comrie was appointed the enlarged Social Club's new steward with his wife the stewardess. His then club Bradford City allowed him to take up the job, but retained his registration, meaning he could not play for City or any other side.

The 1938 Christmas Day fixture, meanwhile, saw a record collection taken of £11 14s 4d on behalf of the Christmas Cheer Fund for the Unemployed. Any lingering festive sprit was doused, though, in January 1939 when Bootham Crescent staged its heaviest-ever home defeat with Rochdale winning 7-0 on a muddy and heavy playing surface. The hosts lost Pinder to injury at 2-0 down in the first half, but he reappeared to play as a bystander at outside-right after the interval, even though supporters were shouting for him to leave the field on account of his helplessness. Joe Firth, who had been transferred to Rochdale from City just a few weeks earlier, scored two of the visitors' goals.

It was reiterated that year, meanwhile, that fans watching games from the Popular Stand would continue to only pay one shilling, which was virtually unheard of at other grounds in the country for a covered vantage point. The first reports of a York City Social Club darts team, playing their fixtures at the ground, also emerged in 1939.

At the end of the campaign, Wass was given a benefit match against Newcastle, having been told his services at the club would not be retained following a 10-year association. He went on to score an own goal in front of a 3,000-strong crowd before also receiving the proceeds from a dance in the Social Club two nights later, with music played by Ted Rowell's band and admission costing a shilling for players and supporters. At the end of the season, it was also revealed that cushion sales at the ground had amounted to £7 9s 3d and band collections had raised a profit of £9 14s 1 1/2d.

Bootham Crescent was a hub for the physical training of young people during the War years. Here one group are put through their paces during a netball session on the pitch and another are attending gymnastics classes

CHAPTER 5

The Popular Stand tunnel serves as an air-raid shelter

"One of the directors had a house next to Bootham Crescent and the house next door to him got bombed."

One of the most sombre moments in Bootham Crescent's history came on Sunday, September 3, 1939 when, the day after War was declared, the players were summoned to the ground by secretary Billy Sherrington, who explained that all football had been suspended indefinitely with the expectation that the club would have no revenue or income. In consultation with chairman William Sessions, the players were given their insurance cards and told they were free to return home. They were then thanked for their services and wished the best of luck in whatever sphere they found themselves.

Preparations for the season had started as normal with a practice match, attended by more than 3,000 people, held in August, along with a League Benevolent Fund fixture against Hull, as numbered shirts made a debut at Bootham Crescent. City had opened the league campaign too with a 2-2 home draw against Chester, in which Billy Allen bagged a brace. Stanley Rous, the secretary of the FA, had been due to visit for the next match at home to Lincoln, meanwhile, as part of a scheduled trip to York.

Many other clubs continued to play friendly fixtures despite the outbreak of War and, a month later, City were admitted into a new North-East division, with half of their ten opponents first or second division teams, from the 82 Football League clubs who wanted to carry on staging games during the War period. The League agreed that clubs could use the services of players who lived or were stationed nearby and, with York being a military centre with the likes of RAF bases at Harrogate, Church Fenton, Pocklington, Elvington, Tholthorpe, East Moor, Melbourne, Dishforth, Topcliffe and Marston Moor on the doorstep, Bootham Crescent would go on to see some of the game's finest talents don the club's shirts during the War period, including legendary Everton and England striker Dixie Dean, goalkeeping great Sam Bartram,

Arsenal centre-half and Middlesex cricketer Leslie Compton, Blackpool and England's George Eastham, Aston Villa and Scotland's Frank O'Donnell and Sunderland and England's Raich Carter. Future Bootham Crescent legend Alf Patrick also played his first game for the club during those War-time matches.

Unlike many seasons prior to the outbreak of War, the club also made a profit during hostilities and a teenaged Terry Fowler was responsible for getting many of those famous names to Bootham Crescent. She explained: "During the war-time, my father felt he ought to do something else apart from running the football club. The army record offices were at what is now the Grange Hotel at the top of Bootham Crescent, so he volunteered to work there. That meant he could easily slip down to Bootham Crescent when needed. He was in charge of the civil section and casualties. A colonel used to look after the army side and, if they weren't very busy, he would say to my father: 'You go down and look after your football club'. It obviously depended on how many casualties there were at the time. I was in my teens as a schoolgirl and, when it was very busy, he used to say to me: 'Try and get me an outside-left for Saturday please'. So, I would ring people like Newcastle and ask if they had anybody who could play for us. It was interesting, I liked it and it worked. I got to know Sam Bartram very well and a chap called Keith Bannister who played for Sheffield Wednesday. He was somewhere local and there were a lot stationed around here during the war. The War-time games worked really well. They got good gates because people wanted something to take their minds off things." With such unprecedented talent at the home club's disposal, extraordinary results were witnessed at the ground as Middlesbrough were seen off 9-5 and Leeds thrashed 8-1.

The tunnel at the back of the Popular Stand, meanwhile, was used as an air-raid shelter for pupils and staff at the nearby Shipton Street School. It was made of concrete apart from the back, which was reinforced to provide adequate protection. Peter Turpin was a nine-year-old Shipton Street pupil who regularly took shelter during the air-raid drills and, looking back, he appreciated the efforts teachers made to create a calm environment. "When the siren went, we were all programmed to hold our partner's hands and told not to run, but to walk at a steady pace and follow the teacher," Turpin recalled. "We went out of the school's back door and walked through the yard, then behind the huge pile of earth near the Shipton Street End and into the Popular Stand tunnel. When we got in there, we sat there and sang. I can remember sitting next to my partner Alan Midgeley and we were all quite happy for half-an-hour or three-quarters-of-an-hour, before we filed back to school after the air raid. It became a bit of a habit for us all after a while and we just did it, whilst always being instructed not to run. As youngsters, I don't think we realised what it was all about and I suppose it was quite exciting, but the teachers must have been a bit concerned, because they were in charge of all the children from the school and there must have been about 80 of us. It was just us and the teachers - our parents were never there - and I remember Mr Lund being the sportsmaster and Miss Hessle was the headmistress."

Players who participated in the war fixtures were initially paid 30 shillings a match, which later rose to £2, with admission fixed at the same pre-War prices, while previously-purchased season tickets were valid for that first campaign. Soldiers in uniform, however, paid a half-price sum of six pence.

The first organised game at Bootham Crescent following the outbreak of War came on Saturday, October 14, 1939 as Sheffield United visited the ground in a friendly as a pre-cursor to the regional league fixtures. It was a notable game also for the appearance again in City colours of Reg Stockill, following his spells with Arsenal, Derby and Luton. He grabbed both goals in a 4-2 defeat with an encouraging crowd of 3,000 turning up.

Middlesbrough visited Bootham Crescent for the first official fixture seven days later and enjoyed a 3-1 victory in front of 4,500 fans. Stockill was again on target for City, although he also conceded a penalty for handball. Within an hour of the game finishing, though, outside-left George Lee was reporting

George Lee scores his 100th peace and war-time goal for York City with a penalty during the Football League War Cup semi-final, second leg match against Sheffield Wednesday

to be medically examined for military service, becoming the first City player to be affected by the declaration of War. He had been given special permission to play in the game, allowing him to report an hour later than scheduled. Allen - the scorer of those two goals against Chester - was the next to receive a call-up.

Just before Christmas, meanwhile, the Hunt Cup charity match between Tom Mitchell's York City XI and York Police was staged at Bootham Crescent with all proceeds going to York Hospital. A rematch was also arranged for early in the New Year. A York Senior Cup semi-final between Tadcaster Albion and York RI and its replay were held at the ground too, as club officials endeavoured to carry on providing a community hub for the city's football enthusiasts. The York Junior Cup, Minor Cup, Half-Holiday Trophy and York Schools' Cup finals continued to be hosted by the ground, along with all the York City Supporters' Works Cup fixtures, with the latter resulting in a £21 14s profit for the club. Dringhouses and York RI also met in a York Minor League title decider and returned for a charity fixture in aid of the NUR Orphans Fund, while the York Schools Sports' finals were staged at the stadium too.

During the summer months, the York City FC Social Club darts' team also organised an open tournament for teams in York, ensuring there was still leisure activity at the ground outside of football. The latter stages of the competition proved so popular that people, who were not Supporters' Club members, needed to get advance tickets to be admitted. Money, meanwhile, was raised to donate dartboards to troops and a women's only tournament was launched as well. The Social Club remained active and, even though membership numbers dropped considerably due to service duty, Saturday night concerts were held there. Soldiers were made to feel particularly welcome with dominoes another popular pursuit.

Bootham Crescent also offered its use for physical training classes after the Central Council of Recreative Physical Training visited the ground to inspect its facilities. Keep-fit classes were, thereafter, organised for two or three evenings a week, designed to train men of all ages, with activities including boxing and an arms' drill with sticks serving as dummy rifles. The Lord Mayor of York (Alderman RJ Pulleyn) joined in the first one-hour drill with 140 other men, aged between 16 and 60. They were put through their paces by former York rugby-league player Gurnos Rees, along with several army and civilian instructors.

With the club committed to staging War-time fixtures, but many of the club's former professional players having work or military commitments, trials were held at Bootham Crescent in August 1940 to run the rule over local amateur players in a Reds v Whites match that also included those from the previous season who were still available for duty. Some local amateurs did, indeed, go on to get their chance to play for City at Bootham Crescent, with two of the first being R Jones, of Dringhouses, and George Mortimer, of York RI. The opening match of the 1940/41 season was again against Middlesbrough, with right-half Matt Busby - the future legendary Manchester United manager - playing for the visitors, who City beat 4-3. Busby was described as having "showed himself a class player" by Citizen in the *Yorkshire Evening Press*. The York Royal Army Pay Corps, meanwhile, formed a team to compete in the York War Emergency League and used Bootham Crescent to play their Saturday fixtures when it wasn't being used by the club.

In October 1940, the ground's first price increase saw the Popular Stand's shilling admission go up by 1d due to a rise in entertainment tax, but members of the forces continued to be admitted for six pence. On Christmas Day, the ground was also loaned out for a representative game between the York Saturday and Midweek Leagues with gate proceeds going towards the Spitfire Fund, which had been launched by Lord Beaverbrook in an attempt to attract the resources to speed up the production of aircraft fighters. A 19-year-old Alf Patrick, of New Earswick, played for the Saturday League XI. International forward Eastham, meanwhile, became the first star player to guest for City at Bootham Crescent in a 3-2 League War Cup victory over Bradford. A small profit of £27 8s 3d was then reported at the end of the season, further justifying the club's decision to carry on hosting games during the War.

In the close season, Bootham Crescent remained active with The Fitness for Service summer campaign again seeing a series of sessions for the Air Training Corps take place at the ground. Physical training exercises were overseen with one targeted at boys aged between 14 and 20. The onus was on developing the fitness of young adults who would eventually join the Services and ball games, relay races and unarmed combat ensured the hour-long sessions were not just treated as "drill nights". Later in the summer, a physical training and gymnastic display, organised by the Rowntree Day Continuation School (a body that provided leisure pursuits outside the national curriculum), saw 400 girls and boys demonstrate their skills on a Tuesday evening in July. It was again aimed at stimulating greater interest in physical training with rhythmic physical training performed by the girls, followed by an exhibition netball game. The boys also gave a gymnastic display, while the Rowntree's Band was in attendance as well for the free event.

A host of internationals, including future legendary Liverpool boss Bill Shankly, meanwhile, played in an Army (Yorkshire Area) v RAF (Northern Counties) match and, in preparation for the 1941/42 campaign, local amateurs were again invited to attend Tuesday and Thursday night training sessions. One player Horwell, from York RI, went on to score all the goals in a 6-0 victory for the Reds against Whites in a pre-season public practice match that included pre-War time City players and former professionals playing as guests.

In November, the English game's most legendary marksman - Dixie Dean - was then donning City colours. England international Dean created a Football League record in 1927/28 when he scored 60 goals in 39 games. A trooper in the War, he was recruited from the Lancers and made his City debut against Gateshead at Bootham Crescent, scoring a "grand" trademark first-half header that "fairly flashed into the net" during a 4-3 defeat. Carter, of Sunderland and England, was the next notable guest to feature for City in January. Towards the end of the season, meanwhile, supporters coming through the turnstiles were donating their own spare clothing coupons - introduced during the War-time rationing period - to help purchase new kit for the club.

One of York's darkest days then saw the Minster city bombed in the early hours of Wednesday, April 29, 1942 in a German reprisal for an attack on Cologne. The stadium suffered slight damage after houses at the Shipton Street End were flattened, with many fans and officials suffering directly or indirectly, as a consequence of the awful devastation.

"Sam Gawthorne - one of the directors - had a house next to Bootham Crescent and the house next door to him got bombed," Irene Hagyard revealed. But, with typical War-time resilience, the ground still staged the Senior Cup final four days later as No 6 ITC beat RAF Linton 2-1.

Both teams lined up to observe a silence in memory of the city's 94 raid victims - ten of whom lived in Bootham Crescent and five in Burton Stone Lane - and the KOYLI Band were also in attendance. The damage to the ground saw the Main Stand pitted with holes from the incendiary bombs but, despite a permit being requested to make the repairs, it was rejected eight months later by the licensing officer, meaning those in seats underneath had to grin and bear any wet weather for the time being.

City, meanwhile, hosted Bradford, as planned, just another week afterwards. A crowd of 2,796 turned up for a 2-1 win which prompted Citizen to write that "York enthusiasts want and appreciate their sport, blitz or no blitz." Those brave supporters were rewarded when Aston Villa and Scotland striker O'Donnell guested for the club in the next game at Bootham Crescent - a Combined Counties Cup semi-final against Middlesbrough. O'Donnell went on to net within half-a-minute of kick-off and headed in a second during a 4-1 triumph in front of a 4,011-strong crowd. City also defeated Halifax 2-0 in the first leg of the final in front of another strong home crowd of 4,710 and subsequently secured their first War-time silverware despite a 4-3 second-leg loss at the Shay.

An army final, between teams from Lumley Barracks, meanwhile, was arranged at Bootham Crescent to raise money for the York Air Raid Distress Fund, as was a match between two works teams featuring ex-Minstermen Malcolm Comrie and Joe Hawkins. Another game in aid of the same charity saw City take on an RAF XI, managed by former boss - Pilot Officer Tom Mitchell. His team was packed with professional stars, including internationals Peter Doherty and Alf Young, although efforts to get Stanley Matthews released from service were thwarted. Supporters were encouraged to pay extra for the programme and the King's Own Yorkshire Light Infantry Band played before the game and at the interval. A total of £100 was raised from a crowd of 1,618 with Doherty hitting a hat-trick in a 5-4 win for the RAF. Future England international Len Shackleton, then just 20 but whose later exploits for Newcastle and Sunderland would see him dubbed the 'Clown Prince of Soccer', scored one of City's consolations as a guest and was described by Citizen as "one of the best War-time discoveries among inside forwards" and a "young player with ideas and should do well".

That summer, meanwhile, the Royal Army Pay Corps staged a sports day at the ground on a Friday night in July, as part of the War-time Holidays-at-Home programme. Prizes were awarded for the tea-and-saucer, hooded horses and fireman's chair races, amongst others. Senior schools and junior schools' sports days were also held at the ground.

After the start of the new campaign, the RAF's Fighter and Bomber Command teams, featuring many English and Scottish professionals, played out a 4-4 draw at Bootham Crescent with proceeds from the 1,400 crowd going towards the 110th Squadron of the Air Training Corps. A match between a Tom Lockie-managed Football League XI and Northern Command was also hosted by the ground, with City left-back Gordon Jones, who was picked up from Dringhouses in 1941, called up for the former. It was the first time a northern third division ground had been chosen to stage a Football League representative side fixture, confirming that Bootham Crescent was now established as a venue deemed worthy of staging such occasions. The Football

League XI finished comfortable 9-2 winners. Earlier, the Auxiliary Territorial Service - the women's branch of the British Army - had given a drill display before the game and at half-time when the West Yorkshire Regiment Band also played. Included in the League XI side was Charlton and England War-time goalkeeping legend Bartram, who had just made his first guest appearance for City in a 4-3 victory over Newcastle at Bootham Crescent, in which O'Donnell scored all four home goals. Bartram was joined in the team by future legends of the game Tom Finney and Shackleton, as well as established star Carter. Finney and Shackleton both scored twice with Carter also on target. A crowd of 5,500 watched the game with receipts going towards the Northern Command Sports Board Welfare Funds. The game took place in October, which proved a great month for Bootham Crescent star-spotters as Arsenal full-back Compton guested for City for the first time and scored twice in a 5-2 triumph over Grimsby.

Some of the best football that had been witnessed at Bootham Crescent was now being played with Bradford seen off 9-1 as six different marksmen made the scoresheet, prompting visiting manager Fred Westgarth to comment that he had not seen anything to equal the display during the War. A second home match with Bradford, meanwhile, was set aside for a collection on behalf of the Football Association's Prisoners of War Fund in conjunction with the Red Cross. It was also announced that a profit of £1,041 was made during the 1941/42 season and, at the annual shareholders' meeting, chairman Sessions announced that one of the first things to be considered by the club after the War should be the purchase of Bootham Crescent.

In January, a City home game was chosen to be broadcast on BBC radio for the first-ever time with the second half against Sunderland commented on from 4.15pm. Sessions encouraged supporters to "see that we have some good cheering coming through over the microphone. It will help the City team as well. So let those far away from the City know, in good cup-tie style, that you are there!" A record War-time crowd of 5,494 subsequently turned up to cheer the team on during a 4-0 win with three saved for BBC listeners during the second period.

That figure was smashed, though, when Newcastle were seen off 4-3 on aggregate and 2-0 on the day in the last 32 of the Football League War North Cup in front of 11,385 fans, showing City's ability to compete on a level playing field with, and even overcome, their north-east superiors during hostilities. Next, Bradford were beaten again - this time 1-0 in the first leg of the last 16

Supporters, including soldiers, perch on the top of the Popular Stand to get a view of York City's Football League War Cup semi-final, second leg clash against Sheffield Wednesday

tie at Bootham Crescent, where record War-time receipts of £686 were taken from an attendance of 10,827, due to an increase to three shillings for stand admission. Popular England international Sailor Brown teed up George Lee for the only effort, which was often City's most-common source of a War-time goal. The Minstermen would go on to complete a 5-1 aggregate triumph.

Supporters for the quarter-final home tie against Chesterfield were then encouraged to get to the ground early with access problems caused by the Popular Stand tunnel's transformation into an air-raid shelter and a reduced number of stewards. Another War-time record gate of 14,007 was attracted, with receipts of £894 and the home side enjoyed a convincing win with Brown and Cecil McCormack on target before the same margin of victory was repeated during the away leg.

Prices for the semi-final, second leg against Sheffield Wednesday, meanwhile, were confirmed by the Football League at a hiked-up price of seven shillings and 3d for Main Stand seats, which were available with a pre-purchased ticket from the ground only. The Main Stand Enclosure price was also increased to 2s 6d. Special turnstiles, meanwhile, were erected in the car park at the Shipton Street End of the ground, where admission was 1s 3d. At the St Olave's Road

61

End and in the Popular Stand, the charge was 1s 6d, although women, boys and members of the forces were admitted for 1s. The cheaper price for the Shipton Street End was to encourage more supporters to walk that little bit further to pay the cheaper price, which helped avoid congestion at the other end of the ground.

Some shine was taken off the occasion, though, when City suffered a 3-0 defeat in the first leg at Hillsborough, having been deprived of the services of Brown, who was recalled by parent club Charlton to score the goal that got them into the South Cup final. But, with Brown back in the side, 16,350 fans still turned up and receipts of £1,398 10s 9d were taken. It represented the club's biggest War-time attendance and many more supporters watched the game perched on top of the Popular Stand. Lee scored from the penalty spot on 34 minutes to claim his 100th goal for the club during the peace and War-time periods, but he was injured and carried off with his assailant - visiting centre-back Walter Millership - subjected to a "great deal of booing". The City marksman did reappear for the second half and played on with a damaged collarbone, but it was the visitors who managed to add to the scoreline at the death, completing a 4-1 aggregate triumph. The cup exploits would help the club report another profit of £2,187 15s 11d, though, over the course of the season. Bartram, meanwhile, played in the RAF Cup final at his new adopted home for the Training Unit against the Fighting Unit.

As the 1943/44 season kicked off, the club announced plans to run a junior York City A team in the local York League, with promising goalkeeper Peter Pickering among those invited to attend Thursday night training sessions at Bootham Crescent, overseen by coach and former left-back Sam Johnson. A total of 35 hopefuls turned up for the first one and admission to A team games was set at 3d, with the first a friendly against the King's Royal Rifle Corps. Local players were also encouraged to attend training sessions overseen by Johnson and Lockie, irrespective of whether they wanted to play for City or not. Around 300 fans, meanwhile, watched the A team's first official fixture at Bootham Crescent, which resulted in a 6-1 home win over Cooke's A. The side was launched partly with the post-War years in mind, with a belief that local talent would need to be relied upon to put together a new team, with a dearth of professional footballers anticipated due to war casualties and retirement. Pickering was in goal for that first fixture and John Lawson, Terry Walker and Eddie Bentall, who went on to have brief post-War City careers, also played. By September, meanwhile, the club had finally received permission to repair the damage caused to the Main Stand 17 months on from the April 1942 bombings, with the work completed by contractors during the following month.

It was not only famous footballers, meanwhile, that were attracted to Bootham Crescent during the hostilities. A game against Bradford in December 1943 brought one of the silver screen's leading ladies at the time to the stadium, although she was not familiar to everybody in City's boardroom, as Terry Fowler revealed. "I remember one funny incident during the war time," Fowler recalled. "There was a very famous film star called Anna Neagle. She was the top star of her day - not a bimbo type, but a serious actress. She played Queen Victoria and those types of roles. She had come to York to some factory for a promotional visit with her husband Herbert Wilcox who was a producer. She was keen on football and an Arsenal fan and asked if she could come to the ground for a game. The chairman at the time was Mr William Sessions and somebody had told him she was a very famous film star so, in the boardroom at half-time when people were having a cup of tea, he said, being a very gracious sort of man and a noted Quaker: 'As one of our guests today we are very pleased to have Miss Beagle'. We all cringed and people started hissing 'Neagle' to him but she laughed and he was completely unaware of his mistake. As a Quaker, he had probably never been in a cinema."

The York Minor League, meanwhile, continued to have a strong relationship with the club and an end-of-season 3-3 draw between champions Dringhouses and a League representative side was played at Bootham Crescent. In July 1944, however, there was a poignant scene in the Social Club when, at the Supporters' Club's annual meeting, a short silence was observed in memory of former player Sergeant Leonard "Taffy" Milner, who had been killed in action in Normandy.

October then saw a City side hit double figures in a Football League recognised fixture for the first time when they thrashed Gateshead 10-2 at Bootham Crescent. GH Hawkins led the rout with four goals, Richard Dix hit a hat-trick, with Fred Scott (2) and Tommy Dawson the other marksmen.

Hull City, meanwhile, used Bootham Crescent as a "home" ground for a fixture against Newcastle when the Boulevard Stadium they were sharing with the rugby team was needed for a Yorkshire Cup tie. West Yorkshire neighbours Bradford also hosted a game against Gateshead at the ground when their Park Avenue venue was required for an FA XI v The Army clash. During this period, changes were made too to entrance procedures at the ground with all boys now told to gain admission through the Shipton Street End of the car park, along with service personnel in uniform, via separate turnstiles.

As the 1944/45 campaign drew to an anti-climax, Bartram brought smiles to fans' faces when, after a long run-up, he converted a 40th-minute penalty during a 6-1 Football League North War Cup victory over Bradford, while Jack Pinder dropped back to guard the net. It was the first of three that Bartram would convert for City after accepting a challenge to assume spot-kick duties. The Charlton legend was also successful twice from 12 yards in the second half of a 2-0 Tyne, Wear & Tees Cup triumph over Darlington with Citizen reporting that he "banged in terrific shots". A busy Bartram played centre back for Harrogate RAF, meanwhile, in the Yorkshire Area RAF Cup semi-final at Bootham Crescent, although he cleared the crossbar with a penalty in that match. In an address to the Social Club, Bartram went on to declare that he had never enjoyed playing for a club more than in York, as War-time football began to draw to a close.

Bartram's biggest fan at the time was future *Yorkshire Evening Press* City reporter Malcolm Huntington who was then an impressionable schoolboy watching his first live matches before going on himself to play for York City boys as a goalkeeper. Speaking before his death in 2017, Huntington recalled: "My first game was on September 6, 1941. It was York City v Leeds and York won 1-0. We had great players like Sailor Brown and Frank O'Donnell playing for the club. I also saw Dixie Dean play for York and there were few bigger names in the game than him back then. My dad took me to every home match after that first game and we stood in the Grosvenor Road end, which is where I got my love of goalkeeping from because I was watching Sam Bartram playing in front of me and decided I wanted to be like him. He was very spectacular and a showman. He used to dive at balls that he maybe didn't need to and he always had a word for the kids outside the ground, where he would sign autographs. He was a hell of a good goalkeeper - one of the best around - and I think I learnt a lot about the position just by watching him. I also remember his penalty taking. The team had missed one and the story was Sam Bartram went into the dressing room and said to Joe Wilson, who was the captain at the time and played at centre half: 'Nobody should ever miss a penalty with that big gaping space to shoot at'. I always remembered what Joe Wilson's words were in reply. He said: 'All right Sammy boy, you will take the next penalty'. He did and he scored and then he scored two against Darlington. He used to set off running from his own penalty box and then he would just whack the ball into the roof of the net. It was a bit like how Geoff Hurst used to take them. He relied on the goalkeepers moving, which they generally did. But it all went awry after the War when he went back to Charlton. They had heard about his penalties and decided he should take one for them. He ran all the way from his penalty area but struck the ball so powerfully that he hit the crossbar and the ball bounced over his head, which must have been some shot with the old leather balls back then. He then set off running and just got back in time to save somebody's shot at his goal and he never took another penalty." Reserve keeper Bob Ferguson also tried the same for City against Sunderland a few weeks after Bartram's first successful conversion against Bradford but cleared the crossbar.

The legendary Bartram also impressed Fowler, who said: "Sam Bartram was probably the best player I saw play for York. He was a brave and acrobatic keeper. My father also liked him. He had a flamboyant style and that was all accentuated by his red hair and green jumpers."

The ground continued to host various different games with the final of the Northern Command Inter-Unit Cup seeing 54th Training Regiment, RAC beat 140th Octu, Royal Engineers 7-1, as Football League players again featured on both sides. In April, an RAF Northern Area team also took on a Polish National XI at Bootham Crescent, with the former triumphing 3-1.

Looking back, Huntington added that the War period at Bootham Crescent provided a great source of escapism for fans and families during a grave period in the history of the world. "Everybody looked forward to the weekend because you always knew there was going to be a good team to watch," he explained. "We turned up wondering which players would be in the York side. Some of them only played once or twice because they were only in the area fleetingly and it was a time when you knew York City could literally beat anybody. They used to put out one hell of a good side and, generally speaking, they always entertained you and I was just like any other young boy then. It was all about the pure enjoyment of being there every other Saturday to watch my home-town team play, while falling in love with the club."

Turpin was another impressionable youngster, who was star-struck by the big names suddenly representing his home-town club. "I remember watching Raich Carter and Sam Bartram and it was quite a thrill for us to see players like them," he explained.

Huntington reasoned, meanwhile, that the players who would go on to represent the club when the Football League programme resumed benefitted greatly from rubbing shoulders with some of the game's greats during that golden age of War-time football, explaining: "Sailor Brown was a very tricky, ball-playing inside-left. He was bandy-legged, bald and small but he made George Lee, who played outside-left, the player he became. He gave him the ball all the time and

George Lee went on to score 100 goals for York City (including 90 during the War) and signed for Nottingham Forest for a then club record transfer fee of £7,500 before winning the FA Cup final with West Brom."

With peace declared, Bootham Crescent could look back on a somewhat golden era for football in the city, but the deaths of players, who had represented the club, were a solemn reminder of the War's human cost. Private Samuel Grenville Roberts (five War-time appearances, one goal), Sergeant Leonard Milner (12 Football League appearances, four goals, plus three War-time appearances), Sergeant Gac Reynolds (13 War-time appearances), Sergeant Alfred Edward Bonass (six Football League appearances, plus one War-time appearance) and Sergeant Eric Robinson (13 War-time appearances, four goals) all lost their lives and each would be recognised in December 2011 when five marble plaques were unveiled to honour their memory before a 7-0 home win against Kettering. The plaques were positioned within the brick work of the main Bootham Crescent offices with bugler Colin Carr playing the *Last Post* after a service was held in the car park in front of them by Rev Steve Benford, of St Luke's Church. Families of some of the players attended the ceremony, along with club directors, officials, players and then manager Gary Mills. Lifelong City fan and Dunkirk veteran Bob Burns had helped club historian Dave Batters identify the players and ascertain their War-time roles - a process that entailed several years of work. The plaques, meanwhile, were sponsored by Mr Burns, Shepherd Building Group, Howard Lewis, James Burns and David Doggett, while the club and its vice-presidents matched their gestures with donations to the Help For Heroes charity. Sophie McGill, City's communications and community director at the time, said: "It was an extremely emotional occasion, and I think learning about the history of five players who made the ultimate sacrifice puts everything into perspective for the current players." Bonass was the last City player to perish due to the War in October when, following the end of hostilities, the transport plane he was in crashed over Tockwith just days before he was due to play at Bootham Crescent.

CHAPTER 6

Fans flock to games during post-War boom

"That's what you did back then - you went bird-nesting, swimming in the Ouse until midnight and sneaked into the football."

With German forces surrendering in May 1945, there was an attempt to restore some semblance of normality as the War finally drew to a close and, as a consequence, national Football League fixtures were originally issued in June. But a decision was subsequently made by the end of July, which had the full support of club secretary Billy Sherrington, to arrange regional fixtures for another season to help make the transition to peace-time football a smooth one. A new fixture list was, therefore, issued on August 4 - three weeks before the start of the campaign.

Player recruitment was of primary importance with a team selected from the West Riding by City's scouts meeting the prospective senior team in a Bootham Crescent practice match that saw Everton and England left-half Joe Mercer also enjoy a run-out, although the new campaign would signal the end of star-named guests and the return to fielding footballers predominantly registered to the club. New Earswick striker Ian Winters was given his chance and responded with a goalscoring start to the campaign that would see him later go on to play in the Football League.

The grouping of teams for the transition season also saw City shorn of the glamorous War-time clashes against Newcastle, Sunderland, Middlesbrough, Huddersfield, Leeds and the Sheffield clubs, who the club had competed successfully against. The reserve team, meanwhile, was reinstated and took its place in the Yorkshire League, with City's York & District League 'A' team disbanded, although the second-string side would still have a strong contingent of young players. Tom Mitchell returned to his position as manager, meanwhile, in September after being demobilised from the RAF and Sherrington was free to give full-time attention to his secretary duties at Bootham Crescent.

City were also back in FA Cup action during 1945/46, with first and second-round ties uniquely played over two legs. A 4-3 aggregate win over Halifax was completed at Bootham Crescent with star-man George Lee scoring in the deciding leg despite only being granted regimental leave from Germany two days earlier and journeying home by boat. Bert Brenen also played in the second leg of the next round at Bootham Crescent against Bishop Auckland, having arrived from army service in South Africa earlier in the week. He was on target too as City won 3-0 and completed a 5-1 aggregate victory. Mitchell's team went on to reach the fourth round after beating Chesterfield 3-2 at Bootham Crescent during extra-time, which was played in the semi-darkness of an early January evening following a 2pm kick-off.

Winters struck in the second half of extra-time to complete a 4-3 aggregate win in front of the club's first five-figured, post-War attendance of 14,207 supporters. It was also the club's biggest-ever midweek gate and fifth-highest in their history. City went on to bow out against Sheffield Wednesday, whose second-leg visit to Bootham Crescent saw one local firm enquire about the possibility of buying the Main Stand's complete ticket allocation - an offer that was turned down. A 5-1 first leg defeat at Hillsborough somewhat dampened enthusiasm for the game and, despite tickets having been sold in advance of the away clash, 10,447 fans still turned up for another heavy loss - this time 6-1.

With players' wages returning to £4 a week - double their War-time level - and entertainment tax eating into almost a quarter of the club's revenue, as football clubs were subject to a higher rate than theatres or music halls, chairman William Sessions revealed that the club must target 8,000 average attendances to meet expectations and added that he didn't feel that was unreasonable in a city with a 100,000 population. The tax was eventually brought in line, though, for the 1946/47 season, as footballers were treated the same as actors and singers.

Former England schoolboy international Jack Pinder, who made a record 173 appearances for the club during the War, was the recipient, meanwhile, of a second benefit match when a crowd of just under 6,000 turned up against Huddersfield. The Lord Mayor of York was among them and he expressed appreciation for Pinder on behalf of his citizens.

In common with clubs up and down the country, there was a post-War boom at Bootham Crescent, as people pursued entertainment in an attempt to recover from the traumas of the previous years. Alternative past-times were still scarce in an era before the widespread ownership of televisions and cars and, in

1948/49, an all-time average club record League attendance of 10,412 would be set and reserve games also attracted 3,000-plus gates.

According to future City star Dave Dunmore, then a schoolboy, the declared crowd size also fell somewhat short of the genuine numbers in the crowd. "I used to sneak in as a kid over the fence at the back of the Popular Stand where Lumley Barracks was," he confessed. "Nobody ever stopped us. In fact, some of the older men used to help us climb down from the fences. That's what you did back then in the late 1940s. You went bird-nesting, swimming in the Ouse until midnight and sneaked into the football. We would have been 13 or 14 - just before leaving school. There were two or three of us that did it regularly. We had to, because we didn't have any money. At half-time, they used to always go around the pitch collecting money on a blanket as well and we used to get two or three pennies that they had dropped and pocket them because that paid for an ice cream on the way home. Alf Patrick was the main man for City and Jack Pinder was still playing. I remember he used to belt the ball into the crowd quite a bit and he was a big, powerful lad. A bit later I remember the likes of Ron Spence at wing half and Alan Stewart at centre half."

With Dunmore eventually moving from his home-town club to Tottenham in February 1954 for a then club record fee which paid for half of the famous Happy Wanderers' side that would humble the White Hart Lane stars in the FA Cup, City were well and truly compensated for the losses - both in pennies and gate revenue. "They bought five players with the £10,750 they got for me," Dunmore pointed out. "They were Tommy Forgan, Ernie Phillips, George Howe, Arthur Bottom and Norman Wilkinson, so I like to think that repaid them."

Patrick remembered the post-War period well too. He started out professionally at the late age of 25 due to the War and would go on to become the only player to score five goals in an official first-team game at Bootham Crescent. But he had already achieved that landmark tally in a 7-0 reserve win over Thorne Colliery at the ground a month before playing his first League game in November 1946. Nor was Patrick bitter about the period he missed out on playing professionally and he loved entertaining the big crowds during the post-War period even if the team did not really prosper. He reasoned: "Lots of fellows lost their lives but I was still lucky enough to get the chance to sign professional forms when I came out of the army in 1946. I remember a headline in the *Evening Press* saying the club could not survive on 8,000 crowds back then, but we had attendances of 19,000 and 20,000 against the likes of Rotherham and Hull. We got some good averages and attendances playing for the reserves that were bigger than some clubs' first-team games even though we never really had a good side. We were almost always in the bottom half of the table during those first few years after the War. I remember one season (1947/48) we won four and drew two of our first six games but we still didn't do that well. We had some good players, though, like Jimmy Rudd on the left wing. If he'd have played with lighter balls, he would have been an absolute genius."

During the early post-War period, meanwhile, considerable improvements were made to the ground. Deeper drainage work was completed, as was the concreting of the banking at the Bootham Crescent End and the Enclosure terracing in front of the Main Stand, despite restrictions in terms of getting the necessary permits, labour and materials. Patrick admitted the work on the playing surface made little difference though. "The state of the pitch was always terrible," he said. "You'd get a bit of grass in each corner, but the rest was just brown mud. They would have never played on it in these days. The heavy leather balls didn't help either. I used to say I was 6ft 6in when I started playing but got shorter and shorter heading them!"

When the team resumed Football League action in 1946/47, following a Whites v Colours practice match in front of 1,000 fans, they followed the same fixture programme they had started in 1939/40, prior to the outbreak of War. Chester, therefore, were the first visitors to Bootham Crescent on August 31. Seven years earlier, the game had finished 2-2 and the teams fought out another draw - this time 4-4. Bill Allen, who had netted twice in 1939 before the match was expunged from history, scored once on his official debut for the club. He was one of four players in the City team who had featured in the last game before the outbreak of War. The others were Bob Ferguson, Sam Gledhill and Fred Scott. City fans were forced to wait a little longer than scheduled,

Having a ball during training in 1947 (from left-to-right) Alex Jackson, Jimmy Rudd, Charlie Bradley, Matt Patrick, Billy Allen, Len Butt, George Lee and Bobby Browne

though, for the resumption of League football as the 3pm kick-off time was delayed by 15 minutes after Chester's train was held up for an hour just outside of York. The referee, meanwhile, failed to turn up after he got stranded in Bridlington, meaning linesman Mr NLC Finch deputised. There was also late disappointment in the game as a 4-2 advantage was surrendered during the final eight minutes with Gledhill scoring a spectacular own goal from 15 yards.

The new admission price for adults was 1s 3d, including pensioners, with the Football League stipulating that the only adult concession could be made for members of the Forces, who paid the same price as boys of 9d. It meant the Popular Stand would no longer be known as the "Shilling" Stand. A seat in the Main Stand, meanwhile, now cost 2s 6d - double that of those in the newly-concreted Enclosure in front of it. To ease congestion and minimise the giving of change, fans were also encouraged to pay in twos or fours at the turnstiles. Season-tickets, meanwhile, were sold for the first time since the outbreak of War, with holders invited to reserve their same seats.

Fred Hemenway was thrilled to be watching League football again with one player standing out during that first campaign after the cessation of hostilities. "Edouard Wojtczak was a Polish soldier who played in goal," Hemenway recalled. "Any ball that came at him below the crossbar, he would take close to his chest because he was one hell of a jumper. He had been a professional ice skater and he couldn't half jump. He was terrific and very entertaining." Wojtczak and winger Eryk Kubicji were both signed by City after being members of the Polish Armoured Division, who were stationed at Sand Hutton. They initially had trials at the club and impressed as a Polish Army team beat a City XI 7-3 during a Wednesday afternoon friendly in October 1946 that was watched by 2,000 people. A Polish band also played before and after that game. Wotjczak would go on to make four appearances at Bootham Crescent, as an alternative to normal first-choice Ferguson. His spectacular acrobatic saves would often be followed by a bow to the crowd and he went on to star in ice shows after the War, once walking on skates from York to London to publicise a show. He also performed mime acts and was an impressionist.

Ferguson and Wojtczak's successor in goal was another player Hemenway rated - Peter Pickering - who would later join Chelsea for £6,750, which was the second-highest fee paid for a keeper at the time. "Peter Pickering was a good keeper too," Hemenway recalled. "I once saw him take a goal kick and it bounced on the penalty spot at the other end. He had a terrific kick on him."

71

Had it not been for a childhood romance, however, with the club secretary's daughter, Pickering might never have got his chance at Bootham Crescent - initially during the War period and then afterwards. "Peter was one of several good goalkeepers we have had over the years and he was one of my very early boyfriends," Terry Fowler revealed. "I met him at a school dance. He was at Archbishop's Grammar School and he walked me home. I said afterwards that I thought I was deliberately targeted because he came in for a coffee and started talking to my father, telling him he was a keen goalkeeper. I think he would have ended up at the club anyway but that's how he got his foot in the door because my father told him to come down for a trial."

But poor results at Bootham Crescent meant not everybody was happy and an unpleasant atmosphere saw ridicule and abuse directed at players, officials and even the press box, as revealed by Citizen, of the *Yorkshire Evening Press*. A record league attendance for Bootham Crescent of 15,485 was still set, however, that November for the visit of Northern Section leaders Doncaster, who left with the points following a 4-1 win. Smashing the previous best figure, it was the first league gate over 10,000 at Bootham Crescent with City's previous highest attendance, outside of Cup ties, coming when 10,120 turned up at Fulfordgate for an Easter Monday clash against Port Vale in 1930.

Patrick had been due to make his debut in the Doncaster match, but failed a late fitness test after he strained a muscle the day before and news of his injury was conveyed on a board that was passed around the ground ten minutes before kick-off. Many were disappointed, having hoped to catch a first glimpse of the local striker in senior action after he had caught the eye with his goalscoring exploits for the reserves. Future legendary commentator Kenneth Wolstenholme, whose famous coverage of England's 1966 World Cup final win would become a part of the country's footballing heritage, did see Patrick's debut, though, when he worked for the BBC at Bootham Crescent during November's home clash with Stockport. Then 26, Wolstenholme provided running commentary from the second half of the game, which was taken by the *General Forces Programme* with the final half-hour also aired on the *Light Programme*. Patrick's 32nd-minute goal in a 3-2 win would not have been commentated on by Wolstenholme, but he will have reported on the second-half penalty that Patrick won for Pinder to convert. By November, new loud speaker appliances had been fitted to the stadium to help guide and advise spectators on big match days after the admission and exit procedures had been criticised against Doncaster.

In that 1946/47 season, a severe winter also saw no games take place at Bootham Crescent between February 1 and March 22. With floodlights yet to be erected and a government ban on midweek football because of the post-War economic crisis, the season was subsequently extended until June 7. An unforgiving playing surface in May, meanwhile, cost Patrick dear at the end of his first season as a professional. "When we started playing again, the pitch was like concrete," he explained. "There were no sprinklers then and I broke my wrist against Oldham. I was off work for about five or six weeks, so I lost money because I had to have a big plaster on." The Supporters' Club Inter-Works competition was also relaunched with a record entry of 50 teams, as fixtures took place at Bootham Crescent.

In 1947/48, Midland League reserve football was played again at Bootham Crescent after the club resigned from the Yorkshire League. Admission charges rose, meanwhile, for first-team matches with Main Stand prices going up from 2s 6d to 3s. A booking fee for life-members to secure their seats was also considered, but not implemented. An additional charge of 3d was introduced too in the Popular Stand to help meet wage, travelling and material costs, bringing it into line with the 1s 6d Enclosure charge, although the other areas of the ground were still available to those who wanted to carry on paying 1s 3d, with such uncovered sections still able to accommodate 12,000 supporters. Main Stand season-ticket prices were also more expensive at £3 10s, but more were sold than for the previous season. Concrete terracing, meanwhile, was added to the St Olave's Road End, which was also repainted in readiness for the new campaign.

Patrick went on to become the first City player to score four goals in a League match during a 6-0 home win over Halifax on August 30, 1947. The striker completed his hat-trick in the first 35 minutes, having also had a goal disallowed for offside during that period. He went on to add a fourth on 77 minutes. Leeds United had previously put a bid in for Patrick and other higher-division scouts were now beginning to flock to Bootham Crescent to cast their eyes over him.

For the visit of Hull City in November, meanwhile, Lumley Barracks' parade ground was used for parking to accommodate the many visiting coaches. One exuberant away fan also placed a model tiger in the centre of the ground before the teams fought out a 2-2 draw.

In April, Tommy Ledgard, who had been employed as a handyman and been part of the ground staff at Bootham Crescent for many years, received the gate receipts from the Midland League reserve match against Rotherham having become seriously ill and lost his eyesight, rendering him unable to continue in his job. Chairman Sessions had appealed to supporters at the penultimate home game of the season to attend the match for Ledgard's benefit. The receipts from a 2,280 crowd went on to total £109, with a collection at the game raising a further £31 and he was given an additional year's pay.

For the 1948-49 season, meanwhile, Monday-night games became the favoured evening of choice for non-weekend fixtures, instead of the club's previous preference for a Wednesday evening. The Monday tradition would persist until the club's first season of English second-tier football in 1974/75.

York City players put through their paces during a training session on the Bootham Crescent pitch in August 1947. Pictured are Bobby Browne, Alex Jackson, Billy Allen, Jimmy Rudd, Matt Patrick, Charlie Bradley, George Lee and Len Butt

Dave Dunmore in Bootham Crescent action during his first spell as a York City player

CHAPTER 7

Alf Patrick scores five in Rotherham romp

"There was no big celebration from me when I got my 100th goal. There was no hugging and nobody would have wanted to kiss some of the blokes I played with."

A historic announcement was made in September 1948, influenced heavily by the healthy £5,000 profit the club had made the previous season with gate receipts at a record high of £16,213. The purchase of Bootham Crescent was announced in the Social Club at the shareholders' annual meeting, bringing an end to 16 years of leasing. It had already been publicly advertised for sale to comply with Charity

Tom Gale, the York City captain in 1948, meets Billy Smith, the skipper from 1922, at the dinner to celebrate the purchase of Bootham Crescent, which took place at the Royal Station Hotel in November 1948

Commission law when the club began negotiations to secure ownership of the land. Chairman William Sessions went on to claim the club owned one of the best grounds in the third division, although he stressed at the time that an average attendance of 10,000 was ideally required for the club to fulfil its potential and push for promotion. The ground was bought for £4,075 with the equipment on it seeing the stadium's overall value listed at £7,204 in 1949. City celebrated the news by defeating Hartlepool 4-0 at Bootham Crescent with Alf Patrick (2), Matt Patrick and Bill Allen the marksmen. A dinner was also held at the Royal Station Hotel, where the deeds were handed to the chairman. Past-and-present directors attended, along with many enthusiasts who had worked for the club over the years and the first captain of the team - Billy Smith.

By now, meanwhile, the York & District Referees' Association were holding monthly meetings in the Social Club - a tradition that would continue right until the stadium's latter years. They also challenged the Supporters' Club to quiz-night competitions.

With home form strong and regular five-figured crowds flocking to Bootham Crescent, November also saw another turnstile incorporated at the Shipton Street End of the car park. Two more no-change turnstiles were added too, making 14 in total at the ground, which was more than at many third division stadia, with the better-supported Rotherham only boasting eight at the time, which was the same number as Darlington.

In November 1948, Alf Patrick went on to create Bootham Crescent history again as he netted five times during a 6-1 home win over third division north leaders Rotherham - a big game that saw the Main Stand's concrete terracing completed before it took place, while the York Excelsior Prize Band played 45 minutes before kick-off. It was an incredible result against a Rotherham side that had won 15 and drawn one of their opening 17 matches. City, though, were showing signs of form going into the game and were in the middle of a run of nine successive home wins - a sequence that would see them score 33 goals and concede just five.

Patrick opened the scoring with his chest on 28 minutes after Jimmy Rudd and Sid Storey combined down the left to create a chance that was snaffled up at the far post. Three minutes after the break, an excellent second goal followed when Matt Patrick sent George Ivey racing down the right wing and he crossed for Patrick to rattle a tremendous right-footed shot into the roof of the net. Full-back Harry Brigham put City further ahead from the penalty spot on 57 minutes and Patrick completed his hat-trick just after the hour mark, finding the net with his right foot following more clever work by Storey. Rotherham went on to reduce the deficit, but Patrick had not finished, outpacing the visitors' defence to score a fine individual effort on 83 minutes. Four minutes later, he grabbed his fifth from two yards out following a goalmouth scramble. He then received a tremendous ovation for his exploits in front of 19,216 supporters which represented a record League attendance for the club, with £1,271 taken in receipts. It was believed the attendance was also swollen by a number of supporters from Hull, who were cheering on the hosts against their title rivals. All those of a City allegiance, meanwhile, were chanting the goals in sequence by the end of the contest. Ald W Dobbie, then Lord Mayor of York and MP for Rotherham, was also at the match, hoping for a draw. Rotherham

Alf Patrick, the only man ever to score five goals during a competitive game at Bootham Crescent and the first to reach 100 career goals for York City there, in action (pictured in the dark shirt) at the ground in January 1952

had been blown away by York's quick-moving, short-passing attack and Patrick might have even scored six times as, after grabbing his first, he had cleared the crossbar in a one-on-one situation.

Recalling the historic haul on his 90th birthday in 2011, Patrick admitted: "I can only remember the first goal but I've still got the Evening Press report on that match and it talks about one of the goals being a 25-yard strike. I don't know how I managed that with the balls we used to play with! You obviously have no thoughts of getting five goals when you put the first one in, but it was just one of those matches and I kept the newspaper cutting: 'A Patrick Goes Nap By Himself'. It would have been nice to get six of the best, but you can't be too greedy, and I'm surprised it was never done again at the ground. I remember going to Rotherham the same season and one of their fans shouted: 'You won't get five again this time, Patrick'. He was right - I didn't get any!"

Fred Hemenway was in the crowd again for that match against the Millers and added: "I once asked him if he remembered his last goal in that game and he didn't, so I told him it went in off his knee, but he used to harass teams to death did Alf. He never gave them a moment's peace and never gave anything up. I don't ever remember him having a bad game."

For Malcolm Huntington, Patrick's historic match stood out as a 'Where were you when Kennedy was shot moment?' as he remembered vividly the reason why he was not at the game.

"Missing Alf Patrick's five goals was one of the greatest disappointments during my time following the club," he admitted. "I was playing for York City boys in the morning at Denaby and, at the end of the match, the schoolmaster gave us a choice after lunch of going back to York to watch York v Rotherham or going to see Sheffield United v Chelsea in division one. I was the only one to put my hand up for going back to York, so we went to Bramall Lane and saw the most terrible match. Sheffield United won 2-1 and there was hardly any incident at all. We then got back to York railway station and, because there were no mobile phones back then, we saw the headline in the *Green Football Press*."

The bigger post-War gates, meanwhile, were creating new problems in terms of access into Bootham Crescent with one *Yorkshire Evening Press* reader writing in to say: "I am one of those unfortunate people having to use the 'Glass Bridge' over the railway. I would like to make a suggestion to save someone in the near future having their ribs crushed in trying to get over after a match. My suggestion is put a line of pipes or tubing, the same as one seen at most crossings, up Grosvenor Terrace at the railway wall side, starting about three feet from the bridge, leaving a space for anyone coming over from the opposite side. The policeman on match duty should stand near and only allow those coming over through the opening, everybody else to go up Grosvenor Terrace and down between the rail and the wall." Such a suggestion was never acted upon with generations of supporters putting their ribs at risk following big home matches.

In February, meanwhile, the area finals of the England and Wales Individual Darts Championship were staged in the Social Club. Back on the pitch, Hull City, led by former England international Raich Carter, beat the Minstermen 3-1 in April 1949 in front of an all-time record League attendance of 21,010. Takings of £1,451 for the all-ticket clash also represented an all-time high at the time. To help supporters from outside the city and to ease congestion at Bootham Crescent, tickets for the game were also sold in advance at Tadcaster Junior Sports Club, Easingwold's Fleece Inn and Oliver's Garage in Norton. The remaining Main Stand seats, which were not taken by season-ticket holders, were sold one evening from the Social Club, as was the norm while, the following night, those wanting tickets for the Enclosure and Popular Stand had to go through the Bootham Crescent turnstiles as on a normal match day, buy their maximum of two tickets and then leave the ground by the normal exits. The game was a sell-out with police authorities determining the number of tickets that could be sold (16,000 to City fans and 5,000 to Hull) to comply with safety measures on crowd control which had been brought in following the 1946 Burnden Park disaster at Bolton when 33 fans were crushed to death. That meant the overall club record attendance against Huddersfield, which might have been broken given the importance of the game to the promotion-chasing visitors, was never in danger of being threatened. To ease access, turnstiles were clearly marked with corresponding colours on tickets and 2,000 people were queuing to be let in when the gates were opened at 1.15pm, with members of the special constabulary called in to help police the game.

Ten minutes before kick-off, a young Hull fan ran onto the pitch and placed a model tiger on the centre spot. In response, a similar-aged City fan sprinted on to put a red-and-white ribbon around its neck. That led to a chain of events where a City supporter then invaded the pitch to hurl the tiger away, before the same Hull fan retrieved it and put it back on the centre spot, only for somebody else with a home allegiance to put a beret on it! Young supporters were also allowed to climb over the rails to get a closer view of the action. Reports, meanwhile, stated that the crowd-control measures meant the ground did not look fully packed out with estimates that another 2,000 fans could have been accommodated in the Shipton Street End alone. Alf Patrick gave City a half-time lead in the match, but an injury to John Brown, which saw him leave the pitch for 38 minutes with concussion before groggily returning to the action, handicapped the hosts' chances and Carter went on to hit the bar, before scoring the second goal and creating the third.

In the summer, meanwhile, with the help of the Supporters' Club, the Popular Stand's lower tier was concreted and 24 steps of concrete terracing were also introduced at the Shipton Street End. That meant concrete terracing was now in place all the way around the ground. A brick-dust running track was also laid in front of the Main Stand. Re-seeding of the playing surface, including getting rid of weeds, meanwhile, meant the first public pre-season, practice match for 1949/50 was played at Stockton Lane's Co-op Ground, where the newly-formed third team would host their Yorkshire League fixtures. The idea was also revisited of extending the Main Stand to encompass the full length of the pitch, with architects consulted and the Supporters' Club offering their help to fund such a venture, which would have increased the overall ground capacity to 30,000. A more modest extension was eventually agreed on and constructed, though, in 1955.

City disappointed during the new season, finishing bottom of the third division north and the feelings of the local fan base were no better highlighted when, over Easter, a Good Friday crowd of 12,330 for Rotherham's visit dropped, following a 3-0 defeat, by more than half to just over 6,000 for a home contest against second-placed Rochdale the next day, seeing takings plummet from £819 to £425.

Towards the end of another unspectacular 1950/51 season, Bert Brenen was awarded a benefit match against Leeds, with a bumper crowd of 11,000 turning up to pay their respects to the club's servant of 13 years. Leeds won 4-0 but Sunderland and England forward Len Shackleton was the star turn with his "back-heel flips" and George Lee also returned to his former club as a guest. The impressive gate meant Brenen received the maximum reward for his services permitted for a benefit match of £750 - the first City player to enjoy that honour.

As part of the Festival of Britain celebrations in May 1951, meanwhile, City entertained League of Ireland clubs Sligo Rovers and Transport, winning 4-0 and 5-0 respectively, with the home crowd getting their first sight during those games of a young right-winger Billy Hughes, who was later to star in the run to the 1955 FA Cup semi-finals. Hughes scored one and set up two against Sligo in front of a modest attendance of 2,260. The match against Transport also only attracted 2,598 fans with Johnny Linaker hitting a hat-trick.

Prices for the 1951/52, season, meanwhile, were increased by three-pence. Future England B international goalkeeper Des Thompson also moved on to first division Burnley in November, having reportedly honed his reflexes by regularly spending hours after normal training sessions kicking a ball against the car park wall in Bootham Crescent and fielding the rebound.

Midway through the campaign, a crowd of 2,544 turned up on a free mid-December afternoon for the first team to cheer York Boys into the last 32 of the English Shield after they beat Bradford. Alf Patrick also became the first City player to reach 100 league goals and he did so in style when he hit a hat-trick during a 6-2 home triumph over Halifax. His second goal racked up the century five minutes after the interval. It was a header from a Hughes corner and led to prolonged cheering before the game restarted.

Patrick does not recall a great on-pitch and post-match fanfare but admitted: "I'm proud of being the first player to score 100 goals for York because other records can be beaten but that one can't and I'm also pleased with a goal ratio of one every other game. I can remember the last one I got on the ground as well. It was against Yorkie - the lion mascot! I put a penalty past him when they had me and Norman Wilkinson on the pitch at half-time a few years ago. Before that Halifax game, I knew I was supposed to be on 98 because there had been a story in the *Evening Press* about it, but there was no big celebration from me when I got my 100th goal. I just ran back to the halfway line. There was no hugging and nobody would have wanted to kiss some of the blokes I played with. After the game, I will have done what I always did and gone to Betty's for tea with my wife and then to the pictures."

The campaign also saw the popular Newark Imperial Carnival Band make a couple of appearances at the ground, during their tour of the country's football stadia. They played for an hour before the game against Halifax, as well as at the interval and would return during following seasons.

Winger Billy Fenton, meanwhile, played his first season for City and received the congratulations of his team-mates and Bootham Crescent supporters as he equalled Reg Baines' record of 29 goals in a season on April 21 after netting twice in a 2-1 win over Barrow. Fenton went on to break the record at Wrexham, although 22 of his eventual 31 goals were scored at Bootham Crescent that campaign. Emerging nursery team Cliftonville, who had provided the club with the likes of Dave Dunmore and Mick Granger, also played Major Buckley's Leeds United juniors in an evening friendly on the ground.

In April 1952, Tom Lockie was rewarded with a testimonial match as City took on a Football League XI side at Bootham Crescent that included the likes of Sam Bartram and Len Shackleton. Arthur Bottom, then of Sheffield United and unknown to York fans, also played in the game. A 14-year-old Barry Jackson, destined to become a City legend, was in the crowd that day too and remembers being dazzled by the "Clown Prince" Shackleton

"I remember Len Shackleton coming to Bootham Crescent for Tom Lockie's testimonial," Jackson said six years before his death in 2021. "Tom was a wonderful soldier for York City and a great servant and Shackleton was brilliant that day. He was hitting balls from behind him from the middle of the park for wingers to run on to. What a player. He was maybe the wrong type of player if you had a big league match or a cup tie and he should have won more England caps but, in benefit games like that one, he was unbelievable to watch."

Patrick played for City when Lockie was first-team trainer and remembered the Scotsman's love for a hot bath and dislike of nicotine.

"Players get showers now but we used to have two baths and Tom Lockie made sure we went in the cold one," Patrick laughed. "There would be seven or eight of us in the thing, whilst he was on his own in the other one. We all used to smoke as well and Tommy used to say 'Make that your last' before games but we had a keeper - Matt Middleton - who used to put a cigarette on the dressing room door frame before the match and, then, he would smoke it at half-time. That's what society was like in those days - a hell of a lot of people smoked."

Lockie's coaching programme was not the most sophisticated either, according to Patrick. "We trained twice a week on Tuesday and Thursday nights," Patrick remembered. "On the odd occasion, through one of Bert Brenen's contacts, we would go to the gym at St John's College or indoors at the Railway Institute but the majority of the time we would be at Bootham Crescent and we would just run around the pitch because there were no floodlights then. We did very little ball work." Every club, meanwhile, largely adopted the same tactical approach with Patrick musing: "I often wondered what would happen these days if teams lined up like we did with two full backs, three half backs and five forwards."

Patrick's pre-match routine, meanwhile, would have also followed the familiar pattern of many a post-War semi-professional. "I worked at Vickers - the optical engineers in Haxby Road - all the time I was playing for City," he added. "My foreman in those days used to moan about me going to chase around a bag of leather and was a bit of a misery. I would get up for work at 7.30am on a Saturday and used to bike to games when I finished at midday. It was about a three or four-mile trip to Bootham Crescent and I often wonder what would have happened if I'd ever got a puncture. I would have been in big trouble. When we played night games, I would also do a full shift at work first. I got £3 a week from City during the season when I first started and that went up to £5. In the summer, we got £2 a week."

Patrick's bike was possibly one of those being referred to by a letter writer to the *Yorkshire Evening Press* in September 1952 when he moaned: "I would like to draw your attention to the unnecessary inconvenience given to patrons leaving the ground by the hundreds of bicycles stored in the parking ground in front of the stand. These reduce the exits to no more than three yards wide. The annoyance is aggravated when the bicycle users struggle, after the match, against the flow of the crowd. Dirty marks on suits and jagged silk stockings are the result and bad language the outlet of struggling home-goers."

The bicycle in the 1950s was an indispensable mode of transport for hundreds of City fans, especially in the rush from work to make midweek kick-offs, which were sometimes scheduled as early as 5.30pm. There was an alternative to leaving your bike at the ground, however, courtesy of an enterprising local shop keeper, as Irene Hagyard revealed: "Me and my husband used to go on our bicycles after the War and there was a lovely lady who had a little shop at the end of Shipton Street. She had a yard and charged us sixpence to leave our bikes in there. My husband's two brothers did that as well and she got quite a few in her yard. It wasn't a bad sideline for her, because you could even get into matches for a shilling in those early years."

Dunmore, meanwhile, had graduated from Bootham Crescent's terraces to the pitch by the end of the 1951/52 campaign - scoring on his City debut at the age of 18 during a 3-0 final-day defeat of Crewe. "I don't remember my goal so I can't say it was a belter because it might have been a lucky tap-in or whatever," Dunmore laughed. "I remember my work-mates being in the crowd more than anything. We worked at Clifton Carriage Works down Avenue Terrace, which wasn't far from the City ground so it wasn't far for them to come. Dick Duckworth was also the manager back then and he was a regimental, sergeant major type. It was clear he was the boss but you knew where you stood with him." The goal was described in the *Yorkshire Evening Press* as "an easy goal as the result of atrocious covering by the visitors' defence" and another possible explanation for Dunmore's maiden professional strike failing to stand the test of time in his memory bank could be that it wasn't his first at Bootham Crescent. Recalling what must have been one of the longest-range strikes ever witnessed at the ground, Dunmore revealed: "The first time I played at Bootham Crescent was for York City boys. I captained them, and I also got the chance to play at the ground in a York Schools' final as well for Canon Lee. We reached a couple of those and Bootham Crescent felt like Wembley back then. I don't remember the goal on my first-team debut, but I do remember scoring there from near the halfway line when I was playing wing half for City Schoolboys. I played left half even though I was right-footed because I could use both feet. It was just a whack up field. The keeper had come to the edge of the penalty area and it bounced over him. It took off after I hit it and the keeper had come flying out of his goal."

Unlike Patrick, Dunmore also enjoyed the support of his employers as he tried to make the grade at City, allowing him to keep on top of his fitness levels with regular visits to Bootham Crescent: "I was given time off for training if I wanted it off and they were good to me at work," he explained. "George Barnes was my boss and he was pushing me, like my dad was. I used to go training two mornings a week, as well as on a night, when Tom Lockie was trainer."

May 1952 also saw England under-14s meet Ireland in the first schoolboy international to be held at Bootham Crescent. The attendance was 16,000 and England, who were captained by future City manager Wilf McGuinness, won 5-0. McGuinnes hit the post with a 25-yard drive and a display was also given by the Newark Imperials Carnival Band at half-time. The game was staged as a climax to the York Schools' FA's golden jubilee year. Refreshments, meanwhile, were sold at the ground for the first time by the Supporters' Club in 1952. Profits were initially small, but grew, even though, 20 years later, it was reported that the elusive £100 figure had not yet been recorded for any individual game.

For the 1952/53 campaign, season-ticket prices went up to £4 10s due to an increase in entertainment tax again. The Football League also set the minimum matchday admission fee at 1s 9d.

In October, Duckworth left the club to take the managerial vacancy at Stockport but, in his last game after the news was made public, his York team beat his new employers 3-0 at Bootham Crescent thanks to goals from Fenton (2) and Dunmore. Duckworth's successor Charles Spencer sadly died the following February with teams and officials lining up in the centre of the field for a two-minute silence before the next home game and City's players also wore black armbands during a 3-1 defeat to Workington.

On the first Saturday in March, meanwhile, with the first team and reserves both playing away, Cliftonville Juniors took on Leeds United Colts again at Bootham Crescent. On Good Friday, the continued interest in local amateur football was also illustrated by the 1,500-strong crowd that turned up for the York Senior Cup final as Poppleton Road Old Boys and New Earswick played out a goal-less draw.

Meanwhile, the Pocklington branch of the Supporters' Club which, having been formed by six people in 1951 had grown to a 200-strong membership two years later, complained of licencing problems at the end of the season that had meant they could not transport themselves on a bus to Bootham Crescent from their headquarters on matchdays. Instead, they were instructed to set off from a point one-and-a-half miles away from their base. Such petty restrictions were a problem for the club, who relied heavily on support from the rural areas around the city, with Malton, Tadcaster and Easingwold also boasting supporters' club branches. Club scout Jack Pinder, meanwhile, arranged a trial match on the ground for 26 players he had spotted within a 30-mile radius of the city, with many invited to train at Bootham Crescent on Tuesday and Thursday nights.

The FA also instructed the club to post notices at the ground warning supporters about their conduct after prolonged booing of the opposition from the Popular Stand during the Southport home game had led the referee to stop the game and ask police to go over and deal with the matter.

Season-tickets at Bootham Crescent in the Main Stand were to be reduced, though, from £4 10s to £4 5s after Queen's Park Rangers secured a reduction in the level of entertainment tax that clubs were charged following a legal challenge. Meshed wire appeared over the players' tunnel too at the start of the 1953/54 season to "prevent any molestation from misguided spectators", according to *Yorkshire Evening Press* reporter Wilf Meek.

The club also agreed to allow the York & District League to stage a match at the ground in September to help raise funds and assist the purchase of trophies and medals at the end of the season. Division one champions York RI beat Senior Cup holders Poppleton Old Boys 3-1, although reports stated the occasion was worthy of a better attendance. In October, meanwhile, 13-year-old Fishergate schoolboy Colin Addison was making his first strides into the game, playing at Bootham Crescent for York City Boys during a 3-2 defeat to Barnsley.

Off the pitch, public transport services to and from the ground seemed to be improving with one correspondent to the *Yorkshire Evening Press*, calling himself "In Hope", declaring that "at the last home match a long fleet of buses were waiting in the Crescent to take supporters home to all parts of the city", as he dismissed one excuse that was being used to explain poor attendances. Tentative suggestions that the traditional Christmas Day fixture against Barnsley might be switched to Monday December 29, meanwhile, were met with opposition from further *Yorkshire Evening Press* readers, naming themselves "Two Saturday Afternoon Workers". Revealing the problems some supporters endured balancing work commitments with following their club in the 1950s, their letter read: "It was stated that Monday will be a general holiday in York, but might I ask for whom? Certainly not the shop workers who seem to get a raw deal every time. When has Christmas Day or any other public holiday failed to attract a good crowd at Bootham Crescent? We think Saturday afternoon supporters get more than a fair crack of the whip. To refer back to the Barnsley match, if it is decided to play this on the Monday, we and several hundreds more like us will have to wait until Easter to see the team we so willingly support whenever possible."

For the first time since before the War, though, the club experimented with an 11am December 25 kick-off, instead of 2.15pm. History confirmed that Boxing Day matches, when public transport normally ran a more frequent service, traditionally attracted 3,000 more fans. The early start did not please some either, with another *Yorkshire Evening Press* letter writer "Loyal Yokel" bemoaning: "You readily admit that a great deal of City supporters come from the surrounding country districts but, I ask you, how many do you think will be able to see the team when the kick-off is in the morning? Firstly, it will mean leaving home early to get there and, secondly, with the match finishing at approximately 12.40pm, what about the Christmas dinner? Apparently, the loyal supporters who travel into York every Saturday, wet or fine, have to suffer for the lukewarm city dwellers." A crowd of only 5,136 - the lowest for an official Football League fixture on the Yuletide date at Bootham Crescent since 1935 - subsequently turned up for a 2-0 defeat against the Tykes although, with the team struggling, gates had dipped in general.

A small section of supporters at the Saturday morning York City Boys matches at Bootham Crescent, meanwhile, were asked to refrain from booing the opposition on their entrance into the stadium and during games, as it is not "in accordance with the York Schools' FA's reputation for sportsmanship and hospitality". The plea was made ahead of a Yorkshire Shield home tie against Sheffield after previous incidences of "bad manners". CS Baxter, president of the Schools' Athletic Association, declared: "The booing that goes on at York City matches is disgraceful and we know that children are natural mimics. I am sure they are just copying older people." HG Raynes, general secretary of the association, added: "It has been pretty bad at boys' shield and cup matches. We, of course, have met the same thing in other towns where we have played, but we want to start this campaign in York. A circular letter has gone around all schools where there are members of the association." The letter stated that the association felt schools must do everything possible to teach boys and girls the principles of spectatorship, with an emphasis on courtesy. "We would like teams which visit York to feel that they are welcome and that their efforts will be applauded generously, so that our schools will be renowned for sportsmanship," the letter explained.

Midway through the season, meanwhile, a cheque for £300 was presented to the board by the Supporters' Club and covered the costs of a wall built on the Popular Stand side to enclose the ground more effectively from Lumley Barracks, following complaints that free access was being made from that corner of the ground. In January 1954, a new auxiliary branch of the Supporters' Club was launched at Bootham Crescent too with fundraising their chief duty and, to this end, a weekly lottery, based on football scores, was launched. Fans tried to predict the results of British fixtures and, in the summer, Australian games, with the possibility of big cash prizes in return for their weekly payment to participate. At its most popular, it was a scheme that required 20 agents to cope with the demands of 1,500 members and raised £1,000 a month for the club and, by 1962, the scheme had raised more than £86,000 but a change was then made with a daily ticket draw replacing the football result predictions, due to competition from the national Football Pools betting business. The auxiliary branch had several headquarters before finding a home in Bootham Crescent's development office. Another popular scheme, meanwhile, saw holidays to the likes of Paris, Rotterdam and London offered as prizes in 1971. The auxiliary branch was also responsible for the introduction of the Rosettes - a group of girls who were dressed in City colours and helped the Jackpot ticket sellers on match days.

In March, meanwhile, Dunmore was ruled out of Tottenham's first division clash at Chelsea after injuring his ankle training with his old team at Bootham Crescent. The young forward had been sold on to the White Hart Lane giants during the season and had already made his debut at Arsenal's famous Highbury stadium, but was still completing his apprenticeship as a machinist in York and training with City rather than Spurs.

At the end of April, a joint benefit match for Alf and Matt Patrick was called off after overseas tours, announced at short notice by other clubs and chiefly Tottenham, meant players scheduled to play in the game had to withdraw. Both players were guaranteed a fixed sum, aside from the game, for their services, with Alf Patrick reportedly receiving £350. He subsequently moved on to Scarborough but was still given permission to train at Bootham Crescent.

A poor season, in which re-election was narrowly avoided, had seen Bootham Crescent's average attendance drop by 3,000, with not one £1,000 gate recorded, whereas three had been in 1952/53. The receipts taken through the turnstiles were, accordingly, the lowest since 1947.

The railway bridge, as pictured in the 1950s, that was the route home from Bootham Crescent for so many fans down the decades

New signing from Nottingham Forest Gordon Brown drives the tractor as his team-mates also prepare Bootham Crescent for the 1950-51 season

CHAPTER 8

Tottenham toppled by the Happy Wanderers

"After the final whistle, the Tottenham players were very generous with their congratulations and said the best side had won."

At the start of a 1954/55 season, which would become forever etched into Bootham Crescent folklore, a concession was provided by the club for old-aged pensioners, who would only be charged the minimum ground fee of 1s 9d for a place in the Popular Stand. The minimum charge was, at the time, set by the Football League and had to be adhered to by its member clubs, but City made the gesture to provide their older supporters with covered protection for the lowest price they could offer, representing a three pence saving on what they would have paid in the Popular Stand previously. The playing surface was also reported to be in its best-ever condition with Bingley Research experts having conducted experiments on it over the summer.

A 6-2 opening day win at Wrexham, during which new striker Arthur Bottom hit a hat-trick, meant a bumper crowd of 10,156 turned up two days later to see another summer recruit Sam McNab score the only goal in the first home match of the new campaign against Hartlepool. But a series of three straight defeats saw the gate plummet to less than 6,000 for a Monday night 0-0 draw with Workington and some unimpressed supporters engaged in slow handclapping, with the club accepting manager Jimmy McCormick's resignation shortly afterwards.

The team continued to struggle during the opening months of the campaign but, on October 16, 1954, during a 3-1 home win over Darlington, City first fielded a side that would become the most famous in their history - Tommy Forgan, Ernie Phillips, George Howe, Gordon Brown, Alan Stewart, Ron Spence, Billy Hughes, Arthur Bottom, Norman Wilkinson, Sid Storey and Billy Fenton - the 11 players who would go on to play against Newcastle in the FA Cup semi-finals later that season. The Happy Wanderers, as they were fondly nicknamed, thrilled City crowds with their emphasis on close-passing attacking football and, on that first game together, *Yorkshire Evening Press* correspondent Wilf Meek opened his match report with the line: "This was the sort of football to pull in the crowds at Bootham Crescent." A crowd of 12,179 attended with Meek adding that the match would not have disgraced the second division. Wilkinson, Fenton and Storey were the home marksmen.

But the famous Cup odyssey was to start with a somewhat fortunate home win on November 20 when neighbours Scarborough were narrowly seen off 3-2 courtesy of goals from Wilkinson, Bottom and Spence, as only a goalkeeping mistake by Frank Hyde ensured the hosts prevailed in front of 10,155 fans. City played in blue shirts and white shorts for the tie and Scarborough in yellow shirts and black shorts with both required to change from their normal red colours due to the rules of the tournament that were still in place then. Alf Patrick did not feature against his old club, as he was suffering from a knee injury, but other ex-Minstermen Bert Brenen, Charlie Ware and Don Barber were in the visitors' line-up. Ware was reported to have excelled in the first half, giving City captain Phillips a torrid time. The visitors also led twice, with winger Barber opening the scoring on 24 minutes after Brown had rattled the crossbar for the hosts. Keeper Mick Granger, deputising for an injured Forgan, had just made a brilliant fingertip save to thwart Gordon Mitchell, but he was beaten when Ware went past Phillips skilfully and crossed to the far post, where Barber bent low to head in. Wilkinson, who had seen an earlier header cleared off the line, went on to level in the 49th minute. He again used his head to net after Bottom, Fenton and Hughes had all combined. Shortly afterwards, both teams hit the woodwork with a corner eluding Granger and the ball bouncing off his crossbar, whilst a deflected Hughes effort struck an upright. But Mitchell nudged the Seadogs back in front on 70 minutes, when a bombardment of the home goal saw several shots charged down before the ball was eventually driven home by the 21-year-old, former England Boys international. With a major shock on the cards, Bottom eased some tension on 80 minutes with a clinical finish from Hughes' pass. Five minutes later, City then decisively took the lead for the first time when a loose ball from a corner found Spence who, from just outside the penalty box, lobbed a left-footed effort over the head of Hyde.

Non-League neighbours Selby Town, meanwhile, also made the second round of the competition and, after drawing Hastings United at home, were offered the use of Bootham Crescent for the game after City were handed a trip to Dorchester Town at the same stage of the competition. The reserves were due to play at Worksop on the same day and York's rugby-league team were at

Castleford, seemingly enhancing the prospect of a bumper crowd if the match was to be moved 15 miles up the road. City's directors also agreed to forego the 10 per cent charge on the gate which would have been permissible under FA rules and would have only sought turnstile steward costs of approximately £10. The proposal was put to the Selby Town committee who, having hosted Bradford Park Avenue in front of 6,000 supporters the previous season, decided to keep the game at Flaxley Road. Explaining that choice, club president Councillor N Reasbeck said: "I do not think we will accept York City's kind offer. We must win this match and by going to York we would throw away ground advantage to gain a few extra pounds. The club committee feels that we can get as many as 10,000 people into our own ground and we do not think that the tie would attract more people to York. We have a duty to our regular spectators and it is because of them the committee wishes the match to be played in Selby." Hastings' players trained instead at Bootham Crescent during the two days before the contest and, on arrival, were even greeted by a blast of the county anthem *Sussex by the Sea* over the public address system. While City were completing a 5-2 win at Dorchester, Hastings went on to enjoy a 2-0 victory at Selby in front of a disappointing crowd of 3,000 fans. Selby officials admitted during their AGM the following summer that the club had made the wrong decision and their financial situation would have been much improved if they had taken up the offer to play at Bootham Crescent.

For the Happy Wanderers, further away wins in the Cup followed at first division Blackpool, who were seen off 2-0 despite boasting the likes of Stanley Matthews and Stan Mortensen in their ranks, and Bishop Auckland (3-1). In between, meanwhile, frustration at a 3-1 home defeat to Barnsley saw "a few misguided stand occupants" hurl their cushions in the direction of the referee, which was also described as "a perfectly fatuous and childish exhibition" in the *Yorkshire Evening Press.* There were complaints, meanwhile, from the visitors' goalkeeper that he had been hit by snowballs during the match on an icy afternoon.

The 3,700 tickets for the Bishop Auckland game were sold in less than an hour to the general public at Bootham Crescent after the Supporters' Club and its auxiliaries had taken up their allocation. People had been queuing two hours before the tickets started to be sold, while Supporters' Club officials JW Edwards, Harry Ward and Arthur Shaw supervised the disposal of tickets.

City were then drawn at home to the mighty Tottenham in the fifth round and put on arguably the finest display in the club's history to triumph 3-1 on a heavy pitch in front of an all-ticket crowd of 21,000 - the limit that was determined as a safe capacity by the police authorities.

Efforts had been made to ensure the sale of tickets was overseen as fairly as possible with night-time shift-workers even getting the opportunity to get one of a limited number of tickets on the morning before they went on public sale later that day. The Supporters' Club, Auxiliary Club and Social Club were also given 4,000 tickets to distribute to their members, meaning City's most-loyal fans did not miss out on the momentous occasion. Tickets for the Tottenham match were sold on the basis of one per membership card, which had to be produced and stamped. That process started the day after the general sale and lasted from Friday to Monday, including at a home reserve game against Lincoln on the Saturday. As ever, season-ticket holders also had the opportunity to reserve their normal places in advance. Nearly 4,000 people, mainly consisting of shift workers or their wives, formed two queues - one for five-shilling admission and the other for 2s 6d - outside Bootham Crescent on the first morning that tickets went on general sale. Almost half went away disappointed - after queuing for hours - with only 2,250 going on sale in that first early batch. Michael and Peter Pink - Easingwold Modern School pupils who were 12 and 11 respectively - were first in line for the 2s 6d tickets, having got to the ground shortly after 6am in the middle of a snow shower that lasted half an hour. By the time tickets went on sale the queue stretched 70 yards down Grosvenor Road. Mrs George Bradley, meanwhile, was reported to have cycled eight miles from Rufforth with food for her husband midway through the morning after he had turned up at 6am after finishing his night shift. The 5s queue also snaked 100 yards down Newborough Street by the time tickets went on sale. Some light relief was provided when City's team, along with Spurs ace Dave Dunmore, arrived for training. As soon as the last of the tickets for shift-workers were sold mid-afternoon, a queue began to form for the final home allocation of 9,500, which went on sale at 6.30pm. Thousands queued for hours around Bootham Crescent, although others only waited in a 10-minute line for 2s 6d tickets at the turnstile near the Shipton Street entrance to the ground. Police were advising fans to join that queue, but most seemed suspicious of its size, which was a pity for them, as many in that line were able to visit the turnstile twice. The biggest two queues for the 5s and 2s 6d tickets extended as far as Clifton Cinema in one direction and to Shipton Street in the other. William Young - a 64-year-old man - queued to get his son a ticket for two-and-a-half hours before collapsing within a few yards of the turnstile. Fans had also arrived five hours before the advertised time of sale for the remaining 200

Main Stand tickets on offer with police counting 200 people from the front of the queue well in advance of the official start, which allowed the remaining disappointed supporters to disperse. By the end of the first day of general sales, it was announced that a 21,000 sell-out was guaranteed with gate receipts of £3,845, as Spurs went on to sell their full allocation as expected. City, though, would only see £906 of that money - the same as Tottenham - with £933 payable in entertainment tax. The rest was eaten up by the work bill for getting the ground fit to cope with a capacity crowd, as well as a compensation payment to Stockport, who hosted City two days after in a re-arranged game that only attracted a crowd of 2,933. Compensation was due to bring the gate receipts in line with the season's average.

Three days before the big match, police announced that they would use walkie-talkie sets to control the flow of traffic to Bootham Crescent, with a large area around the ground sealed off to general two-way traffic on the Saturday afternoon. The routes were clearly signed by the AA, as police also guided motorists into the streets available for parking. Special buses were put on, meanwhile, to transport people to and from the railway station before and after the game. Only buses, taxis and cycles were allowed down Bootham Crescent and there was to be no traffic at all on Grosvenor Road. The traffic scheme lasted from 1pm to 5.30pm and a cycle park was also situated in the car park behind the Main Stand. Chief Constable Mr CTG Carter admitted: "The position of the ground raised difficulties when such a large crowd was expected, but if spectators co-operated 100 per cent with police and ground officials all the arrangements would go smoothly."

A special souvenir programme was also printed and, with the cooperation of the Supporters' Club, Auxiliary Club and Social Club, a total of 10,000 copies were printed, costing three pence each and giving pen-pictures of each team, as well as photographs of many of the players.

In the days leading up to the match, it was hoped the snow fall would protect the pitch from frosting up. The day before the game, meanwhile, a local contractor supervised a gang of men to start clearing some of the snow. Hard frozen lumps of turf, which were regarded the main danger to players, were removed too. Referee George Gibson was one of the earliest arrivals at Bootham Crescent on the morning of the game and had no hesitation in declaring the pitch fit for play, with the proviso that any further snow fall did not make the pitch markings indiscernible. With this in mind, the ground staff had acquired a supply of blue dye, which had to be repeatedly applied to make sure all lines were as clear as possible, as there were further snow showers during the build-up to the match.

Spurs lost Ireland international Jonny Gavin on the morning of the game when he learned his father had died and travelled immediately to be with his family in Birmingham. The experienced Sonny Walters was subsequently drafted in. Bootham Crescent's gates were opened for the match at 1pm and, from 2pm, the band of the 5th Battalion, West Yorkshire Regiment (PWO) played a programme of music. It was still snowing, meanwhile, when Phillips beat Alf Ramsey in the toss-up. Ramsey, more than 11 years before he etched his name into football history by leading England as manager to their only World Cup victory, was one of six full internationals in the visitors' side.

There was little sense of the seismic shock that was on the cards, meanwhile, when the London giants went ahead after only 11 minutes on a pitch, described as difficult and treacherous. Ramsey played in a low centre and George Robb found the roof of the net from five yards. But, after Forgan had made a brilliant save to keep out Len Duquemin's header, City went on to outplay their illustrious visitors with some superb football. Brown was unlucky at a corner when the ball dropped into a pool of water just as he was about to shoot, so he mistimed his effort and couldn't recover in time to get a second chance. Spurs keeper Ron Reynolds also saved magnificently from Bottom, before two deserved goals in as many minutes turned the tie on its head. First, on 29 minutes, Fenton set off from the left side of the halfway line on a crossfield run, with Ramsey trailing in vain pursuit. He then backheeled the ball to Hughes, whose perfect right-wing cross was headed in by Wilkinson. In the next attack, Bottom beat two defenders and passed to Wilkinson, whose fierce shot was parried by Reynolds only as far as Fenton, who slammed the ball into the net. Pandemonium subsequently broke out at Bootham Crescent and the players received a great ovation when leaving the pitch at half-time. After the break, Eddie Bailey's header was cleared off the line by Howe, but Fenton saw a shot whistle inches over and Reynolds saved rather fortunately with his feet from Bottom. Forgan also made a tremendous save to keep out Duquemin's header but City, playing Spurs at their own short-passing game, remained in control and, with 10 minutes to go, extended their lead. Fenton beat Ramsey down the left and his cross was steered into the net by Wilkinson from seven yards. Part-time player Wilkinson - a cobbler by trade picked up from Hull City reserves in the summer - was then only denied a hat-trick against the world-famous London club when his 20-yard drive forced a magnificent one-handed diving save by Reynolds, as the home fans cheered hoarsely and sounded their rattles and bells.

At the final whistle, the crowd swarmed on to the pitch to mob their heroes and celebrate a historic result. Unsurprisingly, the game grabbed national headlines with the *Daily Express* exclaiming: "No fluke - it might have been six." Spurs legend Danny Blanchflower was also generous in defeat, admitting: "York's standard of play left us speechless. They were better in all departments." Ramsey added: "York were the better team and deserved to win. They showed they could play good football on a difficult pitch." The full back went on to win the Jules Rimet Trophy with his team of "wingless wonders" and his aversion towards wide men might well have been triggered by the torrid afternoon he was given by Fenton.

Remembering the game in February 2015, Happy Wanderers' goalkeeper Forgan said: "When we looked at the ground before the start of the game, we thought it would be hard to play the good football York had been playing all season, but we were wrong. We played extremely well considering the conditions and deserved our win. After the final whistle, the Tottenham players were very generous with their congratulations and said the best side had won. I don't remember much about the good save I made from Len Duquemin's header but, if it was in the papers, I will take it! I do remember the atmosphere at the ground being unbelievable. The York crowd certainly made themselves heard. As a player, you knew they were completely behind you and, in a match like that, it counted for a lot. After the game, everyone was ecstatic. In fact, I would say we were a bit cocky. We were saying the sky is the limit."

Commenting on the 50th anniversary of the tie to *The Press* in 2005, Wilkinson remembered: "Billy (Fenton) wasn't a great player but his pace used to frighten people and Alf Ramsey couldn't handle it." Wilkinson also hailed the role of Storey, then 35, who shackled promising youngster Blanchflower, later to become Spurs' double-winning captain in 1961. "As soon as the draw was made, Sid said. 'Danny Blanchflower's mine'," Wilkinson recalled. "He had played with him at Barnsley and told us he knew what he could do. That was a boon for us and Sid didn't let him play at all." On his own role, Wilkinson said modestly: "Two goals was pleasing enough and you just enjoy it as it comes. Billy Hughes dropped one on to my head for the first goal. I got to it before their centre-half and it went in lovely from eight yards. I didn't do badly with headers at any time. Billy (Fenton) scored the second, beating Ramsey to the ball after the keeper saved my shot. He then got away with 10 minutes to go and put a cross in that I turned into the goal. It wasn't really a shot, but it went right into the corner. We didn't really have any stars or internationals, but we just played as a team and were a great side. The ground was a bit iffy, but the snow was cleared away and melted and we adapted better than they did."

Wilkinson had taken over up front from Alf Patrick who, despite his move to Scarborough, was in the crowd to see City knock out the famous London club. "I was at the Tottenham game with my wife and father-in-law in the Popular Stand and we were all packed in so tightly that the fencing came down," Patrick said. "That run was great and they were a marvellous side. There were six internationals in that Tottenham team, including Alf Ramsey and Danny Blanchflower and, while they talk about teams like Bradford beating Chelsea in recent times, York City got to the last three in the FA Cup that season. It was a bit disappointing for me to miss out on all that, because I'd played with half of the team, but Norman had been brought in and he was a good player. I used to tell him you might be a better player than me, but I've got more hair!"

Fred Hemenway, who watched 85 years of matches at Bootham Crescent, was in no doubt as to which was the finest he ever saw from all those fixtures. "That was a great game," he enthused about the Spurs victory. "We saw George Robb, an England international, score first but, then, City got cracking and what a beauty Norman Wilkinson's equaliser was. I remember Alf Ramsey forcing Billy Fenton all the way across the pitch into the right-hand corner because he

Norman Wilkinson makes it 3-1 to York City as the Happy Wanderers knock Tottenham out of the 1955 FA Cup

Billy Fenton puts York City 2-1 up as the Happy Wanderers team knock the mighty Tottenham Hotspur out of the FA Cup on their way to the semi-finals of the competition in 1955. Future England World Cup-winning boss Alf Ramsey, who was given a torrid time by Fenton, is arriving just too late to stop his nemesis netting

would not let him get it on to his left foot. But Billy just back-heeled it to Billy Hughes and he centred it for Norman, who was running in from the corner of the penalty area. He got a lot of his goals coming from that position and he just headed the ball straight into the net in front of us. I've never forgotten that goal. It was terrific. Years later, I used to play bowls with Billy Hughes. I said to him: 'There's one thing that's always puzzled me about that goal. You crossed the ball straight in when Billy Fenton back-heeled it to you, but that wasn't your normal style. You would have normally tried to dribble it into the blinking net'. He said: 'It must have been the right thing to do at the time' and I said: 'It was'. The way that team were playing then, they could have beaten anybody. They were the best team I ever saw at Bootham Crescent. Arthur Bottom couldn't half hit a ball and he always kept his shots down because he got his body right over it."

Hemenway would not have known it at the time but he was probably rubbing shoulders with a future City favourite that day as a 14-year-old Colin Addison was watching the game from the same spot. Addison was later player-manager as non-League Hereford pulled off arguably the biggest-ever shock in the competition's history by knocking out Newcastle and he admits the Tottenham game gave him his first taste of the FA Cup's special allure. "I was there with Barry Jackson and Barry Tait in the Grosvenor Road End," Addison recalled. "I think we were all training with the club on Tuesday and Thursday nights by then. I can still see George Robb scoring at that end and Norman's header. That result definitely made an impression on me about how special the FA Cup was."

97

It was also a memorable occasion for Addison's 17-year-old companion Jackson that afternoon. The man who would go on to make more appearances at Bootham Crescent than any other player in the club's history said: "I was born in Wensleydale, where my father was the village copper in Askrigg, but we moved to York, where I went to Joseph Rowntree School and I grew up supporting the club. I didn't go to too many games as, like any young footballer, I was often playing matches, but I was at the Tottenham game and that York side was a most wonderful set of players. I was stood behind the goal where Norman Wilkinson headed in a magnificent goal. It was a fantastic game and that team was very unlucky not to get to Wembley. Sid Storey was a very good player at the time too and he later became trainer for a while."

Graham Munday, meanwhile, was another in the crowd and remembers Storey turning on the style and Ramsey being all at sea. "Alf Ramsey won us that match because he was too slow," the lifelong City fan reasoned. "He should never have played. I was working down south at the time, but I came back for that game and nobody could touch Sid Storey in the mud either. He could turn a ball on a sixpence and was very clever. There was nothing on him, but he could keep out of tackles and was so mobile. He used to tell me he wouldn't have been any good on hard ground but, on mud, he was a pass master and could place the ball between the keeper and his goal. Billy Fenton also had that off to a tee and used to set off like an arrow, but Alf Ramsey was lost that day. I also remember the captain Ernie Phillips motioning with his hands to tell the team to put the ball in the corners when we were winning."

Sid Storey tracks Tottenham's Tony Marchi with Danny Blanchflower watching on as the York City midfielder inspires his team to a famous FA Cup triumph

One 17-year-old future City player, meanwhile, watched the drama unfurl from a fuming visitors' dugout. Alan Woods - who would become a member of the Minstermen's 1964/65 promotion-winning team - was on Tottenham's books at the time and recalled: "I was 12th man and it was my job to help the trainer Cecil Pointon. I carried the skip out of the coach into the dressing room and put the kit on the pegs that day. If the players wanted anything, I also had to get it as well. I think I was chosen because I came from Dinnington and I could go and see my parents after the match. I was sat on the bench for the game next to Cecil, who was doing his nut. He was annoyed because we had one hell of a team. He would have no complaints if you'd just had a bad game because that happens to all footballers no matter how good you are. But he couldn't stand it if you didn't get stuck in and have a go. He was furious during the game at York and quite rightly so."

Woods reasoned that the pitch proved a leveller but only because of the Spurs' players reaction to it, explaining: "The pitch played a part without a doubt. It was frozen and all the snow had been shovelled off and piled up around the sides but you have to play whatever conditions there are and get on with it. You were often ankle deep in mud in those days, but a lot of the Tottenham players didn't want to know. It was so cold and they were frightened because the pitch was rock hard. It wouldn't have been played now - no way - but York wanted the gate money and any club would have been the same. It was a full house and a great atmosphere but (Tottenham manager) Arthur Rowe wasn't very chuffed. I thought it was over once we got a goal but, of course, it didn't work out like that. I was surprised how well York played, but they were up for it. They got stuck in and had a go and deserved to win. There's no two ways about that and they all did well as a team."

On the miserable scenes in the away dressing room afterwards, Woods said: "Nobody said a word. Only Cec Pointon kept muttering. The players just got stripped off and got in the bath. All they wanted to do was to get out of the place." There was a silver lining, though, for the future Minsterman, who explained: "It was fine for me. If you were in the first-team squad, your salary immediately went up to the £20-a-week maximum wage regardless of what your basic wage was and, at 17, I would have been on £7 then. I was chuffed actually because, if you're not in the team, you don't want them to win or you're not going to get back in. I didn't want them to win and nobody does in that situation if they're honest and I think I was in the team for the next game."

Tottenham's York-born ace Dunmore, though, did not feature in or watch the match, having been hailed from his home town for a reserve fixture back in London. "When I signed for Tottenham, I was still working as an apprentice machinist and had two years of my seven to complete, so I still trained at York and only used to travel down to London for matches," he explained. "Only if I got a week or fortnight off work, would I go to Spurs and train and I was going to be 12th man for the Cup game but we were playing Chelsea in a big match between the first and second-placed teams in the Combination League. We had to win the game, so I went down there to play when they were coming up here. I would have liked to have been involved but Alan Woods was 12th man instead and, unlike them, I ended up with a medal because we finished champions of the Combination."

The former Minsterman was, however, primed for information before his journey south. "They wanted to know about the York players and I told them what I thought as I saw it," he said. "I knew it would be a hard game because City were on a high and on a roll with everything going right for them at the time." As a former player still based in York and training with the club, Dunmore also didn't blame the Happy Wanderers and their supporters for the subsequent ribbing he received. "Tottenham took the defeat in their stride because that's football - you have to take the knocks as well," he explained. "I wasn't training with Spurs at the time, so I didn't get any stick from them for coming from York. All the stick I got was from around here and all I could do was congratulate them. It was a brilliant result. The conditions maybe favoured York a bit because the pitch wasn't anything like the surfaces nowadays when you never seem to get any bad bounces. In fact, back then, players used to help with the work on the pitch. I did that in the summer to get a bit more money at Tottenham when I moved down there."

Dunmore also recalled Ramsey being magnanimous and gracious following his torrid afternoon at the hands of Fenton, adding: "Billy was quick and could hit the ball. Alf Ramsey wasn't happy we had got beaten but he had a lot of praise for the City players and appreciated that they had performed well." Indeed, Ramsey was reported to have congratulated the City players on their performance in the dressing room afterwards.

Future City board member Rob McGill, meanwhile, chose the memorable occasion to watch his first game at Bootham Crescent as a Tottenham fan - having only arrived in North Yorkshire from London a matter of days earlier. Taking up the story, he recalled: "I'd always been a football person in London.

I played a lot and was loosely involved with Tottenham's youth activity, which is what they called their academy back then. I was picked up playing schoolboy football at 14 and went down there, but I wasn't good enough. There were two parts to the youth activity - Edmonton juniors and Tottenham juniors. I started off with Edmonton and didn't make it as far as the Tottenham team, but then a job opportunity came up and I moved to York in 1955 and the first game I ever saw at Bootham Crescent was York v Tottenham in the fifth round of the FA Cup. The teams had never met before and never have done since. The last game I watched before I left London was Tottenham beating Port Vale 4-2 in the fourth round and, afterwards, I told all my friends that I was upping sticks and that the best draw for me would be an away tie at this York City. I started working for Rowntree and, even though it was short notice, because the game took place only a few days after I had arrived, there was a guy who I was working for who was a York City director - Mr (John) Rosindale - and he was able to get me a ticket when they weren't easy to get hold of. I didn't really know anybody in York at that time, so I went on my own and it was a brilliant game. Some of my favourite players like Len Duquemin, Danny Blanchflower and Alf Ramsey were all in the Tottenham team and, because I had picked up some information since moving to York, with the stupidity of youth, I'd actually written to White Hart Lane before the match and told them they ought to look out for this winger Billy Fenton. But I was a converted York fan by the end of the game. I've always believed you should support your local team and I was looking at York as a very permanent move, so that was the start of it all for me. I became a York City supporter on that day, whilst always having that Tottenham connection."

McGill also felt that his new adopted city were worthy winners of the tie and a lot smarter looking than he had imagined, adding: "I was in the end where Norman Wilkinson headed the goal in and it was all a bit incredulous. I was a big Tottenham supporter and I went into that match with the total expectation that Spurs would wipe the floor with them but, suddenly, it all went funny and the impression I had at the end of the game was that York's win was very well merited. Although I was quite biased, York were brilliant that day with the way they moved the ball around. With it being the old third division north days, although this sounds awful, coming up from London I expected teams to be playing with holes in their stockings. I thought it would all be a bit Mickey Mouse, but it wasn't, so that was quite enlightening. It was a very good team for its day and they gelled together."

On his first impressions of Bootham Crescent and the atmosphere it could generate, McGill went on to enthuse: "The ground was packed out and people had rattles, because they were allowed in back then. It was what I'd call real proper football and there was no animosity between the supporters. It was as though we were all part of the same culture and atmosphere. Bootham Crescent was also quite a smart ground then and I was quite surprised how close the fence was to the touchline. It surprised me how close to the play you were and how close you were to all sorts of incidents. I remember an evening match under floodlights later on and a reserve-team full back had come in for a game. It was raining and he was stood on the half-way line just in front of me in the Popular Stand and the keeper hit a great, big, long punt and the ball was moving quickly through the air. As it started dropping, the full back didn't seem to know whether to head it, take it on his chest or control it with his feet and I heard him say: 'Oh, my god'. He then decided to take it on his chest and, as the ball hit him, his false teeth shot out. It was hilarious and those are the sort of things that stick in your mind."

After becoming a club director half-a-century later, McGill admitted that the thrills of '55 could never really be emulated. "The nearest we got to the excitement of that FA Cup run was probably when we got to the new Wembley stadium for the first time in the FA Trophy," he reasoned. "That seemed to generate massive support in the city. Shops were decorated, and people got really involved, although football was probably more hardcore in York during 1955. It was all about the five-and-a-half day week, which everybody worked back then. Children would meet their dads outside the ground on a Saturday after they had come straight from work. It was a real working-class environment and the only bit of entertainment around. The alternatives simply weren't there, so football had a real impact on people's lives, because the cinemas couldn't open until 4pm on a Saturday, and Sunday was a day of observance. I'm very nostalgic about that period and it was a super time when kids would be waiting at the same bus stops as the players to go home, making it easy to get their autographs."

Happy Wanderers hero Bottom, meanwhile, would become an early hero for McGill, who explained: "I started making friendships and a group of us used to go to games from Rowntree. We would stand behind the goal at the Grosvenor Road End and position ourselves where we could just see over the top of the crossbar and we'd wait for Arthur Bottom to break through. That was before teams took an intellectual approach to defending and it would often come down to one man against another man and Arthur Bottom seemed like he knew he was going to score, when he got clear, because he always had a big grin on his face. Which way the team kicked often depended on who won the toss of course and you always wanted to get behind the goal York were attacking so, if you were at the wrong end, it would be a mad scramble to get to the other end of the ground, but we'd run and just get there in time. You'd learn to look for the actions of the ref for a clue that the teams would be swapping ends and then you'd set off straight away."

Billy Sherrington's daughter Terry Fowler also believed the Tottenham Cup shock took top billing in terms of fixtures at Bootham Crescent, even if her father kept his celebrations low-key. "It was probably the best game I ever saw because there were so many stars in their side," she reasoned. "He was delighted afterwards but he never went over the top like some people. He had people ringing him up from all over the country that he'd not seen for years." Sherrington also felt great sympathy for the lengths supporters would go to in their desire to secure a ticket for the club's biggest matches. "He used to feel dreadful when he turned up at the ground at 8am in the morning and people had been queuing for tickets since after midnight," Fowler added. "He felt so sorry for them, especially in the middle of winter."

The result was a fine reward for such loyalty, though, with a delighted Sherrington quoted on the front page of the following day's *Sunday Express*, saying: "The secret? Team spirit. We like to be modest about our football but now we're afraid of no-one in the Cup." It was also reported that a crowd of City supporters joyfully escorted Spurs fans to York station to see them off home. On the same newspaper's back page, meanwhile, under the strapline "The Cup Shock of the Year", the team were described as "the 100-1 Cinderella side" that "thrashed mighty Spurs". Alan Hoby's match report went on to state that the win was "no fluke" and "from the first whistle to the last, they outplayed and outskilled Tottenham", with their passing described "as crisp as pork crackling". He also declared the Happy Wanderers to be "one of the finest teams the third division has ever produced". The pitch, though, was described, as "appalling" with slush on top and ice underneath. He went on to reveal that Forgan put a lucky black cat toy mascot in his goal for the game, as he did for every tie during the run following the victory at Dorchester, with the team having been presented with the gift, trimmed with City colours, by staff of the Bourne Hall Hotel in Bournemouth - the club's headquarters for their second-round match. Captain Phillips, meanwhile, was quoted pre-match as saying: "We use the ball here. We make it do the work."

Fenton also added afterwards: "We thought we would win. We never had any doubts." Hoby stressed too how Blanchflower was "reduced to the stature of another player". As a "tailpiece", it was also recorded that members of the press were given hot water bottles to combat the extreme cold.

In Monday's *Daily Express*, meanwhile, reporter Henry Rose painted a picture of the scenes at the final whistle, writing: "What a sight when it was all over. Hats, cushions thrown into the air and the field black with Cup-frenzied City fans as the victorious players tried to thread their way through." He also described how pre-match he came across Sherrington thumbing through cuttings of the famous 1938 run. The journalist added that, whereas that run had been achieved by "terrific tackling, stamina and refusal to admit defeat", the team's latest success stemmed from "sheer football". Spurs boss Rowe, meanwhile, was quoted as saying the game "was enough to make you weep". The writer added: "It could have been four, five or six with no injustice to the first division club" and reasoned that pit haulage worker Storey should take a bow for his "black-out of £30,000 Danny Blanchflower". Tom Lockie, who had become caretaker manager of the team, also espoused his philosophy on how the game should be played in an interview, saying: "There's only one ball on the field. One side can't have it all the time. We make sure we get most of it."

City would go on to win 1-0 at Notts County in the quarter-finals thanks to a Bottom goal - a game that also saw fans queuing for hours at Bootham Crescent for tickets. The general-public allocation, aside from those tickets set aside for season-ticket holders and members of the Supporters', Auxiliary and Social Clubs, were snapped up in just over two hours. All of the visitors' 11,200 tickets were sold for the massive Meadow Lane contest and, four days afterwards, more than 10,000 turned up to see City overcome Chesterfield 3-2 in a 4.30pm kick-off with Bottom beating Fenton's club record of 31 goals in a season, as a brace moved him on to 33. The record-breaking effort was a simple strike after Wilkinson's shot was parried and Fenton was reported to be the first to congratulate his colleague in the bath afterwards.

Before the first batch of stand tickets went on sale at Bootham Crescent for the subsequent semi-final against Newcastle at Sheffield Wednesday's Hillsborough ground, television newsreel cameramen were there to film the early arrivals. Of those that were forming a queue at 9am - eight hours before tickets were due to be sold - were Mr and Mrs Reginald Duffin, of Acomb. Mr Duffin's place in the queue was later taken by his daughter who, along with her mother, sat on a stool wrapped in a blanket to protect against the wind and snow with flasks of tea for fortification. By midday, there were 50 people in the queue and, by mid-afternoon, there were hundreds present. Many were "huddled under rugs, reading novels and dreaming of next Saturday", reported the *Yorkshire Evening Press*. The following day, when 14,000 ground and enclosure tickets went on sale to the general public, people were arriving nine-and-a-half hours early with 67-year-old pensioners Richard Layfield and Walter Skelton first at the ground. Both had walked to Bootham Crescent after their 7.30am breakfast, having arranged with some of their companions to be served with a snack lunch at the ground. Mr Skelton was not even queuing for himself, but a friend. By mid-afternoon, more than 1,000 people were queuing for the 6s tickets and between 1,500 and 2,000 for the half-crown tickets. Billy Kettlewell, an 11-year-old schoolboy, was at the front of the Enclosure queue with a snack and cold tea in a lemonade bottle. The queues swelled at 4pm with the arrival of schoolchildren, at 4.30pm by those lucky to get off work early and, soon afterwards, by many others as the city's bigger firms and factories closed their gates for the day. By 6pm, when the tickets went on sale, the queue for 2s 6d tickets snaked for more than a mile down Grosvenor Road, Burton Stone Lane and as far as Ratcliffe Street into Scarborough Terrace. It was reported that some people tried to queue jump by meeting friends but were prevented from staying by "bantering remarks of: 'We're watching you.'" All the tickets were accounted for within three hours, but it was believed few people left disappointed with many of those in the queue, when the last of the batch had been sold, understood to be lining up for a second time. The office's phone at Bootham Crescent did not stop ringing, however, during the days before the match with further unsuccessful requests for tickets. Heavy rain also meant the players could not train on the pitch at Bootham Crescent in the build-up to the game, so the majority of their preparation was limited to running sessions on the terraces or work at York Railway Institute's indoor gym.

The irrepressible Bottom was then on target as City forced a semi-final replay by drawing 1-1 against a Newcastle team featuring the legendary Jackie Milburn at Hillsborough. Long queues, which had become a familiar sight at Bootham Crescent, formed again two days later for the Wednesday afternoon replay at Sunderland's Roker Park. More than 8,000 tickets were sold for the 2.30pm kick-off in two hours on the Monday morning, with the intention to then send the remainder - numbering about 4,000 - back to the north-east. But Sunderland granted permission for tickets to carry on being sold between 2pm and 4.30pm and 6pm and 7pm in the Social Club, with only a few left at the close of the day.

The day before the tie, Sid Storey had a fitness test, having missed the Hillsborough clash with a back injury. He trotted around the pitch at Bootham Crescent, touched his toes and loosened up his waist muscles, before declaring: "The back feels dandy." As other players gathered for a work-out on the terraces, children in the adjacent Shipton Street School, meanwhile, started their morning chant of: "We want Bottom!" They only stopped when their hero, with Spence and skipper Phillips, went to the boundary wire and posed for a photograph. No ball was used in the final training session with Stewart having sticking plasters on both knees, which were scratched and gravel-scarred from Saturday's tie. A handful of spectators later waved off the team bus with its familiar red-and-white rosette on the radiator.

It was the Magpies, though, who went on to progress to the final, following a 2-0 replay win at Roker Park. Nevertheless, the run had been an amazing achievement for the joint-management team of Lockie and Sherrington, who had taken over following McCormick's resignation during the second month of the season. Explaining their dual roles, Forgan said: "Tom Lockie was a very good person for the job. Not only did he set the training, he did 101 things behind the scenes. Billy Sherrington was a very shrewd man and was only seen on Friday - payday. He always wore a waistcoat and kept three-penny bits in one of the pockets to make sure you got the right money. Payday was very different for footballers back then!"

The experience probably also gave Sherrington an insight into a job that he sometimes found somewhat unfathomable. "When managers disappeared, he used to take over and he often said he wondered what managers did," his daughter Fowler explained. "He said I know what I do and what the trainer does but I'm not sure what the manager does."

Fowler, herself, was also still helping out with what would now be deemed managerial or club secretarial affairs. "My father had a lot of contacts with Newcastle and Sunderland and I used to ring them up for players," she said. "Newcastle would also call him or me up and say: 'We've got so-and-so, he's not quite good enough for us, but he could do a job for you'. He got a lot of players like that and some did very well. One was Billy Hughes. I used to book the overnight stays as well. I remember organising accommodation at the Bourne Hall Hotel in Bournemouth for the Dorchester game during the 1955 FA Cup run."

A framed picture, depicting scenes from the Cup run, was subsequently hung in the boardroom. But City's Cup exploits had one regrettable consequence - a fixture pile-up which saw them play 11 games in April and, in all probability, caused the club to miss out on promotion. Five of those matches were staged at Bootham Crescent, including a Good Friday top-of-the-table 1-1 draw against Accrington that attracted just under 20,000 supporters, with 3,000 locked outside, including some visiting fans, when the gates needed to be shut. Many managed to find other perches to watch the game from, though, including the crowded rooftops of Shipton Street School. Storey took an early knock in the game and was tended to on the sidelines for 15 minutes. He played on but could not wield his normal influence on the game. A Bottom equaliser did, nevertheless, earn City a point from a bad-tempered encounter. It was the prolific Bottom's 39th goal of an outstanding season - which is still a club record outside of the Midland League era. He could have also set an even greater tally, had he not missed the final eight matches of the campaign after suffering a pulled leg muscle.

The day after the Accrington game, which had seen the then customary Good Friday two-minute silence observed, the Minstermen were back at Bootham Crescent for a clash against Grimsby and, despite dominating, the hosts could only draw 0-0 in front of more than 12,000 supporters, meaning an aggregate attendance for the two matches of 32,265 was recorded, resulting in record gate receipts of £2,853 for one weekend.

The 1954/55 season was also a campaign in which David Meek - son of The *Yorkshire Evening Press'* long-standing City writer Wilf - began a journalism career at Bootham Crescent that would lead to him reporting on Manchester United for 37 years following the death of the *Manchester Evening News'* Tom Jackson in the Munich air disaster. On his thrilling introduction to life in the press box back then, Meek recalled: "My first ever job in journalism was phoning copy over for an ex-Leeds United centre-half called Tom Holley. He was a huge guy who worked for the *Yorkshire Evening Post* and wrote his reports out in long hand. The press box back then was one row of about ten seats and you were enclosed behind glass. If you got sat the wrong side of Tom, you couldn't get out because he was so big, so you made sure you went to the toilet before the match. My dad also had a phone line back then that went direct to the *Evening Press'* Coney Street office and it was a very friendly, family-orientated club. The people who were involved in the running of the club would mix in the boardroom with the press on match days. There was an inner sanctum that we didn't go in but, for the most part, we mingled together and all the directors were friendly. The lady who served the tea was the secretary's daughter (Terry Fowler) and it was that type of club." That good will was not always extended by one particular board member, though, as Meek recalled. "I went on to cover the club for the *Yorkshire Post* and *Yorkshire Evening Post* and my father, who had become a director in 1950, used to have great fun with me," he remembered. "I was still living at home and he would come back from board meetings knowing the team for Saturday because he had discussed it with whoever the manager was. I could never get it out of him or any transfer news or anything, which he took great delight in teasing me about."

Despite going on to write about the exploits of some of the world's greatest-ever talents such as George Best and Bobby Charlton, Meek never forgot the Happy Wanderers' team he had the privilege of watching from the press box. "I was 24 when I started covering York City in 1954/55 and it was a terrific run," he enthused. "They were my favourite team for years and I could always reel the names off. Terry Butcher made bleeding heads fashionable in later years, but Alan Stewart was there before him. He always seemed to get whacked around the head, nose and eyes. He was a real, brave centre half with great determination. At wing-half, they had the balance just right with Gordon Brown a classy player who could spray the ball around and Ron Spence more defensive and able to win the ball. I also loved the way Arthur Bottom played. He was a superb footballer. If he'd had another yard of pace, he would have been in the first division. He had marvellous feet for a big man. He also linked up nicely with Sid Storey who, if he'd have been a stone stronger, would have been in the first division too, because he was really clever and nimble. Then, there was Norman Wilkinson who was a battering ram of a centre forward. They were a good side and they did not fluke any of the results. They deserved to win every tie. Tottenham had an all-star team, including Alf Ramsey. He was a classy full back, but he hadn't really got any answer for York's wingers on the day. Billy Fenton was very fast and I don't think pace was Alf's strongest suit. I can still see Billy flashing by him. My dad wasn't a very demonstrative man but he did let himself go a bit after that match."

Profits from the FA Cup run, along with a Stand Extension fund, meanwhile, saw the Main Stand extended towards Shipton Street that summer, resulting in an extra 360 seats and increasing the ground's seating capacity to 1,350, which was in line with the greater demand for season tickets. The work was undertaken to make provisions for the possibility of higher-division football in the future and the join point, where the last quarter was added, could be seen right up to the final game at the ground. New turnstiles were also added in the car park at the end of the extension and the exit gate was widened. Admission to the Main Stand would no longer be possible from the Enclosure, but from the car park only. Businessmen in York spontaneously launched the Stand Extension Fund as the net profit from the Cup run, after entertainment tax and expenses were deducted, was still reported as being insufficient to cover the £7,000 cost of the work and other associated projects. Those that made donations on the fund's launch were Unwins (York) Ltd (£50), AE Sorrell, York (£50), E Grainger, The Mount, York (£20) and N Kay, York (£4 4s). Mr JE Mummery, manager of the National Provincial Bank in York, was the fund's treasurer. Other subsequent contributions included 25 guineas from the York Pullman Bus Company and a combined total of £745 10s from local brewery companies, such as John Smith's, Hammonds United, Messrs JW Cameron, the Yorkshire Clubs and Hope and Anchor. The Social Club also donated £500, with the Supporters' Club (200 guineas) and the Women's Section of the Supporters' Club (100 guineas) following suit, while City's directors handed over £261 5s. With approximately £2,300 raised by the fund, plans were submitted to York Corporation for approval. Included in the proposals were also ten additional rows of concrete terracing at the Shipton Street End - resulting in 33 in total - to increase its capacity by 1,000. New toilet facilities would be built there too, as well as for Main Stand Enclosure patrons, which were positioned adjacent to the extension. A new watering device, meanwhile, was brought in to improve the playing surface under the supervision of groundsman George Bass. Another scheme - to build a concrete supporting wall at the St Olave's Road End at a cost of several thousand pounds - was held up as no contractor could promise to complete the job by the start of the season in August.

The summer improvements were the most extensive made to the ground since its opening 23 years earlier and were reported as making the stadium the best in the Football League's northern section. One further mooted idea to extend the Main Stand over the social club, which would have resulted in more than 2,000 seats, never came to fruition. Members of the Supporters' Club also carried out their usual maintenance work over the close-season period - voluntarily making improvements to the visiting dressing room and referee's room and painting all areas of the ground. City's players trained at Bootham School in pre-season, as the work was completed.

The average league attendance during 1954/55 had risen to 9,630 with gross receipts amounting to £38,227, compared to £17,930 the previous season.

The Happy Wanderers team back row (from left-to-right): Norman Wilkinson, Gordon Brown, Tommy Forgan, Alan Stewart, Ron Spence, George Howe, Tom Lockie. Front row (from left-to-right): Billy Hughes, Arthur Bottom, Ernie Phillips, Sid Storey, Billy Fenton

CHAPTER 9

A 9-1 win and promotion for the first time

"They throw parties for teams that get promoted now and the players get invited to this and that. We probably just had a few beers and Peter Wragg will have arranged a night out."

The enthusiasm, created by the FA Cup run, rolled over into the next campaign with the average home crowd of 10,291 the second-highest in the club's history despite a final mid-table finish of 11th in the third division north section. Such encouraging numbers came despite a rise in the minimum admission charge to two shillings, as determined by the Football League. City responded to the edict by making 80 per cent of Bootham Crescent's accommodation available at that price, meaning the price to watch from the covered Popular Stand stayed at 2s - a figure that represented double the pre-War admission charge, which was roughly in line with inflation. Rates on the ground, for example, had gone up from £126 to £243. Prices in the Main Stand and Enclosure Paddock, meanwhile, rose to 4s and 2s 6d respectively. The charge for boys remained at 9d, with season tickets costing £4 15s, instead of £4 5s. Nevertheless, Bootham Crescent saw £700 taken within two hours when season tickets went on sale, with the reserved area for members having to be revised three times before the start of the campaign, as the new extension was put to full use. Of the extra three pence on the minimum charge, clubs received two pence with one penny going to the tax man.

New traffic proposals around the ground were also devised by police with bigger crowds anticipated. They included only taxis, special buses, official cars bearing a special label and bicycles being allowed down Bootham Crescent on a match day, while parking was not permitted on Grosvenor Road. Only official cars and team buses were admitted into the car park, the size of which had been reduced by the extension.

The Saturday before the start of the season, the annual public practice match was played, with the work to the ground still being completed. City's semi-final

Cup team played as the Reds against a Blues reserve side and won 5-2 in front of 4,700 fans. In the Meek household, the big attendances led to the kind of family joke that would have been repeated in many where some of those under the roof considered Bootham Crescent a place of worship. "My mother was a big church goer and my dad would ask her how many were in the congregation on a Sunday, then delighted in telling her there had been a few more at Bootham Crescent the day before," David Meek remembered.

The start to an eagerly-anticipated campaign proved an anti-climax, though, with Wrexham winning 3-1 at Bootham Crescent in front of a 12,173 gate. Encouragingly, with future generations of support in mind, an increased proportion of the attendance, though, were boys, numbering 1,600 in total. Two *Yorkshire Evening Press* readers RJ Dumore and RJ Campling were not impressed by some of the young newcomers' behaviour, however, complaining: "We should like to draw your attention to the iron gates at each end of the Popular Stand. On three successive occasions we have been one of the unfortunate spectators who have missed quite a lot of the match owing to the deplorable (dangerous) habit of children climbing on these for a better view. Would it be possible to make a small enclosure for children somewhere on the ground or appeal to the spectators to allow children preference along the rails? Since these gates are such a general nuisance we cannot see any further use for them now that the charge of two shilling is universal for that side. We notice that these could be easily moved without a lot of expense and replaced later if required."

Those that were converging on Bootham Crescent saw just one point taken from the first three home games, however, before debutants Clive Colbridge and Peter Tait were on target in a 3-0 defeat of Hartlepool. In mid-September, however, a resurgent City went top of the table after seeing off visitors Stockport 1-0, courtesy of an Arthur Bottom goal. The result ensured that all three of the club's teams were all leading their respective divisions, with the reserves and the newly-reformed "A" team heading the Midland and Yorkshire League tables respectively. City's "A" team, whose home fixtures were generally played at the Civil Service ground in Boroughbridge Road, also hosted sides at Bootham Crescent when the first team and reserves were both playing away fixtures. Thorne Colliery agreed to switch their home game for the first Yorkshire League contest to be played at the newly-modernised stadium that campaign, with City winning 3-0.

By November, meanwhile, it was announced that the room under the new Main Stand extension would be turned into a players' games room with a billiards table. The following month, then Arsenal captain Don Roper and his wife were shown around Bootham Crescent with the view to him becoming City's new player-manager and he was reported to be impressed with the facilities. Nevertheless, he turned down the opportunity to take charge of the team a couple of days later, reportedly due to business interests in London.

There were more FA Cup exploits too during the campaign, with City winning at second division promotion hopefuls Swansea to earn a plumb fourth-round home draw against top-flight Sunderland, then known as the "Bank of England" side due to their big-money signings. It was the first time the two clubs had met in the Cup and the contest between the previous season's beaten semi-finalists attracted an all-ticket 22,000 crowd. Ticket prices were in line with the Tottenham match the year before and cost 10s for the Main Stand, 5s for the Enclosure and Popular Stand and 2s 6d for the rest of the ground. Priority allocations were also again made for the Auxiliary Club, the Social Club and Supporters' Club, as well as season-ticket holders. With the Auxiliary Club now numbering 12,500 members, the Supporters Club 4,000 and the Social Club well over 1,000, not every member in those bodies was guaranteed a ticket, though, from the 75 per cent home allocation for the 22,000-limit that had been set following consultation with the chief constable and City Engineers' department. Those people who were members of more than one of the clubs were initially asked not to get an extra ticket, which was possible for anybody with dual membership, to give those regulars who were non-members a chance in the queues. Subsequently, though, 6,000 were handed over for the Auxiliary, Supporters' and Social Clubs to be distributed by each group as seen fit. It also emerged that fans who attended the reserve match the week before were, due to their loyalty, considered worthy enough to be "quietly" offered the remaining Main Stand seats for the tie that hadn't been snapped up by season-ticket holders.

Even so, a majority of tickets were still made available for those prepared to queue during the public sale on the Monday preceding the game, when Mrs E Shepherd, of Heslington Lane, made sure she was first in the queue. She arrived 12 hours early at 6.30am wrapped in warm clothes and carrying a flask of tea and sandwiches with only a "red-and-white golliwog" for company. Mr WE Ward arrived soon afterwards with a paraffin stove for warmth, as snow fell at the stadium. By 9.30am, the queue was 50 deep and, at noon, there were 300 in a line that snaked back towards Lumley Barracks. Three hours later, the estimate was 5,000 in a queue that now stretched past the Barracks on Burton Stone Lane and to St Luke's Church with the club believing they could have sold 30,000 tickets, rather than the 16,500 they had been allocated. When the first tickets were sold at 6.25pm, there were loud cheers from a queue that was more than 1,400 yards long, while 70 to 80 people were squeezing through the narrow doorway every minute. A 15-minute walk on icy roads was needed just to go from the head of the line to its tail, which extended the full length of Scarborough Terrace. But, in the space of two-and-a-half hours, 9,000 tickets were sold and many supporters still went home disappointed. The last ticket - a 5s one - went to Mr J Dale after the man in front of him declined the chance to take it, as he had wanted a 2s 6d ticket. At Sunderland, meanwhile, a stampede towards the office, caused by 2,000 people surging forward in a 10,000-strong queue for 4,500 tickets, meant sales were abandoned for another day.

On the day of the game, nearly 100 regular and special police ensured the traffic plan for areas surrounding Bootham Crescent was adhered to. Cyclists were instructed to leave their bikes in the car park behind the Main Stand but could not approach the ground from Grosvenor Road or St Olave's Road in an almost identical approach to policing the game as the Tottenham match the previous season. Only club officials with the requisite pass, meanwhile, were permitted to leave their vehicles in the car park.

The returns of Billy Fenton from injury and Bottom after suspension meant the famous Happy Wanderers' starting XI was selected for the tie, while most of the outdoor training for the game was again done on the Bootham School pitch in Rawcliffe Lane and considerable extra banking was laid down at the Shipton Street End of the ground. The BBC also sent two representatives to the game, with their commentaries on the tie of the round given in sports broadcasts afterwards. With the two kits clashing, contrary to league rules when the visitors changed strip, Cup rules still dictated that both sides found alternative colours, with City playing in blue shirts and white shorts, while Sunderland wore white shirts and black shorts. A special programme printed in the blue-and-white colours of the day was also sold for sixpence. Licences, meanwhile, were given for the Exhibition Hotel, Ye Olde Grey Mare, Corner House Hotel, Bootham Tavern, White Horse, Imperial Hotel, Punch Bowl Inn, Castle Howard Ox and Burton Lane Club to extend their Saturday opening times by an hour to allow supporters to toast victory, drown their sorrows or contemplate a replay after the match.

Snow, which always seemed to greet every big cup tie at Bootham Crescent, had to be cleared off the pitch on the eve and morning of the game, along with small pools of water, but the playing surface was declared "soft but fit" when matchday arrived. Revered former England international Len Shackleton and future Northern Ireland manager Billy Bingham were among the big names in the visitors' line-up. Gates were opened at 12.45pm with music played by the Prince of Wales' Own 5th Battalion West Yorkshire Regiment (Territorial Army). In the minutes before kick-off, City's Robin mascot, carved in wood and painted in the club's colours, was also paraded around the ground and a constant din was raised from bells, rattles and almost everything that could create a noise. Record gate receipts of £4,115 were taken but entertainment tax accounted for £1,005 and other costs meant both clubs only received £907.

When the game got underway, Shackleton rattled a home post and forced Tommy Forgan into a brilliant save, but City were far from over-awed. Skipper Ernie Phillips did so well against Shackleton that the "Clown Prince" seldom tried his trademark tricks with the ball and preferred to pass it on quickly and, in the final analysis, only heroics from Forgan's opposite number Willie Fraser, including when Norman Wilkinson and Fenton tried to scramble the ball over the line late on, kept the score goal-less and earned Sunderland a replay that they won 2-1 at Roker Park.

In the aftermath of the tie, chairman Hugh Kitchin spoke about his desire to increase Bootham Crescent's capacity by 8,000 to 30,000. It was felt improvements to the Shipton Street End then offered the most realistic opportunity to expand. But the addition of terracing at both ends of the pitch was considered, along with the possibility of another stand extension, provision of more cover and new offices for the Social Club. As with all work at Bootham Crescent, all future construction would have been predominantly concrete, brick and steel based, with other clubs, who erected wooden stands and terracing, having run into trouble due to replacement costs. The club also began to formulate plans to install floodlights at the ground, seeking tenders for the job and examining systems installed at other stadia.

Charlton legend and City war-time favourite Sam Bartram, meanwhile, was appointed as the club's new manager, ending an 18-month period during which time nobody had officially filled the position. His first home game - a 3-2 win against Barrow - heralded an enthusiastic welcome over the loudspeaker system.

A scheme to relay home match commentaries to local hospitals had been agreed too, following the example of bigger clubs. It involved extensive wiring work at an estimated cost of £300 and the first game to be broadcast was the December 1 home clash against Darlington with commentaries available at the County Hospital, City General Hospital, Fairfield Hospital, St Mary's and the

Grange. Mr EA King and Mr AW Rogers were the first commentators, with the service extended to the Fulford and Naburn Hospital by the end of the 1950s. Throughout the 1955/56 season, facilities at Bootham Crescent had also been provided for parties of blind students to attend games with the aid of their own commentator.

Famous World Cup referee Arthur Ellis, meanwhile, paid a trip to the ground in April to take charge of the Lucas Trophy clash between the Yorkshire and Lancashire police representative sides. The game attracted a 1,000-strong crowd with Lancashire completing an aggregate victory. A 16-year-old Colin Addison also impressed a watching Bartram with his performance in the York Senior Cup final at Bootham Crescent for Cliftonville. As a result, he was selected for the club's "A" team and scored the equaliser in a 2-2 draw against Wombwell Athletic at Boroughbridge Road. City did win some silverware at the end of the season too, completing a 7-4 aggregate win over Hull at Bootham Crescent to lift the East Riding Invitation Cup in front of a crowd of 8,881. Bartram played in goal for both legs and kept a clean sheet in the decisive 5-0 home victory that saw Bottom hit a hat-trick. Both players' names were then chanted by the crowd as Phillips was presented with the trophy. Bottom did not reappear as he was in the bath, but Bartram addressed the supporters, saying: "You give us the support and we will give you the football."

A 22ft-high concrete wall, meanwhile, was built during the close season at a cost of approximately £3,000 to replace the fencing at the St Olave's Road End of the ground. It was to act as a safety precaution and provided the necessary support for more extensive banking and terracing. Ten additional rows of terracing were subsequently put in place for the start of the new season. Plans to add Social Club and Supporters' Club premises at that end of the ground were also discussed, along with the revisiting of the idea to extend the Main Stand over the social club. At the AGM, meanwhile, record receipts and a profit of £8,453 were reported, meaning the club had an accumulated credit balance of £22,000 with the Bootham Crescent ground and accompanying equipment now valued at £19,832. The Supporters' Club also did well financially with £700 taken at the two tea bars, with the "tea ladies" having served 25,000 cuppas over the course of the season. A third tea bar was proposed for the following campaign. The new wall allowed the ground's capacity to grow from 21,000 to 23,600, but the 1955/56 campaign would see the last five-figured average attendance and boasted the highest all-time aggregate crowd of 236,685. Plans to reconstruct the buildings adjacent to the Social Club, which were mainly wooden buildings incorporating a store room, the Supporters' Club office and the general office were put on hold meanwhile.

Prior to the start of the 1956/57 season, a remarkable crowd of 7,099 watched the public Red and Blues in-house practice match with a youthful Barry Jackson getting his first run out in the club's colours. The 18-year-old defender filled in for an injured Gordon Brown and was reported to have "towered above his colleagues", while giving a "display which did him great credit". All the proceeds, as per normal and in line with Football League rules, were passed on to local charities, who benefitted to the tune of £326. The Fenby Memorial Fund of the York FA, established to assist amateur players who suffered injury playing the game and could not work, received £60 and £50 was given to the Friends of York Hospital to assist the scheme to provide hospital match commentaries.

Initially joining the club as an amateur, Jackson would eventually sign professional terms later in the season and remembers vividly how Bartram gave him his big break. "I signed professional when Sam Bartram was manager," Jackson pointed out. "I'll always remember meeting him because he came to see me when I was working at a farm and, when he asked me to sign for the club, I was actually sat on top of a pile of spuds, because it was potato-picking week in Strensall. Sam wasn't considered successful as a manager, but he was a wonderful fellow and a really grand, lovely man. I had been playing for Cliftonville and people like Arthur Brown and Les Horsley, who was a funeral director, were involved with both clubs. Sam gave me my chance as a professional and I found him ideal for myself, even though some people thought goalkeepers didn't have the ability to organise a team."

Jackson was immediately mentored by the team's famous semi-final heroes. "Most of the 1955 FA Cup team were all still there when I signed and they were wonderful with me, especially the centre-half Alan Stewart and Tommy Forgan in goal," he recalled. "They were really obliging and did nothing but encourage me, which was very helpful. Even though I probably ended up taking his position, Alan Stewart helped me so much and was a superb man. Then, there was George Howe - the full back. What a player. He didn't always have to tackle, because he was so good at showing people down the line and, before they knew it, they had ended up near the corner flag. He was a terrific full back and it was a terrific time to be joining the club. Norman (Wilkinson) was also a very intelligent chap and very good at pulling away from his centre half. He used to always find space on the pitch. He was brilliant at that and a very good header of the ball."

Four-figure crowds for reserve games were also the norm at Bootham Crescent during this period, meaning local players like Peter Turpin - the young primary school pupil who had sheltered at the ground during the War - enjoyed the experience of playing in front of a sizeable gate despite never getting a chance to impress in the Football League. "I was selected for four first-team games, but never played," he recalled. "The part-time contracts you signed meant you got paid when you played and didn't if you weren't in the team, so that sometimes affected your chances of playing when the team had full-time players as well. My dad didn't think football was a profession either, but I did play regularly for the reserves and we got some good crowds. Tom Lockie was the trainer and he was a great Scots lad. I also remember playing with people like Dave Dunmore, Alf Patrick and Billy Hughes, but I had good games and bad games."

Optimism was high at the start of that campaign when a 15,318 crowd turned up for a 2-2 draw against Workington, which represented the club's biggest-ever attendance for an opening home fixture at Bootham Crescent. City could not gain any momentum under Bartram, though, with the gates soon dropping. Nevertheless, to reflect the growing number of people driving to Bootham Crescent for matches, additional car parking had been provided by October in Lumley Barracks for a small charge.

The final-ever Christmas Day fixture staged at Bootham Crescent, meanwhile, saw Bottom, Wilkinson and Fenton net during a 3-3 draw with Hartlepool. Festive clashes on December 25 at that point were still not as well-attended as Boxing Day matches, due to the restricted public transport available.

The season also heralded a 9-1 club record win over Southport.

City were on the fringe of the third division north promotion race ahead of the February 2 clash and Southport were second-bottom, but nobody would have anticipated the final outcome. On a muddy surface, after Southport had a goal disallowed for offside, the hosts forged ahead on 14 minutes when Bottom unleashed a tremendous shot from outside the penalty box following Wilkinson's left-wing cross. Moments later, Southport full-back Peter Lomas was badly injured after tackling Fenton and was unable to play on, which left the visitors to play the rest of the game with ten men as substitutes had still not been introduced into the sport. Bottom went on to extend the lead on 27 minutes, converting a penalty after being brought down. The rampant City striker then completed his hat-trick before the interval, shooting in off the post following Peter Wragg's pass, before also hitting the frame of the goal from a deflected free kick. After the break, Billy Hill went close twice for the dominant home side before Wilkinson headed in a fourth from Fenton's cross. Southport's keeper Jack Richardson made a string of fine saves to keep the score down and Fenton hit a post, before five goals were added between the 75th and 83rd minutes. First, Bottom stabbed in a Hill pass and, from the kick-off, Fenton sprinted through to beat Richardson. Brown then cracked the ball home after Bottom's shot had rebounded to him. Wilkinson added an eighth after mesmerising work by Bottom, and Wragg headed in the ninth. Southport's consolation came on 89 minutes when Howe handled and Wilf Charlton converted from the penalty spot, beating Happy Wanderers' net-minder Forgan, whose memories of that match were still vivid when he was interviewed for the purpose of this book a couple of years before passing away at the age of 90 in 2019. "I always preferred to be in the action and I remember thinking a goalkeeper's job is pretty lonely when there's nothing to do, until they scored the penalty," he said.

Jackson, meanwhile, hit a hat-trick at the age of 18 for the reserves in a 3-1 February victory over Grimsby at Bootham Crescent. He was playing as a striker, which he often did during his early days with the second string.

The planned improvements to the Social Club did subsequently take place in the close season, leading to the demolition of all the existing wooden buildings and the provision of brick-built storage accommodation, offices, an extensive joint committee room for the Social Club and Supporters' Club and a modern tearoom for the latter to serve hot drinks from. The Social Club was also now established as the site for booking coach transport to away games and buying special train tickets for the same purpose. An additional turnstile and new exit gates were incorporated too, meaning the frontage looking on to Grosvenor Road was greatly improved. The Social Club and Supporters' Club again assisted substantially with the £4,000 cost. Provision was also made for the ultimate installation of a floodlight pylon in that corner and a power house for the lights. Concrete terracing, meanwhile, was completed up to the limit of the concrete wall at the St Olave's Road End.

Percy Andrews' benefit match at the end of the season also saw a City side, featuring old favourite Sid Storey, take on an All-Stars XI with Bartram in goal and future legendary Liverpool manager Bill Shankly in defence. City won 3-0 against their ageing opponents with York's Football League referee Peter Rhodes taking charge of the game and a crowd of more than 7,000 attended, which saw £695 raised. Forgan also saved a penalty from Bartram during the game, with Fenton, Hughes and Wilkinson scoring past their manager.

At the start of 1957/58, Bootham Crescent witnessed the rare sight of a goalkeeper on the scoresheet when, having had his hand accidentally kicked in a reserve match by team-mate George Patterson, Mick Granger was taken out of goal and netted as a centre forward in a 4-2 victory over Gainsborough Trinity. Another home reserve game also saw Yorkshire and England cricketer Brian Close get on the scoresheet with a headed consolation in a 3-1 defeat for Bradford City.

Future Arsenal and Nottingham Forest attacker Addison, meanwhile, burst on to the scene at the age of 17 and he remembered his first senior match vividly. He said: "When I was growing up, I used to love going to watch York play at Bootham Crescent with my dad. I'd also played there for York City boys in the English Schools and Yorkshire Shield competitions, as well as for Cliftonville at the age of 16 in a York & District League Cup final when we beat York RI. The local finals always used to be played at your home-town club back then on Easter Monday morning. But I also remember my first-team debut as if it was yesterday. It was a lovely summer day and I was playing number 10 as an old-fashioned inside forward. It was two years after the famous Cup run and a lot of the team were still playing for the club. Sam Bartram put me in and we played Bury, who were top of the league, but we beat them 2-1. My mother and father were in a good crowd and I was a bit nervous and tense."

Eight of the Happy Wanderers' side were, indeed, on duty that day and Addison recalled with fondness the harsh lessons he received from some of the heroes he had watched as a schoolboy just three years earlier. "Nearly half of them were in their 30s by then and had been around a bit," he explained. "Ernie Phillips and George Howe both had long careers before coming to York and I learnt a lot off all of them. It was great experience for a young boy of 17 growing up with them. I scored one or two goals and came in and out of the team. That was all part of the learning process and, when you made a mistake, they wouldn't let you get away with it. I remember Ron Spence shouting 'Colin, what have I told you about holding on to the ball for too long?' and then he kicked me up the backside whilst he was running past me. Ernie Phillips also gave me a clip around the ear once in a game at Bootham Crescent. You couldn't do that these days - the PFA would have been on to both of them - but it stopped me from getting big-headed and kept me on the straight and narrow after I'd scored a few goals. Tom Lockie also wasn't afraid to dish out criticism."

Describing his typical pre-match routine as a teenage hopeful, Addison added: "I would have poached eggs on toast for my breakfast then get on the bus or get a lift with my dad and report to the ground at about 1.45pm. You would find out if you were in the first team or reserves on Friday morning when the sheet was pinned up at the ground and there were no pre-match meals or get togethers then."

City also beat first division Birmingham 3-0 at home that season in the FA Cup although, given the club's giant-killing reputation by then, whether that could be deemed an upset was debatable. The match was played on a Wednesday afternoon in early January with the pitch iced up on the original Saturday date and no refunds made available. Referee A Bond made the decision on the weekend fixture at 11.50am when Birmingham fans were arriving at York railway station on the four special trains and they were incensed by the postponement. It was the only match unable to be played from the 32 third round ties, with Mr RA Bourne, of Stirchley, moaning: "This is ridiculous. They must have known earlier than this. Why didn't they tell us before we left for Birmingham? We have wasted 17s 6d on the fare. It is a big disappointment." The general feeling was the famous Cup tie against Tottenham had gone ahead in worse conditions. A capacity of 23,600 had been set for the fixture, split at the time between 15,000 in the ground terraces, 5,500 in the Popular Stand, 1,750 in the Main Stand Enclosure and 1,350 in the Main Stand. But all of the tickets were not sold for the Saturday match and, despite the remaining tickets being put on sale right up to kick-off in the Social Club, the gate was 19,750.

City were 19th in the third division north at the time, while Birmingham were a mid-table, top-flight team, who had been Cup runners-up and beaten semi-finalists during the previous two campaigns. Conditions were good for the rearranged game with the pitch lightly sanded and City, who were again featuring eight of the players from the Happy Wanderers' squad, dominated the first half. Bottom opened the scoring on 13 minutes when he blasted in after former England keeper Gil Merrick could only get one hand to a Fenton shot. Two minutes later, Wragg volleyed in from eight yards after Wilkinson had teed him up. On 28 minutes, it was 3-0 with Hughes' free kick headed into the roof of the net by Wilkinson. The side received a standing ovation at half-time and, whilst after the break, striker Eddie Brown hit the bar for Birmingham, City's defence stood firm with skipper Phillips and centre-back Howard Johnson in outstanding form. Howe also cleared a Harry Hopper effort off the line and Granger made a magnificent diving save to keep out Peter Murphy's header, as City saw the game out with the crowd singing The Happy Wanderers' theme song from their 1955 semi-final run. The three-goal winning margin remains the club's biggest against top-flight opposition in the competition.

In the fourth round, Bolton's visit heralded the biggest crowd at Bootham Crescent since the War with a capacity crowd of 23,600 watching a 0-0 draw after the public allocation of 8,000 tickets sold within two-and-a-half hours. Record gate receipts of £4,292 10s were taken and, on behalf of licensees in the Bootham area, Mr MM Rossfield successfully applied to York magistrates for an extension of Saturday opening hours so, in his words, "when local supporters come out, they can discuss the merits and win of their team in convivial surroundings". Snow had protected the pitch from frost in the days building up to the game but, when it was cleared off, pools of water began to form, making playing conditions treacherous. The referee declared the pitch fit to play at 12.45pm and a cold crowd were entertained before kick-off by the band of the 5th West Yorkshire Regiment (Prince of Wales' Own). In a game of few chances, with players slipping and sliding throughout, legendary visiting striker Nat Lofthouse had a header cleared off the line by Phillips and did have the ball in the net on 79 minutes but was adjudged offside. City went on to lose the replay 3-0.

The club could not subsequently secure the top-half finish that would have earned them third-tier status either, as regionalised lower-league football came to an end and City were placed in the fourth division. One of the poorest games of the season had seen the team humbled 5-0 at home by Carlisle, with Bottom sent off for arguing with the referee and Forgan suffering knee ligament damage, leaving the hosts down to nine men and with Wragg in goal. Former Happy Wanderer Sid Storey also returned to a warm reception before scoring the first goal in a 3-0 win for Accrington at Bootham Crescent. The poor campaign was reflected in attendances with only 6,427 turning up for the club's Easter Monday fixture at Bootham Crescent.

A late rally almost gave Bartram's men an unlikely reprieve when, faced with four home games in nine days to end the season, they beat Tranmere 4-0, drew with Stockport 0-0, overcame Workington 3-0 and defeated Darlington 3-0 thanks to goals from Terry Farmer (2) and Wragg as the club's campaign was concluded on a Thursday in front of 5,570 supporters. The draw against Stockport proved crucial as the Minstermen missed out on a top-12 place due to their goal average - nine goals would have been needed against Darlington to oust Wrexham and claim the last northern spot in division three. As well as Wrexham, York finished on the same points as Rochdale and Tranmere, who all gained admission into the third division. Bartram's team selection had been queried regularly during the season - a complaint that was perhaps backed up by the form of the reserve team who, regularly featuring the likes of former

Happy Wanderers' Fenton and Forgan as well as emerging talents Jackson and Addison, became the club's first team to complete a whole campaign unbeaten in home matches. The second string's final overall record at Bootham Crescent was won 17, drawn 6, lost 0, goals for 61, goals against 24.

Local cup finals that were traditionally played on the ground at the end of the season had to be hosted at other venues, meanwhile, due to the muddy state of the playing surface. Thirteen home games had been staged in the final month of the season - for City and the reserve team - while a donation of £25 was made to the York Schools FA as compensation. Such congestion, meanwhile, led to the introduction of the Northern Regional League, as the club left the Midland League with a heavy heart, having entered the Football League from that competition. Club officials, meanwhile, decided the playing surface needed to be treated as soon as possible after the end of the season. Accordingly, a series of deep ditches were dug across the pitch as the ground's whole drainage plan was remodelled and the turf was reseeded. The club also purchased a light tractor and several other appliances to improve the quality of pitch care at Bootham

New drainage pipes are installed in 1958

Crescent, and the Social Club assisted with costs. A rotavator was used to dig a great deal of the clay sub-soil out, but the corner patches were left alone, as they were deemed to be in good condition. Wet weather slowed the job down.

City would, then, go on to win a place in the third division by merit as they enjoyed the club's first-ever promotion 12 months later, only losing once at Bootham Crescent during a 1958/59 campaign that owed much to a very strong rearguard, featuring Happy Wanderers' Forgan and Howe, with 20-year-old Jackson outstanding at the heart of defence. Jackson would go on to become the club's all-time appearance record holder on 539 games - a figure that still places him top of the pile today - with friend and team-mate Addison believing his loyalty to the club prevented him from playing at a higher level. "Ginger-top Jacko was not a bad player for a big guy," Addison explained. "A lot of people thought he just hoofed and whacked the ball 60 yards, but he could hit a good pass and play as well. He was a great header of the ball and a great defender who was very strong. He also had great fitness levels and could get around the pitch. It was like having two men back there when Jacko was in your team and I was surprised he didn't go further in the game. I know he had one or two offers to move on and I think he could have gone on to play in the second division and maybe the first if somebody had taken a chance on him."

On the emergence of Jackson, Forgan added: "Barry Jackson was very passionate about the game. You always got 110 per cent out of him. He rarely made a mistake so, when he did, he was very hard on himself." Right-half George Patterson, who played 38 games during the promotion season, was also impressed by the emergence of Jackson and Addison, saying: "Barry was a good centre-half. He was a stopper and a big presence in the middle of the defence, where he won all of his headers. Colin was another good player with a bit of speed who I enjoyed playing with. You could see they were both going to have good careers, although Barry stayed with York."

Jackson, himself, was quick to stress how experienced team-mates helped him as he took his first early strides into senior football, making his debut on the opening day of the season at Oldham, before playing his first competitive match at Bootham Crescent two days later in a 2-0 triumph over Southport. "That promotion-winning team still had a lot of the 1955 FA Cup semi-final side in it, so we had the ability to play some good stuff and people like George Howe really kept me right," he reasoned. "They all weren't scared of rollicking you when needed but were then cheering you on to make sure you learned from the mistakes you made. It was drilled into us as defenders to never be caught the wrong side of your man and you see that happen so much in the modern game."

Jackson, who passed away in 2021, also outlined what a thrill it was to play for City at Bootham Crescent. "Having played for City boys, wanting to play for the club was bred into me," he explained. "I never really wanted to play for anybody else. Then, as you progress, you might think what a fool I've been not moving on, but I had a great time and, with the maximum wage, you weren't a lot better off playing in the top division anyway."

While the back line conceded the second-fewest number of goals in the division, the side were not shabby at the other end of the pitch either with Addison, on ten, one of three players who weighed in with double figures as

Wragg hit the target 14 times and Farmer netted on 12 occasions. Former FA Cup semi-final hero Billy Hughes also scored seven. "We were a very strong side who could score goals," Addison pointed out. "Not just me - we got goals from all different areas of the pitch."

Bartram became the first manager to experience promotion at Bootham Crescent with Forgan admitting he benefitted from having a fellow net-minder in charge, even if his coaching input was minimal.

"As a goalkeeper it was nice to have someone who was such a good player in the same position," the City number one explained. "I couldn't say he would come out and train, but I am sure he kept a close eye on me." Addison, who went on to enjoy a distinguished career in management with the likes of Derby and Atletico Madrid, can also recall little emphasis on coaching. He was grateful for Bartram's insights into the game though and revealed that his former manager, then 45, took every opportunity to get back between the sticks at Bootham Crescent. "There wasn't a lot of coaching in those days," Addison explained. "That came in later. Sam was a big man who had been a great goalkeeper and had played what seemed like about 2,000 games for Charlton. What I used to love about him is he always wanted to go in goal during the practice matches we would have at Bootham Crescent or for shooting practice. He would tell Tommy (Forgan) or Mick (Granger) to have a breather or play outfield for half-an-hour and he would play behind the first-team defence for a little bit instead. He wasn't a great coach - the managers back then didn't really know what coaching was - but guys like him had a great wealth of experience and knowledge of the game that they could impart. It wasn't until I went to Arsenal and worked under Dave Sexton and Don Howe that I realised what proper coaching was about."

Terry Fowler also recalled a story her father told that suggested Bartram was not quite a natural in his new role, revealing: "Sam was very nice and he was a bit mad like most keepers but, when he came back as manager, I will always remember my father saying, on his first day, he came into my father's office and said: 'What do I have to do?' He had never been a manager and wasn't really successful in the job in the end."

A 4-0 home victory over Bradford Park Avenue, courtesy of goals from Farmer (2), Wragg and Wilkinson, had seen City top the table after winning their opening three games - the best start to a season in the club's history at that point. The team's first-ever North v South league tussle, meanwhile, resulted in a 1-0 Monday night triumph at Bootham Crescent over Torquay thanks to Farmer's goal following a 6pm kick-off. A headed brace by teenage inside-forward Addison, who was impressing more by the game, also helped the club return to the top of the table after 10 games following a 4-0 home victory against Crewe. Hughes and Farmer joined him on the scoresheet with Leeds and Newcastle scouts in the crowd watching both Addison and Jackson. The first southern side to win a league game at Bootham Crescent, meanwhile, were Exeter on the final weekend in October when the Devon promotion rivals beat top-of-the-table City 2-0. Soon afterwards, it was announced that the club would install floodlights at the ground for the following season. It was also reported that the Auxiliary Club would donate £13,000 towards the cost.

The promotion push, meanwhile, still hadn't really captured the attention by March time with a 0-0 home draw against fellow high-fliers Coventry only attracting 8,633 fans. A visiting director even suggested the gate would have been 30,000 at his own team's stadium. Only two five-figured crowds were recorded during the whole campaign - on Boxing Day against Barrow and Good Friday when Workington were the visitors. But a 1-0 win at Aldershot in the penultimate fixture of the season meant City were already promoted by the time visitors Gateshead were seen off by the same scoreline after a Hughes goal in the campaign's final game. A Monday evening crowd of 9,015 supporters turned up for the occasion, but Addison revealed that the celebrations at Bootham Crescent were fairly low key afterwards. There were no reports of a lap of honour or any other gesture to celebrate the achievement at the end of the game and Addison said: "They throw parties for teams that get promoted now and the players get invited to this and that. We probably just had a few beers and Peter Wragg will have arranged a night out. He was the captain and a good guy and a qualified coach who first got me interested in coaching." Patterson also remembered no grand fuss following the Gateshead triumph, adding: "You have to work hard to get promotion but there was no big celebration. We were just happy. It was all down to good teamwork. We were all in it together and we could handle ourselves as well."

Charlie Twissell, who scored five goals in 19 appearances during the promotion campaign, remembered that the team's efforts, meanwhile, were not always appreciated by a demanding home crowd. He said: "The supporters were great although there was always somebody who wanted to say something they shouldn't, because they always wanted you to win. I remember one match Barry Tait got the ball and Peter Wragg shot down the wing and kept shouting for the ball. I was sat in the stand for the match and one bloke shouted: 'What the bloody hell do you want to kick the ball down there for?' I looked up and said: 'Are you watching the same match I am?' He said: 'Of course I am. He shouldn't have ran down there - they should have hit the ball down the middle'. I then replied: 'Well what happened to the full back when Wraggy shouted and went out to the wing?' He said: 'He went with him'. To which, I asked him: 'Well, did you see the big hole that appeared?' I sometimes thought people were watching different games at Bootham Crescent. The supporters used to come in bus loads, though, when we were doing well. You saw them coming in from Stamford Bridge and all the other outlaying areas. When you're winning, more come every week as well."

Twissell had been recruited from Plymouth during the early part of the season and recalled a car journey with Bartram that alerted him to the perils of using such transport on the approach to Bootham Crescent at certain times of the day. "I found Sam Bartram alright and I remember him picking me up from the train station in York when I was signing for the club," Twissell explained. "On the way to the ground, we stopped at the lights when I heard a big thump on the back of the car. I said: 'What was that?' He said: 'Don't worry. It's just one of the workers'. It was chucking out time at Nestle and Rowntree and there were bicycles everywhere and what they used to do was put their boot on the back of the car's fender when the traffic stopped, rather than having to rest them on the ground. I'd come up from Plymouth and hadn't seen that before and I thought I'm not going to drive a car around here."

But, despite Bartam's ability as a calm chauffeur, Twissell also confirmed that the legendary goalkeeper's initial managerial success did not come as a consequence of any scientific approach to the game. "The way we were playing, there was not too much emphasis on tactics," Twissell pointed out. "We were just told things like this bloke is good, so watch out and stay on him." Twissell also believed the craft of Wragg came in handy on more than one occasion during the historic season. "Peter Wragg was a right wind-up merchant and a bit of a case," he laughed. "He would have a dig at a player and, then, if we needed a penalty, he would go in the area and they would put him in the air so we'd get one. Then, he'd walk away chuffed with himself. He was a shocker for that. Penalties also seemed to be given more often back then. You couldn't hold on to people in the box like in the modern game." Of the side's other leading lights, meanwhile, Twissell added: "I thought Norman (Wilkinson) was a great player. Everybody used to say he was slow, but what they didn't notice is he slowed the game down to the pace he wanted to play. Billy Hughes was also so relaxed when he played and Barry (Jackson) was strong in defence and didn't want to leave the club because of his mum's cooking. Well, that's what we used

127

to rib him about. Mick Granger was a good keeper, but he was really mad. He was only small, but he was quite bulky and, when he decided he had to go for a ball, he went for it come what may. Tommy (Forgan) was a more sensible keeper though. Barry Tait made me laugh because the first thing he did when he went out, whether he was up against a big centre-half or a little one, was crash straight into them. He wanted them to know he was there even though he was quite small. You had good players like Georgie Howe too and Terry Farmer, who was a quiet sort of lad, but got on with the job and then there was Colin (Addison), who we always felt was born for stardom."

Tom Lockie, the mastermind of York City's run to the 1955 FA Cup semi-finals shakes the hand of Sam Bartam, the first manager to win promotion for the club in 1959 with his players looking on

CHAPTER 10

Floodlit football and the arrival of Bryan "Fossie" Foster

"It seemed a bit strange at first, but the lights were good and playing in the dark created quite an atmosphere."

During the summer of 1959, one of the biggest characters in Bootham Crescent's history was employed on the ground-staff. Bryan Foster had played as a goalkeeper for the club's reserve and A teams, as well as being assistant groundsman at Pocklington School, and duly became head groundsman. He served the club until his untimely death in February 1994, aside from a period between 1971 and 1975 when he took up similar positions with Bury and Preston. The playing surface gained an excellent reputation under Foster, whilst his successor Bryan Horner would go on to be voted Division Two's Groundsman of the Year too in 1999. Foster's early work transformed the playing surface with Addison smiling: "Bryan Foster didn't like you training on the pitch. We used to give him some stick, but the pitch was great compared to the likes of Stockport, Chester and Crewe." Jackson also recalled the arrival of Foster, adding: "Bryan Foster was a rum lad and a real wonderful character. He never wanted you to go on the ground, especially when it was snowing, and he used to get a bit upset at times."

In the summer of 1959, floodlights were installed as planned at a cost of £14,500 with the majority paid for by the Auxiliary Club. Their introduction had been under consideration for several years, but the decision had been delayed due to rules against their use for league matches. Floodlit friendlies had been the only option in the past but, with teams from Scotland demanding a £500 guarantee to play such matches in the 1950s, an unlikely five-figured crowd would have been needed to make the fixtures viable. The General Electric Company designed and supervised the project while Messrs Shepherds of York were responsible for the concrete bases and erection of the four 100ft tubular towers. The electrical sub-contractors were Messrs FH Wheeler of Scunthorpe and there were 24 bulbs in each 1500-watt floodlight unit with the capacity capable of expanding to 32. A total load of 144 kilowatts was used for the floodlighting. An auxiliary lighting system, fed by batteries, was also installed in case of a breakdown, with a power house built in the corner of the ground adjacent to Lumley Barracks because it was the most accessible area to lay cable and link up the system with the North Eastern Electricity Board. Cables were laid under the running track around the pitch and a new white kit was worn for the floodlit fixtures, while nylon goal nets were introduced, as they were regarded as more suitable under lights. With the lights tested after midnight when fully installed on an August evening, it was decided an orange ball would be easier to see than a white one too. Reserve-team evening games would also now be played under the lights. Evening games would generally kick off at 7.30pm after the first official match under lights against QPR had a 7pm start and Saturday afternoon fixtures would all be played at 3pm, regardless of the time of year. One third of the lights were normally turned on to illuminate the ground prior to kick-off and then the remaining two-thirds were switched on as the players entered the field. More work was also done on the playing surface during the summer, with some bad patches still having appeared despite the comprehensive drainage work conducted 12 months earlier. A boys' turnstile, meanwhile, was installed at the Shipton Street End of the ground, with one still operating in the Lumley Barracks corner.

Support was good during the first floodlit matches and City's players had a vested interest in the crowd size with bonus payments on offer for the first time if attendances exceeded four figures. The lights were first switched on for the final minutes of a 1-0 Monday night win against Bury at the referee's request in August. But the first advertised floodlit fixture came against QPR on September 7, 1959. It attracted an attendance of 10,593 and almost 12,000 turned up for the floodlit visit of Grimsby later that month. The reserves' first game under lights also doubled the normal gate receipts for a Saturday afternoon, with more than 2,700 watching an evening fixture against Bradford City.

The QPR match saw the lights christened with a 2-1 home triumph.

City striker John Edgar scored the first-ever goal under the lights, converting a wayward Norman Wilkinson effort with a powerful first-time shot on 38 minutes. The game with Grimsby ended 3-3 after the hosts had led 3-0 with two Wilkinson goals sandwiching a Johnny Powell effort. In between, Arthur Bottom returned to Bootham Crescent for the first time with Chesterfield and was on the receiving end of a 1-0 defeat with Wilkinson getting the only goal of the game to outshine his former team-mate, who was well-shackled by Barry Jackson, as the young centre-back continued to attract transfer attention. Jackson played in those first two floodlit games and, recalling those early night-time contests, he said: "It seemed a bit strange at first, but the lights were good and playing in the dark created quite an atmosphere."

The lights were officially switched on, meanwhile, during an exhibition match that saw Newcastle's strongest team beat City 8-2 on October 28, 1959 in front of 9,414 supporters. An army physical training display by the Northern Command took place prior to kick-off

Former 1955 FA Cup semi-final hero Arthur Bottom returns to Bootham Crescent as a Chesterfield player in 1959 and was on the receiving end of a 1-0 defeat

with local official Peter Rhodes refereeing the game and fellow renowned York whistle-blower Lol Cussons a linesman. The club also invited 200 Auxiliary Club members to the game as guests and gave them two free tickets apiece in recognition of the contribution they had made towards helping finance the cost of the lights. After the game in the City boardroom, Newcastle chairman Willie McKeag highlighted Bootham Crescent's growing reputation in the English game, saying: "Your pitch was fine, your floodlights excellent and you did not deserve to lose by such a margin."

Legendary striker Len White, only placed behind Alan Shearer and Jackie Milburn in the Magpies' all-time goalscorers' list, hit a hat-trick, while Welsh international Ivor Allchurch bagged a brace with England 1966 World Cup squad member George Eastham, Scotland attacker Bobby Mitchell and Bobby Gilfillan also on target. Colin Addison and George Patterson replied at 5-0 and 6-1 down respectively and for the latter - a north-east lad - the game represented a much-cherished occasion. "I came from Sunderland, but I watched Sunderland and Newcastle when I was growing up because my favourite footballer was Len

131

Shackleton, who played for both clubs," he explained. "He was a hell of a player, so it was special for me playing Newcastle. George Eastham played for them that day and he was a good player."

Despite the heavy defeat, it was also a memorable evening for teenager Addison, who said: "It was great to get any chance to show what you could do against first division opposition and I remember Newcastle coming to open the floodlights. They had people like Jimmy Scoular and Bob Stokoe playing and it was great for me, as a young kid, to play against them in front of a big crowd and nice atmosphere. We lost 8-2 but I remember getting a goal and feeling good about that. The floodlit games were something new and I used to like them. Even if you had a small crowd at night, the atmosphere was still good." Addison's fellow local-grown talent Barry Tait agreed that those early evening contests had a special aura and also provided more scope for semi-professional players, such as himself, to hone their skills outside of match days. "The lights were good for part-time players like me because it meant we could suddenly train three nights a week," he explained. "People are used to night matches now, but the atmosphere was brilliant during those first games."

Watching night games under lights was a new experience for the Bootham Crescent faithful too and lifelong fan Fred Hemenway admitted: "It was very strange watching football in the dark and the lights became brighter in later years, but they were still better than some grounds back then. I remember going to Doncaster and somebody said: 'When are they going to turn on the lights?' I told him they were on, but they were only on telegraph poles and they were terrible." Terry Fowler, Billy Sherrington's daughter, also declared: "It was strange at first going in the dark, but we got used to it."

Keeper Tommy Forgan, meanwhile, added that the quality of the lights did present problems for players in his position, but that he also enjoyed the unique atmosphere a night match brought. "I played some games at Hull under lights, so I had a little bit of experience before York got them," he explained. "I found cross balls a bit hard to see at times, but they were the same for everybody. There was always a good atmosphere at Bootham Crescent but playing at night under lights was an added attraction."

Charlie Twissell gained notoriety for smashing Reading's floodlights with a wayward shot as a City player and he was also relieved that he hadn't been asked to erect those at Bootham Crescent, as he had been at his previous club. "I never came close to smashing the floodlights at Bootham Crescent," he laughed. "They were higher up than the ones at Reading at the time. I was also relieved that I didn't have to help the contractors put them up at York, like I had to do when I was an amateur player at Plymouth. I'm afraid of heights, even when I see them on television, so my stomach was churning when I was up there on a platform with spanners and no harness. As a full-time professional, I didn't have to get involved at York. You got a bit of a glare off the ones at Bootham Crescent, but not very often. The atmosphere was different, and it was possibly a bit louder, as all the noise that was being generated came from the crowd, because there was no traffic about at that time of night." Whilst he didn't dismantle the Bootham Crescent floodlights, Twissell did recall striking another target, however, on one highly-satisfying occasion, saying: "Somebody had been giving me stick in the Main Stand during one game. He'd been at me all game and was really winding me up. He was a tall bloke who stuck out and, when a ball suddenly came down that side of the pitch and I was running towards the touchline, I could see him in front of me. I decided to kick the ball into touch and I just got him. I just thought, 'Yes, great' after that. It's not often you can get your own back and, at bigger grounds, you were so far away so you couldn't see, or even hear, the people who were abusing you."

Another highlight in what would prove an otherwise disappointing 1959/60 season came when Edgar scored all the goals in a 3-0 home win over Accrington during a six-minute period, claiming the club's quickest-ever hat-trick in the process. Two minutes past the hour, the former Barnsley and Gillingham forward opened the scoring when he finished firmly after a Twissell pass. On 64 minutes, he picked the ball up 40 yards from goal and, following a purposeful run, finished brilliantly from an acute angle. Then, after Harry Anders hit an upright at the other end, Edgar completed his hat-trick with a perfectly-executed chip. Addison played alongside Edgar in that match and the latter would go on to plunder 17 goals during the season. "John could score a goal," Addison recalled. "He came from Barnsley and was a cool finisher. He was a quiet player, but he got on with his work in training. He wasn't a big guy or brilliant in the air, whereas Norman Wilkinson was as good a header of a ball as I ever played with. I made a few goals for him, knocking the ball into the box." Jackson also admired Edgar's goalscoring instinct, adding: "I remember John Edgar coming to the club and he was a real quiet and very likeable lad, who was good at getting the wrong side of his defender."

The flexibility offered by floodlights, meanwhile, was witnessed when City brought forward their February home match against Newport that season to a Friday night to avoid a clash with York's big Rugby League Cup tie against Hull on the Saturday afternoon. Club officials also used the experiment to see if the new kick-off alternative would boost gate figures, with a feeling that some supporters might stay at home on Saturday to watch sport on television. The subsequent crowd of 7,795 - more than 1,700 up on the previous home Saturday game against Southend and not bettered during the remaining eight home fixtures of the season - suggested there might have been some truth in that suspicion. Those at the Friday night game witnessed a match-winning brace from Edgar in a 2-0 triumph. City also changed the kick-off time of their Saturday home match with Port Vale to 6.30pm to avoid a clash with the Grand National and drew a crowd of 6,415 when three of the subsequent four fixtures attracted gates below 5,000.

A senior schoolboy international, meanwhile, was staged at the ground with England beating Ireland 4-1 in a Victory Shield clash.

The Three Lions team featured Ron "Chopper" Harris, David Pleat and Barry Fry, but a crowd of 10,000 was described as "disappointing" in newspaper reports and organisers had hoped for 15,000 fans. Three thousand schoolchildren, from as far afield as Cumberland and London, went to the game after arriving by train and also enjoying a sightseeing tour of the city. A gymnastics display was staged by York secondary school pupils prior to kick-off and the band of the 5th Battalion the West Yorkshire Regiment also played. Future Birmingham City boss Fry got England's third goal with a close-range header that was dropped by the Irish keeper, but winger Pleat, who went on to manage Tottenham, performed the best of the side's future stars. With York Rugby League club also playing Wakefield Trinity in the Challenge Cup on the same day, extra police were on duty to ensure order was maintained among the crowds.

City's promotion momentum, meanwhile, was proving short-lived and Edgar's historic October hat-trick seemed a distant memory when the club lost seven of their last eight games to make a swift return to the fourth division. Twissell sensed a difference in the matchday atmosphere at Bootham Crescent as defeats, rather than victories, became the norm. "It's hard sometimes when you go up to get in the swing of it," he reasoned. "We started losing and I was thinking to myself should we have got promoted or would we have been better just missing out and spending another season at the top, so we could build on two years of success. It might have been a weaker fourth division the season we went up and, like the FA Cup run in 1955, you can get one-offs but, then, not sustain it. The atmosphere didn't change too much because the lads were still trying, but you could hear the moans at Bootham Crescent as we had been winning the previous season and now it was a different standard, but we were expected to keep winning again. You had to laugh when you heard certain comments, but I felt pressure when I went out there and we were losing. You're worried because you are fighting for your place too and we weren't in the right mood to win home games then."

As results worsened, a 1-0 home defeat to Brentford in April saw a slow handclap, which "swelled in volume", conducted by home supporters during the last 10 minutes of the game. A 3-2 defeat against Southend, when the visitors scored all their goals in the last 35 minutes after Billy Hughes' brace had put the Minstermen in the ascendancy, then meant the odds for survival were not in City's favour ahead of their final contest at home to Shrewsbury. The hosts went into that game trailing Tranmere by a point and knew they must win their game and hope the Wirral side were beaten by third-bottom Mansfield. If Tranmere drew, Sam Bartram's men needed to beat Shrewsbury by a double-figured margin due to their inferior goal average. In the event, the match at Bootham Crescent settled matters regardless of Tranmere's 2-0 triumph at Mansfield, as City were beaten 1-0 following a defensive slip-up when Forgan failed to hold on to a ball in the penalty area and Jackson was watching his colleague as Colin Whitaker nipped in to find the net despite Bob Ramsey trying to stop it with his hand. The crowd got behind City after the goal and Hughes hit the crossbar soon afterwards following a goalmouth struggle. But 34-year-old Shrews player-manager Arthur Rowley, who still holds the record for most career Football League goals on 434, also hit the frame of the goal after lobbing over Forgan.

Hughes, meanwhile, appeared to be tripped in the penalty area in the second half, but the foul was adjudged to have taken place outside the box. Jackson was then sent up front during the final stages to try and pep up a forward line that had been misfiring during the final weeks of the campaign and, even though Wilkinson skimmed the bar with a header, it was all to no avail, as Twissell burst clear late on to squander the best chance of the game when he drove wide.

If City's management team had been getting news relayed from events at Nottinghamshire during the match, meanwhile, Twissell admitted he was not party to it. "If there was the chance to get news from elsewhere, it never got through to me," he pointed out. "I was on the wing and there were no messages being passed on to the pitch like there would be now. That even happens when I play bowls. There are people ringing other clubs to see what scores are elsewhere and what we need to do."

135

For Patterson, the Shrewsbury game proved his last appearance.

He almost scored when his shot was stopped on the goal-line early in the second half, but Bartram acted upon a warning he had issued as the club spiralled into trouble. "Sam Bartram was alright with me at first," Patterson revealed. "I had a good run in the team under him, so I was happy. But, in my last season, he told me and John Powell that we had got to keep the club up or we would be out, so the Shrewsbury game was my last one and I ended up at Hartlepool. It was a disappointing season because, if you go up, you want to continue getting higher up the Football League."

York-born Barry Tait made six appearances that season, having scored in three consecutive games during the promotion campaign after bursting on to the scene at the age of 20. As a future City assistant youth-team coach, who spotted the likes of Richard Cresswell and Jonathan Greening before scouting for Sir Alex Ferguson at Manchester United, Tait felt the step up a level proved as testing for Bartram as it did the players. He reasoned: "I think maybe the game changed and people were getting more technical in their tactics. Sam was not a great tactician and I can't remember tactics ever being discussed properly at York. It was only when I took my coaching badges and worked for Manchester United later in life that I realised what that side of the game was all about. Managers in the Premier League have to be fully-qualified coaches now and that's how it should be."

CHAPTER 11

Getting the better of Gordon Banks
and Leicester City

"I remember John Stainsby's goal. Gordon Banks didn't have a chance of saving it."

Following the third division struggles, trainer Tom Lockie again assumed managerial duties as Sam Bartram left for Luton. On the opening day of the 1960/61 campaign, meanwhile, new singing Alan Woods - Tottenham's 12th man back in 1955 - kicked off a career at Bootham Crescent that was to last six years by scoring one of only four goals he managed in that time. It came at home during a 3-2 opening-day win against Millwall and, recalling his debut, Woods admitted: "I scored and, to be honest, it was a cross. I got the ball on the right wing and thought 'I've got to get it in the box', so I tried to put it on one of our strikers' heads but it bent into the far post's top corner and everybody said: 'Great goal'. We were behind at the time and trying to get a goal by throwing everything into the box so that kind of thing can happen when you're aiming for the far post."

Off the pitch, the ever-helpful and industrious Supporters' Club improved the corner of the ground near the tea bar, by covering it in Tarmac that September. Floodlit matches were prompting complaints from local residents, though, with police officials asking fans to refrain from blocking the entrance to garages when they parked their cars and to be as quiet as possible when leaving the ground, as the constant slamming of vehicle doors was disturbing small children in bed. Fines of ten shillings were imposed for those who did cause obstructions with their parking. City's Boys' team also got to play their first game under the lights during a 6-0 English Schools Shield win in front of 1,646 supporters.

The first-ever League Cup tie was staged at Bootham Crescent in 1960/61, meanwhile, with Colin Addison scoring a spectacular consolation in a 3-1 defeat to first division Blackburn, who had been FA Cup finalists during the previous campaign. In front of 10,933 fans, England international Chris Crowe opened the scoring from the edge of the penalty box for the visitors after 15 minutes but, straight after the restart, Addison swept towards goal and scored with a "scorching shot". Derek Dougan - the Northern Ireland international - netted, though, just past the hour when a cross from England's Bryan Douglas deflected off Walt Bingley to give him a simple tap-in.

The third was added two minutes from time when Dougan outjumped Tommy Forgan to head into the home goal.

Addison, then 20, went on to join Nottingham Forest for a club record fee of £12,000 and believes the new competition, which provided lower-league players with another chance to pit themselves against higher-league opposition, probably played a big part in helping launch his career. "I remember scoring a cracking 20-yard goal in that Blackburn game," Addison recalled. "It was a nice evening for football and I hit the ball and it flew into the net - right over the keeper. I was delighted with that and it might have helped me get my move. There were bits and pieces being written about me in *The People* by a journalist (probably Tom Holley) who used to come to York games." Woods, though, recalled a difficult contest in which the hosts were lucky to escape a heavier defeat, adding: "We got murdered really. Big Derek Dougan was playing, as was Ronnie Clayton who had been England's captain the season before and Blackburn were too good for us. It was as simple as that. We could hardly get the ball and, when we did, we couldn't keep it but, when they had it, they kept it for 10 minutes." On the advent of the new tournament, Woods reasoned: "All the little teams know they have no chance of winning the cup competitions, but it was another opportunity for the club to make a bob or two by getting through a few rounds and, as players, we were just trying to win every game."

Addison, meanwhile, had come through the City ranks under Alf Patrick, who had returned to the club as a trainer. The 1940s and 50s' favourite had spotted from a young age that Addison was destined to make his mark in the game, explaining: "Colin came through the academy team when I ran it for two or three years and you could see he was going to be a good player. He was an inside forward and one of those sorts of players who always seemed to have plenty of time on the ball." Woods also noted the youngster's potential, saying: "Colin was good. He could run with the ball and beat people. He could hit the ball as well and deserved a move."

Bradford Park Avenue, meanwhile, refused to have their FA Cup first-round tie at Bootham Crescent switched to avoid a clash with York Rugby League club's home fixture against Wakefield Trinity. They declined to switch to a Friday night or play later than 2.15pm on the Saturday afternoon as, because their stadium did not have floodlights, they argued the hosts would be gaining an advantage by playing under them. The game ended 0-0, but City progressed after winning the replay 2-0. Another replay win, in which the Minstermen defeated Tranmere 2-1 at Bootham Crescent, set up a third-round home tie against second division Norwich. A 1-1 home draw was followed by a single-goal exit at Carrow Road. Addison's performance in the Bootham Crescent tie against Norwich was reported to have prompted several club's managers into a boardroom huddle afterwards and he subsequently completed his move to Nottingham Forest soon afterwards. A clash with the Grand National, meanwhile, was avoided again as City switched their home match with Stockport to a 7pm Saturday night kick-off and the subsequent crowd of 8,221 was comfortably above the season's disappointing average of 6,900.

In April, the Supporters' Club introduced a new fundraising initiative - a lucky draw - with six-penny tickets being sold at matches. A draw was then made at the interval, with half of the proceeds going to the winner and the other half to the club. A total of £72 was raised on its introduction during a 1-0 home defeat to Peterborough, which attracted the biggest gate of the campaign of 11,768. The 50-50 draw, as it came to be known having started off life as the jackpot lucky number draw, would endure until the final game at the ground and the first-ever winner was an unnamed supporter from Haxby. Soon after the initiative was launched, it was decided that three cash prizes would be handed out - still divided from a share of half of the proceeds from ticket sales.

During the close season, meanwhile, the dip in home gates was reflected in the introduction of a new bonus system at Bootham Crescent for the 1961/62 campaign. Players would receive an extra £1 when the attendance was higher than 7,000, £2 if larger than 9,000 and £3 in the event of an 11,000-plus crowd. Previously, players had only gained a £1 bonus for any five-figured gate.

More ground improvements were also carried out that summer with a section, which consisted of corrugated iron sheeting, at the end of the wall at the back of the St Olave's Road terracing, being demolished and replaced with another wall, as turnstiles were also re-sited. An exit turnstile for people wanting to leave the game early was installed at the same time. A new boardroom, as well as offices for the manager and secretary, were built too under the Main Stand with the work serving as a memorial to Hartas Foxton - the former club director and joint-founder of the York Pullman Bus Company - who had bequeathed £1,000

139

to the club for ground improvements. The changes saw the secretary's office transformed into the new boardroom, while the existing boardroom became the tea room and the tea room was converted into offices for the secretary and manager. A new main entrance was also made into the ground on the site of the old tea room, with the former entrance bricked up. In the St Olave's Road End, a new tea bar was also erected for the Supporters' Club, with the old tea bar switched to the Shipton Street End. Tea-bar takings were now becoming a significant revenue stream and accounted for £871 of the Women's Supporters' Club's season takings of £963. Membership cards were also available from the tea bars at a cost of 2s, along with fixture cards and badges for junior members, costing 6d. During this period, a whist drive was also held in the Social Club every Tuesday night at 7pm, followed by a tombola. Admission to the Popular Stand for the new campaign increased from 2s 6d to 3s, which reintroduced a differential in the price between standing and sitting.

The club broke with tradition, meanwhile, by staging the annual Reds v Blues public practice match on a Friday night rather than a Saturday afternoon, as experiments continued to find possible solutions for dropping crowd numbers. Evening football did, indeed, still seem to be drawing in bigger gates at that point with early-season night matches against Exeter (9,322) and Bristol City (8,379) much better attended than the Saturday afternoon home clash with Millwall (6,859) in between, when the St Leger horse race at Doncaster was deemed a rival attraction. Chairman Hugh Kitchin later revealed that gate receipts were generally £250 higher for evening kick-offs. It was felt that some of the estimated 2,000 people who played local amateur football and those who worked on a Saturday helped swell the night-time attendances, with the floodlit atmosphere seemingly appealing to more people, as the night matches that had previously been played in daylight hours never precipitated any discernible difference in gate size. When Friday-night football was subsequently sanctioned by the Football League, City immediately looked to switch two of their Saturday afternoon March fixtures, only for visitors Darlington to turn down one of the requests.

During the League Cup's second season, meanwhile, City went on to see off the likes of Bristol City, first division Leicester, Watford and Bournemouth to enjoy their best-ever run in the competition, reaching the last eight before bowing out 2-1 at Rochdale. Peter Wragg and John Stainsby scored in the 2-1 victory over Leicester in front of 13,273 fans, beating a 23-year-old, soon-to-be England goalkeeping great with Woods admitting that the Bootham Crescent crowd helped secure victory that night against a visiting team that had reached the FA Cup final six months earlier. "Gordon Banks was playing and there was a big crowd, which made the atmosphere better," he said. "We were used to four or five thousand and gaps all over the ground so, to have a big game like that with 13,000 fans and most of them covered, it makes a big difference to you as a player. I thought evening matches were better too. We tended to get big crowds under the lights and they had only just come in - a lot of clubs still didn't have them. The ground created plenty of atmosphere when it was full and was great under lights. The noise used to echo because the tin roofs were low, especially on the Popular Stand. The fans also sang a lot more and liked night matches themselves. I think it was because they could go and watch matches and have a pint afterwards. On Saturday afternoons, they might have to get back for their tea, but one of the attractions of football is having a drink afterwards and talking about who played badly and well and what the referee was like."

Tommy Heron, having started out at Manchester United, also revelled in the big-game atmosphere generated by Leicester's visit. "I was very fortunate because I never had any nerves when I played," he explained. "I was never affected like that. I used to enjoy big crowds and that was a big game. They had a fair side out, so it was brilliant to beat them - an absolutely first-class night. I had come from Manchester United and I was telling the boys before the game not to be bothered by Leicester and that they were the same as us. I said they all had two legs just like us and that we were as good as they were and that we should just get our heads up and enjoy it. I remember John Stainsby's goal. Gordon Banks didn't have a chance of saving it. John used to get stuck in and wouldn't take any nonsense. They also had a good player on the right wing in John Mitten, but I was quite studious and I would always wait for a player to touch the ball, then I'd be on top of them and nick it and I don't remember him giving me any problems. I think Barry Jackson had his head split open in that game as well, but got stitched up and came straight back out, because that's what he was like. He would have wanted to get back out there. We also had some good football matches against Watford during that Cup run and, when Barry Jackson scored that goal in the second replay against them at Bootham Crescent, you couldn't get hold of him. He was a nice, big lad and very excitable."

Jackson's abiding memory of that cup run remained the bang on his head he received against Leicester, though, along with his father's lack of sympathy the following morning. Recalling the Foxes clash, Jackson said: "Gordon Banks was in goal, Frank McLintock was also in their team and Colin Appleton, who was from Scarborough, was playing for them as well. He was a decent player and was similar to me. He was trying to make a name for himself in the game and he captained Leicester in the 1961 FA Cup final against Tottenham. I had to go off in the match because I had a massive cut eye. Dr McKenna gave me four or five stitches, so I went back on in the second half and I was alright. I remember the following day, my dad said I still had to go to work. He didn't consider professional football to be a full-time job and told me to get on my bike, because I was still serving my apprenticeship at Cooke's. I was a fitting and turning optical instrument maker there and Alf Patrick was my chargehand."

Leicester levelled the scores when City were down to ten men due to Jackson being off the pitch, following his clash with Howard Riley.

Earlier, Banks had done well to hold a first-time shot from Wragg before being beaten by the same player on 24 minutes. Wally Gould swung in a high centre from the right that Banks punched 20 yards away from his goal but Wragg, showing excellent timing and ball control, hit a low and forceful effort that found the net after hitting a Leicester defender close to goal. City squandered an opportunity to double the lead ten minutes later when a penalty was awarded after Stainsby was shoved by Richie Norman as he looked to head another Gould centre. Wragg went on to hit the inside of Banks' post and the ball spun back into the keeper's hands for a fortunate save. But, with Jackson off, Leicester got back on terms after Heron missed a tackle on Riley, who put in a low centre that caused a mix-up in the penalty area, allowing Mitten to scramble the ball past Forgan. The winner came seven minutes from the end, though, with Jackson back on the pitch. Woods sent in a free kick and Wilkinson rose high to power a great header towards goal, with the hard-working Stainsby going on to slam the ball in the net. The crowd rose to their feet at the final whistle but, for Forgan, who would miss the last-eight clash at Rochdale after cracking a shoulder blade the Saturday before in a physical contest against Mansfield at Bootham Crescent, the run came nowhere near matching the excitement levels of the club's knockout heroics seven years earlier. "Although we got to the quarter finals of the League Cup in 1962, nothing will come close to the semi-final days when everybody would stop you and want to talk football," he reasoned. By the Leicester game, meanwhile, a special park for motor cyclists and scooters near Lumley Barracks had been made available on match days, meaning they were no longer left behind the Main Stand.

A late equaliser by Gould at Bootham Crescent in the next round earned a 1-1 draw with Watford and, after another draw at Vicarage Road, the Minstermen won the toss to host the second replay at Bootham Crescent. The Monday-night tie did not start well for City, who were 2-0 down within the first 14 minutes, but a spirited second-half comeback saw South African Gerry Francis reduce the deficit.

Jackson then set up a 76th-minute equaliser for Wragg when he headed down a Heron free kick, before stabbing in the three-yard winner himself two minutes from time. Bournemouth were also seen off at home in the last 16 with Stainsby, who had only arrived at the game 15 minutes before kick-off after getting caught up in traffic following a road accident near Wakefield, getting the only goal of a one-sided game, in which busy away keeper Johnny Best was given a tremendous ovation at the end. A trip to the only other fourth division team left in the quarter-finals - indeed both sides were the sole clubs remaining outside the top two tiers - appeared to present an excellent opportunity to make the semi-finals, but City were beaten 2-1 at Rochdale.

Despite the club's knockout success that season, Heron also revealed team spirit wasn't always the best at Bootham Crescent at the time, with 29-goal top scorer Jimmy Weir an unpopular presence in the dressing room. "Jimmy Weir was a good player, but he had a nasty attitude and wasn't a very good person to have inside the club," Heron pointed out. "He said to me once: 'You don't have much to say, do you?' I said: 'Maybe I don't and I wouldn't tell you when I was going to hit you either'. He said: 'What do you mean?' and I said: 'Well, why are you always shouting your mouth off and saying you're going to do this or that?' I said: 'If I say I'm going to hit somebody, I hit them, so watch out'. Then, in training, at Bootham Crescent, he came across me and I got him. Wally Gould wasn't a bad little player, but he could be nasty too."

Yorkshire Schoolboys, meanwhile, were beaten 7-2 by their Lancashire counterparts in front of a 2,500 crowd at Bootham Crescent in the 45th Roses county match, with York City Boys skipper Trevor Bell in the hosts' team.

Another Grand National clash was avoided with a Saturday 3pm start switched to 7pm for the home clash against Darlington - an important match in the promotion race that City won 2-1 thanks to two goals from Francis in front of a 9,579 crowd. The attendance was the second-highest league gate of the season at Bootham Crescent and was only bettered by the 9,767 that turned up for a 4-0 defeat of Workington in the penultimate home fixture of the season. Eight days later, the campaign ended agonisingly at Bootham Crescent following a 1-0 defeat to Aldershot when a win would have ensured promotion against a team that still had an outside chance of going up themselves.

143

It was a poor performance in a scrappy match from a City team that had taken 36 points from a possible 42 at home. Weir did go close when his first-half chip struck the bar and, at the break, the crowd acted enthusiastically to news that Bradford City were losing at Workington - a result that would see City go up if they could take maximum points. But Robbie Stepney hit the post for the visitors, before going on to head in the winning goal from a 74th-minute free kick.

Remembering the contest, Woods admitted: "That was a disappointment. You think you're nearly there and we were playing Aldershot, who were nothing great, so we were thinking we had one hell of a chance, but it doesn't always work out like that. They played particularly well on the day and we couldn't get the ball in the net. That's how it goes and there's nothing you can do about it."

The result meant City had to wait to see if promotion rivals Carlisle lost their last game, whilst hoping Aldershot or Bradford also failed to win their final matches. All three clubs were still to complete their fixture programmes following the season's final weekend, but Carlisle went on to clinch the fourth promotion spot with a 2-0 Tuesday night triumph against Chester.

Watching on for the first time that campaign was 10-year-old Bubwith boy Chris Topping, for whom supporting City was a family affair - long before he became a club legend. "I didn't go Bootham Crescent as much as I'd have liked to as a boy, but York City was in my blood as my granddad was involved at Fulfordgate," Topping explained. "He was a big fan who was on the committee and he helped the club move to Bootham Crescent, as did my dad. They helped with the transporting of stuff from Fulfordgate but, when I was growing up, my dad was an insurance man who worked on a Friday night collecting money in Selby so, because there were a lot of Friday night home games back then, we didn't get to too many. We also lived about 18 miles away and, in the early 1960s, that was still quite a journey. We got to three or four games a season though. My uncle Herbert was also a big supporter and we all went together when we went. People like Billy Rudd made an impression on me. He was a very skilful little player. I enjoyed watching Gerry Baker too and he was still there when I signed for the club. He was good with me, as was Barry Jackson and I thought that was nice of the older professionals. I was integrated very quickly, which was important and lovely for a shy, country lad. They included me in the various exercises and I never felt out of place. When I became a player, my mum, dad and uncle Herbert would still be there with my girlfriend at the time and they used to all congregate to the left of the players' tunnel. My mum was a massive supporter and it was nice to share everything we went through at the club - the promotions and the relegations - with my family. Later I got to watch my son play there in a local cup final for Cliffe and that was a wonderful moment too."

In the summer of 1962, meanwhile, it was revealed that players would only receive a bonus if the team were in the top four after 12 games, instead of being related to attendance numbers at Bootham Crescent. Several rows of the Popular Stand's Tarmac terracing were also concreted during the close season. The top and bottom rows were already concreted, but the work on the rows in between meant all the terracing around the whole ground was now concreted.

Oxford United, meanwhile, were elected to the Football League and immediately agreed to travel to Bootham Crescent for a Friday night fixture as City were still keen to boost gate numbers where possible. Future Manchester United boss Ron Atkinson was in a visitors' side that won 2-1 at Bootham Crescent in that Oxford clash and he cleared a Gould effort off the line with a diving header while Jackson got the hosts' consolation. The Friday night experiment seemed to prove popular with the York public, as a gate of 5,215 was much higher than the preceding home clash (3,494 for a 0-0 draw with Aldershot), the next league game on the hallowed turf (3,784 for a 2-1 defeat to Tranmere) and, indeed, the season average of 4,515, which represented a post-War low. The annual public practice match had also been played on a Friday evening for the second season running. Gates for reserve-team football, meanwhile, suggested there was little public appetite for such fixtures any more with crowds just creeping into three figures at times. Rather than a potentially profitable public attraction, its sole existence was now to keep players match fit. Crowd revenue for such games had dropped from an average of £100 to £20, although the weekly wage bill of the players taking part would be a little more than the former figure.

One of the coldest winters in the UK, known as The Big Freeze, subsequently saw City play no league football from December 22, 1962 to March 8, 1963 with training generally conducted indoors. Players were often assigned with the task of clearing snow from the pitch during this period, only for more to fall. A practice game was even hosted at Scarborough's Burniston Barracks against Sheffield Wednesday to keep the players ticking over. During the freeze, Bootham Crescent was virtually closed down, with Woods recalling: "Tom Lockie took us to Scarborough to train on the beach once because everything was frozen solid in York. We had to use our cars and claim back the expenses. We

145

hadn't played for two or three weeks and it was good because it was something different getting away from Bootham Crescent. We didn't have a training field and all we mainly did at Bootham Crescent anyway was run around the pitch, apart from the 5-a-side games we used to have in the corner. We used to have some competitive games there and I think there were probably more injuries in those matches than we got on a Saturday. There were one or two scraps and punch-ups too, which was a bit daft when you were playing against mates but, after it had happened, everything was forgotten."

Rudd also remembered the monotony of training, especially when the temperatures plummeted. "During the Big Freeze, we seemed to spend weeks and weeks running underneath the stand on the concrete terracing," he recalled. "They had the braziers on the pitch, but it would thaw during the day and then freeze again at night. We would run up and down the terracing and along the bottom, which wasn't too exciting. Having said that, the training we did often just amounted to a couple of hours running around the pitch." Jackson agreed that training was very rudimentary at the time, adding: "We went to the RI gym a lot during the Big Freeze. The club rented it from them. We'd normally

The Big Freeze of 1962/63 meant the club were without a game for two-and-a-half months and meant the team had to find novel ways at times to get some exercise at Bootham Crescent. Pictured (from left-to-right) are Wally Gould, Tommy Forgan, Roy Ambler, Alan Woods, Peter Wragg and Barry Jackson

go into the corner near the turnstiles and play little five-a-side games and there was always a lot of running in my day as well. We would have been better off practicing with the ball a bit more maybe, but training was more about making sure you stayed fit back then." Heron, meanwhile, recalled that Sid Storey tried to beat the boredom with drills he would put on at the ground. "The pitch was frozen solid and there wasn't a gym as such that we could go to, so Sid took us around the back of the stand at the Grosvenor Road end, where there was a bit of space for him to set up a gym there with exercises for us to do," Heron recalled. "I laugh about it now, because footballers these days don't know what facilities we had to contend with, but we just got on with it. At Old Trafford, we used to have to jump and head a ball that was dangling from string off a part of the South Stand and I remember Sid putting down some plastic bottles in different areas. We would have to sprint from one to the next, touching them and coming back. You would always introduce competition into it as well, by making it one-v-one. We also had to help shift the snow and you missed playing the games. I got to Bootham Crescent OK for training though. The buses were still running from Tang Hall and then I'd walk in from town."

When fixtures resumed in March, Heron responded better than most, scoring two of the six goals he managed in 216 appearances for City during back-to-back home matches against Bradford and Hartlepool. Remembering his unexpected Bootham Crescent heroics, Heron said: "The one against Bradford was from just outside the box and I managed to put it right into the top corner. It was nice to score, and the supporters were really first class."

At the end of the season, meanwhile, club mascot Michael Gabbitas, who had run out with the players for three seasons decided, at 13, that he had become too old for the role. He was presented with a bronze statue from the players and he had collected almost 100 coins that had been tossed by referees before the game.

CHAPTER 12

Jack Fountain match-fixing scandal rocks City

"I remember going to the ground as normal for training and there were half-a-dozen police cars in the car park. I thought what the hell has happened here."

Ground admission rose from 2s 6d to 3s for the 1963/64 season, which was in line with most third and fourth division clubs at the time. The Popular Stand and Main Stand Enclosure charge also went up to 3s 6d instead of 3s, but the Main Stand price stayed at 5s. Boys' admission then rose in September from 1s to 1s 6d. The club also conducted a check to clamp down on the number of adult supporters who were being allowed through the boys' turnstiles, which were designed to cater for under-15s only. Setting a club record by starting the new season with four successive home defeats hardly seemed to represent value for money, though, given the admission increases. Earlier, for the third successive season, the annual Reds v Blues practice match was again played on a Friday evening, although the floodlit fixtures were now attracting similar attendances to those on Saturday afternoons.

The campaign would see City finish 22nd and apply for re-election and crowds again dipped with the home meeting against Oxford four days before Christmas setting a new all-time low gate at Bootham Crescent of 1,653 for a snowy 2-0 defeat, which also represented a fifth successive loss. There were attempts to enhance the match-day experience, though, with the renowned Coldstream Guards band playing before the home game with Chesterfield in October and at the interval. They had other engagements in York that weekend and the move harked back to a past era before bands were superseded by the playing of "canned music". The band also played the *Happy Wanderer* song to remind City supporters of happier times. For the Saturday, November 23 home clash with Aldershot, meanwhile, a minute's silence was observed, and black armbands were worn in memory of President John F Kennedy, who had been assassinated the previous day. City lost the match 2-1.

In a bid to bring more funds into the club, a new Development Association was set up to provide week-day prizes of £10, and £50 on a Saturday. The idea of a prize draw, set up to complement that already being run by the Auxiliary Club, was conceived in a meeting at the Supporters' Club with ex-City favourites Reg Baines, Alf Patrick, Ron Spence, Alan Stewart and Billy Fenton all offering their support for the venture, while tickets could be bought from the club secretary George Teasdale, who was the new scheme's promoter.

Bootham Crescent's billiards room was converted into an office, meanwhile, for the running of the initiative, where agents could pay in their money and tickets were distributed.

But scandal then rocked the club in April when reports emerged that Bootham Crescent had been the scene of a match-fixing attempt back in 1961 during a 2-1 defeat to Tranmere in the campaign that had seen City denied promotion on the final day. Initially, the York player, in a crime that involved players from other clubs including England internationals Tony Kay and Peter Swan, went unnamed with *The Sunday People* holding back the identities of some players - probably to boost sales over consecutive editions - which only led to a very unnerving week at Bootham Crescent.

Half-back and former captain Jack Fountain was eventually identified as one of a number of players implicated in the football bribery investigation exposed by *The People*, but he actually played the Friday before publication at Torquay despite reportedly looking very pre-occupied and worried during the two-day trip to Devon that resulted in a 1-0 away win. On the Sunday morning when his name was made public, though, Fountain was suspended by the club after being called for a "brief interview" at Bootham Crescent by the City management staff of chairman Hugh Kitchin, director Arthur Brown, manager Tom Lockie and secretary Teasdale. He was reported to have looked in a "very distressed condition", as he was taken to a side turnstile to avoid the many newspaper representatives and photographers waiting outside the main entrance, before being driven home to Leeds. York's CID officers also visited Bootham Crescent the following day to carry out their investigations. The allegation was that he received £180 by registered post and his contract with City was terminated, whilst he was banned from football for life and served a prison sentence.

The Evening Press report on the match in question started with the following introduction: "York City mixed such a lot of poor football in their display against Tranmere Rovers that it was not altogether surprising they were beaten 2-1." With Fountain playing at the back, the home defence were also described as being "wide open" as John Frye and Alan Arnell secured the visitors maximum points following Jimmy Weir's opener for the Minstermen. A report of "both wing-halves (Fountain's position on the day) made too many inaccurate passes" also now casts suspicion, as does the following observation: "Fountain got himself into trouble and lost the ball to Gubbins." City did stage a grandstand finish in the game to try and force an equaliser, though, suggesting that Fountain's indiscretions could have still been rendered fruitless by the efforts of his team-mates. A reflective piece two days after the match added: "Fountain just could not time his passes accurately and was more than once late to the tackle." By the Thursday after the game, it was also being reported that leading fixed-odds bookmakers were refusing to pay out on City's match with Tranmere and the Mansfield v Bradford City fixture on the same afternoon. Many £2 and £5 double bets had been placed at odds of 10-1 on a Tranmere and Bradford double by a large number of new clients in Yorkshire. One bookmaker added that in some cases bets were made in the same surname, while some were prevented from putting bigger sums of money on the games due to the general maximum stake limit of £5. In response to the claims, chairman Kitchin said he had no intention at the time of carrying out any inquiry at the club, unless any important new evidence came to light. Manager Lockie added: "It was just one of those bad games, when most of the players in the team were below form. That is how football goes - the uncertainty of the game." William Hill, meanwhile, admitted they would be withholding payment of the bets pending an investigation.

More than 50 years later, Alan Woods recalled vividly the moment when the authorities caught up with Fountain. "I remember going to the ground as normal for training and there were half-a-dozen police cars in the car park," he said. "I thought what the hell has happened here. My only idea was they must have found somebody who had hung himself in the stand or something. I went to go in, but there was a policewoman at the entrance who said: 'I'm sorry, you can't come in'. I said: 'Why. What's happened?' and she said: 'I can't tell you that, but nobody's coming in' so, then, I thought what do I do here? I was just stood in the car park and nobody was there to tell me what to do. A couple more lads then turned up. They asked what had happened and, as I couldn't tell them, I asked the policewoman again and she said: 'I just can't tell you'. Then Ron Spence came out and I asked him what had happened. He said there was an investigation into match-fixing and we had to stay there and be interviewed by the police one by one on our own. I didn't know a thing about it but, when they mentioned it, I said I could tell them two or three games that I was certain were thrown without a doubt. One was at Oldham when we got beaten 3-2 after being 2-0 up (that match was also investigated). Four years after it had happened, and Jackie had been in the nick and done his time, I was walking down the front at Scarborough and, who was walking towards us but him. He was a smashing bloke and a good player who I hit it off with straight away at York and I'd always got on well with him. He had three little girls and a lovely little wife, and I looked at him and he looked at me and cried. He said: 'I'm ever so sorry' and I put my arm around him and said: 'It's gone -

Bootham Crescent was teeming with police and journalists in April 1964 when former captain Jack Fountain was arrested on suspicion of match-fixing relating to fixtures played three years earlier. He would subsequently receive a 15-month prison sentence

there's nothing you can do about it now', but I did say: 'You cost us all a lot of money because we would have probably gone up'. I wasn't too surprised Jack had done it though. In every football club you have a betting gang and the first thing they do in a morning is sort their horses out. It still goes on and has done forever. Jack was one of those. He loved his horses and was always talking about a 2-1 shot at Kempton and he knew whether they had come down from Scotland for the race or whatever. I was never interested. I used to have five shillings on the Pools and that was it."

Billy Rudd, who signed for City shortly after the Tranmere match, also retained vivid memories of an unprecedented day in Bootham Crescent's history more than half-a-century later. "It was a bad scene and not a good atmosphere," he admitted. "I think it all started happening on the Saturday night and I was asked to go in on Sunday morning. There were a lot of reporters about and I remember that Tommy (Heron) and I both escaped them by jumping over the back of the Popular Stand. We were a lot quicker than some, who got caught by the press through the back streets when they cottoned on, but I've never been asked about it since. To be quite honest, I wasn't very happy at the time. Tom Lockie asked us all one by one - at least I hope it was all of us because I'm not sure it was - whether we knew anything. He said that I had played in two games that were being investigated as being fixed. It turned out I had been man of the match in one and scored in the other, so I said: 'What are you asking me for?' I think it was because I was a big friend of Jackie's. I went out socially with him quite a few times. He was a smashing lad, but I know he was broke at the time. He was broken by the whole episode as well and I never saw or spoke to him again. One or two of them who were involved got back in the game, but Jackie was getting on, so it was the end of him. The season before, when I was injured, the club had come fourth and I remember the Aldershot game, when we missed out on promotion, being really disappointing. You often wonder whether that game was one of those fixed as well." Like Woods, Rudd was almost certain that more matches from that era should have come under scrutiny, saying: "I don't think it was a one-off. There was a game at Oldham when we were 2-0 up and absolutely pummelling them. But then, in no time whatsoever when the second half started, we were 3-2 down and I remember Norman Wilkinson saying to me: 'What's going on here?' I said: 'I don't know, but it's not right'. It was still shocking when it came out though and the extent of it, because it wasn't a one-off game. I might have been a bit more understanding if it had been a one-off, but it had been going on over a number of matches when the rest of us were trying to do the best we could."

Heron also felt let down by his defensive team-mate, adding: "I was at the ground having treatment the morning it all came out and I saw Jack there. He said: 'I'm sorry, Tommy'. I said: 'I don't want to talk about it Jack, but I don't know how you can do that to the lads when they are giving their all'. We had some very whole-hearted players like Barry Jackson, Alan Woods, Billy Rudd and Norman Wilkinson, who was a tremendous person and a good example for young people. So, for that to happen, it was really hard to take and those involved must have known they wouldn't get away with it. I don't know how they were found out, but people must have been looking into it. When I saw the police at the ground that day, at first I thought there might have been a break-in, but it was in the papers as well. I know some of the other players were questioned, but I wasn't. It didn't come as a surprise to most of us, as we felt something had been going on. We also saw the reporters outside and I said: 'There's no way I'm talking to those people, because they'll just print what they want'." Heron also sympathised with shocked manager Lockie, saying: "I felt sorry for Tom when the bribery scandal broke because he was a whole-hearted man as well and it set him back a bit. He didn't know the game inside out, but he was a nice man and did his best. He maybe didn't have the authority you need as a manager and that meant he didn't get the respect he should have done from some of the players for the position he was in."

Jackson, meanwhile, recalled having surprise visitors to his Bootham Crescent sweet shop as the authorities arrested Fountain. "After the news came out, it made you look back at other games because there were occasions when you thought what were we doing there," he said. "A few of us had our suspicions. It was still a case of jigger me when we heard about it though. It was a sad time - it really was. Jack was a very good player and the captain. The police came and interviewed me at the sweet shop and that was the first I knew about it."

So many supporters of that era, meanwhile, would visit Jackson's confectionary store, which he opened in July 1963. It was especially popular with young fans hoping to see their hero and the centre back enjoyed meeting them all, saying: "The sweet shop didn't make any money, but I had it about seven years and people would pass by on the way to the ground. It was on the left side going down Bootham Crescent and I had two ladies who would look after it, whilst I was at training or playing. We also sold cigarettes and ice cream and I used to enjoy a chat with York fans." The shop had a sign outside of a player in City's colours coupled with Jackson's name.

In an ironic twist of fate, meanwhile, former City players Walt Bingley and Peter Wragg, who were both initially implicated by *The People* too before having their names cleared, met their old club during the final weeks of the season. Bingley played for Halifax at the Shay while Wragg who, at that time was in the process of suing the national tabloid newspaper, was part of a Bradford City team, whose fading hopes of promotion were shattered by a 1-0 City win at Bootham Crescent. It was reported that Wragg - Bradford's captain - was subjected to a few mild home boos, which were drowned out by vociferous away cheering.

Trainer Sid Storey - a member of the club's famous 1955 FA Cup semi-final side - looks at a waterlogged Bootham Crescent before a postponed game against Gillingham in March 1964

CHAPTER 13

Twenty home wins and a second promotion

"It was Scotland v England and everyone used to knock six bells out of each other. People used to smash you into the turnstiles."

Following the fall-out of the betting scandal, the club were rejuvenated in 1964/65 when the efforts of new signings Paul Aimson and Dennis Walker from Manchester City and United respectively, along with Barnsley winger Andy Provan, saw the average League crowd almost double to 7,185. Evening kick-offs, meanwhile, once more proved the most popular fixtures and, of the campaign's first 10 home games, eight were played at night with the other two matches' attendances in the lowest three of that batch. A night home contest with Bradford City attracted the worst crowd of 3,662, but heavy rain was believed to have reduced the attendance substantially on that occasion. The club also circumnavigated the League rules against charging a reduced price for pensioner admission into games. Powerless to make a concessionary offer for individual matches, they instead sold season tickets at a lower cost to the club's eldest supporters. They were available at £2 10s for the ground and £3 10s for the Main Stand, which represented a saving of 1s 3d and 1s 9d respectively per match. The annual public practice match was again played on a Friday night with a 7.15pm kick-off. Aimson scored twice against the prospective first-team defence and his first goal was a trademark header.

In the opening league game of the season, Aimson and Provan were also on the scoresheet during a 2-1 triumph against Rochdale at Bootham Crescent. A club record 20 league games went on to be won at home (with 15 successive wins in all competitions at Bootham Crescent also breaking the previous best sequence) while five-figured numbers flocked to home fixtures against Doncaster, Tranmere, Lincoln and Halifax. The three latter games came during a run-in to the end of the season that saw all of the final six home matches played at night, providing further evidence that the York public was more disposed towards evening kick-offs, which still always started at 7.15pm. In fact, 14 of the club's home fixtures in total would end up being played at night time during the season.

Provan, having been a bit-part player at previous clubs Barnsley and St Mirren before joining City at the age of 20, revealed that Bootham Crescent immediately felt like home. He said: "I arrived on a Friday night and there was a game going on against a German youth team. I was stood behind the goal to the left and it was the first time I'd ever watched a game from the terraces. I had normally been in the dugout as 12th man, including for big semi-final cup games for St Mirren. It was a different perspective for me and, looking across the pitch, I thought it was a great stadium, so I decided to sign after speaking to Tom Lockie afterwards. I soon realised that I loved York and Bootham Crescent felt like a special place. I was a young lad when I went there, and I had turned down the chance to live in South Africa with my parents, so I was alone. I wanted to be a footballer, so I stayed, and everybody was friendly, which made me feel like I belonged, and I felt settled. I was playing regularly and was part of a team. When I'd been at Barnsley and St Mirren, I was only a youngster and didn't really know or speak to anybody."

Provan's love for his new surroundings was soon reciprocated, after he scored on his debut and quickly became a fans' favourite. "I think I just came in from the right wing and tapped a cross in at the far post, but it was nice to get off to a good start in the team and it was a good, experienced team for me to play for at the time," he said. "Rochdale were also one of those clubs I always scored against during my career, no matter who I was playing for. I got a few against them over the years. In fact, I went on to get the first hat-trick of my career against them for Torquay." He admitted, though, that he was frustrated never to strike three times in a match for City, even though he bagged seven braces - all at Bootham Crescent. Sixteen of his 19 goals during that first campaign with the club also came in home matches and, on that remarkable record, he added: "I always enjoyed going out in front of the fans. The connection between them and us as players was good during the promotion season. We maybe attacked more at home, but we always went out and tried to play the same way, even in away games. It was definitely our home form that got us promoted though and maybe the opposition might have been confident as well when they were at home sometimes. Even though I'd only scored one goal for St Mirren before I came to York, I knew what I wanted to be in the game. I had always wanted to be a centre forward from my school days and had been, until I was switched on to the left wing for Scotland's youth team because they had Jim Forrest, who went on to play for Rangers and Preston, to play up front, but I was still a goalscorer and I used to always cut in from the left, even though I could use both feet. When I came to York, Tom Lockie kept saying to me: 'Stay out wide', but I'd be saying: 'What do you want me to stay out wide for when I can cut inside and score'?"

With Provan, Aimson and Walker providing the firepower, Bootham Crescent was soon transformed into a place to be feared with Woods reasoning: "Everybody was frightened when they came to Bootham Crescent that season. It wasn't a case of teams thinking can we win, it was more a case of can we keep the score down. That's what it's like when you're on a run like that." Doncaster were beaten 4-2 at Bootham Crescent in October with Walker (2), Provan and Aimson the marksmen in front of 11,898 for a fixture that Woods always relished. "We always had a battle with Doncaster and I used to play against Alick Jeffrey," he explained. "He was a hell of a good player. We got big crowds against them and I used to love the games." Woods was also impressed by the impact made by new signings Aimson and Provan, adding: "They were good players. Andy was a dribbler. He could pick the ball up, run at players and beat them. He was only six stone wet through, but he was nippy and quick. Paul was the best striker we had whilst I was at York without a doubt. I felt he was better than Norman (Wilkinson), whose game was purely in the air. Norman was one of those who could jump and hang in the air. That's how he got his goals, but he was finding it harder to run towards the end of his career. Paul was good all-round and a handful."

For skipper Billy Rudd, though, Wilkinson remained the club's eminent footballer a decade on from the FA Cup heroics. "Norman was my favourite player," Rudd revealed. "You only have to look at photographs to see he looked like anything but a footballer. He looked 50 when he was 20 and, with him being a part-time cobbler, his shoulders were hunched because he was bent over the last all the time, but he was brilliant in the air. I remember one of his favourite sayings being: 'When the ball is coming in from a cross, head it the way it's come, because you'll get more power', and that's still true to this day." Rudd also recognised, however, the impact made at the club by Aimson, Walker and Provan, particularly on that night-time triumph against Doncaster. "Paul Aimson was brilliant," he declared. "He was good in the air and a smashing chap - a down-to-earth lad from Manchester like me. Dennis Walker also came in and, over the years at various clubs, I saw a few young players sign from Manchester United who thought they were a bit superior because they had been there, even if they hadn't played for the first team. You had to beat that

157

out of them and that was the case with Dennis a bit at first, but he started to play well and was good for the team. Andy was a little Scots lad and a very tricky player. He could go inside or outside his defender and was a good finisher. They all scored against Doncaster and the atmosphere that night was excellent, as it often was for night games. They were always a wee bit different. There were nearly 12,000 there because they brought a big crowd as they were going well and it was one hell of a night. They had Alick Jeffrey and he was a great player, but we managed to weather his storm early on and ran out pretty, comfortable winners. When we were in full flow, we were exciting to watch, and it felt good playing in that team. There were other talented players as well. Derek Weddle could catch pigeons on the right wing, so we had a good forward line, whilst our defence was sound as well. We had big Jacko at centre half and, if we ever had any problems, he would sort them out, but we used to mainly put teams under a lot of pressure."

Woods was sickened, though, by the racist abuse Walker received at Bootham Crescent from visiting supporters as a black player in the 1960s. "Dennis used to get quite a bit of abuse," Woods revealed. "I don't think it bothered him to be honest, but you got a lot of monkey chanting and I didn't like it. I felt for him. After all, I couldn't help being white, any more than he could help being black."

Tommy Heron, meanwhile, felt the attacking trio were important additions in terms of raising spirit on and off the pitch. "Dennis was a good player, who I knew from Manchester United and Paul Aimson was a class player, who was very good in the air but could play too and hold the ball up," Heron enthused. "Andy Provan was also a top-class, wee winger, who was full of it and made Tom Lockie laugh. He used to say: 'You Scotsmen don't half take liberties.'"

Jackson was excited as well by the manner in which the trio transformed the club's fortunes, citing Aimson's arrival as the key catalyst for success. "Those three made a big difference, especially Paul," he declared. "He was a really good player. You were always very confident when you had somebody like Paul in the side because you knew there was every chance he would get you a goal or two. He was a really, good finisher, who could get a goal out of nothing and it was wonderful to have that in your team. Andy Provan could also catch pigeons and was a real character. It was a good team and people like Tommy Heron did a hell of a job too. He was very bright. People used to say he couldn't defend but he was good enough and was wonderful on the ball. It was probably the best side I played in and the atmosphere at Bootham Crescent was wonderful.

There's nothing better when you get people behind you. It lifts you." On his partners in crime, Provan added: "We all clicked. Dennis used to be shouting all the time, while Paul was very quiet, but very lethal."

A mid-term run of seven consecutive league wins also represented a club record and was completed with a 7-1 Boxing Day home thrashing of Chesterfield when Aimson (2), Provan (2), Weddle, Rudd and Wilkinson were all on target. Aimson's brace took his tally for the season to 20 and four of the home goals were scored in a dazzling second-half, 12-minute period, with the players getting a rousing ovation at the end. It is a game that stood out for Woods, as much for the time of the year as for the emphatic margin of victory. "That 7-1 win at Christmas was great," he enthused. "The crowd loved those games and I used to love fixtures at that time of the year as well. Sometimes, we played three games in four days and it was the same at Easter when you would play Friday, Saturday and Monday. I thought it was great because, when you're young, you can't play enough. We also knew we would get six or seven thousand in the ground. You were knackered by the end of it, but everyone was in the same boat. The clubs did it for the crowds to get the money in. The game was still about money, even back then."

Rudd, meanwhile, remembered how he celebrated the Chesterfield thrashing. "That was a great Christmas," he enthused. "I was living with the stable man at York Racecourse and his wife, who ended up being godparents to my children. Ruth, my future wife, had gone home for the weekend with it being Christmas, so Paul Aimson stayed with me and we had a meal at the house to celebrate a great result. It was one of those games where everything we touched turned to gold and I loved the atmosphere at football over Christmas. We used to have two or three games in four days, but you got on with it. The crowd was always a bit better because they were on holiday. We drew 1-1 at Chesterfield, though, two days later and the management weren't happy. After we'd won 7-1, they expected the same result away from home, but football doesn't work like that. If a team has anything about them after a hiding like that, they will make life difficult for you."

Provan, meanwhile, revealed that boss Lockie even managed a grin at the final whistle of the home contest. "During the 7-1 game, everything we hit went in the back of the net and even Tom Lockie was smiling that day," he laughed. "Tom was the most dour Scotsman ever. He was something different to what you'd expect from our country really and reminded you of John Laurie in *Dad's Army* when he used to shout: 'We're Doomed!' He was a really good manager though and was quite thorough. He would give us a run down on the opposition, even though he was an old-fashioned kind of manager. I don't know if Chesterfield had been celebrating over Christmas for that game, but I know I was the only one who scored in the return match two days later when we drew and that was pleasing as well."

In January, meanwhile, more details emerged about how the Fountain match-fixing scandal had been played out at Bootham Crescent during the court hearing at Nottingham Assizes. Club secretary George Teasdale, giving evidence in the trial during which Fountain changed his initial "not guilty" plea to "guilty", revealed that the latter had rung him on Sunday, April 19, 1964 at the club office about *The People's* newspaper article following its publication that day. A meeting was then arranged between Fountain, chairman Hugh Kitchin, Arthur Brown (the chairman of the players' committee), club manager Lockie and Teasdale. At that meeting, it was stated that Kitchin asked Fountain what he had to say about the newspaper article and the player replied: "It is not true." Brown then asked Fountain about a letter that had been reproduced in the newspaper and the defender replied: "I do not know how they got hold of that." Brown responded: "That is not what I asked you" and Teasdale recalled: "There was a silence for a few minutes and then Fountain said: 'I will admit to the match against Tranmere. That is all. They say I received £180, but that is not true. I have my bank book to prove it.'" Fountain insisted, meanwhile, that no other players were involved, according to Teasdale's account. He would subsequently be sentenced to a 15-month prison sentence. Former Mansfield Town inside-forward Willie Gauld - the ringleader of the betting scam who received £7,240 from *The People* for selling his story - was jailed for four years and ordered to pay £5,000 in costs. It was also revealed that Gauld had met two other City players along with Fountain, but their identities remained anonymous.

In February, new, improved loudspeaker equipment was installed at Bootham Crescent for the home match with Aldershot, which was won 1-0 courtesy of a retaken Walker penalty. That was one of the 15 home games that were incredibly all won from November 7 to the end of the season on April 24, during which time Bangor City were also seen off 5-1 in an FA Cup first-round triumph. Rudd reckoned the secret behind such sustained success was the team's gung-ho approach to matches on their own turf. "My philosophy then, as it still is now, was that home teams should go out and attack to try to win the game," he declared. "Nowadays, people say they don't want to lose because there's a belief there's more at stake. I always say: 'Hang on, there was £4 at stake

An unfit, but stylish, Paul Aimson looks on as Bobby Sibbald, Billy Hodgson, Mick Stainwright, Phil Boyer and Mick Mahon prepare for a home FA Cup tie against Bangor in 1964

when we were playing', because that was the win bonus and you would kick your own grandmother for £4 back then. It was £4 for a win and £2 for a draw and that made a big difference in your pay packet. My wife was always happy when we won. When you go on runs like that - and I had similar ones with Rochdale and Bury - you don't think you're going to get beaten. You still have to do the basics and graft, but you go out there expecting to win."

Heron added that the crowd responded well to their team's successful run of results at Bootham Crescent, pointing out: "They wanted to see their team winning like any club's fans and we got that momentum going, which was great. We had a lot of good home wins and that was because of the ability of the team. I remember beating Newport 5-1 when the snow came down and we could hardly see. They would have abandoned it now, but we carried on and the conditions cleared a bit eventually." Play was indeed suspended in that March match for seven minutes at the start of the second half following a heavy snowstorm, but the game, which was deadlocked at 1-1 at the time, continued after the lines were cleared and City responded best to the conditions. Heron also believed the Bootham Crescent pitch, lovingly and meticulously tendered to by charismatic groundsman Bryan Foster, provided a great surface for the team to showcase their talents. He added: "The pitch was excellent and that was down to Bryan Foster, who was a right case. He used to try and get tips off me and Billy, because we knew people from the stables at York Racecourse. He took great pride in his pitch though. I always remember coming back from a game at Hull and, the next morning, Fossie asked about the match. I told him the pitch had been great, just like his and he said: 'You were the best man on the park, Tommy' because the compliment had made his day."

On the last Friday in March, meanwhile, City won their top-two home meeting with Tranmere to take over leadership of the division. A memorable night saw Weddle hit a hat-trick during a 4-0 thumping in front of more than 13,000 fans - the biggest crowd at Bootham Crescent for four years. With Aimson injured, right-back Gerry Baker played at centre forward and had earlier opened the scoring. The atmosphere was reported to be reminiscent of those great Cup ties in the not-too-distant past, as promotion fever began to grip the city.

The team went on to secure a return to the third division in emphatic style, beating second-bottom Halifax 4-0 in a Saturday night match - a result they needed after Oxford had defeated Darlington 1-0 in the afternoon. The ground, therefore, witnessed its second promotion with City finishing one point behind champions Brighton. Aimson and Woods passed late fitness tests for the game and a crowd of 12,719, including the Lord Mayor, turned up for the occasion, with City storming into a 3-0 lead with only 31 minutes on the clock. The first goal came on 18 minutes when Woods made a forceful run and, after Walker's shot was kicked off the line, Provan converted from the rebound. Seven minutes later, Jackson headed out to Walker, who pushed the ball on for Rudd and, after the skipper threaded the ball through to Aimson, he fired past Halifax keeper Peter Downsborough. Aimson went on to make it 3-0 when he swept home from Wilkinson's ball across goal. The fourth was then scored early in the second half when Provan darted away on one of his elusive dribbles and Rudd headed in before bounding back to the centre line in delight.

Jackson admitted, meanwhile, that he had been as anxious as ever during the countdown to kick-off. "There were quite a lot of fans and a few from Halifax wanting them to win as well," he pointed out. "I always ran to the toilet 20 or 30 minutes before kick-off and I was always a bag of nerves during the hour leading up to games. I think that was healthy, as long as you're not too bad."

Woods remembered that the lightning-fast Archie Taylor, who would sign for the Minstermen three years later, posed the only real threat on the day.

"Archie was their winger and was super fast," he pointed out. "He wasn't the greatest of players, but he should have been an Olympic sprinter - he was that quick. I played with him later on at Boston, but he couldn't be bothered to run by then. Before, though, it didn't matter who you put up against him, they wouldn't catch him. The plan was to clunk him one and I think he eventually got clattered in the 88th minute. It didn't matter though because the problem with Archie was, when he beat you, he generally didn't do a lot with the ball. He would kick the ball and go past you, but his crossing wasn't very good and, on that day, Jacko and Forgy dealt with everything he put in quite easily." As left-back, it was Heron's job, in the main, to deal with Taylor and he claimed he used his brain to nullify the threat. "Archie Taylor was a very good winger, who was like lightning out of the traps, but I used to make him run across the park," Heron explained. "He called me a crafty old so-and-so. He said: 'Why are you showing me inside? You're alright, you're fast'. But I said: 'I'm not running with you all day'. He was the only one who could cause any danger, so I realised I had to use my head. Fortunately, I had a good head on me and I could think about the game, so I was able to handle him."

For Woods, the win also heralded a massive sense of relief, having been a member of the side that had missed out on going up three seasons earlier on the final day. "You always have that fear that it might go wrong again, and you tend to err on the defensive in that situation, but we knew we had to win," he said. "Once we got to 3-0 and 4-0, though, we knew we could push the ball about a bit and you play better when you're more relaxed. The referee told us he was going to blow the whistle a few seconds before he did, because he had reffed us lots of times at York and wanted to give us the chance to make our way off the pitch, but we were still mobbed, and it was great. That's what you play the game for. It's a lot better than the fans booing you off."

Rudd's memory of the happy day did not diminish with the passing of time either and he retained a couple of souvenirs to remember it by.

"I remember my headed goal," he smiled. "When I tell people I scored a lot of headers, they laugh because of my size, but I've got a photograph of that goal. I seemed to be in acres of space on my own. I didn't have to climb or jump in the air either. The ball came in at head height and I stuck it away. The atmosphere was great at the end. All the supporters spilled onto the pitch and there were plenty of champagne bottles knocking about afterwards. I've still got the shirt from that game too. My daughter never believed it was mine, because it looks like a little kid's. She always said: 'How did you fit in that?' I had to be discreet to sneak the shirt out though. You couldn't swap shirts like they do now back then, because they needed to be ironed and washed for the following game. I don't know if we had the same kit the next season, but the club wouldn't have let you keep them anyway. I stuck mine in my bag for a memento, but I don't think anybody else did."

On his recollections of the post-match party, Heron said: "All my family were down from Scotland and we all went up into the stand to celebrate. The fans were all on the pitch and, then, we went in the dressing room, where all the bottles of champagne were opened." Jackson, meanwhile, remembered the glow of success feeling more special than the 1958/59 campaign, saying: "I got a lot more satisfaction out of that second promotion. It was great and we were a better side."

Despite his tender years, Provan insisted he had every confidence that the team would do what was necessary against Halifax. "It was one of those occasions when we knew everything would go to plan," he declared. "We had experience to help us with people like Alan Woods in midfield and Ruddy, who was a little leader and could play a bit. We had confidence in each other and always went out to play well with the aim of trying to win every game. I've still got a photo of me coming off the pitch when all the fans ran on after that game. There are a couple of young lads looking at me in what seems like awe. At the time, though, you see all these faces and are just trying to get off the pitch and get into the safety of the dressing room to start the celebrations. I really enjoyed that, because it was my first taste of success in football."

The celebrations were bigger and better than in 1959, with thousands of fans clamouring for their team to appear in the directors' box, where they acclaimed them one by one. There was a specifically persistent call for skipper Rudd, who had to wait a long time for quiet before addressing the crowd. He went on to thank the public for their great encouragement in the final phases of the promotion fight and praised his colleagues for their great team work. Celebrations then continued in the packed boardroom and guest room, with players, wives, directors and staff all toasting the side's success together. Chairman Kitchin also congratulated the players and expressed his appreciation in a speech.

The mid-60s, meanwhile, saw the half-time scoreboard become disused at the Shipton Street End, but it remained in place as an advertising hoarding. For many years, the scores of different games up and down the country, which were signalled by a letter of the alphabet in the programme, had been hung on two nails or, in the case of York's rugby league team, on four. During the summer of 1965, 300 tip-up seats were also installed for season-ticket holders - the first part of a scheme that would eventually see the whole Main Stand converted in the same fashion. Those who sat in the new area paid seven guineas for their season tickets, with places in the rest of the Main Stand costing six. Football League regulations also set the minimum admission price for an adult at 4s, which was the cost to watch fixtures from the terraces.

The continued preference for night matches saw 15 Bootham Crescent fixtures switched from afternoon to evening kick-offs for the first campaign of third division football in six years - with 11 scheduled on a Friday, three on a Monday and one on a Saturday. QPR and Peterborough rejected a change, though, arguing that their travel distance meant that their visits would require an overnight stay. The Football League also finally sanctioned permission for clubs to offer reduced admission prices for pensioners, with City charging 2s. A pension book was needed as proof at one of the boys' turnstiles, which was made available for the elderly supporters. It was also revealed that £1 bonus payments would be paid to players, per every 1,000 supporters at home games over a modest 4,000 gate. Once more, the annual practice match was staged on a Friday night too but, falling in line with other clubs, instead of the Reds v Blues contests, which had become outmoded, the Bootham Crescent warm-up match was part of a two-game series with Bradford Park Avenue visiting six days after hosting the Minstermen. This match also witnessed substitutions for the first time with two introduced for York and three for Bradford, whilst a big crowd of more than 5,000 came through the turnstiles.

The Minstermen could not build on their promotion success, however, going straight back down with just five home wins seeing the club finish bottom of the third division. It was a strange reversal in fortunes for a club that had been so dominant at Bootham Crescent with Rudd arguing that the ranks were not bolstered sufficiently during the summer and losing at home quickly became as big a habit as winning had been. "I remember us starting well and we won 4-1 at Hull with Paul Aimson scoring a hat-trick but, strangely, after the season we'd had at home to get promoted, we couldn't do anything at Bootham Crescent," he pointed out. "The main reason for us struggling was we'd gone up but didn't invest in the one or two better-quality players we needed for the division above. The club were quite happy to just try and stay in the league. I wasn't and, just as when we were winning everyone was confident, when you start losing, things seem to snowball and, no matter what you do, you can't stop it."

On the dramatic reversal of fortunes at Bootham Crescent, Jackson admitted: "It was hard and an absolute disaster. We didn't know how we managed to lose some of the games. It was also very sad to see Norman Wilkinson and Tommy Forgan leave at the end of the season." Provan confessed that games became much more difficult at Bootham Crescent following the noticeable step up in class, adding: "We were still trying, but we just weren't quite good enough. We were playing against some ex-first division players and kept the same team really, aside from adding a couple of players. Teams like Brighton had former internationals that had signed from Chelsea, so we started losing games and the atmosphere at the ground changed. Bad sides get remembered the same as good teams and you felt like you were letting people down, but that's never done on purpose."

The preference for a shift towards evening football was illustrated further, meanwhile, when a reserve game against Darlington was played on a Friday night at Bootham Crescent as an experiment to gauge crowd numbers, with the half-time score of the first team's fixture at Brighton on the same evening also announced at the ground.

A crowd about 200 larger than a Saturday afternoon reserve game turned up but witnessed a disappointing 5-0 defeat. First-team attendances, meanwhile, slipped from more than 9,000 early in the season to under 3,000, although 19,420 did turn up in March for the visit of Hull City, with many away fans watching from a vantage point on top of the garages adjoining the Lumley Barracks land. The match was switched back to a Saturday afternoon, having been one of the matches rescheduled to a Friday night when the fixtures came out. The decision was made when Hull informed their hosts that they would be likely to bring 10,000 fans for a 3pm Saturday kick-off and that number would be significantly reduced for an evening fixture. The Minstermen lost 2-1, but Rudd recalled the swollen gate presented problems for players, as well as supporters, on their way to the game.

"I can remember coming in for the game and people were saying all the roads in were blocked," he explained. "There was a lot of congestion and people couldn't get to the ground. I didn't learn to drive until my mid-30s, so I used to get the bus with Tom Heron from Burnholme. That would take us into Exhibition Square and we would walk up from there. I enjoyed walking to the ground where it was situated amongst all the houses. It was a lovely location and we had no airs and graces in terms of how we travelled around back then. Luckily,

166

we managed to get to the game in time. There was a good atmosphere, but there was certainly no way we were going to beat them 4-1 again. They were on a good run and their tails were up."

The match also held painful memories, quite literally, for Provan, who had his leg broken in the game, even though he would play another four matches, despite the injury, during the next couple of months. "One of their players came in and kicked me from behind," Provan grimaced. "It broke the outside of my left fibula and I heard it go crack. The trainer came on and asked me to stamp on the floor. I said: 'No' because I had heard the snap. People also said they heard it in the stands but, when I went for an X-ray, nothing showed up and I ended up playing the odd game with a broken leg. People thought I wasn't trying, which wasn't like me because I loved to entertain and take the Mickey. Over the summer, I went to hospital on my own and they told me there was a quarter-of-an-inch gap, where the bones had been rubbing away. The press got to know about it and took a photo of me, which Tom Lockie game me a right rollicking for. He said it made the club look small, but I said I'd told him that something was wrong with me. He kept telling me to go out and play and I was trying to do my best for the club, but I knew I wasn't fully fit. I was in pain every time I changed direction or tried to accelerate past people. They wouldn't give me injections, because they said there wasn't anything wrong with my leg. I didn't like taking tablets either, because I thought it would disguise the pain and end up doing more damage."

Dave Dunmore, meanwhile, had been brought back to the club following the previous season's promotion campaign, as had Irish international Eamon Dunphy. The latter was a former Manchester United midfielder and would go on to gain fame as an outspoken Irish TV pundit, but Dunmore didn't find him an unsettling personality, saying: "Eamonn spoke his mind but he was alright and got on with the lads." The ex-Spurs man was also impressed with Aimson, who managed another 20 goals, despite the side's struggles. "Aimo was a good player and a good centre forward," Dunmore declared. "He was powerful and good in the air with a good shot. I had played against him in the top division when he was at Manchester City and playing on the wing, so I remembered him from then when I went back to York." Provan, meanwhile, thought Dunmore's return to Bootham Crescent was one of the few positives during a difficult campaign. He said: "Dave Dunmore was a terrific player and he was so nimble for a guy of his height and weight. He was one of my favourite team-mates to play with and we got on well."

Forgan left for Gainsborough shortly after that match against his old team Hull, but his clean sheet tally of 120 still stands as a club record and, prior to his death in 2019, he retained nothing but fond memories of his old stamping ground, saying: "Bootham Crescent was always a pleasure to play on. It was a very good playing surface worthy of any club and the crowd were very encouraging towards the players. It was a very compact ground and there was a fine Supporters' Club. By the time my playing days were over, I well and truly felt part of the family."

Another club legend Wilkinson, who had scored nine goals during the promotion campaign, only managed four outings as the team were relegated. His last game was at home to Reading on May 6, 1966 and ended in a 2-1 defeat. The last of his club record 143 goals had come in the 3-0 Bootham Crescent triumph over Lincoln more than a year earlier. In his prime, though, his goalscoring prowess had attracted a range of high-profile admirers to Bootham Crescent and, later in life, Wilkinson revealed: "Don Revie used to come to our matches occasionally and I remember Albert Johanneson being with him once. Albert later told me that he fetched them over to watch how I played."

Wilkinson, as a part-time footballer and cobbler, relied on the generosity of his bosses to attend matches, arriving at Bootham Crescent by train and on foot before later, when he could afford to buy a car, travelling down from the north-east in his Morris Minor. City fan Fred Hemenway, in his early 40s when Wilkinson hung up his boots, believed he never saw a finer City player - before or afterwards - to have graced the hallowed turf. "Norman Wilkinson was the best I ever saw at Bootham Crescent," he declared. "I remember another chat I had with Billy Hughes when we were playing table tennis and he said that, with Norman, you could be sure that no matter where you were, even if you were in a tangle, he would always be there in open space to take a pass off you. You would also see him defending in his own half and the next time you saw him he was in the penalty area at the other end, but you never saw him go. He was one of the game's most under-rated players in my opinion. I remember years later seeing Norman at a game and I said to him: 'When are you going to come back and show these players how to head a ball'. He took off his glasses and said: 'If I take these off, I can't even see the field, let alone the ball." Provan had great respect for the veteran forward too, saying: "Norman was a marvellous man. He didn't look like a footballer. He looked like a headmaster with his bald head but, along with Billy Rudd, he ran the tempo of games and would slow the play down and quicken it up to help the team out."

Woods also departed after 259 appearances for the club but always smiled when recounting happy times at Bootham Crescent. "One of the funniest things I have ever seen came after a game when we'd had eight corners on the right-hand side at Exeter and Wally Gould kicked every one of them behind the goal," he laughed. "Tom Lockie was absolutely fuming and came into the dressing room shouting: 'You must have your bloody boots on the wrong feet'. He was having a right go at Wally and I was laughing like hell behind his back. On our first day back in for training at Bootham Crescent, Tom Lockie said: 'Right Wally, let's get these corners sorted'. He got everything all lined up. Wally was told to put it on the penalty spot and Norman Wilkinson was going to come in from the edge of the area and try and score, but the first three Wally took all went behind the goal and I can see Tom Lockie now - his face was blood red and he was shouting: 'You call yourself a professional footballer? If you can't do that, you shouldn't be in the infant school team. It's simple, lad'. He then put the ball on the ground and, with his big, size 12 army boots on and trousers tucked into his socks, he toe-poked the ball and it went plum on the penalty spot. It even kicked chalk up off the spot. All the lads were falling over with laughter and I said: 'You've not got an argument have you, Wall?' He took Wally off corners after that. I took a couple, but Wally was back on them after a while. He'd just had a bit of a mental block with them for some reason."

Rudd also moved on and, despite being a promotion-winning captain under Lockie, it is clear the two didn't always see eye-to-eye. "I used to have many an argument with Tom Lockie," he revealed. "He wasn't very happy when I first signed, and I did my ligaments in both ankles. I was out for the rest of that first season and he said: 'I spent a lot of money on you and I'm not getting my money's worth'. The specialist said I should get some sun in Spain, but there was no chance of that - the nearest I got was Burnholme! He (Lockie) was a nice fellow, but maybe too nice for the job. He always seemed to survive at the club though. He had been at the club in different guises for more than 30 years and I'm always a little wary of people like that. Managers didn't have a big tactical influence on teams back then either. They didn't tend to have ideas or views. It was basically a case of you're the players and you know what to do, so go out and play. I didn't really take much notice of him by the end and, three seasons after I left, I came back with Rochdale. We drew 0-0 and we ended up getting promoted that season. I came out of the showers after the game and I was towelling off in the dressing room when Tom Lockie, who wasn't York manager by then, walked in. He came over and said in his Scottish drawl: 'You never played like that for me when you were here'. I went ballistic and said to him: 'I must have done something right, because I never missed a game for three years'. He probably meant it in jest, but it wound me up. He gave York all that service though and that cannot be sniffed at even if I didn't think he was up to the job or my type of person because you couldn't get him to commit to much for you."

Rudd had also missed just one home match during the final four seasons of his City career and added: "I think I got a knock the one game I missed, because I don't think I was ever dropped." He did, however, return to the ground several decades later and recalled with a smile a backhanded compliment, delivered in typical Bootham Crescent fashion, by one seasoned City supporter. "I came back as a guest and an old chap in the Main Stand to the right of the directors' box was beckoning me, so I went over," Rudd explained. "He said: 'It's nice to see you, Billy, because you gave me a lot of enjoyment when you were here', which was really nice of him. So, he was building me up and I said: 'Thank you very much. I appreciate that', before he shot me down and said: 'But, of course, you couldn't hold a candle to your uncle'. That made me laugh." Billy's elder relative Jimmy Rudd had played for the club between 1947 and 1949. Following the departures of such key players, Provan had a sense of foreboding about the future, pointing out: "Billy Rudd, Alan Woods and Tommy Heron were all good footballers and very difficult to replace."

One notable moment at Bootham Crescent during that difficult season, though, saw John Pearson become the club's first-ever substitute in an official first-team game on August 27. He replaced Heron against a Grimsby team that included future City boss Charlie Wright in goal and 1990s' England manager Graham Taylor at left back. At the time, substitutions were only permitted because of injury, although Leeds United famously used to suffer a stricken player 70 minutes into every game, leading to a rule change after two seasons, which allowed tactical replacements. Unable to recall the reasons for his substitution, reported as being prompted by a thigh injury, Heron reckoned Lockie might have adopted a similar approach to that of his Elland Road counterpart Revie, as he was fit to start the club's next match. "I don't remember being injured," Heron said. "John Pearson was a winger who had come from Manchester United as well and, as we drew 1-1, I expect Tom wanted to go for it a bit at home. Nobody ever wants to come off but, if things aren't going right, you have to accept it. I don't think your number went up in those early days. They just shouted you off the pitch and I think you headed for the dressing room, because there was only room for about three or four people on the bench."

The next time Heron was replaced, there was no question about it being necessitated by injury, although the lengths the club were prepared to go to in order to keep him on the pitch were alarming. "I set off on a run and pulled up against Oldham and Albert Quixall, who I knew from playing together at Manchester United, started laughing," Heron recalled. "He said: 'Ooh Tommy, you've only gone and pulled a muscle'. It was just before half-time so, when I went in the dressing room, they got me on the bench and the doctor ran his finger over the area and I really felt that. Then, the next thing I knew, he got a needle and stuck it in my leg. I wasn't asked if I needed an injection and they wanted me back on but, at the start of the second half, I went to run and just stopped. I said: 'This isn't right', and Albert said: 'Get off Tommy, you could tear it'. To this day, I've still got a ridge where the needle was shoved in. Sid (Storey) was the trainer, but he wouldn't have done it, because he didn't have a clue about things like that. He was another who didn't get the respect he should have done from some of the players."

On the first Monday in May, meanwhile, Bootham Crescent hosted a schoolboy international between England and Germany. The gates opened at 6pm for a 7.15pm kick-off, with the Rowntree Works Band playing from 6.15pm. There was also a display of vaulting and agility exercises by the York Youth Organisations team. York's nine former schoolboy internationals, meanwhile, were guests at the game. Lyndon Hughes, who would go on to play for West Brom and Peterborough, scored the only goal of the game. The most notable player to feature in the match was future full England international Dave Thomas, who won eight senior caps and played on the wing for Everton, QPR and Burnley. Malcolm Webster (Arsenal), Steve Seargeant (Everton) and captain Geoff Merrick (Bristol City) would also go on to play top-flight football, although there were no notable names in the German side. The attendance was also a disappointing 7,127. During the same month, meanwhile, York League champions Nestle Rowntree were beaten by Middlesbrough reserves in the final of the North Riding Senior Cup at Bootham Crescent. In a Boro team boasting seven players with second division experience that season, Northern Ireland international Bobby Braithwaite was the star of the show in front of a crowd just shy of 2,000. He laid on chance after chance for the north-east professionals, although only two were taken by first-team fringe players Stan Marshall and Terry Garbett.

A period of struggle followed for City, meanwhile, as the club were forced to apply for re-election during three successive seasons under three different managers. In the first of those campaigns - 1966/67 - the preference for evening kicks offs continued with a total of 16 of the 23 home games scheduled to be played at night when the fixtures were released. Some weekend contests were played on a Friday night and others on a Saturday evening, as the club tried to gauge the most popular day of the week for later kick-offs. The gates, ultimately, proved very similar for both. City's annual pre-season practice match was also staged at 7.15pm on a Friday, although it reverted back to a Reds v Blues contest. Eight days later, the league campaign kicked off with a Saturday night 7.15pm clash against Chesterfield at Bootham Crescent.

With gates meaning reserve-team football at North Regional League level was needing to be heavily subsidised, the club also took the decision to join the Yorkshire League, where they were placed in the second division, leading to some very one-sided games for the host team at Bootham Crescent, where the visitors included the likes of Brodsworth, Swallownest and Heeley Amateurs. The Yorkshire League Cup provided a little stiffer opposition with a 15-year-old Chris Topping making his reserve debut at Bootham Crescent in a 5-1 November defeat against Bradford City's second string. Unsurprisingly, he was reported as having "defended strongly". Topping - the grandson of Jack Topping who was a City Supporters' Club stalwart in the club's formative years - also played in a reserve match that saw prolific 20-year-old Pickering Town striker Tony Dobson score all the goals in a 5-0 victory over Doncaster at Bootham Crescent. He immediately signed amateur forms with the Minstermen, while continuing to play in the York & District League for Pickering, who he netted 65 times for in 33 games that season. But he never went on to break through into City's first team, going on to play for Whitby instead. Groundsman Bryan Foster also filled in for the reserves at times during that season at Bootham Crescent. At the end of the campaign, another familiar face ran out at the ground with 1955 FA Cup semi-final hero Billy Hughes captaining and scoring for the Yorkshire Herald during a 2-1 defeat to Yorkshire Farmers in the final of the York Sunday League Challenge Trophy.

Some light relief during that first season back in division four was provided, meanwhile, by the precocious Provan who scored one of the most memorable goals ever seen at Bootham Crescent in a bottom-of-the-table contest with fellow strugglers Bradford Park Avenue. Netting the final City goal during a 3-1 win, he dribbled around the visiting keeper before dropping on all fours, laying on the ground at full stretch and heading the ball into an unguarded net in front of delighted home supporters, with Wilf Meek, of the *Yorkshire Evening Press*, reporting that there was a "few moments lull before the crowd realised it was a goal". Reliving that much-cherished moment and revealing the inspiration behind it, as well as Lockie's grumpy reaction afterwards, Provan said: "I got the ball about three yards from the halfway line and beat their two centre halves and a full back. I then went around the keeper and stopped the ball on the line before getting down on my knees and heading it in. But, when I came in after the game, I got thumped around my head and was given a thick ear by Tom Lockie, although that wasn't too rare, as I had a few off him. Everyone had been saying it was a fantastic thing to do and that they wished they had thought of it. They were all chuffed, but the next thing I felt was a big clunk and Tom said: 'What did you do that for? The ball could have burst before you put it over the line!' At the time I did it, it was spontaneous, but I had read somewhere about a Hungarian called Nandor Hidegkuti who had done it once and thought to myself that would be great to do, so I used to do it in training a fair bit during five-a-side games. I enjoyed taking the Mickey out of people and loved nutmegging players. That was my favourite. In that game, their goalkeeper Pat Liney was on the edge of his 18-yard box after he'd come rushing out and there was nobody near me, so I thought why just blast it in. It was in front of the York fans as well, which meant I enjoyed it even more. I thought Bradford might kick me after I'd done it, but it was the last couple of minutes and, to be fair, I think most of them came up to me afterwards and said: 'Well done.'"

The goal had come in a new all-white strip, with the club changing from red home colours for the first time in 31 years. It was a break from tradition that did not concern Provan, however, who was not as fussy about his appearance as new goalkeeper Mike Walker, who would later find fame as a top-flight manager at Norwich and Everton.

"I never really thought about the change in the kit's colour," he reasoned. "We just went out there and played. It wasn't about how we looked, unless you were Mike Walker, the goalkeeper. Mike was a big man and was immaculate. His wife even had to iron his gloves and he brought his own kit in - all nicely pressed. We used to think: 'Is he going out on to a football pitch or a modelling catwalk?'"

For the visit of Morecambe in the FA Cup first round, meanwhile, a van load of shrimps and rock from the Lancashire coastal town was sent over from the Pennines to give away to supporters as they arrived at Bootham Crescent. Presentation cartons of Morecambe shrimps were also made from the visitors to the City directors, while a monster bar of rock was presented at the toss-up before the game. In return, the Lancashire club left with a 0-0 draw, meaning a replay, which led to a third match that eventually saw City progress 1-0 at Maine Road. City's 1966/67 season failed to capture the imagination, however, of the locals - a fact that was illustrated most starkly by 2,142 turning up at Bootham Crescent to witness a Yorkshire v Durham schoolboys' match six days after only 1,855 had watched City play host to Brentford.

During the close season, meanwhile, the Social Club was used as an examination room for student referees by the York FA, while the Reds v Blues practice match was finally discarded for good with Rotherham visiting instead for a friendly before the start of the new campaign.

Promising junior players were also invited to training and trials at the club by Lockie, with recruitment particularly in mind for the club's Sunday League team Bootham United, which was run by player-manager Ron Spence. A new box for the hospital radio commentaries, meanwhile, was provided by City director Chris Hull ahead of the new campaign. Pools considerations also dictated that City's preference at the time for night games would lead to them playing more home matches on Saturday evenings - with 13 scheduled into the fixtures list in total - rather than Fridays so as not to forfeit the £100 they received for being on the betting coupon. The tea bar, adjacent to the St Olave's Road End of the ground, was now used as a "swap shop," meanwhile, on match days for fans to exchange their programmes, badges and other football paraphernalia, with the sale of scarves and hats in club colours soon following.

A takeover, led by former Football League referee Peter Rhodes, meanwhile, was rejected. Bert Tait - the father of ex-City players Peter and Barrie - was part of a four-strong group of businessmen, headed by Rhodes, who advocated that Bootham Crescent should add money-generating facilities to its site to attract revenue outside of match days. Ideas that were raised included a golf driving range and a dance hall. Tension grew, meanwhile, at Bootham Crescent in opposition to the existing board and, with the team still waiting for their first win of the season following nine games and a 1-0 home defeat to Newport at the end of September, a 100-strong group of young fans started a series of chants in the Popular Stand before marching around the ground and positioning themselves in front of the Main Stand, chanting "Resign, Resign" in full view of the directors. Rhodes' name was also chanted in support of his takeover bid and a group of 200 fans continued their demonstration in the car park afterwards, before being dispersed by the police. They were unprecedented scenes of discontent and club stalwart Lockie became the first City manager to be relieved of his duties in October with the club bottom of the Football League and the only side in all four divisions not to have won a single game from their opening 12 fixtures. The final nail in Lockie's coffin came when former fans' favourite Aimson returned to Bootham Crescent to score the only goal of the game for Bradford City, prompting another car-park protest with calls for the board to resign. Future City defender Barry Swallow also played in that match for the opposition.

Jackson had nothing but respect for the departing boss, though, saying: "Tom was wonderful as a trainer and physio. He was brilliant with treatments and the training side of things. He would have had a job for life if he'd stayed as trainer, but he was quite positive as a manager as well and experienced a bit of success with the club, especially in 1955 and other cup ties. A lot of the success of that semi-final team was down to him. He was down-to-earth and told you what he thought. He was honest and that's all you want really." Provan also had a fondness for his compatriot, adding: "Tom Lockie's departure was a shock because he had done really well when we went up but, all of a sudden, he was on his way. He had taken me to the club and sold it to me, so I really liked him. He was like an old uncle really that you could go and chat to. He was a really nice fellow, even though he didn't have a sense of humour. He hated it, for example, if we wanted to relax before a match and make the atmosphere a bit lighter, rather than sitting there quiet. You would come out with a line or a little joke and he would say: 'Enough of that. Concentrate on the game.'"

Just weeks earlier, future first division top scorer, Manchester United striker and Scotland international Ted MacDougall had been lured to Bootham Crescent from Liverpool reserves by the most unlikeliest of inducements - a salad sandwich, although he did also pocket a pay rise from his Anfield salary! MacDougall recalled: "Nobody had agents back then. When I came from Liverpool as a young lad to talk to York, I brought my mam and Grandma with me and George Teasdale - the club secretary - took us all to some hotel and bought us egg and lettuce sandwiches. My mam and grandma thought that was fantastic, so they told me I better sign for York because they seemed like nice people. I was on £18-a-week under Bill Shankly at Liverpool and York gave me £21-a-week and an extra £3-a-week during the season. I also used to work at the racecourse in the summer to top up my wage. I should have probably gone to a better side from Liverpool's reserves, with no disrespect to York, but I was so naive and, because they gave us a bit of lettuce and an egg, I thought I'll sign for you. I must have learned a little bit, though, because I managed to get a pair of curtains thrown in for my next move to Bournemouth!" Provan also believed that MacDougall might have added a couple of extra international mementoes to his personal collection during his time at Bootham Crescent. "As soon as

York City's new manager Joe Shaw meets the players in the home dressing room in November 1967

Ted MacDougall turned up, he looked like a footballer," the fellow Scotsman said. "I don't know how a footballer is meant to look, but I felt straight away that he could play. He was full of confidence, but we never had any big heads at the club. Ted was very confident coming in from Liverpool, but he was a smashing lad and there were no airs and graces with him or anybody. After I left, though, he took the club bungalow I had had and, three years later, I asked my wife: 'Where are those international jerseys I had for playing for Scotland youths?' because I couldn't find them anywhere. She said she had left them up in the attic of the bungalow, so I phoned Ted up and told him there should be a plastic bag in the attic with two Scotland tops in it. He said he'd not seen them. I said they have got to be up there, but he insisted he hadn't seen them. I think he ended up with two more for his collection, although I'm still looking to claim them back from him, because they will have my number 11 on them."

MacDougall earned his move to the south coast after plundering 15 and 25 goals respectively in the 1967/68 and 68/69 campaigns, but the club finished fourth-bottom in both seasons and the emerging striker said: "It was hard. We applied for re-election both seasons I was there but I kind of established myself because I got 40 goals. We only had 10 or 11 players at the start of the second season because a lot had been let go and some weren't really pros. They got paid but their attitudes weren't the best. It wasn't really a good place to be for a young player trying to get on in the game. The club was a big part of my life growing up and I had good times, but not really for football reasons."

Lockie's successor - former Sheffield United defender Joe Shaw - improved results on the field. Off the pitch, meanwhile, Shaw's players Ken Turner, Phil Burrows, Barry Jackson and Harry Fallon teamed up with club secretary Teasdale to defeat a Supporters' Club team in a quiz on general knowledge and the laws of the game, held in the Social Club. Having enjoyed working under Lockie and his successor Shaw, MacDougall struggled to see eye to eye with Tom Johnston, though, following his appointment in October 1968. "Tom Lockie was a lovely man - a really nice person but I don't really remember him with regards to football, so it was really refreshing when Joe Shaw came in," MacDougall admitted. "He had just finished playing for Sheffield United at centre-half and had got close to playing for England even though he was only 5ft 8in. Joe was also a lovely guy and his assistant Billy Hodgson, who had been a really good player, was nice too. But Tom Johnston was a strange character to say the least. He had been at Huddersfield and came in sucking on his pipe and taking the Mickey out of everybody all the time. He was hard work and I would not have seen him going on to get the club promoted to the second division."

Provan had gone by the time Johnston's reign was taking shape, but he also recalled enjoying working under Shaw, even if his expectations of the squad might have been a little too high. "I got on well with Joe Shaw," he said. "I was 5ft 6in and we were about the same size, which had made him the smallest centre half in England. He liked me and used to say: 'I'm going to play you here, so you can do this and that and I want you to do these things for me'. But, because of where he had come from, he tried to turn us into first division players by doing different things in training. He wanted a wee bit more from us and we were probably not quite the standard he wanted. We were third and fourth division players and that was it during my time with the club, aside from people like Paul Aimson and Mike Walker, who were a class above." Unlike MacDougall, Jackson had no problems with Johnston's management style, meanwhile, saying: "Tom Johnston came to us with a reputation for upsetting dressing rooms, but he wasn't like that really."

Shining a light on end-of-season contract negotiations at Bootham Crescent in the late 1960s, meanwhile, MacDougall added: "You would knock on the manager's door and there were no discussion really. They would always call you son - I think it was because they couldn't remember your name. They would then just say: 'You've done well, we're going to keep you on' and tell you what you'd be paid in the summer and during the season." MacDougall also recalled with a smile the less scientific approach to injury management employed by a member of the famous 1955 FA Cup semi-final team. "Ronnie Spence was the trainer and they did everything in those days," he explained. "He washed the kits and did the massages. What I remember most about Ronnie, though, is whether you had a bruise, knock or twist, he would put Vicks (VapoRub) on it. He never thought about getting a big tub of it though and I always wondered why. He just had ones like your mam put on your chest when you were a baby. Anyway, one day I asked him: 'What does that do for you, Ronnie?' He said: 'I don't know, but you'll never get a cold!' If you got injuries back then, you also just used to put a dirty towel around your knee and put a cup of hot water and then a cup of cold water on it and do that for about an hour. It was ridiculous really."

Despite the club's travails on the pitch, there were some portents for a better future during MacDougall's two-year spell with defender Topping - the first-ever apprentice professional at Bootham Crescent - breaking into the first team at the age of 17 during the first game after Christmas 1968 - a 0-0 home draw with Newport. Topping would go on to become a club stalwart, giving the club ten years of outstanding service at centre back with only Jackson and Andy McMillan having played more times for the Minstermen. He would also be a key figure in the promotion campaigns of 1970/71 and 1973/74. During his apprenticeship, though, he managed to avoid the kind of chores at Bootham Crescent that were expected from the thousands of young hopefuls who followed him. "My dad knew George Teasdale - the secretary - back then and Ron Spence, who was the trainer and very fit for a 40-year-old," Topping explained. "They wanted to start a junior team and initially we played in the York & District League. We played on all the pitches around York before the club entered the Northern Intermediate League. They didn't expect much of me, though, as the first apprentice. I was also very career oriented and my dad spoke to George Teasdale and the manager and explained I was into botany and wanted to be a landscape gardener, so I did the training in the morning, then I was allowed to go to what became Wyevale Garden Centre in Poppleton because I wanted something to fall back on after football and my dad felt the same. I didn't have to clean any boots. I just did my own like everybody else did, so I was lucky in that respect. I also passed my driving test at 17 so I could drive to the ground and then to Poppleton."

Then *Yorkshire Evening Press* reporter Malcolm Huntington also remembered where it all began, rather modestly, for Bubwith-born Topping. "I first saw Chris Topping play for York City's third team on Boroughbridge Road at the Civil Service ground," he revealed. "I remember the game because Bryan Foster, the groundsman, was playing too. He was the club's first-ever apprentice and served the club superbly well. He was very consistent and never had a bad game even if he wasn't brilliant in every match. He was a manager's dream." MacDougall agreed, saying: "Chris came through at a young age and had a good build on him. He was a bit different and a nice lad who had a good career with York. I remember Andy Provan being a good lad too. He was a tricky Scottish left-winger."

Topping also recalled that his willingness to risk his body in the line of duty was questioned by a startled MacDougall. "I remember the ball bouncing in the penalty box in one game and I went for a diving header," Topping said. "It was only a yard or so off the ground and I wanted to put it in the net but couldn't reach it. Afterwards, Ted said to me: 'Why on earth would you risk your head like that?' I said: 'Because it was the chance for me to score a goal as a centre half, so why not?'" Topping's appreciation of botany, meanwhile, also saw him escape the ire of charismatic and fiercely-protective groundsman Foster. "We used to run around the pitch during training, but you wouldn't dare run on it, because you got Bryan Foster's fork thrown at you," Topping explained. "Some did it on purpose to get a reaction, but I didn't get that treatment because I was an agricultural man and I knew what he thought about his grass. It was his week's work to get it pristine and it normally would be. His pitch was his holy grail and he didn't want anybody to go on it. One day, I remember Tommy Ross went on one corner and was messing around. Bryan warned him: 'Get off my pitch', but he stayed on and the fork then came through the air. It missed Tommy thank goodness, but Bryan just said: 'If you go on it again, you'll get the same treatment'. It was funny but could have been nasty."

MacDougall went on to reveal that there was a competitive Anglo-Scottish rivalry at Bootham Crescent, perhaps stoked by Coldstream-born Johnston, that might go some way to explaining the team's indifferent displays on a Saturday afternoon. "Our hardest games were on a Friday morning," MacDougall pointed out. "Behind the (St Olave's Road End) goal, there used to be a piece of Tarmac next to the turnstiles and that's where we played five-a-side. It was Scotland v England and everyone used to knock six bells out of each other. People used to smash you into the turnstiles. Tommy Spencer,

Andy Provan, Tommy Ross and myself would be up against people like Gerry Baker and big Barry (Jackson) for England. Gerry was a good right back and what a character Barry was. I loved him. He had the sweet shop on the corner and a big car so we all thought he was loaded. Nobody else had a car so we didn't really need a car park at Bootham Crescent. I remember Roly Horrey used to come to games on his bike and would take his clips off and park it before matches. Luckily, I lived at Mrs Pink's house in Bootham Crescent, so I was just down the road. I think it was £5-a-week for bed-and-breakfast digs. Tommy Ross was my best man when I got married but only because he had a van. I wouldn't have got to the wedding otherwise."

Despite his tender years, Topping also relished those keenly-contested patriotic clashes, adding: "We don't really like Scotland down here, do we? I used to enjoy those games and they would be brutal. There were no slide tackles obviously, but they were what practice games should be. You got stuck in and passed the ball before you got tackled. You'd put some good tackles in but not silly ones that would hurt people." Provan claimed that it was those who hailed from north of the border that came out on top in the contests, where he would torment a fuming Jackson at every opportunity. "It was like gladiators around there and Scotland always won the matches," Provan grinned. "We had people like myself, Ted MacDougall, Tommy Spencer and Tommy Heron and Barry Jackson couldn't get near enough to me to give me a kick. He was also frightened to come near me, because I used to nutmeg him by putting the ball between his big, wide legs. I would thread it between them and then run off laughing. That's what made me so fast - running away from Barry."

During MacDougall's second season at Bootham Crescent, meanwhile, a partnership was born that would go on to become one of the most famous of its generation in British football. With Bill Shankly having allowed MacDougall to leave Liverpool, Brian Clough sanctioned Phil Boyer's move from Derby County to North Yorkshire. Both forwards would go on to become first division top scorers in the future and represent their respective countries Scotland and England at full international level. They were always at their best operating at the top end of the pitch together, however, whether that was for York or when they were later reunited at Bournemouth, Norwich and Southampton. In 1968/69, Boyer struck nine times as MacDougall plundered 25 goals with the latter saying: "Phil came into my life from Derby when Brian Clough sold him to York for £3,000. I used to call him Charlie and he played as a right-winger at York first before we changed to 4-4-2 and then he played up front with me. I'd also started as a right-winger at York because Tommy Spencer was up front when I arrived. Anyway, me and Phil became room-mates and, although we were never close friends, we loved each other. The partnership was perfect for me because he did all the running and work and I took all the glory. We were like the odd couple. I would dominate him and, in the end, our understanding was telepathic really. You don't get two people working that closely together in football now."

Offering an insight into the pair's different personalities, MacDougall, who emigrated to Florida in later life, cited their contrasting attitudes towards travelling. Whereas MacDougall's career was interspersed with summer spells in South Africa, USA and Australia, Boyer's was largely confined to these shores and the former said: "When we were room-mates later in our career, Phil said that he would love to travel around the world and play like I did. I said: 'Why don't you?' He said: 'I can't'. I asked why and he said: 'Because I've got a budgie'. I couldn't believe what I was hearing, and I said 'So?' He then said that his wife wouldn't leave the budgie behind. Then, a few months later, he told me the budgie had died so I said: 'Right, you can come and play overseas then', but he said: 'No I can't. She's bought another budgie!' He might have a whole flock now. I don't know. The last I heard he was living in Nottingham and we've not seen each other for years but I had great respect for him. He was a good player who could run all day."

Jackson was a big admirer of Boyer, but felt MacDougall flourished more after leaving Bootham Crescent. "Phil Boyer could run for ever," the City stalwart enthused. "I rated him highly. With Ted, even though he was our leading scorer for two seasons, I never felt he really settled and I didn't think we got the best out of him. He did better after he left us. At the time, though, I was thinking if somebody like him could score that amount of goals in an average-to-bad side, which was what we were then to be fair, he must have a lot of qualities because there weren't too many chances being created for him."

In February 1968, meanwhile, Bootham Crescent played host to its first major neutral match when Middlesbrough beat Hull City 1-0 in an FA Cup third-round second replay in front of 16,524. It was staged at one day's notice after Sheffield Wednesday's icy pitch was deemed unplayable and there was no time to print tickets, so supporters were admitted through the turnstiles on a first-come, first-served basis with the anticipated possibility that the ground's then capacity of 20,000 could be reached. Ground staff cleared snow off the terraces and around the lines on the pitch to get the game played. It also resulted in record gate receipts for Bootham Crescent at the time of £4,423, beating the previous best of £4,292, set when City had taken on Bolton in the FA Cup a decade earlier. Derrick Downing, who would later play for the Minstermen, scored the game's only goal. City's share of the gate was 10 per cent after match expenses had also been deducted. During the same month, a new monthly ticket scheme, instigated jointly by a Liaison Committee consisting of directors from the Supporters' Club, Auxiliary Club and Social Club, was launched as a new fundraising initiative with a top prize of £100. A number of young women were also chosen "to provide a little glamour" at the ground on matchdays to help with the scheme, dressed in "smart modern red-and-white outfits", as described by the *Yorkshire Evening Press'* Wilf Meek. They would be known as The Rosettes and would be sponsored by the Supporters' Club. Initially six young women were chosen and they were quickly followed by another half dozen.

In March, meanwhile, the unusual decision was made to increase matchday prices with immediate effect during the tail-end of the season. The prized centrally-located Main Stand tip-up seats would now cost 10 shillings instead of 7s 6d, while general ground admission went up from 4s to 5s. Programmes would also now cost 1s instead of 6d due to a rise in printing costs. All 96 lights in the floodlights were also re-lamped to improve their brightness. April went on to see Stanley Matthews' Port Vale team beaten 5-1 with MacDougall hitting a hat-trick during a blistering seven-minute spell. A gracious Matthews commented afterwards: "A very good show. You played some fine football." World Cup winner Alan Ball was also in the crowd to see his father Alan Ball Senior's Halifax Town side enjoy a 2-1 win at Bootham Crescent the same month.

That summer then saw the club shop - which had stood for many years as a refreshment hut on Platform 8 at York station - opened for business. The Supporters' Club acted quickly when they learned the hut was to be dismantled and, at the cost of 30 shillings plus transport, it was given a new life. Initially, it mainly sold programmes tucked just inside the turnstiles at the Bootham Crescent end but, in following months, it began to flourish with the club extending and varying the items available for sale from cuff links to foreign club badges. Albert Ruddock, the Supporters' Club's social secretary, was appointed club shop manager and was assisted by Douglas Scott and the pair often responded to customers' requests and tried to obtain goods that might not have been part of the available stock, with badges, programmes and pennants from nearly every club in England available. By 1972, the following items were described as the most popular purchases: lapel badges (15p), scarves (60p), bob caps (40p), ties (25p and 62.5p), cuff links (90p), tie clips (50p), photographs (10p), pennants (15p and 25p), key rings (12.5p and 25p), foreign badges (12.5p), World Cup badges (25p) and pens (6p). Goods could also be delivered by post for an extra charge. The hut soon fell into disrepair though and was abanadoned.

June 1968, meanwhile, saw new floodlight pylons erected that would remain in place until 1995. The following season also marked the end of Saturday reserve-team fixtures at Bootham Crescent, as a decision to scrap second-string games and withdraw from the Yorkshire League was made as a cost-cutting exercise. Instead, the club would now field a youth team in the Northern Intermediate League for players up to the age of 19 and they would play home fixtures at Bootham Crescent on Saturday afternoons at 3pm, although fixtures were subsequently switched to Civil Service's Boroughbridge Road ground from October onwards to protect the heavy pitch. Topping played in the first game - a 4-2 home triumph over Sheffield Wednesday at Bootham Crescent, which saw the youngsters receive a standing ovation from a "bigger-than-expected crowd", although the exact figure was never recorded. A gate of 484 was taken, though, for the junior team's next Bootham Crescent clash - a 4-0 win over Grimsby, resulting in receipts of £41 3s. The average attendance for reserve matches the previous season had been 185, equating to receipts of £8 1s 9d.

The club's preference for evening football was at its height, meanwhile, during the 1968/69 campaign with the club asking all of their division four visitors to agree to night-time kick-offs in midweek and at the weekend. Football League secretary Len Shipman was not impressed by the club's plan of action, stating: "The Football League has been built on a tradition of all matches starting at the same time and my committee do not feel it would be advantageous of the Football League if the clubs were to alter from the traditional Saturday afternoon just as a matter of course." But Rochdale's Bob Stokoe was the only manager to object. Explaining his decision to insist on a 3pm kick-off, Stokoe reasoned: "If we play York on a Saturday afternoon we can make do with light sandwiches on the way home. If we play at night we would have to provide dinner and I don't think any additional revenue we might get from a night match would compensate for this." A subsequent Football League ruling, announced in September, then stated that Saturday evening matches would only be permitted in "special circumstances", such as due to a clash with the Grand National or York Races. Saturday night games had previously been preferred to Friday evening kick-offs by the City board, so the club could still benefit from the £100 Football Pools money available for appearing on the coupon. City appealed against the decision to the Football League management committee, citing season-ticket holders, who might be shopkeepers or amateur footballers had made their commitment to the club in the good faith that games would be played at a time when they could attend. Their appeal was upheld for those reasons and, in a survey conducted by the *Yorkshire Evening Press*, 69 per cent voted in favour of Saturday night kick-offs, 22 per cent for Friday evening games and just seven per cent for Saturday afternoons. The crowd level for the start of bonus payments during the season was set at 5,000, with the amount going up for every 1,000 extra supporters through the turnstiles.

The old players' billiards room next to the secretary's office, meanwhile, was now changed into a treatment room and furnished with new electrical equipment, which was presented to physio Anthony Power by relatives of the late Mr RH Stanley. The previous treatment room, which had been attached to the home dressing room, was deemed too small. Part of the new room was still used, though, as a counting room for the club's development scheme. The programme and souvenir shop was also moved from its position next to the tea bar to a more convenient spot in the corner of the St Olave's Road End of the ground. One final facelift saw the badly-corroded, corrugated iron in the Shipton Street End replaced, while young members of the Supporters' Club helped repaint the railings and new white goal nets were bought to replace the black ones.

Pre-season schedules were beginning to change too with Shaw deciding on three friendlies against other clubs, as Huddersfield and Leeds both sent teams to Bootham Crescent, whilst a trip to Albion Rovers was also organised. Boyer and MacDougall played together for the first time in the Huddersfield match that featured former City striker Aimson, while the likes of David Harvey, Terry Yorath and Johnneson were in the Leeds side, as a modern era of attracting higher-profile friendly visitors to Bootham Crescent was ushered in.

A crowd of 5,643 watched the Leeds game, which also saw Don Revie in the away dugout. The practice of handing over the proceeds from pre-season games to charity had also now ceased.

The 1968/69 campaign, meanwhile, saw the hooligan movement that was spreading through English football begin to plague certain areas of the ground, particularly the Popular Stand. Describing the unsocial behaviour, one supporter at the time revealed: "They just race up and down, shouting obscenities, pushing people about and over and never watching the game. It's almost impossible to take your wife to a game now with such things going on." Club secretary Teasdale also fumed: "Most of the trouble has been caused by youngsters. If they misbehave they will be turfed out of the ground, banned if possible and also prosecuted. It is only the decent people we want watching football at Bootham Crescent. Let the yobbos stay away." After a late-October 2-0 defeat to Exeter, meanwhile, three young City supporters were escorted from the ground by police, having left their places in the Popular Stand and marched around to the paddock in front of the directors' box to chant: "Resign, resign" and "We want a manager," with more than two months having passed since Shaw's resignation. The fans were led out of the ground when obscenities were then directed at City's board with one member of the group reported to have been kicked out of matches at Bootham Crescent on four previous occasions. With rumours that members of the unsavoury element were planning a demonstration in front of the directors in which bottles, sticks and bricks were to be thrown, a new chairman Eric Magson was subsequently appointed to replace Derrick Blundy the following week, which led to ex-Grimsby and Huddersfield boss Johnston being brought in as manager.

A switch was made again to revert back to 3pm kick-offs on Saturday instead of the 7.15pm starts for the December, January and February fixtures at Bootham Crescent. With the club expected to be asked to revert to the traditional time by the authorities the following season and gates low, the decision was taken to secure the £100 pools money available for afternoon kick-offs with Saturday-night fixtures now not included on the coupons. Crowds were still higher, though, when kick-offs were switched back to night-time in March.

Johnston's first game in charge resulted in a shock 2-1 home victory over second-placed Aldershot thanks to two Ross goals. Some respite from the on-pitch gloom at Bootham Crescent was also provided in 1968/69 when the club reached the third round of the FA Cup for the first time in five seasons and bowed out 2-0 to first division Stoke after putting up a brave fight in front of 11,129 supporters - the biggest crowd for nearly three years. Topping had only made his debut against Newport the previous weekend in a 0-0 draw that was played on a snow-covered pitch. The visitors even started the first 30 seconds of that game with nine men as two of their players, who had travelled independently from the rest of the team from London, only arrived at York railway station at 2.50pm after their train suffered engine failure and they had to change into their kit in a taxi. The Stoke match, therefore, only represented Topping's second appearance for the Minstermen, as he profited from a suspension for Barry Jackson. "Barry got a ban for being sent off, but he wasn't any trouble off the pitch at all," Topping explained. "He had his sweet shop and was great with the children who came in, but his red card gave me my first chance just after Christmas in 1968. The game was played on a very icy pitch and the reports said I committed myself scarily against Newport - putting my head and foot in where it shouldn't have been. It was my chance to impress for the club my granddad had always supported, and I wanted to make people and my family happy. My second game was against Stoke, who beat us 2-0, but both games were wonderful experiences for a country boy who'd only ever played school football. You don't really believe it's going to happen until it does. I remember Chris Dale getting his chance before me and being disappointed but, all of a sudden, I was playing against Stoke and David Herd, who had played for Manchester United. Terry Conroy played for them and Gordon Banks was in goal, although the nearest I got to him was shaking his hand at the end, as we didn't get down his end very much. We gave as good as we got though, and York were a good cup team then. I was only 17 but it didn't really matter who we were playing, as long as I was playing for York. The chance to play for York and win games for the club where I had been a spectator was great. York City were the main thing for me. I wasn't bothered about myself. If the ball was there to be headed, I headed it. I was a York lad through and through and York were my favourite team."

Stoke also included former England international George Eastham and a goal in each half by winger Harry Burrows settled the tie - the first a swerving 25-yard effort and the second a fine first-time finish in the penalty box. City's best chance of a goal came as the side trailed 1-0, but Banks magnificently tipped over an Archie Taylor strike that seemed destined for the top corner - a save that was even applauded by the home players. MacDougall, meanwhile, recalled having a disagreement with the legendary Banks who was playing in between starring for his country in consecutive World Cup final tournaments. "I remember something happening in the 18-yard box and having a row and a tangle with Gordon Banks," the former Liverpool striker smiled. "I had him on the floor and was dragging him with his legs like a cart. He wasn't too happy and there was a bit of argy-bargy, but you didn't get booked for every little thing like you do today. We got beaten, but there was a good crowd there."

Three months later, it was MacDougall, not Banks, between the sticks at Bootham Crescent when he was needed as an emergency net-minder. It was an experience - during a 3-1 home win over Port Vale - that still brought him out in a cold sweat when talking about it five decades later. "Bob Widdowson got injured and carried off," he recalled. "Unbeknown to me, they had asked everyone in the team if they would go in goal. I felt pretty proud to be asked to go in, but I didn't realise everybody else had said: 'No way', so I went in with no gloves on and I was absolutely terrified. I felt like I'd lost all my positional sense and I didn't know where I was. I couldn't even kick the ball out of my own 18-yard box with a goal kick and I thought I could strike a ball as well as anybody. They also had a lad called Roy Chapman (the father of future Leeds and Arsenal striker Lee) who was one of your typical fourth-division centre forwards in that he battered everybody, and the worst part of the match was when he was going clear through and I had to dive at his feet. My mouth was dry all game and I was in a state of fear. I remember saying: 'I'm never doing that again in my life'. I thought it was awful."

Widdowson had dislocated his shoulder in the 54th minute as Chapman scored his 200th league goal but, despite MacDougall's account of his own performance, he kept a clean sheet and the *Yorkshire Evening Press* reported that he delivered a "competent display". City's normal deputy keepers at the time Gerry Baker and Phil Burrows were both out injured and the fiery game also set a then Football League record for players booked in one match with, by modern standards, a modest five men having their names taken. They were Billy Hodgson and Bill Richardson for the hosts, with Clint Boulton, John James and John King the Vale players reprimanded. That same month, former fans' favourite Provan received a rousing reception from the Bootham Crescent faithful on a bitter-sweet return to the ground following a switch to Chester early in the campaign. "The first time I went back was with Chester and I scored, although York beat us 4-2, which I was kind of half-pleased with," he reasoned. "Chester had made me captain for the night and they all pushed me out onto the pitch and the home crowd cheered me. I thought, 'Wait a minute' and looked around to see none of the boys had followed me and they had stopped by the gate before you went out onto the pitch and let me run out on my own, so I just waved to the fans. Then, I went on to score and they booed me - the little so-and-sos. But I had enjoyed my time at York. It was the first time I had played regularly anywhere, and I played all 46 games during that promotion season."

Malton-born Terry Dyson - the uncle of professional golfer Simon and a former Spurs player - also made his first appearance at Bootham Crescent that season, but it wasn't a happy experience as he missed a penalty during a 2-0 away defeat for Colchester.

A remarkable achievement went on to see six brothers play together in Newton-on-Ouse's 3-2 extra-time York FA Junior Cup final over Cross Keys at Bootham Crescent. The Thompson siblings, included Sid, the eldest at 32, as well as Ray, the youngest at 21, along with Tony, Gary, Alwyn and John. Ray got the winning goal after John had earlier opened the scoring. The season also saw the first matchday programme in 40 years - for the February 24 match against Wrexham - not to be compiled by vice-chairman Wilf Meek due to illness.

There was tragedy, meanwhile, at the final home game of the season - also MacDougall's last for the club - when referee Roy Harper collapsed and died of natural causes during a 0-0 draw with Halifax. "I remember the referee going down around the centre-circle area and one of the players taking the whistle out of his mouth to blow it for him to stop the game," MacDougall said. "I also remember the ambulance coming and him being rushed to hospital."

At just 18, the incident had a profound impact on Topping, who added: "It was a horrible day but, as it happened during the game, you just have to dismiss it from your mind. As far as we were concerned, he had gone off alive and we just thought he had passed out. When he keeled over, I can't remember anybody going up to him because he was the referee and we didn't know him. He was also in the best hands with the St John's Ambulance taking him away. One of the linesmen took over as referee and we never thought anything more about it but, dear me, what a shock it was after the game when we heard he had died. It was awful and frightening. I remember him being a chunky chap with a big body, but he wasn't carrying an excessive amount of weight. He was probably 5ft 10in and 15 stone."

Harper, 45, fell to the ground in the middle of the pitch after eight minutes of the game. Both trainers Spence and Halifax's Harry Hubbick immediately rushed to his help and were followed by ambulance staff and City director Dr McKenna. Whilst an ambulanceman massaged Mr Harper's heart, a stretcher was called for and he was carried from the pitch. He received more treatment under the stand and was given oxygen when an ambulance arrived within minutes, but he was found dead on arrival at York County Hospital. It was the sixth time Mr Harper had been due to referee the match, which had been postponed five times due to the pitch being icebound or waterlogged in addition to clashing with an FA Cup tie against Halifax. He worked for Sheffield steel firm Newton Chambers at the time and was married with an 18-year-old daughter. The game was held up for six minutes, before the senior linesman Bill Johnson took over on the pitch while spectator Eric Blott, a well-known local official, responded to a loudspeaker appeal and took over with the flag. The campaign was also the first that Malcolm Huntington reported on as the *Yorkshire Evening Press'* full-time York City writer. He took over from Meek, who had covered the club for 46 years since its formation in 1922. Huntington, himself, went on to cover more than 2,000 matches for the *Evening Press*, *Yorkshire Post* and *Sunday Sun* and admitted: "It was a tremendously enjoyable career that I wouldn't have swapped with anybody."

Mike Gadsby is wrapped up in a blanket during a 1-0 home defeat to Port Vale in 1969 as former FA Cup semi-final hero Ron Spence (pictured left) administers his sometimes rudimentary medical care as the team's trainer

York City's all-time record appearance holder Barry Jackson in the sweet shot that he opened on Bootham Crescent in July 1963. Fans would go in there to buy confectionary and cigarettes but, more often than not, would use it as an excuse to meet and have a chat with one of their heroes

189

York City's 1968-69 intermediate team board the coach for a pre-season game against Wallsend Corinthians. Future club legend Chris Topping is fourth from the right

CHAPTER 14

Paul Aimson's last-minute header stuns the Saints

"I've got a picture of Paul Aimson's header and he looks like some sort of a big bird the way he hangs in the air."

Following his appointment, new manager Tom Johnston didn't just limit his focus to on-field concerns at York City and, being keen to forge close links with schools, he arranged for tickets to be distributed to pupils for games at Bootham Crescent during the 1969/70 season. Johnston also decided on a kit change, opting for maroon shirts, white shorts and maroon socks - the same colours that the club had donned half-a-century previously. Explaining his choice at the time, Johnston pointed out: "So many clubs play in white, red or blue these days and I found we were having to play in several different strips to avoid a clash. Another reason is I am aiming, along with the staff at Bootham Crescent, to try and change the image of the club. This may go a little way towards this. Now our fans will be associated with the club. So many clubs have red-and-white striped scarves, for example, that you couldn't tell who the fans were supporting." The junior section of the Supporters' Club, which had been formed in 1967, went on to paint the inside and outside of the ground in the new colours.

It was confirmed, meanwhile, by the Football League that Friday and Saturday night games would only be permitted in "very special circumstances" going forward, heralding a return to 3pm football on a regular basis at Bootham Crescent. Johnston also reinstated reserve football with the club welcomed into the midweek North Midlands League. A golden goal competition was introduced at the ground too, with a £15 prize on offer for anybody that could predict the exact timing in minutes and seconds of when City scored at Bootham Crescent. It replaced the jackpot ticket scheme.

Johnston's signing of old favourite Paul Aimson early in the season, meanwhile, saw the Bootham Crescent attendance double for a 1-0 victory over Exeter during the second home game of the season, with 6,200 witnessing the second debut of the prolific marksman, following his return from Huddersfield. Such popularity did not lead to resentment or jealousy among the other players with Topping saying: "Paul was a normal Lancashire lad with no pretence. He was a big friend of (Barry) Swallow's and knew Barry Jackson. He just loved York, so we accepted him back with open arms. We knew we had somebody with a good record, so that was perfect - somebody who loved York and could score goals. Things can get dour and stale and, then, you need somebody like Paul to come in, so Tom paid money to bring him back." It was Mick Mahon, though, who scored the only goal of Aimson's homecoming to send City top of the table at the end of August.

A 3-0 home triumph over Swansea subsequently represented the club's best-ever start to a Football League season with nine points taken from a possible 10 and a new maroon-and-white flag, presented by the women's section of the Supporters' Club, flew proudly over the ground. September, meanwhile, saw the club compete for the first time in the FA Youth Cup, with Bradford City the visitors to Bootham Crescent. The hosts won 2-0 with Kilbride and Wash reported as being on target. An 18-year-old Kevin Keegan, prior to finding fame and fortune with Liverpool, England and Hamburg, also scored twice for Scunthorpe that same month at Bootham Crescent but ended up on the receiving end of a 3-2 defeat, with Kevin McMahon (two) and Mahon the marksman.

In October, a memorable occasion marked Gerry Baker's retirement due to arthritis in his knee, as a testimonial pitched the City team against the 1955 FA Cup semi-final side. A crowd of 3,537 watched a 4-4 draw, with Arthur Bottom the only absentee from the Happy Wanderers' heroes. Colin Addison stood in for Bottom and managed to grab himself a hat-trick, while half-time sub Alf Patrick - another guest player - was also on target. For the City XI, Phil Burrows, McMahon, Aimson and Bobby Sibbald netted, while keeper Tommy Forgan played as a centre forward in the second half for the 1955 legends.

The club were requested to put warning notices up at Bootham Crescent and in the matchday programme, meanwhile, after disciplinary action from the FA following a report that a conker had been thrown at Port Vale keeper Keith Ball and toilet roll hurled at the referee, who was also spat at, during the match between the two teams in October.

Loyal servant Jackson went on to win plaudits for putting the shackles on young Welsh star John Toshack in a 1-1 FA Cup draw at Bootham Crescent against second division high-fliers Cardiff, who were eventually seen off 3-1

Members of the 1955 FA Cup semi-final Happy Wanderers team return to Bootham Crescent for Gerry Baker's Testimonial in October 1969. Pictured (from left-to-right) are Alan Woods, Colin Addison, Norman Wilkinson, Billy Fenton, George Howe, Alf Patrick, Ron Spence, Billy Hughes, Gordon Brown, Alan Stewart and Erine Phillips

after extra-time in a third round, second replay at St Andrews. Typically modest about his handling of the 20-year-old forward, who would go on to become a Liverpool legend after moving to Anfield the following season, Jackson said: "John Toshack was a good player, but not as good as he would become later on. I also always had more trouble with the little forwards, due to my height, rather than the bigger ones."

That Cardiff game would surprisingly prove Jackson's penultimate Bootham Crescent outing with his final appearance coming in a 2-1 defeat to Notts County on January 31, 1970 - a fortnight after he had been sent off at Scunthorpe for an offence that was subsequently deemed worthy of a two-month suspension. His excessive punishment meant Jackson was even forbidden from playing in his own benefit match before being released at the end of the season. He never played professional football again and, after a brief spell with Scarborough, took up a job with the electricity board. As a virtual ever present for 12 years, Jackson played a record 539 times for the club - a tally that remains unchallenged in the history books. He believed he should have had more appearances to his name and would forever feel hurt by the manner in which his City career ended, but did not let it overshadow the good times he enjoyed at Bootham Crescent, saying: "Tom Johnston told me he was going to give me a rest for the Scunthorpe game, as we had come through three tough cup games against Cardiff, but I said I was alright. I ended up getting sent off for nothing because I didn't foul anybody. The game was getting a bit lively and out of hand and this chap - I don't know who he was - fell on the ball and kept it between his legs. I tried to scrape it out and didn't touch him but, the next minute, the referee was sending me off and I couldn't believe it. As I walked off, I was so annoyed, I kicked Scunthorpe's bucket and sponge and it went all over their trainer. He wasn't best pleased, and Kevin Keegan even mentions it in his autobiography because he was a substitute for Scunthorpe that day and thought it was funny, but the eight-week suspension finished me and was horrendous. I didn't deserve it and I was absolutely disgusted. I was 31 and needed to be playing. Tom Johnston fixed up a testimonial for me and Hull City came to Bootham Crescent, which was great. An average-sized crowd was there, but I couldn't play in the game because the FA wouldn't let me, which was diabolical. That upset me so much and, at the end of the season, that was it. The club decided to let me go and I was still only 32. That was hard, especially when you loved the game as I did. I took great joy just from playing for what I considered my home-town club. The ending was bad, but I loved every minute of it, even when things weren't going particularly well, because I was still representing York City and I loved the club. I wouldn't have wanted to play for anybody else and I was very comfortable there. I had longer than any other player has had, but still think I left the club too early."

Second division Hull brought their full first team for the testimonial, with a crowd of 3,120 perhaps lower than might have been the case had Jackson been given permission to play. Jackson, whose benefit earned him £750, gave a half-time speech instead and the match finished 3-2 to the home side with Ian Davidson netting twice, either side of a Mahon goal. The emerging Topping - Jackson's successor in defence - admitted the stalwart's departure was keenly felt at Bootham Crescent. "I took over from Barry, which was a shame, but I could never get too sentimental because it could be your turn next," Topping reasoned. "It did feel strange when he left, though, because he'd been at the club so long with his sweet shop just down the road. He was part of the furniture and fittings really."

Off the field, the York Football Coaching Association had begun to stage their meetings at Bootham Crescent. In April, meanwhile, another England Schoolboys international was staged at the ground between England and Ireland. The Railway Institute Silver Band played before the match kicked off and there was also a 20-minute police dog handling display, with both teams presented to the Lord Mayor of York (Ald R Scobey). England won 4-0 in front of a 5,000-strong crowd with future Arsenal and Sheffield Wednesday midfielder Brian Hornsby bagging a brace. David Price, Steve Powell and Billy Rodaway, who would go on to play for Arsenal, Derby and Burnley respectively, also featured.

Jackson's departure didn't represent the only change at Bootham Crescent, meanwhile, at the start of the 1970s. The *Happy Wanderer* song that had been played at home games since the 1955 FA Cup semi-final run was taken off the play list. Another tradition - the practice of lowering the stadium's flag with five minutes left to play - would also come to an end during the decade as well. A third tea bar had been built, meanwhile, under one of the pylons at the Shipton Street End and a new programme shop was erected. The "Penny on the Ball" scheme was superseded by the "Jackpot" ticket too, as the club looked to improve its revenue-making potential.

With neighbours Leeds United now established as one of English football's leading teams, the club also recognised the effect their proximity was having on gates at Bootham Crescent and asked the Football League to avoid arranging home games for both teams on the same dates. The request was rejected, with City's cause not helped by Huddersfield Town also approaching the League with the same complaint. As a solution, City attempted to switch five of their eight fixtures that clashed with Leeds to a Friday night and that was sanctioned, although a Football League ruling dictated at the time that only four matches from all the divisions could be played on that evening, with Tranmere, in the shadow of Merseyside giants Liverpool and Everton, requesting 20 such switches. A change in evening kick-off times, meanwhile, saw games switched from 7.15pm to 7.30pm, giving fans from the countryside areas more time to get to matches. Admission prices also increased by one shilling, following Football League guidelines. The general ground price on a matchday was now 6s, but children aged 16 and under were able to take advantage of a half-price season ticket offer, with the intention that sons or daughters would be able to sit next to their parent for the price of £4 5s on the tip-up seats or £3 15s on the bench-type seats. Previously, supporters paid the full price for seats in the Main Stand regardless of age. Companies were also invited to buy a season-ticket to be used by different people within the business if desired, as the club looked at ways to balance the books better.

The threat of hooliganism continued to linger, though, with ten Lincoln City-supporting youths, who were wearing boots and suspected of belonging to the infamous Clan group of fans, asked to remove their footwear before being allowed into the ground for an August fixture. The boots were looked after by club officials until the end of the game with a police spokesman adding: "Those concerned were told to come in shoes next time."

City's reserves also won the North Riding Cup by beating Billingham Synthonia in a replay at Bootham Crescent that had been held over from the previous season. Dick Hewitt scored both of the hosts' goals and the team celebrated by downing a bottle of champagne that had sat in the club office since being donated by an Arsenal fan when the team ended a long run of away games without a win during the 1960s.

On the field, the new decade had got off to a promising start at Bootham Crescent and the team would go on to enjoy an incredible club record 36-match unbeaten home run, stretching from January 31, 1970 to April 19, 1971 when Oldham won a vital promotion clash 1-0 in front of 14,321 fans - the biggest gate for five seasons. The form of the team saw the likes of future England and Barcelona boss Bobby Robson, then in charge of Ipswich, visit Bootham Crescent to run the rule over Phil Burrows and Phil Boyer. One of the matches in that run saw Topping and Aimson both grab goals in the last two minutes to secure a thrilling 4-3 victory over Barrow in October when the unbeaten run survived its biggest scare after 18 matches without defeat.

Manager Tom Johnston takes charge of the 1970-71 photo call

Sadly, the 1970/71 campaign also saw "Mr York City" Billy Sherrington - still then club president - perhaps predictably leave his last Bootham Crescent fixture during November in an ambulance, given he would never have missed a match through choice. The game in question was a 5-0 FA Cup replay win against Tamworth with Aimson hitting a hat-trick and, recalling how her family experienced every gamut of emotion at the old stadium, his daughter Terry Fowler said: "My father wasn't able to go to games latterly in his life. He had a heart attack watching a game when he was 80 at Bootham Crescent. He was sitting a few seats away from me on the back row of the directors' box and got up and went down the stairs. I didn't take much notice and thought he was just going down to the toilet. It happened about a quarter-of-an-hour before the end of the game. We all then trailed down and he was sitting on a chair looking dreadful. There were two doctors at the game - Angus MacLeod (the club doctor) and Miles Gibson (a neuro-surgeon from Leeds) who was a director at the time. They both went over to him and realised it was a heart attack, so got him an ambulance. We stayed all night at hospital and didn't think he was going to pull through, but he did and lived another six years, although he was never able to go to a match again and that match was his last game. My mother still went and used to tell him about the match when she got home. The games didn't have the same coverage as there was later when it became easier to follow things. Looking back, my father had other interests and liked all sports. He would watch cricket in the summer and played tennis. But York City was pretty much his life and he had a happy one. The club gave me a happy life as well."

On her father's choices for the best player he saw represent the club at Bootham Crescent, Fowler added: "He liked Sid Storey very much. He was very keen on what he called ball players and, earlier than Sid, he liked Peter Spooner, who was an outside-left. My father also used to say it was essential that you had a good keeper. He maintained you could get away with other people making mistakes but not your goalkeeper and I saw some good ones at Bootham Crescent over the years."

The threat of hooliganism continued to trouble the authorities, though, with the FA Cup third round visit of Nat Lofthouse's Bolton leading to police patrols to hunt down "bovver boys" with anybody wearing "bovver boots" or studded belts warned that they would be confiscated before entering the ground. Bottles and a knife were also taken off fans with one supporter watching the game minus his boots, but trouble still flared up inside the ground 25 minutes before kick-off when three Bolton supporters carried a large Union Jack flag to the centre of the pitch and were escorted off by a policeman. Several City fans then ran to the middle of the pitch, encouraging fellow supporters to cheer the team on. A Bolton fan subsequently emerged from behind the Bootham Crescent goal and knocked one of the home supporters over before attempting to run back into the crowd. Spectators would not let him get back over the railings though and he was held before two policemen grabbed him and led him out of the ground.

Ian Davidson's brace clinched a 2-0 victory over the second division visitors, setting up another classic Bootham Crescent FA Cup tie against first division Southampton, which many would go on to regard as the most exciting ever staged at the ground. Prices for the game were increased with Main Stand seats costing 15s instead of the standard league price of 10s. They were still all snapped up within the first hour of going on sale, although the game was not all-ticket behind both goals, with turnstiles open on the day.

City went into the game mid-table in the fourth division, while the Saints were seventh in the first, but honours would end even in a thrilling 3-3 draw. A goal-less first half saw City outclass their opponents, however, with Hewitt and Burrows both going close.

Paul Aimson's terrific last-minute header secures a 3-3 draw against first division Southampton in a thrilling 1971 FA Cup tie that many regard as the most exciting game that was staged at Bootham Crescent

Davidson also had a strong penalty appeal turned down when he appeared to be hauled down by John McGrath, but an indirect free kick was awarded in City's favour instead. After the break, Aimson called Eric Martin into action with a header but, against the run of play, Southampton went on to take the lead on 66 minutes when Mick Channon's left-wing cross was headed past Ron Hillyard by Jimmy Gabriel from five yards out. Hillyard went on to make a fine save from Ron Davies but was beaten again on 78 minutes when Channon ran clear to net after rounding the 18-year-old keeper despite home appeals for offside. Manager Johnston reacted by bringing Tommy Henderson on for Archie Taylor and he combined with Aimson to set up McMahon, whose header beat Martin with 10 minutes remaining. The visitors looked to have secured victory, though, when Davies headed in a deep Terry Paine right-wing cross on 84 minutes after outjumping Hillyard at the far post. Hewitt blasted a five-yard shot into the roof of the net, however, with three minutes remaining after collecting Aimson's downward header from a John Mackin cross. Bootham Crescent was then in raptures as a towering Aimson placed a magnificent downward header from six yards inside Martin's left-hand post following Mackin's right-wing cross in the last minute of normal time.

An attendance of 13,775 also resulted in record gate receipts at the time of £4,777 6s, with Saints boss Ted Bates enthusing at the final whistle: "What a wonderful game. I was very happy to get to the interval still level. We should not have let our lead slip. Full marks to York though - they played excellent football and deserved their draw."

Topping suggested that the game was a true classic, reasoning that Aimson's header wouldn't have been saved by the world's greatest goalkeeper and could have graced any Cup tie. "My wife still talks about the Southampton Cup game," Topping revealed. "Sometimes, you go behind in a match and nothing has gone for you. It's almost like you've tried too hard but then, if you relax, things come your way and I think that happened during that game. We thought Mick Channon was offside when they made it 2-0 although we obviously never saw a replay, so you just had to accept it even if we grumbled at the time. We then did well to get the game back to 2-1 but they scored again and, with six minutes to go against a first division team, you've got to think that's it. A lot of people actually left after that goal, but they must have heard the first roar and maybe the second roar when they got out of the ground and some would have wanted to go back in. The roar at the end was also wonderful - one of those moments you remember for the rest of your life. I remember Dick Hewitt firing into the top of the net to make it 3-2. Then, there was that Paul Aimson header. I've got a picture of it and he looks like some sort of a big bird the way he hangs in the air. He scored from the edge of the six-yard box and, if you were putting on a coaching session for headers, it would be a wonderful example of how to do it properly. The goal came from a cross in from the right after we had knocked the ball around a bit. It was played in from about five yards inside the touchline, just outside the penalty box. Paul got up so well and the keeper had no chance. It was as good a header as I'd ever seen. He got up so high and his neck muscles were so taut. It reminded me of when Pele jumped in the air for the header that Gordon Banks saved during the 1970 World Cup. Pele headed that one down, but Paul got above the ball and headed it under the bar and in the corner. For me, his was unstoppable. Banks would not have saved Paul's header and that's a wonderful memory. A lot of people had gone home then, and I bet they regretted that. Why would you do that in a cup tie? It was ridiculous." City bowed out 3-2 after another titanic contest at The Dell in the replay, with the hosts securing a fifth-round trip to Liverpool.

The end of an eight-year era, meanwhile, was signalled by Barry Jackson's decision not to renew the lease on The Candy Shop that he had run on Bootham Crescent, where fans would habitually stop off for cigarettes and sweets. Reflecting a changing world, February's home match with Brentford was then the first in which fans were subject to decimalisation at the turnstiles. The charges for general ground admission were 15p for "boys" and 30p for adults, while in the Popular Stand it was 35p, the wing of the Main Stand 40p and the centre of the Main Stand 50p. With beauty pageants at the height of their popularity, as the Miss World contest attracted huge television audiences, Miss York City competitions were also now being staged in the Social Club with Carol Oliver, of Burnholme Avenue, seeing off the challenge of 13 other entrants over the age of 16 to earn the title for the 1971/72 season.

The record-breaking unbeaten spell of 36 league and cup games at home, meanwhile, ended with that 1-0 defeat to promotion rivals Oldham in the season's penultimate fixture at Bootham Crescent, although Topping felt there was a sense of inevitability that the Lancashire outfit would end the terrific run. Remembering City's dominance at Bootham Crescent during that time, Topping said: "A bit of it was down to luck but we were quite a good unit who didn't give goals away and there were a lot of 1-0 victories and draws. I remember a lot of the games I played against Oldham because we seemed to go up and down with them, Bristol Rovers and Bournemouth at that time and you always felt one of those teams might end that run. Later on, they had a lad called Alan Groves. He was a winger who was all left foot, but he was very good. He caused us lots of problems and they were always a decent team like us."

The referee Ray Tinker was stood down from officiating that Oldham game, amid fears that there might be reprisals from Leeds fans at the match who, two days earlier, had seen their team's first division title hopes dashed by a famously controversial Jeff Astle goal for West Brom. World Cup referee Jack Taylor, who had never previously officiated at Bootham Crescent, took charge of the fixture instead. Johnston made his first change in 12 matches for the contest with Albert Johanneson recalled at outside-left for Henderson. With only 2,821 having turned up for a 3-0 home win over Cambridge on March 1, a crowd of 14,321 against Oldham also demonstrated the appetite in the city for watching a successful team. That Cambridge victory had been the second in a winning run of 10 triumphs in 11 games that had seen attendances gradually climb prior to the Monday-night showdown against the Lancashire visitors. Left-back Maurice Whittle got the only goal of the game two minutes into the second half, with his first-time attempt from the edge of the box taking a deflection off Taylor to beat Hillyard. Aimson did have a header cleared off the line a minute after Oldham had opened the scoring and Hewitt glanced a header inches wide at the death, as City attempted to extend their incredible unbeaten record and keep their promotion challenge on track. Oldham, though, finished worthy winners by general consensus.

City's final home match, meanwhile, saw Aimson and on-loan Southend midfielder David Chambers secure a 2-0 win over Scunthorpe, whose 20-year-old forward Kevin Keegan had a penalty gloriously saved after Hillyard flung himself low to his right. Keegan transferred to Liverpool shortly afterwards before going on to win first division titles and the European Cup, as well as captaining England. The victory put the Minstermen three points ahead of nearest rivals Chester in the fourth and final promotion place and despite losing their final two games - both away from Bootham Crescent - City still went up. Lincoln's 2-0 Wednesday night triumph over Chester in the latter's penultimate match meant City could stage a promotion party at Bootham Crescent the following day ahead of their final fixture - a 4-0 loss at division runners-up Bournemouth that weekend. Johnston, chairman Eric Magson and skipper Barry Swallow all gave speeches at the party, where the champagne flowed following a morning training session.

In the summer before Bootham Crescent hosted third division football again, meanwhile, tip-up seats were installed throughout the Main Stand, in place of the remaining bench-style areas, with the work funded completely by the Social Club. Their introduction also meant one season-ticket price of £10 for the coming campaign, although the pensioners' price remained frozen at £4. That payment also still included free admission to reserve and youth-team fixtures staged at the ground. The "boys" season-ticket - sexism still dictated that the term juniors wasn't used - cost £5 with matchday prices 30p for general adult ground admission and 15p for pensioners and boys. In the sheltered Enclosure and Popular Stand areas, where there was no concession for pensioners, the cost was 40p and in the Main Stand 50p. Six mercury bulbs were also added to each of the floodlights, resulting in 120 instead of 96 to improve the lamps' quality and eliminate the dark patches seen on some areas of the pitch. One final ground improvement that summer saw a York City Football Club sign erected on the gates at the entrance to the car park. The fixture list for the new campaign, meanwhile, only included one that clashed with Leeds United.

Scottish club Hibernian were also pre-season visitors to Bootham Crescent as part of York's 1,900th anniversary celebrations. That match, which saw the City of Leeds Pipe Band entertain the fans, caused controversy, though, as the Scottish team demanded an £800 appearance fee, meaning a crowd of between 4,000 to 5,000 was needed for City not to make a loss through the turnstiles. McMahon scored both goals in a 2-1 home win and an attendance of 4,483 turned up.

A highlight of the 1971/72 season came in September when former World Cup winner Nobby Stiles visited Bootham Crescent after City were drawn against Middlesbrough in the League Cup. Stiles could not prevent the second division side going behind to McMahon and Henderson goals but a controversial late goal, that saw loud home protests for handball, was allowed to stand and the teams drew 2-2 in front of 10,700 supporters, before City progressed after a 2-1 triumph at Ayresome Park. They bowed out in the next round at then first division leaders Sheffield United.

In October, Aimson went on to score the fastest-ever goal at Bootham Crescent, as he rounded Torquay goalkeeper Andy Donnelly following a poor back pass by Brian Hill to net just 9.5 seconds into a 3-1 triumph over the Devon team. There was more crowd trouble during a 1-1 November draw with Barnsley, though, when a 100-strong group of away fans vaulted the white fence and ran across the pitch into the Popular Stand. During the same month, Danish first division runners-up Hvidovre, who boasted three internationals - Leif Serensen, Paul Henrik Frederiksen and Heinz Hildebrandt - in their team, became the first overseas side, outside of Ireland, to play City at Bootham Crescent. Hvidovre, whose match fee of £700 was not quite covered by a modest crowd of 2,961 at the Tuesday night contest, also played Bolton on a two-match UK tour. City won the game 2-0 thanks to Eddie Rowles and Henderson goals, with only a string of fine saves by Hildebrandt preventing the hosts from enjoying a bigger victory. York-based Football League referee Vincent James took charge of the game.

Portraits of City players, such as Aimson and Swallow, drawn by former wing-half George Patterson, were also sold at the club shop for 5p before Christmas when, at the club's annual general meeting, chairman Magson admitted: "There was a time when Bootham Crescent was considered to be one of the best grounds in the third or fourth divisions, but I don't think that is true any longer as other clubs have spent large amounts of money improving their grounds. We must do the same in coming years. We have really got to get down to the business of looking after our customers." Improvements under consideration at the time were covering the Bootham Crescent end of the ground and providing seats in the Popular Stand with standing room underneath, possibly by building stilts. The top 13 rows of the terracing at the Bootham Crescent End were also dug up and replaced in January due to subsidence.

Shopkeepers Marjorie Hamilton and Frank Crawford wave their petitions against York City's plan to stage a Sunday market in the car park at Bootham Crescent

Trouble, meanwhile, raised its ugly head again on New Year's Day when eight youths were arrested after fighting on the terraces broke out between rival groups of skinheads during the 0-0 home draw with Bolton. In January 1972, the club then upset local residents with plans to hold a 100-stall Sunday market in the car park, with nearby shopkeepers also launching a petition. One - Marjorie Hamilton - complained: "There will be all the noise and dirt of them putting up stalls. From a traffic point of view there will be danger and the area will be subject to litter and vermin. I think it is disgusting." Newsagent Frank Crawford, meanwhile, added: "My main objection is the value of property. It is bound to depreciate with this added nuisance." But club secretary Teasdale responded: "We had a proposition put to us by Grayshem group of companies. We have given them authority to go ahead and they are now negotiating with York Corporation. I have no sympathy with the residents. I can see their point of view, but we are in business to do the best for York City. This is my job. If the market were allowed it would be quite lucrative for us and help us quite a lot to ease our financial burden. I personally would like to see it take place." The proposal was to make rental of the car park negotiable on an annual basis. On the possible cost of the contract, Teasdale added: "I am not prepared to say. But obviously if it had only been worth a few hundred pounds, we would not have bothered." The venture never materialised though.

City's Monday night February home match with Blackburn, meanwhile, was postponed due to the power cuts affecting the country as a result of the miners' strike. Electricity was being switched off for up to nine hours a day, which meant floodlighting the fixture would have been a problem. Miners had been picketing power stations and all other sources of fuel supply in an attempt to step up pressure on the Government during their pay dispute. The strike also saw several reserve matches postponed.

The 1971/72 season went on to see 17-year-old winger Brian Pollard, already an England youth international by that stage, given his first chance in the senior game during a 2-0 derby-day home win over Rotherham. He received a standing ovation from the home crowd when he was substituted in an important Good Friday clash as the team battled against relegation. Recalling the experience, Pollard said: "I'd never tasted anything like it before. It was a big crowd and there were telegrams waiting for me at the ground from family and friends wishing me good luck. I remember Paul Aimson being very kind to me that day. Back then, he would shout at me to get going before he had even flicked a header on."

Goalkeeper Graeme Crawford played his first games for City that campaign too, following a move from Sheffield United and quickly impressed the youthful Pollard. On the Scottish net-minder's impact at Bootham Crescent, Pollard said: "When we already had a keeper like Ron Hillyard, I remembered wondering why we needed to get somebody else in, but then we saw how good Graeme was and he also helped Ron become better."

Crawford, meanwhile, was an immediate fan of his new surroundings, admitting: "I liked Bootham Crescent straight away. I had left Scotland to go to Sheffield United but only played three games for them because Alan Hodgkinson was an England goalkeeper. When I did play at Bramall Lane, though, it was a bit strange as it only had three sides with a cricket ground there as well and, for me, Bootham Crescent still felt big compared to when I was an East Stirling player. It was a good four-sided ground and I loved it. The York fans were great to play in front of. There were always a few comments but, having them there behind you, was brilliant. A few years ago, I went to a music night at the Victoria Vaults on Nunnery Lane with a friend of mine who plays the trombone and, when I was stood at the bar, somebody tapped me on the shoulder and said: 'Can I buy you a drink?' I said: 'No, you don't need to that'. But he insisted and said: 'I stood behind you for years in the Shippo and I'd really like to buy you a drink'. That's the sort of supporters York fans were."

The welcome Crawford received from some of his team-mates during the notorious five-a-side sessions that still took place on the Tarmac behind the Grosvenor Road goal was not as warm. "Ron Hillyard used to kick lumps out of everybody," he explained. "He was as hard as nails." Crawford quickly became acquainted with the physicality of lower league football in England too, none more so than during a Bootham Crescent meeting with fallen giants and that season's champions Aston Villa, who included infamous battering ram Andy Lochhead in their ranks that campaign. Recalling that challenge, Crawford revealed: "I remember Ray Graydon put the ball down for a corner and Andy Lochhead said to me: 'Are you alright son?' and I said: 'Yes'. He then said: 'You won't be in a minute' and he clattered into me. It was his way of letting me know he was there and, in those days, you expected to get whacked as a keeper. There was a lot more contact." Villa secured a 1-0 April win on their way to the title with £100,000 player Bruce Rioch getting the only goal in front of a season-high crowd of 9,620.

Bootham Crescent old-boys Ted MacDougall and Phil Boyer, meanwhile, scored both goals as Bournemouth won 2-0 to boost their promotion hopes and leave City still in danger of relegation with just two matches to play. MacDougall's effort was his 45th of the season. With all three of the Minstermen's final fixtures at home, a 0-0 Monday night draw against Oldham then meant the club knew they would be safe if they could defeat Blackburn on the following Saturday. A 25-yard John Price effort proved the only goal of the game as the Lancashire side secured maximum points, which left City needing to rely on others to stay up. Two days later, they learned their fate when relegation was avoided as Mansfield could only draw 1-1 with Wrexham in their final fixture.

The Interworks Trophy, meanwhile, had been resurrected during the 1971/72 campaign and was won 3-2 by the Yorkshire Herald against Rowntree's in the Bootham Crescent final. Six Kingsway players, seen spitting and kicking opponents in their 1-0 York Schools' Junior Cup final defeat to Hempland at the ground, were subsequently reprimanded, though, by then headteacher Roy Powell, who said: "The six boys concerned were brought out in front of the school assembly and told in no uncertain manner that they had brought disgrace to the school." Privileges such as school trips and participation in the school seven-a-side tournament were also withdrawn.

The summer of 1972 represented the 40th birthday of Bootham Crescent too and its status as a community hub was still very clear with the Social Club open every day of the week. Saturday, Sunday and Thursday nights were set aside for musical evenings, with singing and dancing encouraged. Bingo was also played four nights a week with whist drives took place on Tuesdays.

For the start of the 1972/73 campaign, the Football League ruled that the minimum general ground adult admission for clubs would be 40p, which was subsequently enforced at Bootham Crescent. The club decided to cushion the blow by making season tickets available behind both goals for the first-ever time. They cost £8, with no reduction for juniors (not just boys!), although the demand was described as "very disappointing" by club secretary Teasdale, with a total of only 30 to 40 sold, which failed to cover the printing costs.

Ambitious plans, costing an estimated £500,000, were mooted, meanwhile, by chairman Magson to expand Bootham Crescent. Included in the idea was a new stand to replace the Popular Stand, more car parking and additional facilities such as a restaurant, swimming pool and squash courts. At the time, Magson said: "This idea is really only at the drawing board stage at the moment. The directors have discussed it at some length and we have great ambitions in the direction. One of the things I would like to see is a new stand with seats to replace the Popular Stand, perhaps on stilts with more car parking. If this were done, then we would have to consider covering one end, so that people who prefer to stand to watch a match would benefit. We have also talked over the idea of restaurants, a swimming pool, squash courts and other things. We are determined to improve so that we will be ready with facilities for second division football, which is our immediate aim." But the scheme was reliant on acquiring extra land from the army authorities behind the Popular Stand, as otherwise there was insufficient space to carry out the improvements. "If we had about an extra 100 feet in depth the possibilities are limitless," Magson pointed out.

An interesting experiment, meanwhile, saw a public practice match take place between the prospective first team and reserves, harking back to the Reds v Blues era. No charge was made for admittance with the game refereed by two officials - Vincent James and Ron Himsworth taking charge of one half of the pitch each. It was Johnston's idea "to create a bit of interest".

The new campaign then got off to an unsavoury start, when chaos broke out in the ground during a 0-0 home draw with Grimsby. Hordes of away fans raced across the pitch and several were escorted away by police, many after being chased across the terraces, as fighting broke out. Some wore war-paint and nearly 100 Grimsby supporters were led out of the ground five minutes after kick-off, along with almost the same number of home supporters, as police dogs were used to try and control matters. More trouble flared just before half-time and 23 arrests were made in total. It was reported that skinheads from Hull also turned up at the match to join forces with York counterparts against the Grimsby trouble-makers. As a consequence of the violent scenes, City announced that there would be a greater police presence at future home games in an attempt to curb the trouble. The police bill subsequently trebled, which placed financial pressure on the club at a time when attendances were not particularly high. Spectators were also now forbidden from transferring from one end of the ground to the other via the tunnel behind the Popular Stand, which would be policed with iron doors fitted at both ends. Transfers from one enclosure to the other in front of the Main Stand were stopped too.

In an ambitious competition, organised by the Supporters' Club, meanwhile, a new Vauxhall Viva car was showcased at the September home game against Bournemouth as the first prize. Entrants were asked to guess how far the car could run on one gallon of petrol. The distance was 41 miles, 354 yards and 6.5

inches, with Harold Charlton, of Hessay, the winner after a forecast that was two yards off the correct figure. A £100 profit was made from the competition with the winner decided just before Christmas.

England youth international Pollard went on to join an elite group of players to have netted five times in a game at the ground, achieving the feat in an 8-1 youth-team victory over Scunthorpe.

Despite the new measures, meanwhile, the crowd disturbances showed little signs of relenting and, during a 1-0 FA Cup third-round defeat to second division Oxford, two visiting fans were taken to hospital after being bitten by police dogs, as officers clashed with away supporters on the pitch, just prior to kick-off. Railings in front of the Popular Stand also collapsed after the away team scored the only goal of the game, which led to minor injuries for two people. The police later offered to cover the costs of one of the Oxford offenders' trousers, after the seat of his pants were torn apart by the dog to the amusement of the watching crowd.

Johnston, meanwhile, survived a January meeting at Bootham Crescent, called by the players who wanted to address the manager's poor communication with the squad as they handed over a list of grievances following the resignation of trainer-coach Billy Horner. Swallow and Burrows represented the players, with Johnston, Magson and vice-chairman Ken Lancaster also in attendance, as the meeting lasted two-and-a-half hours. The City boss commented afterwards: "I've got a great big knife in my back and I'm trying to get it out." Everybody eventually reached a compromise, though, with a new committee formed at the club, consisting of two directors, the manager and the captain, so the players could air their views in the right manner going forward.

City would escape relegation in 1972/73 with a win on the final day as summer-signing Jimmy Seal, who was picked up from Barnsley, secured a 2-1 win at Rotherham. But that was only Seal's third league goal in 31 outings and he managed just one of those at Bootham Crescent, as he struggled to win over a home crowd who would grow to worship his scoring exploits in future campaigns. There was an upsetting explanation, though, for Seal's form, illustrating how life away from the football club can have an impact on the pitch. "It was for a very sad reason," he explained about his barren run. "My mum and dad died within three months of each other and it knocked me for six. I wasn't interested in football or anything. I was only 21 and that's a young age to lose both of your parents. I wasn't playing well but they kept picking me.

I just couldn't concentrate though. I was even thinking about my mum and dad during games, but I eventually got over my loss and started playing well."

Seal's grieving process had not been overcome, however, before what should have perhaps been one of Bootham Crescent's greatest-ever striking partnerships was split up after just seven months as Aimson moved to Bournemouth. "Paul was a mate and a really good lad," Seal recalled. "We knew we could hit it off, but we never really got a chance. We once counted how many games we started together, and it was only eight. When I first met Tom (Johnston) in his car, he said: 'I want you to play with Paul Aimson' and I thought that will do for me because I knew he was a good player and we got to know each other really well. He knew where the net was and was very good in the air. Years later, before he died, he came up to York and me and Graeme Crawford met him in the directors' box on a nice winter afternoon."

Earlier that campaign, Aimson had attempted to persuade fellow 1964/65 promotion winner Andy Provan to return to Bootham Crescent with the restless Wrexham winger even meeting Johnston at the ground before declining the chance to rejoin his old club. "I never really wanted to leave in the first place, but Chester had offered money for me and York had signed me on a free, so it was good business for them," he pointed out. "I remember I could have gone back to York, though, when I fell out with my manager at Wrexham. I even went through to Bootham Crescent, but I had my doubts. Paul Aimson was trying to convince me to come back, because he'd done the same and he said it would be like the good, old days, but everybody says you should never go back and something told me it wouldn't have been right. I was 28 or 29 and I decided to sign for Southport instead and won the fourth division title with them before I went to America. I'd been part of such a good team before at York and maybe I didn't want to tarnish that. I had also been really sad to leave, but the club had given me permission to speak to Chester and part of you then feels that you're not really wanted."

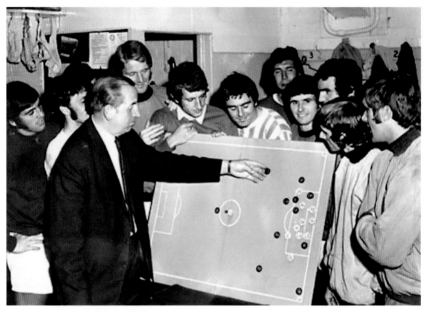

Tom Johnston gets out the tactics board in the home dressing room, as jockstraps dry off in the background

York City's all-time record appearance holder Barry Jackson was released at the end of the 1969/70 season shortly after he had sold his much-loved sweet shop on Bootham Crescent

CHAPTER 15

Tom Johnston takes City up to the second division

"Everyone was on the pitch after the game and it was like winning the Cup final really for us. It was brilliant and a great climax to the season."

In the summer of 1973, new signings Barry Lyons, Chris Jones, Ian Holmes and Ian Butler were made, and the quartet would help lead the club to a historic campaign as promotion meant Bootham Crescent would host second-tier football for the first-ever time. There was also a bit of stardust at Bootham Crescent in pre-season when Nobby Stiles played for fellow World Cup winner Jack Charlton's Middlesbrough side in a friendly that the hosts won 2-1 thanks to goals from Jones and John Woodward. City decided against increasing admission prices for the season despite a rise in VAT, with club secretary George Teasdale reasoning: "Though many clubs have put prices up, ours will remain the same. We are keeping faith with the public and hope that more people will come at the old prices rather than fewer at an increased price."

In September, meanwhile, City decided to advertise for a "disc jockey" to help with the pre-match and half-time entertainment on the public address system. The system had previously been in the club secretary's office, from where basic information had been relayed, but it was moved into the Main Stand so that the person could see the spectators and the pitch when speaking, making communication more natural and easier.

With Jimmy Seal and Jones both ruled out due to injury, John Peachey's goal went on to secure a 1-0 League Cup win over second division Aston Villa, as Graeme Crawford also saved a Ray Graydon penalty, given after Barry Swallow was contentiously alleged to have tripped Brian Little. An exciting third round 2-1 replay victory over second division Orient was then sealed with seven seconds left to play in extra time by a Butler goal. The score had been goalless after 90 minutes, with Holmes earlier levelling after Mike Bullock had opened the scoring. A pitch invasion followed Butler's goal but, after order was restored, referee Bill Castle blew his final whistle just moments later.

Supporters queue for tickets for the League Cup clash against Manchester City, including schoolchildren, despite the kick-off time being changed to a term-time Wednesday afternoon due to the floodlight ban imposed by the worldwide economic oil crisis in November 1973

With a tie against glamour club Manchester City the reward for the winners, the Minstermen immediately announced that the contest would be the first all-ticket affair to be staged at Bootham Crescent since the 1958 FA Cup clash with Bolton. Crowd safety considerations meant the ground's capacity was limited to 19,000 for the game. Supporters who went to the subsequent Southend home league match were issued with a voucher, which would guarantee them one ground ticket for the Cup tie. The resulting attendance was 8,153, smashing the season's previous biggest league attendance of 5,405 against Chesterfield. Southend were beaten 1-0 courtesy of a Jones header, as the team extended their unbeaten run to 16 games and kept an eighth consecutive league clean sheet with Johnston receiving a gallon bottle of whisky before the match as the Third Division's Manager of the Month for October. Manchester City also claimed their full entitlement of 4,700 tickets, including 250 seats, although returned 1,800 the day before the match. Ticket prices were increased to £1 from 70p for a Main Stand seat, which were only available to season-ticket holders. Admission to the ground was 50p instead of 40p, with the Popular Stand and Enclosure prices 75p as opposed to 45p. People were also invited to apply for tickets by post, enclosing their voucher, the correct remittance and a self-addressed envelope. The envelopes had to be clearly marked "Ground, Popular Stand or Enclosure" to ease the process. In the meantime, a 0-0 wind-affected, November home draw with ex-City favourite Colin Addison's Hereford United set a new club record of 17 matches unbeaten.

With a week left to the Cup tie and many tickets already sold, it was then announced that the midweek game would be switched to a 2.15pm kick-off due to the worldwide economic oil crisis, which was leading to power cuts and a floodlight ban, as the Government rationed electricity usage.

The Minstermen would go on to hold Manchester City's superstars to another goal-less draw before bowing out 4-1 in the replay at Maine Road, where 1970s' maverick Rodney Marsh hit a hat-trick. The game pitted Jones against his first club and love with the likes of Colin Bell and Francis Lee also in the opposition's line-up, but Denis Law was ruled out by a cold. An afternoon kick-off, even though it presented traffic complications with the RAC Rally finishing in York at lunchtime, also didn't prevent 15,360 fans from turning up, contributing to record gate receipts of £9,346.50, on a cold and gloomy Wednesday afternoon. The city's schools and factories reported high absenteeism and Jones recalled: "The stories given of how people got off work and school are numberless. I had my hip replaced in 2006 and my anaesthetist said he was at St Peter's school and bunked it with quite a few friends to watch the game. He said the licking was worth it."

Jones also added that, had it not been for the nose of one of his old team-mates, Manchester City would have been on the receiving end of a giant-killing. "Jimmy Seal had crossed the ball into the box and I caught it on the volley with my left foot and thought the goalkeeper Keith Macrae had no chance of saving it," Jones explained. "But it blasted into the face of Tommy Booth and flew off towards the goal line. The memorable quote from Tommy to the press was: 'It caught me on de dose.'"

Chris Topping, meanwhile, was struck by the number of young fans who made it in the ground for the afternoon kick-off. "If you talk to York people who were between the ages of 11 and 16 then, most of them were at that Manchester City game," he explained. "The schools either let them go or took them, which was amazing, and it was a tremendous game. It was strange to see so many children there. I didn't expect that many and there shouldn't have been really. If I had been a teacher at that time, though, I would have used it as a very good educational ploy and maybe that's what happened. They probably told the children: 'If you work hard and get your homework done early, we will look at going to watch York v Manchester City at 2.30pm'.

England forward Franny Lee gets a shot at goal away with Chris Topping looking on during the 1973 League Cup tie against Manchester City

Even the children from St Peter's were there, which you wouldn't have thought would be the case. It was a good game too. Manchester City had an awful lot of class on the field. They had Franny Lee, Rodney Marsh and Colin Bell, who was a fitness fanatic like myself and it was a marvellous feeling taking them on at Bootham Crescent. They were Chris Jones and Phil Burrows' old team too. I was up against Lee, but we didn't always follow people. I was always on the left-hand side but, if the forwards crossed over, we would pass our men on."

Seal remembered a tough contest with few opportunities for the hosts against such esteemed opposition, adding: "They were a very good team with top players like Franny Lee, Colin Bell and Rodney Marsh. Mike Doyle - the centre back - also played for England and he was tough to play against and, while we got a 0-0, I didn't get any chances." The City striker also welcomed the novelty of playing on a midweek afternoon in front of a younger crowd than normal at Bootham Crescent. "It was almost a full house that day and I'm sure some of the kids hadn't told the teachers where they were going," he laughed. "There must have been a few in York with 'colds' that afternoon. You build yourself up through the week in training and, even when you're playing two games, you have routines, but I remember enjoying playing such a good team on a Wednesday afternoon, even though I don't remember us creating any chances." Lyons was not as enthusiastic about the unusual start time, admitting: "That early kick-off put me off a bit because it's a change to the routine and you're not used to that in your system."

Crawford was happy with a clean sheet and believed the hosts could have pulled off a giant-killing. "I felt we did really well against Manchester City and I thought we could have won," he argued. "It was a bit bizarre playing on a Wednesday afternoon, but it was unbelievable how many people turned up and got time off work."

The Minstermen's best chances of the first half saw Peachey, in the team for the injured Butler, force a save and, as Jones recalled, his goal-bound drive smacked Booth in the face. Marsh, Lee and Bell all went close too before the interval. The top-flight visitors then dominated the second half, with Crawford saving well from Marsh, Tony Towers having a chance cleared off the line by John Stone and Bell shooting inches too high.

After the replay defeat, City went on to equal Millwall's 1926 Football League record by keeping an 11th consecutive clean sheet following a 4-0 defeat of Southport, courtesy of goals from Seal, Jones, Brian Pollard and Peachey, although the historic feat was only witnessed by a disappointing 2,712 supporters - the lowest gate of the season. Former winger Andy Provan came closest to ruining his old club's record bid, only to be denied by a fine one-on-one save from Crawford. City drew 2-2 at Aldershot in the next match to miss out on full ownership of the record. Jack Howarth, who had scored the last league goal against City at Bootham Crescent, also ended the sequence by opening the scoring in Hampshire and both goals were headers.

The turnout for the Southport match - well short of the 8,500 chairman Bob Strachan estimated was needed for the club to break even - was blamed on a combination of cold weather, Christmas shopping and the fact that the team had not scored in their three previous Bootham Crescent contests. Having invited the public to give their reasons for non-attendance, the *Yorkshire Evening Press* received a bulging postbag and, giving one explanation for the low crowds, Les Lightfoot, of Ostman Road, highlighted the expense of visiting Bootham Crescent now for the working man on a basic wage. "It costs me 85p to watch a City game and it works out like this - one pint before a game 13p, ten cigarettes 14p, bus fares 18p and admission 40p," he pointed out. Pauline J Kitchen, of Kingsway North, also complained about amenities, pleading: "May I beg to ask the powers that be to improve the ladies' toilets." She also added: "The warm pies go far too quickly and access from the season-ticket holders' stand to the canteen is rather roundabout." R Anderson, of Acomb, agreed with the ladies' toilets issue, pointing out: "A priority is improved ladies' toilets for Main Stand and Enclosure supporters. At present, only one toilet is provided in the Supporters' Club." He then went on to declare: "It is embarrassing telling visiting supporters that there are no refreshment facilities for Main Stand spectators. The public address also needs improving with a varied selection of records, requests, scores, more news etc, thus making the fans welcome." Others were being put off by the rise in hooliganism with Michael Walmsley, of Acomb, pointing out: "The Bolton game was an experience in comparison with which Bedlam would seem like a public library on a Sunday afternoon. We started the game in the middle row of the centre of the Popular Stand and, by half-time, we had been shoved almost down to the front row, near the left corner flag. We could see nothing and hear nothing except the deafening and continuous crash of boots on corrugated iron and we were continually showered with glass rebounding from the roof." The lack of buses running regularly to the ground was another common complaint.

While gates remained modest, Pollard recalled that the club were beginning to attract interest from the television companies, as City's unbeaten run and promotion push gathered pace. "I used to like scoring and one of my best was in a 1-0 win over Blackburn just after Christmas the season we went up," he recalled. "It was in front of the ITV cameras when Keith Macklin had his show. I hit one from 30 yards and it flew into the net. I was also interviewed in the tunnel afterwards but that was never used." Topping, meanwhile, revealed that Pollard's goal would not have made the highlights reel either if he had heeded the advice of his defensive team-mate. "He was about 10 yards outside the area and I shouted: 'Leave it, Polly', but he dashed in front of me and scored," Topping said. "He always jokes about that and I have to concede that it was a bad call on my part."

City's club record unbeaten run of 21 league games ended, meanwhile, with a 1-0 home defeat to Charlton, as Keith Peacock's swerving 13th-minute shot settled matters after he was teed up by ex-Bootham

A bumper crowd of 7,638 attended Bootham Crescent's first-ever Sunday fixture against Watford in February 1974

Crescent midfielder Eamonn Dunphy. The hosts put up a good fight, with a Jones chance cleared off the line and Holmes heading against the inside of a post. But Charlton held on even though centre-half Bob Goldthorpe was sent off for a second bookable offence with 15 minutes to go and keeper John Dunn made a fine save from Seal's header in stoppage time.

As an experiment, the club also played their first-ever Sunday home fixture against Watford in February to examine the impact on attendance figures. Explaining the move, then chairman Strachan said: "We are sympathetic to Sunday football, particularly in the present circumstances, because we feel it will result in an increase in gates. Although clubs voted against Sunday football at the Football League annual meeting two years ago, one has to remember that times have changed, and I believe there has to be some rethinking on the question." Rugby fixtures had, by that stage, been hosted in the city on a Sunday for a couple of years, but supporters who went to the game automatically became members of the newly-formed Robins Club, which was needed to comply with laws governing Sunday sport. Previously, spectators attending a Sunday match had been entitled to get in free but, following the example of Brighton's Dolphins Club, fans received a small ticket at the turnstiles, which acted as a membership for the Robins Club to bypass that legislation. Programmes, which by this time cost 6p, could also only be sold in the ground for Sunday fixtures. The game was the first, meanwhile, for the club's newly-appointed DJ - 23-year-old Phil Eastwood, of Huntingdon Road - and the band of the Yorkshire Volunteers played before the match and during the interval.

Once the action got underway, a very-entertaining match then broke out. Ross Jenkins headed the Hornets in front on the stroke of half-time, but Seal levelled just past the hour after rising highest in the penalty box to meet a Lyons free kick. The Hertfordshire visitors forged back in front through Billy Jennings, but Holmes equalised almost immediately from close range after Watford failed to clear another Lyons centre. City rode their luck in the closing stages, though, with the frame of their goal tested twice - once inadvertently by home left-back Burrows.

The Sunday fixture was a novelty that proved popular with punters, as a crowd of 7,638 attended, which represented a significant improvement on the season's average up to that point. The previous home games had drawn 4,699 and 3,727 crowds, while the Boxing Day fixture against Grimsby had only attracted 5,890. Another Sunday fixture a fortnight later also resulted in a gate of 7,149 as City saw off Cambridge 2-0, although leaders Bristol Rovers rejected a request to play their scheduled Saturday March visit to Bootham Crescent 24 hours later. The Rovers manager Don Megson was keen not to give the hosts the advantage of a bigger and more vocal home gate.

For churchgoer Seal, the date of the Watford game had also presented a problem that Tom Johnston quickly resolved. "It was a little bit difficult for me more than anyone," Seal suggested of the Sunday kick-off. "Tom Johnston said to us a week or two before that we would be playing on a Sunday and asked if there were any objections. I said: 'Yes, me' and told him I went to church. He said: 'Well Jim', in front of everybody, 'if you don't play a week on Sunday, you won't be playing the Saturday after either'. I had meant it half-hearted anyway and would have played, but I just thought, hold on, there are points of view here and I did go to church on a Sunday. It's all about Sunday now for a lot of sports, but that wasn't the case back then. I didn't mention it to anybody at the Methodist church we went to. They might have found out why I wasn't there though!" Topping revealed that there was no other opposition in the dressing room. "I have known of athletes who refused to compete on a Sunday, but it didn't cause a problem or affect us," Topping pointed out. "It didn't seem any different really."

The top-of-the-table midweek home clash with Bournemouth on Wednesday, March 6, was also able to be played under the floodlights, instead of in the afternoon, when a Nottingham company provided a generator, with the Government still placing restrictions on power usage. City officials had approached more than a dozen other companies, but many generators were already needed elsewhere, and Bootham Crescent also had two kinds of lights on their pylons, which further complicated negotiations with businesses.

Voting forms, meanwhile, were included in the Easter programmes as fans were canvassed in a Player of the Year poll for the first time, with the new trophy, contributed by the York Football Coaches' Association, serving as a memorial to Happy Wanderers legend Billy Fenton at the request of his widow Margot. Supporters were asked to base their choices on: 1) behaviour on and off the field; 2) effort; 3) appearance; 4) loyalty to the club; 5) sportsmanship and 6) will to win, with Margot making the presentation at the final home game of the season - a tradition that would carry on right up until the latter campaigns at Bootham Crescent, with Billy's sons also joining or standing in for their mother during later years.

The Good Friday home match with Huddersfield also saw a song played for City fans, recorded by supporters John Bird and Dick Sefton in their Bishop Wilton studio. Sefton played the guitar and organ, with Bird on vocals. Called "The Big Red Band," it included lines such as "We've beaten all the giants, we've beaten all the best, now David is Goliath, we're beating all the rest." The team subsequently scrambled to an unconvincing 2-1 triumph thanks to goals from Holmes and Jones, either side of an equaliser from future City boss Terry Dolan. The team were back in action at Bootham Crescent the following day and suffered a surprise 1-0 defeat to already-relegated Shrewsbury - representing only their second loss of the campaign. The Shrews were captained to victory by ex-City midfielder Laurie Calloway, with Ricky Moir getting the only goal of the game.

Commenting at the Supporters' Club annual dinner, meanwhile, chairman Strachan lamented the lack of space for expansion at Bootham Crescent and admitted: "I curse the day it was ever decided to leave Fulfordgate, although I have no doubt that there were good reasons for doing so at the time."

Promotion was ultimately clinched following a 1-1 draw against Oldham on Saturday, April 27, although the team would have still had two away games left to pick up the one point they needed to secure a top-three finish. The match was played in front of 15,583 - the biggest home crowd for eight years with record league receipts of £5,633 - as turnstiles opened at 1.30pm - 30 minutes earlier than was usual at the time. An hour later, Burrows was revealed

York City's players salute the crowd before going on to clinch promotion to the old second division for the only time in the club's history in April 1974 following a 1-1 draw with Oldham

as the first winner of the Billy Fenton Player of the Year Memorial Trophy after chairman Strachan opened an envelope on the pitch, with Margot Fenton making the presentation.

Cliff Calvert went on to fill in at right back for the suspended Stone against an Oldham team, who were already certain of promotion, but still targeting the title. On a bumpy pitch, conditions were also made difficult by a strong wind. A competitive start saw Oldham defender Ian Wood stretchered off after just three minutes when he landed awkwardly on his shoulder following an aerial challenge with Seal. His injury was later confirmed as a dislocated collarbone. Swallow and old adversary Andy Lochhead, meanwhile, received early lectures from the referee after another clash. The Oldham striker would end the half with a booking for kicking Crawford. George McVitie was then only denied the opening goal midway through the first half by an excellent Crawford save. Trouble also broke out in the Popular Stand, with three youngsters escorted out of the ground by police. Jones went closest for the Minstermen before the interval, firing narrowly wide. The breakthrough then came on 56 minutes when Jones cut in from the goal-line and was fouled by sub Paul Edwards a yard outside the penalty area. Lyons took the free kick and Jones was left all alone to head in high, just inside Chris Odgen's right-hand post from five yards. Two minutes later, Butler rattled Ogden's bar with a great shot and Jones headed over from the rebound. But Crawford had to be alert at the other end to turn a Maurice Whittle free kick behind. On 65 minutes, though, Whittle beat City's Scotsman from a second dead-ball chance. Burrows was penalised for a foul on McVitie two yards outside the penalty box and Whittle curled his shot past the City wall and in off Crawford's left-hand post. Crawford still had an important part to play in the promotion clincher, making an excellent save to push a 25-yard McVitie drive over his crossbar.

The final whistle subsequently prompted a pitch invasion and a lap of honour amid the tumultuous scenes, while City players, along with Johnston, went on to greet the fans from the directors' box as the supporters chanted "Super York." Johnston toasted the crowd with a glass of champagne and, as the bubbly flowed, even the boardroom was opened to other guests, such as members of the press.

Fans invade the pitch to celebrate the 1-1 draw with Oldham that clinched promotion to the old second division in 1974

Goalscorer Jones recalled the match in his autobiography *The Tale of Two Great Cities*, saying: "The first half had a dramatic start when Wood, of Oldham, dislocated his collar bone and was carried off. I felt for the lad as I had experienced a dislocation of the knee before. The tension was electric throughout a first half which saw a lot of goalmouth action but only one real shot by me which went past Ogden's left-hand post. In the second half, I fired a great shot which hit Ogden on the nose and John Woodward blasted the rebound wide. The goalkeeper had to have extensive treatment to his face before he continued. We managed to take the lead from a Barry Lyons indirect free kick. I had been fouled just outside the box on the left-hand side. Barry took it and I got in front of my marker to head it back across goal into the far corner of the net. Next, Ian Butler used his magical left foot to crack a shot against the post, but I headed the rebound over the bar. The game became very tense and Oldham needed to get back into it. Phil Burrows gave away a free kick in the 65th minute just outside the box and Maurice Whittle, who had a great left foot, curled the ball past Crawford into the top left-hand corner of the net. It was a tense finish and both sides were glad to share the honours and take a point each. For Oldham, the Whittle goal had nearly assured them of the title, but we didn't care - a draw was good enough for us and we had achieved promotion. For York City players and fans alike, it was a dream come true. Out of the ashes of near relegation, we had achieved the near impossible and climbed into the second tier of the English Football League. The scenes on the pitch and in the stand were fantastic and people were deliriously happy. For the players, it was exciting to see so many fans beside themselves with joy completely immersing the ground in front of the Main Stand in maroon and white. Every player I talk to from that epic season remembers the thrill and shiver those scenes sent through them at Bootham Crescent that day. I will remember it as the greatest moment in my football life, thrilled that the goal I scored gave so much pleasure to so many loyal York City supporters and gave us players the chance to take on some of the major clubs in the Football League's higher echelons. Nobody can take away the memories of the players and fans that turned up that Saturday afternoon."

Topping also retained vivid recollections of the historic occasion in his sixth season at Bootham Crescent. "We were close and just needed a draw," he said. "Chris Jones gave us the lead but then Maurice Whittle equalised with a free kick. We knew we then had to hang on, but it was wonderful. They were a good side who knew they were and knew we were a good side too. We played each other a lot and the games usually ended in draws or in single-goal victories either way. During the closing stages, the tension was there but, as far as I was concerned, I would run all day and all night to get promotion for York City and Graeme (Crawford) did his bit during a marvellous day. The crowd were on the pitch at the end and it was wonderful. I remember having one glass of champagne, then I just went home with my wife, or girlfriend as she was at the time. My mum and dad were there as well, and my mum wouldn't have been celebrating quietly. She was as thrilled as myself and the team. Such occasions are obviously not as important as world matters, but it was wonderful for me. I then came back to our house in the country and it didn't mean a great deal to people around here. In fact, there are more supporters around there now."

Seal confessed that the joyous scenes at the final whistle were more memorable than the game itself, as he received acclaim from supporters who had doubted his ability just a season earlier. "I honestly can remember very little about the match apart from the final whistle going and thinking: 'Wow, we've done it'," he said. "I'd been at Wolves, Barnsley and Walsall and never had any success but here we were going out into the stand in the directors' box and waving to the crowd, which was immense. The pitch was full. You couldn't see any grass and

I got carried all the way around the pitch. I was shouting to those lads: 'Let me down', but they wouldn't. It had all turned around for me, which was brilliant."

Crawford, meanwhile, recalled having little chance with set-piece specialist Whittle's equaliser, saying: "Whittle used to take free kicks from anywhere and have a shot - even if it was ten yards inside your half he would have a go - so, when you conceded a free kick against Oldham, you would be thinking: 'Where's this going?' and he struck his goal really well. During the closing stages, you then couldn't tell which way the game was going to go and, to win promotion to the second division, was unreal for us players, who had been in the third division and even the fourth applying for re-election. Everyone was on the pitch after the game and it was like winning the Cup final really for us. It was brilliant and a great climax to the season."

Lyons admitted the match itself was little to write home about though. "We finished third in the final promotion place and it was really tense by then," he explained. "There wasn't a lot of football played on that afternoon. The pitches always got hard as you got towards April and it wasn't a classic, but it was nice to get it done by getting a draw. I don't remember setting Jonesy up, but he would be able to tell you about his goal. He and Jimmy Seal were both good finishers in their own ways." A reluctant Lyons also had to be persuaded to join in the post-match celebrations, but admitted he was glad he relented. "I remember going into the dressing room and the crowd were still outside, so the manager said: 'We will go into the directors' box'," Lyons said. "The players went up and I sat there and thought I'm not going up there. Jimmy Seal said: 'Come on Barry', but I said to him: 'I'm not bothered. They will be booing us next year in the second division'. But I did go up and give them a wave and the fans were good. They were all on the halfway line chanting and I was glad I went up."

Lifelong City fan Andy Briggs, then a 12-year-old schoolboy, remembered the final whistle well. He said: "It was the only time I got my dad on the pitch at Bootham Crescent. He didn't agree with pitch invasions, but I managed to drag him onto it with a fair amount of persuasion this one time."

Among the celebrating home fans, meanwhile, was future FA chairman Greg Dyke, who became a City devotee as a University of York student at the time. Recounting his love for the old ground but asserting the need for relocation, Dyke said: "I was a regular at Bootham Crescent when I was a student and my final year was the only season that the club got promoted to what's now the Championship. I remember a winger called (Brian) Pollard who stood out and a very good defence. They were a good side and I went home and away. I wasn't supposed to be biased when I was FA chairman, but I've always had two or three teams I look out for and York are one of them, so I've got fond memories of the ground but, the moment a club moves to a new stadium, the gates go up. There's all this nostalgia about what the old stadium was like but today's fans, quite rightly, want better facilities and they will get that at the new ground. Bootham Crescent was a traditional English football ground and there's only a few left now. They're all wonderful but we shouldn't live in the past. People want to get a drink easily and go to the toilet, which you couldn't do half the time at Bootham Crescent because of the queues."

Seal, now coping better after his double bereavement, blossomed alongside Jones in a manner that was never possible with Aimson. The pair shared 37 goals between them that season with Jones contributing 20 and Seal 17. They became big favourites at Bootham Crescent and, on the success of their partnership, Seal said: "Jonesy came and we hit it off. Chris was adamant that he wanted to try and score as many goals as he could. That was him - the box man. I was the one doing all the work and that's not me being big-headed. I used to have to threaten him on the pitch sometimes and say: 'Come on, you lazy so-and-so'. There were little opposites with us as players and I think that works in football. We knew what we wanted to do in the box as well. Nobody seems to run to the near post to get flick-ons any more, but all the crosses seem to come in low. When we were playing, one of us would make a run to the near post and the other would peel off to the back post. We never stood still because it's easy to mark you then and we got a lot of goals that way."

Topping also felt the new recruits symbolised Johnston's canny knack of pairing together players who would complement each other, declaring: "Tom Johnston was brilliant at piecing teams together. Jimmy Seal did lots of Chris Jones' running for him. But Jonesy would wait in the box until a chance dropped to him and he was the goalscorer we needed, while Jimmy was the worker who went on decoy runs. It was similar with me and Swallow. He would do a lot of the organising and I was the athlete who did the running and a lot of the heading and I was happy with that. The players Tom brought in during the promotion season were also experienced. Barry Lyons and Ian Holmes were opposites but gave us good momentum going forward and creativity. Ian loved to run from our own box to the opposition's box and set up chances or shoot. That was his game. Barry didn't do that amount of running but, if you gave him the ball, he could pass it so well he didn't have to do lots of running and they both got on very well."

The side won eight and drew four of their 12 home matches during the club record-breaking, 21-game unbeaten sequence with Crawford beaten just four times. Midfielder Lyons had joined the club towards the start of that run - initially on loan from top-flight Nottingham Forest - but he confessed the growing sense of excitement at Bootham Crescent persuaded him to drop down a couple of divisions. He also became an instant favourite with City fans after bagging a brace during a 3-1 victory over Aldershot in only his second appearance at Bootham Crescent. "It was a fantastic time to join the club," Lyons enthused. "As the run built up, we started to get crowds of five and six thousand. I had gone to the club on loan and I wasn't sure if I was going to stay for longer than a month, but I enjoyed it so much that I decided to sign, and it was a smashing season. I remember one of the goals against Aldershot being just a tap-in. I was a midfielder, but I found myself in the box. It was nothing special, but it was nice to win a home game and the crowd took to me."

The Football League record of 11 league matches without conceding a goal also included six home fixtures. Not every player enjoyed that run, though, with striker Jones admitting in his book: "Jimmy Seal and me were glad when we finally let one in as we felt the record was becoming an albatross around our necks. The press had started going on about beating the Millwall 1926 record and we were going into our shells as a team and lost a lot of our attacking flair as we started to defend ever deeper." There were two 0-0 draws at Bootham Crescent against Chesterfield and Hereford, as well as single-goal triumphs over Wrexham and Southend on the team's own soil during the sequence and Seal and Jones only scored twice at Bootham Crescent each during the record run with the former admitting: "It did get a little bit defensive. If it came to the last 20 minutes and we'd given it a right go and not scored then we'd take a point, and everybody got behind the ball, but it was a good record and our defence was very good. We had two good defenders at full-back in John Stone and Phil Burrows. You couldn't beat them. Topps and Swall at centre back were great stuff and there wasn't a better keeper around than Graeme. He was a top keeper apart from his kicking, although he was still not as bad as some are today when they need to be able to kick the ball more."

Topping admitted that the emphasis on keeping a clean sheet was almost becoming greater than the desire to get on the scoresheet, as even the crowd started to focus more on the record. "We had to kick a few off the line but that was all part of it because the ball didn't cross the line," he pointed out. "The crowd were almost as excited when we kept a goal out at our end as they were when we were on the attack and that brings pressure as well. The more and more games we went without conceding, the more pressure we felt, but you need a strong defence. Phil Burrows was a very fast left back who was good in the air despite being 5ft 9in. At right back, we had John Stone or John Woodward, who were both reliable. It wasn't just a back five though. There was Jimmy Seal coming back to stop their defenders and Barry Lyons would stop his winger too."

Lyons felt the team still posed a strong threat in the opposition half, though, adding: "We had a very good defence and Graeme was a quality keeper, but we attacked a lot as well and, sometimes, the defence didn't have too much to do. With the record, these things just creep up on you. We weren't aware of it until the sixth or seventh game really and then you just keep rolling along and, as everybody says, just keep looking forward to the next game."

On the secret behind his run of clean sheets, Crawford added: "We had a consistent back four and, if you have that, it really helps. The big thing we had as well was unbelievable team spirit." Supporting Crawford's comments, he and his back four of Stone, Swallow, Topping and Burrows would miss just six games between them throughout the whole campaign. The Scottish keeper added that there were a few close shaves, though, during that record run. "I can remember Tranmere having a penalty that I saved," Crawford pointed out. "I was also beaten a few times by shots, but you had people like Phil Burrows covering for you and there were a few kicked off the line. It would go past me, and Phil would say: 'I got you out of trouble again'. Players like him gave 110 per cent and total effort because they never wanted to be beaten. As the record got closer, I began to feel a bit more pressure and was thinking: 'Is today going to be the day I concede?' and, to a certain extent, it was a bit of a relief when that happened. It was nice while it lasted though and something I never expected to do. I got a lot of credit for it, but it was totally a team effort."

The penalty save against Tranmere was an 88th-minute stop from Willie Stevenson following a wild Stone tackle on Hugh McAuley. Contrary to his attacking team-mates, Crawford also argued: "I don't think we became more defensive during that time. We just played the same and, if it so happened we kept a clean sheet, then it happened." With that record set, Crawford suggested that the club's overlapping, unprecedented unbeaten sequence of league games was rarely discussed. "We never really thought about it," he declared. "We just went out and did our best and there was no pressure. Well, if there was, I didn't feel any. We went out thinking we could win every game, even if we went a goal down. We always thought we could come back and, nine times out of ten, we did. We also had a good rapport with the fans. They were good to us."

City were ultimately never out of the top-three promotion places after beating Southend 1-0 at Bootham Crescent on November 10 thanks to a Jones goal. In March, meanwhile, the team had finished 2-1 winners against fellow high-fliers Bristol Rovers in front of 11,066 at Bootham Crescent. It was a key victory with Topping involved in the incident that saw the latter half of Rovers' famed 'Smash & Grab' striking partnership of Alan Warboys and Bruce Bannister sent for an early shower. "Bruce Bannister was the worst player I played against," Topping grimaced. "I got booked in that famous game against Bristol Rovers at home when Ian Holmes scored the late penalty. I tackled Bannister on the touchline and was late. I didn't mean to be, but he got up and punched me, so he got sent off. He also elbowed me in the return game at their place."

Seal, who had played in front of an average attendance of 3,792 the previous campaign, thrived on the bumper crowds that flocked to Bootham Crescent towards the end of the season. "It was great - absolutely brilliant - especially during the night games," he admitted. "It's a compact, little ground and the atmosphere with the lights on was fantastic, especially when we were attacking the Shipton Street End. I think the fans liked night games more as well. The ground felt like it was full every game because smaller stadiums do look full when you start getting bigger crowds and it made us full of confidence."

Pollard also insisted that the manager deserved a lot of credit for the side's success, arguing: "You can't take anything away from Tom Johnston. He was a wily old manager. What he did cannot be matched by any other manager at York City - taking them from the old fourth division to the second. That was one hell of an achievement with a small squad although we did have competition too. The wingers were good. We had Ian Butler and Dennis Wann who could both play on the left and myself and Barry Lyons on the right. Tom was shrewd and certainly knew how to get the best out of everybody. He also got players in for next to nothing and deserves his place in Bootham Crescent folklore." On Johnston's manner around the club, meanwhile, Pollard added: "He was a little bit eccentric to be honest. He had a great way of telling you if you weren't playing that day. He would tap you on your shoulder as you sat down for your pre-match meal and whisper: 'You can have chips'. I also once saw him walking down the corridor with his coat on fire because he'd put his pipe in his pocket without putting it out." Pollard recalled Johnston's assistant Colin Meldrum providing moments of mirth at the ground too, saying: "Colin liked a beer, or a whisky and I always remember him turning up worse for wear at training once. He was trying to tell us what to do and Tom was behind him shaking his head, but he could still get the best out of us even then."

The ground went on to witness its first penalty shoot-out, meanwhile, when the York City Supporters' Club Interworks Cup was won by BR Engineering Ltd A. They defeated Portakabin 5-4 on spot kicks following a 0-0 draw after extra-time, with Keith Fowler converting the winning effort from 12 yards.

Coach Colin Meldrum checks the weight of youngster Finbarr O'Sullivan with Tom Johnston and senior players looking on as towels dry in the background of the changing room

A fence collapses against Plymputh in April 1974 as the club closes in on promotion to the old second division

Chris Topping, Barry Swallow, Graeme Crawford, John Stone and Phil Burrows scan the record books during the run of 11 successive league clean sheets

Graeme Crawford looks on as City keep yet another clean sheet against Hereford in November 1973

CHAPTER 16

The Y-fronts see off Bobby Moore

"We were the butt of some Y-front jokes, but we had a lot of pride in that shirt."

For the hugely-exciting 1974/75 campaign, it was announced that season tickets would now be available in the Main Stand Enclosure. The move was made with families very much in mind, so they could avoid the growing hooligan element in the Popular Stand. British Rail, meanwhile, admitted they would give consideration, in conjunction with York District Council and the football club, to opening a new platform at Scarborough Terrace on the York to Scarborough line - just yards from Bootham Crescent ahead of the new campaign. It was seen as a method of avoiding hooliganism in the city centre and was welcomed by Peter Corner - the then manager of Bootham Newsagents on the corner of Bootham and Bootham Crescent, who said many shops were being pilfered by visiting fans on their way to and from the ground. It was also reported that a brick, covered in a scarf, had been put through one nearby resident's window. The idea never came to fruition but, in a new move, supporters' coaches from visiting teams were instructed to drop fans outside the ground to avoid trouble elsewhere in the city.

Car parking at the ground, meanwhile, was restricted to officials only, with space having been reduced by the arrival of three Portakabins. It was made clear that there would be no room either for bicycles, mopeds or "invalid cars". The latter caused a problem for police, with the Burton Stone Lane end of Grosvenor Road the nearest point to the ground at which the vehicles could be accommodated. Police had wanted to station their cars there and there was no space either for the "invalid cars" to watch the game from the side of the pitch, as was the case at many grounds at the time. Parking was also restricted to one side of all streets within close vicinity of the stadium, while Bootham Crescent could be used by coaches only.

A record number of more than 1,000 people applied for season-ticket seats for the historic campaign, which was more than double the number for the previous season. The rush was treated on a first-come, first-served basis with fans offered a season ticket in the Popular Stand, which was having seats installed, or the standing Enclosure area once the Main Stand's seating capacity was filled for the first time in the club's history. A total of 1,950 season tickets were sold, compared to the 365 that had been bought 12 months earlier. Seats snapped up second-hand from Manchester City were used to transform the Popular Stand and they increased the ground's seating capacity from 1,000 to 2,762 but reduced the overall figure to 16,529. The last of the 1,999 seats were still being fitted the day before the opening game against Aston Villa, with 900 filled by season-ticket holders. Two refreshment points in the Popular Stand's aisles were also added, whilst other improvements included a new players' entrance, players' wives' room and safety barrier. The Popular Stand had been able to accommodate 5,000 standing supporters before. Plans to cover the Bootham Crescent end of the ground, at a prohibitive rumoured cost of £80,000, never left the drawing board, which upset some spectators who preferred to stand and would now need to do so without any shelter, but Tarmac was laid in the car park to replace the pot-holed cinder surface, which had always been prone to massive puddles after rainfall. The three Portakabins were delivered to provide additional office space with the York City Football Club sign on the gates having to be taken down to facilitate access. One of the Portakabins was used for the Supporters' Club to take bookings for away coach travel and for club souvenirs to be sold. All of the ground enhancements cost £18,000, with the Portakabin buildings leading to an additional £4,305 expenditure.

Other grandiose plans, mooted if City established themselves in the second tier and needed to increase capacity size, never materialised. Included as an idea was the purchase of the Territorial Army and Shipton Street School grounds behind the Popular Stand, which would lead to the ground turning 90 degrees with an untouched Main Stand to then be situated behind a goal. Talk of a double-decker Popular Stand never became a reality either. There was also a suggestion that City might consider relocation to the Thanet Road sports complex in Acomb, with chairman Bob Strachan asking for assistance from the City of York Council and reasoning: "We have very inadequate facilities at Bootham Crescent - no parking worth talking about and a general shortage of space. In Thanet Road, you have a wonderful situation for, perhaps, a bumper sports complex right in the middle of one of the city's biggest areas of population. You already have swimming baths, indoor bowling and an athletics track. It could all be linked with a super stadium... and we may, as a bonus, be able to release some very valuable land in the centre of the city!"

Season tickets for the historic campaign also rose from £12 to £16 in the Main Stand, with the matchday price going up from 70p to £1. Soon after the promotion season ended, meanwhile, City appointed Keith Hunt - a 33-year-old management consultant - as their first commercial manager after he had been working at Bristol Rovers in a similar role, where he had successfully marketed forwards Alan Warboys and Bruce Bannister as "Smash and Grab." He lasted just five months and left in mid-October after clashing with directors and the Supporters' Club but, during that time, he introduced a new match-day magazine-style programme called "Match Mag" at Bootham Crescent and, with the help of former reserve player Peter Turpin, designed one of the most popular and iconic home kits in the club's history - with a white "Y" covering the entirety of a maroon shirt. Turpin was initially sceptical about the choice of maroon, but admitted he was blown away by the kit's appearance, as the players ran out and saluted the home fans during their opening fixture against Aston Villa. "I was a graphic designer and I designed the Y-front shirt," he explained. "I thought it was so obvious - the strong 'Y' - but I didn't like the colour. Tom Johnston told me it was going to be maroon, but I thought it was horrible. But the prototype arrived, and I was in that hell of a crowd for the first game and, when they ran out, it looked superb."

The players were fans of the strip too, with Topping saying: "Keith Hunt was responsible for that and it was a good idea. I was just disappointed we weren't allowed to keep them at the end of the season." Seal added: "I loved the kit, and everyone thought it was great because it was different. We were the butt of some Y-front jokes, but we had a lot of pride in that shirt."

New club ties, scarves and commemorative inscribed tankards in pewter also went on sale to celebrate the club's promotion. The 1974 Club, meanwhile, was introduced for season ticket-holders, who applied for the privilege, which included the use of a lounge bar for match-day refreshments. Hunt also launched a new bingo card initiative with more than £270 to be won weekly, including a first prize of £100. Each card cost 5p. A £30,000 plan to double the capacity of the Social Club, courtesy of a substantial loan from Bass North Ltd, was then revealed by Hunt two weeks before the campaign kicked off, but the club's directors later decided against that venture. It had been intended to host cabaret three times a week at the revamped venue, with applications made to extend the opening hours on match days to 11.30am to 2.45pm, 4.45pm

The players leave Bootham Crescent for a run with York's top middle-distance athlete Walter Wilkinson (pictured in a tracksuit), who was a European Indoor Championship bronze medallist in 1969

to 6.30pm and 7.30pm to 11pm. If permission had been granted, Hunt confirmed that admission to the ground from the Social Club would end, with people needing to come out and enter through their appropriate turnstile. But two new pool tables - believed to be the first of their kind in the city - were introduced into the Social Club.

City's players, meanwhile, were put through their paces during the build-up to the historic season. York's top middle-distance athlete Walter Wilkinson - a European Indoor Championship bronze medallist in 1969 - made sure the players would be fit for the Villa curtain-raiser. Wilkinson, who was also the first Yorkshireman to run a sub-four-minute mile and the first British athlete to achieve that feat before the age of 21, was regularly invited to oversee training sessions at Bootham Crescent, with Jimmy Seal recalling: "Walter was a AAAs track runner and, when people say players are fitter now, it makes me laugh because we couldn't have run any faster or worked any harder than we did and it was all progressive laps with Walter. We would sprint one side of the pitch then jog three sides, then sprint half the pitch and jog the other half, then sprint three quarters and jog the last quarter before doing the whole way round and, just when you thought you had finished, he would say, 'Off you go again'. We did a bit more in pre-season, but he'd come in during the season as well. He was a full-time runner and I think Tom brought him in so he could have the morning off maybe."

But keeper Graeme Crawford always dreaded Wilkinson turning up at Bootham Crescent. "It was terrible," he grimaced. "I was never the best trainer and I hated running. We would run out of the ground and go up to Clifton Ings and back and, as soon as I went through the gates, I thought: 'Why am I doing this?' I didn't understand the point of going all that way just to come back, while Chris Topping was so fit, he'd just be talking to Walter Wilkinson at the front all the way there and back." Crawford was more of a man for short distances, explaining: "We did shuttle runs - or 'doggies' as we used to call them - in the car park on the black ash. Ron Spence used to keep a book with the times in and none of the lads could beat me over 10 yards. Any further though and I was in trouble."

Chris Topping is presented with the Billy Fenton Memorial Clubman of the Year award for the club's first season in the second division in 1974/75. Phil Burrows had been the first winner of the prestigious trophy during the previous season. It was presented on the pitch almost every season at Bootham Crescent afterwards by 1955 FA Cup semi-final hero Billy Fenton's widow and the always resplendent Margot (pictured left) or, as her health deteriorated, the couple's sons

Despite the unprecedented interest in City, four home Saturday matches - against Orient, Southampton, Sheffield Wednesday and Nottingham Forest - were still switched to Friday night kick-offs to avoid clashes with Leeds United fixtures at Elland Road. Midweek games were also staged on Tuesday nights rather than Monday evenings, as had been the previous tradition at Bootham Crescent, with a recognition that the move would give players' bodies more time to recover between matches.

One of Bootham Crescent's most recognisable faces Raymond "Nobby" Clarke died, meanwhile, in September 1974 at the age of 69. For years, he had dressed up as a pearly king for big matches and paraded around the pitch. Recalling Nobby's presence at the ground, Topping said: "He was a nice old chap, who you noticed at big games, like cup ties. It was good that he saw us get promoted and, hopefully, he died a happy man."

On the eve of the most eagerly-anticipated season in the club's history, however, all was not harmonious at Bootham Crescent following a dispute about the withdrawal of car park privileges that threatened a players' strike. As councillor WH Shaw had predicted when the club moved to Bootham Crescent in 1932, the small car park was now proving inadequate, especially for second division football. "The bombshell came the day before we played Aston Villa," Chris Jones explained in his autobiography. "After training Friday, Tom Johnston emerged from his office and announced that there would be no car parking spaces available for the players and wives at the ground. Instead, we would have our pre-match meal at the Clifton Bridge Hotel, leave the cars there and walk to the ground. Uproar, call it what you want, but we thought we had just become third-class citizens, chucked on the muck-pile while the directors played big-time operators without any consideration or discussions with us. Tom Johnston and Colin Meldrum were asked to leave, and the players slammed the door to hold a Bolshevik-style meeting. After 15 minutes of heated discussions, including some asinine ideas like refusing to play and not leaving the Clifton Bridge to the ground, we elected Barry Swallow and Barry Lyons as senior professionals to go and demand a meeting with the chairman. None of us thought that Tom would go out of his way and insist on car park spaces for us, so it had to be the chairman Bob Strachan. When the lads came back, we had been offered three nominated spaces in the car park for the season and designated cars would drive the 12 selected players to the ground. We accepted and duly arrived crammed like cattle into the cars. Promotion to the second division had overawed the directors and they were too willing to look after the visitors at the team's expense. What a nonsense the day before a big game."

The car-park privilege for players would be removed completely in later years and never restored, although Topping was less concerned by the inconvenience than Jones, reasoning: "It was a bit of a minor issue we had with Tom Johnston. I'd have parked anywhere and walked, but Chris wouldn't have wanted to walk very far. In fact, if you ask Jimmy Seal, he would tell you he never wanted to run very far either!" Indeed, Seal was not as upset by the parking disagreement as his striking partner, saying: "It was all to do with the chairman and directors. We had our pre-match meal at the Clifton Bridge Hotel and walked down and I didn't feel that was a problem because I'd always left my car there before anyway. We'd meet up at about 12, have a meal and then have a 10-minute walk down to the ground, which was good for you." Lyons made light of the dispute too, arguing: "It was something for the players to moan about, but it wasn't really a problem. We just left the cars at the Clifton Bridge Hotel and walked down."

With red meat often on the menu at the Clifton Bridge Hotel, a walk to the ground was probably advisable with Crawford echoing Brian Pollard's recollections when he added: "We used to have our pre-match meals at the Clifton Bridge Hotel, where we'd have steak, scrambled eggs or toast and jam. We'd all be sat there on a big, long table and Tom would come

Barry Swallow leads York City out for their first game as a second division club against Aston Villa on August 17, 1974

around and say: 'Just you be careful what you're eating'. Then, he would go to one particular player - and I won't say who - and tell him: 'You can have chips, son'. That was his way of saying he wouldn't be required that afternoon."

The mild-mannered Topping believed, nevertheless, that seeds of discontent had been brewing before the car park dispute, saying: "Tom was a dour Scot, who had strange ways and was very stingy with money. When we won promotion, Phil Burrows asked for a rise but didn't get it. Instead, he got lots of money at Plymouth, but he was one of our best players and Tom should have kept him. We had problems with Tom as a squad and it leaked to the press that the players were revolting against him. Phil Burrows led a bit of that and it was silly things like the showers not getting cleaned. I know we could have done them ourselves, but these little things can become big things, so we had a meeting with the chairman and he spoke to Tom, so it all got sorted out."

Lyons shared Topping's sentiments, too, about simmering unrest at Bootham Crescent, saying: "I found out later that all the players wanted the pay I was on. A lot were saying: 'I want what Barry Lyons is getting' but Tom said: 'No'. Phil was one of the best left backs in the league, so why not reward him? I had come down from the top division and got the same money or a bit more playing for York City, so I was getting quite a bit more than the likes of Phil and Barry Swallow. I didn't tell anybody that, but players found out. They probably went in the office and had a look. I had helped get promotion, but didn't do it on my own and the players were saying: 'I can play as well as he can, so why can't I have the same money?' I wasn't worried about that and, from my point of view, if they wanted me, they had to pay me the wage I was on before and plus. But to say to a lad: 'I'll give you an extra fiver', as Tom would have done, was ridiculous."

Aston Villa keeper Jim Cumbes is beaten by Barry Lyons for York City's first goal as a second division outfit

Some semblance of unity between manager and players had been achieved, though, come Saturday, August 17 when Bootham Crescent staged City's first second division game at home to Aston Villa in front of a 9,396-strong crowd. All 6,000 programmes were sold at the game and, during a 1-1 draw, Lyons scored the first-ever goal at the elevated level as, for two seasons, the ground would also welcome the likes of Manchester United, Chelsea, West Brom, Nottingham Forest, Sheffield Wednesday and Sunderland as league rivals.

The Villa game saw the players receive a huge ovation as they ran out onto the pitch and, urged on by the fans, the home side nearly took a first-minute lead when skipper Swallow headed over from an Ian Butler free kick. Seven minutes later, Villa keeper Jim Cumbes was penalised for carrying the ball too many steps and, from the resultant free kick, Ian Holmes placed a short pass to Lyons, who smashed a low shot through the defensive wall and inside the keeper's right-hand post at the Bootham Crescent end of the pitch. The visitors responded strongly with Crawford making two outstanding saves to deny John Gidman. But Seal went close to doubling the Minstermen's lead on 27 minutes when he rounded Cumbes only to see his shot cleared off the line by full-back Charlie Aitken. Villa levelled against the run of play, though, on the half-hour mark when Ray Graydon headed in from close range. After the break, Swallow and Crawford both worked hard to keep Villa at bay, while Jones and Seal went close to scoring at the other end. Villa also had a goal disallowed and Topping did well to clear two dangerous crosses before Brian Little hit the bar. But the home side also had strong penalty appeals rejected, with a draw representing the fairest final outcome.

Trouble broke out, meanwhile, in isolated incidents away from the ground, but a policeman, stationed on the top of the Supporters' Club with binoculars, helped keep order within the ground. Not everybody was enamoured by the huge crowds now converging on Bootham Crescent, though, with resident Winifred Lewis announcing she intended to dump a bag of empty beer cans at York rates office in protest at the lack of litter bins outside the ground. But most agreed it was a great sporting weekend in York with a record crowd, which might have reduced the Bootham Crescent gate a little, also attending the Benson & Hedges Golf Festival at Fulford, which was won by Belgian Philippe Toussaint.

Villa would go on to finish second division runners-up to Manchester United that season and Topping has fond memories of the historic occasion, saying: "The build-up to kick-off was tremendous. It wasn't often the ground was nearly full and, previously, we'd only really got big gates against teams like Sunderland when they'd bring four or five thousand. There were more than 9,000 there and they were making a lot of noise. We all went out into the middle before the game to wave to the crowd and that was so special. Barry Lyons scored but they equalised, and we had a fair few draws that season. We didn't concede too many goals though and carried that on from the previous season."

Seal, meanwhile, suggested that the result and performance answered some doubts in his mind about his and the team's ability to compete at such a rarefied height. Remembering the fanfare before kick-off and events as they unfurled, Seal said: "We waved to the crowd from the centre circle and all that kind of stuff was just starting to happen in the game. I remember Barry's goal from the free kick being well struck and their goal, which was scored by Ray Graydon, who I knew a little bit from my time at Wolves and Walsall, where we were familiar with the Villa players. Barry's goal was a fantastic moment as we thought we were going to get beaten. We were playing Aston Villa and, whilst it's alright saying you should go out feeling 100 per cent confident, I was thinking they're a good team and I'd have sooner had one of the smaller clubs to start with. But, by the finish of the game, I felt I could compete at that level and that the team could too. You got a bit more time on the ball. They didn't come charging in like they did in the third and fourth divisions. You felt confident to try different things, knowing that the opposition weren't going to come through the back of you. Then later, when we went back down, it was a matter of here we go again."

Crawford was thrilled by the new match-day atmosphere at Bootham Crescent. "That first game in the second division was brilliant," he enthused. "We got a fantastic reception and it was a phenomenal crowd. York had never played at that level and the supporters hadn't seen anything like it. They were really up for it all that season because the only time we normally got to see some of those teams at Bootham Crescent was in the FA Cup."

Lyons enjoyed the pre-match reception from an excited Bootham Crescent crowd, but confessed that the goal was gifted to him by Villa keeper Cumbes. "We waved to the fans and they gave us a good cheer," he recalled. "It was a good feeling going into that game knowing the fans appreciated what you had done the year before. For the goal, we had been awarded a free kick inside the box, but I can't remember why. I usually went over for free kicks and Ian Holmes was standing there. I saw that the wall had been set up with the keeper on one side and the wall had gone too far to the left. There was a gaping gap, so I said to Ian: 'Go and stand behind the ball and just knock it straight to me, not to the right or left'. He did, and I just hit it through the gap and it went in. It was just a basic error by them in terms of lining the wall up and the place erupted when the ball went in. The crowds were great against those big second division teams during that first season. The attendances really bumped up."

A Jones goal then saw City defeat Cardiff 1-0 in their next home match, which was watched by the lowest home crowd of the season of 6,321. The ITV cameras were now regularly showcasing City's matches at Bootham Crescent, meanwhile, with Crawford, five decades on, still owning black-and-white footage of the team's next home match - a 2-2 draw with Notts County in which Seal struck twice. "My daughter got a video of Keith Macklin's highlights for me but, unfortunately for me, it was *Goals on Sunday*, so it just showed all the goals I conceded," the goalkeeping legend smiled. "But we watched the game against Notts County and even my wife commented on the quality of football we were playing. It was unbelievable the way we were passing the ball about. Even though we might not have been as fit as the players now, it was brilliant to watch."

Sunderland's visit in September also witnessed the first all-ticket league match since 1949 when Hull City won 3-1 at Bootham Crescent in front of a crowd of 21,027. Plans to segregate supporters were shelved, though, when Sunderland wanted more tickets than the 6,000 initially given them for the Bootham Crescent End. With the north-east club still wanting more, the City board offered them tickets in the Shipton Street End too, where they could mingle freely with home supporters and it is estimated that around 7,500 Sunderland fans were among the 14,974 crowd that witnessed a 1-0 away win.

As incidences of crowd violence continued to occur, the club also chose to shame City perpetrators by using photographs depicting them causing trouble in the club programme which was, by then, attracting £2,000 in advertisements. Commercial manager Hunt had also put into place a deal, worth £1,500, that would see a Leeds building firm, owned by City fan Peter Gilman, become the club's first match sponsors. Overseas opposition in the form of Icelandic outfit Valur, meanwhile, met City at Bootham Crescent in a friendly, having been in Britain for a week following their 2-1 UEFA Cup defeat to Northern Ireland's Portadown. The hosts won 5-0 with Jim Hinch hitting a hat-trick and Seal and Topping also on target. By the end of October, City fans were in dreamland as their team sat fifth in the table before being beaten 3-1 at home to Bolton.

York City Supporters' Club, meanwhile, were by now hosting Supporters' Clubs from other teams in the National Supporters' Clubs' Quiz Contest. The team, back in 1974, was Dave Batters, Kevin Harper, Dave Stone, Jeff Mortimer, Jeff Simpson and Shane Winship.

The mighty Manchester United's eagerly-anticipated visit then arrived, as almost an early Yuletide present, on the last Saturday before Christmas. Just six years earlier, United had won the European Cup, while City were applying for re-election. But United only edged a tight encounter 1-0 in front of the club's record second division crowd of 15,314, with future City striker John Byrne among the visiting Red Devils fans. By then, the ground's capacity had dropped to 16,637, which was the third-lowest in the entire Football League, with only Hereford and Cambridge United unable to accommodate more supporters. Both ends of the ground had seen 500 knocked off the respective capacities due to crowd safety concerns, with the St Olave's Road End now holding 6,000 and the Shipton Street end 6,100. It was originally announced before a home match with Orient - the first of three Bootham Crescent fixtures before the Manchester United match - that vouchers would be handed out at one of those games, but which one remained unspecified in an attempt to ensure genuine City supporters would gain admission to the big all-ticket clash. Subsequently, though, it was declared that the second of those games - against Millwall - would be the designated fixture. It was the second time the club had used a voucher system, following the Manchester City League Cup tie the season before. A small number of Manchester United fans even chose to miss their team's game against Aston Villa, so they could obtain a voucher. The Old Trafford club's allocation of tickets was also the subject of a programme voucher system. Surprisingly, though, the gate for the Millwall match was the second-lowest of the season up to that point, with a crowd of 6,391. A fixture clash with Leeds was offered as one explanation. Nevertheless, the United ticket still remained the hottest in town and, remembering the occasion, Jones said: "Manchester United were top of the league and they were always going to return to the top flight. It was another bumper crowd of more than 15,000 and I always remember their supporters having a massive police escort from the railway station along Leeman Road, up and over Scarborough Bridge and along to the ground. They did the same for the return trip. Stuart Pearson scored for Manchester United, but I can't say that it was a memorable match."

Topping has not forgotten Pearson's goal that day, though, as the visiting striker stole in front of him to claim the afternoon's decisive touch. "It was a big deal playing Manchester United, but a shame because we lost," Topping admitted. "I was marking Stuart Pearson who scored the goal and it was the speed with which he got to the ball that was frightening. The cross came in and I was going for it, but he got there first." Seal also remembered the thrill of facing the Red Devils at Bootham Crescent. "It wasn't their best team because they were in the second division, but I remember Sammy McIlroy playing and I met him later in life in the boardroom at Bootham Crescent when he was manager of Morecambe," Seal said. "He was a class player - he really was. Stuart Pearson was up front, and the Scots lad Martin Buchan was at centre-half and he was a good player. Playing them must have been even better for the crowd than us though. Fans of other clubs would be asking: 'Who are you playing this week?' and they could say 'Manchester United'."

Lyons, meanwhile, was consumed by the display of colour in the big crowd, explaining: "Against Manchester United, I can just remember Bootham Crescent being red and white. It was the same when Sunderland came and the atmosphere for both games was fantastic. We lost 1-0 to Man United, which wasn't too bad, although some fans were disappointed with that at the time."

Groundsman Jim Smith checks the scaffolding that held the wire-mesh fencing erected at the Grosvenor Road end of the ground for the visit of Manchester United in December 1974

The Manchester United game also saw the designated end for home fans switched from Grosvenor Road to Shipton Street. It was a move that was initially intended as a one-off for the Red Devils' visit, with the Old Trafford club having a reputation for causing trouble. With extra police units drafted in because 7,000 away fans were expected, the decision was made not to have them entering through the car park, where York fans would also be mingling and gaining admission. The switch would subsequently become a permanent feature for home matches from 1976. An application for a new exit route from the ground in the corner that linked the Shipton Street End of the ground with the Main Stand, though, to ease congestion at the end of games and make the ground safer, was turned down by the council, who later advised that it might be permitted on a temporary basis (while City were attracting big crowds), but the cost for the club would have been prohibitive under such circumstances. Entrance to and exit from the ground, therefore, remained only possible from two of the four sides. Despite the United match being sponsored by John Smith's, licensees at the nearby Exhibition Hotel in Bootham and Burton Stone Lane's Corner House Hotel both decided to shut their doors until 7.30pm to avoid potential trouble. The Burton Lane Club in Bootham Crescent also elected not to open until 7pm and many shops and pubs around the ground were boarded up in preparation for the United fans' arrival. Others put security men on their doors. Once in the stadium, meanwhile, the away supporters were also caged in as an 8ft high metal-and-wire fence was erected at the cost of £400 and ran the full width of the pitch behind the St Olave's Road goal, where 6,000 away supporters were accommodated. The measures were in response to some United supporters invading the pitch at Sheffield Wednesday earlier in the month. BBC TV cameras, meanwhile, were scheduled to cover the game for *Match of the Day* but decided not to because of the poor quality floodlights, which would have meant the footage would have had to change from colour for the first-half highlights to black-and-white for the action after the interval. Bootham Crescent's lamps were then made from a mixture of tungsten and mercury, rather than the brighter combination of mercury and sodium, but replacing them would have cost £20,000.

Pearson's goal was scored on 18 minutes following a Willie Morgan centre that wasn't dealt with and the shot crossed the line from just inside the post despite Crawford getting his right hand to the effort. The visitors also had chances to win by a bigger margin. Just five minutes earlier, Brian Greenhoff had struck the home crossbar. In the second half, meanwhile, Crawford pulled off a superb save to prevent Irish international Gerry Daly from finding the top corner. Ron Davies also later saw a chance cleared off the line by Gordon Hunter.

Afterwards, United boss Tommy Docherty was forthright and far from complimentary with his comments on the home performance, saying: "If York are going to get out of trouble, they will have to start playing football. There was only one team trying to do that. York were all kick and rush. It was frustrating for us to play a team like York, but I have played more physical games than that. It was probably hard for them to play because they were under pressure all the time." Responding, Johnston pointed out: "You have to remember that United have spent something like a million pounds. You expect some ability and skill for that sort of money, don't you?"

The game ultimately passed off with little trouble, although one United fan was escorted out of the ground by police after fighting briefly broke out behind the York goal two minutes before the start. But Crawford added that he enjoyed the banter, as he stood just a few yards in front of such sizeable away followings at Bootham Crescent. "In goal, all the fans were behind me and, when the opposition were taking a corner, you were trying to make sure people were marking, but the players couldn't hear me," he pointed out. "The cauldron of noise was unbelievable. But, when the ball was at the other end of the pitch, one of my biggest habits in goal was chewing Beech Nut gum. I would always be going to get a bit out of my bag in the back of the goal and you'd get comments like: 'You'll be in there permanently shortly', but you took that in your stride."

Arsenal, meanwhile, were taken to extra-time in an FA Cup third round replay at Bootham Crescent before Brian Kidd completed his hat-trick in a 3-1 triumph for the Gunners in front of a crowd of 15,362. The attendance heralded a new club record for gate receipts of £9,856, although City were later fined £25 under the Trade Descriptions Act in Selby District Magistrates Court after the admission price for children and OAPs was advertised at 65p, when it was actually £1.25. The club had to pay a Dunnington man, who had complained to the North Yorkshire Consumer Protection Department, back the difference he had paid for four junior tickets. More upset was caused on the night of the game, as hundreds of fans were turned away when the turnstiles were closed at 7.20pm under police orders, with club secretary George Teasdale explaining that those inside the ground had not packed into the terraces correctly despite repeated requests from the police and stewards, as well as over the loudspeaker.

When the action started, the hosts had the better chances to win the tie in normal time, despite Kidd giving the Gunners a sixth-minute lead when he flicked a low shot past Crawford after Eddie Kelly's centre had broken unkindly off Topping. City went on to offer more of a first-half threat thereafter, as Jones and John Woodward both failed to convert one-on-one chances against Jimmy Rimmer and Swallow headed against the bar from a Butler corner. John Radford did, however, head against the foot of Crawford's post on the stroke of half-time. City deservedly levelled on 69 minutes when Lyons was fouled by Bob McNab deep on the right and, after Ian Butler flighted the free kick in, the ball wasn't properly cleared. Swallow knocked it back into the goalmouth and Seal flicked it on, before Lyons rushed in to score with a low shot off the inside of Rimmer's right-hand post. But, in the third minute of extra-time, the London giants were back in front when Cliff Calvert decided to play a 40-yard back pass to Crawford, with the City keeper initially unaware of his intentions. When he did then react to meet the ball, he smacked it against Kidd and it rebounded into the net. More misery was to follow for Crawford in the second period of injury time when a 15-yard Kidd effort trickled between his legs.

There was further agony for Topping, too, after the match as he walked into the car park to drive home. "The Arsenal match was a night game and there was a big crowd," he explained. "I must have been allowed to use one of the car park spaces, because I remember parking my MGB GT sports car in there and it was my pride and joy back then. I remember Brian Kidd being wonderful in that game. He was another tremendous England striker and got a hat-trick. It was a hard game, but we equalised through Barry Lyons, which was wonderful, and Barry was always the man for a big game. But, at the end of the match, everyone wanted to get away quickly because it had gone to extra-time and they took a short cut over the bonnet and roof of my MG sports car to get over the wall of the car park. It was an easy route out for the fans and I had to have the car bonnet repaired because it was a real mess."

Topping was not the only player of that period to suffer a damaged vehicle in the Bootham Crescent car park. The team's success led to sponsorship opportunities with nearby dealers and Seal laughed: "I remember when John Stone and Barry Swallow had been given cars by a local firm. John had got a Ford Capri and they had long fronts. He brought it into the car park to show everybody and crashed it straight into the wall. He parked it where the back of the Main Stand was on the left as you came through the gates. He had never driven a Capri before and didn't realise how close he was to the wall. He gave it a right bang on its nose and we all had a good laugh."

It was a wonder, meanwhile, that there was not further car-park carnage during that era with mini grands prix starting and finishing at the ground. "We used to train up at the university and, as part of the spirit we had at Bootham Crescent at the time, we would race each other in cars there and back," Crawford revealed. "There would even be a big charge to get out of the gates first. You would really go for it and see who gave in. Somehow, there were never any crashes. York wasn't like it is now and the roads weren't busy. We'd also come to the last junction before the gates at the ground at full throttle and everyone would be straining their necks to see if nothing was coming and we could shoot straight across without stopping."

Seal, meanwhile, was also left amused by the reaction of an England World Cup winner to barracking from the Bootham Crescent faithful during that Arsenal replay. Recalling the match, he said: "It was a tough game, but Barry scored the equaliser after I headed the ball to him. It was a really low header and he just tapped it in from about 10 yards. I then thought we had a chance in extra-time until Brian Kidd got a couple more. Alan Ball was playing as well. I'm sure he was the England captain at the time and, for some reason, our fans booed him. It wasn't just York fans doing it either. He got that all around the country just like Wayne Rooney did in later years. I don't think he liked it and he shouted at the crowd when it was 3-1. He said: 'You can all p**s off now. It's all over, so go home'. I just burst out laughing when he said that because I thought it was dead funny, even though I knew I shouldn't, because I would have been in trouble if somebody had seen me. He had been taking all that stick every time he touched the ball and, in that game, I thought he was possibly the best player I ever played against. Kidd was good, but Alan Ball had everything, apart from being good in the air, because he was so tiny. He had respect from all the rest of the players as well. They wanted to give him the ball and the top players always get more touches on the ball. We always seemed to get drawn against the top teams in the cup competitions and that made it harder for us to have a good run."

Lyons still believed the difference on the night was Kidd, who he had encountered in the past on international duty. "It went to extra-time and then Brian Kidd got a hat-trick," he said. "He was a good player and I had met him before when we were both picked for England under-23s at Nottingham. I was substitute, but they didn't have a top coat for me, so I borrowed his jacket to sit on the touchline. I remember we were a bit tired during extra time against them, which was unusual because we trained hard at York, but they overpowered us during that last half-hour."

Crawford, meanwhile, admitted he was culpable for one of Kidd's goals, as Arsenal finished the game strongly. "We were doing really well, then Brian

244

Kidd scored the first goal in extra-time," he explained. "I let one of his goals (Kidd's third) in between my legs. One was definitely my fault and a mistake, but I think the game was over by then and Arsenal had some good players."

Following that defeat, the shock confirmation came that Johnston - arguably the best manager in the club's history - had been released from his contract to take over as general manager at then third division strugglers Huddersfield. Johnston had requested permission to leave before the match and the board of directors, who met with him on the eve of the Cup tie, could not dissuade the single-minded Scotsman. Topping confessed that his departure came as a surprise at Bootham Crescent. "The news just literally broke," he revealed. "There was no warning and Tom wouldn't have wanted that. He had ties with Huddersfield and wanted to go there. It was a shock, though, because we felt there was no reason he should go, but maybe he felt he had taken the club as far as he could. There had been a bit of antagonism with Phil Burrows and a few of the players too about how things were being done in the changing rooms and he'd probably had enough. There was little daft things like the showers always being cold that never got sorted, but he went over night and didn't say goodbye. He was not that type of person. He wasn't a players' manager, but he was brilliant at moulding a team together."

Crawford's views of Johnston were very similar. He said: "Tom never said much. I think he spent all his time watching games and seeing which players could fit into his side. He wasn't the best tactically and his team-talk on a Saturday would be: 'You played these last season and they're just the same, other than two new players' and that was it." Crawford also offered an insight into Johnston's unpredictable nature, adding: "I lived in Sheffield when I joined York and I remember having a game one Saturday and I phoned Tom up because there was two feet of snow. I used to meet a lad called Paul Moloney at Pontefract and we would drive together. When I told Tom, he said: 'Yes. It's the same here, the game is off, but I still want you at the club'. So we scrambled our way through and, when we arrived in the dressing room, Tom said we weren't going to train and that he was going to take us for a good walk to the Ainsty on Boroughbridge Road and back instead. That's what he had got me in from Sheffield for and that was just Tom - you never knew where you were with him."

Seal added that Bootham Crescent was in a state of disbelief following Johnston's departure. "It was a shock," he confessed. "There was no little announcement to the players and he didn't want any fuss, but his record was fantastic, and he got respect from the lads." Lyons has the same memories of Johnston's departure, saying: "He just went and the next morning somebody told us he had left and gone to Huddersfield. It was a shock because you wondered why he would want to. He had put a good team together who looked like they would stay in the second division, which we did. Knowing Tom, though, he probably wanted a bit more money and fancied a change because he had been there six-and-a-half years."

Another convinced that Johnston's reasons for leaving were financial was Crawford, who added: "It was disappointing when Tom left. York had a reputation for not paying the biggest wages. Don't get me wrong, we were always alright as players, but I think the reason Tom went was because of money as he went to Huddersfield when we were in the second division and it was a sad day. People like Phil Burrows didn't get on with him, but he was good to me. He gave me a few rollickings now and again, but I can't remember him ever dropping me. I thought he was alright as long as you didn't beat him at draughts. He used to take his board everywhere and challenge everyone to a game and, to be fair, he never lost because his brain was so sharp."

Johnston had been at the helm since October 1968 and trainer-coach Clive Baker took over as caretaker chief until February 1975 when 37-year-old Wilf McGuinness - the man who had struggled as Matt Busby's successor at Manchester United - was appointed as manager. Johnston stayed for one final fixture before leaving for Huddersfield, as a Southampton team, featuring England strikers Mick Channon and Peter Osgood, were held to a 1-1 draw at Bootham Crescent. For Topping, that meant he relished another chance to lock horns with Channon following the epic FA Cup tie between the clubs four seasons earlier. The City stalwart came out on top too, saying: "Mick Channon was playing at centre-forward and I scored for York, but he didn't score on the day and that was great because I thought he was everything a centre-forward should be. He was a tremendous player and I felt an affinity with him because he was a country boy and liked horses as I did. There was nothing nasty between us, but we went for every header and tackle and gave everything we had got, which you should do. There was a lot of talk about who was the better England striker Mick Channon or Phil Boyer at the time. I played against Phil when he played for Bournemouth and Norwich six times and he never scored against me and I felt Channon was that bit better. He was taller and faster, although Phil was smaller and could get around the field better and I enjoyed pitting my wits against them both."

Crawford also had great admiration for Channon but suggested that the England international was unlucky not to get on the scoresheet in that match. "The standard of shots I faced improved in the second division," the former Sheffield United net-minder explained. "I remember when we played Southampton at Bootham Crescent and Mick Channon went through on his own. I came out to close him down and, when he hit the ball, I thought: 'Brilliant, he's pushed that wide'. But, I watched the ball bend and it hit the outside of the post and went out for a goal kick. It had nearly gone in and I found you couldn't read players at that level as well. They were much more skilful, and you couldn't tell what they were going to do. Some of them, like Channon, were first division players that had come down and they had much more skill than we had."

Indeed, while Channon was kept off the scoresheet, he did deliver the cross that saw Osgood grab the opening goal for the Saints that night. Away boss Lawrie McMenemy commented afterwards, though, about the difficulty any side faced attempting to leave Bootham Crescent with any reward. He said: "I've brought Grimsby, Doncaster and now Southampton to Bootham Crescent and have always found it difficult to go away with anything. It is a compact ground and the crowd gets behind City and lifts them."

Topping revealed, meanwhile, that his first impressions of McGuinness at Bootham Crescent were not favourable, pointing out: "I remember Wilf coming in with a big grey raincoat on and, with his bald head, he looked like Uncle Fester out of the Addams Family. He kept us up, but we were well-placed when he came, and it was the next year when the new players came in that we struggled. Once you get into a slide like that, you've had it. Wilf came and brought his own men like Eric McMordie and Derrick Downing, but they weren't as committed to York as we were. Steve James came in as well and there were two or three Manchester United players that were signed, and it changed the atmosphere around the place. We felt Clive (Baker) should have been manager and that Wilf shouldn't have been there. Clive knew everything about football outside of the top division and liked good football. He knew the lads and would have been an excellent choice." It's a viewpoint that was shared by Seal, who said: "For me, Clive was the best coach by a mile at York City whilst I was there, and we were doing well under him. When he spoke, everybody listened and there was no messing about."

Crawford was no McGuinness fan either, saying: "Going into the second division, we had been stepping into the unknown, but we came away that season thinking we had done quite well and we did rise to the challenge. I believe we should have stayed there, but the appointment of Wilf McGuinness proved to be a bad one. He was a great bloke and coach but, in my opinion, he went about things the wrong way. We had been competing well and doing ourselves justice in that division, but he told us we weren't good enough and started to bring new players in, whilst others left, and things started to go downhill."

Before McGuinness was appointed, Baker enjoyed a 3-0 triumph over Yorkshire neighbours Sheffield Wednesday during his temporary tenure - a victory that saw Butler on the scoresheet and Lyons bag a brace in front of 10,552 supporters. The latter had turned down a move to Hillsborough prior to joining City and said: "Sheffield Wednesday were a strong side and, for some reason, I found myself in the box against them for one of my goals and the goal was empty. I was just sauntering along, thinking I will just tap it in when somebody jumped at me from behind and hit me, but I just managed to touch the ball and it went in. They had brought oodles of supporters having come down from the first division. The season before I came to York, Sheffield Wednesday had offered to buy me for £40,000. I only found out at 12noon on deadline day and transfers had to be done by 5pm back then. After a chat with my wife, we decided to stay at Nottingham because I'd only been there two years but, when it all settled down, I thought it meant that Nottingham Forest didn't really want me and eventually I decided to go to York."

The early days of McGuinness' reign at Bootham Crescent had appeared encouraging when, after caretaker chief Baker signed off with a 1-1 home draw against Brian Clough's Nottingham Forest, the new boss won his first two matches at home against Bristol City (1-0) and Fulham (3-2). "During your first home game as a manger, you just want to get a result and I managed to win the first two," McGuinness recalled. The home victory against Fulham in March was a genuine season highlight with the visitors, who would go on to reach the FA Cup final, featuring England's World Cup-winning captain Bobby Moore at the heart of their defence. Fulham had also gone 13 games without a defeat prior to the game and, along with the legendary Moore, his former Three Lions team-mate Alan Mullery, who ended the season as the Football Writers' Player of the Year, was in the visitors' line-up, as was future City coach Viv Busby.

An electrifying start to the game had the scores level at 2-2 with just 20 minutes on the clock. Jones opened the scoring on seven minutes when he ran on to a cross from Pollard and chipped keeper Peter Mellor. The Londoners levelled four minutes later when Alan Slough hit a low shot past Crawford after riding ineffective challenges by Calvert and Swallow. Then, on 19 minutes, Busby spectacularly found Crawford's top-left corner with a tremendous shot. But, straight from the kick-off, Jones glanced in a header from Pollard's cross. After the break, Jones then charged clear on 51 minutes and, as he was about to shoot, was brought down by Moore for a penalty that Holmes converted in his customary calm manner. Crawford went on to make two magnificent saves to complete a fine double over the Craven Cottage outfit and City's players received standing ovations at half-time and following the final whistle.

Jones unsurprisingly has fond memories of his tangle with Fulham and the legendary Moore, saying: "The game against Fulham was to determine our season and hopefully keep us out of the danger zone of relegation. By then, Cardiff City had joined Sheffield Wednesday as the teams most likely to go down, but it is a lot easier to decide your own fate and win the targeted games. Fulham, whom we had beaten at Craven Cottage on *The Big Match* in October, were one of the sides we needed to beat. I always remember the Fulham games for pitting myself against the late, great Bobby Moore and for somehow coming out on top in the three games I played against him. Having scored two goals at Craven Cottage, I got two goals in the first 20 minutes of the return fixture. For the first goal, Brian Pollard, who was in for Barry Lyons on the right wing, whipped in a cross to the near post and I made the run across two defenders and delicately chipped the ball with my right foot up and high over their keeper Peter Mellor and in off the far angle of the left-hand post and crossbar. The game was an attacking goal-fest and, after Fulham had gone 2-1 up, Brian Pollard was off down the right wing again and fired a cross into the box and I again got across Bobby Moore and glanced a header across Mellor into the net. The crowd was manic and baying for more goals as the game switched from end to end with chances going begging for both sides. I could have had a couple more goals with better finishing and the same went for Viv Busby for Fulham. We carried on in the attacking vein in the second half and, after 50 minutes, Ian Butler beat two men down the left wing and sent me through on goal. I raced down the middle and I was in the process of shooting but got clipped by Bobby Moore in the penalty area and, falling, blasted my shot wide. The ref pointed to the penalty spot and I wanted the goal to complete my hat-trick. I'd also had a good goal disallowed in the game at Fulham that would have completed my hat-trick there. Only Ian Holmes, of our regular penalty takers, was on the pitch as I put the ball on the spot, but I could see Wilf McGuinness frantically jumping up and down as Ian ran up and shoved me out of the way. I looked over to the bench and Wilf looked a relieved man as I reluctantly relinquished the ball to Ian. Holmesy dutifully despatched the penalty, as he always did, and my immediate chance of a hat-trick disappeared. It was a great game to play in though and there were more chances at both ends but none fell to me. It finished 3-2 but it could easily have been 8-6. We all came off to a standing ovation and we knew that the points gave us breathing space at the bottom of the division. We had also completed doubles over both the teams that would make Wembley appearances in 1975's two major cup finals - Fulham and Norwich."

Pollard - the architect of City's first two goals - also gave the legendary Moore a torrid time during the match but modestly put the praise he received afterwards in context, reasoning: "It was good, but it also felt wrong in a way. I can remember going past him quite easily, but it was almost like doing him an injustice because I wasn't really fit to lace his boots. I was getting all the plaudits from the directors afterwards for my performance but, when you think of what he had achieved and done in the game, it all seemed a bit false. I certainly wouldn't have been able to do that to him three or four years previously." Topping also regarded the game as one of the campaign's most memorable occasions, recalling: "It wasn't just Bobby Moore. Players like Alan Mullery and Viv Busby were in that team too, but Ian Holmes took a good penalty. He'd shown that against Bristol Rovers the season before. Bobby Moore was never the fastest and he was even slower by that stage, but he was still cultured and had an aura about him. Chris Jones enjoyed playing against him though."

On facing an England icon, Seal added: "That was fantastic. He was maybe not quite at his best, but he was still a really good player and a legend. Just talking to him on the pitch was special. I can't remember what was said, but we just had a little chat if something had happened in the game and he wished me all the best afterwards." A thrilled Lyons added: "We beat Fulham with all those stars in their side and nobody could quite believe that little old York had done that."

For Crawford, meanwhile, the standing ovation at half-time still stands out as a spine-tingling Bootham Crescent moment. "We got into the changing room and just wanted to get straight back out after that reaction from the crowd, so we could carry on playing against all those good players."

The April home match against Blackpool would then be the first in which the match ball was officially sponsored, with the Supporters' Club paying for it from money raised by their "Golden Goal" sweepstake. But, with three games left, City could not take their first chance to mathematically preserve division two status for another season when they lost 3-1 at home to West Brom - a match notable for the debut of future England captain Bryan Robson at the age of 18. The visitors' £135,000 Scotland international Willie Johnston also opened the scoring.

City would eventually finish a respectable 15th, though, with safety ensured following a 3-1 win at Bristol Rovers in the next game and the historic campaign concluded with a 0-0 home draw against Oldham. That match was marred, however, by more fighting in the ground between supporters that led to 18 arrests, after bottles and cans were thrown as missiles. The average crowd during that first season in the second tier was 8,828 - the highest since 1956/57 - with Seal admitting the atmosphere at Bootham Crescent was intoxicating as some of the biggest clubs in the country paid a visit. "It was fantastic," Seal explained. "Even four or five thousand looked full at Bootham Crescent but, during the first season in the second division, they were all squeezed in and the atmosphere was great. The likes of Manchester United, Sunderland, Norwich, West Brom and Southampton were all coming to us for league games and the attendance numbers were incredible because it was a novelty for the fans as well. Barry Lyons and Ian Butler had played at higher standards for quite a while, so they knew what it was all about, but the rest of us didn't and it was great."

John Ledgeway - a City regular during those heady 1970s days - recalled that the players' performances on the pitch, though, were often more illuminating than the ageing floodlights that season. He said: "I remember York's 1-0 win over Norwich in November that season being the main match on Keith Macklin's *Sunday Soccer* Yorkshire Television highlights programme but, when it got to half-time, they said they couldn't show the second half because the floodlights weren't bright enough and the footage was too dark. Luckily, Jimmy Seal scored the only goal of the game in the first half." Topping saw no problems with the strength of Bootham Crescent's floodlights, though, insisting: "As players, we felt the lights were fine and we just got on with it." If anybody would have been concerned by the supposed darkness if would have been the team's keeper, but Crawford added: "I thought the lights were good compared to what I had experienced in Scotland at East Stirling and I didn't have trouble with them.

Club secretary George Teasdale and office secretary Susan Garrod put reserved signs on Main Stand seats, which were all snapped up by season-ticket holders for the first time ever ahead of the club's first season in the old second division in 1974-75

You went to other grounds and got a bit of a glare, but that wasn't the case at Bootham Crescent."

The TV cameras, meanwhile, were positioned in a temporary gantry situated on top of the Popular Stand and accessed by a perilous climb up a ladder. This would become the norm for future cameramen although, for several months in 2016/17, they were temporarily relocated to the directors' box, while emergency work was applied to the gantry.

The club sign on the top of the car park gates had to be taken down in the summer of 1974 as three Portakabins were delivered for additional office space. Coach Colin Meldrum and forward John Peachey are pictured with the sign

CHAPTER 17

Back-to-back relegations and Elton John
puts the kettle on

*"He dived and, while Chris never swore very much, I remember him calling
Keegan a 'chuffing cheat'."*

Bootham Crescent's second season in division two got off to a bright start
quite literally - after new floodlights had been installed in June on the existing
pylons. Thirty more powerful bulbs replaced the previous 24, but there were
dark days ahead as Wilf McGuinness' tenure began to unravel.

Despite a 2-1 opening day home win over Portsmouth with new signing from
Middlesbrough - Eric McMordie - on target, the rest of City's campaign would
prove very disappointing. Barry Lyons joined McMordie on the scoresheet but
stressed that his fellow marksman was not a popular addition to the squad.
"Eric McMordie was one of Wilf's boys, who had been on trial at Manchester
United," Lyons explained. "I don't think anybody got on with him at York, but
he was picked every game whether he played well or not. That felt like the case
with all the players Wilf brought in and things fell away from then on. Wilf
also tried to be one of the boys and that didn't really work either. I didn't last
much longer, but I had enjoyed those first couple of years playing at Bootham
Crescent. It was a compact ground and the playing surface was good. Bryan
Foster did a good job on the pitch. Night games were always special too with
the atmosphere under the lights, especially with a bit of crispness in the air and
dew on the ground."

Season tickets, meanwhile, had doubled in price for the new campaign in
certain areas of the ground, with the cost for a seat in the Popular Stand going
up from £14 to £24 - the same price as in the Main Stand. But purchasers of
senior season-tickets before May 31 had benefitted from the club's first early-
bird discount offer of £2. Explaining the hike-up in Popular Stand prices, club
secretary George Teasdale reasoned: "These seats have a very good view, are

sheltered from the elements and, in our opinion, are now every bit as good as the Main Stand seats, so we have charged the same price."

Brian Pollard also suggested, meanwhile, that team spirit was rapidly deteriorating at Bootham Crescent under McGuinness, following a flawed recruitment policy. "Some of the lads resented it when Wilf McGuinness brought in his ex-Manchester United players and started replacing players who had taken the club from the fourth to the second division," he pointed out. "We had done all the hard work, but some players were starting to get kicked out and that wasn't very nice. Tony Young was brought in midfield and Steve James at the back. They had the pedigree, but I felt some of them were just there for the money. We had fought to get to the second division and now these players were taking our places. I wouldn't go as far as saying it was becoming a joke by then, but some of the things that were going on, you wouldn't want happening at your football club. I could see that even as a relatively young player still." Topping agreed with Pollard about the changing atmosphere at Bootham Crescent, pointing out: "The Manchester United and Middlesbrough contingent were brought in and, while the likes of Steve James, Derrick Downing, Eric McMordie and Robert Hosker were all good players, York City was not their team. That's what the players from the previous two seasons felt. The togetherness had gone. We had

World Cup-winning captain Bobby Moore jumps for a header as Fulham lose 1-0 at Bootham Crescent in November 1975

something very special in 1973/74 and 74/75. We had a group of players who socialised together, as did our wives. We would have done anything for each other. We'd have risked our lives if we had been at war together and we certainly risked injury. I remember Dennis Wann breaking his leg. That attitude was missing when we started losing and some players had gone. You get into habits and, once you get on a run like that, it's hard to get out of. You almost need a bad refereeing decision to stir the crowd."

During the first half of the season, a rare highlight was provided in November when, following a run of seven successive defeats, the Fulham side, still consisting of Bobby Moore and Alan Mullery, were once more beaten with an Ian Holmes penalty securing a 1-0 triumph. Moore was culpable for the spot kick with his short pass intercepted by Chris Jones, who was brought down by Cottagers keeper Peter Mellor.

The team also showed some fight during the closing weeks, winning four consecutive games at Bootham Crescent, including triumphs over Nottingham Forest and Southampton. Such results suggested that few of the division's leading lights still relished a visit to North Yorkshire and McGuinness maintained: "We had some good games against the bigger teams at Bootham Crescent. I don't think they liked going there because it did not hold a lot of supporters and was a small ground. We lost so many balls but the playing surface was always good. That wasn't a problem." Pollard also felt Bootham Crescent played its part in unsettling some of the big-name visitors during those two campaigns in the second tier. "The stadium and big crowds helped us back then," he admitted. "In a small ground that was so enclosed and tight, the noise was incredible really. The away dressing rooms were not that big either and opposition players might have felt uncomfortable coming to us."

Mick Channon scores for promotion-chasing Southampton in March 1976. City won the game 2-1, but could not stave off the inevitability of relegation

But the fourth victory in that sequence - a 3-1 win over Plymouth that represented the biggest triumph of the campaign - proved little consolation as a win for Carlisle meant the club were relegated with four games still to play. "It was a battle to stay up and you got that feeling that it wasn't going to happen even though we kept plugging away," McGuinness recalled. "Big clubs could buy, and we couldn't compete financially. We needed more of everything - more fans, more players and more money." Despite the late rally, Pollard reckoned the writing was on the wall long before the Plymouth match. Pollard scored in a match that also saw future England striker Paul Mariner, watched on the day by then national manager Don Revie, make the scoresheet and he added: "By that time most of the old players had gone and the atmosphere was very different, but I remember scoring in the Plymouth game because Phil Burrows was playing for them. I didn't get much out of him, though, because you knew that if you went past Phil more than once, he would put you in the stands the next time."

Topping reasoned that the opposition's long journeys might have played a part in the team's late rally in front of their own fans, but also spoke of his pride in still producing his best for the Bootham Crescent faithful despite relegation being unavoidable. "It's always nice to be at home and the fact those teams had to come up from Plymouth and Southampton might have been a factor too," he said. "They can fly or go by train now. Home advantage always counts more when you're on a winning run, but we still wanted to win because it was our team and profession. We still wanted to do our best, even though we knew by then we would be going down to the third division." Graeme Crawford concurred with his old team-mate's views, reasoning: "Coming to Bootham Crescent was still hard for a lot of the clubs. They were used to massive grounds, but Bootham Crescent was compact, and everything was on top of you. Even though it wouldn't have been intentional, they might have been expecting an easy game as well, but we didn't lie down, even when things weren't going right for us."

A 2-2 draw against Chelsea, with goals from Jimmy Seal and Micky Cave in front of 4,914, saw the curtain come down on second division football in York on April 24, 1976 with the club finishing second-bottom above Portsmouth. For Seal, the game represented a final opportunity to lock horns with one of the country's leading talents at the time. "I scored in that Chelsea game when Butch (Ray) Wilkins played and what a player he was," Seal recalled. "Until you play against or train with these lads, you don't really realise what they are like. You really find out how good they are when they're playing for the opposition and

Chris Topping goes in for a header during the last second division match to be staged at Bootham Crescent against Chelsea

he was top drawer. It was sad, though, at the end of our last game in the second division. When you do something like we did with that promotion, the fans probably never thought we could and we had our doubts, but we did it and, then, to go down it was a real disappointment. I still think we were the club's best team ever and that's not me being big-headed. Denis Smith also built a good team, but we were playing at a different standard."

The average crowd that campaign had fallen to 5,189, with as few as 2,857 witnessing a 2-0 defeat to Orient and, on the dwindling attendances, McGuinness said: "Bootham Crescent was a lovely ground - small and compact. I was just disappointed we could never fill it. Those that did come were brilliant though. They really got behind us and were always nice to me."

Crawford recalled the atmosphere at home games changing during that second season in division two, saying: "We had a great rapport with the fans, but they were even starting to get at the likes of Barry Lyons and Ian Holmes, who the crowd loved, and that's when everything breaks down." He never felt that match against Chelsea would represent the final second division game ever to be played at Bootham Crescent, though, saying: "I thought the club would get back up there one day and they have come close a few times. I think Denis Smith's side could have done it with a bit more luck and Alan Little's team nearly got there as well. There's always the potential to get back to a higher level if the structure at the club is right."

Prior to the Chelsea game, meanwhile, Bootham Crescent had hosted an England v Wales schoolboy international seven days earlier. Wayne Clarke - the brother of Leeds striker Allan who would go on to play for the likes of Wolves and Everton himself - opened the scoring for the Three Lions team. Fellow future top-flight professionals Andy Ritchie and Brendan Ormsby also played in the England team, while Kevin Ratcliffe, who would later captain Everton to domestic and European success, was in the Wales side.

The club also crossed swords with Liverpool for the first-ever time that season in the League Cup, with queues for tickets starting to form outside Bootham Crescent from 4am on the first day of sales. But the match fell well short of a full house with Liverpool only selling 450 tickets for a tie that held little appeal for the Merseyside giants, whilst a decision to charge juniors the full adult price put others off.

Emlyn Hughes congratulates Liverpool team-mate Alec Lindsay after he had converted a late penalty, controversially won by Kevin Keegan, to secure a 1-0 win in a 1975 League Cup tie

A controversial 87th-minute penalty, when Topping was adjudged to have fouled Kevin Keegan, secured a 1-0 win for the Anfield side in front of a crowd of 11,897. Alec Lindsay settled matters from the spot and the decision was still being keenly contested by Topping more than four decades on.

"I gave the penalty away, but I thought it was dubious," he argued. "I was beaten again by the speed of Keegan - similar to when Stuart Pearson got the goal for Manchester United. But I went for the ball and he just toed it past me and fell over, which is the sign of a good striker. Chris Jones would have done the same. Diving wasn't brought over by foreign players as people said it was. Franny Lee was tremendous at it. Keegan went down on the edge of the penalty area and we thought it should have been a free kick at worst, but the referee gave a penalty. He didn't book me, though, which was interesting. After the game, their manager Bob Paisley said: 'Never mind if it was in or outside the box, you should look at Kevin Keegan's ankle', but I didn't mean to hurt him. I just caught his ankle as I got my toe to the ball. You can get injured quite easily without having been fouled. In what he said, Bob Paisley also almost admitted it was outside the box and the decision would never have stood up in court." Lyons had a close view of the incident and agreed that Keegan had conned the officials and outwitted Topping, saying: "Chris was a bit naive. From where I was stood, I knew what was going to happen. Chris was chasing him and, as soon as he got to the penalty box, Keegan stopped and ran into him. I could see it coming."

Crawford recalled Topping's out-of-character response, meanwhile, to Keegan's simulation, saying: "He dived and, while Chris never swore very much, I remember him calling Keegan a 'chuffing cheat'. Alec Lindsay took the penalty and I didn't get near it. He hit it well and it was in the bottom corner."

McGuinness also felt his underdogs were the victims of unfavourable officials that night, reasoning: "In those days, I thought the officials leaned towards the bigger clubs and, from my point of view, it shouldn't have been a penalty." Striker Seal was in rare agreement with his then manager too, adding: "That wasn't a penalty and we all knew that. Kevin Keegan dived into the box, but I suppose we would have done the same. Keegan was also brilliant otherwise."

That was a description Seal also bestowed upon England's Ray Clemence who was keeping goal for the visitors that night. "I remember somebody getting the ball to me on the edge of the box and I turned quickly and had a shot," Seal said. "It was going right into the angle but Ray Clemence was the keeper and he didn't just turn it around the post - he caught it. He flew across his goal to dive and what a save. I'll always remember that. It was 0-0 at the time and I was certain I had scored, and they were a top team." Indeed, the chance, following a mistake by Phil Neal, came just four minutes before Lindsay's spot kick. In the first half, meanwhile, Keegan had seen an opportunity pushed on to a post by Crawford, while Jones missed City's best opportunity of the opening 45 minutes, shooting wide after going past Emlyn Hughes.

Regrettably, hooliganism continued to be prevalent during the season, with a half-time pitch invasion by home fans during the 4-1 defeat to table-topping Bristol City in October leading to trouble in the Popular Stand when the perpetrators jumped into the seated area to try and evade the police. Against new leaders Sunderland the following month - a game which resulted in another 4-1 reverse - five arrests were also made after three windows were broken in the Supporters' Club. Unrest had been caused when some away fans were not admitted into the ground for kick-off, due to problems getting them all through the turnstiles. A firework was also thrown onto the pitch and exploded between Crawford's feet as he went to pick up the ball. The attendance was 15,232 - just short of the then 16,627 capacity. There was trouble too when Chelsea visited in the fourth round of the FA Cup with 14 away fans arrested after the whistle blew for the start of the match and led to scenes of "pushing, hitting, shoving, kicking and shouting" after supporters of the London club infiltrated the Shipton Street End. The thrilling 3-2 victory over Brian Clough's Nottingham Forest, settled by Pollard's 86th-minute winner in March, meanwhile, saw visiting fans invade the pitch at half-time in an attempt to run from the Bootham Crescent End to the Shipton Street terrace. They were stopped by police who, despite being heavily outnumbered, made many arrests.

With the craze for pageants at its peak, the Tadcaster branch of the Supporters' Club also held a beauty queen competition in the Social Club, with the management team of McGuinness and Clive Baker fulfilling judging duties. In February 1976, a representative match between the Universities Athletic Union and an FA XI had also seen former England World Cup winners Bobby Charlton and Nobby Stiles enjoy a run-out for the latter at Bootham Crescent, alongside future City scout Harry Dunn - then a Scarborough player. The game ended 2-2.

Despite the ultimate disappointment of relegation, a *Yorkshire Evening Press* reader Denis Heron, of Stockton Lane, summed up poetically what a trip to Bootham Crescent meant to him, as a season-ticket holder in the Main Stand. "Saturday soccer for us is something special," his letter to the newspaper started. "Mum making the coffee for half-time, the drive to the ground, the comments 'Come on dad, we are going to be late', over the bridge into the little sweet shop on the corner, a friendly chat with the lady, a few laughs and then the atmosphere of nearing the ground. Up the steps into the stand as the cheer greets the team. At this stage all the team is popular, even a few Christian names are used! The regular fans are around us. The man from Beverley and his son never misses and he is always there before us. Behind him, a man and his wife shout a greeting, a few laughs with three others regularly behind. One wag pipes up with 'Don Revie is here today, he is having a rest from football'. The realisation that strangers have become friends over a couple of seasons. What does that mean to me? It is part of the enjoyment and may I suggest for the regulars a big part when the team is not doing well. There are never two games alike and even when we go home disappointed there ARE times when the other team is just too good."

City responded to their return to division three, meanwhile, by slashing their prices. The biggest beneficiaries were Popular Stand season-ticket holders who would pay £20 in 1976/77 - a £4 drop with an additional £2 discount if fans renewed before May 31. General ground admission, at either end, was the only price that remained the same, with the match-day cost of 65p the minimum that could be charged under Football League rules. Enclosure season-tickets, meanwhile, were shelved due to the small demand. Explaining the theory behind the cuts, chairman Bob Strachan said: "The Popular Stand has been half-empty most of the season and, obviously, we want to see it full every Saturday. Some people complain that they won't stand out in the rain for 65p a game. Now, we are saying come along and have a seat at a moderate price."

But the following campaign would see the team, now sporting a white jersey with a maroon Y, tumble out of the third division as well with an average league attendance of 2,986 - the first time that crowds had ever dropped below the 3,000 mark. "It was difficult going back to playing in front of small crowds," Pollard confessed.

Second division hero Seal, meanwhile, was offloaded by McGuinness in November and was saddened by the way life at Bootham Crescent had deteriorated under Tom Johnston's successor. "Wilf McGuinness came in and that's what went wrong at the club," Seal declared. "He was a very friendly, jovial chap away from football and was good company, but he brought in Steve James, Tony Young and a couple more who all had a bit of Manchester United history and there was only Steve James who could play. Wilf was hopeless for the team and nobody liked him. He gradually got rid of all that side. Barry Swallow was first and we were all saying in the dressing room: 'Who's turn is it this month?' He liked me for a good while and I was still playing well, but eventually turned against me. Perhaps I had a few bad games - I can't really remember - but if we had kept Tom or Clive, I think we could have kept going in division two. Ian Butler and Barry Lyons were out of the team very quickly - probably because of their age - but they could still play. It broke the heart of that team and the club. I was one of the last to go but that was nothing to be proud of and I just wanted to leave by that time even though I loved the club, because I knew I wouldn't be in the team with Wilf. He used to tell us all these Man United stories and, while they were alright the first time you heard them, we weren't bothered about all that. I left for Darlington, where Barry Lyons, Dennis Wann and John Stone had all gone. We all travelled there together from York."

On the dwindling crowds at the club he had left, Seal added: "When the crowds drop, your confidence goes as well. It's not good and the least thing that goes wrong they are on to you and that's not the best thing to listen to when you've had all the praise before. I always think instead about being in the second division - the Championship as it is now - and turning up for games in a nice, little ground that was full of people. They were the best of times and that is my abiding memory of Bootham Crescent rather than anything I did there personally either. It was a good club to be at during that time - it really was. We were well paid too.

We would get double the wages of a senior worker at Rowntree. It was a good salary but nothing like it would be in that division now."

Seal had not scored at Bootham Crescent for a final time, though, returning twice with Darlington to remind home supporters of his prowess in front of goal. He was also genuinely moved when the Mintermen faithful expressed their gratitude for his past efforts at their club. "The first time I came back to York, we won 2-1 (in October 1977) and I scored but it felt weird," Seal admitted. "A couple of seasons later, I had been injured and hadn't played for about two games, but the manager told me he would make me sub because it was against my old team. I wasn't 100 per cent fit and we were 3-0 down or something so he said: 'Jimmy, go and get warmed up'. I jumped out of the dugout and ran down the side of the stand and the supporters all just stood up and clapped me. It made the hairs on the back of my neck stand up and I really couldn't believe it. It was wonderful, and I got on and scored again. It was so nice to go back and get that reception even though we ended up losing 3-1. When I went back to Barnsley with York, they booed me which made me mad because I had been their top goalscorer when I left them. But the York fans remembered what I'd done for the club and it's nice to be appreciated."

Trouble continued to typify the matchday experience at Bootham Crescent, meanwhile, with a pre-season "friendly" against Oldham leading to eight arrests, prompting prosecuting magistrates' court chairman Mr E Smith to state: "It should be made clear now that courts, the police and, more important, the public are not prepared this coming football season to endure the disorder and hooliganism they had to suffer last year. We want to see an end to it and will be giving the police every possible support to put a stop to football hooliganism."

For the first time, the new season also kicked off with a League Cup tie as Barnsley visited Bootham Crescent for a 0-0 first-leg Saturday afternoon contest. By the end of October, though, fans were chanting "McGuiness Out" after a humiliating 4-1 home defeat to fellow strugglers Northampton left the club rock bottom of the third division. One rare cause for celebration came in January when future England boss Terry Venables' Crystal Palace team were seen off 2-1 at Bootham Crescent in the league thanks to two headers from Chris Galvin. Venables' verdict at the final whistle was: "No complaints. York worked very hard and deserved their victory." Kenny Sansom, who went on to become a Three Lions left-back and Arsenal favourite, also played in the game.

A 1-1 home draw with Reading, however, meant that, barring a 23-0 final-day victory at Portsmouth, the club were relegated, in front of their own fans on the way to finishing rock bottom. After Gordon Staniforth grazed the crossbar in that game, Holmes opened the scoring on 24 minutes with a 20-yard half-volley. But John Murray replied before the break with a thunderous free kick that crashed in off the crossbar to condemn the hosts to back-to-back relegations with a backdrop of "McGuiness Out" chants and slow handclapping from the season's smallest crowd of 1,748. Topping, who went closest to snatching victory in the closing stages when he forced a good save from visiting keeper Steve Death, admitted that Bootham Crescent had become unrecognisable from the ground that had thronged with five-figured crowds just a season earlier. Recalling the pain of relegation back to the old fourth division, Topping despaired: "There were only 1,748 against Reading. They were also fighting to stay up (Reading would finish the campaign relegated with City) and there are no easy games when you're down the bottom. It was quiet at the ground and you could hear all the individual people with big voices in the crowd. You need a cracking goal or the referee making a mistake to get the supporters rallied in that situation and it was horrible and hard work when the crowds went down. I just tried to do my best in every game and, luckily, eventually Tom Johnston saw that I was still performing well in a bad team and took me to Huddersfield in the end. It was nice that somebody wanted me."

Crawford, meanwhile, made his last appearance a month before the end of the campaign, having decided that the atmosphere at Bootham Crescent had degenerated to such an extent that he no longer wanted to be around the place that had been so much fun just a couple of years earlier. Explaining his feelings, Crawford said: "Managers do come in and break teams up, but the players Wilf brought in were not our type and he tried to change things too quickly. Somebody like Steve James was a great player, but the others weren't and they all seemed to come from Man United or were ex-Man United players. I don't like decrying players but, in my opinion, people like Eric McMordie were in it for the money and things just went from bad to worse. Things were going on in training that you wouldn't believe. I was thinking: 'Is this bloke in the real world?' I ended up leaving York City because of Wilf McGuinness. When it came to the end of the season, the club had an option to keep me for another year. Wilf asked me if I was going to sign for next season. I said: 'That depends. Are you staying?' Wilf said: 'Yes', so I told him: 'Then, I won't be here'. They said: 'What do you mean?' and I explained that I wasn't enjoying myself and didn't feel like I was doing a good job for York City in the circumstances. They told me I wouldn't be able to sign for anybody else and that they would keep my registration and I was out of football for a while. Michael Sinclair tried to persuade me to come back, but Scunthorpe then came in and resurrected my career. The club relented in the end and got a small fee for me. It was very difficult in those last couple of years. Nobody likes to see the crowds dropping because it's a sign of something not being right. I was still trying my best, but a frame of mind sets in and you're feeling things are going against you. You become demoralised. It was really bad when the club were relegated, even though we knew it was going to happen. I wasn't playing by then, because I wouldn't sign a contract, but you still had to go and watch, even though I didn't really want to. I also knew, in my own mind at that stage, that I wouldn't be coming back. Even if we had stayed up, if Wilf was still there, I wouldn't have stayed."

McGuinness struggled to find the players to reverse the slide although the addition of 19-year-old winger Staniforth from Hull City at Christmas time had proven a rare, successful acquisition. "Gordon was a livewire who did well for us and it's a pity I couldn't get a few more in like him," McGuinness reflected. Staniforth, himself, revelled in the chance that McGuinness had given him despite the side's struggles as he played his first home game in front of a Bootham Crescent crowd that was ten times smaller than the one that had witnessed him make his York debut. "All I wanted to do was play for Hull City at the time, but I wasn't getting a chance there and then an offer came in to play for Wilf McGuinness," Staniforth explained. "My first game for York was at Sheffield Wednesday where we lost 3-2 in front of 22,000 fans the day after Boxing Day and that was a dream. But coming back to play at Bootham Crescent in front of 2,000 was still brilliant. All I wanted to do was play football and York City gave me that platform. It was better than the reserves and I just wanted to show off and do my best."

Staniforth also revealed that several areas of the stadium, not just Bryan Foster's precious pitch, were used for training purposes under McGuinness. He said: "I remember playing head tennis in the car park, which was made of gravel and dust, but we would put some string across it and argue left, right and centre about who was winning. We had a great time. Graeme Crawford enjoyed playing it and we used to play on a Friday morning because training sessions were always light the day before a game. We didn't do any shape work. We would just jog around the track, do a few sprints and then play some head tennis or go home. The ground was old and scruffy, but it played a big part in our training regime back then and was the focal point for everything because our training facilities were so poor. We went from one place to another and trained on a bit of grass next to the railway line sometimes. At other times, we would just run up and down the steps in the Shipton Street End and the Main Stand."

Recalling the car-park contests, Crawford said: "We would put a net across the car park and play head tennis or volleyball. It was good fun in that car park." Gary Ford, who had joined the club as an apprentice, was also often summoned to join in long head-tennis battles with the manager. "I found Wilf amazing, but what happened at Manchester United knocked his confidence big time," Ford reasoned. "He was great with us apprentices though. He used to get us in the car park, which was made of ash back then, and we'd play head tennis behind the back of the Main Stand for two hours. Every afternoon, Wilf and John Harrison and John Byrne and me would play Two v Two. Our area as apprentices was the away changing rooms. That's where we lived and every afternoon at 2pm, Wilf would shout 'Apprentice' and we thought: 'Here we go, two hours of tennis'. Wilf got really competitive, but we learned from it. It improved your touch and everything and it probably de-stressed Wilf as well."

Ford and Byrne struck together a strong friendship during those formative years, although the former recalled how the future goalscoring favourite's first steps onto the hallowed turf at Bootham Crescent could have been his last. "I remember John Byrne's first day of training," Ford explained. "Me and John Harrison - the other apprentice - had been with the club a week and he was a bit late coming from Manchester. We were doing sprints on the side of the pitch opposite the dugout and we were told not to walk on the pitch because Fossie would go nuts. We had been given kit, but John had his own Manchester United shirt on, because he'd not been issued with any yet and he ran straight across the pitch after coming out of the tunnel. Well, you can imagine Fossie's reaction - a young 16-year-old doing that. I don't think he did anything that one time, but it was so funny because you knew how he would be feeling. That was the first time John Byrne ran onto that pitch and it could have been the last!"

The home changing room was also a social hub when not being used on match days with Staniforth revealing: "Everyone prefers showers now, but the communal bath was great. It took an eternity to fill but we used to stay in there for hours having a chat after training and it was the place to be. I can also remember the boot room past the away changing room at the end of the corridor and there were a lot of cubby holes back then but the lay-out got a bit more organised as the years went on. The physio's room moved two or three times whilst I was there. He had a little room in the right corner of the changing room as you walk in when I first came to the club. It had a bed in it and that was it. I remember having a stiff neck and John Simpson was the physio. He was old school and would just put you on his bed and jerk it quite violently. That was it. There was no chat or notes written down. I also remember the front offices used to be a boardroom, which was quite palatial, while the general manager's room was above the Social Club." Ford, who was on the verge of breaking into the first team, also enjoyed a spot of banter in the bath but, in the interests of hygiene, continued his washing regime afterwards. "They used to put some sort of antiseptic in the bath and it always smelled of that," Ford recalled. "It must have been Dettol and there was always some carbolic soap or something but, after getting out, I used to go in the showers to get clean. As apprentices, after the first-team players had got out of the bath after a game, we also used to get in it and scrub the footballs clean - me, John Byrne and John Harrison. Charlie Wright used to make sure we made everything spotless for training when he became manager. The three of us used to be in the old boot room too with our backs to the wall and one used to knock the mud off, one would put polish on and the other would buff them up. We used to mix it around from day to day as well, in terms of who would do what."

CM Forth, of New Earswick, meanwhile, wrote to the *Yorkshire Evening Press* to bemoan the ageing facilities of Bootham Crescent during that second successive relegation campaign, asking: "Why encourage City supporters to use the Shipton Street End, traditionally reserved for visiting supporters with its inferior facilities, antiquated toilets and a tea-bar where drinks are available only when the water pipe isn't frozen?"

Back in the fourth division, City slashed their season-ticket prices for a second consecutive campaign with, unusually, admission into the Popular Stand now cheaper than standing behind the goal. Explaining the gesture, secretary Teasdale said: "We are very conscious of the fact that there is a lack of covered accommodation on the ground which, in our present financial position, will not be remedied this year. To encourage people to take advantage of the cover we have, it has been decided to reduce the price for a season ticket." The price for a Main Stand season ticket dropped from £23 to £18 and the Popular Stand price went from £20 to £17. For a matchday transfer to the Popular Stand, meanwhile, the cost went down from 25p to 20p.

An Executive Club was also launched, which would see members pay £100 to the club in return for a season ticket, light refreshments at half-time and the use of facilities, including a bar and colour television. It was the brainchild of supporter and company director Sid Moore and ex-City captain Swallow. Executive members would also be permitted to introduce a guest and would have the opportunity to meet players and their wives, as well as opposition players and officials. All City players, directors and officials were made honorary members of the Executive Club and it was on the site of the former 1974 Club, which had operated during City's two seasons in the second division. It was open to members two hours before games and for one-and-a-half hours afterwards. A five-man committee was headed by Moore with Swallow vice-chairman. Fifty per cent of profits made by the new group were to be given to the club, with the other half used to improve amenities for the Executive Club members. Friday night matches also became commonplace again in a bid to avoid fixture clashes with Leeds United.

The club lost the first-ever penalty shoot-out, meanwhile, to decide a first-team fixture at Bootham Crescent during a League Cup first round replay with Rotherham after the two-legged aggregate score was deadlocked at 3-3. With a replay also failing to separate the teams and the score 1-1 after 120 minutes, Pollard, Holmes, Peter Scott, Staniforth and Bobby Hoy all scored from the spot but, after Rotherham had converted their first sudden-death spot kick, Geoff Hutt's rising shot was easily saved by Millers keeper Tom McAllister. At the time, McGuinness was not pleased with the manner in which the tie was settled, arguing: "Tossing up used to be bad enough but this puts a lot of pressure on the penalty-takers and the goalkeepers. But there was a lot of excitement."

September, meanwhile, saw Billy Bremner's All Star XI take the Bootham Crescent field for Swallow's testimonial. Three hours of entertainment was laid on for the crowd, including the finals of a six-a-side competition won by Riccall United and a hot-shot penalty contest at half-time, which saw Dringhouses' Graham Green presented with the York Crime Prevention Mitchell Trophy after beating former City keeper Crawford four times out of five from the spot. In front of a 3,335-strong crowd, which was only bettered in two league games during the season - against Hartlepool with their large travelling contingent on Boxing Day and against table-topping Watford - Staniforth was thrilled at the chance to showcase his skills against the likes of England legends Bobby and Jack Charlton, while Peter Lorimer, Colin Todd, David Harvey and Kevin Hector also featured and former Bristol Rovers foes Alan Warboys and Bruce Bannister - 'Smash and Grab' - were also reunited for the night. McGuinnes played for City as a winger too during the last quarter of an hour. It was a game as memorable as any at the ground for Staniforth who beamed: "I scored a hat-trick in that game. Barry Swallow had got Billy Bremner over and all that lot and I remember John Kay, who was the Hull City manager that let me go, was playing centre-half for them, so I was up against him and it was a case of up yours." Bannister and Lorimer had put the All Stars 2-0 up, but Barrie Mitchell replied before Staniforth went on to strike three times in 15 minutes.

McGuinness was sacked in October, however, as Wright took over the reins with the club destined to apply for re-election. Looking back at his troublesome tenure, McGuinness said: "It was a long time ago but when things don't go well for you, as a player or a manager, it hurts. I still think of York City with affection though because, at Bootham Crescent, they were a small club with a big heart." Staniforth also remembered McGuinness with affection for keeping his spirits high during difficult times. "I found Wilf fascinating," the two-time City Clubman of the Year admitted. "He was crazy, and I probably didn't appreciate at the time what he had achieved in terms of his playing career and following Sir Matt Busby as Manchester United manager. I think he found it very frustrating at York, but he was a character and his tricks with the ball were phenomenal. He was brilliant technically on the training pitch and used to show off juggling the ball and doing all sorts. He would ask the players to try and do it, but we couldn't because he had been such a very good player at a high level. I was very sad when he left because he made an impression on me to get me over from Hull, but it was not a successful time and it probably hardened me to the game of football. It made me realise you have to look after yourself, but he was never down. He was bubbly despite the tough times he had and never bitter. He was always smiling, chatty and doing a trick. We had a good team spirit and all the players got on well with each other even though the results weren't good, and it was a difficult period for the club." Topping, meanwhile, was as non-plussed with Wright's arrival as he had been by McGuinness' reign, saying: "Wilf had to go but Charlie Wright was very pro the former Manchester United players as well because he had played for Bolton. He was the boss of York City, so I did what he told me, but I can't say I liked or disliked him."

With the club in the doldrums, November 1977 seemed an unlikely period for a number-one selling, world-famous artist who, two years earlier had been given his own star on the Hollywood Walk of Fame, to pay a surprise visit to Bootham Crescent. Maybe just as unexpected was that he wanted to see City winger Pollard who, taking up the story, explained: "Everybody had gone off for training, but I was told to stay at the ground. Nobody was there but I was told somebody was coming to speak to me and then I saw Elton John walking towards me in the players' tunnel. It was the first I knew Watford were interested in signing me and he asked me where the manager's office was. I was a fan of his at the time. I think George Teasdale - the club secretary - was in temporary charge then and, whilst Elton John went into the manager's office, I shot off to phone my wife to tell her who I'd just met. Graham Taylor, who was Watford's manager at the time, then opened the door of the office and told me to come in and Elton John was just sat there. They were talking for a bit and I was so nervous it wasn't true. Elton John eventually got up to make us a pot of tea to calm me down, so me and Graham could talk business and I felt I was leaving York at the right time even though Watford were in the same division."

In December, meanwhile, the club's then lowest-ever attendance of 1,284 turned up to watch a 0-0 Bootham Crescent stalemate against Torquay in new boss Wright's first home match. An attempt to improve cash flow then saw a new lottery launched in February with the first draw boasting 1,335 prizes from a maximum 20,000 tickets, giving people a one-in-11 chance of winning something. The top prize was £1,000 with total prize money amounting to £2,200. Other prizes ranged from 50p to £500. Maureen Leslie, having been appointed as the club's first pools manager, was in charge of the new initiative, along with lottery controller Trish Woods. Tickets were sold at a cost of 25p at a number of retail shops in the York district and the main winner was then announced at matches. The launch day also saw a special kiosk erected in St Sampson's Square, where the chairman, manager and players took their turn to sell tickets. Ninety per cent of the tickets were sold for the first draw, which was made by Iris Strachan - the then chairman's wife - at half-time during the home game against Barnsley with Grocers' shop assistant Eileen Fogg taking the top prize. She was not at the game but was given the good news by telephone and then picked up by a club official and taken to the ground, along with husband Ronald, where they were presented with the winners' cheque.

In April, an impressive individual achievement was recognised when Topping was presented with the match ball from his 350th consecutive appearance for the club against Crewe. But the season would end with a match that lowered the club's worst-ever home league attendance figure when a crowd of just 1,229 turned up to witness a 3-0 home defeat to Northampton, meaning the side finished third-bottom. The average league attendance that season was also a new record low of 2,139.

In the summer, the last link to the second division days was then broken when Topping completed his move to Huddersfield for £20,000. He never missed a game at or away from Bootham Crescent during his last seven seasons with the club, racking up an incredible 355 successive league appearances in a total of 463 senior games for the club. Topping was an ever-present during the two-and-three-quarter year reign of the unpopular McGuinness, who said: "Players like Chris Topping should be given rewards. They are the backbone of clubs. You knew what you were getting from him and I'm surprised bigger clubs didn't come in for him." There was no reward for Topping, though. Nor was his farewell marked with the kind of occasion afforded to his central-defensive partner Swallow, whose later actions would see him vilified at Bootham Crescent. "Barry Swallow got a testimonial and I didn't," Topping explained. "I started in 1967 when Gerry Baker was still around and left in 1978 when John Byrne and Gary Ford were coming through, whereas Swallow only did eight years. That still needles me, to a certain extent, that he got one first, especially after what he's done since. When I played my last game at Bootham Crescent, I didn't know it would be, because the move came about in June. I would have liked to have said a proper farewell, preferably in front of a bigger crowd than it would have been, but it would have still been nice to say goodbye, because it was just a case of a headline in the *Evening Press* saying that a York City player was going to Huddersfield for £25,000 and my brother said: 'It must be you or Gordon Staniforth'. My move was then written about for one or maybe two nights and that was it."

The young and impressionable Staniforth was also disappointed to see one of his early mentors move on, adding: "Chris wasn't great technically, but he was reliable in a battle. I was sad to see him leave, but the club was in a period of change and he bettered himself late in his career by going to Huddersfield." Topping, himself, also thought the time was right to end his association with the club he had cheered on from the age of 10 as a fan. "Tom Johnston wanted me at Huddersfield and, thank goodness, because by that time we had dropped down two divisions," he explained. But Topping's affinity with Bootham Crescent never ceased and he fondly remembered all six goals he scored at the ground. There was the one in the second division against Southampton and I also scored against Bournemouth on my birthday at home and against Workington in a night match," he recalled. "It was great for York to win a game because I had scored. That was so nice. The Bournemouth goal was a header and the Workington one was my first ever. I scored that from about a yard. The ball had been stopped on the line. It wasn't classy or anything."

On his incredible club record of playing in 355 consecutive games for the Minstermen, the unassuming Topping said: "It's only like some people never missing a day's work. I had the odd twisted ankle when I was at York, but I just strapped it up and carried on because that's what you did. My dad was a Japanese prisoner of war and came back, thank goodness, so I had to follow that. I was stubborn like him and liked to be involved. Nobody could ever accuse me of not being fit. I could run all day and I wanted York to win, so I would go for every challenge." Despite his proud injury record, though, Topping declared himself unfit when Huddersfield visited his old club the following season and admitted he felt quite relieved that he never had to line up as an opposition player at the ground that was so special to him. "I didn't get to play against York at Bootham Crescent," he said. "I was injured when the clubs played each other during the first season after I left, and I remember walking in to watch the game. That was strange and horrible. We then got promoted and our paths never crossed again. I wouldn't have liked to have played in that game really because it would have felt strange stopping York from scoring. It wouldn't have been a happy day for me, even though I would have done it and kept them out because I was working for Huddersfield. I had a sore knee and was watching with divided loyalties, because I will always support York above all other teams. It was my mum and dad's team, my granddad's team and that of my youngest sister as well."

Indeed, every game Topping played at Bootham Crescent was a family affair. "The camaraderie with each other and the fans was always special," he added. "I had a little contingent in that paddock to the left of the tunnel, including my mum and dad, my uncle and, sometimes, his wife and son. They also got to know the people around them, so there were around 20 of them in a group eventually."

Clive Baker gives treatment to Peter Scott in January 1976 when the physio bench was still situated in the home dressing room

Brian Pollard, Peter Scott and Mick Cave show off their platform shoes and flares after a game is postponed in January 1977

Gordon Staniforth, George Hope and Gordon Hunter watched by new trainer John Simpson in July 1977

A fan tries to sneak a peak of the action as a behind-closed-doors friendly against Middlesbrough takes place in August 1975

Manager Wilf McGuinness holds a pre-season, dressing room meeting in July 1975 with vice-chairman Gordon Winters looking on

CHAPTER 18

Sponsored kits and Jeff Stelling's 9.30am drinking sessions

"Fossie treated every blade of grass as if he was married to them."

Michael Sinclair subsequently took over as chairman during the summer of 1978 and one of his first decisions was to introduce a new home kit of red shirts, navy blue shorts and red socks, with the Y-front shirt dispensed with. A new club badge, featuring Bootham Bar, also featured on the strip, while the ground was painted red, white and blue to cover up all remaining traces of maroon. It took 100 litres of paint to complete the three-month job inside and outside the stadium and was undertaken by trainer John Simpson, along with then apprentice professionals Gary Ford, John Byrne, John Harrison and Andy Leaf. A handful of loyal supporters also assisted, including Eric Thorpe, who hadn't missed a home or away game for 12 years at that point.

Match-day programmes would also be given to fans free of charge for the first time and, early in the season, a designated section for disabled supporters was created in front of the Enclosure. Club secretary George Teasdale, meanwhile, stepped down after 17 years of working "65-hour weeks" at Bootham Crescent. His assistant Shane Winship would eventually become the Football League's youngest secretary at the age of 21 a year later, having worked in the club's offices since leaving school six years earlier. On Teasdale's departure, Winship had been made responsible for the launch that summer of the Travel Club, which would provide transport from Bootham Crescent for away games after taking bookings at the ground. Trips to Wembley for England matches were organised too. The club decided against switching any Saturday afternoon matches to Friday nights, though, having felt avoiding clashes with Leeds United games at weekends was making little difference now to numbers through the turnstiles.

A new club shop was then opened in September. It was situated just inside the entrance to the car park and opened for match days an hour before and an hour after kick-off, with Anne Granger the manageress. Newitts, the York sports

The new club shop opens in September 1978, situated just inside the entrance to the car park. At the time Newitts, the York sports outfitters, paid the club an annual royalty and had the sole right to reproduce the club's new motif on a large range of goods

outfitters, paid the club an annual royalty and had the sole right to reproduce the club's new motif on a large range of goods. Items on sale included scarves, hats, car stickers, lighters, combs, beer glasses, coffee mugs, T-shirts and key rings. An adjacent programme shop was opened two months later. It sold a wide range of Football League, Scottish League and non-League publications as the demand from collectors grew higher. The club also applied to the council for permission to lay a five-a-side football area on its recently resurfaced car park. Under the plans, a 6ft high, chain-link fence on top of the car park wall was to be erected to stop balls going into the backyards of houses in the neighbouring Newborough Street. It was intended too to fix floodlights along the top of the fence with covers to deflect the glare onto the two pitches and away from the houses. As part of the scheme, the three Portakabins in the car park would have needed to be re-sited and a fourth added. Another new initiative, meanwhile, saw autographed footballs kicked into the crowd by City players before the October home match with Scunthorpe as a "thank you gesture" to the fans.

Fortunes finally improved on the pitch too, with a top-half-of-the-table finish and a run to the FA Cup fourth round as goals from Gordon Staniforth and Kevin Randall saw off second division Luton in a 2-0 Bootham Crescent triumph along the way. Neighbours Scarborough were knocked out at home in the second round during a first game between the two clubs in more than 20 years with the visitors accounting for an estimated 3,000 supporters in a crowd of 7,870. The Seadogs' fellow non-League outfit Blyth Spartans had earlier forced a first-round replay before being knocked out in the north-east. All three ties captured the imagination of the Bootham Crescent crowd with Staniforth recalling: "I remember the Scarborough FA Cup match really well. We won 3-0 and I scored twice. They were non-League but there were almost 8,000 fans there and their supporters helped nearly fill the ground. When I scored at the Shippo End, they were all in there as well. It was the first time the clubs had played each other since the 1954/55 run and the FA Cup meant everything to me as a young kid. With the atmosphere, those were the games you wanted to play in and I loved it. I also remember Blyth Spartans because they brought a lot of fans as well. Alan Shoulder was playing for them just before he got his move to Newcastle and we drew against them before winning the replay up there. We also beat Luton and they had some good players in their team that had played at a high level like Alan West and Bob Hatton. There were others like Brian Stein, Ricky Hill and Mal Donaghy who would become top players and I always looked at the team sheet before games to see who was on it because the bigger the names the better. I wanted to play against them and, when the big teams came to Bootham Crescent, I saw it as a big challenge that I used to love. The ground played its part in our success during those games and we proved that by doing well against the bigger teams there. They were coming down to little, old Bootham Crescent and I always talk about little, old York because it's a nice place and people don't expect you to do this, that and the other so, when we did, it was brilliant and a big shock to other teams. There were obviously some big results after my playing days that proved the same. I think teams come to York expecting the club to be too nice and it was the same with my teams when I coached at York College too." The Luton game would have been the first at Bootham Crescent to be featured on BBC TV's *Match of the Day* highlights programme, but heavy snowfall led to the tie being postponed despite the efforts of 150 volunteers who had turned up at 6.45am hoping to help clear the pitch and get the game on. The subsequent victory landed the club an away tie at Brian Clough's reigning league champions Nottingham Forest, who went through 3-1.

During the club's January annual meeting at Bootham Crescent, it was subsequently announced that 96,000 new shares in the club would be issued. A £54,000 loan that had been made to the club by the board of directors to cover losses made in the 1977/78 season was converted into shares, but 20,000 were also offered to the general public, who could become part-owners of their club. Shares would cost £1 each and were issued in minimum batches of £25. The eccentric Bryan Foster, with a cold winter leading to multiple postponements, put out an appeal, meanwhile, for flame-throwing equipment to clear snow and ice from the pitch and the terraces. He went on to acquire three flame throwers with help from York firms Taylors, Houghton's, Orton's and Newitts and managed to get a February home game with Bradford City on.

Journeyman winger Neil Warnock, however, endured a difficult time at the club during the campaign. Brought in by Charlie Wright from Barnsley at the age of 29, he was identified as a potential leader on the pitch, but the future

Premier League manager would only make one league start - during a 1-0 defeat against his former club at Bootham Crescent - before being released mid-term. As an example of the influence the cantankerous, recently-appointed director Douglas Craig was already wielding at the club, Warnock - never one to shirk away from a confrontation himself - was deemed surplus to requirements after directors made it clear they did not rate him. "I had one or two battles over the period with Douglas and we fell out a couple of times," Warnock recalled. "I was made captain by Charlie in pre-season but, then, I contracted flu and wasn't fit to play. He desperately wanted me to play and, when I came back from the doctors on Friday morning, he had me taking set-plays in my trousers during training. I played and, then, after the game, he told me on Monday that there were people inside the club who didn't think I was good enough and he was going to have to let me go. It was probably the most short-lived captaincy there's ever been in football. I shouldn't have played for him and, because I did, I ended up getting sacked but that did drive me on when I left there. It made me determined to prove myself as a manager and come back to haunt them. In fact, that spell taught me a lot about management. Charlie was really overweight, and I remember thinking that, when I got older, there was no way I was going to be embarrassed by the condition I was in."

Wright's condition might have been linked to his off-pitch habits as Sky Sports former *Soccer Saturday* anchorman and *Countdown* presenter Jeff Stelling could testify. During that period at Bootham Crescent, Stelling was just starting out in his broadcasting career and he smiled: "I covered York for Radio Tees as a cub reporter between 1977 and 1980, which meant fortnightly drives to Bootham Crescent in the company Hillman Imp to speak to the manager. The visits were never less than interesting as the manager was larger-than-life Scot, former goalkeeper Charlie Wright. My first meeting with the big man was pretty daunting. I was in my first job in radio, just 22 and in awe of managers and players alike. I arrived at 9.30am and Charlie put me at ease with the offer of a drink. 'Coffee would be great', I responded. No chance. Charlie stretched to the side of his desk and pulled out a crate of Newcastle Brown Ale. So we sat drinking Brown Ale at 9.30 on a Thursday morning and this became the pattern of my visits to York. I remember once having to spend a couple of hours sleeping before I dared to head back to the studios after a couple of Newcy Browns. I know Charlie had a reputation as being abrasive, but I never found that. He was always welcoming and helpful."

His morning tipples with Stelling probably served as a release from the day-to-day stresses of Wright's first managerial job with Staniforth remembering

Future Premier League manager Neil Warnock (pictured fifth from the left) with fellow 1978 summer signings Peter Stronach, Roy Kay, David Loggie, Jimmy Walsh, Steve Faulkner, Barry Wellings and Andy Leaf

a man who, unlike his predecessor McGuinness, struggled with the pressures presented by the Bootham Crescent job. "Wilf had been great, but Charlie was strange and all I remember was him walking around with pressure on his shoulders," Staniforth revealed. "He used to love me and what I did, so I was pleased with the relationship we had but, looking back, there were no tactics, plans or strategies other than trying to score more goals than we let in. We just went out and played and sometimes that worked, but sometimes it didn't."

A year after Warnock's departure, meanwhile, he made his first steps into coaching and would go on to lead Huddersfield to 2-0 and 3-0 victories on his first two visits to Bootham Crescent as a manager in 1993 and 1994. Despite his struggles as a player at the time, however, Warnock retained an affection for the intimacy of Bootham Crescent and an admiration for a playing surface, lovingly cared for by the inimitable Bryan Foster. "It was a lovely club and the playing surface was great thanks to Fossie," he smiled. "He treated every blade of grass as if he was married to them. He used to say: 'What are you lot doing on here?' He did a fantastic job though and was a great bloke. I also remember, as a player, you were right close to the stands at Bootham Crescent and you could hear every word said to you - good and bad at that time!"

York-born 17-year-old Gary Ford replaced Warnock, meanwhile, in the latter's one start for the Minstermen. It was only Ford's fourth-appearance of 428 for his home-town club and Warnock admitted that there was good competition for places on the flank back then. "I was a brainless, flying winger," he laughed. "Then there was Gary who was a good young lad full of energy and Gordon Staniforth was doing quite well when I was there too." Ford recalled Warnock's

City career as short and sweet, but still memorable. "I'm the reason he didn't play much because we played in the same position," Ford joked, before adding: "He was a character and a Jack the Lad, and he used to sell fruit and veg at the club. He had a shop or a market stall and used to bring the food to the ground and sell it out of the back of his car. He was coming towards the end of his career and wasn't as quick as me. You could see he might make progress in the game, though, because of his character."

Staniforth and Warnock became good friends during this period with the Minstermen as the latter also used his chiropodist skills to tend to the former's feet. Before both went on to pursue careers in coaching and management, they would regularly discuss their views on the game at Bootham Crescent, normally with Warnock's pet dog for company. "Neil Warnock was a big-time Charlie but I got on with him," Staniforth said. "He was a chiropodist and he did my feet. He took his gear around with him and would shave my hard skin off. He was brilliant at it too. He had the gift of the gab as well, but he had one of the shortest spells I can remember any footballer having at any club. He used to lead training and was a fitness fanatic, but he was a bit of a bully and he had that reputation later in life. I wouldn't have predicted that he would become a millionaire manager and, as a player, he was an average right winger, who enjoyed training and was full of himself. He used to bring his dog to every training session and put him in the car. Sometimes, we would have a break and me and him used to sit in the car park talking football all the time and we would eat a sandwich, whilst he would feed his dog on the back seat at the same time. It was a nice dog - a black border collie. You could see a little bit of what he's taken into management, but it was literally a case of him coming in, scraping his boots, feeding the dog and then he was gone."

One other memory of the Bootham Crescent car park that has never faded for Staniforth involves the Great British eccentric Foster. "I remember Fossie walking through the gates into the car park one morning and he got on his knees and kissed the floor, then got up," Staniforth smiled. "I don't know whether he knew if anybody saw him, but he was taking the Mickey because he would often mumble and grumble about not being able to do this or that. He was just making his point that Bootham Crescent was the Holy Grail. The pitch was OK but typical of pitches in those days. There was not the technology around then to help groundsmen, but we still didn't have many games postponed."

Ford, meanwhile, has vivid memories of the unglamorous life he led as a City scholar, recalling: "John Simpson used to train us, and he was a physiotherapist, but he was ex-army and it was like being in the forces. You had to be at the club at 8.30am and, while saying things needed to be cleaned with a toothbrush sounds stupid, that's what we had to do. We had to clean all the boots and the changing rooms, but the first job was painting the corridor floor. We also trained with the first team and had to grow up quickly. When I got into the first team at 17, I would play a full match and then clean the changing rooms afterwards, but it was character building."

Staniforth managed to hit the club's first league hat-trick in more than seven years, meanwhile, during a 4-0 triumph over Port Vale, taking his tally to 19 for the season. Despite still having three games left to play, he failed to reach 20 but also expressed his pride at lifting the Billy Fenton Memorial Clubman of the Year Trophy for a second successive year. "I never got 20 goals in my career because I was never a prolific scorer, but that Port Vale game was a halcyon day for me and I got my goals by working hard to be in the right place," he recalled. "Winning the Billy Fenton Clubman of the Year twice and receiving it on the pitch was brilliant as well. That was special and meant a lot to me. I was living in Pocklington at the time and I had to build a fireplace with York Stone to put it on because it was so flipping big!"

Coinciding with Ford and Byrne's emergence, City were awarded a grant of £18,000 by the Sports Council to institute a youth development scheme at Bootham Crescent and former City favourite Barry Lyons was appointed the club's first full-time youth coach in June 1979. Lyons relished his new role at the ground he had graced, enthusing: "It was wonderful, and I enjoyed it. I set up the first youth side. There had been youth players before, but they wanted a full-time youth set-up. I came for an interview with Charlie Wright but didn't get the job at first. It was given to somebody who had come out of university and was from Cardiff (Gareth Powell), but he couldn't get on with life in York and didn't get a full quota of players, so I was appointed in the summer and we had trials to get some local lads in to make a full squad up. We played as the A team, which was the third team really after the reserves. I also got some good lads from Barnsley and Middlesbrough. We did well, and I remember playing Middlesbrough in the quarter-final of a cup game. We lost, but the lads played so well. John Byrne and Gary Ford were both around then, as were others like John Bentham and Tommy Stanley. I used to have the lads six days a week and we would be training or having team meetings. It was good, but then Charlie Wright got the sack and the board asked if I would take the first team until the end of the season." Lyons' Colts team, who went on to become the York & District League's division five champions, would also finish the campaign by beating Dunnington 1-0 in the final of the York Junior Cup at Bootham Crescent.

Family season tickets were also introduced, meanwhile, for the first time. It meant that two adults and two children could attend every home match at a price of £70 or £79.85 (after the June discount price had elapsed). Players' Club season tickets were offered for the first time too, giving supporters who paid £60 access to the players' lounge before and after games and a seat in the Main Stand. A later government hike in VAT meant a season ticket for the Main Stand went up to £37.25 or £30 by the discount deadline. The 1979/80 season also saw Bootham Crescent celebrate City's 50-year anniversary in the Football League with chairman Sinclair declaring that Bootham Crescent was "one of the most attractive grounds in the third and fourth divisions". Wright helped in that respect by always insisting on the red, white and blue paintwork being kept fresh and smart, with loyal supporter Thorpe even appointed on to the club's full-time staff with his job to take charge of ground maintenance. For the first time ever, meanwhile, all the players' kits were sponsored, with Newitts - the city's main sports equipment and sportswear shop - having their name featured on the shirts. The match-day programme was also now being financed by advertising revenue. There was confusion at the first home game of the season, though, as City went out of the League Cup following a 3-2 first-round, second-leg victory at Bootham Crescent against Mansfield after extra-time. That tied the aggregate scores at 3-3 and many left the game expecting a replay, but the new away goals rule meant that Mansfield progressed to the next round.

A star-studded rock 'n' roll spectacular at Bootham Crescent, featuring pop idols from the Swinging Sixties, then flopped with a £6,000 loss recorded as only 750 of an anticipated 7,000 audience attended the open-air concert on the last Saturday in August. Acts included Wayne Fontana and the Mindbenders, Billy J Kramer and the Dakotas, Joe Brown and the Bruvvers, Jimmy James and Alvin Stardust. The event had cost £12,000 to stage and was organised by Hugh Bowman - the owner of Feelgood Discount Records in Goodramgate and a City vice-president. Disappointed with the turn-out, he said: "People have told me that the city needs entertainment, so I thought it a good idea to hold a rock 'n' roll concert at the football ground. One minute they want in and the next minute they knock it. I've never come across a city like York and certainly won't hold one here again." York police also received 130 complaints about the noise from residents as far away as Haxby, Clifton and Rawcliffe Lane. More than 35 policemen were drafted in for the four-and-a-half-hour concert, but there was no trouble from a mainly young audience.

The club received a major boon, meanwhile, when former Scotland and Leeds star Peter Lorimer signed for Wright during the close season from Toronto

Scotland international Peter Lorimer scores against Port Vale – one of the seven goals he contributed at Bootham Crescent during a short stay in the 1979/80 season

Blizzard, where he was then plying his trade. He would go on to score seven of his nine City goals at Bootham Crescent, but the team finished the campaign eighth-bottom and his last game - at home to Tranmere on March 1, 1980 - saw him sent off. Recalling that "sad" end to his six-month spell with City, the 1974 World Cup midfielder said: "It was nothing really. I remember running into the corner and their player (Eddie Flood) tackled me a bit too hard. I was going back to play in the American League the following week and he went for me. I was a bit annoyed because I didn't want to get injured. I rode the tackle and then pushed him down when I got up, so the ref gave me an early bath. It was disappointing, and I wasn't happy about it because I wasn't a player who got sent off and it was nothing really, but it was a consolation that it didn't affect anything. I was going back to the States anyway so the suspension was irrelevant, but it was a sad way to finish after enjoying my time at the club. I always thought there was a really good atmosphere at Bootham Crescent the way it was tucked away amongst all the houses and the playing surface was always immaculate thanks to Fossie. The fans responded well to me and I think they appreciated me going to York. It would have been easy to turn down the offer and just train back in the States, but I wanted to help the club. I was in between seasons for Toronto in the American League so came to York to keep my fitness up as well. Charlie Wright called me out of the blue. I didn't know him then, but somebody must have told him I was available. He was very demanding, and training was good. I lived in Wetherby, so it was nice and local

281

and only half-an-hour to travel in the morning. Everybody, from the directors to the groundstaff, was nice and treated me really well, which made my time at the club really happy. Fossie was also a great character. I had a racehorse at the time and he was always asking me in the dressing room for any tips I might have got from the stables. He wanted to know what was happening in the racing world."

Staniforth admitted he was thrilled and shocked to share a dressing room with Lorimer, explaining: "I was getting frustrated and might have said one or two things to other people about needing to bolster the squad. Then, lo and behold, there was a right deal done and Peter Lorimer walked through the door. He was a legend to me because I was young, and I thought he was fantastic. The nearest we had got to a superstar before was Peter Scott because he played a handful of Northern Ireland internationals, but Peter Lorimer's arrival boosted our profile no end and, whilst I wouldn't say he won us games on his own, his free-kick taking was legendary and I really enjoyed playing with him." Childhood Leeds fan Ford was also a little star-struck by Lorimer's arrival, saying: "My dad took me to Elland Road to watch Leeds from the age of five so, when Peter Lorimer came to play for us, that was great for me. He was a nice man, who was down to earth, but he was my hero and it was amazing when he walked through the door. I was only 18 and I was playing alongside him. I had to do his running because he didn't run a lot, but he could pass and strike a ball better than anybody else."

Goalkeeping favourite Graeme Crawford, who had been brought back briefly in January 1980 and made his second debut against Crewe at Bootham Crescent with future Liverpool legend Bruce Grobbelaar his opposite number, was given sore wrists, however, by Lorimer's legendary shooting power that saw him nicknamed "Thunderfoot" during his spell in the States and "Ninety Miles An Hour" by Leeds fans. "Peter Lorimer was great, but I used to hate training with him," Crawford explained. "He used to blast balls at you and his shots would knock you back. Charlie Wright had brought me back to the club and I got a great reception, but I wasn't around for long because Charlie got sacked and Barry (Lyons) was put in charge. It was difficult then because we had played together, and I understood that he wanted to put together his own team, so he brought Eddie Blackburn in." The spell proved a great opportunity for Crawford to renew old acquaintances, though, with groundsman Foster still providing the laughs and hurling his pitchfork around at players and manager alike. "We had red ash around the pitch and we would occasionally go for a loosener on match day and I remember, during my first spell at the club, Bryan Foster throwing a garden fork at Phil Burrows because he cut the corner," Crawford laughed. "Fossie shouted: 'Get off my pitch at him'. It would have killed him if it had hit him. I never got that treatment, but Charlie Wright did one day after I had come back as well. I remember Fossie was lining the pitch with whitewash and we were doing set-pieces. Charlie took a corner and, after he hit the ball, it smashed into the whitewash. Fossie chased him out of the car park for that."

Lorimer, meanwhile, only had vague recollections of his seven Bootham Crescent strikes that added to a career haul of 309 professional goals for club and country when asked for his memories four years before he passed away in 2021. "I know I scored a couple of free kicks (one in a 3-1 home victory over Hereford was reported as a "tremendous 28-yard free kick that was thundered through the defensive wall" by then *Yorkshire Evening Press* reporter Malcolm Huntington, another came in the 5-2 FA Cup rout of non-League Mossley and a third in a 5-1 defeat of Port Vale was also described by the newspaper scribe "as a 25-yard thunderbolt and worth the admission money alone"), but I can't really remember them," he admitted. "I'm not one for looking back too much but, obviously, every time you put the ball in the net you get a lot of pleasure out of it." But the two-time league championship winner does remember how emerging teenage striker Byrne caught his eye during his City stay. "There were some good young players coming through and I enjoyed helping them," Lorimer said. "John was one of them and you could see he was going to be a good player. When you've been around at clubs, you can tell these kind of things, and I'd been at Leeds and seen lots of young boys come through. He was the best York had at that time and he went on to have a good career. When I saw him, I thought straight away that he was a higher standard than York. He was a very talented, young player with natural ability and a good attitude towards working hard at his game."

Staniforth also spotted the burgeoning potential of the future Republic of Ireland international, adding: "John used to clean my boots and you could see he was definitely going to be a great player and maybe me leaving paved the way for him to come through, which was a good thing. He was only a raw kid, but he always had talent and had something about him. He would still be a great player in the current era with his skills and swank."

Lorimer's first match - a 2-0 home defeat to Peterborough in September - saw the attendance swell to 3,102, which was the biggest gate of the season at that point and would only be beaten in the league during Yorkshire derbies against

Doncaster, Bradford and Huddersfield. A crowd of just under 2,000 also saw City lift the North Riding Cup following a 2-1 win against a Middlesbrough team, who boasted £700,000 in talent, including big-money signings Irving Natress, Terry Cochrane and Jim Stewart. David Loggie and Steve Faulkner got the Minstermen's goals.

In a bid to boost crowds, City went on to offer cheaper admission into one area of the Popular Stand for the home match with Scunthorpe at the start of October. The cost for a seat in the "Z section", nearest to the Shipton Street End, was reduced to £1.30 for adults and 75p for juveniles and pensioners, compared to the normal respective prices of £1.60 and £1.05. Transfers could normally be made from the Shipton Street End to the "Z section" for an extra 50p - mainly catering for standing fans who might want cover in the event of inclement weather. The club even considered removing 200 seats to provide sheltered standing accommodation, which they were coming under increased pressure to provide, but decided not to after following police advice. The price cut had little impact on gate numbers in any case, with the Scunthorpe match attracting the lowest home crowd during the first three months of the campaign.

There was also a landmark occasion in mid-February 1980 when girls football was staged at Bootham Crescent for the first-ever time with Mill Mount beating Burnholme 4-1 in the final of the *Yorkshire Evening Press*-sponsored York City Five-a-Side Schoolgirls' competition. Christine Watling (2), Trish Wells and Ann Smith were on target for Mill Mount, with Fay Harding replying for Burnholme. The five-a-side tournament became an annual event with boys' teams also taking part. It was played in the car park, though, rather than on the hallowed turf.

The ground's floodlights, meanwhile, were improved to meet Football League requirements at a cost of £20,000 in the summer of 1980 with Staniforth's six-figure move to Carlisle paying for the work, as well as a new gas boiler, after chairman Sinclair admitted the old oil one had been held together by "prayers and chewing gum for some time". By making the floodlight enhancements, which saw the bulbs become three times more powerful, City matches could now be televised in colour. The new lights were similar to those that had been installed at rugby league club Hull KR, with York firm House and Son awarded the contract for installation. A total of 12 two-kilowatt bulbs were fitted on each pylon. Other work done during the same close season included refurbishing the home dressing room, converting the boot room into a referee's room and turning the old referee's room into a new medical room.

The floodlights were officially switched on by ITV personality and former Wolves player and Northern Ireland international Derek Dougan, prior to a pre-season friendly game in August 1980 against Grimsby, which was refereed by Keith Usher, who would later become club secretary.

Despite the club struggling for long periods of Staniforth's first three-year spell as a Minsterman, meanwhile, the former England schoolboy international cannot remember anything but positive support from the Bootham Crescent faithful. "The fans were great with me because they could see my honesty and graft," he said. "I should have scored more goals, but I tended to set them up more. I wasn't a natural goalscorer, but the fans liked the fact that I wanted to get involved. I think the crowd understood when I left, because I was a young kid wanting to better myself but it's funny how many players always come back to York. I went up and down the country but came back here and the city, club and ground are in my heart because I was given my first steps in the game I love here."

The 1979/80 season was also when a seven-year-old Guy Mowbray, who would later garner a reputation as one of the country's finest commentators with ITV and *Match of the Day*, first watched his home-town club at Bootham Crescent. On those early memories, City supporter Mowbray said: "My first match was against Peterborough in September 1979 and we lost 2-0 (the game mentioned previously as being Lorimer's debut). I don't remember anything about that game other than going with my brother in the Shipton Street End. I can remember watching us beat Portsmouth later that season, though, because it was my eighth birthday and we took a couple of friends along as well. We saw the goal (scored by Derek Hood) go in because we were behind the goal. I also remember their goalkeeper because it was Peter Mellor, who had played in the Cup final for Fulham. Later, I would go to games with my mates and I went to pretty much every home game once I was in secondary school at Huntington, as well as a few away. I would walk to the game with my friends down the side of the hospital and, for the League Cup tie against Bradford in 2015, I found myself walking to the ground that way for the first time in ages with a friend of mine who was ticking off the 92 grounds. I asked him to walk slowly so I could take it all in again. When I was young, that walk always seemed to be teeming with people, as did the bridge over the railway after games. The myth was always that you could be carried over that bridge without your feet touching the stairs because it was that busy. When I went with my mates, we used to stand in the Shipton Street End in the back-right corner because my dad, who had been going since the 1930s and was in the biggest-ever crowd, told us you could see all the pitch from there. I think he was also trying to make sure we didn't get caught up in the throng behind the goal."

With Lorimer gone, City fans watched their team finish bottom of the old fourth division the following campaign under ex-playing favourite Lyons. Fans also had to pay 14 per cent more for a Main Stand season ticket that season, with the price going up from £30 to £34. But, following a £25,000 loan from John Smith's Brewery, the Social Club was revamped at a total cost of £30,593 in a two-month period from the end of June to the end of August, with the creation of a lounge bar in addition to the existing main Supporters' Club room. One bar served both rooms and the size of the club was increased from 160 square metres to 284, with photographs depicting the club's great FA Cup runs and the 1970s' second division hey-days displayed on the wall.

The Junior Reds Club was also launched, with a fee of £1 for the season meaning under-16 members only paid 70p to get into games instead of the full adult price of £1.30. Meetings with players, film shows and football tournaments were also staged at the ground for members of the new group. The Gabbiadini brothers - future City professionals Marco and Ricardo - were two of the first members and played for the Junior Reds football team. A first Junior Reds meeting, meanwhile, saw manager Lyons give members a talk at Bootham Crescent before they enjoyed two football films. That was followed by a visit and talk from Leeds United players Eddie Gray and Arthur Graham and regular meetings with City players took place, normally after the youngsters watched a reserve game at Bootham Crescent. In August, a 12-year-old Marco Gabbiadni and Railway Institute's Stephen Burrows were also chosen by City's then youth-team coach Kevin Randall as the outstanding players at the York Crime Prevention Soccer Competition, which had become an annual event at Bootham Crescent. Ricardo, meanwhile, became the first Junior Reds member to lead the team out as a mascot for the December 27 home match against Rochdale after his name was pulled out of a hat to win that honour. Mascots for the remaining games that season were decided in the same manner, while older Junior Reds members took their turn to be ball-boys. During its first season, the Junior Reds attracted more than 700 members and Colin Sanderson would gradually assume responsibility for its running. In its 1980s hey-day, the Junior Reds also staged Christmas parties in the Social Club every year, which were attended by all the players.

During January, City's new-look Social Club secured an hour's extension to their opening hours despite objections from 12 residents in neighbouring

Newborough Street and Bootham Crescent. A one-year music and dancing licence was granted for 1am instead of 11pm with meals to be served too, although there were provisos. Vehicles could only be left on one side of the car park and not alongside the wall adjacent to the houses, with a car park attendant supervising. No live music was permitted after 11pm either and all music had to stop at 1am. A total of 42 residents went on to sign a petition against the licence. James Race was to run the club, although he pointed out there would be no 'pop groups', just a resident pianist and, occasionally, live entertainment from a singer or a comedian. The club were also instructed to add extra insulation around the walls to reduce noise levels and no windows or ventilation ducts were to face Newborough Street. In November, the Social Club hosted the first York City Supporters' Club Individual Sports Quiz when a field of 40 was whittled down to 12 finalists following a 70-question written examination. Whist, darts and dominoes Social Club teams were also competing in the York Social League and hosting home fixtures at Bootham Crescent.

November saw one of the country's greatest-ever sporting legends play at Bootham Crescent, meanwhile, when then England cricket captain Ian Botham ran out as centre forward for Scunthorpe reserves in a North Midlands League Cup tie. Botham helped the Iron win 3-2 after-extra time, although he was described as "rather slow and unfit", while showing enthusiasm. The following

Cricket legend Ian Botham plays for Scunthorpe reserves at Bootham Crescent in November 1980. He played at centre forward, but was reported as looking unfit. The visitors won 3-2 nevertheless

campaign Botham would return to Bootham Crescent for a first-team fixture but was an unused substitute.

February saw former England stars Jack Charlton and Stan Mortenson invited as guest speakers to the first York City Sportsmen's Dinner at the refurbished Social Club, with referee Neil Midgley the master of ceremonies. There was capacity for 130 diners and the night was a men-only event. Ex-Yorkshire and England captain Brian Close and Sir Alf Ramsey's former England assistant Harold Shepherdson were also booked for a similar function in April. Sponsors were sought for the speakers with Bill Bonney, a York painting contractor, doing the honours for the Charlton and Mortenson night.

In between, as an experiment to assess the impact on gate numbers, City gave away 700 tickets to the 40 schools that replied to an offer of free admission to the Wimbledon home match for children accompanied by a paying adult. An attendance of 2,026 saw the visitors' Alan Cork score the only goal of the game. It was the only crowd that rose above the 2,000 mark during the final six home fixtures of the campaign, even though the club also admitted juveniles in for free on production of a *Yorkshire Evening Press* coupon for subsequent Bootham Crescent clashes against Crewe and Bury, for whom future Everton and Wales legend Neville Southall starred in a 1-0 away win. The final home game of the season against Northampton, meanwhile, attracted only 1,167 supporters, which represented the lowest-ever league attendance at Bootham Crescent. Losses of more than £33,000 were subsequently made over the campaign. City were beaten 2-1 in the Tuesday night contest against the Cobblers, with 17-year-old Steve Senior making his full debut and Byrne scoring the hosts' consolation.

Early in 1981, a gym, costing £46,000 and measuring 60ft long by 40ft wide, was built at the Bootham Crescent End of the ground in the corner closest to the army barracks, near where the small wooden programme hut, which had also served as the club shop, had been. City received £14,559 from the Sports Council and £20,000 from the Football League Improvement Fund to help towards the costs. The remaining £11,500 needed to build the gym was covered by fundraising activities by the York City Development Association, which was headed by chairman Ian Hardy. One venture involved people buying tickets containing any one of the seconds in a 90-minute match on them. They were available for each quarter of the season and there was a prize of £25 if the person's second corresponded to the first goal in a game and £10 if it corresponded to the last goal. The building of the gym also involved excavation of some of the banking at that end of the ground. Ford believes, though, that the gym was used less frequently than the "Cloggers Corner" area it had replaced, where in-house, small-sided battles had continued to be staged right through the generations. "It used to be just like a backyard there before the gym was built," he explained. "It was just ash and we used to play five-a-side there. It was called 'Cloggers' Corner' and, at 16, you were pushed up against the brick wall. Tommy Stanley was taken on as an apprentice the year after us and came from an old mining village, but he still remembers being kicked and frightened there. When Wilf McGuinness was manager, he also employed a lot of ex-professionals from bigger clubs who were tough lads and didn't give a hoot. They thought kicking us around was part of our education. When the gym was built, we didn't really use it a lot. There was a multi-gym in there and some weights and, maybe, if there was bad weather, we'd go in there and use the weights or play a bit of three-a-side, but St Peter's school gym was better really, and we used to go there."

Despite finishing bottom of the Football League, admission prices went up for the following campaign with ground admission now £1.50 - a rise of 20p - while Main Stand season tickets were £45. City received permission, meanwhile, to add another refreshment kiosk at the Bootham Crescent end of the ground. Bobby Charlton was the club's next Sportsmen's Dinner guest in June and others to follow in 1981 included comedian and former Doncaster defender Charlie Williams and ex-Liverpool captain Emlyn Hughes. Shane Winship, was also appointed as the club's first-ever sales executive and the new proprietor of the Social Club with Race resigning due to health and family reasons. The sales executive role saw Winship run all the club's commercial activities other than the lottery.

For 1981/82, Friday night matches were also experimented with again, as four home fixtures were switched from Saturday afternoon kick-offs. Lyons also brought in a player who subsequently became one of the most cherished to ever pull on a City shirt. Making his presence felt immediately, Keith Walwyn became the first City player to top 20 league goals in a season since Paul Aimson 11 years earlier. His first appearance at Bootham Crescent came in a 1-0 pre-season North Riding Cup win against Guisborough Town. Ford was on target, but *Yorkshire Evening Press* reporter Huntington noted: "Walwyn could become a favourite of City fans with his all-action battling type of game, which should give a few problems to opposition defences."

But the move for the powerful striker almost fell through as chairman Sinclair baulked at Chesterfield's £5,000 valuation and the Saltergate club's Ernie Moss was actually Lyons' first-choice target, before he opted for his understudy. Recalling the conversation he had in the Bootham Crescent boardroom about Walwyn, Lyons said: "John Byrne trained so hard and, then, it would come to a game and he used to fizzle out after 75 minutes. Nobody could understand why. It was probably nerves because, physically, he trained as hard as anybody. Suddenly, though, everything clicked, and he was a super player for 90 minutes. Him and Keith Walwyn ripped people apart. I wanted a big striker who could take the weight off John, who was very skilful but couldn't cope early on with the strength needed in division four. I said that Keith wouldn't score many goals, but that he would help bring John Byrne into the game and I thought he was the perfect partner for him. The chairman Mr Sinclair initially said we couldn't afford him and then he said we will have to buy him on the tick and that he would only pay £4,000, even though Chesterfield wanted £5,000. He went on to score 20 goals that season despite what I'd said, and I never thought that would happen because he looked awkward at times, but everyone loved him."

September's Friday night home match with Northampton, meanwhile, saw two blind supporters enjoy the opportunity to follow the game via a headphone link to a pair of stand seats for the first time. City donated the seats for the season as part of a link-up with York Lions, who financed the equipment with the commentary provided by the York Hospital Broadcasting Service. An unusual arrangement for a League Cup derby tie against Sheffield United then saw the entire Popular Stand and the Bootham Crescent End of the ground reserved for away fans only as a crowd of 4,750 witnessed a 1-1 draw that saw the Blades progress 2-1 on aggregate.

Even with Walwyn and Byrne leading the line, however, the club's home form was dreadful with a run of 14 Bootham Crescent fixtures without a home win setting a club record that would stand until the old ground was demolished. Brian Pollard, who shared right-wing duties with Lyons in the legendary 1970s' second division team, returned for a second spell at the club in the midst of the sorry sequence and recalled: "When I came back, the club were in a similar situation to when I first signed and that's not to say I was the main reason for the improvements both times. They were struggling a bit, but I was grateful for the opportunity to sign a monthly contract. It was weird at the time though. Kevin Randall was also there and had a spell as manager, but it just wasn't happening for him." Byrne also recalled the side's struggles at Bootham Crescent during that season - in complete contrast to what was to follow when only a single league game was lost in front of the Minstermen faithful during each of the subsequent campaigns. Reflecting on the difference, Byrne said: "We had good players back in 1981 and the nucleus of that Championship-winning side was already there but it just never clicked at that time. We didn't have the team spirit and camaraderie that came later when the likes of Denis Smith and Viv Busby arrived. We used to go out for a few beers to build that back in our day but that's frowned upon now. You do need that winning mentality they brought though. That hadn't been there for a long time and they gave us belief. They certainly turned my career around and there's definitely a massively psychological aspect to the game. If you are on a winning run, you get into that winning mentality. You go out onto the pitch knowing you won't be beaten and the opposite is true when you're on a losing streak. I remember in the Championship side I thought I was going to score in every game but that wasn't the case during that run in 1981/82. As a young 20-year-old player, I had the pressures of just wanting to do well, rather than being afraid because of the run we were on, but I remember never really seeing eye to eye with Kevin Randall at the time too and that didn't help."

Ford reasoned that an ever-changing team also played a part in the home travails. The likes of Stuart Croft, Alan Waldron, Graeme Hedley, Gerry Sweeney and Gerry Fell all came and went following brief spells at Bootham Crescent, while others such as Ian McDonald, Billy McGhie and Malcolm Smith left during the campaign. "It was about confidence and I don't think we ever had a settled side," Ford explained. "Most teams had small squads back then and it was pretty much the same 12 every week, but older pros were coming in and not staying for long."

In Walwyn, though, Lyons had found a forward who could act as a minder for rookies Ford and Byrne with the former saying: "Big Keith looked after me and John and, if there were any problems, he was there. That made you relax, because there were a lot of characters and hard men in the game back then, but they were more worried about him than they were us. I remember our old keeper Eddie Blackburn coming back to play us for Hartlepool during the championship-winning season and my job then was to keep putting the ball in the box. Keith scored both goals in a 2-0 win that game and Eddie said all he could see when he was coming for a cross was Keith's eyes and he was thinking: 'Oh no'. But Keith was the nicest man you could ever meet. He didn't mean any harm. He was just brave."

Lyons eventually lost his job, as did his brief successor Randall, but the former was a bit puzzled with the timing of his dismissal. "I don't know why they didn't sack me the season we had finished bottom," he reasoned. "The following season we got off to a good start before the poor home results, so I was surprised when the decision was made. I was in the office and just about to come out when I saw the chairman coming towards me and Kevin Randall behind him with a big smile on his face. The chairman told me that he had decided that I was going, and that Kevin was taking over. He was my right-hand man, but I just thought get on with it. He said he wanted to be called the manager, not the interim manager, but he didn't last long. The club later asked me to stay on as youth coach when Denis Smith was made manager, but it was difficult. There was an atmosphere with Denis and, if I had been manager, then I don't think I would have wanted somebody there who had done the job before in the background chatting, not that I would have done." Looking back at his spell in charge, Lyons admitted he experienced managerial highs and lows at Bootham Crescent, explaining: "Initially, I enjoyed it. The club looked certain to finish the season I took over in the re-election zone, so everybody was happy when we put some results together and got out of it. Fans took to me at first and there were chants of 'Barry Lyons' Red-and-White Army' and I suppose that was nice, although it was a case of enjoying it whilst I could, as it eventually turned to boos. That was difficult to take, but you get used to it and just have to not let it become a problem. We set off quite well the season we finished bottom but, all of a sudden after Christmas, the chairman decided he was going to get rid of players. He paid off our top scorer Terry Eccles, without my knowledge, just to save a few bob on national insurance. There were others as well and the players were then looking around at training, thinking who's next, which made it hard to motivate them."

Lyons, meanwhile, was not the first or last City manager to enjoy working with loveable rogue Foster, even if his love for a bet and inside knowledge meant he wasn't always on hand. "Quite often when I needed him for something, I couldn't find him, but he would be up in the control box at the back of the Main Stand," Lyons explained. "I only found out in later years that he had a direct phone line to a jockey in Malton, who was giving him tips. Some of the players were mad on gambling, especially the goalkeeper Eddie Blackburn. He was always pestering Fossie for tips, but I don't think many came in."

Prior to Smith's appointment, results improved on the club's own soil under caretaker chief Barry Swallow with a 6-0 victory over Crewe representing the club's biggest home win since 1964/65.

292

George Bodley serves his final day as a turnstile operator in 1982, having ushered people into games at Bootham Crescent and Fulfordgate

Scotland international Peter Lorimer runs out for a game during his short spell at Bootham Crescent in the 1979/80 season

Stanchions were added to the goalposts at Bootham Crescent in the 1970s

An aerial view of Bootham Crescent in 1983

Girls' football was played at Bootham Crescent for the first time in February 1980 when Mill Mount won a Five-a-Side Schoolgirls' tournament Pictured (from left-to-right) are Ann Smith, Kathryn Sanderson, Trish Wells, Christine Watling and Mary Lowery

CHAPTER 19

Denis Smith and Viv Busby begin to shake things up

"All I could see when I got the ball was backsides. Nobody wanted it and that was a culture shock."

Stoke centre-back Denis Smith was brought in during Barry Swallow's caretaker spell in charge and went on to become Bootham Crescent's first player/manager the following season. Smith's City career could have ended almost before it began, however, following an eye-opening debut during a 3-1 Bootham Crescent defeat to neighbours Hull. "Playing Hull was a local derby and a big game, but it was a totally different type of football to what I had been used to," Smith admitted when recalling his maiden City outing. "I was knocking little balls down with my head and making short passes and people weren't expecting that at all. All I could see when I got the ball was backsides. Nobody wanted it and that was a culture shock. I remember Barry Swallow being in charge and I had an awful match, so I said to him: 'If you want to get rid of me, I'll go back now.'" Powerhouse striker Billy Whitehurst was on the scoresheet for the visitors that day and York-born future England manager Steve McClaren also ran the match from midfield.

The following month, meanwhile, former City favourite Graeme Crawford showed he could still do the business at his old ground. "When I left York, I came back to Bootham Crescent with both Scunthorpe and Rochdale and got a great reception," he reminisced. "When I returned with Rochdale in April 1982, we'd only won once away from home in six months, but we got a 2-1 victory and I saved a penalty from Derek Hood. I used to travel with Terry Dolan who was playing for Rochdale then and, on the way over, we were chatting about the game and joking. Terry said: 'What will you do if York get a penalty?' I said: 'I will stand right in the middle and won't move because the last two penalties I've seen Hoody take, he's just blasted them'. Unbelievably, they got a penalty and, just as he put the ball down, I said: 'I'm not moving, Derek'. Anyway, he blasted it and it hit me on the chest and we always have

Denis Smith delivers a team talk to his players in 1983

a laugh about that on the phone now. It was a bit strange, though, because I would have rather been playing for York still. But they still gave me a good clap and I never really got abused as such."

When Smith took over the reins with Viv Busby as his assistant, he insisted he wanted to play home matches on a Saturday afternoon, whereas Lyons had enjoyed Friday-night games because it meant he could scout players the following day. Smith also made rebuilding a defence that had shipped 91 goals the previous season - more than any other Football League side - his first priority. Ex-Bournemouth and Blackburn goalkeeper Roger Jones was brought in, along with full-backs Chris Evans and Alan Hay from Stoke and Bristol City respectively. After a cash bid for promising Stoke youngster Steve Bould was turned down, ex-Birmingham and Walsall defender Ricky Sbragia was also signed to play alongside Smith at centre back. John MacPhail would replace the boss eventually after being recruited from Sheffield United later in the season, but not before receiving a defensive masterclass though. Remembering the first match he watched at Bootham Crescent - a 5-2 New Year's Day triumph over Darlington - MacPhail laughed: "When I was going to come to York from Sheffield United, the plan was that I would replace Denis because he was going to retire but, the first game I saw there, I was told to go upstairs and watch a proper centre half. He meant himself obviously and he went on to score twice and the team won 5-2, so I didn't want to show my face in the dressing room after that! But he signed me the following month and it was a great time to come to Bootham Crescent. Denis was changing things. Viv was a great coach and Denis would become a good coach."

Recalling his defensive surgery, Smith said: "Ninety-odd goals had been conceded the previous season, so there was obviously something wrong. Eddie Blackburn was in goal and he was a shot-stopper who had been the Player of the Year, but I prefer my goalkeepers to come for the crosses and lower the number of shots they have to face. Roger Jones was class. He could make saves if he needed to do but he was never in the wrong position to start with. I played during that first season because we needed somebody to organise and talk at the back. Viv packed in and stayed in the dugout because I thought we were OK for goalscorers but, once I got John and Ricky in, that was me finished." Sbragia, meanwhile, almost decided against a move to York after initial talks with Smith at Bootham Crescent, saying: "Denis said he wanted to have a look at me and offered me a three-month contract. I said: 'No' and that I couldn't commit to York for three months. I said: 'Give me one year and I will come and live here', which is what I did. That's how it started, but I've been here ever since, and I'll never leave now, because I love York."

Sbragia added that he was immediately impressed with the personnel at Bootham Crescent, including existing players and his fellow new recruits. "Playing with Denis was good for me and then John (MacPhail) came in," Sbragia pointed out. "We also had Alan Hay at left back and Steve Senior on the right. We were all in our 20s, but good hungry players with an abundance of experience. I had played 190 games before York and most of us had done that, so we were experienced pros, but young experienced pros. You then had the likes of Keith Walwyn, John Byrne, Derek Hood and Gary Ford who were already there. Denis had a spell as a player first, so he'd assessed what he needed and, with Viv Busby there as well, it was a good place to be. All the staff were friendly, and Michael Sinclair also ran the place as a good, family club where everyone was on a similar wage. We didn't have somebody on £50,000 and somebody on £10,000, so there was no jealousy. Michael Sinclair ended up launching me a little bit when I went into coaching by helping me along financially because it was very expensive to pay for fees and you dropped your wages by 50 per cent when you went from being a player to a coach. Gestures like that meant everyone there wanted to play for the club. We didn't expect to go up in that first season. There was just a determination not to be near the bottom again, but we trained really hard that summer, then did a lot of football and unit work to gel us together. Maybe we were a bit hesitant about our chances during the first six games of that season, but our confidence grew and we all got on so well. There was nobody we actually feared, although we did far better than we thought, and Denis and Viv made coming to work fun, while still teaching us the basics and having good discipline. We also had exceptional players. The front three of Keith Walwyn, John Byrne and Gary Ford were terrific and you had Brian Pollard as well, so there was a good combination of youth and experience in the attacking positions. We probably only fell short that first season because of the squad's low numbers. That played a part when suspensions and injuries came along, but we started to get that continuation in terms of quality players in the coming years with the likes of Marco Gabbiadini, Mike Astbury, Keith Houchen, Brian Chippendale and Alan Pearce coming through and you had the confidence that whoever was coming into the squad was of the same quality as the person they were replacing. Not many players left either. The break-up only really happened years later when Denis left for Sunderland. There was also a social side, which was important too. We would go to the pub for an hour or three on a Tuesday afternoon if we didn't have a game and you got to know people and what they were thinking that way. Denis used to buy the first round, so you made sure you all got there on time. Some of us were married and some of us were single, but the group was always together, and I can't remember it ever blowing up in the dressing room. Denis and Viv were usually very constructive, and I can't recall an occasion when the players fought each other. Even though there were some strong characters in that squad, we won and lost together, and we probably just needed a bit more belief during that first season, although we had it at home."

Aside from the addition of Sean Haslegrave in midfield, the positions in front of the back four were largely filled by existing professionals whose talent had remained untapped. Ford fell into that category and, having spent his formative years scrapping for results, was impressed by Smith's reinforcements, pointing out: "They were still quite young, except for Roger, but his experience was amazing. He didn't have to move, and I don't think he ever dived. He just walked across and picked the ball up because his positioning was so good. One of the best signings was Sean Haslegrave though. He kept me and John (Byrne) on our toes. He was on at us constantly and you need that help. We didn't get it before from the older players. They were just ticking over and were not hungry."

Future FA Cup finalist and World Cup striker Bryne was even on the verge of being discarded due to an apparent, undiagnosed allergy to the Bootham

Crescent playing surface. On his inherited aces, Smith added: "I was a big fan of Byrney from the start. I'll never forget one of my first days at the club. We were playing five-a-side football in the gym and I was struck by the ability of a young, blond-haired lad. I couldn't understand that the club were trying to get rid of him because he was allergic to the grass. We found out it was hay fever and you could see he had talent. He just needed encouragement. But, when I had him as a manager, I used to fine him 50p, which was a lot of money for him back then, if he didn't pass when he needed to, because he used to try and beat four players and shoot from bad angles. I also remember saying to Big Keith after the last game of the season, when I didn't know I was going to become manager, that he should be looking to play a lot higher because he was a handful. Technically, he could be awful at times, to be perfectly honest, but his power was incredible, and he could score goals. He was one hell of a beast, but the nicest possible beast you could come across because he was a lovely man. On the field, though, you could put a cross in and he'd score then you'd look and there would be three opposition players flattened in the box, but they wouldn't have known what had happened, because people just bounced off him. Brian Pollard, Gary Ford and Derek Hood were all there too and Malcolm Crosby wasn't even in the side when I came to the club. They didn't understand the game how I had been led to understand it and their talent wasn't being used."

After the upheaval of recent years, Ford also welcomed a consistency in selection as he and fellow former apprentice Byrne both began to flourish together in the first team. "We were a steady side and we didn't move around," Ford pointed out. "We all stayed in the same positions and knew our jobs. With me and John, I didn't have to look to see where he was - I just knew and that takes time to happen. We were also getting that bit older and more confident. You rarely go onto a pitch knowing you are going to win, but we felt like that at home." Winger Pollard felt the new management team made an immediate impact, saying: "Denis and Viv came in and turned everything around with the addition of a couple of players and they were a bit more professional. Ricky Sbragia and John MacPhail came in. John had all the pace and Ricky's positional play was second to none. Roger Jones also wasn't the tallest or most agile goalkeeper, but he was always in the right place. They all made the existing players more professional than they had been before too. I knew John Byrne and Gary Ford as apprentices during my first spell at the club so was aware they had potential. Keith Walwyn was as raw as they come but, if you'd put a barn door in front of him, he would have gone through it. He was also a lovely bloke too. When he wanted to run, he could run, but his physical presence was usually enough. Centre-halves couldn't have liked him and that included Denis Smith, who Keith used to batter in training. When Denis and Viv first came to the club and were playing, they also led by example because they were good players."

On the importance of midfielder Haslegrave's recruitment, meanwhile, Smith added: "Sean Haslegrave was a massive signing because he was a character who brought the lads together. He must have had four or five birthdays a year because he was always asking for permission to get the lads together for a drink, but I didn't mind that." Smith was open to trying new things at City as well and, during his first close season, agreed to be a question-and-answer panellist, along with Peterborough boss Martin Wilkinson, as a big screen was hired to show the World Cup final in the Social Club. Clifton Without Junior School teacher Lindsay Rice also joined the club's staff in an honorary capacity to invite junior Minor League squads and school football teams to attend home matches as guests of the club.

The 1982/83 season, meanwhile, represented the club's diamond jubilee and marked the 50th anniversary of the move to Bootham Crescent, with the scorer of the club's first-ever league goal at the ground half-a-century before - Tom Mitchell - invited as a guest for the opening match of the season against Torquay. JW Cameron & Co sponsored the game in another link to the club's first Bootham Crescent fixture, with the company having bought the Scarborough and Whitby Brewery Company in 1953 from John Hunt - the man who cut the ribbon to officially open the stadium.

Although Smith's first game as manager at Bootham Crescent was a modest 1-1 draw against the Devon club, played in front of only 1,737 supporters, the team would become nigh-on invincible at their home arena that campaign with one run of 13 league and cup wins reaping 47 goals. In fact, a 0-0 home draw against Swindon on March 26, 1983 saw City fail to score at Bootham Crescent for the first time since February 6, 1982 - a sequence of 30 games. Eventual champions and then leaders Wimbledon were the only visiting team to take maximum points all season - following a 4-1 reverse in October - but seventh-placed City would end the campaign with the best home record in the division. Sbragia remembered the challenge Wimbledon posed as Dave Bassett had begun to assemble a Crazy Gang, including the likes of goalkeeper Dave Beasant, that would go on to ply their trade in the country's top division and lift the FA Cup in 1988. "Wimbledon had good players physically and technically, who were well-suited to that division," he said of their lower-league credentials at the time. City never dwelt on such rare setbacks at home, though, with Sbragia adding: "Whatever happened on Saturday, we would talk about on the Monday and then drive up to Clifton for training, but we never went back to it after that. It was gone and history. Denis and Viv always focussed on encouragement, because you knew when you hadn't played well."

Walwyn led the way for City that season with 24 goals and the average league crowd of 3,243 was the highest since the second division days. That gave Smith great pride after almost a decade of footballing decline in North Yorkshire. "Coming from Stoke, I had never heard of rugby league, but the rugby club were getting bigger crowds than the football club when I joined the club, so it was important to look at what they were doing, and we needed to become more entertaining," he reasoned. Ford also welcomed the surge in spectators at the ground. "It was mad how the crowd went up from just over a thousand," he admitted.

The team were denied a victory at home to Peterborough in September of that campaign, though, as future England keeper David Seaman saved a Derek Hood penalty during a 1-1 draw. Describing the incident, *Yorkshire Evening Press* reporter Malcolm Huntington said: "Hood sent Seaman the wrong way, but as the goalkeeper dived to his right, he brought off a freak save as the ball hit his legs and went for a corner." Seaman endured a mixed afternoon, throwing the ball straight out to Ford for City's goal and making a misjudgement that Walwyn almost capitalised on. The future Arsenal shot-stopper was also described as making fine saves, though, from Mick Laverick, Byrne and Walwyn. In October of that season, a firework display was held to celebrate the centenary of the *Yorkshire Evening Press* newspaper at Bootham Crescent, with thousands attending. Members of the York Youth Gymnastic Display team also performed before the fireworks, as did the band of the Ist Battalion The Duke of Wellington.

With job-less numbers rising all over the country, at the end of October, City also halved the admission price to 80p (in line with the cost for pensioners and Junior Reds) for fans who produced an unemployment card. October also saw the club's first-ever Player of the Month prize - a gold watch - awarded to Sbragia. The new competition was sponsored by a different company each month with Smith Brothers plumbers' merchants the first business to get involved. In the mid-2000s, Preston & Duckworth's would run a Player of the Month competition jointly with *The Press* newspaper, where the winner would again receive a watch, as would the fan chosen to make the presentation on the pitch before a game. The supporter was chosen randomly from those who voted for their man of the match via email to *The Press's* office - a poll that contributed to the award, along with the newspaper's ratings at games. During the final years at Bootham Crescent, the prize changed to a framed photograph, but it was still presented by a supporter, with the man-of-the-match polls conducted on social media site Twitter.

Back in January 1983, the club's first Sunday home fixture in nine years attracted the highest league gate in more than seven for the visit of Scunthorpe, with 7,097 coming through the turnstiles. Chairman Michael Sinclair and manager Smith, though, maintained that they were not in general favour of playing on the traditional day of rest. "I am not very keen on Sunday games, as I like to spend the day with my family," Smith pointed out. There was a feeling that the attendance was always going to be high too, regardless of when it was scheduled with City having won seven games in succession at home and Scunthorpe fourth in the table. City won the match 2-1 with Walwyn and Ford netting.

A new record for gate receipts of £17,300, smashing the previous best figure of £9,165, was subsequently recorded when 9,909 witnessed the Minstermen beat then league leaders Hull City 1-0 with Byrne heading in the winning goal. Around 3,000 Hull supporters made the trip and future England boss McClaren was again in the visiting side, along with Brian Marwood and Gary Swann, who would go on to play for Arsenal and the Minstermen respectively. The Tuesday night contest was not as enjoyable for nearby residents, though, with windows smashed on houses in Shipton Street, Scarborough Terrace, Newborough Street and Upper Newborough Street, as hooligans went on the rampage. In fact, only 15 windows were reportedly left intact on Scarborough Terrace, with front doors also kicked off their hinges, shop window displays strewn across the road and cars overturned, as 50 away fans caused £3,000 worth of damage. The following Saturday's home match against Chester saw an appeal launched to help those affected by the vandalism, with fans asked for donations on a blanket that was carried around the pitch at half-time.

At the end of the season, 64-year-old physio John Simpson played the last 90 seconds of his testimonial against Leeds, meanwhile, at Bootham Crescent in front of 3,066 supporters. Apprentice 17-year-old professional Alan Pearce scored with his first touch in a senior game for City during a 3-2 triumph for Leeds. Marco Gabbiadini had earlier netted as the Junior Reds Supporters' Club beat their Leeds equivalents 4-1.

Internal improvements, meanwhile, were made behind the Main Stand at Bootham Crescent in the summer of 1983. A Vice-Presidents' Lounge with a bar was built, along with a new extension to the Main Stand entrance incorporating a lounge and office accommodation for the club secretary and lottery staff. The work was funded by John Smith's Tadcaster Brewery Limited and cost in the region of £25,000, while the extension was designed by York architect Ronald G Sims. With the club embracing executive spectator hospitality, the Vice-Presidents' Lounge would be situated above the admin office and behind the directors' box. The lounge also initially accommodated visiting managers and VIP visitors, while the two Portakabins in the car park were sold, which created seven more parking spaces for vice-presidents and match officials.

A ladies' football coaching session at Bootham Crescent taken by Malcolm Crosby

A crowd of just under 10,000 crams into the ground for the home match against Hull in April 1983

An aerial shot of Bootham Crescent in 1983

CHAPTER 20

Walwyn and Byrne fire Centurions into the history books

"Once that team got going, they believed they were going out there and were going to win. The crowd believed that too."

York City etched an indelible place in the Football League record books in 1984 following a campaign that never saw them outside the top-two positions in division four on the way to becoming the first English club to rack up more than 100 points in a season after the switch to three points for a win. For the second successive campaign, Bootham Crescent witnessed just one home league defeat - a 3-2 loss to Torquay in November - which ended a 13-month unbeaten run on their own soil in the league. Kevin Young, making his debut for the Devon club following a £5,000 move from Burnley, scored the winning goal five minutes from time for the visitors, who also included a teenaged, future England international defender Keith Curle in their team, playing on the wing. The goal was greeted by astonished silence from home spectators and, despite the historic campaign, that result still irritated Denis Smith, who said: "Losing always rankled me whether it was in a practice match or a five-a-side game. I don't think that had been the case at York for a few years before. I only enjoyed winning and couldn't see the point in playing otherwise. Once that team got going, they believed they were going out there and were going to win. The crowd believed that too."

Indeed, the fans turned up in their numbers and, by the beginning of November, City put back the kick-off for their Tuesday night match with Wrexham from 7.30pm to 7.45pm in an attempt to get all of the supporters into the ground following the congestion problems caused by gates that had doubled in size. The move was sanctioned by the Football League and, after being reported as improving matters, was implemented at further evening games during the season. Jack Dunnett, chairman of the Football League, also officially opened the new Vice-Presidents' Lounge and Main Stand extension prior to the game.

January, meanwhile, saw legendary commentator John Motson and the BBC's famous *Football Focus* cameras visit Bootham Crescent to interview Smith and Viv Busby. The following month would see beer company Hansa agree a shirt-sponsorship deal for the rest of the season and the logoed kits debuted at the 1000th league game to be staged at Bootham Crescent - a 2-0 triumph over Darlington with John MacPhail and Gary Ford, who was making his 250th appearance for the club, the marksmen. MacPhail fondly remembered the fun atmosphere at Bootham Crescent during the historic campaign, saying: "John Byrne had ability and great feet, while big Keith (Walwyn) was awkward and a handful. He would hit the ball and I don't think even he would know where it was going sometimes. Brian Pollard and Gary Ford were on the wings supplying crosses, while Sean Haslegrave and Malcolm Crosby gave the team great experience in midfield. Then, at the back, there was Steve Senior, Ricky Sbragia, myself and Alan Hay in front of Roger Jones. Everybody got on with each other and there were no superstars because nobody would have allowed anybody to behave like that. There wasn't a single bad apple. The camaraderie and fun we had there was fantastic. It was a place filled with laughter and it was a good team that Denis and Viv had gelled together. They just gave us the leeway to go out and play."

Fans also flocked to Bootham Crescent with a new cup competition for teams in the bottom two divisions - then named the Associate Members Cup which would later become the Football League Trophy - attracting 5,837 for a first-round 2-1 defeat to Hull, with Steve McClaren scoring the winning goal. That attendance has never been beaten since for a City fixture in the competition - home or away. The club also charged a higher admission price than for league games, with the cost £2 for standing instead of £1.70 and £3.50 for a seat instead of £3. Two home fans were arrested at the game, but there was nowhere near the same level of trouble that had marred the previous season's meeting between the two teams. In March, the club staged a morning kick-off for the first time since 1969, with the home match against Swindon brought forward to 11am to avoid a clash with York Rugby League Club's Challenge Cup semi-final against Wigan at Elland Road. Attempts to switch the game to Friday or Saturday night had been vetoed by the league, but Swindon agreed to the early kick-off. The theory was it would allow sport supporters in the city to watch both matches, either in person or, in the case of the rugby match, on television. City beat Swindon 2-0 thanks to goals from Walwyn and Ford in front of a 3,341 crowd (the lowest at home since the last Saturday afternoon match before Christmas) and moved nine points clear of nearest rivals Doncaster with a game in hand, while the rugby club pushed Wigan close before losing 14-8.

A 1-1 draw, meanwhile, against eventual runners-up Doncaster in April attracted a Sunday crowd of 11,297 - the biggest at Bootham Crescent in eight years since Chelsea's 1976 visit in the FA Cup, resulting in record receipts of £20,725, with every seat in the ground sold, along with the visitors' full allocation of 3,750 tickets. The match also saw a dividing fence erected in the Popular Stand to separate supporters of the two teams. City missed out on a club-record equalling run of seven straight league wins in the match, with the visitors forging in front when Glynn Snodin beat Jones at the far post after a free kick was headed on by Ernie Moss. Two minutes later, Rovers keeper Dennis Peacock saved a penalty from Byrne, who took responsibility when nominated player Steve Senior decided against taking the spot kick. But the scores were levelled when Peacock charged 35 yards out of his goal and was left helpless as Ford comfortably beat him to Alan Pearce's long pass through the right channel and lifted the ball into the vacated away net. Ford admitted that he enjoyed the mid-80s' derby tussles with a Doncaster side, who included brothers Ian and Glynn Snodin - both destined to play top-flight football. "I remember scoring that day because one of the Donny supporters ran onto the pitch and was straight in front of my face," Ford recalled. "All I could smell was beer, but the police ran on. It was intimidating because I didn't see him coming and he was just there. I also had Billy Bremner, who was a big hero of mine and Doncaster's manager at the time, walking towards me at the end of the game and I thought: 'Hello, what does he want?' He just said: 'Will you come and play for me next year?' I wasn't tempted, though, because we were the better side at the time. There was not a lot of difference between the two teams. I think we were just more consistent. The Snodin brothers were playing for Donny back then and I was always up against Glynn, who was their left back. We used to have a battle and knew we were in for a battle every time we played each other. We respected each other and were both at the top of our games. I also remember for one of those big matches against them, I was walking down to the game from where I lived in Leeman Road and a Donny supporter pulled up because he was lost, so I got in his car and he gave me a lift. I don't think he believed I was playing, but he maybe spotted me on the pitch."

Ricky Sbragia also enjoyed the dust-ups with Doncaster back then, saying: "I still bump into their centre-forward Colin Douglas now and we talk about those games, because there was a rivalry between us and them. They wanted to challenge for the title as well and it wasn't far off being a derby match. That's how we treated it and we always gave the opposition respect, but knew we were stronger than them physically. We were a big team with myself, John MacPhail,

Keith Walwyn and Keith Houchen. We knew the Donny games were vital to win because, if we got six points from those matches, that would move us away from them. The crowds against Doncaster were also brilliant. You were definitely aware of just how many were there and could see that it was a bigger crowd than normal. That made you appreciate the importance of the game, because why would 11,000 people be there otherwise? It was the closest derby we had at the time and we always felt they would be up there so, when we played them, we knew it would be a decent attendance. Normally a big gate at Bootham Crescent would be 6,000 or 7,000 and I remember Sean Haslegrave when he was going out to warm up before the game saying: 'I'm going to go in the far-left corner, just so their fans can give me stick now and I can get it out of the way'. But there was no fear in the dressing room. Everybody was comfortable with who they were working with and the build-up was always comfortable, even though we knew those games were the ones we had to win. We knew the fans probably wanted to win this one a bit more than the others maybe, because of how many were there. But, five minutes into the game, you tend to forget about everything else and you're focussed on the match. You would get an impression of it again with the noise when a tackle went in or something happened off the ball that we hadn't seen, and the crowd reaction was bigger than normal. It's a great feeling when you're winning games though and we had the belief we could beat most teams, especially at home."

Yorkshire Evening Press reporter Malcolm Huntington had begun to believe the side were virtually invincible on their own soil too. He said: "I remember Denis Smith saying he wanted teams to be frightened to death when they stepped off the bus coming into the ground and it did seem a bit like that because they won a lot of games very comfortably that season. You never thought they were going to be beaten and they used to whitewash teams. Roger Jones was also the best keeper I saw at Bootham Crescent, other than Sam Bartram." Pollard agreed that the team felt indomitable on their own soil, saying: "We thought we were going to win every game back then. We got the record number of points, but I'm not sure the atmosphere was better than in the 1970s' second division days because we had bigger crowds back then and the atmosphere was always incredible when both ends were full."

The final three home games all gave City supporters big reasons to celebrate however. First, the formality of promotion was mathematically guaranteed following a 4-1 Good Friday triumph over Halifax with Byrne hitting a hat-trick and Walwyn also on target. Fans piled onto the pitch after the final whistle to lead celebratory chants in front of the Main Stand. Walwyn's brace past former

City team-mate Eddie Blackburn then secured the title in a 2-0 home triumph over Hartlepool with three games still left to play. The result also marked a club record-breaking 29th league win. With six minutes to go in the game, fans had started to congregate on the touchlines, chanting "Champions" and singing City's recently recorded song "Here We Go", which had been written by York musician Bob de Vries, who had been the lead singer in the punk band Cyanide. As the game entered its final throes, supporters from the Shipton Street End were standing almost up to the goal-line and, when the whistle went, another pitch invasion ensued. The team, along with Smith and Busby, went on to join in the festivities from the directors' box and the party continued in the players' lounge for a further two hours, where the champagne flowed. Finally, Byrne, Derek Hood and Ford netted as City also broke the 100-point barrier following a 3-0 Bootham Crescent victory over Bury.

It was fitting that Ford scored the final home goal that season with Huntington revealing: "We used to go and see Denis Smith at Bootham Crescent on a Thursday for his press conference where he announced the team and, once, he said: 'It will be Gary Ford and ten others'. He was always the first name on Denis' team sheet because of his graft." Indeed, from October 1981 to April 1986, Ford only missed one match at Bootham Crescent. "The one home game I missed during that run was because of chicken pox," he explained. "You didn't want to miss a game because you had your basic wage and, if you played, you got a bit more money and, if the team won, you got a bit more money. The squads were also smaller, so you were told to 'run if off because we need you'." Ford was delighted, meanwhile, to draw a historic campaign to a close at Bootham Crescent with the Centurions' third goal. He said: "The Bury game was the best of the lot and I've still got the TV clip from that match. It was very rare that Byrney crossed the ball for me to score - it was normally the other way around - but he did that game and it was probably the first time he'd set me up. It was brilliant when everyone ran on the pitch as well."

The match provided a bitter-sweet memory for Pollard, though, who was left out of the team, despite playing 35 games and scoring seven goals that campaign. He never played for the club again with Smith offloading the popular attacker without an explanation. "It was like a celebration every week back then, but I wasn't picked for the Bury game and was told by Denis that he would be letting me go," Pollard remembered. "He's never given me a good reason for that and it spoiled everything for me. It took a lot of the shine off and that was a shame because I didn't have a bad season. If you gave 100 per cent, the crowd would always back you at York. They gave players a lot of stick if they didn't, but I'd like to think I always did."

John MacPhail salutes the crowd as he makes his way through the pitch invasion at the end of the final game of the historic 1983-84 season against Bury

Sbragia admitted that the squad felt they would be promoted as champions halfway through the season, so the 100-point challenge became a big focus during the team's run-in. The match against Bury, though, would also prove the only one City's talismanic centre back missed all season after he had helped safeguard a 1-0 victory at Mansfield the game before, when his professional foul, which were only punishable with a yellow card back then, was nevertheless enough to earn him a suspension for the historic final home fixture.

It meant, like Pollard, he was forced to watch on from the sidelines, having celebrated going up and winning the championship in the previous two home contests. "Halifax was usually a tough one and a bit of a derby," Sbragia recalled of the promotion-winning contest. "They also had good players like Paul Hendrie, but we had so much belief that, even by Christmas time, we thought we were going to win the title. It was just a matter of when we were going to get presented with the trophy and that wasn't arrogance - it came from having such a strong belief. We felt we were the best team in the league and had the ability to break teams down. We had that belief we would always score and, when we went behind in matches, we just thought we've got to do a bit more now. You have that bunch of games at Easter that can be crucial, but we had come to a stage where we knew nobody could beat us and that everything was going in the right direction, so it became a case of how many points we could get. As we kept winning games, that became a big thing for us and we wanted to get to 100 points. I was suspended for that Bury game because I'd got booked in the match before at Mansfield. It was 1-0 to us at the time and their player was going through and I thought I'll bring him down. I knew I would get suspended for the last home game, so I was a bit gutted. But it had been going through my mind and I was thinking: 'Should I bring him down?' and I decided: 'Yes', because he could have beaten Jonesy. Denis would have been happy with that as a professional foul, but it took me out of the team for that Bury match, which was difficult because it was the only game I missed all season and I knew we would be getting the Championship trophy and all that. It was for the team though and that was more important than me. We might not have got 100 points if I hadn't done what I did (the team went on to lose their last game at Hereford, so Sbragia's foul could, indeed, have proven the difference between accumulating 99 points and 101) and you were encouraged to take people out in those situations. I still really enjoyed the occasion, but it would have been nice to play in that match. I also felt for Brian Pollard, because it's never nice to be dropped, but it made me realise these are the decisions managers have to make and that I might have to do the same in the future. I don't know why Denis dropped him and we were a bit surprised. Sometimes, it can be a power thing. He might have been showing that he was in charge and the manager. For most of the season, the whole team were fit and that helped in terms of not chopping and changing. The back four was near enough the same all season and we were fortunate that we didn't get injured."

Smith, meanwhile, spoke of the pride and joy he still felt, almost four decades on, at achieving all three landmarks at the club's home stadium. He said: "Doing it in front of our own crowd was the main thing and it was great to get everyone wound up. We won promotion fairly early and then the league, but the 100 points target gave us something still to play for because that's in the record books now and nobody will ever be able to take that away from us. We were the first to get over that mark, which is brilliant for a club like York. It was also fantastic to beat Bury 3-0 in the final home game because, if the team didn't let a goal in, I was happy. We were good at celebrating too and we had a good time that night." Ford, meanwhile, recalled how Smith urged the team to celebrate each landmark that season - promotion, the title and passing 100 points, saying: "We celebrated quite often, and I think we celebrated after each of those last three home games. We had a good social side and Denis encouraged that at the right time. He would tell us to go to the Bootham Tavern if we'd had a hard training session on a Tuesday and there was no midweek fixture." Ford also revealed how the players would toast their successes and recover from their rare failures in the Social Club with supporters after games. "We always used to have a drink in the Social Club after a match and you knew where different people would be in there because they were always in the same spots," he smiled. "Bootham Crescent was a community back then and an escape for so many people. Everyone was involved. The fans knew the players and even Denis would say after the match: 'Right, everyone get to the social club'. You had to go in the bar. My dad loved Bootham Crescent and he was in the bar before and after games. He was with me, the players and the fans in there. There was a big connection with the supporters."

Sbragia also recalled that close connection between players and fans at the time, saying: "We were never away from the supporters. We were doing a job they would probably have loved to do, but everybody mixed together in the Social Club. Everyone knew the players and their families as well. That's changed a bit at all football clubs and, even then, you got the odd punter who wanted to give you a bit of stick, but you just got on with it." The board were also a supportive presence at Bootham Crescent with Sbragia adding: "Michael Sinclair gave us all a tankard and I thought that was brilliant and a nice thought. We had got the medals, but that was a nice little surprise that none of us expected and they were waiting for us on the bus in boxes after the last game of the season at Hereford. It was a really good period to be at the club and it was probably the best group of players I have worked with in all my time in football. I had won promotion at Walsall before, but it was nothing like it was at York. We understood the club had limits financially and, whilst you're not always happy about that, we knew why that's how it was, because everybody was in it together. We knew they were doing the best they could for us and the management and the board were good and always very approachable."

MacPhail concurred, meanwhile, that passing 100 points felt like the biggest accomplishment, reasoning: "It was a fantastic achievement to get more than 100 points because no team had ever managed that before and Denis wanted to do it." There was also personal recognition for the Scottish defender as, despite strong competition from all areas of the pitch, he was presented on the pitch with the Billy Fenton Memorial Trophy as Clubman of the Year - an award that he also picked up the following season. On that honour, he said: "It was great to receive the trophy in a stadium packed full of fans - much better than it would have been at a dinner in a hall somewhere with a few hundred people there."

In tremendous scenes at the final whistle against Bury, the new obelisk-style fourth division Canon Trophy was presented to skipper Roger Jones by Football League management committee member Ian Jones, who was also the chairman of rivals Doncaster, on scaffolding, which had been specially constructed in front of the directors' box for the occasion. Earlier, 40 autographed balls had been booted into the crowd 15 minutes before kick-off by City's players to set the tone for a carnival atmosphere during the bank-holiday Monday contest. Two more club records tumbled as City moved on to 95 league goals for the season and completed their 11th double of the campaign. A 2-1 final-day defeat at Hereford meant they went on to finish the season with 96 goals.

Against Bury, Keith Houchen's pass teed up Byrne for the first goal, while Hood curled in a free kick following a foul on Walwyn to double the advantage on 25 minutes. The crowd then surged onto the pitch when Ford prodded in a third with a minute to go after his initial header had been blocked on the line following a jinking Byrne run. Referee John Hunting, who retired after taking charge of the FA Cup final later in the month, then restored order before sparking off another invasion when he signalled the end of the game by taking the ball off Jones as he was about to clear. An overwhelmed Bury had not even managed a single shot on target.

The players subsequently jumped on an open-top bus, which left Bootham Crescent at 5.45pm after the game and was driven through the city by Happy Wanderers legend Sid Storey to the Mansion House for a civic reception. City fans had seen their side score in every home game for the first time ever during a single season and Sbargia admitted that he never felt putting the ball in the net was going to be a problem at Bootham Crescent that campaign, saying: "Viv always encouraged us to play, but mainly in the other half and, that season, everything gelled, and everybody was hungry. We had excellent attacking options and we always knew we had goals in us. Keith (Walwyn) was immense and out of this world. I would have hated to play against him. It was hard enough in training. You could hit him, but it wouldn't bother him. He was such a game man and I don't think we would have been the team we were if he hadn't been there. He was a massive focus for us, because we always felt he would never give anybody a free header and would upset defenders. I used to call him 'The Wedge', because he was always in there battering people. He took the bruising, but John Byrne was an instrumental player as well, because he would pick up the second balls and play and, if you couldn't go to Keith, you went to Byrney instead and could trust him. They really complemented each other and the great thing at the back was, if you were under pressure, you could just play it long and Keith would win the ball and that allowed you to push up the pitch as a defence, because we played a bit of offside as well, back when it was a straightforward rule. Then, you also had Gary Ford and Brian Pollard down the wings. Off the ball, we were 4-4-2 but, on the ball, we were 4-2-4, especially at home. Gary Ford and Steve Senior had energy to burn on the right, as did Alan Hay and Brian Pollard on the left. They had great understandings and got on well off the pitch as well. Gary Ford and John Byrne had terrific feet and Sean Haslegrave and Malcolm Crosby could also cover the ground and were battlers. Sean would say: 'I will go in and commit myself and you can pick up the loose ball'. While we always felt we could score goals from open play, we got our fair share from set-plays as well and could all score. We all chipped in with at least three or four a season from the back and set plays were vital, because we knew we could make our height advantage count with them."

Sbragia also outlined Walwyn's importance to the team in defending dead-ball deliveries with his gazelle-like, near-post leaps also a familiar sight during those heady days at Bootham Crescent. "We used to put Keith at the near post for corners and told him to just head everything, because we knew not many balls were going to clear him," Sbragia explained. "We used to zonal mark, which Denis had brought in and was a bit different. I'd only done a wee bit at Blackpool before, but some players would mark and some would line up across the six-yard box but, when Keith was on the near post, the ball would have to be that far in the air to get over him and, if it did, you might have Roger Jones coming for it depending on the flight. If people tried to get the ball over both of them, it was probably going to go out of play and it was very rare Keith lost anything in those situations."

The historic title success was, indeed, a great squad effort, considering only 18 players were used the whole season - with just 16 of those starting matches. It was also achieved despite charismatic groundsman Bryan Foster's attempts to keep the team off his prized playing surface with Sbragia laughing: "Sometimes we trained on the pitch, but Fossie was never happy about that. I remember one day Denis said: 'I'm going to go on the pitch on Friday'. It was Thursday and Fossie said: 'No, you're not'. Denis said: 'Yes, I am', so we went on and, as we went out, he was cutting the grass to the left, so we went right. Fossie then got to the centre circle and just left the lawnmower running and walked off the pitch. It went straight into the net, which was brilliant."

The club received £8,000 as fourth division champions, £2,000 for finishing the season as top scorers and Canon - the Football League's sponsors - also awarded the club an additional £1,000 for reaching 100 points, adding to an overall profit of almost £15,000 that was made over the course of the campaign.

As the only man to play in both sides, Pollard is arguably the best-qualified person to comment on which was the better team - the historic centurions or the 1973/74 promotion winners who went on to play in the old second division? His answer is pretty categorical. "Without any disrespect to any player in the 1983/84 team, I think the 1970s' team would have beaten them," he declared. "I was in both and I think a lot of people who watched both would agree. The 1970s' team got into the second division. The 1980s' side didn't, and I don't think they would have done, even if the players had been kept together. If somebody asked me which team I'd want to play for in a match between the two sides then I would have gone for the 70s' lads because I felt we played better as a team. There were similarities though. Both teams played 4-4-2 and had similar wingers who could also defend well." Asked which team-mates he would have taken first to play alongside him from both golden Bootham Crescent eras, Pollard added: "If I could pick one player from the 70s' team, it would probably be Phil Burrows. I knew how good he was because I played against him in training and I never saw anybody give him a roasting. He was a physical specimen and stood out for me although the two lads up front were good too. Sealy did all the running and Jonesy tucked them in but they both seemed to end up with about 18 goals every season. From the 1980s' team, you would take big Keith (Walwyn). He took some beating and was so physically imposing. That side had lots of good players technically, but Keith could get you a goal out of nothing. You could just hit a hopeful ball up to him and he would beat three players, get on the end of it and then set somebody up or put it in the net."

Generations of City supporters, meanwhile, were well aware that the team always chose to kick towards the Shipton Street goal in the second half of games ever since the tradition of supporters switching ends was phased out in the mid-1970s and statistics from the historic 1983/84 campaign make interesting reading. Of the 14 times, Smith's men attacked that way after the break, the hosts won 13 and drew one of their games. On the nine occasions, they finished the match at the other end, they won five, drew three and lost one.

Brian Pollard scores past future England keeper David Seaman in a September 1983 clash against Peterborough

Keith Walwyn heads in a typical goal against Newport in April 1986

CHAPTER 21

Keith Houchen's penalty sends Arsenal packing

"Keith Houchen rolled home his penalty - and all hell broke loose. The rattle did overtime."

Back in the old third division, prices went up from £1.70 to £2 for ground admission, £2 to £2.50 in the Enclosure, £2.20 to £3 in the Popular Stand and £3 to £4 in the Main Stand. But the cost for pensioners and Junior Reds members was frozen at £1 and the programme remained free. Despite growing demand for the introduction of season tickets in the Shipton Street End, meanwhile, club secretary Tom Hughes reasoned that the numbers interested would still not be high enough to make that offering practical in that area of the ground. He said: "It would involve the club in considerable cost and would be virtually impossible to administrate. If there were 500 or more fans who would be prepared to buy a ticket before the season started, we would give serious consideration to it. I suspect the numbers would be considerably below that. We have only four turnstiles at the Shipton Street End, one of which is for Junior Reds and pensioners. If we had a gate for season-ticket holders as well, that would leave two turnstiles to get perhaps 4,000 people through and that would be out of the question on big match days. Clearly, season-ticket holders wouldn't want to queue with everyone else to get in. If there are 500 fans who want season tickets for about £35 to £40 for the Shipton Street End, then I hope they will get in touch with me but, if there are only 50 to 100, then it simply wouldn't be a practical proposition."

The reserve team, which had been disbanded, was also reinstated as the club entered the Central League, with most home matches taking place on a Wednesday night. During the summer, meanwhile, the Popular Stand was re-roofed and some of the seats were replaced in a project that cost just under £30,000. Following the success during the previous two seasons of switching a local derby to a Sunday kick-off, City also pushed back two games by 24 hours - against Doncaster again and Bradford City. By the summer of 1984, the once-thriving Supporters' Club was in decline though. Membership had dropped from 700 to 150 in seven years and the club had now taken over many of its former duties at Bootham Crescent, such as running the tea bar, the Travel Club and the programme shop. Two new tea bars - one in the Shipton Street End and one at the Grosvenor Road End just outside the Social Club - were also introduced for the new season.

The team subsequently made a great start to the new campaign and went top of the table following a 1-0 home win over Bristol Rovers in early October thanks to a Keith Walwyn goal. By then, City had won six and drawn two of their opening eight league fixtures but lost a little momentum when one of the finest strike partnerships Bootham Crescent had ever seen was split up, as John Byrne was sold to QPR a fortnight later. On his departure, Smith said: "Once players start getting sold, others start thinking what about me. The problem when you're a smaller club is, if you have good players - and John was exceptional - then they are going to leave sooner or later. It's not right for them to stay either. I wouldn't have wanted him to go, though, because it's amazing how good a manager you become when you have good players."

Byrne had played against then first division QPR just weeks earlier in the League Cup, with the first leg at Bootham Crescent seeing a return to home fans being permitted at both ends of the ground with City supporters filling a section closest to the Social Club at the Grosvenor Road End and the followers of the London club given the other section and seats in the Popular Stand. The decision was made to ease congestion at the car-park turnstiles with a big demand for admission expected from home supporters, while few were expected to travel from down south for the Tuesday night first-leg fixture. City lost the tie 4-2 in front of a 10,012 crowd, with the kick-off delayed to ensure everybody could be admitted for the start of the game. Gary Bannister (2), Terry Fenwick and Wayne Fereday netted for the visitors to secure victory, despite equalisers from Keith Houchen and Walwyn.

Changes were made for the following Tuesday's visit of then league leaders Bristol Rovers, with the Enclosure turnstile at the Shipton Street End becoming a ground turnstile to provide four points of entry rather than three. Crush barriers were also erected to separate supporters in front of the turnstiles at that end of the car park and home fans continued to be allowed in the same section of the Grosvenor Road End. Although there would be more good times to look forward to in the FA Cup, Gary Ford believed that Byrne's departure curtailed the club's chances of continued progress up the Football League. "We could have made another step, but John went and then others started to leave," he explained.

Smith's team would eventually fall away to eighth but other highlights at Bootham Crescent included a 7-1 thrashing of Gillingham - the club's biggest win for 20 years - which saw Houchen hit a hat-trick, Alan Pearce bag a brace and Walwyn also net. That game, meanwhile, saw the York Nomads Society - an unofficial supporters' club - ask fans to sign a "free speech" petition after Bootham Crescent officials had banned the selling of their magazine *Terrace Talk* at the ground on match days. The publication, edited by Frank Ormston, represented the start of the fanzine movement at York, which was beginning to spread at clubs up and down the country.

Houchen, an emerging Marco Gabbiadini and November signing Dale Banton tried to fill the void left by Byrne with Smith adding: "In the promotion season, Houch played more games in midfield just off John and Keith because he wasn't as good as them, which is quite a statement considering that he went on to make a big name for himself by scoring in the FA Cup final and playing at the highest level. Dale gave us a bit of pace and Marco was just a baby then - a powerful baby, but just starting out." Gabbiadini was embarking on a career that would see him go on to command combined transfer fees approaching £3million but, despite his clear potential, he was not spared any of his apprentice duties. The former Nunthorpe Grammar School pupil and future Premier League striker and England under-21 international recalled: "When I started, there were five of us as apprentices and it was hard work. We did a lot of the jobs that needed doing. I used to ride in on my bike in a morning and, when we got to the ground, we would have to sort the kit out, which meant getting it from the laundry and putting it out in the dressing room. Crosser (Malcolm Crosby) was our coach back then and, for the second part of our day, we would all cram into the back of the minibus with the first-team players and go to training at Clifton Hospital where, from time to time, some of the patients would come out and try to join in. After training, we would then go back to the dressing room and our real work would start. We used to have to tidy up the kit because it would be everywhere, and the dressing room was a mess, so we'd bag everything and take it down to the laundry. We'd also have to clean the dressing room, including the bath, and scrub all the corridors. Then, you started on the boots and cleaned them. I used to do the manager's and coaches'. We used to have a couple of laughs and pranks, but you stayed in the same kit all day until the jobs were finished and never got fed. There was no obligation on you to eat the right stuff and I used to take a packed lunch with me because that's what my dad did going to work as a scaffolder. At the end of the season, we used to paint the fencing around the pitch and we also used to have to paint a blue hoarding board in the David Longhurst End that meant you had to climb up the floodlight pylons to get to it. The club would get closed down for health-and-safety violations these days for having us do that. The best thing you could probably say about it was that it was character building, but it was part of being a young footballer and it all acted as a bit of an incentive, because I didn't want to do it for two years and it didn't take me long to start getting involved with the first team. I then signed my first pro contract and, whilst I still had to do some jobs, they weren't as bad or as regular. I've worked with young footballers since then and they don't leave grounds until 4pm or 5pm, but it's because they are having double sessions and working on their skills and techniques or having extra sessions in the gym. We were leaving at a similar time, but we were cleaning and scrubbing, although we did used to try and escape to the little gym that had been built not long before. That was our little hiding place. It was an unusual shape, though, for five-a-side because it was square, so we invented a game called 'Batter'. We had little goals in opposite corners and you only had one touch to score or protect your goal, so you were blocking the ball or shooting. It was actually very good shooting practice for me at that age, but you often came away with Mitre logos imprinted on your legs from when you had got in the way of somebody's blast."

For Gabbiadini, the thrill of making it as a professional, at the place where he had grown up watching as a fan, also provided great motivation. "I used to go to Bootham Crescent as a kid and get a Z-Stand transfer," he explained. "You could pay your 50p at half-time to get a better view of the team kicking the other way, because they would leave the last bit on the right-hand side of the Popular Stand open for transfers from the Longhurst. I used to watch Keith Walwyn and all the lads I went on to play with, which was great for me. The ground always created a good atmosphere when things were going well and it's the little things I remember like going to the chip shop down the alleyway when I was a supporter."

The average attendance of 5,550 that first season back in the third division was City's biggest since 1974/75 with the 10,442 that turned up for the March visit of eventual champions Bradford - a game the Minstermen lost 2-1 with Martin Butler getting the consolation - representing the last time a five-figured league crowd would be witnessed at Bootham Crescent.

In the FA Cup, City also reached the fifth round for the third time in their history. Newcastle Blue Star and Walsall were both seen off in early rounds at Bootham Crescent before the club were pitted at home to Arsenal after the

Gunners defeated Hereford in a replay. At the time, City were mid-table in division three and the Gunners were fifth in the first division. Even though Northern Ireland legend Pat Jennings had fallen out of favour and England's Graham Rix was injured, the Gunners still boasted eight internationals in their team on the day and their line-up was worth £4.5million, compared to the £19,000 that had been spent to assemble City's starting XI. The club also took the unusual measure not to increase ticket prices for the tie before the identity of the opponents had been confirmed, as a gesture of gratitude for the fans' support, with a priority voucher system in place for a Saturday afternoon home match against Swansea long before the much-postponed Highbury replay against Hereford was concluded.

Tickets, for voucher or season-ticket holders, then went on sale the following day, with all Main Stand seats snapped up in half-an-hour. All tickets for the Popular Stand were also sold before it had been confirmed whether the visitors would be Arsenal or Hereford, as were all of those in the Enclosure by the end of the first day of general sales. Arsenal eventually saw off Hereford 7-2 four days before they visited Bootham Crescent.

Gabbiadini recalled that the onus on him to help smarten up Bootham Crescent in the build-up to that big game was even greater than normal. "I remember bumping into (legendary television commentator) Brian Moore in the corridors the day before, because he was doing his research and it was a bit like when the Queen is coming to town," Gabbiadini said. "Everywhere had to be spotless, because a top team were coming, along with the TV cameras. He was obviously a really familiar face at that time and I remember turning around and just saying: 'Hello Brian', because I was a bit star-struck."

Volunteers help clear snow off the pitch to ensure that the big FA Cup clash against Arsenal can be played

Around 200 supporters helped groundstaff work hard to ensure the game went ahead by clearing three inches of snow off the pitch on the morning of the tie, with groundsman Bryan Foster arriving at 5.45am and the volunteers at 7.30am. Straw had also been placed underneath canvas sheets in the goalmouths and centre circle to try and protect the surface from frost. "The odds would be against it taking place now," City boss Smith recalled of the scenes that morning. "The staff were all out - myself and Viv Busby too - but it was about the supporters basically, along with the groundsmen." Houchen added: "There was a lot of snow on the pitch. They had put canvas sheets and straw along the top. Come the matchday, all that had to be cleared off. That was the thing about the FA Cup in the old days that you never see any more. The whole community, and all the supporters, used to get involved. They would be out on the radio for volunteers to come to the ground and clear the pitch to see if we could get the match to go ahead. I remember the referee inspecting the pitch, with the linesmen and the different managers. The players were out there having a look and you wouldn't have been surprised at all if you were getting back in your car and driving home." Ford also admitted: "Nowadays, it wouldn't have gone ahead, but they got games on for the supporters in those days. It wasn't as bad as people said either. Early on, it was difficult, and I remember slipping for a shot, so I'll blame the pitch for that, but it got better."

Arsenal boss Don Howe, meanwhile, was confident the game would be off and *Yorkshire Evening Press* reporter Malcolm Huntington recalled: "I remember their manager wandering about saying: 'Give the referee a cigar and let him get his feet up and have a coffee. It's not fit for play'. The referee decided it was fit for play." City had a different mindset to their illustrious opponents with Ricky Sbragia saying: "No-one on our side grumbled about the pitch."

Scotland international Charlie Nicholas, reportedly the highest-paid footballer in British football at the time, was in the Arsenal side on the day and admitted most of his team-mates wanted the tie postponed.

"Being from Scotland, I was used to tight, little grounds and smaller stadiums, so I knew the game could be a banana skin," he said. "The conditions were difficult. It was a really icy day and we felt that was a problem for us. Apart from being solid, though, the pitch was decent. It wasn't rutted, it was just brick hard. Quite a few of the English boys thought it would be off, but I was saying, in my experience, the people from this far up north, similar to Scotland, would come to the club and help get the game on. It was a big cup tie and they knew the pitch could be a leveller, so they were doing everything in their power to get the game on. We were there an hour-and-a-half before kick-off, but we couldn't get onto the pitch, because everyone was clearing the snow off it and it was packed at the sides of the pitch. There was a lot of hay around as well. We came out for the warm-up and we couldn't string two passes together. Don didn't want to play the game and none of us did either, because there was no chance of getting the ball on the floor and passing it. In the team talk, he said it was going to be a back-to-front football match and, if we matched their hard work, we would go through. All our moulded boots and pimpled shoes had been brought up, but that didn't work to be honest. The York boys wouldn't have had anything like that, but they still did the business."

Confidence was also coursing through the veins of the City team. "I know it seems ridiculous to say we thought we would have a chance, but we did," Smith pointed out. "It was the way we were playing and there was a total belief in the side." Sbragia also felt playing the tie at Bootham Crescent added to the team's belief, saying: "We always felt that we could beat anyone at home. The pitch was really tight and there were some conditions that really helped. They didn't fancy it." His defensive partner John MacPhail, meanwhile, recalled the Gunners' manager was not enamoured with the decision to play the tie, adding: "I remember Arsenal not being happy at all. They were whinging. Don Howe made it clear they weren't pleased with the state of the pitch straight away because they didn't think they'd be able to play silky football on it." Houchen added: "We weren't overawed by anything. Denis and Viv had us set up to have a go at them. We certainly weren't saying: 'We'll keep the goals down', or anything like that."

TV coverage was provided from a camera positioned on a mobile crane for the first time at Bootham Crescent. The cameras would subsequently document that City adapted better to the tricky, icy pitch in front of a crowd of 10,840, which resulted in record receipts for a tie that would also be watched by millions on *Match of the Day* later. Arsenal had returned 1,000 of their tickets, but the home sections were a near sell-out. When the action got underway, Paul Mariner's header was saved by Mick Astbury and Tommy Caton fired a free kick wide. But City soon settled and Houchen went close after good work by Alan Hay and MacPhail. Eighteen-year-old Martin Butler, meanwhile, was prominent and, after one of his forward charges was halted, Ford shot wide. Pearce also headed off target from a Walwyn centre.

On his side's start to the game, Smith said: "I think they were shocked by the intensity of our play. The work rate throughout the team was incredible. We closed them down far quicker than they would have expected, and they struggled." Sbragia remembered feeling optimistic about the side's prospects at the interval. "We pressured them," he explained. "You could get away with murder in those days and, physically, we dealt with them. As a back four, we felt really comfortable. At half-time, we felt: 'We are in here. We can win this game.'"

Following the break, Arsenal threatened when Astbury was forced into fine saves to deny Mariner and Tony Woodcock, but Caton had to head Walwyn's lob off the line at the other end. Butler also shot over from the edge of the box after a positive forward surge and Houchen narrowly failed to get on the end of a Walwyn cross after a strong run by the striker. Nicholas was substituted on 77 minutes having made little impression on the tie and the former Celtic forward left the pitch ready to settle for a replay. He said: "I got taken off and I can't remember threatening. The ball just went from back to front a lot and York were a match for us with their energy and power. When I came off at 0-0, there was a sense among most of us that we were really up against it. If we could have walked away with a draw, we would have been absolutely delighted although, with 20 minutes to go, I thought we might be fitter than them."

With the tie looking poised for a Highbury replay, though, there was last-minute drama when City launched an attack down the right involving Walwyn and Butler and, as the latter crossed into the box, Houchen went down just inside the 18-yard area under a challenge from midfielder Steve Williams. Recalling the incident, Houchen said: "It was a crazy, needless foul. I always wondered if he got fined for it or what his manager said after the game. It was probably ten yards outside when he first started to foul me. He had switched off and got a little bit lazy. We were in a really threatening situation. He realised I had a yard on him and, if the ball came in, I was going to have a chance of getting on the end of it. I think he fouled me again just as I got towards the box. I could actually feel his arms and legs all over me as I was coming into the box. In the old days, it was all well and good being honest and staying on your feet but, if it is a foul and if it is a penalty, make sure you get the penalty. He was hanging all over me. I thought: 'I'm going to go to ground here anyway'. We went down in a clatter of arms and legs flying. Straight away, you are looking. 'Where's the ref? Has he seen anything?' I always remember, as I hit the ground, and he fell with me, I looked across and the ref was just coming into the box and he was actually putting the whistle to his lips. Then, it was: 'Where's the ball? Where's the ball? Let me have the ball.'"

Amid the bedlam at the Shipton Street End, Houchen calmly found John Lukic's bottom right-hand corner as the keeper dived in the opposite direction. Commenting on the 30th anniversary of the game, Houchen said: "I really loved taking penalties. I always called them a free goal. My wife, Yvonne, was in the stand that day. When the penalty was given, there was all the commotion and the crowd were going mad. Arsenal were very professional, and they held it up for three or four minutes. She was watching me all the time everything was going on and she said: 'You looked like a little boy stood on the edge of the box waiting to take the penalty'. She thought: 'You are stood there all on your own and everyone is just waiting for you to knock it in the net. What if you don't?' People say: 'Did you pick your spot? Did you decide and not change your mind?' I think I used to put the ball down and just trust instinct. In my own mind, up until a couple of paces before I hit the ball, I wasn't sure myself whether I was going to go bottom or top. With that one, I did give him (Lukic) the eyes. I was lining up and looking down at the right-hand corner and looking and looking at the right-hand corner. As I've hit it, I am looking at the right-hand corner and cutting across it to hit in the left-hand corner while off he went in the other direction. It was a sweet enough strike. It was right in the corner and it was the type of penalty where, if he had dived the right way, I am not really sure if he would have been able to save it."

MacPhail also scored four penalties that season but was happy for Houchen to assume the responsibility on this occasion even though, like the spot-kick hero's wife, he admitted it did cross his mind how everybody would feel if the chance wasn't taken. "It was definitely a penalty and a fantastic finish by Houchy," MacPhail pointed out. "I had confidence in him, but I did think, if he misses, that would be a nightmare. He slotted it in well, though, to the goalkeeper's right." Ford, however, was less certain about the referee's decision, saying: "I thought it was a dodgy penalty. It was 50-50. Keith says he didn't dive but, whilst it put him off running into the box, I thought it was a nudge. That was all. Houchy was very confident in front of goal, though, so I had confidence in him scoring - definitely." From the visitors' dugout, Nicholas felt the referee had made the correct call, admitting: "It was just a clumsy challenge. Steve would have debated it, no doubt, but I don't think he had an argument really and it was despatched well by somebody who was on his way to making a big reputation for himself in the FA Cup."

With the ecstasy came a spot of agony for Houchen during the ensuing celebrations. "There were people up on the floodlights and, when the penalty went in, the crowd absolutely erupted behind that goal," he remembered. "I ran

Keith Houchen wheels away in delight after converting the penalty that knocked mighty Arsenal out of the FA Cup in 1985

Keith Houchen is mobbed after converting his famous penalty against Arsenal

towards them in the snow and Keith Walwyn was the first one who got me. Cor, he hit me - bang - right in the back of me. He was twice the size of me, 16 stone, and down we went, and I don't remember much after that because I think everybody else came in as well. It was such an achievement for everybody - a massive cup upset."

The Guardian perfectly captured the moment in their match report, which read: "Keith Houchen rolled home his penalty - and all hell broke loose. The rattle did overtime." Former West Ham and England midfielder Trevor Brooking, meanwhile, was forced to backtrack having, just seconds earlier, commented on the professional job Arsenal had done in securing a replay as he worked for Radio 2 in a cramped Bootham Crescent press box. MacPhail, meanwhile, could not resist a little dig at Mariner and Woodcock in retaliation for some earlier taunts from the England internationals. "Me and Ricky had been giving Tony Woodcock and Paul Mariner a hard time by kicking them all game and, with about four minutes to go, I remember them saying: 'Wait until we get you back to Highbury, we'll put seven past you," MacPhail explained. "At that point, we thought it would be ending 0-0 and both teams would have settled for that and seen it as a job done. There hadn't been many chances at either end, but Houchy then got the penalty and scored it and I remember running back to our half and saying to them: 'We won't be going back to Highbury now lads'. The scenes at the end were unbelievable too. It was like winning the league in one game. We had beaten Arsenal which, for a small club like York City, was almost unheard of."

The final whistle was blown after Hay's corner - City's first of the game - was caught by Lukic and Ford felt the home side were the hungrier team on the day, even though his marker - then England international Kenny Sansom - was one of the few visiting players who demonstrated a will to win. "I thought we were the better team," Ford declared. "We just wanted it more, although I remember Kenny Sansom was left back and he wanted it. Tommy Caton did as well. You could tell the ones that did. They are the top players. Sansom just wanted to bomb forward and you found the better full backs had the confidence to do that, which makes it difficult for you to bomb forward, so I had to do more defensive work than I would normally do in that game. We went straight to Oscar's Wine Bar afterwards, where we normally met up for a night out, because the owner had said, if we beat Arsenal, he would give us all bottles of champagne. Sean Haslegrave's nickname was 'Bubble', because champagne is all he drunk, so he was happy."

Watching everything unravel from the Arsenal bench, meanwhile, Nicholas recalled: "I remember being sat in the dugout and we were just frozen cold with a sense that we knew this was going to happen to us. There was a bit of anger from Don afterwards but, when the performance was broken down, the almost farcical conditions gave us a bit of a soft excuse when we were deservedly beaten. I think he made us do lots or running for two or three days, though, as a punishment." Nicholas did, however, find somewhere at hand to drown his sorrows. Whether "Champagne Charlie" shared a tipple with Haslegrave is unlikely, but the Glaswegian revealed: "I went into the bar afterwards and had a quick beer. I don't think we were supposed to and were probably meant to look down and depressed on the bus, but I had a pint before I got on. There were a couple of us that did. Everybody in there was happy after such a big cup shock at home and we decided to join them. I had never been stung by a result like that in my career and it was a bit of a turning point. It made me realise these things can happen to anybody. Everyone still talks about it. When FA Cup draws come along and York's ball is picked out, they normally add: 'who famously beat Arsenal in the 1980s', and I start to think: 'Yes, I know, I was there'." Proud manager Smith, meanwhile, had the last word on the day, declaring: "I demanded passion and commitment and I got it."

Gabbiadini confessed that he was inspired by the buzz around the club at the time, adding: "I remember all of us being together at the club waiting for the Cup draw on Monday lunchtime and that was great as well. I was a young lad about to go into a great squad of York City players which was fantastic for me and it's amazing how many went on to become good coaches. Malcom Crosby was great in reserve matches as well. He was brilliant and talked to you so much." Only vandalism, with windows in nearby streets smashed, marred a terrific day in the sporting history of the city as Mary Fennell, of 60 Newborough Street, revealed in the *Yorkshire Evening Press*: "I was shattered with glass when the window was put through. It was terrifying, and I was still taking splinters out of my hair two days later."

The subsequent draw landed the club with a plum home tie against European champions Liverpool. It attracted an all-ticket crowd of 13,485, including 4,000 from Liverpool, with the office staff of Hughes, Sheila Smith and newcomer Tricia Westland inundated with requests for tickets. Prices were again kept at the same level although the matchday programme, which was free at the time, would cost £1.

A voucher scheme was again devised and a bumper crowd of 10,940 turned up for a league game against Wigan, with an estimated 2,500 locked out. Massive queues built up 90 minutes before kick-off for that match and the car-park gates behind the Main Stand were closed with hordes of people also spilling into side streets. Fans were even given the opportunity of watching the game from the Wigan end, but without the chance to obtain a voucher, after all 9,500 had been snapped up. Kick-off was subsequently delayed by 15 minutes. Ford scored during a 2-0 triumph and revelled in the unusually high attendance for a run-of-the-mill league clash. "It (the voucher scheme) was a great idea," he said. "The bigger the crowd the better. It was a good result as well because Wigan had a good team then. Bryan Hamilton was manager and he took me to Leicester a year or two later and maybe that game was why."

Ticket sales for the game were brought forward by two hours from 10am when just under 10,000 fans turned up, armed with their vouchers. The queue stretched for almost half-a-mile around Burton Stone Lane and about 1,000 fans were left disappointed with the vouchers issued having offered priority for a ticket, but no guarantee, and the last of the 8,500-strong home allocation was sold at 11am.

An injured Houchen, the hero against Arsenal, missed the Liverpool tie, which kicked off amid an electric atmosphere with the game producing a new club record for gate receipts of £29,138. A dozen police horses were brought in, meanwhile, in an attempt to avoid the scenes outside of the ground that had occurred following the Arsenal match when just three were on duty. All police leave was cancelled, with officers from other divisions drafted in too. Determined to prevent a pitch invasion, as also happened against Arsenal leading to four arrests, the club put up a high fence behind the Grosvenor Road goal, where the Liverpool fans would be standing. The plan was for the fencing to be temporary but, ultimately, it would not be dismantled until the early years of the new millennium. It did not prevent supporters clashing on the pitch after the final whistle either, with police struggling to control the situation as 400 City fans charged onto the pitch and some taunted Liverpool supporters who broke down the fences to confront them. A total of 11 arrests were made during the subsequent fighting.

Sixty tons of straw, obtained from Malton farmer Alec Bulmer, was placed on the pitch to protect it from the frosty weather ahead of the 1985 FA Cup tie against Liverpool

In an effort to get the game on, during the days leading up to it, a hundred rolls of Polythene, each measuring 25 metres, were bought for £1,800 so falling snow could be swept off and the pitch protected from frost. Then, 60 tons of straw, obtained from Malton farmer Alec Bulmer, were laid down for the same purpose with the whole Gabbiadini family part of an army of volunteers who started turning up at 6am and helped Foster work under the floodlights to make sure the playing surface was ready for kick-off. "It was a good day and a big occasion," Gabbiadini recalled. "As apprentices, we watched the match in the paddock behind the dugout and helped clear the pitch of all the straw after the combine harvester had been over it. My mum and dad also joined in and our little dog was there as well. It was all hands to the pump. I remember after the pitch had been cleared about two hours before kick-off, the TV cameras arrived, along with a producer who was really smart. He looked like a city gent with really, shiny shoes and he was stood near the halfway line, as Bryan Foster, who was a bit of a legend in football, was painting the lines purple. He was doing it with a brush and he used to always chunter and moan to himself while he was working. Anyway, TV interviews were taking place and this guy shushed Fossie as he was getting close to the cameras. Fossie just looked at him and carried on his way, painting two lines of purple stripes over this guy's shoes." Extra seats were also set out in front of the Main Stand to cater for the legions of press reporters and broadcasters at the tie. A total of 35 needed to be accommodated with the press box only having a capacity of 22. Highlights of the match were to be shown on ITV the following day, whilst it was also

329

transmitted live in Scandinavia. Touts, meanwhile, were asking for up to £30 for £2 tickets outside of the ground ahead of kick-off.

Recalling the scenes even prior to a ball being kicked, Smith said: "It was incredible. The place was bouncing for about an hour before and a good while afterwards. We could have sold the ground out twice over, but the board didn't put the prices up and tried to ensure everybody could come. People thought we couldn't do it again after beating Arsenal but, when they saw the team get going, they soon realised we could give Liverpool a game too." Home-grown talent Ford summed up the confidence running through the side ahead of the tie when he insisted: "I wasn't bothered by nerves. When you're younger, you have no fear. If I'd been older, I might have done, but we were at home and felt we had every chance."

MacPhail also reckoned City fans turned up with a belief that they might witness another special moment of FA Cup history. He said: "The atmosphere was electric. It was packed out and the fans seemed to sense that something might happen again after the Arsenal match. I thought we were a bit unfortunate too. We might have sneaked a win on another day which would have been unbelievable because they were obviously a good side." Sbragia also recalled the buzz of anticipation in the days leading up to the tie and right up to 3pm as both teams prepared to do battle on a firm pitch. "I can remember the build-up and rush for tickets," he said. "You'd be coming in for training and all the fans were there. That made it hit home what a big draw it was obviously but, while you couldn't say it was just another team, it was quite strange because we weren't nervous or feeling any pressure. The Cup was a release from everything and we had nothing to lose. The weather also helped. That was a big factor for us. The fans cleared the pitch and I remember going in on the morning and thinking this is hard. We had leather studs at that time and we used to scuff them deliberately to take the cap off, so the nail would be poking out and that gave you a better grip. I can remember they were complaining before the game about the conditions not being acceptable. We could hear they weren't happy and Denis would come into the dressing room and feed us more stuff, which

Alan Hay, Alan Pearce, Brian Chippendale and Mike Astbury train on the straw laid down to protect the pitch before the Liverpool FA Cup tie in February 1985

made us think this might be a chance for us. We knew we needed them not to be at their best and did think the pitch could be a leveller. As a team, we played really well, because we knew everyone of us had to be 100 per cent and play to the top of our game."

The crowd would have been bigger but, by the early 1980s, cracks had appeared in the concrete wall that had been built at the back of the Bootham Crescent End in 1956. The rear of the terracing, therefore, had now been cordoned off and the capacity reduced to less than half the 28,000-plus attendance record set in 1938. When the action got underway, John Wark shot wide for the visitors from 20 yards early on, but Butler went on to see a seventh-minute effort ruled out for offside after charging on to Derek Hood's through ball. It was a decision Smith was still determined to contest 30 years later. "I didn't think it was offside," he insisted. Sbragia agreed, adding: "Martin Butler was caught offside, but I thought it was on." It was a decision that, following frenzied celebrations, was roundly booed by home fans and the TV highlights did, indeed, confirm that Butler was clearly onside, and that referee Peter Willis signalled a goal before spotting the linesman's raised flag.

During a first-half performance deemed worthy of a standing ovation by home supporters at the break, Sbragia's header also called Bruce Grobbelaar into action. The deadlock was broken on 52 minutes, though, when Anfield legend Ian Rush scored following a free kick that was conceded by Walwyn for a foul on Kevin MacDonald. Gary Gillespie then cracked a long ball forward that was helped on by Kenny Dalglish's head and Rush turned quickly to smash a 15-yard effort past Astbury. Recalling the ability of the legendary marksman, Ford said: "I remember seeing how sharp, lean and quick Ian Rush was and it does go through your mind: 'Oh, he's a bit different'. When they went ahead you did think: 'Here we go', as well." Sbragia admitted that he felt he was at fault for the Wales legend's opener, saying: "For their goal, I think I thought Dalglish was going to win a header, but he didn't make a clean contact on it and the ball ended up going between my legs and Ian Rush was through. You could never switch off against players like that. In other games, you could for a little while and have a little think about things. In that game, you had to be totally focussed all the time. We also knew about turning them and playing the conditions by going long and big, because there was no way we could outplay Liverpool."

Rush's effort was the first goal City had conceded in nine games, but the hosts fought back strongly with Walwyn heading just wide. MacPhail still had to react brilliantly to clear a Steve Nicol header off the line after he had beaten

Astbury, but Walywn then went close again with a header at the other end, before Bootham Crescent went wild when the hosts equalised with five minutes to play. Pearce's free kick from the left, awarded when Nicol fouled Butler, was knocked back into the middle by Ford and, following an almighty scramble that saw Sbragia shoot against the crossbar that Walwyn then struck

The John MacPhail shot that led to Ricky Sbragia's equaliser against Liverpool in the 1-1 1985 FA Cup draw

with his header from the rebound before a MacPhail shot clattered off Grobbelaar's legs, Sbragia lashed the ball into the net. The modest marksman, meanwhile, admitted his famous strike could have ended up anywhere. "I remember Keith was causing mayhem in the box and the cross that came in from Gary Ford wasn't a great one," Sbragia said. "It was a bit flat. I volleyed it and I'd never volleyed anything in my life, but it hit the bar. Then, I could see

Ricky Sbragia celebrates his equaliser against Liverpool with fellow centre-back John MacPhail

Keith coming in and he headed it against the bar. Then, Monty (MacPhail) had another chance kicked away before the ball just came to me and I wasn't really thinking anything then. It fell to my left peg and my left peg could have taken the ball anywhere but, luckily, I just banged it in and I can remember the roar and people jumping on me. A bottle of Guinness hit me on the head too. Somebody from the Liverpool end hurled it at me, but I just got on with it because of the euphoria of what had just happened. You dream of getting a goal like that. I had seen players get goals against big teams before and you think 'God Almighty' and then it happened to me. It was probably the best feeling I'd had in football at that time. Denis was then telling us to keep our concentration. It would have been nice to go on and win but, from the club's point of view, a replay was great because it got them more money."

Smith, meanwhile, insisted that he always suspected his side could level against their legendary visitors, especially from dead-ball situations where defenders Sbragia and MacPahil were always a menace. "Even though they got in front, I knew we were always a goal threat and that we could be dangerous at set plays with Ricky and John because the delivery was so good," he explained. "I remember the ball bobbling around forever for the equaliser and, while John used to score more, Ricky could turn up when it mattered and centre backs should score goals. Their job is to go up in the penalty area for set-plays and there's no point sending them up there if they're not going to contribute. John was very good at it and went on to get me 18 goals in a season at Sunderland." MacPhail had vivid memories of the contest and added: "When Martin Butler went through and scored, we thought it was a goal, but the flag went up and, while it was like the Alamo at times and I remember clearing one chance off the line, I felt we deserved the equaliser. I remember hitting the shot and Grobbelaar saving it, but Ricky just got the bits and put it in the net. Everyone went bananas then, as did the fans - they were all jumping for joy."

Steve Senior gets in a tackle on Liverpool's Ronnie Whelan in February 1985

Irish international Ronnie Whelan later had a goal

mysteriously disallowed during a pulsating finish, but City had their replay and, despite the crowd trouble at the end, it did not spoil another great day in the club's history - certainly not for a 12-year-old Guy Mowbray, who got firmly wrapped up in Cup fever that season. "I went to the Arsenal game with my sister who was five years older than me," he said. "We watched from the Enclosure just behind the dugouts, so we were right in the heart of it. For the Liverpool game, I did go behind the goal in the Shipton Street End despite what my dad had told me in the past and, for me, those two home games against Arsenal and Liverpool will always stand out. They were the sort of occasions that made me think I would like to be involved with something like this. I remember queuing for tickets for the Liverpool game and getting to the ground at about 5.30am. They were queuing right around the corner by the Barracks and down Burton Stone Lane. It was February and we got there before it was light, and we did that for two years running because we drew Liverpool again but, on both occasions, some people had been out there all night. The only other time people did that in York was for the Newitts sale in January."

For one City fan, meanwhile, Sbragia's equaliser was a somewhat bitter-sweet experience as MacPhail explained: "There was a bet on with my mate Alister McLean who was from Scotland and owned Oscar's Wine Bar at the time. In the round before, he had said, if we beat Arsenal, he would pay for 48 bottles of Moet Chandon champagne for the lads. A lot of the players lived out of town though, while myself and Alan Hay were living with Alister at the time in a big house just around the corner from Bootham Crescent, so we pretty much drunk the lot. We went there most Monday, Tuesday and Wednesday nights and shared a bottle. He then said he would double that bet to 96 bottles if we beat Liverpool in the next round and, apparently, he went white when we equalised. It's perhaps a good job we didn't win, though, because me and Alan would have probably become alcoholics!"

Recalling his part in the scrappy leveller, the angry reaction of Liverpool's supporters and his subsequent belief that City could go on and win the tie, Ford said: "All Denis ever said to me was: 'Get the ball in the box' constantly and there was a big scramble before Ricky put the ball in. I remember a glass bottle hitting Ricky on the back when we were celebrating. It had been thrown by one of the Liverpool supporters and they were evil and hostile, but I don't think he was hurt and it was very rare you got that end full, so when we scored it was mad. The place went nuts and I was thinking about the chance of a win. I definitely thought we could do it after that goal. We had just beaten Arsenal and thought we could beat anybody. We wanted to win rather than going to

Anfield and felt we were going to. Even in games like that, we knew we had a chance at Bootham Crescent because it's all about confidence, but I remember Ronnie Whelan, who was a real grafter, having a goal disallowed and that was it. We didn't celebrate the fact that we were going to Anfield because we just wanted that win and it was a bit of a let down after beating Arsenal, because we knew our chance was at home. It's more like a day out when you're going somewhere like Liverpool."

Despite Rush getting on the scoresheet, meanwhile, MacPhail was satisfied with the way himself and Sbragia had fared against one of the world's most-feared strike forces at the time. "I had played against Dalglish before when I was at Dundee and he played for Celtic and he was one of the best players I'd ever seen," MacPhail declared. "He could go right or left. Rushy didn't particularly do anything and I thought we played him quite well but, if he was in the 18-yard box, you knew you always had to be aware of him and he ended up scoring their goal despite being quiet for most of the match." Summing up the challenge City had faced, Ford declared: "They were the best team in the world at the time and you could see their professionalism. Kenny Dalglish was probably the best player I ever played against. How he found himself space and time was so clever."

Goal hero Sbragia was also impressed with Dalglish and Rush - on and off the pitch - even meeting up with the latter the following day. The Scotsman said: "Kenny Dalglish was a hero of mine and both him and Ian Rush were brilliant. They didn't moan once the game was underway and, even afterwards, they were good when we shook hands. They didn't act like they were above us and I think that was the Liverpool philosophy anyway. A lot of teams like that would tend to ignore you, but I remember Alan Hansen and Gary Gillespie being friendly as well and they all handled it really well. My dad came to the game with my two eldest brothers and they had never seen me play. When I started in football, they just left me on my own to get on with it. My dad came to Birmingham for my debut against Manchester City at home, but the Liverpool match was the second one that he saw. I went to the Cross Keys pub on Tadcaster Road afterwards with them because I knew the owners Kevin and Diane. We had a couple of beers and I got a phone call on Saturday night from the press saying Ian Rush was staying overnight in York so, on Sunday, I met him, and we had a couple of photos at Clifford Tower taken together. I've still got them, and he was fantastic when I met him - a lovely bloke." Looking back on the contest as a whole, Sbragia added: "The whole game is a bit of a blur, but I remember Phil Neal just coming forward all the time and they had a lot of corner kicks. The game just passed so quickly, maybe because they were passing so quickly! I only really reflected on everything afterwards and then you think: 'Oh, my God, we did enough to get a replay at Anfield'. We used to force the issue on teams, but it was the other way around in that game and we set up a different way to normal. They were all world-class players. I remember going into the ground on Monday thinking we're going to Anfield and that was good because we had another big game to look forward to and I still have mementoes from that match that I will be giving to my grandchildren."

Gracious visiting boss Joe Fagan summed up the game, while sipping a cup of tea in the away dressing room after his team had left for the players' bar. He said: "It's us who have had to battle for a draw, not York. I was not surprised by what York achieved. They are a good-calibre side. They didn't sit back and allow us to dominate and were obviously determined not to let us do what we wanted. York were good value for their draw and deserved what they got." Almost 8,000 fans subsequently made the trip over the M62 for the replay, but the Minstermen were swept aside 7-0. Fans had queued for tickets from 4.30am at Bootham Crescent, not wanting to miss out, even though there was the option of paying through the turnstiles at Anfield.

City also enjoyed their best-ever run at that point in the Football League Trophy, then sponsored by Freight Rover, reaching the Northern Area quarter-finals before bowing out 3-2 to Lincoln at Bootham Crescent. Attendances in the oft-maligned competition were still respectable with 4,010 watching that tie and 3,891 witnessing an earlier home victory over Chesterfield. The loss to Lincoln irritated Smith, who would have loved to see his City team tread the hallowed turf of English football's world-famous home. "That side would have graced Wembley," he argued. "They were an outstanding group and I didn't go into any cup competition not wanting to win. Getting to that final would have been a great day out for the players and fans."

Just a fortnight earlier, meanwhile, 17-year-old fledgling Gabbiadini had been given his first-team debut as a substitute during an otherwise, long-forgotten 3-0 home defeat to Bolton. On that experience, Gabbiadini admitted: "It wasn't a great game and, by no means, the most memorable debut ever. I don't really look at it as my debut, as I was only brought on with 20 minutes to go when the team were 3-0 down. I think Denis said something like: 'Go on and win the game for us, son'. I didn't get much of a reception, as I think most people had started to make their way home, so it was a low-key start for me. It was still quite an achievement, though, because I was a late starter as an apprentice, having gone back to Nunthorpe School to do my A levels, so I didn't start with the club until November and I made my first appearance in March." Surrounded by larger-than-life personalities at the time, Gabbiadini also stressed that you had to survive to thrive at Bootham Crescent during such a successful era. "The first-team dressing room was full of characters at that time and, if you were cheeky to somebody like Keith Walwyn, he would throw you in the bath," Gabbiadini laughed. "Some today might describe what went on as bullying in the work place and I'm sure some felt it was back then and were affected, but you had to stand up to it and I didn't mind. You had to learn to thrive in that environment and I enjoyed confrontation. You also had beers in the dressing room at the end of games. All that changed during my career. Beers on the bus back from away games were also phased out because the need to rehydrate properly was recognised. But, when I started out at York, all you ever used to drink was tea. Everything seemed to revolve around it. There would be big enamel jugs of it in the dressing rooms and it would always come out at half-time. Managers would also get somebody to fetch a cup for them during the first half. The apprentices would have to clean the jugs out in the bath as well."

Gabbiadini also remembered the Social Club still being a great venue for players and supporters to mingle with one another after matches. He said: "The players and supporters used to mix together, and the lads used to go in the bar after games until about 7pm on a Saturday. Nobody went off in separate directions at the end of the match. We were all different age groups, but you would start your Saturday night, whatever your plans were, by having a drink with the lads and fans."

A 1-0 home win over Brentford at the start of March was also notable for the match-winning debut of joiner Tony Canham who, at the age of 24, had been drafted in on a non-contract basis from Harrogate Railway. His 42nd-minute header would prove the first of 70 goals he netted for the club in 413 appearances, placing him seventh in the all-time list for games played. The Sunday home derby with top-of-the-table Bradford City that month, meanwhile, highlighted the extent of the 1980s' hooligan epidemic, with police seizing items such as Stanley knives, a flick knife, a length of chain, a metal spike and several nails by using metal detectors at the away turnstiles.

The summer of 1985 also saw improvements made to the ground - the need for which had been highlighted by the big crowds of the past two seasons. Only two of the four sides of the ground at Bootham Crescent remained available for entry and exit with home supporters also funnelling through the car park to get into the Shipton Street End.

The work, costing £100,000, included the installation of eight new, more compact turnstiles at that end of the car park. Previously, there had only been four on a wall near the Shipton Street corner. Both dressing rooms were refurbished with new baths and showers, whilst a new referees' changing room and physio treatment room were built. New toilets were built at the Shipton Street End and the club shop was erected in the car park. The manager's and accounts office were also moved, and the press box relocated next to the directors' box in a two-seated vertical row of desks that would still be in place until the ground was demolished. Hospitality suites were added too, but a longer-term plan to extend the Main Stand at both ends and install 600 new seats never came to fruition. The hospitality boxes were built into the Main Stand, looking out onto the car park and not the pitch, as would be the case for the duration of the club's remaining time at Bootham Crescent. Final touches to the new dressing rooms, meanwhile, were being made right up until the eve of the opening match of the season at home to Plymouth. With Bootham Crescent largely made of concrete, brick and steel structures and not wood, the cost of safety measures imposed on clubs following the tragic Bradford Fire Disaster at the end of the season did not impact on City either. Highlighting the club's commitment to ensuring supporters' safety, Hughes also revealed that all locks in the ground were controlled by one key with he, the police, control stewards and the groundsman all having copies. The cost of the club's revamping exercise was illustrated in the yearly accounts when it was revealed that almost £170,000 had been spent on sprucing up facilities. Broken down, £55,000 was used on better toilet accommodation, £25,000 for exit gates at the Shipton Street End, £42,000 on turnstiles, £25,000 on perimeter fencing, £3,000 on stand seats and £23,000 for fire exits and stairs. For the first time, the club also introduced season tickets for terraced areas of the ground.

City subsequently got off to another good start in 1985/86 and a 17-year-old Gabbiadini helped secure an opening day 3-1 victory over Plymouth with a goal on his full debut - the first of a senior career that would see him hit the back of the net 274 times in total. Remembering the day vividly, the future England under-21 international said: "I had a really good pre-season and I had to dislodge some really good players like Dale Banton, Keith Walywn and Ian Butler to get a place in the side. Banno was the record signing so, for me to get in the team for the first game of the season, was really pleasing. The team was announced the day before the game and I had my pictures taken for the press. That feeling of making the first XI for the opening game of the season was great and stuck with me throughout my career, because I managed to do it 18 seasons running from 1985 to 2002. I took pride in that, because it meant you were in the managers' good books. The game against Plymouth was also more how you think a debut should be, than that first time I had come on as a substitute. I scored, got booked, got injured and had to go off and it was like everything happened to me in that one game. For my goal, I got put through which, with my pace, I tried to do a fair bit. A lot of teams tried to play the offside trap back then, but I ended up one-on-one with the keeper and just hit it underneath him. It was a decent goal, but there were no histrionics when it went in. We didn't practice moonwalks or dancing around the corner flags back then. Denis Smith would have probably headbutted you if he'd seen you doing that. I just think I did the classic celebration of one finger in the air and then ran to the Main Stand where my mum and dad were to acknowledge them. They came to all the games and loved it at Bootham Crescent. I ended up turning my ankle later in the game though and had to go off."

City were still second behind runaway leaders Reading by the end of November, having equalled their second-highest ever league win the previous month with a 7-0 home thumping of Darlington, which saw Canham score a hat-trick. It was the club's biggest victory since the 9-1 thrashing of Southport 28 years earlier and earned the club £500 from then league sponsors Canon for becoming the first third division club to reach 25 goals for the season. The game before, a Houchen brace and Banton effort had seen off Bolton 3-0 with Mowbray, then 13, getting the same insight into the matchday experience as legions of other schoolboys have enjoyed down the years. "I remember being a ball boy because you took your turn once a season to do that as a Junior Red and I've still got my programme from the game against Bolton when Sam Allardyce was playing for them," Mowbray reminisced. "I remember being in the corridor before the match near the changing rooms and seeing Keith Walwyn and being in awe of him, but he was so nice to me, as was Keith Houchen. My first heroes were Keith Walwyn and John Byrne. Big Keith was just such a gentleman but an absolute giant of a man as well."

Stronger perimeter fencing was installed at the insistence of the police, meanwhile, towards the end of October, but plans to introduce it at the Shipton Street End of the ground never came to fruition. City had not suffered any pitch encroachments during the season, but the clamp down on crowd disturbances across the country was being imposed by local authorities. Police objections to alcohol being served in the club's sponsors boxes before, during and after games, though, were overruled by York's licencing magistrates. A steward would be on the door separating the three boxes, which accommodated up to 15 people each, from admission into the ground, ensuring no drinks were taken out. The magistrates had also exempted the Social Club from the restrictions of the Government's new Sporting Events (Control of Alcohol Act) the previous month, which allowed drinks to be bought immediately before and after matches. Police had wanted the Social Club to be closed during the hour leading up to kick-off and the hour directly afterwards. City showed a zero-tolerance attitude towards the continued threat of hooliganism, though, with Mick Gregory, of Tang Hall, the first to fall foul of a new policy of issuing three-year bans following an incident in the Social Club. He failed to turn up when given an opportunity to appeal and explain himself in front of the Social Club committee. The ban applied to "the ground and all surrounding club premises".

Home form remained good throughout the campaign with 16 wins and 49 goals, but an indifferent spell mid-season and patchy away results saw the team ultimately finish the campaign seventh. A rare defeat at Bootham Crescent saw eventual title-winners Reading edge a 1-0 victory on a November afternoon when former York RI and Rowntree's shot-stopper and future Sheffield United number one Andy Leaning played for the club in a ground that he had forged an emotional connection with from an early age - the same kind of love affair shared by members of countless different families through the generations. "I could have joined the club as a 16-year-old, but my father made me do a joinery apprenticeship, so I thought my time had passed," Leaning explained. "I played for York RI and Rowntree's instead, but my chance came again when I was 22 after Mick Astbury got injured in a game against Bristol Rovers in 1985, so I made my debut at Newport. But, being a York lad, my first game at Bootham Crescent was special. My dad had taken me there as a kid and the first football match I ever saw was York v Cardiff in the FA Cup in 1970. It was fantastic as a young lad when the bigger games were played there. I remember watching York v Manchester City (in 1973) and Arsenal (in 1975). I also watched all the second division games against the likes of Manchester United and Aston Villa and they were terrific. The atmosphere on a Saturday afternoon was great and Bootham Crescent is where I got my love for the game really. I can still smell the pipe smokers. It was about the whole experience of coming into the ground and the excitement of watching a live football match. We had season tickets in the Main Stand and would sit with one of my dad's mates. There was not the same level of exposure as there is now on TV. The only live football you saw was local football. Apart from that, there was *Match of the Day*, which you weren't always allowed to stay up for, *Sportsnight*, which was definitely on too late on school nights and, then, there was Keith Macklin's highlights on a Sunday afternoon. I'll always remember going there as a kid and watching football is a big thing for a dad and a lad to do together. My dad was a football person and it was just considered natural that you would go and watch your local football team, so it was a big thing for me to make my first appearance as a York City player there even though we lost 1-0 against a Reading side who weren't bad. To play there, with my dad watching in the stand, was great because he was a die-hard fan - an absolute stalwart supporter. You never forget those first football matches you go to and the excitement that goes with it, so it was great to then get the opportunity to do what I'd always wanted to do when I was younger when I would get back from games and practise on the back lane."

Leaning's debut eclipsed what he had previously felt might represent his footballing pinnacle when he played as an amateur on the ground. "I did get the chance to play at Bootham Crescent for York RI once in a Minor League Cup final and my ambition, at that time, was just to play on a first-team pitch," he confessed. "All of a sudden, I found myself in the goal that Graeme Crawford played in and he was my idol at the time. I remember how he used to run onto the pitch and he always had a red Newitts bag with his gloves in, which he used to throw into the net. When he went past his six-yard box, he used to make a little mark there as well and, for that game, I went through all those daft little things because you take notice of all that when you're a kid."

On the Bootham Crescent crowd's reaction to seeing one of their own play for their team following his graduation to the professional ranks, Leaning added: "There was myself and Gary Ford in the team and, sometimes, it can be harder for local boys because, while the crowd are behind you, it's almost as if a bit more is expected of you and that brings a bit more pressure. But, at that time, Denis Smith and Viv Busby were a fantastic management team and the whole atmosphere they had created at the club was great for a young player. They were both very inspirational."

There was more FA Cup magic, meanwhile, with the club negotiating four home ties against non-League quartet Morecambe, Whitby, Wycombe and Altrincham to reach the last 16 again. Morecambe were seen off in a replay at Manchester City's Maine Road after a 0-0 draw at Bootham Crescent, but the other three were defeated at the first time of asking, with a Whitby side, featuring former Leeds United stars Eddie Gray and David Harvey, beaten 3-1. Liverpool were then paired with City again in another fifth-round clash at Bootham Crescent. In a bid to ensure that, this time around, tickets were

The queue for tickets to see Liverpool at Bootham Crescent for a second consecutive season bends well down Burton Street Lane

Linda Collins, of Selby, shows off the programmes she needed to buy to get priority access to tickets for the Liverpool FA Cup tie in February 1986

guaranteed for the club's most-loyal supporters who were not season-ticket holders, vouchers had been printed in the programme at the start of the season. Under the terms of that scheme, fans would receive a ticket in return for bringing along the match-day programmes from three of four designated home games during the season - against Plymouth on the opening day, Bolton in October, Brentford in November and Wolves in January. Seven days before the match, Liverpool sent former European Cup-winning boss Bob Paisley to watch City's 3-1 home league defeat to Derby County and, for the latest meeting, the mid-February pitch was hard and heavily-sanded having been covered with plastic sheeting during the run-up to the match.

City started the tie brightly when Banton raced on to a Ford through ball but dragged an excellent 12-yard chance inches wide of Grobbelaar's right-hand post. Dalglish, now Liverpool's player-manager, then started to become more prominent and saw a shot on the turn held by Leaning. City continued to have the edge, however, with Grobbelaar saving in typical breath-taking fashion when he tipped over a cracking edge-of-the-box half-volley by MacPhail after

Simon Mills goes in for a tackle on legendary Liverpool striker Ian Rush with Craig Johnston looking on during the 1986 FA Cup tie

Gary Ford opens the scoring against Liverpool in February 1986 with Bruce Grobbelaar floored and Jan Molby looking on

Home fans celebrate Gary Ford's goal against Liverpool in February 1986 with Mark Lawrenson pictured in the foreground

343

Andy Leaning is beaten from the penalty spot by Jan Molby during the 1-1 FA Cup draw against Liverpool in February 1986

Steve Senior is controversially penalised for handball under pressure from Craig Johnston with John Wark looking on for Liverpool in February 1986

Walwyn and David McAughtrie had combined to tee up the chance. It was an opportunity MacPhail felt might have written him into FA Cup folklore with the former Sheffield United defender remembering: "When it left my boot, I thought it was going in the top corner, but he was a very agile keeper and made a great save."

The visitors were happy to reach half-time level and, after the break, Banton also headed just over. A lively Rush, though, was thwarted by the alert Leaning as he bore down on the home goal. He also escaped the back four's attentions for a second time soon afterwards and might have won a penalty when he went over an outrushing Leaning It was Smith's men, though, who forged in front on 61 minutes when Canham lofted an up-and-under into the penalty area, Banton headed it on and Walwyn, occupying several visiting defenders, laid the ball to Ford, who smacked a 12-yard, first-time drive just inside Grobbelaar's left-hand post. The ensuing joy was short-lived, as City held the lead for only four minutes after Sean Haslegrave fouled Sammy Lee and Dalglish floated the resulting free kick into the penalty box, where Steve Senior was dubiously penalised for handball under pressure from Craig Johnston. Jan Molby subsequently rolled the spot kick into Leaning's bottom-right corner, as the City keeper started to dive in the opposite direction. "I wasn't happy when we conceded straight away but you have to understand who we were playing against and they will have known that we would be at our most vulnerable after scoring," Smith remembered. "I didn't think it was a penalty at the time and still don't. Jan used to strike the ball reasonably hard so, while you always have a chance, the odds were against Andy."

Ford is still irritated by the penalty decision too, adding: "The most annoying thing about that match is we got cheated. It was never a penalty. Steve Senior was off balance and Craig Johnston was leant on his back. It could have been a foul the other way. The performance was very similar to the Arsenal game. I thought we deserved to win, but I think the referee bottled it in front of their fans at that end. We were the better side in both games that season because the referee bottled it at Anfield too." Nor was Ford daunted by his one-v-one battle against the Merseyside giants: "I played against Alan Kennedy in the first game and Jim Beglin in the second one and, to be honest, they were average. When I think of the battles I had against Glynn Snodin for Doncaster, I would have put him above them and left-back was probably their weakest area."

Rush went on to chip over the bar after being sent clear by Wark with five minutes left to play and Dalglish later complained about the state of the pitch being "diabolical and dangerous", although he admitted it had been the same for both sides. Thirty years later, a bullish Smith, meanwhile, reasoned: "The pitch helped at times in the Cup runs because it wasn't the most conducive for good football but good players, whether you're in the higher divisions or not, deal with that. John Byrne certainly did when he was at the club and there was nothing wrong with Liverpool's pitch, but we almost won there in the replay, so it's all down to your mentality. It's the same when some people complain about bad dressing rooms and I don't believe in all that. If you go in and the toilets are smelling and everything, then that should be good enough reason to turn the opposition over. That was never the case at Bootham Crescent and

345

we updated as much as we could, but Kenny loved complaining. He was one of the nicest blokes you could meet when you got him on his own and had a drink together, but he was different near the media. I had no problems with him and he would have probably just been trying to put some pressure on the referee."

MacPhail also remembered Dalglish's objections, saying: "I think Kenny was whinging about whinging and Alan Hansen wasn't happy about the pitch either. They thought it was awful and that the game shouldn't be played. Kenny said it was too bumpy and there was too much sand on the pitch, but those Liverpool matches ended up bringing in a lot of money for the club and built a lot of things like the executive suites. It was a real bonus for the club to draw them two seasons running and get replays at Anfield." Ford, meanwhile, reckoned the playing surface was not anything unusual, given that era's standards. "The pitch was very similar to what it had been against Arsenal, but it was still better than some places you went to back then," he claimed. "I played at Derby's Baseball Ground when there was no grass on it and it was just a heap of mud. Kenny Dalglish was a constant moaner and I think he put pressure on the referee when he was doing it. It's probably why they got the decisions they did in both matches."

Mark Lawrenson was in the visitors' side that day and admitted he felt the match should not have gone ahead, having renewed acquaintances with Foster, who had been groundsman at Preston when he had been a player there. The BBC television pundit said: "The game shouldn't have been played. The pitch was frozen, extremely icy and rutted. I'm sure good old Fossie had been up all night making sure it was even more rutted and it was dangerous. I felt like Bambi on ice. When the referee said the game was on, I was thinking back to a Cup match with Preston when we'd been knocked out 3-2 in similar conditions, if not worse, at Scarborough, but we managed to get through this one - just. We knew these games were tough, but there's a massive difference between the pitches players play on now and what they did back then. Even my local non-League team Southport have a great

Groundsman Bryan Foster covers the pitch in straw for protection against the frosty weather ahead of the 1986 FA Cup tie against Liverpoo

playing surface now, so things have changed for the better, but you still get upsets." Despite Dalglish's public comments, behind closed doors in the dressing room Liverpool's approach to the tie in such conditions differed from that of Arsenal the previous year, as Lawrenson explained: "Kenny moans every day anyway but, to be honest, you would do about a pitch like that as a manager because, wherever you go, you want a level playing field, but the backroom staff's attitude was conditions like this are part of life's experience and you have to get on with it."

Liverpool defender Alan Hansen gets closed down by Keith Walwyn, who the European Cup winner admitted he did not relish facing during two successive seasons

Lawrenson, who is pictured twice losing his footing during the televised highlights, also revealed that the Merseyside giants had come to North Yorkshire prepared - well, in a manner. "We had all-weather training shoes - and that's the best way to describe them - that came out for rutted pitches," he explained. "They were kept in a special box in the boot room at Anfield and only brought out when a pitch was rock hard. They came with us to York, but nobody would have their own. There were about 15 or 16 pairs and you'd have a mad scramble to get a pair that fitted you. I'm a size eight-and-a-half, but I was playing in size 10s that day and you just had to make do." Nor were there collective groans, Lawrenson pointed out, when Liverpool's legends learned that they would have to visit Bootham Crescent for a second successive season. "I missed the first time we drew York because I had a slight hairline fracture on my leg and Joe Fagan told me to go and have a week in Majorca, but nobody moaned when we were told we had to go to Bootham Crescent again," he said. "We could have been drawn away at Manchester United and, while we knew it would be tough going to a lower-league team, we knew we should have enough to go through and the team was also full of characters. There were no egos and we didn't fear for ourselves going to places like Bootham Crescent so, once we'd seen the pitch, it was a case of it is what it is, let's deal with it."

On his reunion with the irrepressible Foster, meanwhile, the then Republic of Ireland international smiled: "He took his cap off when I went over to see him, and he did that with most people when he wasn't throwing pitchforks at them for stepping on his pitch. He was a great character and what you saw was what you got with him. He'd do anything for you really, especially if you gave him a bottle of Scotch!" Lawrenson's defensive team-mate Hansen was also in for a reunion of sorts, having gone head-to-head with City's bruising great Walwyn a year earlier. Remembering the Scotsman's thoughts about that prospect, Lawrenson added: "I knew all about the Keith Walwyns of this world because I was the third division boy, who had come up from the lower leagues with Preston. I'd played against the likes of Andy Lochhead, Wyn Davies and all sorts, so I knew what to expect from Keith and I knew him from the past. But I remember when we went to York the second year and Alan Hansen saw Keith Walwyn's name on the team-sheet and he said to me: 'Oh great, I'd forgotten they'd got him and he's on my side as well, isn't he?' For most of my career at Liverpool, it was me who took care of those types of characters while Alan handled the other forward, but I just said: 'Hey ho and good luck', because I'd been told I was playing right back."

Instead, Lawrenson was tasked with keeping Canham quiet but the City winger went on to set up the game's first goal. On that responsibility, the Liverpool man added: "I was up against Tony Canham. He was clearly a fans' favourite and he was really tricky. He had a low centre of gravity and he was flying down the left wing, whilst I was struggling to stand up on an icy pitch in boots that didn't fit me." Contrary to the modern-day obsession with over-analysis of the opposition, Lawrenson and his Anfield team-mates would not have been briefed on the threats posed by the likes of Walwyn and Canham either. "The only time in my eight-year career at Anfield a member of the opposition was mentioned before a game was for the 1984 European Cup final when Joe Fagan told us that their captain Agostino Di Bartolomei was a really good passer and that, whoever was nearest to him when he was on the ball, would just have to try and stop him," he revealed. "Otherwise, it was always about us. We were expected to know what we were in for and we did, even when we went to places like York. Excuses were never tolerated, and nobody would have dared moan if they'd got a whack in the face from somebody because that's what you knew you were going to get against a lower-league team."

What that season's double winners did get was a genuine contest and Lawrenson still has admiration for the way the team and their supporters acquitted themselves in the tie. "We hadn't been playing particularly well and York and their fans were buzzing," he admitted. "They were really good at stopping us playing and we couldn't get going. The supporters probably thought, when York went 1-0 up, we've got a chance of winning here, but we got away with it after we were awarded a dubious penalty and I think York's goal gave us a kick up the backside. We were then lucky at Anfield as well. There was nothing wrong with Keith Walwyn's goal and, when the ref disallowed it, me and Alan Hansen looked at each other and had a little chuckle because we knew we'd got away with it." Lawrenson went on to reason that, when Senior was penalised for handball, he had no doubt about heavyweight maestro Molby's ability to level the game, saying: "I had complete faith in Jan sticking the penalty away - absolutely. He probably never received the acclaim and recognition he deserved in the game because he replaced Graeme Souness for us, but he was a great player. The biggest problem for him that day would have been walking from the halfway line to the penalty spot to take it!"

Smith, meanwhile, hailed Leaning's performance in his first season as a professional and reasoned that Ford's goal illustrated the wide players' ability to weigh in with goals. He said: "Andy was a good keeper and one of the reasons I ended up leaving York because there were a couple on the board who wanted to get rid of him and I didn't. Gary Ford scored that day and all our wingers, including Tony Canham and Brian Pollard, could get on the scoresheet." For Leaning, the tie represented a tremendous transformation in his fortunes over a 12-month period. "The previous year I had played for Rowntree's against Nunthorpe in the North Riding Cup and I'd had a decent game," he explained. "It had gone to extra-time and, when I got back in the car, I put the radio on and they were just going over to Bootham Crescent because the penalty had been awarded that Keith Houchen put away against Arsenal. Mick Astbury was at the other end and, whilst I was obviously delighted for him and the team, I couldn't help but think that could have been me. Upset is probably not the right word, but I was left with that feeling that it could have been me playing at the other end. Then, they drew Liverpool in the next round and, at that point, I decided to get myself really fit. I was playing decently for Rowntree's and I was fortunate enough to get some reserve games at the back end of that season at Bootham Crescent. The club were short of a keeper to play for the last three reserve games and I remember I was working in Leeds in a room on my own when the telephone rang. I left it because I thought it's obviously not for me but, then, it rang again, and it was Viv Busby and he asked me to play for the reserves, which I did. We played Sunderland and I had a decent game and Viv said: 'Why don't you play in the last two matches as well?' They went well for me too and I was offered a contract for the following season so, a year after thinking what could have been, I was actually playing against Liverpool."

On the eve of the tie, Leaning admitted that honouring the club's proud reputation in the Cup crossed his mind, as he recalled games he had witnessed at Bootham Crescent and had been told about by his father. "I was like a kid in a sweet shop building up to that Liverpool game," he enthused. "We'd played Derby at home the week before, because they were down in that division at the time and the club was a nice environment to work in. Denis and Viv had brought an excitement to it. We were expected to get results and wanted to get results because we had a decent team. I was also brought up with the knowledge that York had a great Cup pedigree because my father told me all about the 1955 run and, as soon as we got on that pitch to play, I couldn't wait." Once the action started, though, Leaning admitted to feeling a little star-struck when he stared at the other end of the pitch and saw a multiple League Championship and European Cup winner between the sticks. "You want a touch early on in games like that to get you going and I think I did get one," the City keeper recalled. "I seem to remember it was a quiet game because of the state of the pitch. It was a difficult surface to play on and, as a keeper, you had to be spot on, but I was looking at the other end and thinking I can't believe I'm on the same pitch as Bruce Grobbelaar because he was one of my heroes. He was as flamboyant as ever on the day. He played as he usually did. He made saves and kicked the ball as though there was nothing wrong with the pitch. It was a surreal situation wishing each other all the best before the game, as you always do as keepers. Then, it's just a little wave and you're down to business. There was nothing else said beyond that. He had a job to do and so did I. Once that build-up to the game is over, you just want to get on with it and, once the game starts, you're concentrating on that. It was a great atmosphere although the pitch wouldn't have been played on in this day and age."

Leaning impressed as much as his famous counterpart on the day and, on denying the country's most potent striker Rush to provide the platform for Ford to give the hosts a shock lead, he said: "I remember the ball went over the top and Ian Rush was brilliant at latching on to situations like that. He was in the prime of his life, but I came out and got a block on his shot. Gary Ford then scored in the second half and we were in dream land. Then, you're thinking what if and could it be, because it would have been one of the greatest shocks of all time." Ford has fond memories of his goal, reciting how the man he usually sent in crosses for teed him up for the opener. "It was another unusual moment because Keith (Walwyn) passed the ball to me and it was normally the other way around," he laughed. "He laid if off and I just hoped for the best. I don't think I placed it. I just closed my eyes and hit it, but the crowd's reaction was a bit surreal. You don't really realise what you've done at the time. It's just a case of let's crack on once you're playing and becomes a normal game."

But the lead proved to be so very short-lived and Leaning still harbours doubts about the penalty the Merseyside giants were awarded and recalled his feeling of helplessness as one of the coolest players of his, or any, era stepped up to take it. "First, they got a free kick, which I didn't think was a foul," Leaning argued. "The ball then got put in the box and Steve (Senior) was penalised for handball as he was falling backwards. The ref pointed straight to the spot, but it was controversial, and I had no chance with the penalty in front of the Liverpool fans. As soon as he (Molby) hit it, I immediately thought that's going in. There was no back-lift, which is how he played. I've got a picture of it at home and I'm grasping thin air really. He just got it out of his feet and hit it. After that, there were a few chances at either end, and a draw was a fair result."

Recounting the swift turn in events after Ford's goal, MacPhail added: "Going ahead against a team like that was almost unheard of. You are expecting them to score first as had happened the previous season and they probably upped the ante after that. I remember Steve going up for a header and the referee giving a dubious penalty, but you can't do anything about that. You can argue all day with the referee, but it won't change his mind and, while Andy's a big unit, Jan Molby stuck the penalty away well." Smith's reaction at the final whistle, meanwhile, highlighted the confidence that was coursing throughout the club at the time. "I remember at full-time, Denis said we must keep believing because he was sure we could go on and win the tie still at Anfield," Leaning said. "We almost did too." With the previous year's thrashing at Anfield in mind, Ford was a little cautious in his post-match interview. "The television people spoke to me on the pitch afterwards," he recalled. "I said to them that, as long as it wasn't 7-0, I'd be happy."

Gabbiadini was being used sparingly at the time and missed out on a chance to take on Liverpool, as Smith opted for experience, but he was again an interested and inspired onlooker, explaining: "I wasn't disappointed to miss out really because you know, as a young player, you will be in and out of the team but, watching the match, did put a bit of fire in my belly. It made me realise these players were as normal and down to earth as we were and similar characters to those in our dressing room. You saw they were just human beings when they came to Bootham Crescent. I remember Ronnie Whelan wasn't playing and he was in the bar, having a pint with my mum and dad before the game. They were stars who you saw on TV every week, but it made me think there was nothing stopping me playing at the same level as them. When I saw the lads match them on the park, it then made me think that even more."

Even though there was an away allocation of 6,500 tickets, fans started queuing in freezing conditions from 2am during the early hours of the morning when they went on sale for the Anfield replay, which Liverpool subsequently won 3-1, but only after extra time and a second-half Walwyn goal - that would have been the winner - was disallowed. The Merseyside giants went on to win the final and completed a league and cup double against neighbours Everton with Johnston admitting in the Wembley programme: "We were very fortunate, and York gave us two hard battles."

A second trip to Anfield also pleased the boardroom with Smith pointing out: "The club were delighted with the replay because it meant lots of money and it paid for a lot of work on the ground. Stadiums all over the country weren't great back then, but Bootham Crescent had still been a step down for me coming from Stoke's Victoria Ground. The offices were Portakabins in the car park, but we got new ones after the Cup runs. As we went along, we spent the money on the stadium and that was sensible because having good working conditions helps. It means people enjoy going to work more. There was work to be done all around. Possibly the first improvements we made to the dressing room was just putting some coat hangers up. It was good to give the physio some room to do his job properly too, because he had done his work in the middle of the dressing room before. Bootham Crescent was a good, old-fashioned football ground where rival sets of fans could stand on the terraces at each end of the ground. You could hear them as well because of how close they were. We tried to improve it as much as we could without taking away the character."

Ball girls were used at Bootham Crescent for the first time in February 1985 and selected from the Junior Reds Club. Pictured (from left-to-right) are: Helen Richardson, Sarah Pullon, Lisa Morris, Kerry Mangan, Carol Wright, Louise Brown, Liz Hopwood, Jackie Spencer, Sarah Mangan, Nicola Nowell, Louise Addinall and Sharon Thirlway

CHAPTER 22

Beating Chelsea and losing to Caernarfon

"I remember pulling in at Bootham Crescent with Alan Little and we both sniffed the air. It smelt of chocolate. In Hartlepool, we'd just been used to smog."

For the 1986/87 season, improvements continued to be made to Bootham Crescent with video equipment installed, and crash barriers strengthened and Ricky Sbragia admitted he was pleased to see Bootham Crescent spruced up. "I remember a big, new bath coming in and the seating and toilet areas were made better, which is all credit to the club," he pointed out. "That gave us a bit more comfort and it was nice to see the money going back into the club. They did the front of the club up too and brought in the executive boxes and they did things like that when there was a windfall. We also had little lockers underneath us in the dressing rooms and we got dressed there before training, not like later years when they had a separate complex, so it was always our base and it was nice for us to see it become a bit smarter."

The new season witnessed another excellent result, meanwhile, against higher-division opposition - this time in the League Cup - as first division Chelsea were seen off 1-0 thanks to a Tony Canham goal. The London side would subsequently go through to the third round on aggregate after winning the second leg 3-0 at Stamford Bridge. But first blood was drawn by City after Sbargia's long diagonal ball to the left set up Canham for the winning goal in the Bootham Crescent tie on 50 minutes. The City winger went on to round Chelsea keeper Eddie Niezwiecki and found the inviting net despite Doug Rougvie's attempts to prevent the ball from crossing the line.

Chelsea were not the world power they would later become following Russian billionaire Roman Abramovich's arrival in West London but still represented a notable scalp at Bootham Crescent with Andy Leaning keeping one of the most potent strike forces at the time off the scoresheet. "We had beaten Sunderland the round before, which was a good result and we were then up against Kerry

Dixon and David Speedie at Bootham Crescent," he recalled. "It was another test and another good night. I enjoyed it and it was all part of the cup fever we were thriving on at Bootham Crescent around that time. We expected to get results when we pulled out these ties against the big clubs. That carried on when I left against the likes of Manchester United and Everton and that cup pedigree has always been there." Having watched the famous Arsenal triumph and two Liverpool contests from the sidelines, meanwhile, Marco Gabbiadini made the first XI against Chelsea and admitted that it was an eye-opening experience, with England international Dixon and Scotland striker Speedie at the other end of the pitch. "I remember running around in circles a lot and getting a bit of a runaround in that match," he explained. "I received a lot of guidance from some of the senior players and they were telling me to calm down and let them have the ball a little bit, which was something I wasn't used to doing, so it was a different experience to anything before. People like Ricky (Sbragia) helped me in that Chelsea game. We were playing against big names like Kerry Dixon and Micky Hazard and it was my first taste of that."

Sbragia had more experience in such situations but, nevertheless, enjoyed pitting his wits one more time against top-flight opposition, saying: "We played well against Chelsea. We felt confident enough to believe we could beat anybody at home because we were a decent side. There had been some changes in the team by then and, maybe, they thought it would be a formality. The pitch was in great nick too and, whereas Liverpool came and gave us a bit of respect, maybe Chelsea under-estimated us. We were always up for games like that and the crowd was good. It was a night game and I liked them when there was a wee bit of moist on the ground. We went into it with nothing to lose and knew that we could get a bit of recognition in games like that. They are always good for younger players, although Chelsea showed their class in the home game."

In November, meanwhile, Gabbiadini became the youngest City player ever to score a hat-trick, claiming the match ball at 18 following his treble during a 4-1 home triumph against Darlington in the Football League Trophy with strike partner Keith Walwyn also hitting the target. Gabbiadini netted on six, 19 and 36 minutes to also become the first man to grab a first-half treble for City at Bootham Crescent since Paul Aimson more than 15 years previously. Recalling that historic night, he said: "It was in the days when there was no back-pass rule and people used to play the ball back to the keeper from the halfway line and at least one of my goals came when I intercepted one of them. It was quite a big night for me, as I wasn't playing that regularly and I think I've still got the Mitre Delta somewhere."

But the same season saw City on the receiving end of an FA Cup upset when Caernarfon Town, whose players were paid £30-a-week, became the first non-League side to win a replay at Bootham Crescent, clinching a 2-1 triumph despite Canham reducing the deficit with 11 minutes to play. City had 19 shots on goal compared to the Northern Premier League visitors' five, but Austin Salmon opened the scoring on 10 minutes following a misjudgement by keeper Neil Smallwood and went on to tee up Steve Craven, who netted a second from the edge of the penalty box. John King, who would later lead Tranmere into the Championship play-off semi-finals three seasons on the trot, masterminded the victory and his dugout rival Denis Smith was magnanimous in defeat, at least outside of the home dressing room, explaining: "That was great for them. You can't gloat over what we had done to Liverpool and Arsenal and complain when the tables are turned on you. That's football. You have to take it on the chin and start again. There's not much else you can do. It wasn't nice in the dressing room afterwards, but I had to pat their players on the back and wish them all the best. I also found out, when I became manager of Wrexham later on, that there are some good players in Welsh football because they take a lot of lads from Manchester and Liverpool."

Gary Ford recalled the players incurring the wrath of Smith at the final whistle, saying: "Denis used to get angry for a minute, then that was it. He was fine after that, but there was a furious minute after he initially walked through the door, then he calmed down." Sbragia, meanwhile, confessed that City might have underestimated Caernarfon, having mistakenly believed that they had avoided the potential for a banana skin in Wales. He said: "I remember, at their place, Caernarfon had turned all the showers on at 1.30pm after our kit had been put out and, when we went to put it on, it was all wet from the steam, so we thought we had done the business when we managed to get them back to Bootham after that. But we didn't perform, and they also deserved credit, because they were better than we thought. You have to be clinical in games like that and we weren't on the night. Then, they scored, and it gave them something to hold on to and work harder for. I think Denis lost his temper and read us the riot act after that one and we were poor. It was totally a bad night and one of my last games I think."

In the league, another good start had been made with the club second at the end of September, but the team's form nosedived after that. A 3-1 New Year's Day triumph over fallen giants Middlesbrough, with Walwyn (two) and Martin Butler on the scoresheet in front of 8,611 fans at Bootham Crescent, proved a rare highlight, although the visitors' 21-year-old, future

England international still caught Smith's eye that day. "That was a good result and it was a big achievement to cope well in that division against clubs like Middlesbrough," Smith reasoned. "I remember they had a young centre-half called Gary Pallister playing who I tried to sign for York. He was just coming through and, after we beat them, I wondered whether they would let him go." Leaning also remembered the Boro clash as a welcome boost during a tough campaign. "That was good," he confessed. "We weren't playing too well and needed a result. I remember we checked into the Royal York Hotel the night before and it looked to all intents and purposes that the game could be called off because there was really heavy rain the night before, but the game went ahead on a glue pot really. We went 2-0 up early on and that settled our nerves a bit because they had a good team. Tony Mowbray was the captain and they also had Gary Pallister and Stephen Pears, who was good in goal. Mowbray scored to make it 2-1 just after half-time but we got a third through big Keith for a comfortable win in the end and it was an exciting game." Another future England international - winger Stuart Ripley - also played in the match, which represented the first-ever Football League meeting between the two clubs.

City still needed a point, however, from their final game at home to Notts County to stay up. Butler's 67th-minute solo goal, as he dribbled past keeper Mick Leonard and defender Wayne Fairclough before finding the net, earned a 1-1 draw despite Richard Young's injury-time goal for the visitors and Bolton Wanderers went on to suffer relegation to the Football League's bottom tier, as City narrowly avoided being involved in a relegation/promotion play-off during the only season that system was used in the English game. It was Ford's last game for the Minstermen and he admitted, after all the good times he had at Bootham Crescent, it was a struggle to get the result needed to secure safety. "It's hard when you're down there," he explained. "You don't have that confidence as a team. My confidence was gone by then as well. It doesn't help when you're only on a one-year contract and coming towards the end of the season because you're thinking have I got a job and that's not healthy. You are nervous, and you shouldn't have those nerves. You don't have the confidence to play how you want to do and just start doing the basics. The team had gone from thinking they could beat the best team in the world to not fancying our chances against Notts County at home. It was time to go. I had done 10 years and the club didn't want to move on and go where Denis wanted. With the addition of another couple of players, I felt we could have been in the Championship."

The likes of Walwyn and Sean Haslegrave bid farewell too after that final game and Sbragia hung up his boots. Walwyn had thrilled City fans at Bootham

Crescent with his goalscoring exploits and remains second only to Norman Wilkinson in the club's all-time goalscoring list on 140 goals. Centre-back Sbragia, meanwhile, took up a new role at Bootham Crescent. "I was given the youth-team manager's job and it was completely different for me," he recalled. "I was still training with the first team at first but, three or four games in, I said to Denis to be fair to everyone I wanted to do it full-time. I had done some badges anyway and, even when I was 17 at Birmingham, I had done a bit of coaching. I also completed two years of a four-year joinery course at Blackpool and did a bit with Tetley's in a pub but didn't want to do that with having children. Then, I had a bit of luck, when Mal Crosby went to Kuwait at the same time I was having problems with my back, so the youth-team position was available."

The Notts County clash also represented the last game in charge for City's management team of Smith and Viv Busby, who departed for Sunderland that summer. On the end of a glorious reign and era at Bootham Crescent, Smith said: "People had started cherry-picking our players, so it was like getting promotion when we stayed up. We showed around that time we could also grind out results when we needed to. I didn't know the match against Notts County was going to be my last game though. I got a call from Sunderland when I was on holiday in Magaluf and things started happening from there. I had been trying to sort out contracts with players, but they knew we had gone as far as we were going to get, and they were getting better offers."

Leaning also departed after being surprisingly released by the club. "It definitely felt like the end of an era," he recalled. "Everyone left and mostly went on to better things. I still feel if that side had been kept together, we could have made a push for promotion that season, but John MacPhail went to Bristol City and there seemed to be a demise after that. I saw Denis at the end of the season and he said he wanted me to stay, but the board had told him they wanted to go a different route. He said, however, that there were other clubs interested and I signed for Sheffield United after a trial with Everton. It was a surprise, though, that I hadn't been given a new contract."

MacPhail had left at the end of the previous season having been unhappy with the manner in which Smith handled his contract negotiations at Bootham Crescent. "I asked for a rise of £50 and a two-year contract, but Denis said to me York City don't give them out and you can only have a one-year deal," the Scotsman explained. "I said that's fine because Terry Cooper had asked me if I'd like to go to Bristol City. Denis then told me he wanted £60,000 for me. I wanted to stay because my wife was from York, but it ended up going to a tribunal and it was the first one Brendan Batson was involved in as he had just started with the PFA. Denis brought lots of newspaper clippings along about how I had been the man-of-the-match against Arsenal. But Brendan Batson said to him: 'If he's that good, why don't you give him a £50 rise and a two-year deal. That's nothing'. Terry Cooper had been willing to pay £30,000 for me but I ended up going there for £13,000." MacPhail's fondness for Bootham Crescent never diminished, though, with the former Dundee defender enthusing: "It was a great ground with the big, long tunnel and, because it was small, when we were winning, it created a good atmosphere. It was a warm place. The people were very friendly, and we always used to go in the bar afterwards, which was great. It was a real family club. It was just like a second home to us as players. It was that intimate."

Former Exeter, Plymouth and Blackburn boss Bobby Saxton subsequently took over the managerial reins with only Derek Hood left from the 1984 title-winning team. Jeff Miller, meanwhile, arrived as physio - a role that he would fill for just under 30 years. But it was disclosed that the club had made losses of £65,000 during the 1986/87 season and the start of the next campaign confirmed what most people feared - tough times were ahead. Saxton inherited a side with just two professionals signed on contracts and the team did not win a league game until a Halloween 1-0 home victory over Chesterfield. Dale Banton was on target to secure the points after the team had failed to win any of their first 15 contests.

On the task he faced as Smith's successor, Saxton said: "Whatever happened between Denis and the chairman is between them, but I took the job because I wanted it. Denis had left to go to Sunderland and the bulk of the players also went due to freedom of contract, so we were starting from scratch. I had to basically get a full squad of players together to keep York in the division. I also had to sell Marco Gabbiadini to Sunderland for £80,000. Denis wanted him, and we wanted the money. We hadn't got a squad and it's hard to get players to come to your club when you're in that situation. As a manager, you want to pick and choose but, when you're trying to get better players, they do that too. I worked for ten or 12 different clubs in my career and York was a very good one. For me, though, it was just a case of being at the right club at the wrong time and it was a battle, but I still enjoyed it and the board were excellent behind the scenes." In his new role, Sbargia witnessed Saxton's struggles first-hand. "I remember coming in the first day and Bobby Saxton only had five players," Sbragia pointed out. "Bobby was begging, stealing and borrowing to try and get people in, so the players he was getting were maybe not ones he necessarily wanted, but he needed to fill the squad. The club had been decimated at that time and he admitted later, when we were coaching at Sunderland together, that it was very difficult for him."

Gabbiadini's career, meanwhile, was on an upward trajectory that would see him eventually ply his trade in the top-flight and he can clearly recollect how Saxton informed him that he would be moving on and his initial deflation when he learned the identity of his suitors. "You never really had a plan back then," Gabbiadini reasoned. "There was no pathway laid out for you and we didn't think like that in that era. You just tried to do as well as you could, but Denis had left, and the club was in crisis. All those players who had enjoyed those good years were not particularly looked after by the board, so it was really tricky for Bobby Saxton and he looked almost shell-shocked. People in the game talk and have a really high regard for him, but unfortunately we didn't see a lot of what he could do at York and that was a shame. We had a shocking start to the season and I had only scored one goal in eight league games. Then, one day, Bobby rang me and asked me to go back into the club. When I arrived, he then walked me onto the pitch and into the centre circle, where he said: 'There's a big club in for you'. That got me excited and I was thinking Manchester United or Liverpool so, when he said Sunderland, I was a bit disappointed because they were in the same division at the time and we had beaten them in the League Cup the season before. It turned out to be a perfect move though. I was playing at a level I was comfortable with and for a club who were on the up. I also hit it off with Eric Gates straight away. People say I was always going to leave and play for Denis but, when Bobby took me out onto the pitch, that was the first I knew about it. I hadn't spoken to Denis since he had left, and it was in the days before people had mobile phones. People also felt you had a choice but, back then, it was the club who often told you what you were doing."

One positive during Saxton's reign was the Bootham Crescent crowd witnessed youngsters Steve Tutill, Gary Himsworth and Andy McMillan all make their first strides into the pro game. McMillan, who would go on to make more appearances at Bootham Crescent than any other player aside from Barry Jackson, made his debut as a half-time replacement for David Spofforth during a 2-2 home draw with Mansfield three days after Christmas in 1987. He was on the dole at the time and playing Sunday League football in Hull but was called upon as a non-contract player due to an injury crisis that meant eight players were unavailable and led to the club unsuccessfully applying for a postponement on the eve of the game. Recalling his debut, McMillan, who helped the team

Sunderland supporters climb up the floodlight pylon during the troubled March 1988 Bootham Crescent clash

Police open a gate in the fencing to prevent a crush in the away end after Sunderland supporters were let in without tickets for the troubled Bootham Crescent clash against Sunderland in March 1988

A Sunderland supporter aims a kick at the match ball during a break in first-half play at the troubled March 1988 clash

Sunderland fans spill onto the pitch during the troubled March 1988 clash

Then club secretary Keith Usher is embroiled in the trouble during the March 1988 clash against Sunderland

recover from 2-1 down to earn a share of the spoils in a much-improved second-half display, said: "Because the lads were struggling a bit, Bobby Saxton dragged a couple of them off and I was on. I had come in from Hull so did not really appreciate how successful the club had been before, but the atmosphere around the place was sombre at the time and I think there were only about three players there when I signed. I wasn't too bothered about that back then though. I was making my debut and I can still smell the dressing room. I would have run all day and I can actually picture myself at 19 getting down the wing."

Another rare highlight saw Smith and Busby's Sunderland beaten 2-1 at Bootham Crescent in front of a 9,000-strong crowd. At the time, City were bottom of the table with four wins from 37 games, while Sunderland were second and destined to finish the season as champions. Ex-City pair MacPhail and Gabbiadini were also in the visitors' team and the game kicked off amid a Cup-tie atmosphere.

Goalkeeper Scott Endersby and centre-back Tutill, returning to the team after three months out with an ankle injury, helped keep a confident Roker Park outfit at bay during the opening exchanges. But it was City who forged ahead on 34 minutes when Gary Howlett found Ian Helliwell and the big striker cut in from the left before firing in a shot that hit both posts and then crossed the line. Endersby made several fine saves to preserve the hosts' lead before a magnificent second goal was added on 75 minutes. A pass from Helliwell sent Himsworth raiding down the left wing and his cross was met by Banton who headed into

Sunderland supporters invade the pitch and break the goalposts at the end of a troubled contest in March 1988

361

the roof of the net. Seven minutes later, Sunderland reduced the deficit through Colin Pascoe from close range after a backheel from Gates, but City saw the game out with Tutill having kept a tight rein on close friend Gabbiadini throughout. Gabbiadini saw a late penalty appeal rejected when he went down under a Tutill challenge just outside the box and Gordon Armstrong also saw a headed goal disallowed for an off-the-ball foul on Endersby during the frantic final throes.

At the final whistle, hundreds of pitch-invading Sunderland supporters took out their frustration on the Bootham Crescent goalposts by breaking them and the offenders also fought with police. Earlier, the match had been halted for four minutes when 150 visiting fans had spilled onto the playing arena. Two policemen were injured and 32 arrests were made, which led to then Lord Mayor of York Malcolm Heppell lobbying the Sports Minster for a supporters' membership scheme. City club secretary Keith Usher was also attacked as he tried to help restore order. Guy Mowbray, meanwhile, was in the crowd that day and recalled: "That was a fantastic win but there seemed to be as many of their fans as ours at Bootham Crescent and they were everywhere, not just in the away end."

Saxton has vivid memories of the victory too and the part an 18-year-old Tutill played in it. He recalled: "It was an achievement to beat Sunderland bearing in mind our situation. It was chock-a-block that day and the support from Sunderland was fantastic. Steve Tutill obviously still had a lot to learn about the game, but he had all the assets. He was pacy and good in the air and, at the end of that game, he was absolutely shattered and could hardly make it off the pitch. He gave us more than 100 per cent that day and that was the type of lad he was." On keeper Endersby's heroics and match-winner Banton, Saxton added: "Scott Endersby was lively and quick. I always liked my keepers to be agile and we managed to take him in from Carlisle. Dale Banton was also a nippy striker, who was sharp and busy."

MacPhail remembered vividly the reaction of Smith at the final whistle, saying: "On the day, we didn't produce our best football and Denis was livid going back to the club he had left and getting beaten. He was a bit of a psycho when he lost games. Steve Tutill did well against Marco and he was a good centre-half who went on to have a good career at York. It just wasn't our day." The bruises from Gabbiadini's reunion with Tutill lasted longer than the pain of defeat against his old club, even if he felt he might have received more protection from the officials. Recalling the match, Gabbiadini said: "I remember the referee being particularly bad and we didn't get many decisions. We had a good season and didn't get beaten many times and only lost a handful of other games, but Tutts kicked lumps out of us that day. He was a physical player and a stopper, and those types of players could get away with murder back then. It wasn't one of my best games, but you have to take days like that on the chin and move on to the next match. York were just about relegated at the time and I was sad to see them go down but, that season, we were taking 3,000 supporters to wherever we could. The away support was incredible, and it was every home team's cup final almost, but you have to deal with that. It was a bad day at the office, but we didn't have many during our 46 league games that season. It wasn't the end of the world and I was never one of those players who said they went home and kicked the cat and never spoke to their wife and kids for three days. Even after defeats, I would just treat it as a game of football and move on to the next one."

Smith, who was booed before the game as he posed for pictures, argued there was an air of inevitability about the Black Cats' defeat and was just pleased the safety mechanism he had insisted on, when fences were put up at the ground, averted a possible tragedy. Police later defended their decision to allow Sunderland supporters into the ground without tickets on the day and Smith said: "I think everything was built up for us to get beaten that day. It was very hostile coming back, but I was just happy that, when the fences had been put up at York, we had put handles on them. I had been a supporter myself and, when it's a full stadium, you need to have somewhere to go if there's a crush. With the handles, they could go on the pitch and there might have been another problem that day if we hadn't insisted on having them and I'm proud of that because it probably saved some lives." Gabbiadini, though, was not a fan of the fences, even with the safety measures, saying: "I remember the fences being up and to see them go out of the game was a positive."

As a home player, McMillan recalled being thrilled with the atmosphere generated by the big attendance, even if many inside the stadium were from the north-east. "I think half of that crowd were from Sunderland," he said. "I'd been at Hull before and Boothferry Park was a massive, open stadium whereas, at Bootham Crescent, everything was quite confined, and the fans were quite close to the pitch. That created a real buzz and it was a fantastic place. When I saw it packed out for the first time in that game it made me think what we could have at the ground and we were lucky enough to pack it out a few times again over the years."

Remembering the scenes at the final whistle, Saxton revealed that one man felt very differently: "They dragged the goals over and Fossie (Bryan Foster) wasn't happy seeing them on his pitch." Saxton added that the colourful character of groundsman Foster, who was awarded with a gold watch for his long service that season, also provided moments of levity during his difficult tenure. He said: "Fossie was the biggest character at the club. What a boy he was. We used to have a tactics board in the dressing room and we had a lad called Jim Branagan, who was a right back. I remember coming in after a match that we had lost, and Jim had been responsible for a goal. I think he miskicked the ball, so I had a pop at him and he said he had made the mistake because of a bobble on the pitch. Everybody looked at each other after he said that because they wanted to know how Fossie would react. It was his pitch and he went mad. When we came in for a debrief meeting on Monday, I went to the board and there was a big message pinned up on it: 'Branagan, you could not play on a ****ing bowling green'. Jim came in and held his hand up and we left the note there for a week." A young McMillan, meanwhile, was always too smart to incur the wrath of City's eccentric groundsman. "Fossie was an absolute legend," he smiled. "I remember the gaffer's office and that door in the tunnel was always open. Fossie would be sat with his feet up on the gaffer's table watching the racing. The gaffer would also be sat opposite or on the sofa and the banter you could hear would be great. He was a lovely man, but he would throw pitch forks - not near you but at you - if you walked on his pitch, but I never did. I respected him because I knew he was quite a good shot with them. It was old school and he got his job done. His pitch was always immaculate, and he had the club at heart and was just a character who all the players loved."

Despite Foster's award-winning playing surface, the club went on to finish second-bottom on goal difference above old rivals Doncaster, racking up then club records for the fewest wins in a season (eight), most defeats (29) and fewest points (33 or 25 under the old two-points-for-a-win system). The lowest victory tally was eventually beaten in 2016 when the club dropped out of the Football League for a second time. Despite there still being six games left to play, relegation was confirmed for Saxton's men following a 2-0 home defeat to Grimsby, who would also end the campaign relegated. Billy Stubbs and Paul Agnew scored the Mariners' goals. Given such a fate had been inevitable for several weeks, if not months, the game did not particularly stand out for McMillan, who was also, at the time, concentrating on making his own strides as a fledgling pro. "We knew we were getting relegated that season," he explained. "It was just a case of it's happening, and the talk was about preparing for the following season. I was just a young footballer and it's only when you play more games that you realise how big these games are."

Not even the return of club favourite Gordon Staniforth, who was plucked out of retirement from the pro game two months into the season, helped halt the slide. Commenting on what he found following his return to Bootham Crescent, Staniforth said: "I had been the manager of the Buckles Inn on the A64 and I loved being involved again. I was paid £70 a match as a part-time player and it was great for me but Bobby had lost it completely. His tactics were get the ball and boot it as far away from our goal as possible and that's what we'd do in training. He had a decent career but couldn't handle struggling players or teams and he struggled. Otherwise, not a lot had changed at the ground. The car park had been tarmacked but that was about it. It was a swansong that I thoroughly enjoyed though." Staniforth also saw some reason for optimism with the emergence of McMillan and Tutill. "Andy and Steve were both honest York players who wanted to do well every game," Staniforth pointed out. "They were reliable 7/10 players. I always said to my York College students: 'If we can get most of the team on 7/10, we will do well'. It's when you get a few fives you're in trouble, but Tutts was a colossus and Andy was as fit as anything. He could get up and down and was a great player. It was good to see them go on and have good careers."

In March of that relegation season, meanwhile, a public meeting had voted to go ahead with a plan to "Roof The Shippo". Subsequently, after that Easter Monday loss to Grimsby, a committee was elected in the Social Club to raise the money to construct the roof. Fundraising events included a series of sportsman dinners with one attracting several members of the 1955 FA Cup semi-final team and the 1974 promotion-winning side. A total of £1,500 was also raised as 70 people, including chairman Michael Sinclair and the playing squad, completed a four-mile sponsored walk around the city walls. Later, a pre-season friendly against Middlesbrough in 1989 saw all the proceeds donated to the fund, along with those from the sale of then club historian Dave Batters' *York City: A Complete Playing History* book. Club secretary Usher went on to arrange for a new executive box to be perched behind the Shipton Street End and it served as a rallying point for the appeal. It was stocked with items of football memorabilia, which were regularly replenished by fans donating articles for sale, and provided a steady matchday income.

In July, meanwhile, an American football game was played on the ground as part of the York Festival. It pitted two American Air Force, UK-based teams Alconbury Spartans and Lakenheath Eagles against each other with the latter 1987 UK champions and European runners-up. The Brighouse-based Conquest Alliance marching band, who were also national champions, added to the party atmosphere, while, ahead of the main event, York's modest, fledgling gridiron team - the Yorvik Vikings - demonstrated some of the moves and rules of the game, which had risen in popularity due to six years of TV coverage on Channel Four. In a match that was described as "dull" by the *Yorkshire Evening Press* with defences on top, Spartans emerged 7-0 winners in a low-scoring contest. Quarterback Kerr sprinted in for a three-yard, converted touchdown, representing the only points in two hours and 50 minutes of play. The crowd was also reported as "sparse", but fears that the pitch would be severely damaged proved unfounded.

The summer then saw the long-serving Hood released and awarded a testimonial in November but hope for improvement followed when Saxton was given £100,000 to spend and close-season captures included keeper Chris Marples (£28,000) from Chesterfield, ex-Coventry City centre-back Kevan Smith (£35,000) and midfielder and new skipper Steve Spooner (£29,000) from Hereford.

A bad start to the season was made, however, and a 2-1 home defeat to Scunthorpe in mid-September dumped the club to the bottom of the Football League, prompting Saxton's resignation. Explaining that decision, the beleaguered boss said: "I used to go through five stages as a manager, trying various options to turn things around. If I got to the end of the fifth and the situation hadn't improved, then I would think perhaps it's me and the best time for a fresh face to come in, so I told Michael Sinclair, the chairman, I had tried plans A, B, C, D and E. First of all, as a manager, you try and put your own stamp on things. Then, if you're on a bit of a rocky road, you see who you can bring in to the team from within the group to change things. If that doesn't work, then you look to see who you can sign from outside. Then, you might look at changing the system and then the way you train. That wasn't easy at York though because we didn't have a proper training ground. Sometimes, we would have a game of cricket in the car park with the staff." Despite a torrid tenure, though, Saxton still harbours fond memories of the club and Bootham Crescent, saying: "I loved the old-fashioned charm of the place and the pleasure of driving into the car park, parking up against the wall and going into a little office. It was a neat and tidy ground in a nice area and a very, very good football club. The name itself was special. It's like Roker Park was for Sunderland. I don't think people will ever forget Bootham Crescent."

John Bird took over almost a month later after Barry Swallow had again held the fort in a caretaker capacity. The new boss had impressed when his Hartlepool team won 3-2 during the first game at Bootham Crescent following Saxton's departure, prompting the chairman to sound him out about the managerial vacancy afterwards. "After we beat York 3-2 at Bootham Crescent, Michael Sinclair had a word with me in the boardroom," Bird revealed. "York were struggling but I knew Bobby Saxton quite well and knew they'd spent a bit of money. At Hartlepool, I'd had no money, but we ran York ragged that night. We were doing quite well in the league and Michael Sinclair asked me how I'd done that. I said I'd got my players working very hard and busting a gut for me every week and it was as simple as that. The following week he approached the Hartlepool chairman about me and I took the job because the set-up and facilities at York were a lot better. Alan Little came with me as well, as my coach. We'd worked together at Hartlepool and I remember pulling in at Bootham Crescent with him and we both sniffed the air. It smelt of chocolate. In Hartlepool, we'd just been used to smog." Little was just as taken by his new surroundings, adding: "My first impression of the ground was how clean and tidy it looked, compared to Hartlepool."

Results were better under Bird, who sold Banton to Walsall for £80,000 and recruited Shaun Reid from Rochdale for £35,000. The team even had an outside chance of reaching the play-offs during the final week of the season before finishing mid-table. Bird adopted an abrupt manner in his attempt to reverse the club's fortunes, shaking things up a little at Bootham Crescent. "The players were shocked when Bobby Saxton went," he explained. "Michael Sinclair told me the players liked him a lot. In my first meeting with them, I said: 'You all seem upset'. They said: 'We are'. I said: 'Bobby Saxton's a good bloke'. They said: 'Yes, he's a great bloke'. I then said: 'Well, he was a good friend of mine and you lot certainly helped him didn't you because he's on the dole now and you're all here in work'. After saying that, I walked out. Michael Sinclair said: 'What are you doing?' I said: 'Leave them. I'm not having that. It's no good them feeling sorry for themselves'. They were the ones on the field and that was my first team talk."

Bryan Foster supervises York Rugby League groundsman George Marwood as the rugby posts go up at Bootham Crescent for a Challenge Cup tie against Leeds in 1989. It was the first time rugby had been played at the ground

York's Challenge Cup first-round clash against Leeds

In January, meanwhile, rugby league was played at Bootham Crescent for the first time when York's Challenge Cup first-round clash against Leeds was staged there. It earned the football club £3,000, but the whole exercise wasn't without its complications, as the machine to dig out the three-foot holes required to secure the longer rugby uprights broke down, meaning groundsman Foster had to resort to manual spadework. Protective of his pitch as ever, Foster said at the time: "I have been told that rugby does the grass less harm than football, so we will just have to wait and see." A crowd of 11,347 - rugby league's biggest of the day - went on to witness a 28-9 Leeds win. The Wasps, as they were then known, gave away ten needless points in the opening quarter with Phil Ford claiming a try, converted by John Bentley and, after Stewart Horton kicked a drop goal for York, Carl Gibson was allowed to scoot over. But an upset looked possible when that deficit was reduced to 10-9 on 51 minutes as Horton's try was converted by St John Ellis, who had earlier landed a penalty. Hope was swiftly extinguished, though, from the resulting kick-off when Paul Mulherin was controversially adjudged to have knocked on and the visitors won the resulting scrum, allowing Australian Test star Andrew Ettingshausen to touch down in the corner. Further tries were added by Bentley and Lee Crooks, with another Great Britain legend Gary Schofield also in the visitors' team.

Then record losses of £190,000, meanwhile, were made during the season, although the club did not carry an overdraft thanks to interest-free loans from directors plus a £100,000 share issue, which saw chairman Sinclair's family company Mulberry Hall underwrite virtually the whole sum. Staniforth also returned to head a new scheme that was being rolled out at clubs up and down the country and would grow in size and scope during subsequent years. "Football in the Community had been piloted in the north-west and we started it at York," he explained. "It was perfect timing for me to get out of the Buckles Inn. I was licensee of the Social Club at Bootham Crescent and the Football in the Community officer at the same time. Everything we did was new, so it was exciting. We had a blank sheet of paper. I had three or four trainees, who

Gordon Staniforth, the club's first community liaison officer, led a scheme in 1989 that saw unemployed adults dance on the pitch with residents from the Merlin House Residential Home for the Mentally Handicapped

came off the dole to do some coaching. We also did tea parties and old-aged pensioner bingo in the Social club every Wednesday. It was great, and I loved it because it was a new start for me after football but gave me the opportunity to still be involved in a game, which I couldn't leave, because I find it infectious." In later years, Staniforth would also gain a new matchday perspective at Bootham Crescent when he worked as a match analyst for the Press Association. On that experience, he added: "I thoroughly enjoyed working in the press box because I enjoy watching football. Some ex-pros can't and find it frustrating or fall out of love with the game. I never have done and watching matches increased my knowledge of the game. I was seeing things and putting things right on the pitch in my head and looking through the eyes of a coach. It was very sad when the club moved out, but stadiums have to be multi-purpose and work seven days a week. Bootham Crescent had become so old and decrepit, but it holds so many fond, fond memories."

Wayne Hall, a 20-year-old recruit from Hatfield Main, meanwhile, enjoyed his first outing at Bootham Crescent during the penultimate game of the campaign, coming on as a substitute during a 2-1 home defeat to Cambridge. It was to be his first of 438 appearances for the club, placing him fourth on the all-time list and, remembering his debut, Hall said: "It's every boy's dream and I was fulfilling it. I can remember not being overawed at all and I just got on with it. It was quite a big step up, but I thought I settled in quite well. I'd

369

already played in quite a few reserve games and John Bird wouldn't have put me in if I wasn't ready."

The 1989/90 season resulted in another mid-table finish with fortunes not helped by an injury to new striker David Longhurst, who was bought from Peterborough for £30,000 only to be sidelined after just four games. One notable contest in an otherwise generally mundane campaign was the Littlewoods Cup second round tie against top-flight Southampton, who included a 19-year-old Alan Shearer in their side. Shearer limped out of the action in the second half at Bootham Crescent, but went on to bag a brace in the deciding away leg, as the Saints completed a 3-0 aggregate victory. Even though Shearer was kept off the scoresheet during a 1-0 victory for Chris Nicholl's men at Bootham Crescent, McMillan could appreciate the future England captain's potential, saying: "Alan Shearer was a handful. He was just a young kid but his movement, pace and eye for goal was exceptional. When, we went to The Dell to play them, it was very similar to Bootham Crescent. It was very confined, and you could hear every word from the crowd."

Rod Wallace headed in the only goal of the match at Bootham Crescent late on despite a linesman's flag being raised for offside, while his twin-brother Ray was sent off just moments later, on 88 minutes, for barging into a linesman. Earlier, Iain Dunn had missed a one-on-one chance against Saints keeper Tim Flowers and Howlett saw a shot cleared off the line by former England defender Russell Osman. Spooner was also thwarted by Flowers when played clear by Helliwell. After the break, Marples kept out a fierce Shearer shot after the chance was created by Saints legend Matt Le Tissier, who went on to provide the cross for Wallace's winner.

Off the pitch, the "Roof the Shippo" appeal suffered a blow in early 1990 when the council rejected an initial planning application. A few months later, the assigned, two-year fundraising period was reached with insufficient funds collected but, as the target was still in sight, it was decided to extend the appeal by a further year. April 1990 also saw a clock in the club's colours placed on top of the Popular Stand. It was presented to the club by the family of Phil Dearlove - a young City fan who had died the previous June following an accident at home. Dearlove was described as a City fan in the "truest sense", supporting the club through good times and bad, whilst using all his lieu days and holiday time as a British Rail signalman to work around his shifts, so he could make home and away games. He had been taken to matches from the age of four by his father and had often stated that, if he ever won the pools, he would give some money to the club.

With the "Roof the Shippo Appeal" in mind, meanwhile, attempts to persuade England to play a warm-up match against City at Bootham Crescent before the Three Lions headed off for the 1990 World Cup in Italy proved fruitless. The audacious bid was made after the national team had played a friendly against Aylesbury the previous year, but then manager Bobby Robson did have the grace to ring City's club secretary Usher to apologise for not being able to find time for the fixture.

For only the second time in the club's history, the team also won more away games than at home during the campaign. That had last happened in 1946/47 with Little admitting: "We inherited a situation where the team was not playing well at home. The players seemed to be more comfortable and relaxed away from Bootham Crescent, even though the crowd weren't really difficult to play in front of, compared to the likes of Hartlepool."

A cameraman and his young helper watch on from the roof of the Social Club as Tony Canham tussles with Grimsby in November 1989

City players enjoy an aerobics and dance exercise class in the Bootham Crescent gym

David Spofforth on boot-cleaning duty in September 1984

Physio Jeff Miller weighs Chris Marples on the return to pre-season training in 1988

Alan Little (left) and John Bird arrive as the new management team in 1988 with the whiff of chocolate in their nostrils

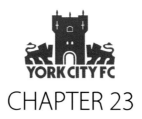

YORK CITY FC

CHAPTER 23

David Longhurst's tragic death on the pitch

"I remember thinking I hope that's not what I think it is, but they then started pumping his heart and it was one of the saddest moments I've ever seen in my life."

The 1990s' would eventually herald a record six successive campaigns in the third division but not before initial struggles and, overshadowing everything, was the tragic death of 25-year-old striker David Longhurst after he collapsed on the pitch due to a rare heart disorder during a home match with Lincoln on September 8, 1990.

David Longhurst scores against Colchester in January 1990

Longhurst had made an exciting start to the season and, against Lincoln, came close to scoring twice in the opening minutes and twice more before the first-half's midway point. It was immediately clear something serious had happened 44 minutes into the game, however, with worried players from both teams anxiously appealing for help from the sidelines and one City player running over and shouting to the bench: "He's not breathing." Soon afterwards, a message from the PA system announced: "I am sorry to announce the game has been abandoned due to the seriousness of David Longhurst's condition. Please leave the ground in an orderly manner."

Former club director Dr Angus Mcleod, along with medical officer Robert Porter, had tried to give the player mouth-to-mouth on the pitch but, by the time he was taken into the treatment room, they could still detect no pulse and he did not respond to being defibrillated. Some stunned team-mates sat

Fans gather at the car park gates anxious for news on David Longhurst after the Lincoln game was abandoned

around the edge of the pitch in tears as the reality of what had occurred became apparent and 200 fans stood in silence outside the ground as the ambulance taking Longhurst to York District Hospital pulled away. The late Malcolm Huntington, who was reporting on the match for the *Yorkshire Evening Press*, could always recall the tragic occasion vividly. He said: "I can remember exactly where it happened just outside the penalty area at the Shipton Street End. I had an awful feeling that something very serious had happened straight away because I had seen the referee Roy Harper collapse and die on the pitch many years before. You see people rolling about when they are trying to kid people but, when somebody collapses and they're not moving, it's a terrible sight. I remember thinking I hope that's not what I think it is, but they then started pumping his heart and it was one of the saddest moments I've ever seen in my life. He was a very gifted player with a lovely touch who held the ball up well. His mother and father heard about it on the radio coming back from a holiday in Scotland, which was terribly sad too. It preyed on your mind for a long time after that and everyone at the club was very sombre."

John Bird, meanwhile, went from preparing his team for a division three match to contending with the saddest moment of his managerial career. "It was tragic, and I've thought about it all many times since," Bird said. "It was unbelievable really. We had signed David from Peterborough when Mark Lawrenson was manager there and he was a really good player, so I believed he was a really good signing. He was as chatty and bouncy as he always was before the game. The ex-Leeds striker Allan Clarke was Lincoln's manager at the time, because I can remember going into their dressing room and telling them. David just went down and I thought he was injured. We went into the dressing room whilst he

Chris Marples is in tears as he leaves Bootham Crescent following the death of his team-mate David Longhurst

was being treated and I remember saying to Iain Dunn: 'David's injured out there, so it's your chance and you've got to take it'. We didn't know what was happening outside until the secretary Keith Usher came into the dressing room as we were holding a team meeting and I'll never forget telling Alan Little to get him out of the dressing room because I didn't want him in there - it wasn't the secretary's place. So, Alan squared up to him to usher him out, for want of a better word, but Keith fought against it and said you've got to come out here and dragged me out. He then told me what had happened, and I couldn't believe it."

Recounting his memories of Longhurst and the tragedy, Little added: "The boy was on a mission that season. He was on fire in pre-season and it felt like it was going to be his time. He had written a motivational piece of writing on his shirt about what he wanted to achieve, and we'd seen no indication of what was about to happen that day. No medical equipment available to the physios back then would have detected it. I remember the run he made down the side of their back four and then he went down in the box. Nobody knew why at first and we thought he was injured but the old doc went out with a young Dr Porter and it became apparent what had happened. I remember both doctors coming in and making an official announcement. They were upset, like we all were, and had tears coming down their eyes because they couldn't save him."

Bird also remembered vividly the moment Longhurst's parents arrived at the ground. "David's mother and father had been on a caravan holiday and were coming back to watch the game on their way home," he explained. "They had contacted Keith (Usher) to say they were stuck in traffic and that they wouldn't make kick-off, so they actually arrived just after the game had been abandoned, which was awful. It was an absolutely shocking day." One of Bird's first thoughts in the aftermath of the tragedy was to inform the man who had recommended Longhurst to him - future Premier League manager Phil Brown. "I'd had great reports about him when he'd been on loan at Halifax and I checked up on him with Phil Brown, who had played for me at Hartlepool and Halifax," Bird recalled. "When I told Phil I was thinking about signing David, he said: 'You've got to sign him', and I always remember after the game I phoned Phil. He was on a coach coming back from a game because he was playing for Bolton by then and he was absolutely devastated." It was also the manager's duty to break the horrific news to his squad. "The scenes were terrible," Bird said. "I always remember Chris Marples taking it badly. There was a glass door to the toilets in the dressing room and - I wasn't really going to mention this - but, when Keith Usher told me, I don't know what made me do it, but I put my fist through the panel and David's death cast a shadow on Bootham Crescent for a long time. We were all shocked and there were flowers everywhere and we, more or less, closed the ground down and didn't play our next game. There was no bereavement counselling or anything back then, but people were donating money and the stand was built in David's memory."

While details from many of McMillan's 492 City matches would become vague with the passing of time, his memories of the terrible day his close friend passed away in such shockingly sad circumstances always remained very vivid. "It was very close to half-time and I think the ref just said: 'Right, we'll make it half-time now'," he recalled. "You could just sense the way medical staff were behaving that something wasn't right, and the paramedics were also out there. Then, suddenly, they were telling everybody to get away from him. I honestly didn't think he would pass away because that's the last thing you think about, but we knew, deep down, that something was wrong. Everybody was asking if he was alright, but we felt that he would be put in an ambulance, taken to hospital and then he would be fine. John Bird tried to get on with things as normal but, when he went back out and came in again, he was as white as a ghost. He had a tea cup in his hands and threw it at a mirror or a pane of glass - I can't remember which - before saying: 'He's passed away'. Then, it was just meltdown and you could hear his girlfriend Vicky screaming down the corridor and that was the biggest thing for me. It was awful, and it made the hairs stand up on the back of your neck. My wife, who was my girlfriend at the time, was trying to console her but she was trying to get into Jeff (Miller)'s room. I can't remember if they got in or not. We used to go out as couples so were quite close and she was heartbroken. I don't know if they would have got married, but they were very close and had been together for a number of years. I know his parents were on their way to the ground too and heard their son had passed away on the radio which must have been terribly devastating, as I can appreciate now as a parent myself. It was a real tragedy and a terrible time at the club."

Wayne Hall, who was only 21 at the time, also played in the game and, like fellow full-back McMillan, his memory of the tragedy did not dim with the passage of years. "The whole thing is still quite vivid in my mind," he admitted. "It was a very hot day and he was on fire actually - running everywhere. He had just made another run then, all of a sudden, I remember turning around and he had collapsed. The physio and paramedics ran on but, when they carried him off, we all feared the worst. The game was abandoned and rightly so. There's more to life than football. What happened made everybody realise football is a game and nobody should lose their life playing it. We found out after that he had a heart defect and there had been no suggestion of that whatsoever. He came from Peterborough and had all the tests they did back then, but they hadn't picked up his condition. It affected quite a lot of people afterwards - a lot of players and all the backroom staff. I remember John Bird coming in to tell us and he was really upset, and we were all devastated. He was a good player with a good touch and also a good goalscorer. He was a bubbly lad too - one of those who was the real life and soul. He was really good in the dressing room, made fun of everybody and was really sharp with the banter. He settled in really well at York and it was as if he had been there for years to be honest. To pay the respect York did by naming a stand after him was the right thing to do."

McMillan also recalled Longhurst lighting up Bootham Crescent with his personality during his short spell at the club, as well as stressing that nobody ever suspected he had the heart condition that would cost him his life. "He was one of life's

Club commercial manager Sheila Smith takes flowers to the David Longhurst tribute on the car park gates

characters," McMillan smiled. "I used to live on Newborough Street just behind the ground and he used to stay with me. He would eat Corn Flakes straight out of the box with his hands. He didn't bother with milk or a spoon. He was just a good guy who made me laugh every time I looked at him and everyone loved him from the people in the offices, to the players and the fans. He was bubbly and great to be around. Nobody suspected he had heart problems because he never had any ailments. He was a fit, young man who worked hard in training and did all the running with no issues or complaints." Even before the Shipton Street End was renamed in Longhurst's honour, McMillan also revealed there were early signs of his friend's spirit living on at Bootham Crescent. "I'll tell you one of the strangest stories about Longhy," he revealed. "He used to love going into town and having a bottle of Super Stein in Oscar's. I remember, in the days after he passed away, all the lads having a few beers together and we were pretty upset so we came to the gates at the ground and put a bottle of Super Stein out where the scarves and flowers were and we all raised our glasses to him before saying how much we would miss him. And, no word of a lie, when we came back the next day for the memorial service, the top was still on, but half of the beer was gone. There must have been ten witnesses to that and it was surreal. It was as if he had his last swig of Super Stein and left the bottle there. I don't believe in those type of things, but to see that was strange and pretty scary stuff. Maybe the sun had got to it - I don't know - but he used to love going out with the lads and the banter we had, and he was sorely missed."

Little was touched, meanwhile, by the reaction of the club's fans to the popular striker's death. "The passion of the fans came out in the aftermath," he declared. "The gates at the ground were covered with flowers and there were other things like bottles put down there too. It was very emotional, and the stand was a great tribute to the boy. He was a big loss and I'll never forget the cheeky smile he had - he was a bit of a character."

Admitting his friend's death had a profound impact on the squad during the aftermath, McMillan also stressed that there was no form of counselling available to assist the players in their grieving. "What happened to David shouldn't have happened and it cast a shadow over the ground," he explained. "I was numb because I knew him so well. I wasn't just losing a team-mate, I was losing a close friend. He hadn't been at the club that long, but it was one of those instances when you just click with somebody. He was three years older than me, so we were a similar age, but he was more like an older pro because he had been at four or five clubs and he looked after me and made sure I was alright. It wasn't a good season after that. Suddenly, football doesn't matter, and you listen to some of the comments now from people in the crowd and think to yourself it doesn't really matter - it's a game of football. We were also left to deal with it pretty much. We had a club chaplain at the time and he offered support, but I wasn't a church goer and I think, if it happened today, there would be plenty of professional people to help you out." Little agreed with McMillan, saying: "We had the vicar and he offered to speak to all the players individually when he felt the time was right, but there was probably not as much professional support as you'd get these days."

Nigel Pepper, meanwhile, had only signed for the club that summer at the age of 22 and admitted his new team-mate's death cast a shadow over that period of his career, saying: "I can't remember my first game at Bootham Crescent. I probably would in normal circumstances and the reason I can't is because it was only my third home game when Longhy died. That's what dominates the memories of the start to my York career. I have strange recollections because me and TC (Tony Canham) are in the foreground having a laugh and joke about something on the TV footage that was filmed while the game had stopped and Longhy was being treated in the background. You just didn't think about things like that happening and it's a horrible memory." Pepper also recalled the moment the news was broken in the changing room. "We found out from John Bird," he explained. "Someone came in and said something to John and he just put his hand straight through the glass on the door into the shower room. He just said: 'He's gone' and it was horrific. He was still a young, fit bloke, but you just never know. It's something you never forget and is still there as clear as day, but you have to move on. You've got to get on with it and get through it, not through a lack of respect, but you just have to do. It was a horrible thing to go through at 22, but I wasn't a kid and, if it happened today, it would be just as horrible. We beat Doncaster in the next game and, while you're professional anyway and want to win every game, what had happened added to that desire and it wasn't just for that one game. We didn't stop thinking about him after that."

Pepper also declared that the newly-roofed Shipton Street End, named after Longhurst, became a fitting legacy. "That was a great tribute and gesture for him to be respected that way," he said. "It was a massively, horrible thing for the club to go through and whatever funding that was needed came in pretty quickly. The roof at that end definitely added to the atmosphere too. At Bootham Crescent, it was like the fans were on top of you and, if you were kicking towards the Shippo End in the second half on a wet Tuesday night, you always thought you were going to score with that atmosphere and York fans cheering you on from all three sides around you going forward. We tended to try and kick that way in the second half because it was psychological, especially if you were chasing a result. I loved night games anywhere I played but, while Bradford City have a fantastic stadium, the stands were big and set back away from the pitch. Having the stands close in around the pitch at Bootham Crescent helped build the atmosphere. The better you played, the more rowdy the crowd got and that drives you on. I can't think of anything better than a wet Tuesday night at Bootham Crescent. It was always a great surface as well and the club were forever getting awards for the pitch. It maybe deteriorated and got a bit boggy and sandy towards the end of the season, but it was brilliant to pass a ball on when it was wet and dark."

The impact of Longhurst's death in football was far-reaching, touching former team-mates, managers and supporters. It also left a profound impression on the opposition players, as future City assistant manager John Schofield revealed, having played for Lincoln that day. "It was a very, very sad day for everybody and I can't begin to imagine what his family went through," he said. "I was playing in the centre of midfield and what sticks in my mind is, as I was travelling across the pitch, David Longhurst was behind me and, as he ran past our right-back Paul Casey, he went down as though he'd been fouled. I was thinking at the time I'm not sure that was a foul and I can't remember whether a free kick was awarded or not. After that, everybody came on and was seeing to him and, God bless him, he never moved again. It was just before half-time and, when we came off the pitch, we weren't really aware of what had happened. Then, Allan Clarke, our manager, came in and said: 'The game's been postponed because their player has passed away'. It was said as matter-of-fact as that because I think Allan was in shock and all of us, as players, were. It was unbelievable because you don't imagine that when you kick off on a Saturday that something devastating like that is going to happen. It took a few days to get over it for us as opposition players, so God knows what it was like for the people who played with him on a regular basis and were friends with him. It put everything into perspective as regards the job we do as, when you go to work, you don't expect to see a fatality. Later in life, when I went into coaching, my first job was looking after the academy and youth team. It was when the LFE (League Football Education) were just getting involved and heart screening was being introduced. There were a lot of people questioning whether we needed it at meetings but, with having been so close when somebody lost their life on a pitch, I was able to say what I had personally experienced and that how important it was to get screening right. It had to be the way forward because people's lives are more

Long-serving youth coach Colin Sanderson looks at the floral tributes to David Longhurst on the side of the pitch prior to the player's memorial service

important than football. You can also overcome these defects and little conditions now. You can take medication and there are ways around it to give people the chance to still have a safe, active life."

John Uttley - a City supporter since the 1970s - admitted Longhurst's death represented the saddest day he had experienced in football. He said: "That was a very low moment. I can remember going to the club shop at half-time and seeing the ambulance in the car park with David's girlfriend shaking as she tried to drink a cup of tea. Then, when we went back into the ground, the news came over the tannoy that the game had been abandoned due to the serious situation. It was an exceptionally sad day that put everything into perspective and I can remember getting back into the car with Radio York playing classical music rather than reporting on football."

A memorial service, held at Bootham Crescent eight days later at 3pm on a Sunday, was attended by more than a thousand City supporters.

Wreaths and bouquets were laid along the pitch, with Longhurst's parents, brother and girlfriend all present - the latter going onto the playing field to lay a single red rose before the beginning of the service, which was conducted by Canon John Armstrong. A minute's silence was first observed, before the York RI InterCity Band accompanied three hymns, including footballing favourite *Abide With Me*. Skipper Shaun Reid also gave a speech to pay his tribute, before Longhurst's cousin Leonora Truskin read out the poem *My Last Party*. Afterwards, Longhurst's brother Mark was presented with the match ball from the day, signed by all the City players. A collection, meanwhile, raised £1,144 towards the Shipton Street Roof appeal.

Fans pay respect to David Longhurst at the Bootham Crescent Memorial Service

Goals from Ray Warburton, Ian Helliwell and Canham went on to ensure that City defeated old rivals and table-toppers Doncaster 3-1 in the next home game - a fortnight on from the tragedy. It earned the club the Barclay's Performance of the Week award and, on the motivation behind that triumph, McMillan said: "We might have had a bit of a chat in the dressing room, but I don't think there was any tactical talk at all. It was all about let's do it for Longhy. That was it and that was our inspiration to go out there and we also had some good players in that team." Little detected that resolve among the squad, pointing out: "After the initial shock, there was a determination among the players that they had to push on and do something in his memory, although it took a while to get the smiles back around the place."

The side would go on to struggle for goals in Longhurst's absence with Helliwell's return of seven equalling the club's lowest top-scorer tally for a season but the likes of goalkeeper Dean Kiely, midfielder Steve Bushell and Jon McCarthy were all seen in action at Bootham Crescent for the first time. McCarthy made his debut soon after the tragedy as a striker but recalls the shadow that hung over the club. "I remember that whole period and what effect it had on everybody and the physio," McCarthy said. "All the talk was of how well Longhy had been playing. Everyone believed he had been in the zone before his death." Bird believed marksman Longhurst's absence was felt as keenly on the pitch as it was off it, adding: "Ian Helliwell was a great asset to have with his head, but he wasn't a main goalscorer."

It was clear, though, that Bird had found a reliable last line of defence in Kiely, who quickly became a crowd favourite before later playing in the Premier League and winning international caps with the Republic of Ireland. "Dean Kiely was a hell of a signing from Coventry, where he'd been kicked out," Bird pointed out. "He was a bit skinny and frail, but we put him in quite early. He had good hands. They were like glue because the ball used to stick to them."

University graduate McCarthy, meanwhile, retained vivid memories of his introduction to life as a professional at Bootham Crescent. "I'll never forget my full home debut," he said. "We beat Darlington 1-0 in the FA Cup, so it was a derby game and I was going up against old-fashioned centre-halves because I was a striker then and the atmosphere was good. I remember running out for the game and there was a bottle of whisky. Some players would have a little drink before the game. Tony Barratt was one who liked to do that and that's what it was like back then. Afterwards, I remember Chris Marples sat naked on the side of one of the big baths with a cigarette in one hand and a can of beer in the other. There would always be 24 cans of Hansa waiting in the dressing room afterwards if we won, but nothing if we didn't. That was my introduction to professional football and, it's fair to say, I hadn't quite expected that. But I ended up seeing both spectrums of the game because, later, with managers like Trevor Francis and Steve Bruce at Birmingham, it was the time when psychologists and nutritionists were coming into the game." McCarthy also witnessed his first incidence of flying teacups in the home dressing room at Bootham Crescent, explaining: "John Bird would always put out a tray of tea at half-time and I remember all the cups being odd - none of them were the same. Anyway, at half-time in one of my early games, we were losing, and he was banging the table and every one of them smashed. He then went to throw the tray like a frisbee at somebody - probably Chris Marples - but it hit him on the shoulder and then caught me straight on the head. He didn't mean to do it and, as a young player, I wasn't going to say anything. Some of the lads were hammering me for not saying anything and some stuck up for me."

Pepper, though, revealed that he was spared Bird's fury when he was, incredibly, sent off for a third time against the same Darlington team in one season. After seeing red in league and FA Cup games against that season's champions, Pepper was dismissed during the Bootham Crescent return league fixture in February

1991. Retelling the extraordinary turn of events, Pepper said: "Before that game, something had been written about the chance of a hat-trick in the press, but that third one was ridiculous. It was in the 89th minute and a straight red that was an absolute load of rubbish. It was for a tackle on John Borthwick and, when we signed him about 18 months later, he showed me the mark on his leg, which we had a laugh about because he was a great bloke and a funny, funny man. I'm not saying it was a fair tackle - it might not have been - but it wasn't a straight red card. I had a lot of red cards in my career and some were right and stupid, but some were absolutely laughable, and I felt the referee was looking to send me off that day. I'm absolutely certain the referee had it in his mind that I had been sent off against them twice that season before, but it was just one tackle in the 89th minute and I didn't get in trouble with John (Bird) afterwards. John was as tough as old boots so, if you had been sent off for dissent or spitting in somebody's face, I dare say he would have pinned you up against the wall, because he was that sort of bloke - a great guy. If you were going in for tackles and getting sent off, though, after genuine attempts to win the ball, he wouldn't fine you or anything. I wasn't more fired up or anything against Darlington, so I've no idea why it happened like that and I don't think I ever got sent off against them again. It was just that one season and it was ridiculous."

YORK CITY FC

CHAPTER 24

The Shippo gets a roof and a poignant new name

"It was good sometimes to look to my right during games and see all the fans in there on a buzzing night below David's name."

Vic Longhurst stands in front of the stand named in the memory of his son at the Leeds United friendly that acted as the official unveiling of the newly-roofed David Longhurst Stand

At the end of the 1990/91 season, work started on the new covered stand at the Shipton Street End of the ground a month after planning permission had been granted and three years after supporters Chris Forth and Frank Ormston had launched the Shipton Street Roof Appeal Fund with the blessing of the directors. After gaining the approval of the player's family, a David Longhurst Memorial Fund had also been set up with donations added to the money that had already been raised for the roof appeal. Many supporters of Longhurst's former clubs organised fundraising events too. In Scunthorpe, a disco raised more than £1,000 with the organiser's employer doubling the donation. Visiting supporters also often gave generously, with many handing over the £1 change from their admittance money. Fanzines, including Rangers' *Follow Follow* and Bradford's *City Gent*, donated copies that were sold to help the appeal too. The Football Trust, meanwhile, contributed 50 per cent of the £150,000 cost of the roof, which was built by John Laing Construction. Fans got their first look at it during the opening game of the 1991/92 season - a 1-1 draw with Gillingham. But it was officially opened by City president John Greenway MP for Ryedale and Vic Longhurst, David's father, who pulled the cord to reveal his son's name before a 2-2 friendly against Leeds United on October 14, 1991 in front of a 4,374-strong crowd. Leeds, who would go on to be crowned top-flight champions that season, fielded a strong side with Lee Chapman opening the scoring before Wayne Hall drove past John Lukic to level. Steve Hodge quickly made the score 2-1, before Shaun Reid levelled the scores for a second time and Tony Canham hit the post late on as the hosts searched for a winner. Along with his parents, David's brother and other family members attended and £20,000 was raised to go towards the costs of paying for the building of the roof.

Following one of the most distressing incidents in his life, Andy McMillan sought some solace over the years from the club's tribute to his popular team-mate, adding: "It was pleasing the club did what they did with the David Longhurst Stand and the fans raised a tremendous amount of money and put a lot of effort in to pay for the roof. It was good sometimes to look to my right during games and see all the fans in there on a buzzing night below David's name."

Michael Sinclair stepped down as chairman, meanwhile, with Douglas Craig, a retired civil engineer, who had been on the board for 13 years, taking over. Craig immediately hit out at Robert Gibb, the chairman of club sponsors Flamingo Land, after he had claimed there was a crisis at City and proposed a takeover bid. In his riposte, Craig snarled: "The truth is that York City is one of the best-run clubs in the third and fourth division. We own our ground, which is one of the best in the lower divisions and our overdraft of less than £100,000 is also one of the lowest in division three and four. We will be having no further negotiations of any kind with him about York City." The overbearing Craig could be just as confrontational from the directors' box during first-team or reserve matches, never refraining from directing abuse at his own club's players.

386

Before Craig took over as chairman, even club legend Gary Ford had been subjected to one such tirade. "Michael Sinclair used to come into the changing rooms and Douglas Craig did too, but he would shout at you from the directors' box and he did that to me once," Ford explained. "I responded, and I got called into the office by Denis (Smith). I don't think Denis was too bothered, but he'd been told to do it." Craig's tirades worsened when he became chairman, with 1990s' favourite Nigel Pepper insisting: "You can't have that. It's up to the manager to shout at the players. It wasn't his place to do that."

Centre-back Paul Stancliffe, meanwhile, was signed from Wolves as preparations for the 1991/92 season were made, but a poor start to the campaign saw Bird lose his job following a 1-1 Associate Members Cup (Football League Trophy) home draw against Carlisle in front of 957 fans, which was, at that time, the smallest-ever recorded attendance for a first-team fixture at Bootham Crescent. Three decades later, Bird still bore the scars, meanwhile, from the manner in which Craig handed him his P45 that night. "We'd drawn a few games early on and were near the bottom, but I'd made some good signings in the summer," the ex-Hartlepool chief said. "The problem was we had injuries, but I still thought it was going to be my season. I was enjoying the job and had put my staff together and got some good players in. One was Paul Stancliffe at centre-half, but he was injured. By that time, I had brought in Nigel Pepper and Ray Warburton too from Rotherham and Wayne Hall after I saw him on a rainy night in Frickley when I couldn't face a horrible journey to another game I had planned to watch. We'd also taken Jon McCarthy from Hartlepool, signed Dean Kiely after Coventry released him and had some very good young players coming through like Andy McMillan and Steve Tutill, so it was a massive blow when I got the sack. I knew we hadn't started well but pre-season training had been good, and I was dying for the injured players to get fit. The Carlisle match was a terrible game at a time when I was really wanting to lift things. It was boring fare from both sides. I remember being in the boardroom on stilts looking on to the car park after the game and I stood there admitting to a couple of directors that the game wasn't too good, but they said: 'It's alright. We'll get it sorted. It's only early days'. But, at that point, a few fans walking through the car park saw us in the boardroom and started chanting 'Bird Out' and I thought: 'Oh no'. Shortly afterwards, I got sacked in the car park. As I went to go home, I got followed and Douglas Craig said: 'I think we better call it a day'. I thought that was going to be my season, so it was annoying. We'd worked hard in pre-season, got some good players in and the staff were right, but it only takes five or six results and then you've lost your chance and can't retrieve it."

Bird was not alone in his admiration for the squad with some very interested high-profile visitors to Bootham Crescent during his reign. "Liverpool watched Ray Warburton," he revealed. "Kenny Dalglish came to have a look at him and he was a good, classy defender but injury problems held him back."

McCarthy revealed that the players were not as surprised by Bird's sacking as the manager himself, having been made aware of the fans' feelings after trudging off the pitch at the end of the match. "I remember being in the dressing room after the game and hearing all the fans outside in the car park chanting 'Bird Out,'" he explained. "It wasn't nice, and I can still sense the atmosphere. There was an inevitability about what was going to happen. It was my first taste of that type of thing, but there was a feeling from the older lads that we had let him down and he was probably going to get the sack." Pepper had been another Bird recruit and, on his sacking, he admitted: "It was a low point and sad. He had signed me, but managers don't get any time and there wasn't much difference between the squad John got together from the one that went on to do better and progressed. Given time, who's to say he wouldn't have done exactly the same, but management is a fickle business and you can soon lose your job."

John Ward, formerly Graham Taylor's assistant manager at Watford and Aston Villa, took over with McMillan, then 23, immediately impressed by his impact at Bootham Crescent. "John Ward was a breath of fresh air and I loved everything he did," McMillan admitted. "He wasn't the biggest man but, when he walked into a room, he had a real presence and he knew how to talk to people. He knew when to put arms around people and when to give them a rollicking, without it being blatantly obvious that's what he was doing. Communication is a big part of the job and he would know your birthday, your wife's birthday and your son's birthday. He knew everything, including where you lived, and he would call your kids by their first names. I would have run through the brick wall in the changing rooms for him. He never told you what to do on the pitch, but he wanted a certain style of play. He wanted us to pass the ball, but he said, if you keep making the same mistakes, then we've got to have discussions. You never wanted to make a mistake for him and, if you did, you didn't feel like you were just letting yourself down. You felt you were letting him down, which was the worst thing ever." Fellow full-back Hall was also an instant fan of the new boss, explaining: "John Ward came in and changed quite a lot. He had worked with experienced managers and coaches. He was the breath of fresh air York needed at the time and that's no disrespect to John Bird before him or Alan Little afterwards. In fact, Alan learnt a lot off John because he had done an excellent job."

Progress under Ward was steady initially, though, with only the occasional highlight such as a McMillan goal from the halfway line against Crewe - one of only four he would score at Bootham Crescent in 12-and-a-half years at the club. "David Beckham got one from the halfway line a few years later and he got all the rewards," McMillan joked. "Mine was a bit of a crossfield pass though that I shanked, and it went in the top corner. It was from the far side in front of the Popular Stand and I was looking to find Ian Blackstone on the far post. I claimed the goal at the time but admitted over the years that it was a complete fluke."

Hall, meanwhile, provided another memorable moment when Bootham Crescent hosted its first live televised game - a second round Saturday night FA Cup tie against Tranmere in December 1991, which finished 1-1 in front of the new Sky television cameras. The popular left-back, known as 'Ginner' due to the colour of his hair, cracked in a 25-yard humdinger to earn the Minstermen a replay on the Wirral, although his finish proved more polished than his post-match interview. "All I remember about that night is it was absolutely freezing, and, for the goal, the ball hit a bobble," he smiled. "I was going to shoot anyway but I think that helped me because it meant the ball dipped over the keeper. Otherwise, it would have probably gone straight into his hands. I was also interviewed by Sky afterwards. They showed me the goal and, well, what do you say? I just said that I hit it and I think they were probably a bit disappointed with my interview. They probably thought I was quite boring, but I wasn't used to it. I'd come in from non-League football and suddenly I was playing in front of the TV cameras. I remember the day after was market day and I was in York and one of the stall owners came up to me and said: 'You scored that goal last night, didn't you?' I said: 'I don't know what you mean'. He said: 'I was watching Sky and the guy who scored looked just like you'. But I said: 'No, you've got the wrong man and walked off'. I've not got a copy of the goal or the game, but my friends have seen it on YouTube so it's there if I ever want to look at it. I got mobbed by a few players and it was a good goal, but I didn't get too many, so I thought they were all brilliant. I was just as happy when I scored a tap-in against Rotherham at Bootham Crescent." City received a £30,000 cheque from the new television company for staging the match, which saw John Morrissey give Tranmere the lead before Hall's spectacular equaliser. Chris Marples, meanwhile, made a brilliant save to prevent former Liverpool striker John Aldridge from winning the tie.

The club would go on to finish fourth bottom for a second successive season, but a crowd of 7,620, including 4,849 from the visitors, led to record gate receipts of £33,000 for the penultimate home match against Burnley, which resulted in a 2-1 defeat. Blackstone tapped in after a McCarthy shot was parried on the stroke of half-time in that game, but Burnley fought back and grabbed a late winner through John Francis to clinch the title and prompt a mass pitch invasion at the final whistle. The away fans were celebrating an end to seven seasons of football in the basement division - the only period in their history that the Clarets had plied their trade at that level. But McCarthy also felt it was an important chapter in the Minstermen's subsequent revival too, pointing out: "There were almost 8,000 fans at Bootham Crescent and I never realised until years later, when I was teaching in Lancashire, that it was such a massive game in their history. The programme from the game is really revered in Burnley. It was their first promotion for a long time and I remember the atmosphere being terrific going out for the warm-up and then just before kick-off. They beat us, but that whole experience gave us a taste of things and gave us confidence because we did well against them. It was a big night for them, but we held our own, so it was quite a significant occasion for us too because, going into the next season, we had coped with playing in front of a big crowd at Bootham Crescent."

New floodlights, shorter in height at 27.5m but twice as powerful, were also installed at a cost of £122,000 at the end of the season. They were supplied by Thorvill Electricals of Staffordshire, with the old pylons, which had been 30m high, finding a new home at York Railway Institute Football Club's New Lane premises.

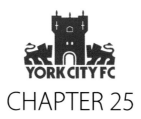

CHAPTER 25

Gary Swann sends City to Wembley

"When the goal went in, you could feel how excited people were about going to Wembley and we knew we had to make sure we made that happen."

The 1992/93 season would become one of the most memorable in the club's history, culminating in a first-ever trip to Wembley and promotion following a play-off final victory over Crewe. Striker Paul Barnes' £50,000 arrival from Stoke City would prove an inspired addition to the squad and he got off to the best possible start, making the scoresheet, along with Ray Warburton, during his debut - a 2-0 home triumph against Shrewsbury on the opening day. Recalling that high, the ex-Potter said: "I was trying to get into the team at Stoke, but York came along and paid a bit of money for me, so I knew I was going to the club with the intention of being played. I wanted to play first-team football and was looking forward to the challenge. I knew, if I performed, I would be in and around the team and it was great to be playing in a proper match rather than for the reserves, so it was nice to get off to a really, positive start. That's good for a goalscorer. Fans always tend to take to goalscorers and it's important to hit the ground running. That game wasn't just good for me either. It was a good start to the season for the team because there were a few other new players that day too."

Andy McMillan was an immediate fan of his new team-mate, pointing out: "We used to keep clean sheets all the time, but couldn't score so it was a great bit of business by John Ward to get Paul Barnes in. He made a huge difference. He didn't just score goals either. He linked up play and got his big, fat backside in the way so people couldn't get the ball off him." Nigel Pepper also appreciated the impact Barnes made at Bootham Crescent, saying: "The difference between a lot of teams in that division is goals. Barney didn't do a lot else, but he was a fantastic goalscorer. He was never going to track back or defend corners, but he was paid to score goals and he was brilliant at that. He had a great awareness of where he needed to be. It's difficult to say he didn't make the difference to that team, because we had a decent side with a good defence, good goalkeeper and good players throughout the team. When we added a guaranteed 20-goal-a-season striker to that, we knew we would be fighting at the top end of the table rather than at the bottom. That's what Barney did for us. He was a brilliant signing. Even though he didn't cost a massive amount of money, it was a fair bit for York, but he was well worth it."

Pepper, who would finish his City career as the club's record scorer of penalties with 19 converted from 22 attempts, suddenly had a rival for spot-kick duties however. He explained: "I was on penalties, but I kept getting suspended and the thing was, when the team got one and I was out of the side when he scored it, there wasn't much I could say when we were both on the pitch for the next one. I had to wait until he missed one, then I would take them back. But, then, I would get suspended again and it was like that for two or three years." Pepper quickly became renowned for his reliability from the spot, although he recalled one occasion - in 1993/94 - when the goalkeeper outwitted him at Bootham Crescent.

"I remember having one saved at Bootham Crescent," he grimaced. "It was the only time a goalkeeper conned me for a penalty. It was Martin Hodge, who was very experienced by then, in a League Cup tie against Rochdale and he stood two-thirds to one side and left a small gap at the other side. I thought: 'He's not going to con me. I know he's going to go to the big side but, if I hit it properly, he's not going to get there anyway'. But, as soon as I put my head down for the run-up, he set off. I still went the same way and he got there and turned it around his post."

Paul Barnes celebrates one of his four goals against Scunthorpe in March 1993

Among Barnes' 21 goals during his maiden campaign as a Minsterman, meanwhile, were four in a 5-1 Bootham Crescent triumph over Scunthorpe when he became the first player to manage that individual feat for 32 years in blizzard conditions on a Saturday afternoon in February. Barnes went on to pull the leg of the future Premier League and international defender he was pitted against that day many years afterwards, explaining: "Matt Elliott went on to coach my lad (Harvey) in Leicester's academy and he played at centre-back for Scunthorpe that day. I still have a bit of a laugh with him about that match. I think, at the time, I was going through a bit of a lean spell so, to get four goals in one game, was a great feeling, especially being up against a defender like Matty, who went on to have a great career and played at the top level with Scotland." Recalling Barnes' four-goal blast, team-mate McMillan added: "He tore Scunthorpe apart. He got four goals and didn't do anything else in the game, but he knew where the back of the net was, and you need people like that to win you games."

Many of Barnes' efforts were teed up by Jon McCarthy, who felt both the striker and manager Ward were key figures as the club engineered an upturn in fortunes. "John Ward came in and turned the place around with his coaching and man-management," McCarthy reasoned. "That was a massive lift for us and adding Paul Barnes proved the difference. We'd never got hammered before and all those games we had been losing 1-0, we were now getting draws in and all the matches we'd been drawing we were winning. Paul Barnes got 21 goals and Ian Blackstone also got double figures from the wing. We had the spine of a good team with experienced players such as Paul Stancliffe at the back and Gary Swann in midfield, as well as youngsters like myself, Dean Kiely, Andy McMillan and Wayne Hall."

The McGill family - long before becoming owners of the club - were also big Barnes fans with Jason and Sophie now joining dad Rob at games and establishing a new supporters' group. "I introduced Jason and Sophie to it," Rob McGill explained, prior to passing away in 2021. "We lived in Farlington at the time and we started a supporters' group up called the Farlington Reds. We would stand together, as a little group, behind the Shipton Street goal. One season, we gave away a prize, which was a dinner for two for the first player to get a hat-trick and it went to Paul Barnes. It then got to the stage where I couldn't stand up, so we started sitting in the Popular Stand. They both started going to games very early in life. I think Jason was only six for his first match and we made going to games a family occasion with (Jason and Sophie's mother) Carole coming later in the end. They both went through the usual stuff of supporting Manchester United initially, but I said: 'You don't support Man United, you support York City' and it went from there. They became devout supporters and that was it."

Rob's wife Carole, meanwhile, regarded her early days supporting City as halcyon times that were never quite matched when the family watched from the directors' box. "I came into it after my mum died in 1993," she explained. "Before then, they all left me on a Saturday and I used to go shopping with my mum, but they didn't want to leave me on my own any more after she passed away. I used to like the chips with peas on top from the kiosk and I had always been a York City supporter. As a little girl, I used to get the footballer cards from the newsagents and my favourite player was Alan Stewart. I had a crush on him, even though he was quite an unlikely heartthrob. I got his autograph and I've still got it. We made the autograph books at school. I never liked being in the boardroom though and I wanted to go back to where we started, because I found it a bit artificial. You had people just coming for the hospitality and it was difficult if we had lost and had to go back in to say well done, because you didn't really want to."

A 17-year-old Scott Jordan, meanwhile, recalled how the squad's senior pros of that era helped him make the often, unsettling transition from apprentice to first-team debutant even if he was too young to celebrate with them. "I came on as a sub against Rochdale for two or three minutes that season, but I only touched the ball once," he recalled. "My first start was in the FA Cup against Stockport not long after, when I got a last-minute call-up because Nigel Pepper was injured. Stockport were a big team and had giants like Kevin Francis and Andy Preece in their side. I was living in digs at the time and all the other lads in the house had gone off to play for the youth team, so I was there alone until 1.30pm stewing really. I think, when you're a local player, the crowd are watching you more and, when you do something well, they respond a bit more. They want you to succeed and the FA Cup creates its own atmosphere too. Stockport were in a higher division, so it was quite a decent fixture and experienced players like Paul Stancliffe and Jon McCarthy were a great help to me. We got beaten 3-1 but I got one of the man-of-the-match awards after the game and it was a crate of beer. I was only 17, so I was thinking what will I do with this. I didn't think we would be allowed to drink it back in the digs, being under age, so I ended up giving it away to someone." Just a week before that Stockport game, the Family Stand - a new designated section in the Main Stand

had been opened and sold out for a 2-0 home victory over Barnet after manager Ward had run the London Marathon to raise money for the project.

The Family Room, which was housed behind it, was opened a year later and served half-time refreshments for adults and children. In later years, lunch was served in the room for the players at times after training and it was often used as the location for pre-match and post-match press conferences. During the club's sponsorship deal with Nestle, it was also garishly decorated with pictures of Smarties.

York-born Swann, meanwhile, had arrived at Bootham Crescent at the same time as Barnes and, at 30, was playing for his home-town club in a stadium he had first visited as a fan, before playing there several times as a schoolboy and then as a visiting professional. On those memories, he said: "My dad used to take me to the ground in the 1960s and 70s and I remember watching Barry Swallow wear the old kit with the Y on the front. I also used to play at Bootham Crescent in junior cup finals for Dringhouses and Leeman Road and played there for City boys for a year before joining Hull City. It was great to play under floodlights for the first time at the age of 12 or 13. As a kid, it felt like Wembley and was certainly better playing a final there than at Joseph Rowntree. I remember they would open the Shippo End, before it became the David Longhurst Stand, and you could smell the cocoa wafting in the air that people were buying. I played in midfield or defence and Gary Ford used to also be in our Leeman Road side with Aiden Butterworth, who went to Leeds, up front scoring all the goals for us at Dringhouses. When I became a pro, I also played at the ground quite a few times for Preston and Hull, which was obviously a local derby, and we had always done alright. It's always been a really confined stadium with everybody close to the pitch and, with it being my home town, I used to have my brother, parents and family watching. My parents still lived in Acomb, so I always wanted to produce a good performance there. When I came back to York, I'd won promotion at Hull and Preston, so I wanted to do that at my home-town team as well and I remember the three of us coming in at the start of the season - myself, Paul Barnes and John Borthwick."

Alan Little, who had been assistant to John Bird and Ward, subsequently took over from the latter after he left for Bristol Rovers in March 1993 - a decision that was forced on him in McMillan's opinion. "I always remember him telling us when he was leaving for Bristol Rovers," McMillan explained. "He was sat in the home dressing room in front of all the players in floods of tears. He didn't want to leave the football club, but Douglas Craig wouldn't give him another contract. He said Bristol Rovers had offered him a three-year contract on £70,000-a-year so he had to take it. We could obviously appreciate that, and he shook everybody's hands and walked out. He was a fabulous guy."

On the surprise announcement, Pepper admitted: "It was a shock. He was an absolutely fantastic manager, coach and person - everything really. I have a lot of respect for him and, when he left, the club was in a great position."

Ward's number-two Little, meanwhile, had not expected to be thrust into the hot-seat at all and nor did he feel he would take the reins for long. "It was a total shock when John Ward left," he confessed. "I understand why he did, though, because he needed to do what was right for him and his family and it was a good move for him. I also felt I'd only have the job short-term. I never thought it would lead to the length of tenure I had, but I had no fear. I never did with football and I think the fact that nothing affected me was my biggest strength."

Attacking talisman Barnes thought the transition at Bootham Crescent was seamless, saying: "Everybody had respected John and he was probably the best manager I played for. Along with being a great coach and manager, he was also a real gentleman. But Alan was already around the club and everybody respected him too. He was a decent guy who expected you to work hard. He didn't ask you to do anything you couldn't and managed how he played himself by demanding 100 per cent from everybody on the pitch and in training. He carried on from where John had left off and had a good squad of players." Offering his views on why the transition was seamless, Little said: "I had a great relationship with the players and I think that's why we carried things on for those last 10 or 11 games. We all socialised together and went in the Social Club afterwards for a couple of drinks with the wives and kids and I think that's how it should be. It's important to do that. It's also important not to fill yourself with a load of beer but, after a couple of drinks, you often get to know your players better and they might open up more and share things with you that they wouldn't otherwise. We just rolled along and went with the flow during that period. We had no fear about who we were playing next because we had a good group of players."

Pepper, meanwhile, found a kindred spirit in Little, who had been a tough-tackling, whole-hearted midfielder himself as a player. "Like John, Alan was a great bloke who I also had a lot of time for, so I was chuffed to bits for him when he took over and did well," Pepper explained. "He had been a tough player and was a great motivator of a team. I enjoyed playing under both of them, but they had two very different personas. Alan gave teams desire and was the sort of manager you wanted to play for. John was more calm, calculated, technical and tactical."

A goal from Swann - Ward's pre-season signing from Preston - on 60 minutes, making him literally the hero of the hour, subsequently saw City seal a 1-0 aggregate play-off semi-final win over Bury at Bootham Crescent. Barnes sent an inch-perfect cross in from the left flank after turning his marker and Swann, who had timed his run to perfection, beat Bury sweeper Ian Hughes to the ball and headed powerfully into keeper Gary Kelly's top right-hand corner from close range. City had started to raise the tempo following a sterile first half and, after Swann's goal, Blackstone had the chance to make the final throes a little more comfortable for home supporters. But, after being sent clear by Tony Canham on 86 minutes, he saw Kelly grab the ball off his toes. It mattered little, though, despite Bury sending centre-back Alan Knill upfield to try and save their season and City prevailed in front of 9,206 fans, which was the biggest crowd since the visit of Liverpool in February 1986. The crowd also shattered the previous record for gate receipts at Bootham Crescent, set the previous season against Burnley. That windfall of £33,000 was smashed by a new figure of £46,459.50.

Remembering the historic occasion, a professional Hall insisted he was not distracted by the considerable gate, adding: "I never really took much notice of the crowd size. I wouldn't be able to tell you how many fans were at any of the big games we had at Bootham Crescent because I was that focussed on playing, doing well for the team and not letting myself down." McCarthy, though, recalled the nervous adrenalin coursing through the veins that night, saying: "There was a great atmosphere - I know it's a cliché, but it really was electric. I remember feeling great relief when Swanny eventually broke the deadlock. He scored with just over half-an-hour left and, as the minutes passed by, I was just thinking we can't concede now. When the goal went in, you could feel how excited people were about going to Wembley and we knew we had to make sure we made that happen. You could feel the tension every time the ball went near our goal because the fans were nervous and couldn't contain themselves."

Barnes also had vivid memories of the match, adding: "I remember Dean Kiely having a great game in the first leg and we were fortunate to come away with a goal-less draw. I also remember the second leg well. There was a great atmosphere and I can remember crossing the ball for Swanny to put a header in the net. We were then desperate for the whistle to blow and, when it did, it was a fantastic feeling as lower league players, knowing you were going to play at Wembley. It was a massive boost for everybody at the club. There was a pitch invasion and we all celebrated together in the directors' box. It was all during my first year as a regular first-team player, so they really are fantastic memories." About Swann's unlikely emergence as a goalscorer - he had not netted all season but went on to hit the target in the play-off final too - Barnes said: "Swanny was a great team player, who got up and down the pitch and, when it mattered, scored a couple of very important goals. He would have been well down the list, though, if you'd have asked me who was going to be our goal hero in the play-offs. We had people like Jon McCarthy, John Borthwick, Nigel Pepper and Tony Canham. There were six or seven you'd have put ahead of Swanny and I'd have probably put Steve Tutill in front of him too."

Swann, meanwhile, joked he was equally as surprised to receive a pass from Barnes, adding: "Barney wouldn't even pass to you in training. He was the striker who wanted to score the goals and we let him do that. On that occasion, though, he provided the cross out on the left for me. He played it in and I was running towards the goal, trying to get there before their centre half and I managed to glance it past their keeper in front of the David Longhurst Stand. I then remember running along the front of the stand and seeing everybody jumping up and down with their faces lit up. That was great because I knew what it meant. Barney was shouting at me to go over to him on the left, so I did and said: 'Thanks very much for passing it for a change'. The place just erupted after the goal and everyone was singing and chanting but, at the same time, we were concentrating on making sure we got through those final minutes.

Two Mr Blobbys join in the celebrations after York City fans look forward to seeing their team play at Wembley for a first-ever time following the 1-0 play-off victory against Bury in May 1993

Then, the final whistle went, and it was great to feel that elation and relief. I was so proud to help get my home-town club to Wembley." Swann also insisted he always felt he could deliver on Ward's belief that he would score goals for the team following his summer arrival, saying: "It was strange how things had gone because I'd got double figures the season before at Preston but I had been setting up everybody else and every shot and header I had just wouldn't cross the line. I was always looking to try and get goals and, with me and Nigel Pepper in midfield, we were always taking turns to get in the box, while the other player would sit but it was just one of those things. The ball wouldn't go in for me. In that situation, you just carry on doing what you can for the team and concentrate on performing well and doing your job to the best of your ability. We were on a winning streak and there were other players scoring like Paul Barnes, Jon McCarthy, John Borthwick and Nigel Pepper. Pepp was getting his free kicks and penalties from midfield, so it wasn't a big problem that I wasn't scoring, as long as I helped keep them out at the other end and kept providing chances for others. It all changed though in those final two games. Against Bury, we knew how important the game was and had done the job at their place with a 0-0 draw. The longer the game went on, we also knew we would get some good chances and, luckily, one dropped to me."

Hall claimed he shared Barnes' surprise at Swann's belated emergence as a goal hero, saying: "He would have been very, very low on my list of potential match-winners. In fact, about as low as me, but Swanny was a very good, experienced player who came in and did a great job sitting in midfield." Swann, though, recalled Hall actually forecasting his match-winning status. "We had a fight to get into the dressing room and I remember following Paul Stancliffe in and he turned around and said to me: 'We've done it - the two old codgers are going to Wembley', Swann revealed. Ginner also said: 'I knew you would do it today'. He had said before the game that, because I hadn't got a goal all season, I would score the winner and he reminded me of that."

Little was delighted for Swann too, saying: "He had come to the club with a reputation for getting goals, but hadn't got any up to that point. He knew what the game was about, though, and it was great to see him score in front of the Longhurst. That was fantastic for the supporters behind that goal. The final whistle was something special too. We had a lot of chances and were the best side in the second half. It took a long time to break them down, but we deserved it overall and it was a cracking night." For Andy McMillan, who had become accustomed to the club struggling at Bootham Crescent since his emergence as a young talent, the whole atmosphere of the old stadium had been transformed. He said: "We had some great nights building up to Wembley. Night games were always special, and I don't think you could beat them at Bootham Crescent. I remember the ground was rocking against Bury. It was packed. I lived in Elvington at the time and I had to leave early to make sure I got to the game in time because we weren't allowed in the car park. We had to park in the streets and walk in, which I could understand. The club needed to make corporate money and those people want to know they're getting a parking space. We absolutely battered Bury that night too. I think, if we had got five goals, that would have been a fair reflection of our dominance and their goalkeeper was outstanding."

Kiely, meanwhile, at the age of 22 and not knowing then that he would go on to play for the Republic of Ireland and in the Premier League for Charlton, Portsmouth and West Brom, admitted the Bury game represented the pinnacle of his career at that point. "Bootham Crescent is where I made my senior debut and played my first professional game, so I've got fond memories of the place," he explained. "I had come to York from Coventry to get in the side, but the team were near the bottom of the Football League at first. The following season we made a real good fist of things though and did really well. With the Bury game, it was great to be part of something that was successful. I remember we were pretty strong at home that season (the club only lost two league games at Bootham Crescent) and we had got some momentum going into the game. The away end was full, and the ground was jam-packed, which made for a great atmosphere. I was lucky enough to go on and play in front of 75,000 crowds but, back then, that was a fantastic experience for me." Aside from Swann's goal, Kiely also believed the former Preston midfielder added valuable know-how to the side, reasoning: "Swanny brought different attributes to the team. There was a great blend of young and experienced players and he belonged to the latter group. He came in and helped us out, before scoring those vital goals."

McMillan never forgot the sense of collective elation at the final whistle either, adding: "I remember everyone running on. We knew they were coming on when the final whistle went and, if it's your fans, that's not an issue. It must have taken me half-an-hour to get from the far side to the tunnel. Then, we went in the dressing room and came back out into the directors' box and everyone was singing Tina Turner's *Simply the Best*. The place was rocking and I remember Nigel Pepper getting hold of the microphone and singing his heart out which got everyone going even more. Most people I speak to still buzz off that game." Pepper's memories of the occasion were less vivid, but he is not surprised by his

Tina Turner rendition, given his fondness for belting out songs in the changing room. He said: "I can't remember too much about the game, other than, whilst I was never nervous in a game, I was a little wary when we were leading 1-0 because, although we were winning, I knew if they got a goal they would be through (the away-goal rule was employed in the play-offs until 2000, but only after extra-time). We didn't have a cushion, but it was a perfect Wednesday night game. I loved night games more than Saturday afternoons and afterwards was brilliant in the directors' box when all the fans came onto the pitch. I don't remember singing, but I was probably doing something stupid. I loved singing and did it every day. I remember Guy Mowbray recording me singing once when he commentated on our games. He was interviewing somebody in the changing rooms and I was coming out of the showers singing *Sittin' on the Dock of the Bay*. I think he put it on the radio a couple of times, bless his cotton socks. We had a lively dressing room, which was great, and I hadn't really experienced anything like that night against Bury in my career. We got promoted at Rotherham, but I played ten games and you had to play 12 to get a medal, so that was a bit of a downer. We hadn't gone up at that point, but we were going to play at Wembley and knew we had a very good chance of winning. It was a huge thing to get to Wembley. As a player, there are three or four things that jump out at you in your career and that was probably top of the tree, just in front of the other big nights we had at Bootham Crescent."

Hall also had fond memories of the post-match celebrations, saying: "I remember the fans coming onto the pitch and then going into the stand afterwards. It was a great night and absolutely fantastic for the fans. They had stuck by a club that hadn't been doing well previously and it was great to give them something to celebrate at last." Kiely revealed that his feet literally didn't touch the ground after the final whistle, explaining: "It was a massive deal getting to Wembley and everyone spilled onto the pitch. I remember getting carried off by a wave of people and rightly so. The fans deserved to be sharing that moment with us. The ground had seen some big Cup wins over the years, like against Arsenal, but it had been a while since the supporters had witnessed success over the course of a season. It was a real positive experience for me too. I had come down to York to play first-team games, so to push on and contribute to promotion was fantastic."

Little also declared that the quality of his team's performance that night was still clear on a second viewing a generation on. "I was given a tape of the Bury game, but I never watched it again until 10 or 15 years later on YouTube and, after about 25 minutes, I thought this isn't a bad game, you know," he enthused. "Some of the football we played was terrific and it was a fantastic move for the goal that Paul Barnes ended up laying on."

The excitement grew, meanwhile, at the ground as City's first appearance at the famous national stadium beckoned. "We were still training in the build-

Jon McCarthy and Alan Little board the Wembley-bound bus in the car park ahead of the 1993 play-off final against Crewe

up to Wembley because the final was ten days after the semi-final," McMillan explained. "There were people queuing up Grosvenor Terrace for tickets and, in training, everybody was being careful. They didn't want to get injured. The gaffer didn't name the team, but we had a very stable side back then, so everyone had an idea and Alan made training very light-hearted, short and sharp." Kiely also recalled how Little kept everybody focussed on the task ahead, saying: "The wait for Wembley seemed like an eternity but all the talk was, now we had got there, we have to finish the job off. We didn't want to end the season as gallant losers, and Alan Little did really well. He had taken the reins from John Ward and ran with it. The players were also low maintenance. We all knew our jobs and got on and did them."

On his attempts to keep minds focussed at Bootham Crescent, Little added: "There was a lot going on in the build-up to the game. We had all the suits and shoes to hire and it was quite difficult because there were one or two players who didn't know whether they would be in the side, so I decided to name it on the Thursday. People were a bit edgy and it was getting a bit niggly in training, as players were determined to show they should be playing at Wembley, but you have to be careful with injuries when it gets like that."

The Minstermen would go on to gloriously beat Crewe on penalties at Wembley. Good times had returned to Bootham Crescent with Kiely making fine progress in goal, McMillan, Stancliffe or Paul Atkin, Tutill and Hall forming a reliable back four, Swann and driving force Pepper offering midfield steel, McCarthy and Canham providing skill and pace down the flanks and Barnes being ably supported by Ian Blackstone and Borthwick in attack. The squad also headed back to Bootham Crescent swiftly to celebrate with a modest supper laid on for the historic victors. "After Wembley, we came straight back to the ground on the bus and into the Social Club for pie and peas because that's the way we were," Little explained. "We were happy to be back in York and didn't want to stay around in a Wembley hotel."

For one player, the celebrations carried on late into the night after he was "kidnapped" from Bootham Crescent. "I remember when we came back from Wembley and a car picked Steve Tutill up outside the ground," Pepper explained. "He had given the penalty away and I think he thought he was being kidnapped, but they took him to a party in Fulford. He didn't even know who they were!"

The average home attendance that campaign had also gone up from 2,506 the previous campaign to 3,946 - the highest figure for seven years. On the contrast in the matchday experience at Bootham Crescent, McCarthy commented: "When I first came to the club, we were getting 1,500 fans for some games but that went up to 4,000 and coming out to that size of crowd every week was great. We used to always kick towards the home end in the second half and it spurred you on, especially as I was attacking down the right wing in front of the Main Stand."

The junior team also reached the FA Youth Cup quarter-finals that season before being beaten by Manchester United. Future first-team keeper Andy Warrington was in between the sticks for the talented teenage team and recalled: "We beat Newcastle and Coventry in the FA Youth Cup at Bootham Crescent and went on to play Manchester United at Old Trafford. That was an achievement for one of the smallest clubs in the League and we all lived together. I roomed with Graeme Murty, who got a fantastic move to Reading. Then, Richard Cresswell and Jonathan Greening came through and Nick Culkin - the keeper after me - went on to sign for Manchester United. It was a bit of a production line back then." Jordan also remembered the excitement of playing at Bootham Crescent under the lights for the first time during that FA Youth Cup run and as he broke into the reserve side, even though cost-saving measures meant the pre-match warm-up was often conducted in near darkness. "As a youth team, we didn't do that well in the league, but we had a good run in the cup," he said. "Players who didn't feature much came in and did well. It was different for us playing at night too, because we were used to playing on a Saturday morning. I played quite a few games with the reserves when I was a first-year YTS as well. You were playing against older players and under floodlights, which was new and felt special. But it was also strange, because we used to warm up in the dark, as the club would only put one light on until right up to kick-off because they wanted to save electricity, so it was quite eerie when you first went out."

Ricky Sbragia insisted he had full faith in his youngsters as they faced bigger clubs in the competition, including in players who would not subsequently make the grade. "We had a good team," he declared. "The Northern Intermediate League was a decent standard and we'd played Newcastle before in that. Coventry were a bit different because we hadn't played against them, but we had a lad called Andy Bowker and he was a flying machine, who caused them problems. I think he went into banking when his three years were up, but he was always a threat. He was an intelligent lad, but quite strange as well, because he would break his boots in one at a time. He would say I'll break the right one in this week and, then, the left one in the next game, which puzzled us. We often went for clever lads, though, because you were judged on your education results so, if you had a choice between two players, we tended to go for the one who could take information in." Sbragia admitted he might have approached the home ties differently with hindsight, though, pointing out that he probably underestimated the sense of occasion connected to playing at Bootham Crescent for the first time. "I could have done it better," he reasoned. "Looking back, I should have had a couple of days' training with them on the pitch before, if Fossie (Bryan Foster) would have let me, but we just went straight into it. The crowd wasn't anything great, but it was bigger than what they were used to on the open fields at St John University or York RI. It was our FA Cup and the one you went for. Manchester United see it as the biggest prize in youth football and we had to look at it as the same at York City. Doing well in the league was great, but the FA Youth Cup was national. Going as far as we did was a good achievement for what we were. We always set out to be difficult to beat and, when I left in 1994, we were top of the Northern Intermediate League. We beat Hull 5-1 with Richard Cresswell, Jonathan Greening and Scott Jordan playing and I knew it was a really good team. We had a small nucleus of players - a bit like the 1983/84 team - who played week in, week out, even though we lost some to the reserves."

Warrington, meanwhile, believed Sbragia deserved a lot of credit for the run, as he took his first steps on a coaching career that would see him work for Manchester United, Sunderland and Scotland. He also took great pride in ensuring Bootham Crescent looked its best at all times, which meant long working hours for Warrington and his fellow apprentices. "Ricky Sbragia was a massive, massive inspiration for me as a youth coach," Warrington admitted. "Having somebody like him supporting you gave you a big boost. He was hard-line and a tough taskmaster though. You knew if you had stepped out of line with him, and he made sure you did all your jobs. He was a hard man to please when you were cleaning the dressing rooms. We also had to wash the kits because there was no kit man and we cleaned and swept everywhere. We didn't leave until 4.30 or 5pm and it was just part of growing up and being part of a team. We learned so many life skills. If something was dirty or out of place, nobody left until it was sorted, so everybody mucked in together to get things done. Some complained but they were probably the kids who didn't make it. Ricky's youth teams brought a lot of money into the club in terms of transfer fees and probably paid for a lot of things around Bootham Crescent."

Jordan also recalled his long hours as an apprentice, which he never begrudged and even enjoyed, with a couple of memorable pranks and time-saving measures employed to try and knock off early perhaps explaining why City's home kit might not always have looked pristine during that historic campaign. "We had to clean the boots, changing rooms and kits," he explained. "If you cleaned something and he didn't think you'd done the job right, then you'd have to do it again. We came in before the players and wouldn't leave until 5pm most days, but it was probably the best time I had as a footballer. I remember we put a few lads in the tumble dryer and turned it on for a laugh once. One was a lad called Nick Gosling, but he was stuck in there when Ricky came in and he wasn't impressed. You also used to push everything into the washing machine as tight as you could because, if you couldn't get it in, it meant you would have to do another load. It was hard to shut the door and the kit never washed well because there was no room for anything to move. You also used to have to put cards in it and wait for the cycle to end before you pulled one out and put another in. Sometimes, though, we would take the cards out earlier and that could get it all done 20 minutes quicker. It was a friendly ground though. You went to away grounds and the changing rooms were often cold and damp, but Bootham Crescent was never like that. They were always clean, and I know, because it was my job to make sure they were for two years. You got used to every part of the ground as a YTS apprentice."

Sbragia, himself, confessed he has felt compelled to apologise to many former City apprentices for his hard-line stance, saying: "I think I was very tough at the time and also used to try and play the game for them. Later in my career, I didn't tend to do that and I let them learn the game, but I was a bit of a taskmaster back then, I must admit. I would have a go at them and I used to run my finger over the top of the ledges, because I knew they wouldn't bother with those, but they were good really. I bump into a few of the old York apprentices now and I tell them I must have been awful when I was your coach. They just laugh and say I was strict, but it instilled discipline in them and I got them pro deals, which I suppose was the case. I was also a novice thrown in at the deep end when I got the job and I just thought about how it was done when I was a young player at Birmingham. It was just all about running to get as fit as possible back then and I do apologise to them when I see them now. When I went to Manchester United, Darren Fletcher even said to me later: 'I can remember the rumours about you and that you were very strict and demanding, but you're nothing like that'. When I went to Manchester United, I was also told to make sure it was the best five years of the kids' lives and that they loved coming in. I stopped shouting at them after that, because I realised the main thing is to pass on all the knowledge you have got." Sbragia also displayed his softer side at times, adding:

"There was a lad called Big Tony, who we took under our wing at the time. I think we first came across him up at Clifton and he was quite poor, but he used to watch us train and loved it. We used to let him have a bath every Friday. We pretty much closed the club down for him, so he could have a proper wash and I would tell the apprentices: 'You've got ten minutes before Tony gets in the bath' and that used to speed them up a bit. We would give him ten minutes in there and he loved it. He also used to help us with the kit and the lads really loved him. We gave him a sandwich and a cup of tea as well and you would often see Fossie sat in one dugout and Tony in the other. We tried to look after him a bit."

Sbragia's tough love would lead to a conveyor belt of young talent that would never be matched at Bootham Crescent, even if one future golf star slipped though the net. "I thought I was a good coach, before I learned the difference at Manchester United, but my job was to get the players pro and I did that," he reasoned. "We had people like Richard Cresswell, Nick Culkin, Graeme Murty, Jonathan Greening and Lee Morris, so we had some good assets. We also had Simon Dyson, the golfer, in our Centre of Excellence, but his dad came to me and told me he was packing in. He was a great cricketer as well, but his dad told me he had a wee chance of playing golf. I said: 'Okay. All the best'. That conversation took place in the little gym, but we had a fair bit of success with people like Steve Tutill, Nigel Costello and Gary Himsworth coming through as well. We also lost a couple. Curtis Woodhouse - the boxer - went to Sheffield United, but we got a small compensation fee for him and we had an abundance of players that got into the first team." Sbragia also introduced important changes to the structure of youth football at Bootham Crescent, explaining: "The one thing I found really difficult during my first year, after I'd gone into coaching in November, was we had 30 schoolboys, but could only take on nine scholarships so, after that, I decided we had to get the numbers down. My reasoning was that, if we were only taking on nine, then why not choose your nine at 14 and keep them until they were 19? That was the plan and it's what we did. We ran dual teams, so we had 18-man squads."

Jordan admitted, meanwhile, that watching the first team secure a Wembley appearance at Bootham Crescent served as an added incentive for him to make the pro grade. "We always sat behind the dugouts for games and, after that match, we stayed out to watch all the players go into the directors' box because it was a big celebration with the club getting to the final," he explained. "We did the same when Burnley won promotion at Bootham Crescent because you wanted to see what it was like when you achieved something as footballers."

Nigel Pepper scores a penalty against Torquay in September 1992, as the club makes preparations to install seats in front of the Main Stand

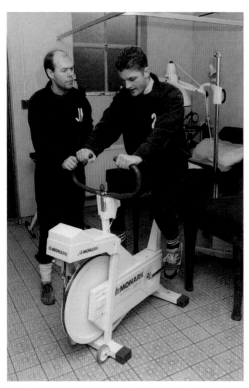

Ray Warburton on a new exercise bike is monitored by Jeff Miller in the physio room in 1993

CHAPTER 26

Knockout blow for Sir Alex, Cantona and Beckham

"Eric Cantona was staring straight at me and I remember thinking, for a second, what am I doing here?"

Alan Little's team went on to reach the play-offs during their first campaign back in the third tier, finishing fifth - the club's highest position since the old second division days. Future World Cup final commentator Guy Mowbray also took his first steps towards a glittering career in broadcasting at Bootham Crescent that season. Taking up the story, he revealed: "My first report of any kind was at Bootham Crescent for Club Call (the premium rate phone line that provided club news, match commentaries and interviews). It was for a game against Brentford in 1993 that we lost 2-0. The season before, I had watched Wayne Hall score the winning penalty at Wembley and I had been working in London for a bank but had decided to move back to York. I wasn't really enjoying it and my dad had rang me up and asked me what I wanted to do. I'd always dreamt I would become a footballer and was kind of still hoping somebody would spot me, but my dad said that boat had sailed. I was 21 and, frankly, wasn't good enough anyway, but I decided I'd like to do something in the game so, naively, I wrote to all the national broadcasters hoping they would need somebody and got no replies. The only response I got was from John Temple who was doing Club Call for York, Leeds, Hull and Hartlepool at the time, so he said I could shadow him and, if I picked it up, I could cover for him because he needed some help. I had tickets for Manchester City v Liverpool the day of that Brentford game and told John I couldn't make it, but my dad told me to get back on the phone, so I did and started covering York and Hull matches. It was a pleasure to work at the club in those days. Bootham Crescent was so friendly, and you got to know everyone. My first interview with Alan Little must have been rubbish, because I had no interview technique back then, but I remember him being really patient and so good to me. Keith Usher (then club secretary) had his critics, but he was always great with me and had the club at heart. He also often put up a fight against Douglas Craig on certain issues, which not many people knew about or, indeed, did at the time."

The club ultimately missed out on a second successive trip to Wembley, drawing 0-0 against Stockport in front of a Sunday home crowd of 8,744 - another new record for gate receipts (£55,000) - before losing the second leg 1-0. Bumper league gates against Hull (8,481 for £49,366) and Burnley (8,642 for £50,034.55) had also bettered the previous record earlier in the season. Heavy rain had put the Stockport match in doubt three hours before kick-off, but it went ahead, and City missed three gilt-edged, first-half chances to seize

Burnley fans find a perch for the best view at Bootham Crescent in April 1994

the initiative in the tie. In the 17th minute, a Gary Swann pass sent Ian Blackstone clear but, unluckily for him, the ball got stuck in a puddle and he had to check before getting it on to his preferred left foot and trying a chip, which was turned away for a corner by visiting keeper John Keeley. Moments later, Keeley made a brilliant diving save to keep out a flashing header from Tony Canham following Blackstone's cross. Paul Barnes also went on to fire over as he charged through on Keeley's goal. At the other end, Wayne Hall was then needed to head Mike

Wayne Hall heads a Stockport effort off the line during the 1994 play-off, semi-final

Flynn's effort off the line just past the half-hour mark and Dean Kiely also made a great save to deny Chris Beaumont. Another great opportunity for the home side was spurned, though, four minutes before the break when Keeley parried a Barnes shot, leaving Blackstone with a yawning goal, but his weak finish allowed the Stockport keeper to recover and gather. The score might have been 4-2 at half-time, but City lost their way a little in the second period and didn't manage another shot on target. At the other end, Kiely saved well from Beaumont who, along with Kevin Francis, also fired too high with only the City net-minder to beat, as honours ended even.

The 1,320 away tickets for the Edgeley Park decider still sold out within hours of going on sale, even if Jon McCarthy admitted more than 20 years later that he felt the chance to win the tie diminished after the Bootham Crescent draw. "That was a wet night and they were a good, big team," he explained. "They had Kevin Francis at 6ft 7in and Jim Gannon was a strong player too. They were direct and dangerous at set-pieces and, when we didn't get ahead in the first leg, I remember coming off thinking that maybe we had missed our chance. It would have been an unbelievable achievement to get up through the play-offs again. Steve Cooper came into the team that season and did a really good job, but he was probably the only real change, so Alan (Little) did well. He didn't change much and carried on what he had learned from John Ward. He deserves great credit for what he achieved as manager and the millions he brought into the club selling players, but he wouldn't have courted that. If we had gone up, we would have probably been targeting the bottom teams to try and stay up and, whether we could have survived, might have depended on the club investing money into the team."

Hall, though, continued to believe in the team's ability to reach Wembley for a second successive spring after the Bootham Crescent stalemate, reasoning: "They were a very good side at the time with a few players who went on to bigger and better things, but there was nothing to be over-awed about. We definitely had the confidence to go out and think that we were going to win against them, because we'd had a good season, and all felt we could win the play-offs again. We still fancied our chances going to Stockport for the second leg, as it was quite a good ground for us. We'd got good results there a few times but, like the home leg, it was 0-0 until right to the very end. It would have been nice to go up to the next division and see how the club could have done if we'd kept everybody, but that didn't happen, and people started to leave after losing that game." Swann also felt the 0-0 home draw didn't diminish the team's hopes of getting to the final, reasoning: "We threw everything at them because we knew we had to try and nick a lead, but I still thought we could sneak a result there."

Manager Little, meanwhile, was left to reflect on missed opportunities during the first leg at Bootham Crescent. "Ian Blackstone could have had a hat-trick," he claimed. "He had some great chances, but we didn't score, and I had a feeling they would be dangerous and tough to beat at their place. They had a big team with people like Kevin Francis and we ended up losing 1-0 at their place after a rare Paul Stancliffe mistake. They were two cracking games though and that team came so close to making the next step up." Illustrating the team's belief at the time, Nigel Pepper was another who still fancied the team's prospects for progress after the home leg, reasoning: "You think you're up against it, but you know it only takes one goal away from home and you're right back in it. Then, the home team has to do something special, because they hadn't got an away goal, so I still felt we had a chance."

For Andy Warrington, his daily chores as a youth-team scholar, meanwhile, included a painful afternoon, as he helped prepare the pitch for the Stockport play-off clash, which resulted in spilt blood on the Bootham Crescent playing surface. "A group of us YTS apprentices were getting the pitch ready for the play-off semi-final by raking the six-yard box with the groundsman," he explained. "I was shattered, because we'd been working all day and I ended up sticking the pitch fork right through my big toe. I went straight to see Jeff Miller and had to go to hospital. There was a trail of blood from the six-yard box, to the players' tunnel and into the physio's room." By then, Bryan Horner had replaced Bryan Foster as groundsman following the latter's untimely death from a heart attack just three months earlier. But the eccentric Fossie was still terrorising players in his final years with Warrington revealing: "I remember Fossie chucking a pitch fork at Chris Marples. He had gone on the pitch and Fossie ran right across it chasing after him. He missed him with the fork and Chris carried on running out of the ground at the away end."

Pepper also recalled Marples incurring the wrath of Foster, saying: "Bryan Foster was absolutely nuts. I can remember coming out of the gym once and Chris Marples walked across the pitch. Fossie through a pitch fork at him and it flew just past him and stuck in the pitch. On another day, it could have gone through his leg. Chris Marples didn't think it was that funny, but it was hilarious. Fossie was a funny, funny bloke. After a game, he used to fix the pitch in his wellies and donkey jacket and, then, he would come out around town with us in the same gear." Nor was former midfield hardman and boss Little spared the Fossie treatment. "I remember his pitchfork would come flying at me if I stepped on the field," Little recalled. "He threw it at everybody, but he was a brilliant, down-to-earth, old-school character, who said what he thought. He also tended that pitch with his own hands, more or less. He didn't have much machinery back then, just a 46-inch cutting machine. The verti-drainer only came along after he had passed away. He would put the divots back in on his own and I used to have to ask him if we could get on the pitch for quarter-of-an-hour's work. He'd say yes but throw the pitchfork down and walk off. He'd then come back and be on the pitch repairing the divots whilst you were still trying to train around him."

Barnes, meanwhile, was irritated by the home leg against Stockport and disappointed that some of the team's players would not go on to perform at the level their talents deserved following the aggregate defeat. He said: "I remember the frustration of not scoring a goal against Stockport. It would have been great to go back to Wembley just a year after being there and a credit to the team and management. When you look back at that side, there were so many good players. Wayne Hall was a bit unsung, but he always did a sterling job. You probably wouldn't have got a better right back than Andy McMillan in many of the leagues at the time either and I'm sure, if he'd got the chance to play at a higher level, he would have taken it. Myself, Nigel Pepper, Dean Kiely, Jon McCarthy and, later, Graeme Murty all went on to bigger things and I think there were a few others in the team who could have done. Coming from Stoke into the lower leagues, it was also great to play with some of the characters we had at York and we had some fantastic senior pros like Tony Canham, who was in his testimonial year. Ian Blackstone was also great to play with. He was a non-League player who got a chance to play in the League and he grabbed it with both hands. He gave the club real good service."

McMillan also remembered thinking the tie might have been lost after the Minstermen failed to take advantage of a one-sided home leg, though, saying: "We should have been three or four up at Bootham Crescent and their keeper did really well again. He was pulling off saves left, right and centre and there were chances galore. If we had got two or three up, with our ability to stop the opposition scoring, that would have given us a really good chance of getting to Wembley in the second leg and we wanted to get there again to give those fans who hadn't been able to go the first time another day out. It's a real shame we couldn't take a lead to Stockport because I thought we were the better team and, when we came off after that home leg, I felt 0-0 might not be enough, especially with the number of chances we had created. We should have killed the game off at our place." Kiely, while happy to keep Stockport off the scoresheet, also remembered feeling slightly unsatisfied at the end of the first leg. "I was pleased with the clean sheet because I placed a lot of importance on that and I can't remember being very busy or over-worked," he pointed out. "We were well-drilled as a unit, but we were a little disappointed we couldn't get our noses in front and take a lead to Stockport. We felt like we'd done half a job and, as it turned out, there was little between the two teams over both matches, other than Chris Beaumont's goal at their place."

The Stockport game was the last Swann was to play at Bootham Crescent, but he retained fond memories of his period there as a City player, adding: "We used to play a lot of head tennis in the gym - myself, Barney, Ginner and Andy Mac. I also always remember we would all jump into the mini bus in the car park every day and Alan (Little) would drive us to the training ground."

Impressively, only 13 league goals were conceded that campaign at Bootham Crescent, which represented a club record. Kiely, McMillan and Tutill were all ever-presents, and Hall missed just one game during the season. "The defence was very stable," McMillan said of the reasons behind the back-line's Bootham Crescent defiance. "It didn't change much, and we were very rarely injured. Now and again, Stan (Paul Stancliffe) knew he had to step out and step back in, because he was in the latter stages of his career and, then, Paul Atkin would come in. Stan was a great organiser who knew the game well and understood it. He talked to us young kids, like myself, Steve Tutill and Wayne Hall, who were all roughly the same age and were playing with youthful exuberance, and he would rein us in. Stan would shout: 'Where are you going?' and 'Come back here'. It was all about being organised and having a determination not to let the opposition score a goal. Having somebody like Deano behind us helped too. I knew he would get a move - maybe not to the level he ended up at - but that was great for him. He was a good shot-stopper and good for me because he was a leftie, so all his throw-outs came my way. Poor Ginner (Hall) got about three a season." On the secret of that defence's success, Hall added: "Everybody knew what each other's strengths and weaknesses were. We were very organised and Stanny had lots of experience and talked to people. He was getting on in years but, what his legs couldn't do, his brain would make up for and he would drag people around. Dean would also shout a lot behind us and was an excellent goalkeeper who made some great saves, although I didn't realise we conceded so few goals at home that season. That wasn't bad really, was it?"

Kiely, meanwhile, derived great satisfaction from the club's impressive goals-against tally at Bootham Crescent, adding: "I was very proud of that. I've been ribbed during my career for knowing exactly how many clean sheets I've kept, and it was great to be part of a team, at that stage of my career, that was trying to push up the divisions. We wanted to make an impression on the next division. We were not going up thinking we're a little club, so this is going to be tough, as quite a few teams do in that situation, believing it's a step too far. We wanted to keep the momentum going and we did. That shows the mentality of the players and the club at that time. We didn't just want to hang around and be relegation fodder. We were well-organised and well-drilled as a team. We weren't a pushover and made Bootham Crescent a difficult place to visit. The fans' reaction to seeing their team get promoted and play a better standard of football in a better division was good, so it was a good place to be and there was a good blend of players in defence. Andy McMillan was probably one of the best players around in the lower leagues at the time. Wayne Hall was really tenacious and a very good one-on-one defender. Steve Tutill had false teeth like me, which shows he put his head in where it hurts for the team. He was a real, robust centre-half and a great man to play behind. Importantly, Paul Stancliffe also came to the club from a higher level and imparted his knowledge and know-how to others. He linked up well with the likes of Steve Tutill and Paul Atkin and certainly helped me a lot in terms of telling me where he needed me to be and how I needed to be connected to the back four."

McCarthy reasoned that the impressive goals-against column at Bootham Crescent was also a team effort, saying: "Paul Stancliffe was a key player in that record, but we were also solid in front of him. I'm not taking anything away from that defence, but we were all as defensive minded as we could be. We were a strong 4-4-2 and got everybody behind the ball. Alan would always tell us to tuck in narrow if we lost the ball and we were very difficult to break down as an eight or nine. Everybody seemed to play 4-4-2 then and we always did very well matching up other teams. We had an outstanding keeper in Dean Kiely and Paul Stancliffe would have had everybody tucked in. He knew where to be and formed good partnerships with Steve Tutill and Paul Atkin. They were good players with a defensive-minded four in front of them too. There were some good players as it showed when some of us moved on, like myself, Dean Kiely, Paul Barnes and Nigel Pepper. There were also others that were underrated and people like Andy McMillan and Wayne Hall must have come close to getting moves as well." On that back-line's strengths, Little added: "We had people like Stancliffe and Tutill, whilst Andy McMillan was a dream player and Wayne Hall was a worker who got up and down all the time. He made mistakes but had the desire to recover and put them right. We also had wide men in Graeme Murty, Tony Canham and Jon McCarthy, who could go forward and get back. Andy McMillan was great on the overlap too and Dean Kiely was a massive player for us."

That summer, meanwhile, the Main Stand was extended downwards by demolishing the standing Enclosure section and adding extra seats down to ground level. The work cost £220,000 and necessitated extending the Main Stand roof forwards to help keep the rain off the new seating area.

In 1994/95, the club would then go on to finish ninth in the table with a 2-0 home win over eventual title winners Birmingham proving a highlight. The Blues had the best unbeaten run in Britain at the time of 25 matches and included the likes of Steve Claridge and Mark Ward in their side. But McCarthy headed in the first goal just past the half-hour mark and, on 73 minutes, teed up Canham for the second. It was a match that McCarthy reckoned was of great personal significance for him. "I scored one of my favourite goals in that game," he explained. "We beat them 2-0 and they'd gone 20-odd games unbeaten under Barry Fry. That match probably led to me getting a move there later, because I scored and set one up for Tony Canham." McCarthy did, indeed, move on during the summer with Little acknowledging: "We never replaced players like Jon McCarthy, Paul Barnes, Dean Kiely and Graeme Murty. The club didn't think it was right to splash out big salaries to keep them either and the side started to break up."

After the pitch's drainage system had collapsed in February, meanwhile, new pipes were laid in May, including the main drain across the pitch at the David Longhurst Stand End and 14 feeder pipes. Running the length of the pitch, the pipework cost £11,000 with Philliskirk & Sons, of Green Hammerton, the contractors. A water tank would later be added close to the social club in the late 1990s to help further maintain the quality of the playing surface.

The following campaign then heralded one of English football's biggest-ever shocks, as City dumped Manchester United out of the League Cup, then sponsored by Coca-Cola. Having earned worldwide headlines by winning 3-0 at Old Trafford in the first leg after a Barnes brace and Tony Barras' goal, the Minstermen completed the job at Bootham Crescent, clinching a 4-3 aggregate win.

The Red Devils included all their big guns for the second leg with the likes of Eric Cantona and Peter Schmeichel back in the side, but Scott Jordan's goal during a 3-1 defeat sent City through in front of a crowd of 9,386, with record receipts again registered and estimated to be in the region of £63,000. French superstar Cantona was returning for his first game after receiving a nine-month ban for karate-kicking an abusive Crystal Palace fan and he was booed by City supporters every time he touched the ball. An extra 180 police officers, meanwhile, were drafted in for the contest, although only six arrests were made - three for being drunk and disorderly, one for a public order offence, one for criminal damage and one for unlawfully selling tickets. Warrington also made his debut in the game at the age of 19 with Kiely injured and missing his first game since December 1992. The full United team on the night was Schmeichel, Gary Neville, Steve Bruce, Gary Pallister, Lee Sharpe, David Beckham, Paul Scholes, Terry Cooke, Ryan Giggs, Cantona and Andy Cole. Roy Keane and Phil Neville also came on as substitutes. "They put all the big boys out, so there could be no excuses for them," then manager Little insisted. "Their team sheet was scary, but all I remember before the game was my eldest daughter coming down to give Alex Ferguson some chewing gum in the tunnel, because they'd seen him using it all the time on the television. My wife and two girls thought the world of him back then."

Pepper, meanwhile, insisted he was thrilled by the visitors' team-sheet, rather than being intimidated, reasoning: "You want to play against players like that and, then, it was a matter of this is what it is and, if we are going to progress, we had to make sure we beat them over the two legs. What a night for the crowd it was to see their full-strength team out, down at Bootham Crescent. That's not going to happen every week." Eventual goal hero Jordan admitted that the build-up to the second leg was probably a little more daunting than the night itself, saying: "The build-up on the day wasn't too bad. We went to a hotel before, which we didn't normally do for home games, then got to the ground early. It was different because there were so many cameras there, which we weren't used to. I didn't feel any nerves, though, to be honest. I was just looking forward to it more than anything and remember feeling more nervous in other games. It was maybe in the days leading up to it that I remember just running through corners and free kicks and, when you were told who you would be picking up, it did make you think we'll get hammered and, because we had won 3-0, there was a bit of pressure. Three-nil seems a lot, but it's not if a team score twice early on as they did. Andy Cole was really sharp from the start. You sometimes don't realise how quick some players are and he was. They had picked the best team they had available at the time and we were just trying to catch our breath at the start. Luckily, when we got the goal back, that settled the game down a bit. If we hadn't, they would have possibly got a few more, because we were hanging on a bit at that stage and the first 20 minutes were a struggle but, the longer games like that go on, the better you feel, and you enjoy it more. Everyone just wanted it so much, because you could sense how close we were to pulling it off."

Warrington confessed it was a surreal time for him, as he was thrust into the spotlight before he had even played a minute of professional football. "I had been at Hull three days before as a matchday squad member because it was in the days when you could only name three substitutes and a goalkeeper

Alan Little watches on with Alex Ferguson in the background during the League Cup second leg clash against Manchester United. An injured Dean Kiely also watches on from the bench after discharging himself from hospital with a fractured cheekbone

wasn't always one of them," he explained. "Deano broke his cheekbone, so Paul Baker went in goal and I never really thought about what that meant. I thought the club would probably bring somebody in, but Alan Little told me on the Monday that I would be playing, so there was a lot of press coverage, but Alan didn't really build the game up. He was very down to earth and told me to just go out and do what I'd been doing in the reserves. I think he purposefully played it down because it doesn't really get any better than making your debut against Manchester United as a 19-year-old lad. With a 3-0 lead, people had started thinking we should really be knocking them out, so it was a bit of a surreal feeling. Being my debut, I didn't really know what to expect. I'd only played reserve games at Bootham Crescent and nothing prepares you for playing against those names." Standing shoulder to shoulder - or a little lower in Warrington's case - as the players waited to run out at Bootham Crescent was an experience in itself. "Lining up in the tunnel was unbelievable and I was nervous," he admitted. "I remember coming out of the home dressing room and looking to my left down the corridor to the away dressing room and I was looking straight at Peter Schmeichel - I was at his chest level!"

Early goals from Scholes and Cooke saw United claw back the aggregate deficit to 3-2 after just 14 minutes of the second leg. Warrington had made a fine early save from Cole, but Scholes swept a low 10-yard shot past him after collecting a left-wing cross from Cantona. Moments later, Cole and Giggs combined down the left to tee up a chance for Cooke that he calmly converted from a similar distance. But Barnes saw a decent attempt pushed onto a post by Schmeichel and then, six minutes before the break, he cut inside Pallister and rode a sliding Bruce challenge, before he and Jordan both swung a boot at the loose ball 15 yards from goal. Television replays confirmed that the latter got the decisive touch as the ball rolled into a beaten Schmeichel's bottom-right corner. The visitors, who were destined to do the domestic double that season, signalled their intentions in the tie during the second half by introducing Keane, who

Tony Barras does battle with a 20-year-old David Beckham during the 1995 League Cup clash against Manchester United

had not been risked from the start due to a suspected hernia problem. He quickly flashed a shot wide and Cantona also missed the target with a volley from Scholes' cross, while Cole found the sidenetting as the Red Devils pressed. United did manage a third goal on 80 minutes when, after Beckham picked out Cole in the box, the ball ricocheted kindly to Scholes just inside the penalty area and his shot spun into Warrington's bottom-right corner with the aid of a deflection off Barras. Scholes went on to narrowly miss the target with a hat-trick chance, but United could not force extra-time and the fourth away goal that would have put them in the ascendancy. A cramping Nicky Peverell, meanwhile, agonisingly squandered a late opportunity to wrap up matters when he shot wide of an empty goal from an acute angle after intercepting Gary Neville's back pass to Schmeichel with Jordan screaming for a square pass. But it mattered little, as referee Jeff Winter's final whistle heralded joyous scenes.

For Warrington, memories of the game remained hazy, but he recalled certain moments, where he was pitted directly against two of world football's greats from that era - Cantona and Schmeichel. He said: "I don't remember that much about the game, but I do remember the referee (Jeff Winter) pulling me up for a back pass when Andy McMillan chested or kneed the ball to me. There

419

Debutant Andy Warrington sticks up an arm to claw away an Eric Cantona free kick for Manchester United during the second leg of the famous aggregate League Cup victory in 1995

was an argument about that and I was annoyed but, then, I put all the lads on the line for the free kick and stood straight in front of them. Eric Cantona was staring straight at me and I remember thinking, for a second: 'What am I doing here?' He looked like he would smash it, but he tried to dink it over me and I managed to claw it away. It then landed at Andy Cole's feet, but I managed to kick the ball away. Very late in the game, they also got a corner. It was taken in the corner between the Main Stand and away end and it was probably David Beckham that took it. Anyway, I looked over to my right and Peter Schmeichel was five yards away. I was thinking: 'Oh no, here we go'. He had scored in the UEFA Cup a week earlier but we managed to deal with it." Warrington and his City team-mates were mobbed by incredulous pitch-invading home fans at the end, which denied the debutant keeper the chance of acquiring a cherished memento. "The scenes were unbelievable at the end," Warrington admitted. "None of us had experienced anything like it. It was a great feeling and all the supporters were on the pitch. We were mobbed, and you couldn't blame them. It was a massive, massive occasion, but it meant I never saw anybody from Manchester United after the final whistle. They had got off the pitch as quickly as they could, and my biggest regret was that I never got Peter Schmeichel's shirt or saw him after the game. I was gutted about that, but it was all a bit surreal, including looking up to my mum and dad in the stand. Then, when we got into the dressing room, everyone was jumping on each other and celebrating in the two big baths. They are really good memories. We then had a day off but were in the following day to prepare for a home game with Wrexham on Saturday when I kept a clean sheet in a 1-0 win on my league debut, so it was a great week for me."

The unfortunate Kiely, meanwhile, also made it out of hospital to watch the game and participate in the post-match mayhem. "I didn't see Deano until after the game in the dressing room," Warrington remembered. "He had been in hospital but discharged himself and still had his band on. His face was still massively swollen, but we had a bit of a chat and he would have been disappointed because it was a big match for him." Kiely, though, insisted he felt no bitterness at his misfortune and was desperate to get to the game and cheer his team-mates on, saying: "I had my nose broken, my eye sockets fractured, and my teeth knocked out at Hull, so it was a pretty bad injury and the timing of it wasn't the best. Put it this way, it ended my modelling career, unless somebody wanted me to sell their goalkeeping gloves for them! On the night of the second leg, I remember being in York District Hospital and I asked for permission to discharge myself. They agreed, so I stuck my tracksuit on, walked over the railway bridge and into the ground. I still had double vision, but I wanted to see the lads and wish them all the best, especially Andy, rather than lie in a hospital bed just a quarter-of-a-mile away. It wouldn't have felt right not to have gone down and shown my support and I enjoyed the game. It was a terrific atmosphere and it was great that we were able to get through. People maybe thought it would just happen after we won 3-0 at Old Trafford, but they were wounded by that result and put a decent complement of players out. The fact that the lads completed the job showed what a purple patch that era was for the club because we went toe-to-toe with them and got through. Andy did really, really well on the night too. After the game, I couldn't really join in the celebrations much because of my face, so I went back to the hospital after congratulating the lads."

Indeed, summarising on the game for ITV's *The Big Match* highlights programme, former Liverpool and Scotland star Ian St John, who was sat alongside commentator John Helm, said: "He looks as though he's gone 10 rounds with Frank Bruno," as the cameras panned to the battered Kiely in the dugout during the game. But Jordan, who had come up through the ranks with Warrington, never felt that pitching the fledgling keeper in for his debut against Manchester United would be an issue, adding: "I didn't think anything of it. Deano had got injured, but I never thought for one moment that Andy would struggle, and it would be a problem. He was second choice, but he trained with us every day and there was no shame in being behind Deano."

First-leg hero Barnes added that he felt the two-week gap between the stratospheric result at Old Trafford and the return leg contributed to a frenzied excitement at the stadium. "There was a bit of a gap between the two legs, so we had a couple of days to calm down after the Old Trafford win, but there was so much media around the ground after that result," he said. "On the night of the game, there were chairs all down the side of the pitch for the press and it was a game that had gripped the imagination." Sitting in the home dressing room beforehand, Barnes was also reassured by Little's calm manner, although reality struck home when Alex Ferguson's starting XI was announced. "Before the game, Alan was very level-headed," Barnes pointed out. "He rarely got excited and just tried to make sure we were focussed on the job in hand. He just said let's be nice and safe at the back and keep a good shape. He also told us not to panic if we went a goal down because we had proved before that we were good enough to cope with them. But, when we saw the team sheet, you couldn't help but have a little chuckle to yourself. We knew they would be coming at us full throttle with all guns blazing. Eric Cantona and Peter Schmeichel were back in their side but to go up against those players - even if it's only once - is why you play football."

Hall echoed Barnes' sentiments, relishing the challenge of tackling some of world football's greats on the Bootham Crescent turf, rather than being fearful of that prospect. He said: "The atmosphere was bubbling up a long time before kick-off and it was a special, special night. Just walking into the ground, there were masses of people there and you knew it was going to be a big night. I was excited and, even though we were 3-0 up, I still didn't feel any pressure was on us. I was just looking at it as another game. Alan just told us to go out and enjoy it and make sure we gave a good account of ourselves. He told us it was a good game to play in and asked us to try and be better than the man we were up against. They had all their big guns out and we knew we had a great game on our hands, but it was a fantastic experience to play against such quality players. Even being on the same pitch was special in terms of watching them and how they performed. It was great to see Eric Cantona's name on the team sheet because you want to play against players like that - definitely. You want to pit your skills against the best you can and try and compete to the best of your ability. It just proved to you that, given the chance, maybe you could step up to that level and, although we lost 3-1, we still went through." Hall was struck by the presence of some of the Red Devils' legends, though, explaining:

"I remember being surprised by the size of some of their players. Eric Cantona was massive. On television, he just looked like a stocky striker, but he was gigantic. Gary Pallister also filled the tunnel, along with Peter Schmeichel."

As Warrington locked horns with such huge names in his first senior match, Barnes was impressed by the fledgling keeper's response, reasoning: "Making your debut is a big moment for any keeper but for the opposition to be Manchester United must be daunting, but he did really well. He just got on with it and wasn't over-awed. He also had some experienced players helping him out and it was the first game of what turned out to be a good career for him." Hall was another, meanwhile, unsurprised by the manner in which Warrington coped with the magnitude of his debut. "I travelled up to training with Andy every day and I knew what he was capable of and knew he was a good keeper who was mentally strong enough to go in and enjoy the game," the former City left-back explained. Little felt the same way, adding: "Andy grew up in that game, but he was a big lad and a good keeper and, as a young player, he never worried me going into that game."

Barnes, though, admitted that when Warrington was beaten twice during the opening exchanges, he was concerned the floodgates might open. "I think everyone feared the worst when they scored two quick goals," he reasoned. "It was immediately a case of having our backs to the wall and I was starting to think how the tie could turn around quite quickly, but we always had confidence in our ability as a team. We also knew we had good players and it's a credit to the guys that we didn't panic and a fantastic achievement to come through it on a great night." Hall shared Barnes' trepidation following Scholes and Cooke's goals, confessing: "They scored a couple of early goals and you're starting to think: 'Oh dear, where's this going?' But we knuckled down and, when Scott scored, it settled a lot of nerves and, after we mobbed him, we started playing our game again."

Pepper agreed that the task looked sizeable following United's two early goals, but Jordan's goal came at a timely moment in the tie. "When they went 2-0 up, I don't think there was a player on the pitch that thought we had a chance at that point," he confessed. "Even our goal was a strange one with Paul Barnes and Scott Jordan both trying to claim it after looking like they'd kicked it at the same time. I still don't know who they gave it to now, but it was a relief when it went in." Barnes, meanwhile, claimed he was a boot-lace width away from being credited with the goal that swung the tie back in City's favour. "I remember standing right next to Scott Jordan and I was trying to boot the ball

Paul Barnes and Scott Jordan (number 11) both appear to claim the vital League Cup second-leg goal against Manchester United with a crestfallen David Beckham also pictured. Television cameras subsequently proved that is was Jordan who got the decisive touch

at the same time as him," Barnes smiled. "When it went in, I felt pure relief and the noise from the crowd was fantastic. That goal totally changed the outlook of the game and took a bit of pressure off us."

McMillan laughed at Barnes' claims that he almost got the vital touch ahead of Jordan. "He would claim any goal - even in training," he smiled. "He tried to claim Scott Jordan's goal, but it was definitely Scott's." Jordan also revealed that, even during the celebrations, Barnes tried to strike up a bargain, so it would be his name on the scoresheet. "I hadn't seen the goal for a few years, but my son has downloaded the clip from YouTube now," he said. "I remember me and Paul Barnes going for the same ball and it wasn't even a great shot. It just trickled past Schmeichel and was one of those, if I had struck it better, he would have probably saved it. When the ball went in, it was more a case of relief. I didn't have the energy for a big celebration and it was still the first half, but I was thinking I reckon we can do it now. Barney tried to claim it because he was on a goal bonus as part of some sort of boot deal I think. As soon as I scored, he said 'I scored the goal, OK, and I'll give you half the money'. I never heard anything else though and it wasn't mentioned again. If he thought he'd scored, he wouldn't have said that though and he didn't get a touch."

Paul Barnes plots a way past Manchester United centre-backs Gary Pallister and Steve Bruce during the 1995 League Cup clash

Despite the old ground erupting, Jordan insisted he did not let the elation distract him during the ensuing minutes up to half-time. "I remember all the fans jumping on each other when the goal went in," he said. "It was full, which you never got at Bootham Crescent and looked really packed and playing in front of a full ground made a massive difference. It was much different to playing an ordinary league game. I think the fans raised their game as well to show the Man United supporters how loud they could be, but I just got on with the game after the goal. I was only 20. If it had been later in my career, I might have taken it in a bit more. I wasn't thinking it could be the last time I played against a team like that, but it was." Remembering Jordan's vital scuffed goal, Little laughed: "I think Scott Jordan's bobbly shot bounced about 20 times before it crept in the bottom corner. Then, it was a case of adding up in your head what they needed now to win."

Any premature fervour was also quickly doused by Little when the players returned to the home dressing room at the interval with Barnes recalling: "At half-time, Alan told us to calm down and keep our shape because they would be trying to get back in the game. We knew what we had to do, and all the team

425

were determined not to undo all the good work we'd done at Old Trafford." Recalling the same team-talk, Hall said: "Alan was trying to calm everyone down and told us to keep on playing the way we were and to enjoy it, while telling us to try and win our individual battles again."

Goal-hero Jordan, meanwhile, was just pleased to get a rest, explaining: "At half-time, I think we were just glad to have a breather because everyone was shattered. I was on the left wing and playing against Gary Neville. I had played against him for the youth team when he played at centre half and, although he's not very big, he would win every header and that's what he was like on that night too. He never let up for somebody who played football at the highest level and was playing at York. In fact, they were all the same. None of them wanted to be beaten and you could see that, but there was nothing over physical. It was just a good, competitive game and there wasn't a bad tackle or any verbal stuff all night. At half-time, it was a case of let's just relax instead of getting wound up and thinking too much about it. We were just concentrating on making sure it was more of the same in the second half." Little, meanwhile, confessed: "I can't remember what I said at half-time and I could have said anything - I don't think it would have sunk in at that point!"

After Scholes' second goal dragged United back into the game, Barnes admitted the hosts were forced to fight a rearguard action before wrapping up the famous triumph. "In the last 10 or 15 minutes, our backs were against the wall but, over the two legs, we deserved to win because we could have scored more at Old Trafford," he argued. Hall agreed, adding: "That last 10 or 15 minutes seemed very long but, while people might say we scraped through, at the end of the day, we beat one of the best teams in Europe over two legs. I remember all the fans then running on at the end and you don't mind that because they want to pat you on the back and say well done. It was great to see the ecstasy on their faces because they'd been through a lot over the years and deserved that moment." Jordan also confessed: "We were really hanging on during those last 10 minutes and the final whistle came as a big relief. Every time they went forward, they looked dangerous and, at the other end, Peter Schmeichel seemed to catch every corner. He was coming out to the edge of his box and then throwing the ball straight out to start an attack."

It was the end of a night that Barnes believed left an indelible mark on the club's history, adding: "There was a lot of emotion in the dressing room afterwards. There was also relief at finishing the job we had started at Old Trafford. It was a great night for the club and will stand out in York City's history long after we have all passed on." Little added: "I can remember everyone getting on the pitch and it was absolutely unbelievable. We got battered but got through it somehow. Then, afterwards, in the changing room, we cracked open a crate of the cheapest lager available in York. Whenever we won, (then club secretary) Keith (Usher) took care of that and that's what we always got brought in."

Goalscorer Jordan, meanwhile, was suddenly the focus for masses of camera lenses at the final whistle. "The photographers came over to me and the picture that came out looked like I was in shock," he recalled. "Then, in the changing room, it was like we couldn't believe it, but we had done it and were celebrating. It was a longer night at the ground than usual, because it was one interview after another one and there were so many people wanting to talk to you. I got *The Sun* the next day and all the newspapers had the same picture of me. As a club, we'd never been recognised on that level and given that amount of praise." Little remembered both himself and his players suddenly becoming box-office news with the nation's television cameras and assorted media outlets converging on Bootham Crescent during the coming days. "For three days after, the players were on fire and we couldn't keep them away from the ground," Little explained. "There was a lot of attention on the players, as well as myself. We had a lot of TV people at the ground and nobody was used to it. I was on breakfast TV playing with the change in my pockets one morning and there was somebody waving his hands around telling me to stop it. But the Man United game took so much out of the players and we didn't have a big enough squad to rest them back then. They couldn't recover from the whole mental toll of those two legs and we dropped down the table."

Barnes added that the United players were magnanimous in defeat even during later years. "I really enjoyed playing against Gary Pallister and Steve Bruce, who was also at Birmingham when I went there," Barnes pointed out. "I always had a laugh with him about that tie. It wasn't just me pitting myself against them two though. It was great watching Ginner (Wayne Hall) going past Ryan Giggs a few times. All their players were really good before and after the games. They weren't mardy, and I even remember Paul Parker saying to me that we'd get good moves after our displays and it wasn't long after that I signed for Birmingham. I always enjoyed playing at Bootham Crescent though and had a good rapport with the fans. I have fond memories of the ground because it gave me the lift I needed in my career. The crowd was right on top of you and that's not normally the case with newer grounds now. You could always hear comments from the fans and that used to make me laugh. When I came to the club, they were crying out for success and I was pleased that, for a period of two or three years, we managed to give them a bit. The fans responded to that and loved that period, as the players did too. It was a super club to be at back then."

McMillan also recalled Kiely trying to convince the management staff that he could play on the night, saying: "Deano discharged himself for the game and wanted to play but his face had been smashed in and was really swollen. He also had a black eye with stitches in the side of his head, but he declared himself fit. There was no way he could play though, and Andy did really well on a great occasion for him." McMillan, meanwhile, was tasked with keeping the 21-year-old Giggs quiet - a challenge that proved fairly torturous. "I remember looking at the team sheet and thinking Jesus Christ, they've brought the big guns out," he grimaced. "Cantona came back, as did Roy Keane, Paul Scholes, Gary Neville and Schmeichel. I came up against Ryan Giggs and he was so quick. He actually seemed quicker with the ball than he was without it and I didn't know where he was going. I would show him the line and he would run down the line. I'd then show him inside and he would come inside. You always try as a defender to get the upper hand but, against somebody like him, you had no chance. As soon as you thought you were going to get a tackle in, he would lay the ball off and would run circles around you. I am a Manchester United fan and Paul Scholes was also my idol and favourite player of all time, so just to play against him was great. I've also got a picture in my boy's bedroom of me when a corner is being taken and I'm just staring at Eric Cantona at the near post, even though I'm not even marking him."

Pepper, who lined up against Scholes on the night, also shared McMillan's admiration for the England international at the final whistle - even if he was responsible for the City midfielder's booking that evening. "Paul Scholes was brilliant that night," he said. "He got me booked, though, by taking a little dive. "I had gone in for a tackle and pulled out, but I still got booked for it. He was such a good player though. He was one of those who you used to watch and think: 'Well he doesn't do that much' but, when you're on a pitch with him, you see his movement. He was here, there and everywhere and always wanting the ball." McMillan also admitted that he feared the worst after Scholes and Cooke's early goals left the illustrious visitors trailing just 3-2 on aggregate with more than three-quarters of the second leg to play. "You feel 'here we go' in that situation," he explained "They're going to turn the screw now. Luckily, back then, there were no stats for possession and passes completed because I think the numbers would have been quite high, but we just defended really hard. There were other Cup games, like against Everton the next season, when I thought we were the better team by a long way, but Manchester United were a different class that night and difficult to play against, but I enjoyed it and it's an experience I will always remember."

McMillan went on to describe his reaction to Jordan's goal as one of bewilderment rather than elation, saying: "I didn't even celebrate. I remember thinking he's just scored past Schmeichel and, then, trying to work out in my head whether they needed two or three goals now. I realised it was two and then thought: 'Oh, my God' and just ran back to our half to concentrate on organising everything to keep them out." Having quelled any response from United before the break, McMillan and his team-mates headed for the dressing rooms but the City right back revealed: "I can't remember the team talk at half-time but, knowing Alan and having worked with him for ten years, it would have probably been along the lines of: 'Listen, the opportunity is there, now go out there and take it' and we did."

As United refused to go out without a fight, though, McMillan also recalled a tense finale to the tie after Scholes made the aggregate score 4-3 on 80 minutes. "That last ten minutes was very difficult and they should have got another goal in the 87th or 88th minute," McMillan pointed out. "I think Giggs whipped a cross in and Scholes was millimetres away with his shot. We probably knew then, when that didn't go in, that it was going to be our night." That was confirmed moments later with McMillan confessing: "It was pure relief at the final whistle and the fans came on the pitch again. Today, the stewards are told to stop that from happening, but I don't really get that. Maybe there's an argument for protecting the pitch and player safety, especially with a club as big as Manchester United, but players want that connection with the fans at moments like that. You need to have that bond with people. After a great result, you want the fans to celebrate it as much as the players and they want that involvement too. I still speak to people who say I was hugging you after that game. I don't recognise them, but it's great they'll never forget that. The place was buzzing and then you get the music blaring and that's the way it should be, but that's been lost a bit. I also remember sitting in the dressing room in my normal place for games with my head in my hands afterwards and, the next minute, there's champagne being sprayed about. I've got pictures of that and it was a great occasion for the club and everyone involved."

Having experienced the euphoria of reaching Wembley in 1993 at Bootham Crescent, McMillan added that the feeling after overcoming Manchester United represented a different form of elation. He said: "Bury was a big celebration but beating Man U was more of a relief. We won 3-0 at Old

Trafford, so were in a position we never expected to be in and knew we had an opportunity to go through. I remember being in a hotel before the first leg and there was talk of keeping the score down to 11. No word of a lie, that was the number mentioned. They were going for the Premier League and were a great team with a great manager, while we were struggling in League One at the time. But, after getting that result, you think we should really go on to win the tie at our place." Pepper expressed the same sentiment. "There was a lot of relief more than anything after the game," he said. "We knew we had been up against a top team and, let's be honest, we were given a runabout in the second leg. It was a bit of a tonking, but that goal was enough, which was brilliant."

McMillan went on to reveal that the household names were not queuing up to offer their opponents congratulations. "I didn't get to speak to any of them afterwards," he explained. "They left very quickly and weren't happy and you don't expect players of their level to take defeat against a League One club very well. They don't like losing and that's why they're at the top of their trade. They have a desire and determination to win football games." Jordan recalled, though, that the Red Devils were thwarted in their attempts to make a quick getaway by a surprising oversight. "Nobody got a shirt from them at the end of the game because they got straight off the pitch," he confirmed. "But I do remember that they were all on the bus and couldn't leave because the tax on it had run out. One of the supporters had pointed it out and they had to stay a bit longer whilst it was sorted out."

David Meek, though, did reveal that Sir Alex Ferguson was very generous in defeat on a poignant night for the Manchester United correspondent at the ground where his father had reported for four decades. "He greeted me by saying: 'Well that was a win-win situation for you, wasn't it?'" he recalled of Ferguson's immediate reaction on seeing the experienced journalist. "He knew my York family background and said: 'Whichever of us had won, you would have something to be pleased about'. I said: 'Yes, exactly'. He complimented York on playing well though and that it was a good, tidy game so he had no complaints about the result. He thought his team had acquitted themselves properly in the second leg. In the first game, he had felt some players took York for granted, but he believed his team had the right attitude at Bootham Crescent. He had been pleased with how his players started the game and just put the aggregate result down to the vagaries of cup football. I was one of the lucky ones that night because I got my seat in the press box, whereas some of my colleagues were sat on chairs around the pitch. The way the scoring went made it a good exciting cup game and I thought of my dad at the final whistle.

It was a classic case of the haves being beaten by the have-nots and, considering all the years he had been involved in football in the lower divisions and even the Midland League, he would have enjoyed that night."

Little, meanwhile, revealed no words were exchanged between himself and the legendary Ferguson at the final whistle. "Alex is obviously not a great loser, and nothing was said at the end of the game, but I got to know him later on when he came to open our training ground and he was always a gentleman," Little explained.

Amid all the memories of the good times he enjoyed in management, Ferguson, who started watching the game from the directors' box just behind Bobby Charlton before moving to the dugout after Jordan's goal, also retained vivid recollections of his team going out of the Coca-Cola Cup at Bootham Crescent in an interview for this book in 2016. Despite the 3-0 deficit going into the return leg, the Red Devils boss had every faith that the tie could be rescued and picked his star-packed side with that intention in mind, saying: "In the first leg, we had played some of the young players and Pat McGibbon got sent off on his debut, which was a blow for him and me, as we were related because his father was a first cousin of mine. But, going into the second leg, I was confident because I always was with the kind of players we had and, if you're 3-0 down to any team, it requires serious team selection. It was also Eric Cantona's first game back from suspension, so it was a big night for him and a big night for the club to get him back after such a long time. We didn't want to be knocked out and knew, if we got through, it would be a chance to get Eric more games in the competition too."

Ferguson also recalled the build-up to the Bootham Crescent leg, as he placed a wager with his captain in the away dressing room just before kick-off on a night of historical significance, as one of the world's most famous and prolonged court cases reached a verdict. He said: "It was the day of the decision on the OJ Simpson trial and, while the players were getting ready for the game and I was doing my team talk, Steve Bruce said: 'Boss, wait a minute, the decision on the trial is coming up'. I said to him: 'He'll get off'. He said: 'No chance. He's guilty'. So, we had a little bet and it got raised to £20 and the news came through just after he had shaken my hand." Former American Football ace and actor Simpson was, indeed, acquitted of the murder of his ex-wife Nicole Brown Simpson and her friend Ron Goldman.

On the atmosphere that awaited his team, as they ran out of the players' tunnel, meanwhile, Ferguson admitted: "You could feel everybody was a bit excited -

that's for sure. When Manchester United go to play a lesser club, that team are always looking to achieve something that will go down in their history books and good for them. It's great that we get these upsets in cup football." A shock was the last thing on Ferguson's mind, however, when Scholes and Cooke's early efforts saw the hosts' aggregate winning margin narrowed to just one goal. "Of course, I thought we were well on our way at that point, because the players had done what they had to do," he pointed out. "We had started the game well and scored two early goals, but York were galvanised by the goal just before half-time and, then, their manager could tell them how well they were doing, having gone in with a two-goal advantage."

When Scholes scored for a second time on 80 minutes, though, Ferguson remained optimistic that the visitors would still progress into the next round, based on his team's tradition for conjuring up late goals. "At Manchester United, scoring late, away goals was a big part of the club's history so, going into the last 10 or 15 minutes needing one, was not an unusual position to be in, but it didn't quite work out on this occasion," he reasoned. Ferguson maintained, however, he was gracious in defeat, adding: "I had invited York's staff into my office for a drink after the first leg, which I always did with the opposition manager - win, lose or draw - because I felt it was the proper thing to do. I never talked about the game we'd just played, but football in general and who they were playing next. I acted no differently after the second leg and I congratulated York on their achievement. I had learned a long time before that, as manager of Manchester United, you had to accept defeat with dignity and it was never right to be churlish in those situations."

Future England under-21 international and top-flight striker Richard Cresswell celebrated his 18th birthday during the first leg at Old Trafford and, as a City apprentice who would make his first-team debut later that season, he was at Bootham Crescent to watch the club complete the job, admitting the tie made a big impression on him.

Future club director Sophie McGill, then a teenage fan, celebrates the aggregate League Cup victory over Manchester United with fellow supporters

Nicky Peverell and Paul Barnes toast knocking Manchester United out of the League Cup

"It was a fantastic night and it inspired all of us, as young players," he said. "Graeme Murty (who played in the first leg) and Scott Jordan, who were a couple years older than us, were in the team and it made you think this is what I want to do. It was an amazing victory over two legs and will never be forgotten in the club's history. I was Steve Bushell's boot boy at the time and, after the Man United game, we were all hanging around in the corridor waiting outside the dressing rooms to see which players were coming out. I remember seeing Eric Cantona and it gave me a taste of what can happen in football. That team was a good side with the likes of Jon McCarthy, Paul Barnes, Dean Kiely and Andy McMillan in it. It was a team you could be proud of and what you always want at York City. There were two fast wingers and a centre forward, who didn't do too much outside the box but, if you gave him a chance or two every game, he would score you 20 goals a season."

For then six-year-old City fan Liam Wright, the night was also made all the more memorable as he enjoyed the honour of being the home side's mascot for the night. "I used to go on the Travel Club bus with my dad from the age of four onwards," he explained. "My first game was Stockport at home in 1993 and I went to Burnley for my first away game not long after, but I can't remember those matches. Because James Richardson, who ran the club shop at the time, knew how big a fan I was, he managed to swing it for me to be the mascot against United and, whilst I can't remember much about the game itself, I can remember the build-up and the celebrations at the end. I was only six at the time and I was definitely nervous, but more excited really. I remember walking into the changing room and it wasn't like when I was mascot again at Oldham away. There was no daft music blasting out or people joking around. It was a bit quiet and, whilst at Oldham they made a real fuss of me, there was none of that either. I couldn't really understand it at the time but, now, I obviously realise that it was the biggest game of their lives and they were totally focussed. I also clearly remember being stood in the tunnel with Colin Sanderson to my left as the players came back in from their warm-up and I'm kicking myself now because Cantona walked past me and put his thumb up, but I wasn't interested

433

in him. Andy Cole also went through and I just didn't care about all their superstars. I just wanted to see Nigel Pepper, because he was my all-time hero. I then remember leading the teams out with the referee and being on the pitch at the end with everybody else celebrating."

A sporting Bobby Charlton, meanwhile, maybe had the last word on the evening's seismic shock, conceding: "York did great." United's visit also coincided with the debut for a set of new dugouts at Bootham Crescent. They were supplied by Sutton-on-the-Forest company Minster Windows and hurriedly erected in the two weeks prior to the big match. Both were glazed with unbreakable polycarbonate with other fittings made from maintenance-free plastic. They replaced the old brick structures.

City were subsequently knocked out at QPR in the next round and the team went on to flirt with relegation, finishing one place above the drop zone with Kiely moving on to Bury at the end of the campaign.

He always retained a great love for his first home stadium due to its intimacy though. "I liked the fact that fans stood behind both goals because you felt connected with them," he explained. "It was great when the away end was full because you wanted to send them home disappointed. You could also build a rapport with supporters in the David Longhurst End and you got used to the familiar faces that stood in the same places every week. You wanted to send them home with a smile."

The team went on to struggle again in the league during the following season as the highlight was another League Cup giant-killing, again completed at Bootham Crescent, over an Everton team containing eight full internationals. It was the first and last occasion the Toffees played at Bootham Crescent. After Neil Tolson netted in a 1-1 first leg draw at Goodison Park, he also got the ball rolling during a 3-2 home triumph with Gary Bull and Murty joining him on the scoresheet in front of 7,854 fans.

During the opening exchanges, Gary Speed headed over for the Merseysiders before a 21-year-old Murty dragged an edge-of-the-box shot wide after exchanging passes with Bull. Neville Southall also gathered a 20-yard Adrian Randall drive, whilst Andrei Kanchelskis fired across the face of Warrington's goal. Everton then nudged themselves in front on 24 minutes when Joe Parkinson's poorly-struck long-range shot looped up off John Sharples and Paul Rideout volleyed past Warrington as the ball dropped to him eight yards out. But City levelled just before half-time when, following a poor punch by Southall, Randall raided through the left channel and sent in a low cross that was prodded in from seven yards by Tolson. Paul Stephenson went on to fire into the sidenetting and, at half-time, Everton introduced 17-year-old sub Michael Branch, who went close to putting the visitors back in front with a 25-yard effort that just floated over a beaten Warrington's crossbar. Tolson shot narrowly wide from a similar distance after bringing Pepper's raking forward pass down on his chest just before the hour mark and the hosts' second goal did arrive when a pinpoint pass out of defence by McMillan, who was enjoying an outstanding performance, sent Stephenson sprinting down the left wing. He then cut inside and curled

Graeme Murty scores against Everton legend Neville Southall during the League Cup victory in 1996

a shot against Southall's left-hand post with Bull following in to tap into the inviting net. Southall went on to parry a Pepper drive after he had been fed on the overlap by Murty's clever backheel.

Tolson's lob also narrowly missed the target with Southall stranded following another brilliant long pass by McMillan. Everton briefly rallied with a deflected Anders Limpar effort flashing just over, Speed's overhead kick bouncing wide and Kancheslskis dragging a chance off target. City had a third goal, though, with three minutes left on the clock when Stephenson lofted a high ball forward from his own half for Murty to chase. He brushed off England left-back Andy Hinchcliffe and then nudged the ball past an advancing Southall from just inside the penalty box. With City supporters chanting "We Want Four," Everton then grabbed a stoppage-time consolation when Speed diverted a mishit Branch shot past Warrington from six yards with his heel.

But City were deserved winners on the night with visiting boss Joe Royle admitting: "They played well, scored three goals and could have had more. They deserved it." Cheeky and derisory chants of "Are You Scarborough in Disguise?" belted out of the David Longhurst Stand, just as they had done 12 months earlier during the aggregate triumph over Manchester United and, for Warrington, beating the Toffees even eclipsed the previous heroics against the Red Devils. "I really, really enjoyed the Everton game, as I played in both legs and felt it was more of a personal achievement," he reasoned. "We went through on aggregate against Manchester United, but lost the game I played in and I think the Everton game meant a bit more for me." He also ensured that he did not miss out on a souvenir from the game this time around, revealing: "My hero was Neville Southall. When we played the first leg at Goodison, I remember being in the tunnel trying to focus on the game but all I was saying was: 'Can I have your shirt after the game?' I wasn't going to miss out on his and he said: 'Don't worry, we'll sort it out after the second leg'. I said: 'Don't forget' and he said: 'I won't, and I'll see you after the game'. We obviously went on to beat them and I knew he would want to get off the pitch as soon as possible, but I saw him after during the cool down and he gave me his shirt, which was great. It was my first bit of memorabilia from football and I still have it framed."

Pepper added that he believes the Everton match stands alone as the most complete team performance at Bootham Crescent during his seven years at the club. "Like the night we got to Wembley, Everton also jumps out for me as being special," he explained. "We should have had eight goals that night, because some of the football was brilliant against their full team. I struggle to remember a better performance by us at home and it was a special night in terms of how we played, the crowd reaction and everything. In my opinion, we did to them what Man United had done to us at our place the year before. We looked like the team from the higher league. Against Man United, we got through, but we took a tonking. Against Everton, we more than deserved what we got from the game. Everybody there will agree it was the right result and nobody could argue with the scoreline at the end."

Warrington also believed the triumphs over Manchester United and Everton were both inspired by the atmosphere generated by Bootham Crescent, adding: "The fans were close in and Premier League sides don't always relish coming to really tight, compact grounds that are full to the rafters. I remember there being benches down the side of the pitch with reporters on them, along with the lads who weren't in the matchday squad, because there weren't any spare seats in the ground. Anything that could be sat on was being used. You probably wouldn't be able to do it these days due to health and safety and, if a ground as small as Bootham Crescent is packed, then the atmosphere is fantastic. It was the same when I played for Rotherham at Millmoor and for Doncaster at Belle Vue and the atmosphere the night we played against Manchester United was brilliant." Hall also stressed the role Bootham Crescent played in inspiring the victory, reasoning: "The ground was quite compact and the fans being close to the pitch helped us because they were quite vocal and loud. It was another great night."

McMillan was named man of the match against Everton but revealed that he came really close to missing the game with an agonising neck problem that he hid from physio Jeff Miller and everybody else at the club. "I had done my neck in, but I sneaked off to the chiropractors in New Earswick on the day of the game, which I don't think Jeff knows to this day although he might have guessed there was something wrong by looking at me," McMillan explained. "I kept it quiet though and didn't tell anybody. The chiropractor had some wooden balls and was rubbing them on my neck with all sorts of other stuff, but I couldn't move it and felt physically sick. I was in so much pain and couldn't even drive properly because it was agony turning my head left and right. I told him I'd got a game that night. I didn't explain who I was, and he didn't know who it was against, but he said: 'There's no way you'll be able to play'. I thought: 'Of course. I'm going to play' but, when I got to the ground, I remember warming up and I still couldn't move my neck. It had properly locked and I thought I'm going to have to say something but, then, I looked around and thought: 'It's Everton, so no way. There's not a chance I'm going to miss this game' and, to be fair, it eased because the adrenalin's there and it gets you through or maybe the chiropractor had made it better and it loosened off by the time the game started. I ended up being man of the match and won a mountain bike. The prize had just changed from a television. I really enjoyed the game and it was probably one of the best I had for the club."

It was not the first time that he had hidden an injury at Bootham Crescent either. "I remember playing for six or seven weeks with a pulled groin," McMillan explained. "I used to sneak into the toilets with tape and wind it around my groin, then put my shorts back on. Nobody knew about it and I couldn't feel a thing because the tape was so tight. I would play and then hide back in the toilet afterwards to take it off and try to keep quiet, because obviously my hairs were all stuck to it. You did that because you just didn't want to miss games. You don't make nearly 500 appearances playing injury free. I don't think that's possible and, if you wanted to play, you just played with injuries. I didn't want to miss any games. I think I went on a run of 150 consecutive games (McMillan went 156 league fixtures without missing a match from October 1991 to March 1995). People rotate squads now but, if you had told me I was getting rested in the early 1990s, I would not have had it. If you thought you were playing well, there's no way you wanted resting - not a chance." He also reasoned that it was easier to hide injuries back then, during the less rigorous approach to pre-match warm-ups. "I used to be the last one to get changed 20 minutes before kick-off," he explained. "Up to then, I would be sat in my suit reading the programme. Then, I would just go out and run to the far side to sign a few autographs for the people who always want them. Then, I'd ping a

The goalscorers against Everton Graeme Murty, Gary Bull and Neil Tolson celebrate Bull's goal

few balls about with Ginner and Jon McCarthy and that was it. I think the long, structured and regimented warm-ups these days are sports science gone mad to be honest. I think players know themselves what they need to do before games."

The passage of time did not dim McMillan's recollections of the Everton tie either. He said: "I remember hitting a crossfield ball to Paul Stephenson and Stevo did his magic on the left wing but his shot hit the post and Gary Bull slid in to score. I always remember Graeme (Murty) sliding towards the David Longhurst Stand too with everyone piling on top of him after he scored. It's probably why he had back trouble later in his career! But it was a great night for him and that was your typical night game at Bootham Crescent. The place was rocking, and the ground played its part in those games. They were the best nights ever with a bit of dampness on the pitch, mist in the air and fans there who had been at work and were relieved to come and watch. It was so loud and, even just walking in before a game, was a great experience. I would get to the ground an hour-and-a-half or two hours before kick-off and there were people there already at that time. For games like that, there used to be more than a thousand people around two hours before a game and you could feed off that. Sometimes, it could take you an hour just to walk through the car park to the door after signing autographs and having a chat. I still saw some of the same faces 20 years later too, when I came back to the club as a coach."

McMillan pitted his wits against Swedish international and ex-Arsenal winger Limpar on the night and remembered an enjoyable duel, saying: "Andrei Kanchelskis made the occasional brief foray over and I was glad when he went back to the other flank, but Limpar had good quality. He wasn't a Kanchelskis or Giggs in terms of pace, but he had really tidy feet and could see a pass and use the ball well. It was a joy to play against him and he was really nice and complimentary after the game. There were links made after the game that I was supposed to be going to Everton, but it was just rumour again. That was never an issue for me though. I was quite happy at York and was enjoying myself." While McMillan had been happy to let fellow full-back Hall contend with Kanchelskis, the Fiorentina-bound Russian international had a strange request on the night. "Andrei Kanchelskis was like lightning but, 10 or 15 minutes into the game, he came up to me and asked me not to kick him because he thought he was leaving and he did end up going to Italy a few weeks later," Hall revealed. "I wouldn't say I went out to kick anybody anyway. I always tried to compete fairly and, when he came near me, I still went for the ball. I can't remember him beating me to any challenges, but I made sure I didn't get too tight to him because I knew, if he spun past me, his speed was frightening."

Guy Mowbray commented on both the Manchester United and Everton ties, as his talents were beginning to be recognised by the local radio stations. "I did a little bit of stuff for Radio York at the time of those games but, back then, Barry Parker was so well-ingrained as the York City commentator that I mainly did the occasional Scarborough game and York Wasps rugby league match," he explained. "I did cover the Everton and Manchester United games, though, at Bootham Crescent as Minster FM's sports editor and they were fantastic nights. I remember being in the corridor waiting for interviews after the Manchester United game and it was a bit surreal because the Premier League had really taken off by then and people like Eric Cantona and Peter Schmeichel had become really famous, but here they were in the tunnel at Bootham Crescent having got knocked out of the Cup on aggregate. I also remember the celebrations after the Everton game, which we deserved to win. I was working with Ivan Ash and remember his bit of commentary when Graeme Murty scored. He compared him to Sonic the Hedgehog! Afterwards, I asked Graeme what he could remember about the goal and he said he could remember every step. He said he was thinking: 'Oh, there's England's left-back Andy Hinchcliffe and I've just gone past him' and then: 'Oh, it's Neville Southall, one of the world's top goalkeepers, and I've just scored past him!'"

Recalling the decisive goal and another giant-killing, Little added: "I remember Graeme Murty breaking through from the middle of the park and it was a great finish. I think Everton were going through a lean patch at the time and it was a good time to meet them (following an opening day victory over Newcastle, the Toffees had failed to win any of their next seven matches). Our pitch could also be difficult at times and the open away end wasn't nice for visiting fans, so they weren't always in the mood to get behind their team. Our fans made the atmosphere at those games something special, though, under the lights and everybody was excited." Pepper felt the tie provided the springboard for Murty to go on and enjoy a distinguished career that would see him play Premier League and international football. "I know Graeme Murty went on to do good stuff but, for me, when you look back at his York career, that was the game that defined him," he reasoned. "It wasn't just his goal that night, it was the way he played, because he was brilliant all game against top-quality players. He showed his own quality and it was the catalyst for him to go on and do what he did. I think it made everyone take notice because it was against a team like Everton, rather than Darlington or somebody - no disrespect. He was head and shoulders above everyone that night and it was a huge platform for him to go on and do well."

Mowbray, by then, had also become a regular victim of one of the club's biggest pranksters of that era, recalling: "I used to be sat at the back of the Main Stand and Nigel Pepper would try to knock my phone off the desk during the warm-up. He was remarkably accurate, and I would often catch it or head it back but, sometimes, when I wasn't looking, he'd catch me off guard and hit me." Cresswell, who had played in the first leg at Goodison, was an unused substitute for the return match, but was still wrapped up in the victory. "I was itching to get on, but it was a tight game and I was a young kid. It was another great night and there were never really any like that there again," he reasoned.

The following month, Bootham Crescent bore witness to two of English football's future stars when Michael Owen and Rio Ferdinand played for England under-18s in a Sunday afternoon international against Northern Ireland. Both were virtual unknowns at the time but Owen, who was just 16 and on the front cover of the programme, made a big impression, less than two years before playing for his country at the World Cup finals, by scoring all the goals in a 4-0 win. Future stellar centre-back Ferdinand was also reported as "assuming control of the midfield".

The celebrations begin after knocking Everton out of the League Cup in 1996

Ferdinand sent Owen sprinting clear for his first goal just two minutes in, with the then Liverpool youth-team striker rounding Irish keeper Glynn Clyde to open his account. Moments later, he drove a left-footed effort high into the roof of the net for a sparkling second goal. Eight minutes after the break, he then sharply flicked in a Mark Perry header for his hat-trick and, after Northern Ireland's future all-time record goalscorer David Healy saw a 64th-minute penalty saved by Luke Weaver, Owen converted a spot kick of his own after being tripped.

A crowd of 842 had witnessed one of England's brightest stars in the making and, afterwards, purring under-18 national coach Dave Burnside hailed Owen's display, declaring: "You don't often see genius but, if you look at his record from under-16 through to this level, he is the most prolific goalscorer in international football. He is one of the most exciting forward talents I have ever worked with." McMillan was among the fans at the game, adding: "It was a really good coup for the club to get that match. I remember walking to the ground and sitting there watching and thinking these aren't bad. I remember a kid scoring four goals but didn't even realise, until this interview, that it was Michael Owen. I was just going to the club to watch football because I loved the game, but I remember watching him and thinking he's decent."

Scholar Cresswell was in the crowd again to see Owen's striking masterclass but, as an aspiring forward himself, insisted he wasn't daunted by the standards needed to become one of the country's top attackers. "I went to watch that game and he was unplayable - absolutely rapid," Cresswell recalled. "I remember everyone speaking about him in the stand. He was absolutely tiny, but everyone was saying: 'He's going to be the next England forward', which he was a couple of years later. With his pace, nobody could get near him, but I wasn't intimidated by how good he was at that age. I actually thought, deep down, that I can do that, because I was very single-minded." FA chief executive Graham Kelly, meanwhile, praised Bootham Crescent's staging of the match, saying: "It's a lovely playing surface, while the ground administration has meant we have been very well looked after."

As an example of how driven he was as an apprentice, meanwhile, Cresswell revealed how he and fellow youth-team player Jonathan Greening, who would go on to win a Champions League winners' medal with Manchester United in 1999, would put in the extra hours at Bootham Crescent during the evenings. "To make it at any level, you need to have that passion for the ball and, on a night-time, me and Jonno would be playing head tennis against each other in the gym and wanting to kill each other," he laughed. "So, is it coincidence that we went on to have decent careers? We were getting two hours' extra training without even knowing about it. It was a bit of fun, but there was also plenty of banter and arguing. Whoever lost sometimes wouldn't speak to the other person for a day or two and we were doing that off our own backs. I don't know whether kids would do that now. Maybe they wouldn't be allowed because of health and safety." Cresswell also added that he was learning valuable life skills under youth-team coach Ricky Sbragia. "EPPP brought in rules that meant the scholars weren't allowed to do jobs anymore, which I think is absolutely disgusting because kids come to clubs and don't know how to lift a brush," he bemoaned. "At 16 and 17, I was head boy and kit man. I had to oversee everyone and, if somebody hadn't done one job right, Ricky would come for me. He used to get a coin and scrape it along the bath and say: 'Do it all again'. He would be looking for any bit of grime and he'd put his finger across door frames as well, but I can see why he did it. He was making the point that your standards had to be high in everything you did. He was trying to give us responsibility. At 16-years-old, I had to pack the first-team kit every week after I'd washed it. I'd be doing that every Monday after training with a first-year scholar, because there was no kitman back then. It made me nervous every week, but that was good, because it meant I made sure I never made a mistake with the kit. I'd be there until about 6.30pm before going home to our digs just around the corner. On match days, I'd then put the kit out and roll the socks up, while (physio) Jeff (Miller) went through his checklist with me. You can't imagine that happening now and we also painted the boot room and cleaned it out and swept the stands as well. Now, kids can clean boots, but only if they want to. The FA have taken all that responsibility away. They argue it's just cheap labour, but we were learning to grow up quickly in a tough environment."

In July 1997, loyal-servant Tutill's testimonial against Middlesbrough went on to draw a crowd of 7,123, with visiting boss Bryan Robson handing £4.5 million summer signing and England international Paul Merson his first outing for the club. The game ended even after an eight-goal thriller with Tolson, Cresswell, Rodney Rowe and a guesting Barnes on target for City, while Danish international Mikkel Beck (two), former Manchester United left-back Clayton Blackmore and Craig Hignett replied for Boro. Having received in the region of £31,000 from his testimonial, Tutill moved to Darlington early in the following campaign, which would also see promising youngsters Greening and Murty move on to Manchester United and Reading respectively. Pepper left for Bradford, meanwhile, at the end of the 1996/97 campaign, but not before marking his farewell Bootham Crescent appearance with a goal that he now admits was a fluke in a 3-1 victory over Preston. "I knew I would be leaving by then and it was a strange time, but I don't want to say too much about that," he said. "Some things had been said and a few clubs showed an interest in me. I claimed my goal against Preston was a great diagonal chip into the top corner, but I had actually tried to smash my shot and the ball clipped the defender's foot before sailing over Bobby Mimms, who was the keeper. I knew him from when I was at Rotherham and he was hammering me, saying I couldn't claim that."

Pepper moved on feeling that the club were starting to slide backwards, as a result of past player sales, while team spirit at Bootham Crescent had also deteriorated. "When we were doing well, we used to go out and drink together on our Wednesdays off or played golf together," he pointed out. "We were a real team. That's why we did well, and I think we could have gone on to achieve more if the club had invested just a little bit, instead of letting people like Paul Barnes and Dean Kiely go. It wouldn't have taken a fortune and that team could definitely have gone again. A lot of us went on to play at a high level and did well, so I believe we could have played in the Championship for York and that would have been special. It was time for me to move on when I did though. A couple of bigger clubs had come in for me, but I would have stayed, without a shadow of doubt, if the club had looked to press on. If you get rid of Paul Barnes, you have to bring another Paul Barnes in, or you're not going to keep moving forward. The same applied with players like Dean Kiely and Jon McCarthy. If you keep those three and myself, we had a good nucleus and there were players still there, who were good, solid professionals, like Wayne Hall and Andy McMillan. Every club I went to, including Bradford and Aberdeen, I used to tell them Andy Mac was one of the best footballers I had ever played with. I told them he was one of the fittest lads and best passers of a ball I had ever seen. He also had pace and just needed a little bit of a nasty streak - maybe a little bit of what I'd got - then I think he could have gone right to the top and played for England. He was that good. If I had been a newspaper reporter, I would put him down for 8/10 every week, because you knew he would never let you down. He was somebody you would always want in your team as a manager."

Pepper's ties to Bootham Crescent were never severed though and, in later life, he was a regular at the ground in a work scheme that helped rehabilitate young offenders. On the important role the ground played in that process, Pepper said: "A lot of kids I work with have got nothing constructive in their lives but, after taking them to Bootham Crescent, which was a punishment because they had to pick up litter after watching the games, you would be surprised by how many got a little buzz and wanted to play football or get involved. They would go off and try and join a club or we would try and get them fixed up with some training, so they were doing that instead of hanging around car parks and streets getting up to no good. Some were York City fans but didn't go to watch them because they might not have been able to afford to, so it was great to let them experience seeing their side live. They were going to work but watching their team as well. There were also lads who had never been and, for the first game they went to, they would just sit there with their heads down but, three or four games in, they would be jumping up when York scored. It was a fantastic project. The McGill family and York City were brilliant helping to set that up for us and we did it for about six or seven years. The scheme was finished because of council cuts, which was a real shame as it helped massively with their rehabilitation. It also amounted to thousands of hours of community service completed. I'd like to think it could be revived because it was cost effective too. I used to take six kids at a time and, if you worked the hours out, it was more worthwhile than a lot of the stuff we do."

Cresswell, meanwhile, scored his first goal at Bootham Crescent during a 2-1 defeat against Luton in November 1997, having failed to net in his first 25 home games. During that period, he had been loaned out to Mansfield and the young striker, who would go on to join Sheffield Wednesday for a club record fee of £950,000, confessed the going had been tough at times in an unforgiving home arena. "It wasn't all sunshine and roses," he explained. "When you first get in the team, you go through some rough spells and you have to get over those speed bumps. It all went well at first, but then the team started struggling a bit and the lads got a bit of stick and I took some too. If you gave the ball away, for example, how are you going to react when somebody is booing you, shouting at you or telling you that you're rubbish or something less polite? You need to have mental strength to deal with that and it's all about how you come back from adversity. The experienced players and Alan Little helped me through it. He handled that very well, because he would put me in and then take me out for a bit and put me on the bench. I also ended up going on loan to Mansfield in the division below to get my confidence back. I was quite selfish and driven and, when I returned, I thought I'm going to prove you wrong. Scoring was a good feeling and it was always the dream to get my first goal at Bootham Crescent in front of the Longhurst. I remember it going in - and it was a good finish to be fair - but then thinking: 'How do I celebrate?' I'd already scored away, but getting the first one at home is still a big thing. There was no better feeling to have that adrenalin rush at 20 and I still crave it now because it's fantastic and it was great the following season when I got 19 goals."

Marco Gabbiadini, meanwhile, had suffered few problems finding the net since leaving Bootham Crescent a decade earlier but, after returning to his first club and making a second City debut during a 1-1 home draw with eventual champions Watford in February 1998, he couldn't hit the target in front of the Minstermen faithful during his homecoming and was released at the end of the season, before going on to plunder more than 50 goals for Darlington over the next two campaigns and 91 more in total before retiring. Explaining the reasons behind his struggles, Gabbiadini said: "York were doing quite well, but it was a strange time for me. I had suffered some injuries and, after leaving Derby, I'd had a spell in Greece, then had a bad experience with Chris Kamara when he was manager at Stoke, so I was at a bit of a low point even though I was quite fit. I got injured in my first game back, which was really disappointing because I had been having a really good game. It was against Watford, who were flying in the league, but we drew 1-1 and I won the penalty that Tony Barras scored by getting brought down. But I got kicked in the second half and I was never right after that, so it spoiled my time back at the club. I also remember getting my teeth smashed in at Bootham Crescent. I was on all fours looking for them. I looked like Sylvester the Cat in the cartoon and I was thinking: 'Oh, my god, this is just getting worse'. It wasn't a particularly happy time, and Alan Little thought I had come to the club with the injury. He didn't speak to me until the end of the season, which left a bit of a sour taste and I ended up at Darlington. Coming back to York would have been ideal and I was quite excited by the prospect of coming back to my home-town club, so it's a shame it didn't work out, because it still felt like home. The roof had gone up on the home end and that made a difference, but part of the charm of Bootham Crescent was you went back there and not much had changed. I even went back before the club moved to the new stadium and took a picture of sunset over the Popular Stand."

Gabbiadini also noticed the potential of some of the young players beginning to break through at Bootham Crescent during his brief second spell with the Minstermen. "There were some good players at the club back then," he pointed out. "Graeme Murty had established himself and Jonathan Greening and Richard Cresswell were coming through as well. I still see them quite often and Jonno says to me: 'You used to scare me'. I think it was because I was 30 and I had played quite a lot of football. He was a bit wary, but I hope that was

An aerial shot of Bootham Crescent in May 1998

in a positive way and because he was in awe of me maybe, because they both went on and had terrific careers. You could see they were quite decent then and people were already talking about them."

In March 1998, for the first time, fourth officials displayed the number of minutes that would be added on at the end of each half on an electronic board, acting on the instructions of the referee. Manager Little was then granted a testimonial that July after six seasons at the helm. It was against a Middlesbrough team including England legend Paul Gascoigne and attracted a 6,215 crowd. Gazza, just weeks after being left out of England's World Cup finals squad, played the entire first half, with former City favourites Barnes and McCarthy returning to play for City on the night.

In a 3-1 away win, Cresswell's header beat Australian international keeper Mark Schwarzer to cancel out Neil Campbell's early goal. Campbell and Colombian striker Hamilton Ricard went on to seal victory.

Warrington was in the City side that day and recalled: "Gazza wanted to try and score past me from the halfway line, but he didn't manage it." On the England great's visit, Hall added: "Gazza was just barmy and a cracking

Scott Jordan gets ready to replace City's number eight with physio Jeff Miller ready to signal the substitution three years before the advent of the electronic board in 1998

England legend Paul Gascoigne mesmerises City midfielder Steve Agnew with his mercurial footwork during Alan Little's testimonial in 1998

lad. My son needed an Achilles operation when he was younger, and Gazza signed a Get Well Soon card for him after I'd mentioned it before the game. Nothing was too much bother for him and I remember him having a right laugh with Andy Warrington. He said he was going to chip him from the halfway line and Andy never left his goal-line after that. There was another occasion where he was near the corner flag with two or three players around him, but he came out with the ball laughing because that's how good he was."

On facing the 1990s' icon, then fledgling forward Cresswell said: "He was unbelievable and such a character. I can't remember him getting up to any antics, but it was great to be on the same pitch with such a great player. He would talk to you all the time on the pitch, saying things like: 'Well done, kid, keep going'. He was such a positive man and a genius on the ball. I thought the way he used to protect the ball with his arms was great as well. He used to hand people off like a rugby player, whilst he was running with the ball and I've never seen anybody else do that. It was perfectly legal. It wasn't a foul and he used his arms better than anybody I've ever seen, because nobody could get the ball off him." Little, meanwhile, was touched by the big attendance, adding: "It was a nice day and a reward for the service I had given. I gave the club everything I had every day I was there, and it was great for me to see such a good crowd come out."

447

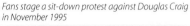

Fans stage a sit-down protest against Douglas Craig in November 1995

Alan Little sits among the rubble after the wall in front of the Main Stand had been knocked down following the 1994 play-off defeat to Stockport with seats set to be installed in the Enclosure section. Despite how it appears, the renowned football hard man had not acted in frustration and battered it down with his own hands. It also meant local cup finals could not be played at the ground that year

Alan Little squats inside a hot-air tunnel designed to thaw out the pitch

York City commercial assistant James Richardson and Dinah Smith at the opening of the refurbished club shop in April 1997

A view from the corner of the Popular Stand in May 1998

CHAPTER 27

Andy Dawson bags winner against Manchester City

"I'm going to sit and watch you parade around Bootham Crescent in a pair of shorts with a tail hanging out of your backside."

The 1998/99 season would prove to be City's last as a third-tier outfit at Bootham Crescent as the club were relegated, even if the team still continued the trend of defeating fallen giants at their home stadium, as 7,527 turned up to see goals from Gordon Connelly and Andy Dawson defeat Manchester City 2-1. Debutant Dawson had come on as a substitute and won the game with his first kick in professional football on 84 minutes.

Earlier, it had taken the hosts just 82 seconds to forge in front when Martin Garratt freed Richard Cresswell and his low cross was missed by Neil Tolson but slammed in from 15 yards by Connelly. The visitors levelled just past the half-hour mark in fortunate circumstances when Craig Russell's speculative shot from way out on the left looped over Bobby Mimms after clipping the shinpad of Tony Barras. But Dawson had the final say. Accepting a shrewd pass from fellow sub Rodney Rowe, he curved a 15-yard shot around a defender and beyond keeper Nicky Weaver.

Two decades later, home-grown talent Dawson, born in Strensall, still remembered every second of the day, including the build-up for a game that seemed more important than the average league fixture. "We were treated to a pre-match meal at the Jarvis A19 Hotel, which was unusual," he recalled. "It was like we were treating the match as a special occasion. At that point, the team had not been announced and it was only on arrival at the ground that I was told I had made the bench. It was very noticeable, before the game, that lots more people were around Bootham. Both sets of fans were very vocal throughout the match and there was a different buzz in the air. I was performing consistently well in the reserves and that had got me on the bench on numerous occasions for the first team in that season, including the very first game. I remember the first-team coach Derek Bell and manager Alan Little making quite a fuss that I had made the bench, but I still thought it to be another occasion I would not get on. I was not particularly nervous, as I thought I would probably not make an appearance as there were other players on the bench that were normally used in front of me." Dawson's memories of the events that unfurled, as he watched from the dugout were just as vivid. "The first half was end-to-end, but York appeared to dominate the opening minutes," he said. "Martin Garratt was playing well in midfield and Richard Cresswell was very busy. We went ahead 1-0 with a goal from Gordon Connelly and, from thereon, it was quite open. Man City got a deflected cross in over Bobby Mimms, but neither team dominated the second half and the game could have gone either way."

As the game entered its final throes, Dawson got his surprise call from manager Little, leading to a bout of butterflies. "Gordon Connelly got a knock and he couldn't shake it, so I replaced him," Dawson said of the moment he was summoned for his senior debut. "Alan told me to warm up as I was going on for Gordon and then I got nervous. I also didn't expect to play right wing, as I only ever played right back - even in the reserves. The only instruction I got was to do what I did in the reserves and to run my socks off for the rest of the game. It was definitely a mixture of nerves and excitement when I got on and I felt tired after my first run, as I had used up a lot of nervous energy." Of the moments leading up to the goal that secured his place in Bootham Crescent folklore,

meanwhile, Dawson admitted he might easily have been a villain rather than a hero. "I remember my first involvement was to defend a Man City corner where the person I was marking almost scored from a header," he said. "It just went wide, and I thought I better buck my ideas up. From the resulting goal kick, we worked our way up the pitch on the break where we won a throw in the Man City half. I remember making a 60-yard sprint

Andy Dawson gets mobbed after scoring the winning goal against Manchester City with his first kick in professional football

to support Cres and Rodney (Rowe). I shouted Cres to ask for the ball. He ignored me and threw it to Rodney who held the ball up on the edge of the six-yard box. I remember me and Cres made the same run, but I was just in front. Rodney then laid the ball off and it fell to me more favourably and I remember thinking, as I was being closed down, don't smash it - just hit the target. It was my first touch in professional football and I deliberately side-footed it into the far corner with my left foot. Nicky Weaver did get a fingertip to it and I didn't see it hit the back of the net as I had already turned to celebrate."

On the reaction of his team-mates and the City supporters to his goal, Dawson enthused: "I ran off and Martin Garratt was first to get hold of me and shouted a few expletives. Then, everyone piled on. After they got off me, I looked for my parents in the Main Stand. I didn't spot them but waved anyway. My brother was also in the Longhurst with his mates. I was very aware of the crowd going crazy and it did not calm down for the rest of the game. Any contribution I made, I was being cheered. At the end of the game, I felt a mixture of excitement and relief. Relieved to have finally made my debut and over-excitement at what we had just achieved. I was trying to calm down, but the adrenalin was set in. There was a lot of singing in the dressing room afterwards and everyone involved came up and congratulated me with a ruffle of the hair. I remember laying in the team bath by myself and being the last person out of the changing room. I went straight from the dressing room for an interview with Chris Kamara, who was there doing a special for Sky Sports on Cres. That was followed by a few radio interviews and a press interview with Alan Little just outside the dug out." Dawson's celebrations carried on well into the evening with the full-back recalling: "To celebrate that night, I went to a restaurant in the city with my mates and was recognised by a number of Man City fans. They came over and, whilst I was worried I was in for a spot of trouble, they actually shouted me and my mates to a couple of rounds of drinks. I had numerous conversations that evening and met lots of people who wanted to talk about the game."

The result is often referred to as the nadir and lowest point in the Manchester club's history when placed in context with their current standing as one of the world's wealthiest and this country's most-successful clubs. That recognition is something Dawson still enjoys, saying: "It always seems to get a mention as a pivotal moment in Man City's history and I'm proud of that. Even living in Australia now, the match crops up from time to time, especially given where Man City are now." Dawson would only go on to play another 31 times for his home-town club, but retained a fondness for Bootham Crescent, saying: "The playing surface was great. I always looked forward to playing as you could play some good football on that surface. The fans were always good for a song as well and could be heard all around the ground. You were close enough to them to hear all comments too - good and bad. It was a great club to be a part of and, as a kid, I always had a great sense of pride in being able to represent my home town. I will always remember my times there and especially my professional appearances. I could probably recall something about every game I played in at Bootham Crescent."

The Manchester City game would prove loyal servant McMillan's final win at Bootham Crescent and he remembered the occasion well, saying: "That was unbelievable. I remember thinking why the hell are Man City in this league. They had a phenomenal following. They packed out the away end and I think they were in the David Longhurst Stand as well. They took over everywhere, but it was one of those days when everything clicked into place for us. We weren't expected to win, because we were at the wrong end of the table, but it was another one of those good days at the club. Andy Dawson was that daft he probably didn't realise he had scored himself. But he was a good, young lad who wanted to listen and learn, and he should probably have gone on to play more games than he did."

Recalling the victory over a club that his family had strong ties to, the previous conqueror of the visitors' cross-city neighbours Scott Jordan added: "It was a good, hard game and they were a strong side who shouldn't have been in that division. My cousin Stephen Jordan went on to play for Manchester City and my dad supported them, so it was a big thing for him to see me playing against them. I remember the pitch not being the greatest at the time and there wasn't much grass on it, so there wasn't much football played but we always felt we could beat anybody at home and it was often the easier teams we slipped up against." Jordan was not surprised, meanwhile, by Dawson's emergence as an unlikely match-winner, explaining: "You don't always realise it's a player's debut because you train with them every day and might have played in the reserves with them too so, when they come into the first team, you just expect them to get on with it. You have faith that the manager wouldn't just take a risk and throw anyone in and that they believed whoever played would be good enough." Cresswell had fond memories of the game too. "I remember Andy Dawson scoring that goal," he said. "He cut inside with his left foot and scored on his debut. It was his only ever career goal but not a bad one - to get the winner against Manchester City."

But, while the Manchester club would go on to win promotion through the play-offs, a run of five straight defeats at home would send the Minstermen tumbling down the table and Little was relieved of his duties with player-coach Neil Thompson taking over. Cresswell, by then an England under-21 international, also left for Sheffield Wednesday with his last game a 3-1 home loss to Wigan in mid-March. He had scored 19 goals by that point, having struggled to hit the target

Richard Cresswell in action during the 1998 victory over Manchester City

in previous campaigns and his form had seen scouts from the highest divisions regularly converge on Bootham Crescent. On that experience, Cresswell added: "I scored twice against Luton and that game stands out because they were two really good goals. The speculation started then, and I heard about Leeds, Middlesbrough and Manchester United all being interested. It becomes quite hard then concentrating on your game because you're thinking what's happening and where am I going? But, then, Sheffield Wednesday came in, who were doing very well at the time in the Premier League. I didn't know I was leaving when I played against Wigan and, after the game, I was picked up in a car to go and play for England under 21s. I ended up leaving on deadline day - March 23 - and Sheffield Wednesday's physio was also England's, so that helped get the deal done by fax in the hotel. When I left, I thought I was leaving a good, steady League One club. The board and fans might have lost sight of where the club should be and maybe felt we should always be up near the play-offs in that division, but the timing of Alan's sacking proved to be the wrong decision. I can remember being really disappointed when he lost his job. We were going through a bit of a tough patch, but we were never near the bottom. I felt it was a knee-jerk reaction and I remember thinking that's so unfair. I had one game after and then left. I thought, at the time, his sacking was a big mistake and I watched the results come in every week after I had left. I went on to score the winner against Liverpool for Sheffield Wednesday at the end of the season and, then, came in after the game and heard that York had been relegated and I was devastated. Everyone was asking me what was wrong because they thought I'd be elated after the game, so I had to explain to them."

Little remained the longest-serving manager at Bootham Crescent since Tom Johnston left for Huddersfield in 1975 but admitted he did feel on borrowed time before he was told his fate. "The team had taken two points from 10 games, so I felt the writing was on the wall," he reasoned. "I still hoped the York directors might show me some loyalty and that would see me through, but I was called into the boardroom, where all the directors were and the chairman (Douglas Craig) said what he had to. I then stood up and shook all their hands and said that I had nothing but respect for them. I knew my time was up and I had enjoyed working for them. They had been good to me and there was no suggestion of what would happen with the chairman a few years later. I still have great memories of my time at the club and, when my daughter got married in York a few years ago, myself and Derek Bell came away from the reception and walked down to have a look at Bootham Crescent, but the place was all locked up. It was a great place that felt like home. It was comfortable and a nice, tidy place to be. There was also a lot of spirit in that Main Stand, which you are closest to as manager." Nor was the drama during Little's reign limited to the football pitch and boardroom. "When I was manager at York, I always said that my door was open to anybody who wanted to come in for a chat and I remember one day a mother turned up with her daughter and a baby in the back of the car, insisting that the baby belonged to one of my players," he recalled. "I asked her who it might be, and he was single at the time, but I spoke to him in my office and it eventually petered out into nothing and was all sorted. The lad did look a little shook up and sheepish for a few weeks afterwards though."

The Wigan game - McMillan's 492nd for the club - also unexpectedly proved his last following a subsequent fall-out with Thompson and Craig, who threatened to withhold his registration as a player the following season even though it was clear the manager wasn't going to select him. "I didn't think it would be my last game at all," McMillan reflected on the Wigan defeat. "I felt pain in the back of my knee and didn't feel right at half-time, but I never thought I would then have the fall-out I had with Thompson. The lad stayed at my house and we drove into training together and we used to talk about players not thinking he would get the job. Next minute, he's the manager and he stabs me in the back, which was very hurtful. He was somebody I thought I could trust, but all the time he was plotting my exit out of the club and that was disappointing. I've seen him on a few occasions since and not spoken to him. I won't do until he apologises. There are ways of doing things. I had been at the club for 13 years. I thought maybe he saw me as a threat. I remember being sat in the stand and the fans were singing for him to go and for me to play, so I think he had to find a way of getting me out. Douglas Craig was out of order as well. He didn't need to do what he did. I never gave him any issues. Every time the club offered me a contract, I signed it. Never once did I say I'm not signing that. I never argued about wages or appearance money. Then, all of a sudden, one man changes his whole opinion of you. I had spent so long somewhere that I never wanted to leave and had shown loyalty. Maybe you expect to get it back but, at the time, there was none. It was bitterly disappointing what happened and the way it happened. I wouldn't wish it on anybody. I understand it's only a game of football, but it was also my livelihood and he was taking money off me that I needed to pay my mortgage. I didn't think the way they did it was necessary, and it left a bitter taste in my mouth. There was no need for him to threaten me with never playing football again and that, if I stayed, he would make my life incredibly difficult. He's shown his true colours ever since and he could have killed the club. He and a number of those on his board certainly gave it a good go."

Craig and Thompson's belligerence meant, at the age of 30, McMillan remained the player who racked up the second-highest number of games at Bootham Crescent, falling 47 appearances short of Barry Jackson's record in all matches. That still rankled with the South African-born defender, who argued: "I think I should have got the record. I went up to Scotland to play for Ayr and should never have gone. I knew Neil was never going to last with the style of football he wanted to play and the players he was getting in. No disrespect to them, but they weren't footballers. They were big lads. He didn't think you had to play football at that level. I retired after going up to Scotland because my heart wasn't in it any more. What happened killed my enthusiasm for the game. I didn't touch a football for a year or two. I then played a couple of games for Pickering, but I was wasting my time. I wasn't enjoying it. I felt I could have played for another three seasons and wanted to get past the record, create a new one and then start coaching at the club and work my way up, but I had to leave before eventually going back."

Manchester City would also get their revenge with a final-day 4-0 defeat at Maine Road, in front of a crowd of 32,471, sending the club down and bringing an end to the longest-ever sequence of consecutive seasons in the third tier following the six-campaign stretch. Paul Emblen's 83rd-minute goal for Wycombe at Lincoln saw the Minstermen drop into the relegation zone for the first time that season and the club went down on goal difference. A 1-0 defeat to Bournemouth at Bootham Crescent the week before, with James Hayter on target, had been just as instrumental in City's downfall after seven points from a possible nine at home looked to have secured a position of safety. Dawson admitted there was a feeling of shock at the club for many weeks afterwards, saying: "We had got some decent results at home towards the end of the season that we maybe didn't expect, with wins against Millwall and Blackpool, as well as a draw against Stoke. I was in the starting line-up quite regularly and those results, and the way we played, made us feel that we were going to escape the drop. It actually felt that we could win every game. Even though we went to Man City last game and lost, we still thought we would be safe from relegation, but it was Wycombe's late goal that sent us down on goal difference and everyone was completely gutted."

City have never managed to reach the same level again and McMillan reasoned that his Bootham Crescent nemesis ought to carry the can for that late-season slump, saying: "It was poor and Thompson has to take a lot of blame for that because we weren't in the bottom four all season, although Alan had probably seen out his time at the club too because, sometimes, it's best to walk away."

Whilst it was the end of one era, though, a new chapter was beginning in lifelong fan Steve Ovenden's matchday experience at Bootham Crescent. Costumed mascots were just starting to become an integral feature in stadia across the country and then magistrate Ovenden donned Yorkie The Lion's outfit for six years after approaching the club with details of how he would tackle the job if he ever got the chance. It did not take long for that opportunity to materialise, as Ovenden recalled: "The first mascot was called Shippo and a woman called Sarah (Pullon) did it, but I'd been writing silly letters to the club for quite a while about what I felt the mascot should be doing after watching them at other clubs. I was invited in for a chat and was told the job was mine. It was May 1999 when I made my debut during the last home game of the season. It was a big match and they wanted the mascot involved. We lost 1-0 against Bournemouth and, if we'd have won that match, we'd have stayed up. I had to wait a while for a suit that was made to measure, though, so the one I wore for that first game was held together by safety pins when I put it on. Later, Nestle paid for and sponsored a new costume. The chocolate factory was very supportive back then, before they became more national orientated. It was branded and that's why the mascot's name changed from Shippo to Yorkie. I used to throw chocolate bars into the crowd until somebody said you might injure people, but we were never throwing them like a javelin. It was always underarm, and we'd lean over the barrier of the Shippo, but it was stopped because somebody might complain."

For Ovenden, it was a real thrill to be wearing the colours of his team on the hallowed turf that he had seen so many of his heroes tread during the past 20 years. He added: "I'd been a City fan since the 1977/78 season when I first started going with my uncle. When I was a boy, my football team used to get knocked out in the semi-finals when the finals were held at Bootham Crescent. Then, during the two years we got to the final, it wasn't hosted at Bootham Crescent, which meant I had never played there so, to put the kit on, albeit dressed as a lion, lead the team out and be the first on the pitch to hear the crowd go mad was out of this world and I was doing it every other Saturday. I was only going to do it for one game, but it was really good, so I decided I wanted to do it the next season. The next match was Swansea at home and it was a sunny day, so it was sweltering in the costume. Roger Freestone was in goal for them and he was the keeper for Wales at the time, but I messed about with him and had a chat a couple of minutes before kick-off, as you could back then. One minute I was watching these players from the stand and the next minute I was part of it and that was mint. I was running out with them and kicking a ball about at Bootham Crescent and that was the stuff of dreams for me. It started as a joke to begin with but, once I was in that moment and celebrating wins with the managers at the final whistle, after 20 years of supporting the club, I loved it. I also enjoyed the interaction with kids. They thought I was magical if they were under seven or eight, or they wanted to punch and kick you or try and take your head off when they got a bit older."

Like any childhood City fan, Ovenden had his own unique memories of what Bootham Crescent meant to him during his formative years and later on. "My uncle used to take me when I was seven or eight and we used to cycle to games with the commercial manager Maureen Leslie's husband Gerald," he explained. "We weren't really typical football supporters. I was there with two 60-year-old men and Gerald used to bike along with a cravat on. At half-time, the tea would come out, but it wasn't just drunk out of a flask and plastic cups. He would get the China out and pour it for us in the front row of the Main Stand. My uncle used to say: 'What do we look like with him?' But what a man he was and they're such happy times when you're a kid. I did that right up to my 20s and it was a real family experience. We'd bike down and have a pint in the Social Club before the game and Gerald would carry the China on his bike - I don't know how he did that. He then left it for Maureen to take home in her car, because we went to the Working Men's Club over the road for a few pints before biking home. We had some real laughs and I don't think that kind of thing happens now at modern grounds. You won't be able to replicate a night at Bootham Crescent with the lights on and trees and houses in the background either and, even though I appreciate it was time for a change, it was just a magical place."

Explaining his typical matchday routine as Yorkie, Ovenden added: "I would get to the ground at about 1.30pm and be in my kit for 2, then do a bit in the car park, which was another unique thing about Bootham Crescent. You weren't just walking around concrete blocks there, like you do at Scunthorpe and other places. I would be in the car park, near the gates, kind of encouraging people to go into the club shop, but never in a pushy way. I'd just wave at people for half-an-hour, then go into the tunnel, take my head off for a breather and have a drink. I'd then take the mascot for the day onto the pitch at about 2.30pm and we'd kick a ball about with a player, whilst I'd also try and gee the crowd up and walk all the way around the pitch, shaking hands and having my picture taken. Then, the referee would blow his whistle and a lot of them used to give the kid the pound coin they used for the toss-up. I shook hands with all of the captains as Yorkie, even people like Roy Keane. Well, he shook my paw. I used to go back in the tunnel at 2.50pm and have a little chat with the mascot and, then, the referee would press the buzzer and the players would come into the tunnel. I'd be stood there at the front with the kid and, sometimes, teams would be swearing, yelling and bawling and there was proper intensity, so I'd just be saying to the mascot: 'It's alright. You'll come out with me and we'll run out to the middle and clap to the crowd' to take his or her attention away from all of that. I used to get Christmas cards written to Yorkie the Lion and so many grown adults have now got pictures of me with them when they were kids. They still come up to me and talk about when they were mascots and they will remember that for the rest of their lives. I was part of that and totally by luck really."

Yorkie's mischievous streak would also see him sabotage the team's pre-match preparations on occasions. "During the warm-ups, if the team was doing alright, I used to mess about with them and run off with the ball or take shots at the keeper," Ovenden explained. "I just used to find something to do to make the crowd smile. In the professional era, where everyone wants to be seen to be professional, that might be frowned upon, but surely you've done all the work you need to have done by that stage during the build-up to the game. The players would be laughing too, because they didn't know what I'd be up to next. It did become harder, though, because it's like any trend - once you've seen a gag, it's not as funny if you try to repeat it."

Bootham Crescent also played host to the likes of future England stars Joe Cole and Michael Carrick as a crowd of nearly 1,000 watched an FA Youth Cup last-16 clash against tournament favourites West Ham.

The game ended 1-1 with Christian Fox grabbing a spectacular 85th-minute equaliser from 25 yards, following Michael Ferrante's first-half opener for the Hammers. Fox was also sent off in stoppage time for handball, but goalkeeper John Mohan saved Carrick's resulting penalty. The goalscorer would go on to make 77 senior appearances for the Minstermen but had a strong recollection of his first big game on the hallowed turf, saying: "As a team, it was our first taste of playing in front of a big crowd. The Main Stand was almost full, and I remember feeling a mixture of nerves and excitement. The atmosphere was always amazing under the lights for a midweek game and the playing surface was perfect. I think it was one of the best in the league back then and the chance to play on the first-team pitch gave everybody in that team memories they will have for a lifetime."

On the challenge of pitting his teenage talents against future England pair Cole and Carrick, meanwhile, Fox added: "Joe Cole showed glimpses of what he was about in that first game, as did Michael Carrick. Those two stood out, but they had other good players as well (the likes of Stephen Bywater and Richard Garcia went on to enjoy notable careers and 10 of the team would become professionals). In the replay that we lost, Joe Cole had an absolutely ridiculous game. He was so sharp, and nobody could get near him, while some of the tricks he was pulling off were the kind you would try in training but wouldn't dare attempt them in a match. He was a year younger than everyone back then as well." Fox earned England youth international honours himself and recalled his own contribution at Bootham Crescent during a night in which the final result looks some achievement with the benefit of hindsight. "My goal was a 25-yard shot into the top corner quite late on, but it was a mixed night for me, because I went on to handle the ball on the line and got sent off, so I was really relieved when Carrick's penalty was saved and, looking back, we didn't too badly," he reasoned. "West Ham had a great reputation for young players at the time and they went on to win the final 9-0 on aggregate over two legs against Coventry, but five of our side were also taken on professionally, including Lee Bullock and James Turley."

In the summer of 1999, meanwhile, Sophie McGill was appointed as the club's first public relations executive, with a remit to transform Bootham Crescent into a fan-friendly venue for 21st-century football. City also announced a record profit of £1,274,202 for the year ending June 1999, swollen due to the transfer of Cresswell, but the operating trading loss amounted to £483,000, even though gate receipts broke the £500,000 barrier for the first time. The Bootham Crescent payroll was £1,427,028 at the time with repairs and safety work costing £45,000.

During the same summer, the board received the backing of shareholders for a move that would reportedly save the club's assets in the event of liquidation. The assets, primarily Bootham Crescent and the Wigginton Road training ground, were transferred to a holding company - Bootham Crescent Holdings - whose board members Douglas Craig, Barry Swallow, Colin Webb and John Quickfall now assumed ownership of them. Terry Fowler - the daughter of former club secretary and president Billy Sherrington - was one of the few people present to voice her concerns about the switch, saying: "I inherited my father's shares and went to the shareholders' meeting when Douglas Craig was chairman. It was when he wanted to set up Bootham Crescent Holdings and I protested. I was the only woman in there. I said that I couldn't see any point in doing it. I didn't trust him. He said: 'What do you know about running a football club?' I said: 'Probably more than you do', because I had been involved in it all my life. He might not have known who I was, but I don't think that would have made a difference anyway. He was an arrogant man and it was obvious what he was doing, and he went on to make a lot of money out of it."

McMillan's testimonial against Leeds, meanwhile, took place at the height of his dispute with Craig and Thompson, sadly tarnishing the occasion for the City legend as he was even dragged off the pitch by the manager. Recalling the game, McMillan said: "Leeds were going to bring their first team up until about two weeks before when they got an offer to go to Ireland, so it was Leeds' young lads and a bit of an anti-climax. There was all that going on with the board and Neil still too. I got told I was only going to play until half-time in my own testimonial match, which obviously didn't go down well either. I remember him taking me off, but I should have said 'I'm not coming off, this is my night, not yours'. So, Thompson ruined that as well and my head wasn't in the right place." Looking back, though, McMillan was still able to remember all the laughs and good times he had at Bootham Crescent, including during a two-year return to the club in 2014 as academy manager. "Kevin Dixon was one of the funniest guys I have ever met without even speaking," he revealed. "He

Andy McMillan salutes the crowd at his testimonial against a Leeds United XI

was just daft. Alan Pouton was funny with his spotted hair too. I don't know if he thought leopard spots and bleached blond hair was fashionable or it was for a bet but Trigger, as we called him, was good mates with Paddy Atkinson and, if he asked him to do anything, he would have done it back then. Tony Canham and Nigel Pepper used to also batter everybody. It was brutal and, once they got hold of you, you might as well have given up because they bounced off each other and went for you."

He also had great memories of one of the finest right-wing partnerships witnessed at Bootham Crescent. "Jon McCarthy was a great footballer, but I still wind him up about the number of runs I would make outside of him, only for him to drive inside and give the ball away," McMillan smiled. "Then, he would turn around to me and say: 'Off you go' and I would have to run back but, to be honest, he would always end up putting me in at the right time." As one of a select band of players to enjoy the honour, McMillan added that he never tired of hearing the City fans chant his own song: "Andy Mac is our Right-Back." "It's great to hear that when you're playing," he enthused. "It makes you buzz and I still hear people sing it occasionally now. The chant also came back when Andy McWilliams was here."

In October 1999, meanwhile, England's under-15s took on their Northern Ireland counterparts in front of more than 2,000 fans at Bootham Crescent. Future Three Lions full internationals Glen Johnson, Darren Bent and David Bentley all played in a 2-1 win for their country, with York-born defender Chris Kamara - the son of former Minsterman Alan and then on the books of Nottingham Forest - making his England debut at right back. Sammy Clinghan, who would later play for the likes of Forest, Norwich and Coventry, opened the scoring for the visitors, but Ciaran Donnelly, who drifted out of the professional game after a spell at Blackpool, levelled and Michael Gordon got the winner before also going on to make just 19 appearances for Wimbledon in the senior game. Kamara did not make the grade either but returned to North Yorkshire to play semi-professional football with Selby Town.

A struggling Thompson, meanwhile, lasted until February 2000 when Terry Dolan was brought in as manager. The club stayed up, but Bootham Crescent witnessed its biggest turnover of players during a season up to that point, with a then club record 35 used throughout the campaign. Losses for the season were £700,000 with chairman Craig admitting the club had "gambled a bit". The wage bill was £1,635,736 and it transpired that City had one of the worst wages/turnover ratios in the history of British football at that point. Mark

Sertori was an example of such excess with the 32-year-old, lower-league journeyman having been recruited for a five-figured fee and handed a two-year deal. The Bootham Crescent faithful never warmed to him, though, with Ovenden, as the man inside Yorkie The Lion's costume, recalling: "Mark Sertori was much-maligned. It wasn't his fault the club paid Halifax £25,000 for him but, when the team was announced, I used to stand with him and, when the crowd heard "number six Mark Sertori", there would be boos. Before the game, I used to joke about who would be topping the boo-ometer and he used to tell me to get lost."

The last home match of the season - a dead rubber against Halifax - provided unexpected levels of entertainment and drama, meanwhile, as the visitors had three players - Paul Stoneman, Alan Reilly and Craig Middleton - sent off and Yorkie the Lion almost came to blows with the Shaymen's captain. Remembering the spat, Ovenden said: "I used to nick lots of water bottles because they were all lined up together behind the goal and I would squirt the crowd with them. Everyone loved it. On that day, when we scored our second goal, I was stood near the goalpost and I squirted the crowd but some of it probably went in the goal area and their captain Graham Mitchell later claimed I had hit him in the face. I didn't know about any of that at the time. The game went on and they lost 2-0 with eight men (James Turley and Scott Jordan scored). Afterwards, I was waving to people with my thumbs up because we'd won and was absolutely buzzing. Then, almost panto-like, the crowd were shouting: 'He's behind you', so I turned around and Graham Mitchell started swearing at me and pushing me towards the Shipton Street End. I was in panto mode and almost falling over dramatically but he said: 'If you ever do that again, I will kill you'. He had completely lost it. I told him to grow up and that I was a 30-year-old bloke dressed from head-to-toe in a furry outfit like a fancy-dress freak. Then, he started again and was pulled away, so I turned around to the crowd, waved them goodbye and went down the tunnel before going to the club shop to get changed, where somebody said I had to go see the club secretary Keith Usher about what had just happened. I thought: 'Don't be so silly', but I went to see him, and he said: 'I'm not joking, Steve, the referee wants to see you. This is deadly serious'. So, I went and knocked on the door of the referee's room. He told me that Graham Mitchell had ran half the length of the pitch to confront me. I told him I had no idea why he reacted like he did. He said he would not normally bother reporting an incident like that, but he was being watched by a Football League assessor and, that if he didn't, it would have repercussions for him. He went on to tell me that his day job was a policeman and that a complaint had been made. I was working for the Crown Prosecution Service at the time, so I was starting to worry. He said that Graham Mitchell had told him I had urinated on him. I said that's rubbish and there's no way I could have done that and told him to look at the costume. I said he might have got hit by some water, but the referee continued to keep a straight face. He then went on and said: 'I understand you work for the CPS and you will, therefore, be familiar with the law so, if identification is an issue, we will need to have a parade'. I was still a bit shocked and not sure where things were leading, but then he said: 'It might be a problem though finding 11 other people dressed as a lion' and I realised he was taking the Mickey. It all got in the papers though and was on the front page. Luckily, they just laughed at work because it was at a time when magistrates were seen as a bit grey and dull, so it showed we were human and it gave the club a bit of profile as well. My only concern was Cyril the Swan had got in a spot of trouble and Swansea ended up getting fined £1,500, which was a big deal when they were still in the old fourth division at the time. I knew I hadn't done anything wrong, but I was thinking this isn't good if the club get disciplined, especially with my job. Thankfully, nothing further came of it."

The 2000/01 season saw the club dice with relegation from the Football League again and a 3-0 home defeat to Exeter left the team at the foot of the table in mid-February. Thirty-eight players were used during another turbulent season, which proved the last in City colours for fans' favourite Wayne Hall. "I wasn't in Terry Dolan's plans," the Wembley hero said of his final days at Bootham Crescent. "He wanted shut of all the players who had been at the club for a long time and wanted to make sweeping changes rightly or wrongly. I'd had quite a few injuries, but it was still disappointing that he got somebody else to tell me I was being released at the end of the season."

The football was also unattractive under Dolan with Ovenden taking it upon himself to provide some fun at Bootham Crescent in his lion costume. "There was more fun with Yorkie in adversity," he reasoned. "With Terry Dolan, we were always in the bottom half of League Two and, because the football was poor, I used to try and give the fans a bit of a laugh and some entertainment. I used to dance and gyrate with the cheerleaders and rub my thighs like the comedian Vic Reeves, because I wanted to make the adults laugh, as well as the children. It was borderline appropriate, but it was pantomime humour and a lot of that goes over kids' heads. People took more notice of those type of things when the team were doing badly because, when they're doing well, everyone's only interested in the football and they are there for the match. I used to have a bit of a thing with the keepers as well. As daft as it sounds, you could lean on the goal post during games back then. Sometimes, the referees would ask you to step away, but you could often have a chat with the away keeper and take the Mickey a bit. I used to have a massive ball and, whenever their keeper was coming to the Shippo End for the second half, I would put it on the 'D'. I would be waiting for them on the penalty spot and then I'd go in the goal. The ball was really heavy and, while some of them scored past me, not many did, so I could take the Mickey out of them and get the crowd on their backs. But they had to join in really or they would get more stick, and most did. Alan Fettis, our keeper at the time, would never kick it, though, because he knew how hard it was to score. I remember one spell where the team hadn't kept a clean sheet for so many games, so I got a bed sheet from somewhere and, when they did keep a clean sheet, I chucked it over him. He said: 'What are you doing?' I said: 'I thought you wanted a clean sheet'. I used to join in the celebrations for most of Jon Parkin's goals too back then, because he was a nutter."

Probably the highlight of that season came before it even kicked off, with Manchester United visiting Bootham Crescent for a friendly as part of the deal that had taken City goalkeeper Nick Culkin to Old Trafford five years earlier. Roy Keane scored both goals as the Red Devils won 2-0 in front of a 9,003-strong crowd with Paul Scholes also hitting a post. The attendance would not be beaten during any of the subsequent years at Bootham Crescent and, remembering the unprecedented anticipation the pre-season match attracted, Fox said: "That was the only time I played at Bootham Crescent when it was a full house. We'd been training away at Keele for a pre-season get together and we travelled back on the day before the game and that's when we found out who they were bringing. The manager Terry Dolan named myself, Steve Agnew and Kevin Hulme as the three-man midfield and theirs was David Beckham, Roy Keane, Paul Scholes and Ryan Giggs, which was probably the best in world football at the time. It was us three against those four and we were just giggling when the manager read out their team."

Fox, who was just 19 at the time, admitted the match was an unsurprisingly, one-sided contest with many of the Red Devils, who had completed the Champions League, Premier League and FA

David Beckham is mobbed by supporters as he steps off the Manchester United team coach for the pre-season friendly in 2000

464

Christian Fox is tracked by Roy Keane during the pre-season friendly against Manchester United in 2000

David Beckham plots a way past Mark Sertori during the pre-season friendly in 2000

Darren Edmondson gets shirty with Ryan Giggs during the 2000 pre-season friendly

Cup treble a year earlier, taking it easy on the hosts. "It could have been 10-0," Fox reasoned. "They were going clear through with the keeper and trying to chip and nutmeg him. Roy Keane got both goals, but I was impressed by all of them. I remember Denis Irwin being unbelievable at full-back and it was great to play in that game. It goes down as one of my best memories playing at Bootham Crescent and people still ask me about that game and playing against those players." While his team-mates might have indulged in a little show-boating, consummate professional Keane was not one for any light-hearted antics and Fox added: "You have this idea of him being big and strong and he wasn't how I pictured him because he was actually quite small. He was a ferocious tackler though. People always talked about him being the leader too and the other players were actually calling him 'boss' on the pitch. That was the respect they had for him."

Whether Keane - or indeed the hosts' groundstaff - approved of team-mate Beckham's plans for a quick getaway from Bootham Crescent is another matter. "David Beckham had become a superstar by then," Fox explained. "He was married to Posh Spice and he wanted to get away quickly after the game, so he asked if he could land a helicopter on the pitch, but the club refused." Club mascot Ovenden, meanwhile, was receiving surreal requests for photographs from some of the game's biggest names at the final whistle. "I was a massive fan of our defender Peter Swan at the time, so I wasn't that bothered about David Beckham, Roy Keane or any of them," Ovenden recalled. "But one of the funniest things was when I came down the tunnel after the game and they were all there with their girlfriends, wives and kids and the children of Manchester United players all wanted their photographs taken with me!"

Injury meant Swan would only play two more competitive games for the Minstermen during a spell that saw him make 11 outings in total for the club and the ex-Leeds and Hull defender's fitness problems led to one of the strangest requests ever received by Yorkie The Lion prior to that meeting with the Red Devils. "It was a real shame that Swanny only played for us for three months and then got injured, because he was mint but, towards the end of his career, he was rolling up fat everywhere and the club didn't have big enough shorts for him with the new kit having just arrived," Ovenden explained. "He ran over to me before kick-off and told me: 'You're going to have to take your shorts off'. I said: 'What are you on about?' He said: 'Well are they XXL or whatever?' I said: 'Yes'. He said: 'I need them, then'. So, we're having this conversation at the side of the pitch and people were wondering what it's all about. I told him: 'You can have my shorts. That's absolutely no problem and I'll just go down the tunnel and take them off for you'. He said: 'Well what are you going to do?' I said: 'I'm going to sit and watch you parade around Bootham Crescent in a pair of shorts with a tail hanging out of your backside', because it was sewn into the shorts. He swore at me and did manage to get some that fit him in the end, but that was great."

Middlesbrough had also visited Bootham Crescent for Hall's testimonial with Hamilton Ricard scoring both goals in a 2-1 triumph for the visitors. The beneficiary, though, recalled his embarrassment at being ignorant of testimonial etiquette, revealing: "It was a brilliant night - just fantastic - but, in my naivety, I never realised that you got taken off in your testimonial so that the crowd could applaud you and you could show your appreciation back. Instead, I just jogged off and Paul Stancliffe gave me a rollicking for that. I thought I'd just been taken off because I'd been rubbish in the game. But my best memory of the night is walking onto the pitch with my sons and daughter in my arms - that was really special."

The club, meanwhile, made an undisclosed and unsuccessful bid for the Territorial Army Barracks site adjacent to the ground behind the Popular Stand, and Bootham Crescent also hosted three matches in the 2001 UEFA European Under-16 Championship, including France's 2-0 win over Russia in a quarter-final watched by 557 spectators that featured future Liverpool striker Florent Sinama Pongolle. In an earlier group game at the ground, outstanding Dutch captain Wesley Sneijder had curled a free-kick against the post during a 2-0 triumph for his team over Poland. Fellow future 2010 World Cup runner-up Nigel de Jong was also reported to have starred in a 0-0 draw against Russia, who qualified for the knockout stages in front of a 689-strong North Yorkshire crowd.

Club legends Norman Wilkinson, Alf Patrick and Gordon Brown watch a game against Luton in October 1998

467

Kevin Keegan signs autographs prior to his Fulham team winning 3-0 at Bootham Crescent in February 1999. He had been named as the new manager of the England national team just nine days earlier but combined both club and country roles until the end of a season that culminated in relegation for the Minstermen

Fans stage a Red Card Protest against Douglas Craig in the David Longhurst Stand during September 1999

Hollywood actor Ray Winstone meets Yorkie the Lion in the car park at a game against Brighton in September 2000

The first incarnation of the club's lion mascot was called Shippo with Sarah Pullon underneath the outfit

Yorkie the Lion entertains fans with his antics, as he feigns injury during a match against Bury in February 2003

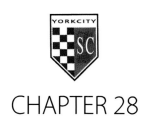

CHAPTER 28

Eviction and extinction threats of Craig and Batchelor

"He was smoking on the bench, but he actually came on."

A record loss of £1.2 million was reported for the 2000/01 season during the annual meeting of Bootham Crescent Holdings, held in December, when Douglas Craig also made the shock announcement that his board intended to resign at the end of the season and invited any parties interested in acquiring the club to contact him. Craig added that the club's overdraft limit would be reached in February 2002 and that the board would only provide additional security for sufficient funds to complete the season. He went on to state that any new owner would not be required to make any payment but would need to undertake certain obligations.

A public meeting was subsequently held at Temple Anderson Hall on January 7, 2002. Over 300 people, including captain Chris Brass, were there, with a unanimous decision taken to form a Supporters' Trust. Paul Rawnsley - a City fan with specialist football finance knowledge through his work with Deloitte and Touche - chaired the meeting and said: "We must not let York City die and must do everything we can to ensure the club survives for future generations." Two days later, another bombshell was delivered when it was announced that Bootham Crescent - the club's home for 70 years - would close on June 30, 2002 with any buyer required to vacate the ground by that date. Talks over a move to Huntington Stadium had been held and it was disclosed that the club would quit the Football League at the end of the 2001/02 season if no buyer was found. The capital needed to buy the club and ground was reported to be £4.5million.

Hugh Kitchin, chairman of the club in the 1950s, found Craig's actions hard to understand, pointing out: "Directors in my day did not regard it as their club to make money from. We were merely looking after it on behalf of the public of York and district." A thousand fans attended the launch of the Supporters' Trust on February 1, 2002 at the Barbican with ITV commentator Jon Champion - a City fan - hosting the meeting that saw the likes of 89-year-old club legend Jack Pinder and York-born, future England boss Steve McClaren in the audience. The pressure group Friends of Bootham Crescent, whose spokesman was Ian Savage, also did a tremendous amount of work with the Supporters' Trust to organise emergency fundraising projects. Whereas the Trust had to operate with a modicum of diplomacy in their negotiations with Craig, there were no such restrictions for FOBC and, explaining the body's purpose, Savage said: "When I heard Douglas Craig's announcement, I was in utter shock like most people. It wasn't just him saying he wanted to sell the club or that it wasn't financially viable in the state it was in, he was saying he would close the club down and sell the ground off for houses and that would be it, so three or four of us decided to form the Friends of Bootham Crescent. We were a group of like-minded individuals - a rag-tag little bunch really - who all knew each other and were discussing the situation. At the time, the Supporters' Trust were doing their level best to try and save the club, but there were certain things they couldn't do and say. We wanted to be the militant arm of things. The Trust would never have encouraged people to protest outside the offices of Persimmon against their plans to put houses on the football ground for example. Nobody ever got hurt or injured at our protests, but we were determined that we would say what needed saying. We were an independent body who weren't answerable to anybody. Fortunately, the media gave us a platform to deliver the messages we wanted. Suddenly, we were being interviewed on Sky TV and the radio, which was an interesting experience, but something had to be done. People, like Steve Beck, as chairman of the Supporters' Trust, were doing a terrific job trying to save the club, but he had to be very careful with the kind of things he said. We didn't."

Two major bidders for the club emerged. One was led by the York Rugby League duo of John Stabler and Russell Greenfield. The other came from John Batchelor - a self-styled motor racing tycoon and owner-driver of the B&Q-sponsored Honda Integrity Racing team, who competed in the British Touring Car Championship. Batchelor subsequently took over the club in March, 2002, promising to make City "the most unusual team" in the Football League. He voiced his plans to conquer the New York City and American markets. Batchelor also announced that he had struck a three-year sponsorship deal with Persimmon Homes for an undisclosed fee, which would be split between the club and his racing team.

Almost incidentally, the team finished the season 14th - their highest placing since being relegated back to the bottom division in 1999. A welcome FA

Cup run also saw the team drawn at home to Premier League Fulham in the fourth round. The Cottagers' owner Mohammed Al Fayed generously donated his team's share of the club record gate receipts to the Supporters' Trust which, with a crowd of 7,563, amounted to £25,000. The gross takings were £73,000, which beat

Legendary Dutch goalkeeper Edwin van der Sar comes under pressure from Lee Bullock during the 2002 FA Cup tie that saw Fulham owner Mohamed al Fayed donate his team's share of City's club record gate receipts to the Supporters' Trust

the previous highest figure of £64,000 for the 1995 League Cup, second leg meeting with Manchester United, although VAT, policing, stewarding, an FA payment and other matchday costs meant the eventual financial boost for the club was somewhat reduced.

Earlier, Colchester had been beaten at Bootham Crescent in a first-round replay, which saw the first penalty shoot-out take place in the competition at the ground. Following a 2-2 draw in which Brass and future Premier League manager Graham Potter had netted, extra-time failed to separate the teams and Alan Fettis went on to save spot kicks from Scott McGleish and Karl Duguid, while Potter, Brass and Nick Richardson converted from 12 yards for the hosts. Fettis' save from Duguid proved the match-winning moment and spared Michael Proctor from taking City's fifth penalty.

Amid all the off-pitch turmoil, meanwhile, future England squad member David Stockdale was serving his apprenticeship at Bootham Crescent, where it was business as usual for the young scholars. He had nothing but fond memories of the period, despite the strict regime of another demanding youth-team coach Paul Stancliffe. Remembering those formative years, Stockdale said: "I'll never forget the very small sports hall in the back of the away end. We used to do afternoon sessions in there and circuits with Paul Stancliffe. All the lads who were staying in digs would also come back at night and play a game called 'Garages', which was a lot of fun. We had a good few laughs. There would be around ten of us and you would split into two-man teams. All five sides had a garage, which was a small goal. You had lives and you had to try and score in other people's goals, while protecting your own at the same time, so you had to get the balance right between the two. It was a lot of fun and got us out of the digs for a couple of hours. You got a sweat on too and the losers would either have to buy some sweets or do extra jobs the next day. We also used to do our college work on Monday and Thursday afternoons in the little room that was upstairs next to the club shop and we spent 99 per cent of our time at the ground. We used to clean boots just inside where the players' entrance was as well, so that was a meeting point and I knew every inch of the ground. I can still picture it all now. You had your jobs to do and that's just the way it was. You had to come back at 2pm if you were on laundry duty and put all the washing into the dryer. It taught you that, if you didn't make it as footballers, you would be ready for the hard graft required in most jobs. You never got to go home before Paul Stancliffe saw that everything had been done to his satisfaction. We had to stay and do the toilets again if they weren't clean and, as I went on in my career, I always told the young lads they were lucky that they don't have to do anything these days. It was a good upbringing at a smaller club. It taught me a few valuable life skills too - like when my goalkeeping gloves stuck to the inside of the dryer! It was tough being away from home at 16, but we all learned a lot."

Stockdale also had vivid recollections of the matchday experience and duties for a Bootham Crescent apprentice at the turn of the century. "I watched my first games at 15 behind the dugouts," he explained. "The higher up you were in the youth-team hierarchy, the higher you got to sit in the stand because you couldn't see anything on the front row. We also had our ball-boy duties sometimes and I soon lost count of the number of times I had to climb through that hole at the back of the Barracks to get balls back. On match days, you would have to get things for the ref too and mop up the changing rooms and corridor afterwards. Whenever famous players came to the club with the big teams in pre-season, I'd take real interest in them as well and try and see what boots they were wearing and that kind of thing."

For the 2002/03 season, meanwhile, a new sign was erected at the entrance to Bootham Crescent car park, declaring the stadium to be the home of York City Soccer Club as part of Batchelor's plan to market the club in the USA. A new strip also incorporated a black-and-white chequered design on the sleeve in a move to promote his motor-racing interests. Batchelor's behaviour at Bootham Crescent was becoming increasingly bizarre and he even came on as a 90th-minute substitute for Aidan O'Kane during a 4-3 pre-season home defeat to part-timers Bracknell, in which both teams ran out to the theme tune of reality TV show *Big Brother*. At the time, Batchelor was popular having seemingly rescued the club from the clutches of Craig and his eccentricity initially endeared him to the Bootham Crescent faithful with his introduction to proceedings heralding a standing ovation and his two touches of the ball greeted with cheers. When he was tackled, the aggressor was also booed, but Christian Fox confessed that the players were beginning to have their suspicions about the larger-than-life new owner. He said: "We had chequered flags on our shirts that season because he was promoting his racing team and I remember that Bracknell game. He was smoking on the bench, but he actually came on and it was like the footage we've all seen of Boris Johnson trying to play football. He was going in for challenges that he shouldn't have been, and it was all a bit of a publicity stunt, which was usually the case with him. The one good thing I remember him doing was bringing Luther Blissett to the club because he was a brilliant coach, but Terry Dolan and Adie Shaw didn't get on with him, so there was a bit of a divide."

Savage also added that Batchelor was initially a very popular character around Bootham Crescent before alarm bells started to sound. "The initial feeling with John Batchelor was that he was the saviour, but there were a lot of false promises and bare-faced lies in some cases," Savage pointed out. "He said he had bought the club and land, but all he had done is paid £1 to own the club. He had no means to buy the ground and had taken a large amount of money that was intended for the football club and invested it into his racing team. He later went on record admitting he had lied and, whilst I don't like to speak ill of the dead, the way he conducted himself at York City was pretty disgusting. We had a lot of contact with him at the start and he was quite friendly. He came across as a really nice chap, who was amiable, and he liked to socialise with supporters. He was always in the Social Club buying people drinks and that was part of his charm offensive and why people took to him, I think, but everything started to unravel and it became clear he was pretty much a con-man."

Brazilian Rogerio Carvalho and Argentinian Nicolas Mazzina were also signed to add some continental flair at Bootham Crescent, but both were limited to a handful of unspectacular substitute appearances. The home of York City was rapidly becoming a setting for surreal farce with Fox adding: "There was a link-up with a certain agent and, one day, five or six South Americans rocked up on trial. They were not up to the level they should have been, but a couple got signed and they were on decent contracts. Sometimes, Rogerio showed moments of brilliance but, at other times, he looked like he'd never played the game. It was a total change for them too. I remember one of them not speaking any English and the other interpreting for him. They didn't end up playing many games." Savage, meanwhile, recalled the buzz of anticipation that initially enveloped Bootham Crescent following the exciting, but ultimately hugely anti-climactic, South American experiment. "Rogerio was a really strange one," he said. "He was billed as an incredible player, but nobody had ever heard of him and you couldn't find any reference to him on the internet. There was nothing to suggest he had played at any kind of decent level, but the club shop stocked up on yellow Brazil shirts with his name on. Mazzina only played a handful of games, but he looked a bit better."

Batchelor also announced plans to launch a new rugby-league team following the demise of York Wasps and revealed that he wanted to build a new stadium at Clifton Moor. Ian McAndrew was subsequently appointed as a new director with his role to oversee the move from Bootham Crescent. The Supporters' Trust, meanwhile, unveiled their first elected board members. They were Sophie McGill, Paul Rawnsley, Terry Herbert, Kirsten Gillies, Steve Beck, Graham Kilby, Richard Willis, Michael Shannon, Michael Brown, Richard Snowball and John Catton.

The revelations began to come thick and fast, though, with Persimmon Homes, having acquired 10 per cent of the shares in Bootham Crescent Holdings, announcing they were submitting planning applications for 93 homes on the Bootham Crescent site, while Batchelor went on to brand council planners as inept and shambolic as he ran into problems regarding the proposed new ground. Craig subsequently resigned from the football club board but remained as chairman of BCH. In October 2002, half-price season-ticket sales were being offered by Batchelor for the following campaign, leading to concerns about the club's financial situation and the Supporters' Trust responded that month by declaring their intention to secure full ownership of the club.

By November, Batchelor's stunts to attract revenue into the club included bringing former fans' favourite Jon McCarthy back for what turned out to be one game only - a 3-2 triumph over Leyton Orient at Bootham Crescent. On that experience, the popular winger said: "That was weird. I was just recovering after breaking my leg three times, but John Batchelor rang me up and asked me to come in and train with the club. I did, and he wanted to offer me a contract, but he wasn't really interested in me as a player. He just wanted to put something on the gate for the next game. The money he was offering wasn't good and wouldn't have covered my travelling expenses really, so I couldn't do it. It would have cost me more in petrol than I'd have been earning, but I told him I'd play the next game for nothing. You could see he was mad. He had everything painted in red and white at the ground and, being more

Club legend Chris Topping participates in the releasing of 93 balloons before the Swansea FA Cup tie in 2002 in protest at the plans for 93 houses to be built on Bootham Crescent at a time when the club had no relocation options

experienced, I didn't get a great feel for him. It was really wrong what he and Douglas Craig did to the club but, on that day, we won 3-2 and then Carlisle came in for me and I ended up playing for them in the next match at Bootham Crescent, which was very strange."

As absurd scenes became common place at Bootham Crescent, Batchelor then took to the microphone at half-time during an FA Cup tie with Swansea and announced he would hand over control to the Trust, only to change his mind 24 hours later. His revelation came after the Friends of Bootham Crescent, accompanied by club legend Chris Topping, released a symbolic 93 balloons from the pitch during a peaceful protest. "I remember that game being a freezing night and we were protesting against the ground being sold for housing," Savage explained. "There were going to be 93 houses built on Bootham Crescent, so we released 93 black helium balloons at half-time on the pitch. Batchelor was really helpful and helped us organise it. Then, after the balloons had been released, he grabbed the microphone and said he was going to hand the club over to the supporters the next morning. There was a big round of applause as we all thought we were moving on to the next stage in the club's history, but he didn't do that and, a few days later, the club went into administration and it became clear there were serious debts. He had taken us for a ride."

On November 28, 2002, the club entered into a creditors' voluntary agreement in a bid to survive. Players' pay packets at Bootham Crescent had been delayed for a second month running and a considerable amount of money was owed to the Inland Revenue. The PFA subsequently stepped in to ensure the squad's salaries were paid but, as Fox explained, every player was well aware of the

Yorkie the Lion joins in the Save City fight

severity of what was unfolding at Bootham Crescent. "The PFA got involved when we weren't getting paid so that was resolved, but it was a horrendous time for the players, the fans and the city," he recalled. "I remember everyone presumed that was it for the club."

At Leeds Combined Courts, it was then announced that the club had just five weeks to find a buyer to avoid being declared bankrupt. The league game against Swansea City on January 18, 2003, therefore, was being billed as potentially the last ever at Bootham Crescent. An injection of £92,000 from the Trust staved off that threat at the 11th hour and, boosted by a £50,000 donation from lifelong fan Jason McGill, the owner of Malton-based business JM Packaging, a formal bid to take over the club was made.

On the first weekend in February, the home match against Lincoln was then designated as a Fans United Day, with supporters of other clubs showing solidarity during a series of rallies in the city centre, arranged before the game. Awful weather meant the game was postponed due to a waterlogged pitch, but the day still proved a success with Savage saying: "Fans came to York from all over the country to support us. A group of Wimbledon fans came up to show their support and donated some money, as did lots from other clubs, which was fantastic. The game was postponed because it threw it down that day. We had turned up at 8am on that Saturday morning to hold a rally in the city centre and Frank Ormston was heavily involved. We all got soaking wet and heard at 1pm that the game was off, but we still raised a lot of money."

Another crucial deadline saw supporters raise more than £50,000 in 72 hours, including a staggering £20,000 in bucket collections at the home game with Bury on February 22, which was attended by 4,115 fans. Savage will never forget the unity felt at Bootham Crescent on that day as the supporters demonstrated a remarkable refusal to let their club die. "We stood at the gates at every match and shook buckets," he recalled. "We'd then go to somebody's house and count it and the people at the bank really enjoyed it when we walked in with a load of coins for them on a Monday morning! It was a big fundraising effort, mainly led by the Supporters' Trust. It was magnificent how everybody came together. You saw everything at those collections from young kids raiding their piggy banks and putting all the money they had saved in, to other people who put notes in and not just one, but several. People were in tears because they didn't want to lose the ground and see the club go bust. Dave Potter (who later became a Supporters' Trust board member) was one of the regular bucket shakers and he had more than one grit-in-the-eye moment as people told him what the club meant to them. The money raised went well into five figures and there was a great feeling of unity. A lot of people who didn't know each other became great friends and started socialising with each other, so I suppose you could say Douglas Craig brought a lot of people together."

The club's administrators eventually agreed to the Trust assuming control, although debts of £1.85 million were revealed. Of that figure, £890,000 would be needed to honour players' contracts with £98,000 owed to the taxman. The Inland Revenue eventually agreed to accept 63p in the pound and the Supporters' Trust took over the club on Wednesday, March 26, 2003 with Beck as the club's new chairman and Sophie McGill, Brown, Jason McGill and McAndrew also on the board. Terry Doyle joined them soon afterwards as finance director. Along with many other City supporters, Savage was at the ground to herald the great news. "I remember it was a week day when the administrator called a meeting at Bootham Crescent to announce that an agreement had been reached for the Supporters' Trust to buy the club out of administration," Savage said. "A lot of fans turned up and many couldn't get in. People had taken time off work to see this happen and, when the administrator said: 'I'm very pleased to say York City is now in the ownership of the Supporters' Trust', there was a huge cheer and round of applause. The administrator went on to say: 'I've never received that kind of reaction for doing my job', and somebody chirped up: 'Don't worry mate, it's not for you.'" The York City Soccer Club sign was immediately dismantled and a 2-0 home win over Southend, courtesy of goals from Lee Nogan and Lee Bullock, saw the club jump up to third in the table after the first match under Trust ownership. Savage recalled the sense of occasion at Bootham Crescent, adding: "That was a good game and going into the top three made it a perfect day. We were the new rightful owners of the club and there were a lot of people on the microphone celebrating the fact it was our club."

John Quickfall, meanwhile, resigned from his position as a director of Bootham Crescent Holdings, who still owned the stadium and training ground. He said at the time: "I should like to make it clear that I will not make any personal profit out of my shares in BCH. It is my intention that any such profit, which may become due to me, will be put towards securing a new home for the club." It later transpired that he had made a donation of more than £20,000 to the Trust.

Batchelor was gone but, having only acquired the club for £1 from BCH and channelled all £400,000 of the Persimmon Homes sponsorship money into his racing team, walked away with a profit of £120,000 despite taking the club into administration. He also admitted that he had agreed, on his takeover, that the club would vacate Bootham Crescent at the end of the 2002/03 season. He had effectively ripped up the club's 25-year lease agreement with BCH. None of the £42,500 he had collected in half-price 2003/04 season ticket sales could be recouped either. Incredibly, amid all the mayhem, the club almost reached the play-offs. Dolan was relieved of his duties, however, at the end of the season with captain Brass becoming the Football League's youngest manager since 1946 at the age of 27.

The club, meanwhile, managed to reach an agreement with Craig, extending their reduced lease arrangement at Bootham Crescent for a further 12 months until May 2004 and plans proceeded to develop Huntington Stadium, although there were mounting problems to bring the ground, which was home to the reformed rugby-league club York City Knights and the city's athletics club, up to Football League standard. It was subsequently disclosed that staying at Bootham Crescent was the preferred option and that the club were investigating ways of making that possible.

The David Longhurst Stand unveil a Save City banner at the FA Cup tie against Fulham in 2002

The increasingly absurd John Batchelor poses as Austin Powers on the hallowed turf

Brazilian Rogerio makes his home debut as a 90th-minute substitute against Boston in August 2002

York City's players observe a one minute's silence to mark the death of legendary striker Keith Walwyn at the age of 47 in 2003

Dastardly pair John Batchelor and Douglas Craig share a joke during a December 2002 press conference in the Nestlé Family Room

John Batchelor shares his unconvincing vision for a new stadium at Clifton Moor

Macabre supporter Stephen Gartside poses as the Grim Reaper after the club had entered into a creditors' voluntary agreement in a bid to survive

John Batchelor's controversial York City Soccer Club sign is dismantled following the Supporters' Trust takeover in March 2003

CHAPTER 29

A first relegation from the Football League

"We should have had tomatoes thrown at us and been spat at, but that's not testimony to myself, it's testimony to the fans at this football club."

The following season would herald a significant victory off the pitch, but one of the biggest-ever setbacks on it, as ownership of Bootham Crescent was once more returned to the football club, but Chris Brass' team finished the campaign relegated to the realms of non-League football. Both dramas would be played out during the second half of a season that had started with rookie Brass guiding the team to victory during their first four league fixtures.

With the club still facing eviction at the end of the campaign, Douglas Craig announced at Bootham Crescent Holdings' annual general meeting in January that the company's directors would accept a payment of £2million for the club to buy back the stadium and the two training grounds at Wigginton Road and next to the Bumper Castle pub. Craig estimated that the figure might rise to £2.6million should Persimmon require compensation if their legal agreement to build houses on the ground, which had been entered into with BCH, was not to be honoured. He also warned that he would be unwilling to extend the lease further - beyond the end of the season - while defending his decision to transfer the club's assets to BCH in 1999, arguing: "The football club would not be in existence at all if I had not done what I did."

At the beginning of February, it was then announced that the club had negotiated a deal to stay at Bootham Crescent. A joint statement from BCH and Persimmon Homes revealed "an agreement has been reached in principle to enable the football club to continue to play professional football at Bootham Crescent". Delighted club director Jason McGill - the key figure in brokering a deal - said: "We are delighted to have reached this agreement. It has taken much hard work and many sleepless nights, but we have achieved our aim of ensuring York City has a home for next season and for the future." Ian McAndrew's efforts in putting a feasible plan together to move to Huntington,

Player-manager Chris Brass announces to his squad in the Social Club that York City had reached an agreement to stay at Bootham Crescent

which had remained the only option for the club's survival for some time, were also recognised, while Trust board member Paul Rawnsley said: "Great tribute is due to Jason McGill and those around him (Steve Beck, Sophie McGill and Terry Doyle) who have supported the aim of staying at Bootham Crescent."

Brass also heralded "wonderful news", while the significance of the agreement was not lost on Friends of Bootham Crescent founder Ian Savage, who declared: "It was so important to get that deal. The ground holds so many memories for York fans. I'm relatively young compared to some supporters, but I've seen us win promotion there, beat Arsenal, complete a two-legged victory over Manchester United and hold the great Liverpool team of the 1980s to draws there twice. There have been a lot of big games played there and great players like Keith Walwyn, so there's a sentimental attachment to the place and, if the club had not saved Bootham Crescent, there would literally have been nowhere to play. The old Ryedale (Huntington) Stadium had been looked at as one solution but it wasn't suitable for league football at that time, so that deal was vital to the future of the football club." On the enduring appeal of Bootham Crescent, whilst acknowledging the need for relocation, Savage added: "If you took one look at Bootham Crescent, anybody could see it was falling apart. It was a warts-and-all experience, and everybody knows going to the toilet there wasn't a particularly nice experience but, even though it was a bit of a dump, it was our dump and we loved it. It was like an old shoe that fits perfectly, but old-fashioned grounds are few and far between now and everybody knew that staying there was never a viable long-term solution. Friends of Bootham Crescent was never about saving Bootham Crescent at all costs. It was about

Club directors (from left-to-right) Steve Beck, Terry Doyle, Jason McGill, Sophie McGill and Ian McAndrew celebrate the deal that allowed York City to regain ownership of the ground from former chairman Douglas Craig and end the threat of eviction

making sure that York City had a sustainable home to play football in and, hopefully, that will be the case at Monks Cross for years to come, even though I understand it would not have been everybody's first choice."

Despite being knocked back four times over a six-month period, the club, spearheaded by a determined Jason McGill, had eventually managed to secure a £2million loan from the Football Foundation, through the Football Stadia Improvement Fund, which was used to acquire 75.89 per cent of BCH's shares. That included buying all of Persimmon Homes' 20,000 shares, while Craig received a £1,084,000 pay-off and fellow directors - disgraced former defensive hero Barry Swallow and Colin Webb - both pocketed £172,661. It meant they received 11 times more than what they had paid for their £1 shares and Craig, Swallow and Webb still retained a combined total of 8.5 per cent of the shares. The initial conditions of the Football Foundation loan, which would be relaxed in future years with further negotiations, stated that the club must identify a site for a new stadium in 2007 and obtain detailed planning permission by 2009 to avoid financial penalties. The loan gave the club overall control of Bootham Crescent, the training ground at Wigginton Road and the land near the Bumper Castle pub. Once plans for a new stadium were in place, it was stated that the loan would be converted into a grant to assist in

483

funding relocation, which was more in line with the normal purposes of the fund. Persimmon, meanwhile, would retain an option to acquire the land for housing at 90 per cent of the market value.

As the club's immediate future at Bootham Crescent was being secured, the outlook was beginning to look less promising on the football pitch. On January 10, Carlisle were beaten 2-0 at Bootham Crescent with the hosts then lying 10th in the table and 18 points clear of the relegation zone. But the team subsequently failed to win any of their final 20 games, picking up just five points as they finished bottom of the table and were relegated to the Conference. Key players Lee Bullock and Jon Parkin were both allowed to leave the club before the situation became irreversible. Parkin even returned to Bootham Crescent to get on the scoresheet for new club Macclesfield, with fellow former Minsterman Graham Potter also on target during a 2-0 triumph in April that saw the hosts drop into the relegation zone for the first time and the visitors climb above them. Christian Fox, who only played a minor role during his final campaign at Bootham Crescent, mainly witnessed the slide from the Main Stand. "I was injured for most of the season, but I watched every home game and you could see what was coming in a way after Christmas," he reasoned.

Jon Parkin and Graham Potter are pictured either side of a screaming Graeme Law, with both scoring goals for Macclesfield in a crucial April 2004 contest that plunged their old club into a relegation zone that they would never climb out of prior to dropping out of the Football League for a first time

"The club got in a rut, lost a couple of players and lost some key games to teams around them."

The 2004/05 season - which marked the golden anniversary of the Happy Wanderers' charge to the FA Cup semi-finals - would now be spent as a non-League club. Relegation was confirmed at Doncaster and, the following weekend, there were tearful scenes as a 2-1 home defeat to Leyton Orient signalled an end to three-quarters of a century of Football League action in the city. Stuart Wise scored the hosts' consolation - the club's last goal in the Football League for eight years - but he turned down the offer of a new contract

Byrne and Walwyn (the late Keith's son Matt) are reunited for the Past Players' festival in 2004

in the summer to return to his north-east roots and work in a factory. "We'll be back" read one defiant banner on the sad occasion, although when the old ground would stage a Football League fixture again, if ever, was uncertain, while supporters invaded the pitch at the end but, perhaps surprisingly, not in anger. They chose to declare their continued support for Brass and the board, clearly grateful for their efforts to ensure they still had a club to support. An emotional Brass was amazed by the fans' response, saying: "We should have had tomatoes thrown at us and been spat at, but that's not testimony to myself, it's testimony to the fans at this football club. They are intelligent. Events in the past are not being used as excuses, but they certainly have not helped the cause. I hope the players have also realised what the club means to the fans, because they will get an even better reception when they actually win something."

Young defender Chris Smith, then 22, was among the players subsequently released by the club who, as a small but still significant consolation, reported an £83,000 profit for the year ending June 30, 2004, compared to the 12-week operating loss of £332,338 that had been racked up honouring existing contracts a year earlier during the first three months of Trust ownership.

There had been brief respite from the alarming slide into non-League football in March when a Past Players' festival was held at Bootham Crescent. Marking the 20th anniversary of the historic 1983/84 centurions' season, members of that team took on players from the Wembley-winning side of 1992/93, with the latter triumphing 6-4. A crowd of 850 watched the game, which was poignantly kicked off by Keith Walwyn's youngest son Matt. City legend Walwyn had passed away the previous April and 13-year-old Matt, then a Blackburn Rovers academy player who would later become a Saint Kitts & Nevis international and score the winning goals for Kirkham & Wesham in an FA Vase final at Wembley, bagged a brace in the match after taking his father's place in the team alongside John Byrne. The event was attended by 40 past players and was organised by City fan and former Football League official Graham Bradbury. It also served as a celebration of the club securing ownership of Bootham Crescent from Craig's holding company. An estimated £5,000 raised on the day, meanwhile, contributed to the £60,000 costs incurred by the abortive Huntington Stadium plans. On the day's success, then director of communications Sophie McGill, said: "We are absolutely delighted with the turn-out. We would have been happy with 500, but it was great to see so many people here. But most of all, it was absolutely tremendous to see all those great players back here at Bootham Crescent. It will be a big contribution to the £60,000 needed for the Huntington Stadium costs, especially when combined with the takings from the club shop, where there were people queuing up outside for the 25 per cent sale, the grand raffle and the bucket collections before and during the game." Walwyn's widow Liz was at the match too and added: "It's been a hard and emotional day, but I was so proud of Matthew. Just seeing him run out in his dad's shirt like that was amazing and his dad would have been so proud of him playing the way he did. I would like to thank John Byrne for looking after Matthew and really taking him under his wing. Keith would have loved that. I have a lot of fantastic memories of York and it was lovely to see everyone again. I also want to thank the fans for all their support."

Just one day after the club bid a final farewell to the Football League following a 0-0 draw at Swansea, Bootham Crescent also hosted a Fans' Match. Originally, the idea had been proposed in the summer of 2003 when it was billed as possibly the final game to be staged at the ground assuming Craig carried out his eviction threat. An auction to take part in the match, which was organised by Yorkie the Lion's alter ego Steve Ovenden, was subsequently held at the Open Day before the start of the 2003/04 season. The Open Day was, by now, an annual event at Bootham Crescent, offering the chance for fans to mix with players and the manager in relaxed surroundings before the serious action started. It was a chance for fans to get autographs and some years public training sessions were held, while other attractions included ground tours, barbecues, bouncy castles and a range of stalls manned by supporters' groups. The auction in 2003 took place in the Social Club and was to decide the 11 successful bidders who would win a place in Brass' "home" team, with a reserve amount of £70 per person required to cover the cost of supplying kit. A total of £2,815 was subsequently bid. Another auction, also held at the Social Club, on a Friday night in February saw £7,325 shelled out for places in former play-off final winning manager Alan Little's "away" team. The combined figure surpassed the Supporters' Trust's £10,000 target, while a raffle decided who would be each side's substitute and the honour of being Yorkie the Lion for the day was also auctioned off.

On the much-anticipated day of the game - thankfully not the last at the ground - each successful bidder enjoyed the chance of experiencing what it was like to be a City footballer first hand. They were all welcomed by then chairman Steve Beck at the players' entrance and ushered into their respective dressing room, where they changed into a kit bearing their name before receiving a team-talk from their manager - Brass or Little. After a warm-up session, the teams then lined up for a souvenir photograph before the match was played over two, 25-minute halves. Kevin Atkinson smashed in a spectacular, last-minute goal from 25 yards to clinch victory for Brass' home team, whose keeper Ian Surgeoner also impressed on his way to a clean sheet. Local jewellers Preston & Duckworth, then the sponsors of the Player of the Month award, also donated £100 watches as man-of-the-match prizes for each team. Brass took part in the game himself, along with Little's 1993 Wembley heroes Andy McMillan, Wayne Hall, Jon McCarthy, Ian Blackstone and Gary Swann.

The view from the away end in January 2004

Former manager John Ward was a reluctant winner as Cheltenham took three points to intensify City's relegation concerns in 2004

York City's new player-manager Chris Brass gets to grips with Leeds striker Alan Smith during a pre-season friendly in 2003

Christian Fox poses for a picture with Great British Circus stiltwalker Andrew Wild

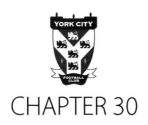

CHAPTER 30

Billy McEwan cleans toilets and flushes away negativity

"I wanted to entice players to the club, but they wouldn't have come whilst it was such a dump, so we tidied it up and gave it a coat of paint."

Following a 2-0 defeat at Aldershot, York City won their first home match as a Conference club and first at Bootham Crescent for seven months after beating part-time Tamworth by the same scoreline thanks to goals from summer signings Paul Groves and Paul Robinson. Unfortunately, that did not prove the catalyst for better fortunes, though.

A subsequent 1-0 defeat against Accrington Stanley was only notable for the home debut of future top-flight star David Stockdale. He got his chance at the age of 18 after Chris Porter was sent off and went on to turn in a man-of-the-match performance. Stockdale's memory of that game, however, was sketchy, with his first-ever competitive outing at Bootham Crescent - a 1-0 FA Youth Cup home win over Hull a year earlier - leaving a bigger impression on the young hopeful. "I don't remember as much about my first-team home debut, as I do the first time I played on the pitch against Hull in the FA Youth Cup," Stockdale explained. "Bryon Webster scored the winning goal in extra-time with a 25-yard volley and I'd always wanted to play on the pitch, because it's special when you're 17. I'd sat and watched so many times and was even on the bench for a couple of reserve games at the age of 15. The pitch was really nice at that time too - lovely and green. We'd see it every day and you'd be thinking it could be me on there one day. We would watch every single game on it and we all wanted to get on it to show people what we could do. We also got in the big baths together afterwards. We had cleaned them so many times, but it was our chance to finally use them." Stockdale also remembered the initiation ceremony he was subjected to after making his first-team breakthrough, revealing: "When you made your debut as a YTS, they made you do naked press-ups in the shower on top of a scrubbing brush that was strategically placed. That would be frowned upon now, but it was harmless fun and put smiles on people's faces, which is important."

In the next home game - a 0-0 draw with part-timers Northwich - City fans were given a reminder of better days when former play-off hero Jon McCarthy returned to Bootham Crescent at the age of 34. During a match that was also notable for being on-loan signing David McGurk's first of 333 appearances for the club, City's supporters saved their greatest encouragement for one of their past legends. "I came back to York and got a great, great reception every time I touched the ball," a grateful McCarthy recalled. "I remember flying down the wing once and putting a cross in and the York fans were applauding me. That was nice. I was also playing at right back, so they saw a different side of me. I wasn't the same player that people remembered, but I was still competent and that meant a lot to me."

The atmosphere at home games was now becoming tetchy with the good will towards Brass following relegation having dissipated as his team struggled to adapt to Conference football. It proved an eye-opening experience for young rookie McGurk, who was quickly recalled by parent club Darlington at the end of his one-month loan spell. "It wasn't the best time to come in," McGurk admitted. "The crowd were a bit hostile and restless. They were starting to get on the team's backs, because the season hadn't started too well. I can remember hitting a long ball straight out of play and the crowd started booing. One of the more experienced lads - it might have been Brassy - then told me to keep my head up. But I knew it wasn't me they were booing really - it was the style of play. We had worked on putting the ball in behind defences during training but, by the end, I was thinking do I play how I want to do or do I follow instructions. As a young defender, though, we'd drawn 0-0 and got a clean sheet so it was a solid enough debut. But, when I told people at Darlo that the fans had been booing, they just told me to complete my month and get fit, because it wasn't a great environment to be in."

The sign in the background spells the end for Chris Brass during his last game as manager against Forest Green

Further lows followed as only 15 Leigh RMI fans bothered to turn up to watch their team gain only their second away point from a possible 42 following a 1-1 draw. Brass was then sacked as manager as his position became untenable when he was booed whenever he touched the ball during a 3-1 home defeat to Forest Green Rovers.

1980s' legend Viv Busby salutes fans after returning to the club as a coach in September 2004. He subsequently had an unsuccessful spell as caretaker manager

Visiting striker Charlie Griffin hit a hat-trick and home fans even resorted to cheering on the visitors, while slow handclapping their own players. Stockdale was saddened by such scenes and Brass' subsequent dismissal, adding: "I always remember he used to take the pressure off us as players. No matter what the crowd were doing, he said that him and Nogs (assistant Lee Nogan) would take the flack."

Denis Smith's former assistant Viv Busby, who had returned to coach the team, subsequently took over as caretaker manager. There was brief talk of "Busby's Babes", as high-flying Carlisle were seen off 2-1 at Bootham Crescent with seven of the hosts' players aged 19 or under on the pitch by the final whistle. Kane Ashcroft, Michael Staley and Lee Grant were all given their full home debuts and were joined by Stockdale and Sean Davies in the starting line-up with Lev Yalcin and Graeme Law also introduced from the bench. Believing the victory illustrated the potential of the club's young players at the time, Stockdale felt it was a shame that none of his contemporaries - other than future Championship campaigner Byron Webster who was an unused substitute that day - went on to better things like himself. "Carlisle brought about 1,500 fans and that game is still a highlight for me because it was a win that was achieved with my mates," Stockdale recalled. "It did surprise me when some of the other lads didn't progress in the game as well. Michael Staley was a really good defender and I think, if he had got a chance, he could have gone on from there. He was a modern-day defender, because he was good with his feet and able to play the ball out. He had a clever mind as well and he stood out for me. Lee Grant

491

was very good too and I remember later playing as a trialist for Fulham before I joined them, and he was trialling for Barnsley, before he drifted out of the game. Lev Yalcin was a very good player too and played for Turkey under-21s but was unfortunate with injuries. The Conference is also a tough place to be for young players. You need a certain mentality because it's a man's game." A grim 2004 ended, though, with chants of "You're Not Fit to Wear The Shirt" belting out of the David Longhurst Stand following a 2-1 defeat to Burton.

In January 2005, a deal with Nestle Rowntree was subsequently struck to raise the £100,000 needed to meet the shortfall in paying off the BCH directors, Persimmon Homes and stamp duty involved in repurchasing Bootham Crescent for the club. In recognition of their contribution, the ground would be renamed KitKat Crescent for two years. The deal was crucial, but the change of name did not curry favour with everybody. Then club historian Dave Batters said at the time: "My initial reaction to KitKat Crescent is 'dear me' and I don't like it. To me, Bootham Crescent will always be Bootham Crescent. The name is steeped in more than 70 years of history and has a nice ring to it. I feel a lot of sadness about the name change, but it's a

The car park sign is replaced to reflect the ground's name change to KitKat Crescent in 2005 following a two-year sponsorship deal with Nestle

sign of the times I suppose. Yorkie Crescent would not have been brilliant, but it would have been better." *The Sun* national newspaper delighted in the new name, however, even naming a chocolate footballing XI with manager Keith Curle-y Wurly in charge of the likes of Hernan Toffee Crespo, Robbie Flake and Gary Revel.

A 2-0 defeat at home to Aldershot soon afterwards saw Billy McEwan brought in as manager to replace Busby. The new manager had actually watched Busby's final game in charge as a paying punter and felt short-changed, saying: "I came to watch York the match before I got the job and I stood behind the goals with my wife. She was quite excited because she thought we were going shopping in York, but I took her to Bootham Crescent instead. We decided we wanted to sit down for the second half and it cost us an extra £2. It wasn't a very good game and, when I spoke to Jason McGill and was offered the job, I told him you owe me £2 because the different view wasn't worth the money. Jason and his family were nice people though and it was a pleasure to work for them."

492

McEwan immediately set about smartening up a neglected Bootham Crescent, cleaning the toilets himself during his first week in the new job after being disgusted by their condition. Remembering his efforts to spruce up the stadium, McEwan said: "It was an old ground, but that was no excuse for the lack of cleanliness and hygiene. I wanted to entice players to the club, but they wouldn't have come whilst it was such a dump, so we tidied it up and gave it a coat of paint. I got my sleeves rolled up and got the players helping as well." He also swapped the positions of the home and away dugouts to be nearer to the David Longhurst Stand and "closer to the York fans" to encourage lots of vocal support. On the importance of making that connection with the fans, McEwan explained: "I wanted everyone united at the football club. I wanted to hear the fans roaring the team on and, if we moved the dugout nearer to them, they could probably hear me shouting from the bench too."

McEwan succeeded in keeping the club up with a 2-1 home win over eventual champions Barnet proving instrumental after goals by Kevin Donovan and on-loan Doncaster defender Jon Maloney. "That was a big win for us," McEwan recalled. "They were flying at the time so, from a confidence point of view, it showed we could get on the right track." Four days later, a 1-0 home defeat to Exeter saw Amy Rayner become the first female referee to take charge of a game at Bootham Crescent. The penultimate home match of the campaign - a 0-0 draw with Dagenham & Redbridge - was livened up, meanwhile, by a stunt from club mascot Yorkie the Lion. By now, Steve Ovenden was sharing match-day duties with Alex Bedingham, who decided to cycle into the stadium, down the touchline, past a bemused McEwan before coming to a halt with a skid next to Darren Dunning, as he prepared to take a corner for the home team. Recalling that incident with a laugh, Ovenden explained: "Somebody had said to Alex: 'Get on your bike, Yorkie', so he actually cycled in during the match, which was a first."

City went on to end a sorry season with their biggest home victory for more than ten years as Farnborough were thrashed 4-0 - a result that said more about the quality of the opposition faced though. The club later announced losses of £83,568 for their first campaign of Conference football at Bootham Crescent.

But McEwan built a young, exciting side for the following season and a 5-0 home win over Altrincham in mid-September - the biggest triumph at Bootham Crescent for 22 years - saw the team sit second in the table. Summer signings Clayton Donaldson, Joe O'Neill and James Dudgeon were joined on the scoresheet by a rejuvenated Andy Bishop and youth-team graduate Bryan

Stewart. After years of decline, there was a feeling that McEwan was on the precipice of bringing success back to the club. "When I went there, there was no confidence in the players," he explained. "They were struggling but, after staying up, we restructured the whole squad and I got players in on trial in the close season using my contacts in the game. We had a good look at them and built a decent, little squad. I wanted to entertain because I think, if people are paying money to watch you, you have to be positive."

McGurk had returned to the club at the start of the season and noticed the marked contrast at Bootham Crescent under McEwan, compared to his short spell during the previous campaign. "He wanted everything to look smarter around the ground and that included us as players," McGurk explained. "We wore suits to games, which was quite new for a lot of players. He wanted the whole place painted and the toilets cleaned because he wanted the players to feel at home. His argument was that, if you bought a new home, you wouldn't want mould in it. He had a professional outlook on everything from top to bottom and he turned the club around with his professionalism. He could be quite ruthless, though, in training and the way he wanted to play. If you didn't stick to that, you were normally out of the door and out of the club. He could fall out with players but, I think, in the long term, most of them would agree he made them better players." Not everybody was a fan of the new regime at Bootham Crescent, however, with Stockdale arguing: "It was a bit of a dictatorship under him and a case of his way or the highway. Top coaches adapt to players. They obviously have their own way of thinking, but they work on coaxing players towards that. With Billy McEwan, you were either in or out. There were no grey areas and I don't think you can be like that with young players who need guidance. Tactically, he was quite good, but in terms of man-management he was miles behind the game."

Prior to Christmas, McEwan's young side wobbled with six defeats during a seven-match sequence without a win. One of the losses - a 2-1 FA Trophy exit at Bootham Crescent to Conference North part-timers Northwich - proved a then 20-year-old Stockdale's final appearance for the Minstermen. Being substituted at half-time also proved a humiliating end to his City career - something that would forever rankle with the talented goalkeeper following his eventual release from the club. "He had already brought me on at half-time for Chris Porter at Morecambe a couple of games before but, unless a keeper is injured, I don't think you should ever substitute them no matter how badly they are playing," Stockdale argued. "By all means, drop them for the next game but, by replacing them during a match, it conveys a total train wreck to the other players. I don't think it's fair on the other keeper going on either. They are coming in cold and you're thinking: 'Right, do I have to do something straight away'. It's hard for the other players to be calm as well when they know they are playing in front of the second choice now. You've not had time to work with the defence, so they lose a bit of certainty. When he made the decision against Northwich he just said: 'You're coming off'. We shared a few words and that was the last time I played for York City, which is still really disappointing in my eyes. I'll never forget how good the fans were to me though and one of my favourite memories was getting a good clap from them when I walked back out at Bootham Crescent with Andy Bishop, having represented the club for the England non-League team. I am still in contact with people there and friends with members of the Harrogate Minstermen. All the way through, even during the bad times, I felt the fans supported me and I used to love going into the Social Club to mix with them after games. I also did a question-and-answer session in there with Graeme Crawford which was special and, even though I got brought off at half-time in that final game, the supporters seemed to have seen something in me, so I will always have a soft spot for Bootham Crescent. It was a place I'd have loved to have gone back to as a player. That was my biggest wish whenever cup draws were being made."

Club legend Crawford also recalled giving Stockdale a pep talk in the Social Club. He said: "I went down to Bootham Crescent to do a fans' meeting with David Stockdale just after Billy McEwan had taken him off at half-time. He had played for the England non-League team not long before and he was auctioning off his gloves from that match. I still had my old green cotton gloves and, as a laugh, I took them to the auction as well and said: 'I've brought them just in case you need them for Saturday's game'. He looked at them and couldn't believe what they looked like. What had happened to him had done his confidence no good at all, but I told him not to give up and said there were so many other clubs out there and his situation at that time was all down to one person's opinion and, whilst one manager might not rate you, another will. You could see he had talent and I was chuffed to see him go on and do what he did."

The club's poor run was brought to an emphatic end when a Boxing Day crowd of 4,921 saw City see off neighbours Scarborough 3-1 with Porter back in goal. After Brian Wake had given the visitors a first-half lead, goals from Bishop, Donaldson and McGurk provided a measure of revenge after the Seadogs' double over the Minstermen the previous season. The introduction of inspirational midfielder Manny Panther, who had been sidelined by injury during the poor run of results, proved a turning point on 38 minutes. He replaced a crocked Terry

Barwick to a crescendo of noise and, by half-time, Bishop had drawn the team level. On his nerve-tingling reception from the Bootham Crescent faithful, the Scotsman admitted: "I will always remember that game. I had been out injured for about six weeks and the

Clayton Donaldson scores against Scarborough on Boxing Day, 2005

team had struggled a bit. Scarborough was the big derby game and we were 1-0 down in front of a big crowd. I came on and the whole place went a bit mad and then, a minute after I came on, I went in for a hard challenge and clattered somebody and the crowd got going again. We scored a few minutes later and went on to win 3-1, so I have fond memories of that game. Even now, I still get messages from York fans wanting to talk about it. Once you get that sort of reception, the game becomes easier and I think it lifted the rest of the guys and the team as a whole. It definitely stands out in my career as one of the most memorable moments. It was a good atmosphere for a proper derby and it was a shame when Scarborough were demoted, and that fixture was lost."

McGurk's goal, meanwhile, was his first for the club - at the end of the ground every City player wanted to score. "We had gone through a bit of a bad period," he recalled. "It was a big derby and the fans weren't happy, because we didn't play well in the first half. But we turned it around in the second. I remember the ball flicking off my head for the goal. Darren Dunning put a free kick in and he did not see it touch me, so he went off celebrating as well. He was saying: 'It's my goal', but some of the lads had seen it touch my head as well. It was great scoring in front of the Longhurst and it was packed out that day." McEwan, meanwhile, was delighted to see so many fans in the ground, adding: "The crowds were starting to go up by then and the supporters were believing in the team again. That was our local derby, and, like the fans, I wanted to enjoy watching my side play good football. I wanted people to start coming to York City again and start talking about us and I think they were after that game."

The fixture proved the last North Yorkshire contest to be staged between the sides at Bootham Crescent, however, following the demise of Scarborough as a club. Supporters would miss the matches, although McGurk felt the fixture's significance had become a little over-stated. "It was probably built into something it wasn't really," he reasoned. "There was a lack of rivalry back then with most clubs in the Conference, though, so the atmosphere was a lot better than most matches. There was a big away following and the game was treated as a derby but, when you look at it now, York v Scarborough isn't a big game. I just think, in the Conference, our fans were looking to make games more interesting. I had played for Darlington at Bootham Crescent and that felt like a bigger fixture. They used to take about a thousand fans and that's when the old stadiums came into their own with terracing behind both goals. Those type of games, when both ends were full, brought out the best in me. They felt like bigger occasions." For future Championship marksman Donaldson, who had been plucked from Hull City reserves, the attendance represented the largest he had ever experienced and he revelled in playing in front of a crowd double the norm at Bootham Crescent then. He said: "It was Boxing Day when everybody was off work and a game that all the fans wanted to go to. We always got good crowds at Christmas time anyway and it made you think about the potential of the club if they turned up every week. The place was packed, and it was an amazing crowd, especially in the Conference. It was a local derby and you could sense the rivalry between the two sets of fans, particularly in a small ground like Bootham Crescent and that made us want to win the game for the supporters."

Bishop, meanwhile, became the first City striker since Paul Aimson 34 years earlier, to hit a first-half hat-trick in a league game during a 5-1 thumping of Forest Green Rovers in February, but an Easter Monday 2-0 reverse against Halifax, in which ex-City midfielder Steve Bushell netted for the visitors, saw the team fall short of a play-off place.

In the summer of 2006, fan ownership at Bootham Crescent then came to an end when the Supporters' Trust membership voted by a 78 per cent majority to relinquish ownership to Jason McGill's Malton-based company JM Packaging. Crucially, protections were put in place to prevent the ground ever being taken out of club ownership again. McEwan's side subsequently made a strong start to the following season. After a 0-0 opening day draw at Bootham Crescent with Exeter, the next four matches were all won. The Exeter fixture also witnessed a significant ceremony when the newly-refurbished Vice-Presidents' Lounge, which overlooked the car park and club shop and could be accessed by stairs next to the Main Stand turnstiles, was named after legendary forward Keith Walwyn following a competition by *The Press* newspaper to suggest a player worthy of such a tribute. Walwyn was a clear winner and his widow Liz officially opened the lounge, along with her husband's former team-mate Keith Houchen and *Press* reader and competition winner Dorothy Elliot. An emotional Liz said afterwards: "It's a fantastic tribute to Keith and it's hard to put into words how I feel. Keith would have been absolutely delighted and I am sure he was smiling down on us today. Keith played for other teams but he regarded York City as his club."

A 0-0 home draw with Stafford Rangers went on to herald the professional debut of another player who become a Championship regular and scored a winning goal for Scunthorpe at Wembley. Martyn Woolford, who was then 20, had only joined the club from part-timers Frickley hours before the transfer deadline, but was introduced by McEwan as a second-half substitute even if, by the player's own admission, he did not even look the part as a pro footballer at the time. "I can always remember turning up from Frickley with my shoe laces tied as tight as I possibly could, and it was the first time I had ever worn a suit," Woolford recalled of his arrival at Bootham Crescent. "My collar was all over the place and I think Anthony Lloyd came over and fixed it for me. The lads must have been thinking: 'Who the hell is this guy?' I took a lot of stick, but it was just their way of making me feel welcome and I will never forget my debut. It was my first taste of professional football and, coming from Frickley, it was a pretty big step up to be playing at Bootham Crescent, but I was excited more than anything else. I wasn't daunted. It had all come about really quickly and, sometimes, you don't get the chance to sit back and think, which is maybe a good thing because you just go out and play your game. I'll always remember the fans behind the goal at York. They never stopped singing. It was constant, and they always created a good atmosphere." In his next home game, Woolford scored his first senior goal during a 3-2 defeat to Morecambe and, while thrilled inside to achieve such a landmark, footballing etiquette dictated that, as his team were losing, he had to keep such excitement contained. "We were 2-0 down and the ball was played over to the back stick," he said. "I wrapped my foot around it and it went back across the goal and in. I then remember not knowing what to do with myself. I wanted to celebrate, but the rest of the lads were trying to get the ball out of the net because they wanted to get back into the game and get on with the rest of the match. It was still a great feeling to score on my full home debut. It was also in front of our fans, which made it that bit more special."

The team's mettle, not to mention McEwan's patience, was later tested by the visit of eventual champions Dagenham & Redbridge in late November. The Essex side's 10am train from London was delayed and the game kicked off an hour late, by which time some City fans had gone home. McEwan also claimed that Darren Craddock's pre-match hamstring injury could have been caused by the constant warming up and down. The hosts ended up losing 3-2 and the furious Scotsman was incandescent afterwards with McGurk recalling: "With his professionalism, he could not understand how any team could decide to travel to a match on the day from so far away and end up turning up late. They then took the three points as well so that didn't help his mood. He went mad and called them a pub team. When we went back there later in the season, they had put Dog & Duck on their dressing room door."

Donaldson also recalled McEwan's mood, adding: "Billy McEwan was going ballistic in the changing rooms and wasn't happy at all, nor were we as players. The game should have been postponed really after we were made to wait an hour for them. I played with Sam Saunders at Brentford later in my career and he was playing for Dagenham that day and always had a laugh reminding me about that game. They were flying, and we were up for the game, as the supporters were, but that delay took something away from the occasion. We scored early on, but I think the delay ended up affecting us a lot. They got on top and ended up going back on the train with the win." Panther added that the whole saga led to a state of confusion at Bootham Crescent and said: "I don't know if that would be allowed now. We were all asking: 'Are they coming up or not?' We were getting conflicting reports and Billy was saying it was a joke and a disgrace. The referee was telling us the game would still go ahead, but it was bizarre and quite surreal. I'd never been in that position before and never was again where a team was so late for such an important game. Typically, they then went and won the game and Billy wasn't happy. As players, we had been trying to keep focussed during the delay and not let it affect us mentally, but I think it did in the end. It was weird, because we were hearing the half-time scores from the other games before we even kicked off. It was very unprofessional on Dagenham's part. Billy McEwan had high standards, even though the club were in the Conference at the time. We all wore suits to games and he was big on discipline and time-keeping. He would never have dreamt of getting a train up from London to York on the morning of a game. He always tried to do his best for the team by getting overnight stays for long journeys and couldn't believe what was happening."

Outlining the difference between his professional approach and that of Dagenham, McEwan said: "I tried to do things correctly because I had been at big clubs like Sheffield United and Derby, so I knew all about the importance of preparation in terms of giving your team the best chance of getting a result. I asked for more overnight stays when we were going to London because you don't want to be rushing about and running the risk of getting caught up in traffic or suffering delays on trains. You spend all week training for a match, so why then get your preparation for it all wrong on the day?"

A 5-0 victory over Crawley, meanwhile, provided a moment to cherish for Panther as he scored for the only time in three seasons as a home player at Bootham Crescent - in front of the David Longhurst Stand. It was the third of the afternoon and the former Partick and St Johnstone midfielder recalled: "It was a tap-in. I slid in and just got there. We absolutely battered them and were 3-0 up at half-time. It's a good memory for me as it was great to get a goal and I was always trying to score one at the home end. I used to love it when anybody scored in front of the David Longhurst Stand because it was always full, and the atmosphere was so good. You wanted to make those fans happy and celebrate with them. They were always singing and getting the flags out and that made for a great atmosphere. We were on the cusp of going up when I was there and I would have loved to have been part of the team that did get promoted. I was very envious of that, especially considering how close we got to Wembley back then. The fans always stuck by us when I was there and I can imagine they would have been great during that period."

Donaldson went on to land himself in hot water with McEwan early in the New Year when news emerged that he had agreed to join Scottish Premier League side Hibernian during the summer and the club would not receive a penny for his departure due to a loophole in the different interpretation of the Bosman Ruling north of the border. Then Hibs manager John Collins - the former Celtic and Scotland midfielder - was even refused entrance into Bootham Crescent by a livid McEwan when he wanted to run the rule over his new signing, with an embarrassed Donaldson recalling: "I remember all that and heard all the commotion going on. John Collins said he was coming to the game to watch me but couldn't get a ticket. He got in eventually, but I think he had to buy one. Billy McEwan was not happy that I'd signed a pre-contract with Hibs and that was how he reacted in those sorts of situations, but he did well with the resources at his disposal and signed some good players. You have to take your hat off to him for the way he turned the club around."

Perhaps in preparation for life after Donaldson, McEwan signed a raw Northern League rookie Richard Brodie, who had impressed against the club during a narrow 1-0 FA Cup victory at Newcastle Benfield Bay Plastics. Brodie scored on his debut in a 4-0 triumph at Altrincham, but he failed to net in any of his first 10 appearances at Bootham Crescent and recalled that it took a while for him to win over the Minstermen faithful during his first of two spells with the club. Remembering that tough baptism, he said: "It had been an honour playing for Benfield against York in the FA Cup. I knew all about the history of the club so when, all of a sudden, I realised Billy was interested in signing me on my first professional contract, it was a privilege and a confidence boost. He and the club gave me an opportunity to change my life and that's what happened. Coming from non-League, I was doing the only thing I'd ever wanted to do as a kid. I had some hard times at first and the fans were on my back a bit. At Bootham Crescent, the fans were so near that, even if there were 3,000 there, you heard things clearly. My first 18 months were really difficult and I went through some hard times and good times. As a player, you can get a massive feeling of how a game is going by the reaction of the crowd and that rubs off on you. If things aren't going well and the crowd gets restless, you start getting nervous and that's when you have bad touches. In time, though, I saw Bootham Crescent for what it was - an old-fashioned, traditional football ground with good people. In the end, the fans were brilliant to me and I ended up being a crowd favourite and that came through hard work."

Drainage problems at Bootham Crescent that campaign did not always assist McEwan in his attempts to play fast, attractive football, though, with more points collected on the road. But, having finished 15 points adrift of Dagenham, McGurk reasoned: "The pitch probably didn't help us, but I don't think we quite had enough to win the league that season. We got to the play-offs and I probably think that would have been the case, even if we had the best pitch in the league. But it was certainly detrimental to players like Clayton Donaldson and Martyn Woolford. They were two of the most skilful and quickest players in the league, so you could understand their frustration with it." Donaldson was, indeed, not enamoured by the troublesome turf, adding: "The pitch on that far side from the dugouts always seemed waterlogged and definitely affected us. Every time you tried to play down that side, the ball got stuck in the mud and it was like that for most of the season. It restricted us, because we wanted to pass and play football. You also want to do well in front of your own fans, but our away form ended up being better. I think we'd have finished higher in the table if the pitch had been decent."

Panther also found the playing surface heavy going, adding: "The drainage wasn't very good in the corners of the pitch, where it was like a swamp, although it did get a bit better as the season went on." McEwan admitted the state of the pitch also played on his mind - especially the night before games. "The board were very supportive, and we tried to get the pitch better by spending money on it because I wanted to play a passing game on the floor, rather than hoofing the ball as far down the pitch as possible," he reasoned. "But the drainage wasn't very good, and I used to be nervous every Friday night when I turned the weather forecast on because, if rain was predicted, I knew the pitch would be a mess and the game might be postponed. Our away record was excellent because the pitches we were playing on were generally better."

In the event, a 1-0 home triumph over Oxford, courtesy of Neal Bishop's goal on the final day of the regular season, secured a play-off spot. Morecambe would be the opponents in a two-legged, semi-final with the first game, at Bootham Crescent, a contest that City dominated, only for it to end goalless. For the hosts, Craig James had a free kick saved, Steve Bowey missed the target twice and visiting keeper Steven Drench denied Woolford and Panther. But the result could still have been worse with Morecambe's Wayne Curtis missing the best chance of the game, firing over from two yards in the 73rd minute. Curtis was not as profligate in the return leg, bagging a brace to secure a 2-1 aggregate victory for Morecambe, who would become one of the first two sides to play at the redeveloped Wembley stadium as a consequence.

In hindsight, McGurk admitted that the failure to score at Bootham Crescent during the first leg proved the team's downfall. "The first legs in all the play-off games I played for York always seemed to be similar," he said. "They were very cagey, and the Morecambe game fell into that category. We'd played each other twice already, so knew exactly what each other were about and there weren't many chances in that game. It was a great atmosphere and they brought a few fans. It was vital for us to get a goal at home and, looking back, we needed one, but they were a very solid team and we would have liked to have created more chances in the match. We kept another clean sheet, which was four in a row, but a couple of mistakes cost us in the second leg and the fact that we missed out on playing in the first game at the new Wembley meant we were even more gutted." Panther felt the team should have won the home game but did not feel despondent at the end of the 90 minutes, reasoning: "I thought we were a better

Clayton Donaldson takes on Morecambe defender Chris Blackburn during the 2007 play-off, semi-final first leg clash

team than Morecambe, although playing them was always a tough game for us. We really believed we were going up that season and I still felt pretty confident after we drew 0-0 in the home leg because we had been the best side comfortably. We gave it our all and had quite a few chances. It was just one of those nights when we couldn't get a goal."

Donaldson, who ended up with broken ribs in the second leg after a clash with Drench, also recalled a bruising battle with future Morecambe manager Jim Bentley and the equally uncompromising Chris Blackburn at Bootham Crescent. He said: "They were a very physical side and we'd always said that about them. I remember being in a battle for the full game at home. I was trying to use my pace and energy to get around and behind them, rather than fighting with them because that was their strength, so I was trying to keep away from them. I thought we played a lot more direct than we normally did in that game and that played into their hands, but I still felt we did enough to get the win. We were easily the better side, but they held on by the skin of their teeth. I think they came for a draw, which made it all the more frustrating. We had lots of chances and the players were a bit disheartened in the changing room afterwards and disappointed because we hadn't taken a lead in the tie. I thought we could still get the win away from home though. I didn't think that would be a problem. We hadn't lost, and I thought we still had a great opportunity. We had a decent squad and were really unlucky not to go up that season."

For Woolford, there was personal disappointment on top of the team's frustration at not establishing a first-leg advantage with the talented winger feeling he did not perform to his highest standards. "I remember their keeper making a save from me, but I also remember thinking I hadn't played well or performed to my best at the time and that we could have done better as a team," he admitted. "We were hoping for a better result but, at 0-0, we still thought we were in the tie and had every chance of winning at Morecambe. It wasn't the worst result in the world and I think it was one of those games when neither side wanted to lose knowing they had another fixture to go at it. It was a better result from their point of view and, whilst it was nice to be playing in a play-off semi-final after a good season, maybe if we'd taken a little lead to their place, it might have been a different story." Woolford's abiding memory of that night, however, is of the energy created by the home fans, explaining: "I can remember the atmosphere and will never forget that group of fans behind the goal. Half the time, when you looked over, they weren't facing the pitch. They were turning around singing to each other, but they always created a good atmosphere at games and that helped us. The noise levels were as loud as I heard at other clubs I played for. When I left York, the fans at some teams expected a lot more of you and, if things weren't going too well, they could quite easily turn against the team at times. I can never remember a time when the York fans turned against us. They were always 100 per cent behind us, which is important for a team that wants to do well. You need a crowd that will stick with you through thick and thin, rather than getting edgy."

Brodie, meanwhile, only made a late cameo from the bench in the home leg against Morecambe, but the night still left a big impression on him. "I remember coming on and it was the first time I'd played at the ground when it was that full," he explained. "The atmosphere was great, and it was all new to me, so I wanted to get on, but it was also just a privilege to be part of a club pushing to be back in the Football League where they should be. There was maybe a bit of disappointment because we wanted to get a home goal but, the way we'd been playing away from home, we still felt we had a chance." Despite the first leg ending goal-less, McEwan could not hide his pride in the players or delight at the 6,600 attendance, saying: "It was a fantastic performance. I thought it was the best we ever played, and I was sat in the dugout grinning like the Cheshire Cat for most of the night. We did everything but score. They had bodies on the line and we had plenty of shots, but just couldn't break them down. The football we played in the first half was unbelievable and we had more than 6,000 fans there, which was great. All I could see were red-and-white shirts around the ground and I'd always said, from day one, my ambition was to fill the ground and it was a good feeling to see so many supporters. Although we didn't win the game, I felt we'd done the city proud. To then lose the tie in the manner we did at Morecambe was really disappointing, because I firmly believed we would go there and beat them."

The second leg proved Donaldson's last appearance during his first of two spells for City before he left for Scotland, but he still had fond memories of Bootham Crescent with a penalty against derby rivals Halifax, converted in front of a jubilant David Longhurst End to complete a personal brace and a 2-0 win on the final Saturday before Christmas in 2006, standing out in particular. He said: "Being from Bradford, I got a lot of stick from their fans before and during the game. I also had friends from Halifax who were texting me and telling me they were going to beat us, but I ended up with the bragging rights. I scored the penalty to win the match in front of our fans and that shut them up. The atmosphere and energy from that end of the pitch was electric. We always went that way in the second half and you looked forward to that because the fans drew everything out of you. They definitely felt like an extra man and I loved scoring and celebrating in front of them."

A poor start to the club's fourth non-League season followed as a much-changed McEwan team, without the likes of departed key men Donaldson and Neal Bishop, marked the club's 75th-year anniversary at Bootham Crescent with a 3-2 home defeat to Rushden & Diamonds, losing in front of their own fans for a third consecutive game for the first time in the Conference era. On the impact of losing key players, McEwan argued: "Clayton Donaldson could get you a goal out of nothing and it's difficult to replace players of his calibre. Neal Bishop also went out of the club, which was another disappointment but that's football - you have highs and lows." The Rushden game was televised live on Setanta Sports, whose behind-the-scenes approach to broadcasting included footage of the half-time team talks, only for an irritable McEwan to refuse to let the cameras in the dressing rooms. But the Minstermen chief, whose team were still playing attractive football despite the adverse results, did appreciate the exposure the Irish broadcasters were giving Bootham Crescent and the club, even if he didn't always agree with their methods. "It was highlighting the type of football we were playing, so that was good from York City's point of view," he reasoned. "I wasn't too happy with them coming into the changing rooms and listening to half-time team talks, but you've got to move on with the times. They were trying things out to see how it would go, but it didn't really work."

For Brodie, there was also personal satisfaction, as his first goal at Bootham Crescent was captured by the cameras. Remembering the moment, he said: "It wasn't a classic. I think it went through their keeper Paul Bastock's arms and legs and he probably should have saved it, but it was the lucky break I needed and a big relief. It was in front of the Longhurst and gave me an extra boost, although I still had a long way to go in terms of knowing what it took to be a professional. I've still got all the match highlights and my grandmother always kept a programme from every game I played in and put them in shoeboxes." A wide-eyed Brodie also welcomed Setanta's presence at the ground and their novel approach to broadcasting. "It was new to most of the players being on the television at that kind of level," he reasoned. "Some of the older lads, who had been at bigger clubs, had experienced it before, but I remember Billy was not a fan of how they did it. I was still learning about things and I just thought it was nice, because it meant all your friends and family, who couldn't make it to games, could watch you on television. I also enjoyed the way they did it. I thought it was interesting for people to find out what goes on in dressing rooms. There were some things that shouldn't be recorded, but people liked seeing what the majority of things were like."

The next time City were broadcast to the nation was a happier occasion as the club ended a 16-year wait to record their first win in front of live television cameras. Alex Meechan scored the winning goal in a 3-2 victory over Halifax, with the club having lost six and drawn three of their previous encounters on the small screen. McGurk was not impressed by the intrusive cameras at Bootham Crescent, though. "I wasn't a fan of that at all," he confessed. "I thought it made a mockery of our league. It wouldn't have been done in the Premier League, so why do things differently in our league? I don't know who agreed to it, whether it was the Conference or the clubs, because the players and managers wouldn't have done. I remember I thought it was getting too much when the cameras were there for the toss-up. It might have been nice for the viewers to get an inside perspective, but not for anybody trying to run a professional outfit. The cameras they used to put in the corners of the dressing room were massive and you were always aware they were there. I don't think they should have been around when the manager was giving his team talk. I remember the game against Halifax and they were interviewing Billy McEwan on the touchline when we scored. They wouldn't have dared approach Jose Mourinho during a game, so why our manager?"

Panther was more forgiving about the intrusion, as it opened up new areas of Bootham Crescent to the viewing public. He said: "It was different and new for the fans to see inside the changing rooms. It was quite refreshing at the time and, for me, being a Scotsman in England, it was a good way for my family and friends, who couldn't make games, to get an idea of what Bootham Crescent was like. They were always impressed by the size and noise of the crowd." Woolford also welcomed the greater exposure Setanta provided both for him and the club. He said: "It was a different experience for myself and it was exciting at the time because we were still a non-League team. I'd just had my first taste of professional football and the next thing I was on television. I suppose looking back it was strange having cameras in the dressing room, but I didn't know any different back then and I was happy with it because I'd never been on television before. All my friends and family got to see me playing at Bootham Crescent too. It gave you that extra bit of fire to do well."

FA Cup fourth qualifying round visitors Rushall Olympic were seen off 6-0, meanwhile, in the club's biggest win since 1985. The victory included a ten-minute hat-trick from substitute Craig Farrell. It is a game that was not remembered as fondly by Brodie, though, who made way for Farrell just before the hour mark after struggling against the Midlands minnows. It was a career nadir at the time with a section of the home support greeting every header won and pass completed by the 20-year-old forward with a sarcastic cheer and highlighting each mistake with a cruel jeer. Recalling how he felt after being subjected to such treatment from Bootham Crescent's harshest critics, Brodie admitted: "I can remember being substituted against Rushall Olympic, having not played well and getting some stick and I just wanted to curl myself up into a ball and cry, but I stuck at it after that and had to be mentally strong."

Two humiliating back-to-back home defeats, though, cost McEwan his job with a 1-0 FA Cup reverse to Havant & Waterlooville followed by a 3-1 league loss to Salisbury. McGurk was disappointed to see McEwan depart, even if his dismissal did not come as a surprise with his demeanour around Bootham Crescent having changed. "We'd won well at Grays a couple of weeks before and, as a player, you hear rumours that he might have got the sack if we'd lost that game," McGurk revealed. "Around about that time, I remember him also looking nervous for the first time in the dressing room. That wasn't like him and it made you think the rumours were true. I wanted to go on a run to keep him in his job because I enjoyed playing for him, but it seemed like the writing was on the wall after those two home defeats. It was a difficult time. The team was not as young and dynamic as it had been. He had become a victim of his own success in many ways. Players he had brought to the club and improved had moved on and he was expected to find replacements. Havant were actually a good team. When you lose to a team from the league below, it never looks good, but they went on to beat Notts County and Swansea and scored twice at Liverpool that season. They had some good players, who went on to bigger and better things like Alfie Potter, and Richard Pacquette, who later played with us, was also in their team at the time. But I remember going 1-0 and 2-1 down against Salisbury and it never looked like we could get back into the game. The belief had gone."

Panther also recalled the dejection that existed in the changing room at the time, confessing: "The Havant game was demoralising. We weren't doing too well in the league so were looking for a decent run in the Cup. They actually weren't a bad team going forward, but there were no excuses. It was a horrible game and we couldn't get going. The Salisbury match was another bad, bad game and Billy had hit a sticky patch that he just couldn't get out of. We weren't getting the rub of the green either, because we were still playing really good football but couldn't win a game. You hear the chat that he might get the sack as players, although it was still a bit of a surprise when it did happen." Woolford was saddened, meanwhile, by the departure of his early mentor, adding: "I remember that period and it wasn't going great. It's never nice to see somebody lose their job, especially someone who had given you your first chance in professional football. I was disappointed personally and, even though we weren't doing too well, we had also raised expectations following the season before."

For McEwan, the FA Cup defeat proved the most painful and the one he reckoned ultimately sealed his fate. "We had that many corners against Havant & Waterlooville I lost count and, for them to then hit us on the break, I think that cost me my job, which was a big disappointment because I didn't want to leave the club," he explained. "It was a big decision and a sad day for everybody - for Billy McEwan and for Jason (McGill) and his family." Brodie, meanwhile, admitted he was left shocked by the change at Bootham Crescent, adding: "That was a tough period. I didn't know what would happen or the procedure in such circumstances at all. He had signed me, so I didn't know whether I would be out of the door. I didn't know who to talk to or what to do. Some of the older lads might have seen it coming but, as a young lad, I didn't really have an opinion. I was just taking everything in."

McEwan's assistant Colin Walker went on to take charge, initially on a caretaker basis, with the team having lost eight of their 12 home fixtures in 2007/08. There was initial success for Walker who, following a 2-0 home win over Weymouth, became the first City manager to end a calendar year with five consecutive wins. Champions-in-waiting Aldershot were also seen off 2-0 in the new year, having only managed one shot on target at Bootham Crescent. Brodie and Woolford were on the scoresheet having been thrown together as an exciting young strikeforce by Walker with the latter revelling in the new partnership, saying: "I did enjoy it. I was scoring quite a few goals and it was nice to link up with him. He was easy to work off. He dragged players away and stretched defences, which allowed me to find little pockets and get my shots away." Brodie was a fan of the new partnership too, saying: "I enjoyed playing with Wooly. He went on to do better things than I did and, sometimes, you need that bit of luck. Wooly was a breath of fresh air, though, as a person as well as a player. He was a Yorkshire lad, which was quite rare at the club then and it was good to play up front with someone of his ability. I remember my goal against Aldershot. Nicky Wroe crossed it in and I headed it in at the far post."

Walker's record-breaking unbeaten start to his managerial career at City would end following his 15th game in charge - a penalty shoot-out home defeat in the Setanta Shield to Northwich. The former New Zealand international also guided the team into the semi-finals of the FA Trophy, but City could not quite overturn a 2-0 first leg deficit in Torquay at Bootham Crescent. A Chris Todd own goal reduced the arrears on aggregate, but Onome Sodje had an effort wrongly disallowed for offside, while Mark Robinson and Woolford both had strong shouts for penalties turned down.

Defeat meant missing out on an estimated £400,000 windfall and another final at the redeveloped Wembley stadium, with McGurk recalling the pain he felt in front of a supportive and colourful home crowd. "Even though the Morecambe defeat hit me harder, I was still desperate to play at Wembley," he said. "It was a boyhood dream and I wasn't to know what was around the corner and whether I would get a chance again. I had actually pulled my calf against Exeter in a match between the two legs against Torquay and wasn't fit for the home game. I didn't train at all before the second leg, but I got through it. I declared myself fit because I was so desperate to get to Wembley and, once the adrenalin got going, I was fine. We were attacking the Longhurst in the second half and the fans were brilliant, which was a massive boost to us. The flags and banners were out, and the games always felt bigger before kick-off when they were out. The supporters built that up and it got better as the years went on. I thought it added to the atmosphere at games because the fans loved it. I remember Chris Todd's own goal and you could feel the supporters trying to suck the ball over the line. Any game when the Longhurst was full was always special. I felt we scored more goals going that way and it would be interesting to know whether that was the case. You knew the fans would get behind you at that end of the pitch and every player wanted to score in front of them. That feeling was better than anything and I'm a fan of the old-style terraces with the atmosphere they generate. I ended up playing up front at that end myself for the last 10 minutes against Torquay and was just running around everywhere. I remember Pars (Dan Parslow) being back on his own at one point and up against three of their players. We were throwing everything at it and it was like being back at school again trying to get a goal. At the end, I don't think I have ever come off a pitch as tired. It was a massive blow. When we had got a goal back, we felt as though we could do it, but it was another chance to reach Wembley and to be one of the first players to play there gone."

Panther also saw a spectacular effort saved late on that would have taken the tie to extra-time and he added: "Torquay were a horrible team to play against and the away leg was a miserable game. We didn't play too badly, but we gave ourselves an uphill battle for the second leg, although we went on to play really well at home. Colin had given the team more freedom to play after taking over from Billy and we got a goal back and were right back in the tie. I nearly scored in the last minute with an overhead kick, but the keeper just tipped it over the bar and it was so unfortunate that we couldn't clear that final hurdle to Wembley again. I was desperate to get there, and all the lads were gutted afterwards. We didn't have a chance to get in the play-offs that season, so it was the one thing we were going for and it wasn't to be." Woolford also shared his team-mates' despair at missing out again on a trip to the national stadium. "You don't get many chances to play at Wembley," he reasoned. "Luckily, I did later in my career but, at the time, you think: 'Is that it, have I just fluffed my last chance of getting there?' and it's heart breaking. It's a huge prize to play at Wembley and something you will always regard as one of the biggest achievements in your career. Against Torquay, while we weren't saying it at the time, we lost that tie in the first leg. But there was still a fight in us to try and stage a comeback and we showed how much we wanted it in the home leg."

Panther also recalled the part the fans played in trying to overturn the first-leg deficit, including the use of flags and flares. "When flares get thrown on the pitch, it can distract you, but the flag displays and smoke did add to the atmosphere," he admitted. "When you can see the fans are giving it a good go to get behind the side, it does give you a bit of a boost." Brodie, meanwhile, was only introduced in the 57th minute during the return leg having fallen out of favour under Walker. On the disappointment of being on the periphery during another failed bid to play at the national stadium, he said: "It was hard watching from the bench, but I don't know if I was ready to start games like that then. Maybe I was, but Colin had put that doubt in my mind. There was a chance of getting to Wembley and we knew that could change our lives. I managed to do that during the years after, but it would have been nice to have done it then. I thought we could and should have done too, but it ended up being another kick in the balls. It's how you react to these things though and the club did bounce back."

The season then petered out, although history was created at Bootham Crescent during an April fixture that had looked as mundane and meaningless as they come prior to kick-off. Unfashionable Woking were the visitors and 22-year-old referee Ross Joyce, who actually worked for the North Riding FA as a trainer of officials, sent off three home players, reducing the Minstermen to eight men on 82 minutes. With the team leading 2-1 courtesy of a Sodje brace, Joyce gave right-back Craddock and goalkeeper Tom Evans their marching orders for dubiously-conceded penalties on 63 and 70 minutes respectively. Midfielder Stuart Elliott was then also sent for an early shower when he intervened after Giuseppe Sole, who converted both spot kicks for the visitors, appeared to strike Woolford in the face and only received a caution for that crime. Brodie, who was shown 26 yellow and two red cards during his first three-and-a-half years with the Minstermen before picking up nine cautions in 21 games during his second stint in 2016, managed to stay on the pitch despite having his name taken on 24 minutes and joked: "For once, I wasn't the one in trouble. Two of my mates - Stuey Elliott and Darren Craddock - were though and I've never played in a game like that again. I don't think I was ever in another side that had two sent off let alone three and I remember a lot of our fans leaving in disgust."

There was more bad news to follow, meanwhile, when the club admitted defeat in its plans to relocate to land adjacent to Nestle's Wigginton Road factory. Jason McGill, now club chairman, also added that time and financial constraints made the geographically-appealing York Central site an unviable option too, with land costing £2 million an acre and the development expected to take another 15 years to complete. As the following season started, a boost was provided, though, when the City of York Council agreed to take over the onerous annual £138,000 Football Foundation loan repayments while land behind York Racecourse, known as Bustardthorpe, became the latest site to come under consideration as a possible location for a new community stadium. In the Social Club, meanwhile, the first York Minstermen Beer Festival was held and would be staged annually for the following four years.

Yorkie the Lion arrives at the ground on a bike during a match against Dagenham in April 2005

Liz Walwyn – the widow of legendary striker Keith - opens the newly-named Keith Walwyn VIP Lounge with Keith Houchen and competition winner Dorothy Elliott looking on

Billy McEwan writes personally to season-ticket holders in May 2005 from the boardroom

511

David Stockdale and Graeme Crawford compare goalkeeping gloves

The 75th anniversary of Bootham Crescent is celebrated with the releasing of 75 balloons in August 2007

Billy McEwan buys a brick for the wall in the car park where supporters could also join in the fundraising venture and pick a message of their choice

An aerial picture of Bootham Crescent in February 2007

CHAPTER 31

Richard Brodie sends the Longhurst into a frenzy against Luton

"I then saw Tyler coming out and smashed my shot into all the toilet rolls."

Despite talented winger Martyn Woolford moving on at the start of the 2008/9 campaign, Colin Walker then equalled a club record when a 2-0 home win over Woking, courtesy of a Danny Bunce own goal and Daniel McBreen's first-half strike, saw his side still unbeaten eight fixtures into the season, matching the efforts of Denis Smith's 1984/85 side. One of those games saw City share the spoils in a 1-1 draw against Histon despite preparations for the game being hindered by the most unusual circumstances the day before. A suspect package was delivered to the ground on the Friday morning, addressed to former chairman Douglas Craig and containing white powder. It was opened by then club secretary Nick Bassett and the ground was subsequently sealed off at the front gates by police for more than five hours, while they and City officials waited for the arrival of forensic investigators from Leeds. It was subsequently confirmed that the powder was Paracetamol, while the package was also tested for fingerprints.

The Histon draw was one of five during Walker's record-equalling sequence and, despite just prevailing 4-2 in a penalty shoot-out Conference Cup victory against Mansfield - watched by the lowest-ever crowd for a first-team Bootham Crescent fixture of 608 disregarding Covid-19 restrictions - performances and results worsened. The poor form led to Walker's departure and a

Manager Colin Walker speaks to a police officer after the ground was sealed off for five hours as a suspect package, addressed to former chairman Douglas Craig, was examined by forensic investigators. It was eventually found to contain Paracetamol

reprieve for Richard Brodie, who had been loaned out to Barrow. Brodie argued that Walker's problems began when his demeanour changed at Bootham Crescent, as he made the transition from assistant to manager. "Initially, it started off well for him but, then, he stopped becoming Col and wanted to be called gaffer," Brodie explained. "He had changed. People get manager's jobs and try to be something they're not, but I don't understand why they have to change and do things differently. He was never going to be Billy (McEwan) and Col never got another manager's job after York, so I don't think it really worked. It changed for me straight away after he left. I had played for Barrow at Weymouth on the Saturday and then was asked by Neil Redfearn, who was caretaker manager for one game, to come back and play for him the following day and I went on as a sub at Bootham Crescent for a Sunday match."

Martin Foyle was swiftly appointed by the Minstermen - a decision that would transform Brodie's career, as the former Port Vale chief turned the struggling rookie into a prolific marksman. On the pivotal moment in his Bootham Crescent fortunes, Brodie revealed: "I'll never forget Martin Foyle's first talk with me. He told me that I looked like a little boy lost who just needed guiding. He did that for me and went on to help me massively throughout my career because I would normally speak to him twice a week." The size of Foyle's initial task was highlighted, though, during his first home match - a 1-0 loss against a Grays Athletic side that had lost their previous ten away games. City were booed off and one Grays supporter chose to celebrate the end of his club's losing streak in the most literal way possible, invading the Bootham Crescent pitch with just a strategically-placed sock to spare his blushes.

The club went on to announce worrying losses of £413,000 for the year ending June 2008, while revealing that wage salaries had swollen to a total just under £855,000, which represented 74 per cent of the club's turnover. JM Packaging continued to fund the club who, under Foyle, were beginning to mount another tilt at FA Trophy success. An extraordinary third-round replay against Kidderminster was settled by penalties at Bootham Crescent with all 22 players left on the pitch at the end of extra-

Michael Ingham saves the 26th penalty of an incredible penalty shoot-out against FA Trophy opponents Kidderminster, in which all of the first 25 spot kicks were converted to create a record for a professional game in England

time converting from the spot initially, including teenage debutant Josh Radcliffe. Mark Robinson and Simon Rusk went on to score from 12 yards again before Michael Ingham saved from Justin Richards to secure a 13-12 shoot-out success. Earlier, Richards had cancelled out McBreen's 74th-minute opening goal. A superstitious Foyle refused

Daniel McBreen helps book York City's first-ever visit to the new Wembley stadium with a goal in the 2009 FA Trophy semi-final, second leg clash against Telford

to watch any of the 26 spot kicks, while the FA later confirmed that no two teams had ever converted the first 25 penalties during a professional shoot-out in England.

Brodie added that the marathon contest also presented problems in terms of getting back to his home in the north-east that evening. "That was just ridiculous and a crazy night," he explained. "Me and Andy Ferrell (the north-east based future City midfielder who was then playing for Kidderminster) actually missed the last train and had to stay overnight at The Groves Hotel. Robbo and Simon Rusk did well that night to score both of their penalties because that presents problems as you're wondering whether you should go the same way and what the keeper is thinking. I remember there being some really good penalties. Their centre-back Mark Creighton put one in that stuck in the stanchion if my memory serves me right."

McBreen's brace went on to see off Havant & Waterlooville at Bootham Crescent in the quarter-finals before AFC Telford made the journey up to North Yorkshire, trailing 2-0 after the first leg of their semi-final tie with the Minstermen. Rusk and Ben Purkiss had scored the goals in Shropshire, while Brodie and McBreen went on to secure a 4-1 aggregate victory with Andy Brown's late consolation for the visitors counting for nothing. Party poppers were handed out in the directors' box prior to the final whistle and fans invaded the pitch. Archbishop of York Dr John Sentamu then joined in the raucous celebrations as players, management and board members jumped up and down in the directors' box in front of jubilant City supporters. Remembering the joyous scenes, then director Rob McGill smiled: "We used to get the Chablis in for the Archbishop. That was his favourite tipple."

On an emotional afternoon, as the club secured only their second-ever visit to Wembley and first to the rebuilt stadium, manager Foyle admitted at the time: "I probably didn't realise what it means to the people who work within the club, but there's been a few crying who have seen the good times, but more bad times." For David McGurk, who was brought on as a 69th-minute substitute, he recalled a straight-forward, triumphant home leg after the previous Wembley heartbreaks. "We'd done the hard work away from home," McGurk recalled. "I was on the bench for the second leg and was brought on when we were home and dry when there was no pressure. We'd played three at the back in the game at Telford and played it again at Forest Green during midweek in between the legs but it didn't work. We got battered and were lucky to get away with a draw, so we changed system again for the second leg and I was a sub. When I came on, it was all quite relaxed and routine. With half-an-hour to go, the fans knew we were going to Wembley and it was a carnival atmosphere."

Brodie felt that the celebrations began even earlier when he scored the home leg's opening goal. Remembering the historic day, he said: "Firstly, I was surprised by how many Telford fans were there because I hadn't realised how well supported they were, but it was a carnival atmosphere really. For my goal, Ben Purkiss went down the right and cut inside. I then hit a shot with my left

Goalkeeper Michael Ingham and chairman Jason McGill celebrate reaching Wembley in the directors' box following the 2009 FA Trophy semi-final triumph over Telford

516

foot and it was bending away from goal, but it hit the post and went in. That put us 3-0 up on aggregate and meant we could play with no fear because, as long as we weren't stupid, there was no way we were going to concede three against a team from the division below. We could relax, pass the ball around and do a few tricks. The fans were also feeling just as relaxed." On the party that started at the final whistle, Brodie added: "It topped anything I had experienced in the game at that time. It wasn't just about getting to Wembley. It was also nice for York City to get a bit of success, which they deserved after so long in the doldrums. From my point of view, it was also great to have that bit of success, having come through the tough times I'd had at the club. I remember being in the directors' box and I was pictured on the front of the *Non-League Paper* with champagne and the chairman had his arm around me. The Archbishop of York was celebrating with us as well. He came to the hotel with us before the game and was a great character and it was quite funny when you'd see him on television as well. I remember having a good chat with him in the car park after the game."

McGurk joined in the jubilant scenes at the final whistle but, with the threat of relegation still looming and his starting place at Wembley far from assured, he did not get wrapped up completely in the moment.

"At the final whistle, it was the first time I'd experienced fans on the pitch at Bootham Crescent and it was good to see them enjoying the occasion," he recalled. "We were also able to get off the pitch, because it was before the time of camera phones really and there was no need for hundreds of selfies. But, whilst I enjoyed the celebrations, my first thought was I've got to fight to get back in the team now and, more importantly, I wanted to get back in because we were in a relegation battle. Shaun Pejic and Pars (Dan Parslow) were playing well but I got in because Shaun played at full-back in the final and Mark Robinson was left out."

The club still flirted with relegation, however. McBreen went on to end his terrible 21-hour-and-46-minute wait for a league goal during a vital 1-0 home win over Eastbourne that lifted his team out of the drop zone going into the final week of the season. A 2-1 home win over Forest Green, thanks to teenager Adam Boyes and a Terry Burton own goal, on the last Tuesday night of the season then meant the club only needed one point from their final two fixtures at fellow strugglers Weymouth and Lewes. They laboured their way to four and went on to lose 2-0 to Stevenage in the Trophy final.

That season also saw the end of regular reserve fixtures for seven years at Bootham Crescent, as the club withdrew from the Pontin's League. Organised second-string football would only be reintroduced under Jackie McNamara following the club's second relegation from the Football League in 2016 for two seasons, although the home fixtures were largely played at the Wigginton Road training ground, other than when Bootham Crescent was used if the former was waterlogged.

In the summer of 2009, meanwhile, Foyle immediately set about improving matters for the following season and a strong challenge in the league was complemented by a good FA Cup run. After a part-time Bedworth team, featuring future City hero Matty Blair, were beaten 2-0, Crewe Alexandra became the first Football League club to be beaten by the Minstermen as a Conference outfit. A five-goal thriller at Bootham Crescent saw substitute Richard Pacquette level the scores on 85 minutes and, two minutes later, Brodie claimed his second of the game - a goal fit to win any tie after he started and finished a move that saw him burst powerfully into the penalty box and repel three challenges before lifting the ball over Crewe keeper Steve Phillips. For Brodie, the goal represented a career highlight. "When I was asked to name my favourite-ever goal in programmes at other clubs, I said that I've got two and they were both scored for York at Bootham Crescent," he revealed. "The first was the one against Crewe and I remember it well. We were 2-1 down but Richard Pacquette equalised and, then, even though some people say my right foot is just for standing on, it somehow worked that day. I remember running and holding off Patrick Ada and then Mat Mitchel-King was there, but I went around both of them and stuck the shot in. It was the first time I had come up against a Football League club and I ended up getting the Player of the Round

Richard Brodie looks like he can't quite believe what he has just done atter being mobbed by team-mates for scoring a stunning, winning goal in the FA Cup against Crewe

award. It was another step up the ladder for me. My other favourite goal was still to come - the one against Luton in the play-offs."

McGurk took most satisfaction from the manner of the victory rather than the result's shock value, reasoning: "It wasn't necessarily special because they were from a higher division, it was more to do with how the game panned out. The tie swung one way and the other and, to get two in the last five minutes, was an unbelievable feeling. The FA Cup ties are massive games and you always look forward to the draws. I remember Pacs scoring and, at that moment, I think most of the team were glad to get a replay. Then, when Brodie scored the winning goal, that elation for the players and fans is something you can't replicate. You only get that on a football field." City eventually bowed out of the competition at the third-round stage following a trip to Premier League Stoke. The club also announced that a modest profit of £30,000 had been made during the year ending June 2009, largely due to the sale of Woolford and the Trophy final appearance.

Foyle's team continued in a rich vein of form and a 4-1 home triumph over Hayes & Yeading United, courtesy of goals from Chris Carruthers, the unstoppable Brodie (two) and Kevin Gall, set a new club record of eight consecutive league wins. There was a poignant contest in the FA Trophy, meanwhile, when City's Bootham Crescent tie against David Longhurst's home-town Corby saw both sets of supporters mark the 20th-anniversary of his tragic death on the pitch by laying wreaths in front of the stand named in his memory. A Ferrell penalty went on to secure a 1-0 win for the hosts. But a suspension for Brodie would derail City's automatic promotion push and, without him, the club lost their first game at Bootham Crescent in 24 fixtures - a surprise 1-0 defeat to Eastbourne.

Off the pitch, meanwhile, it was mooted that Bootham Crescent could be redeveloped as an alternative to moving stadium. The idea, which was again dependent on acquiring the Ministry of Defence land behind the Popular Stand, never reached the drawing board like many others.

A memorable 5-0 home win over AFC Wimbledon would go on to secure a play-off place and provided a fine tribute to 1955 FA Cup semi-final hero Sid Storey, who had passed away in the run-up to the game. Brodie hit a first-half hat-trick and, looking back, enthused: "I got three goals in 19 minutes. Two of them were penalties and I scored ten that season by going to the goalkeeper's left every time. It was great to get a hat-trick to secure our play-off place. We were 4-0 up at half-time and they took one of their centre backs off, which was a sign of how good we were or how bad they were. I also remember the game before when we got a last-minute penalty against Altrincham after Greg Young brought me down and the score was 1-1. Their keeper Scott Coburn came out and said: 'Do you remember your last penalty against me and which way are you going to go this time?' I told him you'll find out in a minute because that's how cocky I was at the time and I put it in the top corner. Graham Heathcote was their manager at the time and, after we ran towards the dugouts to celebrate, he tried to volley the ball at me."

A tense play-off, semi-final first leg encounter against Luton then ensued at Bootham Crescent. Fans in the David Longhurst Stand put on a colourful and spectacular flag display - their biggest yet - with Brodie admitting such demonstrations of support made a huge impression on him. "York City were the only club I played for whose fans have done that," he pointed out. "The bar had been set by them during the Torquay Trophy semi-final, then it was raised 12 months later against Telford and in the FA Cup tie against Crewe, but it was taken to a different level again against Luton. When I walked out, the hairs on the back of my neck stood up and I know that's an old cliché, but it was true. It was a feeling I'd never had before, and I was definitely nervous, although I always got nerves before games and I think that's a good thing. I'm superstitious too and I remember going to that game with my aunty and uncle because it was a Thursday night and we found a 10p piece on the train. I kept it and took it to every other game I played in."

Brodie displayed no nerves, though, when he pounced on 89 minutes to grab the only goal of the game. The 22-year-old striker burst clear after a ball forward skimmed off the head of Luton centre-back Shane Blackett. He then fired firmly into Mark Tyler's bottom left-hand corner to score his 37th goal of the season. Recalling the game and his dramatic late contribution, Brodie said: "After the great atmosphere that had been whipped up by our fans before kick-off, when the game started we got absolutely murdered. If it had been a boxing match, they would probably have stopped it as a contest. Inghy (Michael Ingham) had to make a couple of good saves and I hadn't had a chance all night. Then, all of a sudden, we had a free kick. Their defender Blackett misjudged his header and that did me a favour because it slowed the ball down. I then saw Tyler coming out and smashed my shot into all the toilet rolls. I didn't even know if it had gone in or hit the back boards but the reaction of everyone was unbelievable. It was the first time I celebrated differently, instead of putting my arms up in the air (in his trademark Angel of the North pose). Sometimes, you think I'll do this or that if I score but, when you get a goal like that one, it all goes out of the window. I just ran to the corner flag and then the lion mascot jumped on me and all the players piled on too. All of a sudden, we were going to Luton with a 1-0 lead that we didn't really deserve, which was fantastic. Scoring a goal like that in the last minute in front of the David Longhurst Stand was great. Seeing how much it meant to those supporters was fantastic and a bit emotional. It was a really special feeling."

Guy Mowbray, just a matter of weeks before flying out to cover the World Cup finals for the BBC in South Africa, had a perfect view of the strike, remembering: "Those Manchester United and Everton games were top nights and the only one that came close for me in recent years was the home leg against Luton in the play-offs. I deliberately went behind the goal for that match with my mates and, when Brodie scored right at the end, I must have moved a mile and I loved that." Reflecting on that memorable contest, McGurk reckoned terrific team spirit was responsible for a victory against opponents even he felt might prove superior. "I thought they were a lot better than us on the night and they were on top for long spells of the first leg," he admitted. "I remember getting to 60 minutes and they were playing in front of us from right to left and I thought we won't win this semi-final. I felt they were too strong and a better team, but we had great spirit. I still keep in touch with a lot of the lads from that era and I think that togetherness got us over the line in that tie. Their front four was probably the best in the league. They caused all sorts of problems but (left-back) James Meredith probably produced his best performance of the season against Claude Gnakpa. Ben Purkiss also played well at right back and I remember Luke (Graham) and myself being over-worked at times with so many shots and headers to defend and clear. We could also rely on Michael Ingham when we had to, and everybody was throwing their bodies in the way of the ball. In the back of my mind, though, I remembered how we hadn't got a goal against Morecambe in 2007 and, because we had shown we could hang on to a lot of 1-0 wins that season, I knew it could be vital if we got one. It was the busiest we had been all season, so the feeling when the goal went in was unbelievable and the roar from the York fans was the loudest I'd ever heard. I think everyone knew what it meant because, as well as they had played, they had still not been able to break us down. My body was drained after the game, but everybody had recovered in time for the second leg. The game at Luton was then a perfect performance in terms of not giving anything away."

It was little surprise that Brodie earned his team the first-leg advantage, although McGurk did confess that the quality of several of his strikes that season was unexpected. "I didn't think he was capable of some of the goals he was scoring," McGurk explained. "He wasn't the best trainer in the world or the most technical, but an 11v11 situation brought out the best in him. He had pace and strength and could finish but, when he was also scoring delicate lobs, we were all wondering where's he pulled that out from. But that's what happens when you're at the top of your game. He was the most potent striker in the league and everybody hated him and playing against him. He wound opposition fans up and he was probably responsible for a lot of the rivalry with Luton." Brodie, himself, remembered a period in which he felt almost invincible. "I was playing with absolutely no fear and had nothing to lose," he explained. "I'd had some hard times before when the fans probably didn't rate me and were thinking: 'What has Billy signed?', but I always had a belief that I could score goals and then I just started scoring goals that were outrageous. Foyley actually said to me: 'Can't you score a tap-in?' and had me watching his goals on YouTube. They were going in off his backside and he was getting goals just by throwing his body at them. He was actually teaching me how to score bad goals. I think it worked, because I ended up getting a goal against Kidderminster with my chin from a yard out after a corner at Bootham Crescent. Ranks (Michael Rankine) was also a big help to me that season and it was a great feeling going out onto the pitch thinking the team was never going to lose and I was always going to score."

City were far from a one-man team under Foyle either in 2009/10, with the backs-to-the-wall 1-0 victory over Luton typical of a season in which that result became commonplace. "We were strong defensively but we were helped by having two banks of four," McGurk pointed out. "Even the wingers, like Alex Lawless and Chris Carruthers, could tuck in, get back and help the full backs. We then had Richard Brodie and Michael Rankine who caused havoc and all sorts of problems up top. They got an awful lot of goals and did not get that much support from midfield or defence in that respect. Sometimes, the football was not too entertaining, but we were well-drilled, and all knew what we were doing."

Club director Rob McGill and wife Carole, meanwhile, admitted that the Luton victory was one of their most enjoyable moments having made the, sometimes, uncomfortable transition from Popular Stand supporters to the boardroom. "Going into the boardroom scenario, everything became different," Rob admitted. "Viewing football as a director was not as attractive. As a supporter, you go and watch and, if York lose, you walk down the road all upset but, being involved in running the club, you're always thinking of the cost of losing that match. It's always about finance and funding, which takes a lot of enjoyment out of it. When games got postponed at Bootham Crescent, that was hard as well, because you have to look at cash flow. But I enjoyed that game. Luton had an air of superiority about them. They came in with the attitude that they were a big club and rightly so, to an extent." Remembering victory being all the more sweet due to the rivalry that was arising between the two clubs, Carole added: "The Luton night match was special. The chairmen from Stevenage and Oxford both came to support us to show solidarity against Luton. There was a real them against us feel to the night and it was a real fight. You could really sense that. Their directors were flaunting it before, thinking they were going to absolutely beat us out of sight, as if it was a forgone conclusion that they would win, and that night was about sticking it up them."

City would go on to win by the same margin at a hostile Kenilworth Road thanks to a Carruthers goal, before missing out on promotion back to the Football League following a 3-1 defeat at Wembley to Oxford.

Richard Brodie celebrates the late goal against Luton that gave his team a crucial advantage before heading to Bedfordshire for the second leg of the 2010 play-off, semi-final

Richard Brodie can't hide his delight after scoring in the FA Trophy semi-final win against Telford

The coach prepares to leave Bootham Crescent for the trip to Wembley in 2009

City's squad celebrate the FA Trophy semi-final victory over Telford in the difrectors' box

Chairman Jason McGill and then Archbishop of York Dr John Sentamu with the charity shirt the team went on to wear at Wembley in the 2009 FA Trophy final

CHAPTER 32

Rotherham crushed 3-0 at start of Gary Mills revolution

"You could see we were starting to build something."

During the summer of 2010, the club announced for the first time that their preferred location for a new stadium site was now at Monks Cross, where Huntington Stadium, the then council-owned home of rugby league side York City Knights and the city's athletics club, would be demolished and a new arena erected. Other possible options, put forward by the City of York Council, included redeveloping Bootham Crescent; land at Hull Road next to the University of York's Heslington East campus and the Mille Crux and Nestle North site off Haxby Road. Monks Cross was regarded as the most achievable in terms of cost and time frame, with the possibility of adjacent enabling developments to assist funding.

On the pitch, an indifferent start to the new campaign saw Richard Brodie sold to Crawley at the end of August and Martin Foyle resign. After Andy Porter and Steve Torpey had spells in temporary charge, Gary Mills was then brought in as manager from Tamworth. It was a sad departure for Foyle, although David McGurk quickly noticed the potential for progress with Mills at the helm. "We still weren't conceding many under Martin Foyle because we always had our two banks of four, but we weren't creating as many chances and Richard Brodie had gone," said McGurk, as Foyle made way for a new era at Bootham Crescent. "We then played a lot better football when Gary Mills came in and were still solid with Inghy (Michael Ingham) as reliable as ever. You could see we were starting to build something."

Mills' reign started with a 1-1 draw against Bath City at Bootham Crescent, with Michael Rankine's first-half penalty cancelled out by the Gloucestershire strugglers and the former Nottingham Forest midfielder recalled: "I remember getting a few comments from behind me, which you get all the time, like: 'It's got to be better than this' but, in that first game, it was just a matter of

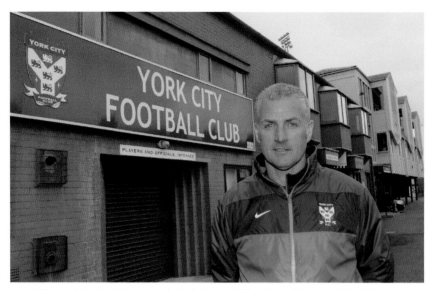

Gary Mills is unveiled as the club's manager for the first time in 2010 outside the Players and Officials' Entrance

getting over to the players and everybody at the football club how I work and how I wanted everybody to pull together. It might not have happened by that first game, but it happened very quickly." Indeed, Mills soon began turning the club's fortunes around, with a 3-0 mauling of League Two promotion hopefuls Rotherham providing another memorable FA Cup night at Bootham Crescent. Rankine bagged a brace in the first-round replay and set up the other goal for Chris Smith, who had been brought back to the club as captain by Mills. For McGurk, it was another memorable evening under the Bootham Crescent floodlights. "There was a big away crowd again, which all added to the occasion and made such nights special," he explained. "I thought we had actually played better in the first game and were unlucky not to get the win. I remember them having some good chances in the first half and we could have been 2-0 or 3-0 down but we got the first goal and their body language changed. Ryan Cresswell - their centre-half - got injured in the warm-up and he was a big loss for them, because a young lad came in and Michael Rankine bullied the two centre halves for the whole game. He got his goals and helped get us up the pitch with one of his best performances for the club."

Recalling an important night in restoring belief at Bootham Crescent, Mills added: "Rotherham were right at the top of League Two at the time, but I remember that we should have won at their place, before bringing them back

526

to Bootham Crescent for the replay and Michael Rankine was on fire during that second game. I think the FA Cup was a chance early on in my career at York to get some confidence and team spirit into that side. We got stronger and stronger after that win and it certainly didn't do us any harm. My job then, as it always will be, was to get the belief into players that they can play. If they can't, I won't waste my time and I'll find them somewhere else to play. I love man-managing players and I think I got the best out of that group of players who had probably been struggling in my first season, before making some changes."

The Minstermen would go on to meet Premier League Bolton in the third round and bowed out 2-0. But Mills' team also began to mount an unlikely push for the play-offs, with a 1-0 triumph over Histon, courtesy of Jamie Reed, representing a ninth successive home win. The brave bid for a top-five place ended, though, in the club's penultimate fixture as City failed to score for the first time under Mills during a 0-0 draw against Cambridge. The club record, set by the likes of Dean Kiely, Andy McMillan, Steve Tutill, Paul Stancliffe and Wayne Hall in 1993/94, was equalled, however, with just 13 home goals conceded in the league.

Two youngsters enjoy a kick about in Grosvenor Road outside Bootham Crescent in January 2011

The five ex-York City players killed in action during the
Second World War are honoured with bugler Colin Carr
playing the Last Post after a service by Rev Steve Benford,
of St Luke's Church in 2011

City's players and staff celebrate being drawn
against then Premier League outfit Bolton
Wanderers during the FA Cup third round in 2011

A volunteer shovels
snow to try and get
the pitch in playable
condition for a match
in December 2010

A frosty Bootham Crescent in December 2010

CHAPTER 33

Double Wembley winners take club back into the League

"The feeling around the football club at the time was magical and something to cherish."

The beginning of what was to become a historic 2011/12 season did not get off to the most promising of starts at Bootham Crescent, with back-to-back home defeats against Telford and Alfreton in August. David McGurk retained a belief, though, that the team would come good under Gary Mills, saying: "We were all confident and some of the football was unbelievable. Teams would sit off us though and we had to find something different to counter that because there was a danger of passing the ball around too much. We needed to penetrate as well and not just play in front of teams."

Manager Mills, meanwhile, felt those early reverses provided an important wake-up call. "Telford only won one away game all season and it was against us but, as a football manager, sometimes those little reminders are what it takes, so you don't get complacent," he reasoned. "A little kick up the backside here and there for the players and myself doesn't do any harm. Unfortunately, to get it, you have to suffer a defeat that you might not be expecting. There were a few people in the stand that maybe thought we didn't have what it takes to get back to winning football matches but, when you lose games, it's for a reason and then you have to put things right."

Results picked up in the autumn, while Oakgate's planning application was submitted for a new stadium at Monks Cross with chairman Jason McGill outlining the repercussions if it was rejected. He warned: "This is our last chance and only realistic opportunity of getting a community stadium for York. Without this stadium, the club could be homeless, and we would certainly have to go part-time the season after next, which would be disastrous for the club and the ambitions of our supporters."

City went on to score six goals in a league match at Bootham Crescent for the first time since 1985, seeing off Braintree 6-2 with Ashley Chambers (two), Paddy McLaughlin, Jamal Fyfield, Jason Walker and Adriano Moke all on target. The game also represented the highest aggregate scoreline at Bootham Crescent since the 9-1 triumph over Southport in 1956. The prolific Walker later scored a sensational overhead kick in a pulsating 2-1 home triumph over Grimsby. At the time, it became one of the most-watched strikes of its kind since Pele's *Escape to Victory* effort, attracting 165,000 views on *YouTube* within a week.

Communications and community director Sophie McGill, meanwhile, hit out against the objections of city-centre retailers towards the Monks Cross community stadium enabling developments, saying: "Personally, I believe it is ridiculous to state York City centre will be destroyed by the existence of Marks & Spencer and John Lewis stores at Monks Cross. It is utter nonsense. What about the 1,000 jobs and £87 million-investment this development will bring to York in this time of austerity when additional employment is essential and should not be turned away?" Former council leader Steve Galloway also claimed that objectors were promoting "distorted arguments fuelled by vested interests".

Back on the pitch, the team set a club record when six different players made the scoresheet during a 7-0 home triumph against Kettering. Jamie Reed (two), Jon Challinor, Matty Blair, McLaughlin, Chambers and Moses Ashikodi all netted during the club's second-biggest victory ever. The manner of those thumping triumphs over Braintree and Kettering thrilled Mills, who explained: "I loved those results and will always love winning like that. People tell you it doesn't matter how you win, but I disagree with that. As managers and footballers, you are in the entertainment business. It's not always possible, but we got that team playing like I wanted them to do with lots of chances being created and, on those two occasions, the ball went in the net more often than it didn't. In other games, we were solid, and we were strong with that side of the game as well, so we could defend as well as score goals. I felt confident that we could beat anybody and that was building up in the dressing room. When we crossed that white line, not only did we believe we weren't going to lose, we felt we were going to win most of our games."

But it took a scrambled, stoppage-time Challinor equaliser to prevent City falling at the first hurdle in the FA Trophy to part-timers Solihull Moors, during a 2-2 draw at Bootham Crescent. While the late leveller was greeted

Jon Challinor scores the stoppage-time equaliser against Solihull Moors that ensured the Minstermen remained in the FA Trophy during the double Wembley-winning season

with vigour by City fans, the players had more than one reason for lamenting a midweek replay at Solihull with McGurk revealing: "That was a strange game. The last thing everybody wanted was a replay because we didn't want to go there on a Tuesday night. We had also planned our Christmas party for after the match in Newcastle and the manager had told us it would be cancelled if we drew. At half time, he then said that if we lost it would be cancelled as well. We all knew the importance of Jon's goal when it went in but, if you look at the footage, nobody celebrated because we were desperate to get another goal, so we could go to Newcastle, but there was only 30 seconds left and the game ended in a draw. Afterwards, the gaffer then asked one of the young lads - I think it was Michael Potts - 'What do you think? Should I let you go on your Christmas party?' Pottsy didn't know what to say. He didn't want to be in trouble with the manager or his team-mates, but the gaffer let us go and we responded by winning the replay 3-0."

Mills chuckled at that memory, but also stressed the significance of Challinor's goal and an early tactical reshuffle in that match - both of which he felt helped shape the rest of the club's season. "I always say that 92nd-minute Jon Challinor goal set us up for what we went on to achieve as I felt the FA Trophy played a major part in getting us promoted, because playing at Wembley the week before the play-off final was a major, major plus for us," Mills pointed out. "I also made a big decision just before half-time in that game when I took Andre Boucaud off and I don't think he spoke to me for about two weeks afterwards. He was probably our best player at the time, but I remember saying to (then assistant manager) Darron (Gee) that we needed to take Andre off if we were going to get back into the game. We needed to be a bit more offensive and get forward from midfield quicker. I also wanted us to be a bit stronger and forceful in there and we ended up getting promoted with three defenders - Dan Parslow, James Meredith and Lanre Oyebanjo - in midfield." On relenting after his Christmas party warning, Mills explained: "I'm not a manager who gets players in on a Sunday morning and runs them around a track. I like to build up a trust with them and I couldn't fault any of the players' work ethic that day. They had shown their desire to win the game, so I let them have their night out."

City subsequently saw off Ebbsfleet 1-0 at Bootham Crescent thanks to a Blair goal during the next round. Victory at Grimsby went on to secure a semi-final meeting with Luton and the terse rivalry that had developed between the two clubs meant the first leg at Bootham Crescent proved a typically, tempestuous contest. Reed opened the scoring on 14 minutes from the penalty spot after Jake Howells was sent off for deliberate handball. Visiting midfielder Keith Keane also saw red for a second bookable offence on 55 minutes but, despite playing the rest of the game against nine men, Mills' side could not add to their advantage and were even booed off at the final whistle. It was a reaction that Mills railed against afterwards and, with the passage of time, he added: "Fans can react that way. They are frustrated if their team is not winning against a team that have gone down to 10 men and, when the opposition only have nine, they feel you should win 4-0 or 5-0, but Luton made it difficult for us. They put eight players in the middle of the park and we couldn't break them down to get a second goal. I didn't want my players abused, booed and jeered off. I wanted everybody behind them, but it was just a reaction at the time and I knew that taking a lead to Kenilworth Road would be good enough."

 A 1-1 draw subsequently saw the club secure another trip to Wembley after Blair's 90th-minute header. Afterwards, Jason McGill stressed how important such achievements were to try and balance the books while the club plied their trade in the Conference at Bootham Crescent. He said: "It's no secret the club loses around £300,000 at Bootham Crescent every season to keep running a full-time professional side, a youth team and a community department. At the start of a campaign, we know those will be the losses if we do not get to the Trophy final, the third round of the FA Cup or, of course, promoted."

His sister Sophie McGill, meanwhile, circulated a shocking slideshow of photographs to councillors and MPs illustrating the need for new sporting facilities to replace the club's decaying Bootham Crescent home. The then communications director compiled a PowerPoint presentation, entitled "Bootham Crescent The Reality", with the help of club photographer at the time Tommy Outing and it was distributed to all the key decision makers ahead of the City of York Council's meeting to discuss Oakgate's planning application to build the new stadium at Monks Cross. The dossier confirmed the club spent £50,000 annually on ground repairs which, in the words of stadium

A picture used to demonstrate the poor condition of the dressing room baths as part of a slideshow presentation, given by then club director Sophie McGill to councillors and MPs in March 2012, to highlight the need for a new stadium

development director Ian McAndrew, only provided an "Elastoplast" solution to perennial problems. Included in the eye-opening album were shots of condemned areas of the away end, unhygienic changing facilities and the rusting directors' box. Mention was also made of the limited disabled facilities and the lack of any baby-changing provisions. The view, meanwhile, from the club's infamous three hospitality boxes, which looked out onto the car park and terraced houses rather than the pitch, was used as further evidence of how the club's income generation potential was stunted. Explaining the purpose of the slideshow, Sophie McGill said: "It is to show people unfamiliar with the ground the current state of our facilities and why a new community stadium is so desperately needed. The dressing room facilities are unsuitable for our own players, but also for those of the opposition. The facilities we provide for opposing team's directors, as well as local dignitaries such as the Archbishop of York, are also a poor reflection on the city as a prime tourist destination and Bootham Crescent does not lend itself to attracting a family audience either. This means it is a struggle to develop the next generation of support. Bootham Crescent represents sport in York and we feel our premier stadium reflects badly on the city and gives visitors a poor impression of York, while smaller towns and cities with arguably less national importance than York, such as Chesterfield, Telford, Burton, Colchester and Swansea, all have modern sports stadia they can be proud of. Statistics show that a new stadium leads to a 30 per cent increase in attendance figures and usually sees an uplift in success on the field, which benefits the morale of a city. Surely York deserves better than a decaying Bootham Crescent and the out-of-date Huntington Stadium?"

A picture of the condemned area of the away end used as part of a slideshow presentation, given by then club director Sophie McGill to councillors and MPs in March 2012, to highlight the need for a new stadium

533

Back on the pitch, former favourite Richard Brodie returned to Bootham Crescent in early April to score the only goal of a close contest that saw Fleetwood move to within a single win of clinching the title. He raced on to a pass from future England international Jamie Vardy, who did not get a single sniff of goal despite having netted 32 times that season prior to kick-off, before charging past home defender Chris Doig and drilling in a powerful low shot - the type City fans had seen on countless occasions in the past. Despite the euphoria of the moment - as Brodie celebrated in front of the travelling supporters - the striker admitted the feeling did not match that he had experienced when scoring important goals for the home team at Bootham Crescent. Commenting on his successful return as an opposition player, Brodie said: "I remember first coming back with Crawley and I knew I would play in that game because Steve Evans, who was the manager then, had a theory that players always did well when they went back to their old clubs, but I didn't have the best of days. I was gutted not to be starting for Fleetwood, because we needed to win to pretty much confirm the title. I got some stick whilst I was warming up from the home fans, which I didn't think was deserved and Scott Davies - who was the Fleetwood keeper that night - said the first 20 minutes after I came on was one of the worst performances he'd ever seen. But, then, I cut across Chris Doig and scored. It was a great moment to celebrate the goal in front of the Fleetwood fans, knowing it had all but won the league, although there was an element of not wanting to do it against the club that was so special to me. It didn't feel as good as scoring an important goal for York at Bootham Crescent either and didn't match that goal against Luton. With York fans, their club means so much to them and you couldn't really say that about Fleetwood or Crawley. They got a bit of money and then ended up with two to three thousand fans from somewhere. York fans have gone through hard times and some of them have been there since the year dot. York's result is still the one I look for first, not Fleetwood or Crawley's. Bootham Crescent and the club will always have a special place in my heart. The fans were great, and I will never forget them singing my name six years after I left when I went to watch the team lose 6-0 at Portsmouth in the away end."

A play-off spot was subsequently secured in the penultimate league fixture at Braintree and City signed off their regular season with a 1-0 home triumph over Forest Green after Moke's late goal. Goalkeeper coach Paul Musselwhite, who was filling in for the injured Michael Ingham, set two new club records, meanwhile, prior to the start of the play-offs. At 43, he became the oldest player ever to play for the club at Bootham Crescent and he also became the first keeper to start his City career with three consecutive clean sheets.

In the play-off semi-finals, City then hosted a Mansfield team that had won 13 of their last 15 games in the first leg. Wrexham, who finished 15 points clear of City, were the scheduled semi-final opponents right up to Moke's 82nd-minute strike against Forest Green, and Mills admitted that he had minor reservations about facing the Stags due to their aggressive style of play. "I can recall saying to Darron (Gee), it looks like Wrexham, but then it was Mansfield instead and I knew they would be difficult to play against, because Paul Cox always sets his teams up to be very direct and to play for long throws, set plays and corners," Mills pointed out. "That's tough, because you cannot switch off for the whole 93 minutes. We did in the first leg and conceded from a long throw early on but, the funny thing with that team, is I always knew that, when we went a goal down, we would come back and get a draw or a win. I felt the same at Wembley against Luton, when we conceded after a minute. Bootham Crescent was also rocking in that Mansfield game, which was a great feeling and drawing 1-1 didn't worry me either. I knew we could go to Mansfield and create chances and I also knew, with the way we were defending, we could keep a clean sheet."

During that tense first leg at Bootham Crescent, Ingham was back in goal as the honours ended even. Ross Dyer headed the Stags in front midway through the first half, but Exodus Geohaghon's own goal, following a Challinor cross, levelled the scores before the break. Mansfield also suffered a significant blow when 30-goal top scorer Matt Green was sent off for two bookable offences,

Mansfield defender Exodus Geohaghon puts through his own goal in the first leg of the 2012 play-off semi-finals

meaning he would be suspended for the return leg. At the time, Mills played down the importance of Green's absence for the second leg but, in an interview for this book four years later, he confessed: "I was pleased he was suspended, because he's a good player. I'm not one to go public and say that, because that makes my team look a bit weak talking up the opposition and I didn't want to make that a reason for why we could go on and win the game. It was never about any other team for me and never will be. I didn't really mention that he was suspended for the second leg. It was always just about us."

Another Blair header in extra-time at Field Mill clinched a 2-1 aggregate victory, leaving the club to contemplate two trips to Wembley on consecutive weekends. Goals from Blair and Lanre Oyebanjo saw Newport off 2-0 in the Trophy final. In between the two games, planning permission was also obtained for the community stadium at Monks Cross, leaving the stage set for the club to clinch a historic, nine-day hat-trick. Describing the atmosphere at Bootham Crescent during those heady days, Mills enthused: "The feeling around the football club at the time was magical and something to cherish, because you don't get moments like that very often, but we all lived through them together. There was a lot of work put in by everybody that season and, to get the stadium news in between the Trophy and play-off finals, made it feel like everything was falling into place. We had a great day in York celebrating the Trophy win and, then, the players had a bit of time off, before coming back in and preparing for another trip down to London."

Mills' team delivered with goals from Chambers and Blair securing a 2-1 victory over bitter rivals Luton, who had forged in front after just 71 seconds through Andre Gray. Bradford, not Braintree, would now be visiting Bootham Crescent during the 2012/13 campaign. Promotion had also been secured with an average attendance of 3,097 at Bootham Crescent, representing the highest figure during that first Conference era. An open-top bus parade that left from Bootham Crescent and ended with a civic reception at the Mansion House went on to see thousands of people line the streets to celebrate the club's wonderful achievements.

City players and staff leave Bootham Crescent on the open-top bus that celebrated their double Wembley-winning season of 2011/12 and promotion back to the Football League

CHAPTER 34

Richard Cresswell returns to spearhead a battle against the drop

"About 10 players jumped on my back to celebrate, but I was still running, and it was an emotional feeling."

The biggest opening-day crowd at Bootham Crescent for 19 years witnessed York City's first fixture back in the Football League, with 4,591 flocking to a home meeting with Wycombe Wanderers. Gary Mills' side subsequently suffered their heaviest defeat for 18 months, however, with goals from Matt Bloomfield, Sam Wood and Stuart Beavon seeing the visitors sweep into a 3-0 lead after 53 minutes. Jason Walker replied with a goal every striker welcomes - the ball going in literally off his backside - but it was not enough to prompt the kind of comeback that had typified the previous season.

A "gutted" Mills remained positive at the final whistle, saying: "I don't think they were any better than us. They scored with a deflection and a cracking goal in the first half." Years later, Mills' memories of the momentous occasion had not diminished. "It was a big game that the club had been waiting for for a long, long time," he said. "It was a special day and just a shame we didn't win it. They scored a worldy goal and it was clear we

Jason Walker scores York City's first goal of their second spell as a Football League outfit, with an effort that goes in off his backside during a 3-1 opening day defeat to Wycombe in 2012/13

had stepped up a level, because that didn't happen as often in the Conference as it did in the Football League. You always want to win the first game. We didn't, but I still had that feeling at the final whistle that we could win games at the higher level and we started quite well after that. The fact that we were running out onto the pitch as a Football League club and not a Conference side was also still a great feeling. It meant I had achieved what I wanted and had been asked to do. It was the reason I got employed and I still have special memories of that time. I carried on watching DVDs of that 2011/12 York City team to motivate myself as a manager."

The club's results did pick up but, despite seeing Oxford off 3-1 in August to record the team's first home win back in the Football League, form at Bootham Crescent remained patchy and, by autumn, a new club record was equalled when the team went four matches in a season on their own soil without scoring. That run was concluded by a 4-0 Johnstone's Paint Trophy drubbing against Coventry, following mistakes by recently-recruited PFA chairman Clarke Carlisle and Scott Kerr. City went on to be booed off the pitch following a 3-0 reverse to AFC Wimbledon in November as Mills' Wembley heroes suddenly looked less invincible. A 4-1 home romp against Bristol Rovers - the club's biggest Football League win since 1995 - lifted spirits in December with Ashley Chambers bagging a brace. Promotion contenders Burton were also seen off 3-0 at Bootham Crescent on New Year's Day with Walker, Paddy McLaughlin and Matty Blair the marksmen, but it proved Mills' last win during his first spell in charge at the club, with his team six points short of the play-off positions at the time and 12 clear of the relegation zone.

Losses of £467,000 were announced, meanwhile, for the double-winning Wembley season with 96 per cent of income at Bootham Crescent being spent on an estimated £1 million in playing costs, including salaries, transfer fees and bonuses. That was deemed the cost of promotion to the Football League with a total of £2.2 million in operating losses racked up during the eight years as a non-League outfit from 2004 to 2012.

A 2-0 home defeat to that season's surprise League Cup finalists Bradford then marked the end of Mills' tenure in March with James Hanson and Garry Thompson on target. It was the club's 11th game without a victory and left the Minstermen with just three wins from 18 matches and one goal from open play in nine encounters. Despite those statistics, David McGurk confessed that a sense of shock still engulfed the Bootham Crescent home dressing room following Mills' dismissal. He said: "It was hard to believe, and I didn't see it coming, even when he did go. There were rumours, but I thought there was no chance of that happening. I thought he would still be at the club no matter what. We were still playing good football, but you could see the confidence of the young players, who had been flying and got us up from the Conference, draining away as the results dipped. It was the first time in their careers they had experienced that, and they did not know how to come through it. The gaffer tried to change things, but they didn't really work, and the home form was suffering. I still would not have thought that Burton game would have been his last win in charge and we'd even had team meetings during that lean period without the manager. We were making the point that, whilst it might not seem we are in trouble because we were about ten points clear of the relegation zone, we could easily get dragged down. But, no matter what we were doing, trying and saying, nothing was working. I still don't think we would have gone down with Gary Mills, but the chairman made the right choice because we stayed up."

The sack came as a bitter surprise, nevertheless, to Mills, who admitted he never anticipated his dismissal either. "I didn't see it coming - absolutely not," he sighed. "I remember the game before. We had gone to Rotherham and they equalised to get a draw in the 92nd minute. I thought we were playing some good football, but we were getting draws that might have been wins. It was a sticky period, but I was certain we'd come through it. Nobody wanted us to be on that run, but things can't be good all the time. Unfortunately, for me, the people at the top wanted somebody else and, although I was disappointed by that, I don't bear grudges. I knew we had to start winning games, but I never thought I was about to lose the job that I loved, although I knew something was wrong because the chairman had stopped kissing me!" Mills, who would later return for a second spell as City boss, will always retain a fondness for the setting of some of his greatest triumphs as a manager, though, saying: "It was a proper football ground. People talked about the new stadium all the time I was at the club, but it was a ground that I fell in love with. I'm old school in the way I manage and the way I like my players to work. I'm also old school when it comes to the old stadiums. I was brought up with them and you got a really good atmosphere at Bootham Crescent, which you sometimes don't get at newer stadiums."

City were hovering just four points above the relegation zone when Mills left. Ex-Northern Ireland and Norwich chief Nigel Worthington took over, but early results were not encouraging. The team drew 0-0 with Rochdale during his first home game in charge with a 90th-minute shot by on-loan midfielder John McGrath proving the hosts' only on-target effort. Prior to an April 1 home meeting with Plymouth, the team had gone three months and 16 games without a victory - a run that had seen the club plunge into the bottom two and in real danger of becoming the first promoted Conference club to go straight back down from the Football League. But the side went on to make fools of anybody writing off their chances of survival.

Chambers and Richard Cresswell, who Worthington had brought back to the club on loan from Sheffield United, were the first-half marksmen in a 2-0 triumph. On his return to the club 14 years after he had left for top-flight football with Sheffield Wednesday, Cresswell said: "The place hadn't changed at all and it was like walking back in time. The chairman rang me and said would you be interested in helping us stay up. I thought: 'That's a lot to put on me' and lots of things were coming into my head, including stuff like my kids being at school in York and what it would mean for them if it all went wrong, so I said I would speak to Nigel (Worthington). He said he wanted me to come in and help the team hold the ball up and I knew then that I wanted to make an impact, not just out on the pitch, but in the dressing room as well, to make the players believe in themselves and get the best out of each other. I wanted to help vocally and physically. My game had changed by then and I was more of a target man. We didn't play good football during that spell, but we ran and battled. I don't think I had ran so much for a long time during those few games I played and, if you have somebody who has played at a high level doing that, it can bring everybody on and that's what it seemed to do. The players started believing in themselves and we got some great results."

On the thrill of being back on the scoresheet at Bootham Crescent, Cresswell added: "I think my reaction showed how much the club means to me and my family. About ten players jumped on my back to celebrate, but I was still running, and it was an emotional feeling. I was thinking I am part of this and I can help the club get where they want to be. It felt like the most important goal I had scored for the club because, when you're young, you don't realise how important the club is to the city and fans, but you do when you're older. I felt that, if the club went down, it might be another ten years before they could get up again so, when I scored, it felt like such a relief and was an amazing feeling. I remember going up with the keeper and thinking there's no chance he's going to get there before me and I headed it in. Platty (Tom Platt) should have scored first from the corner and I remember shouting to him: 'I've got your man'. I blocked his marker and he had a free header, but the ball just bounced up and I put it in and, after that win, we got some momentum." At the back, McGurk had a more comfortable afternoon than expected and could sense the tide beginning to turn under Worthington, saying: "I remember the game before at Bristol (Rovers) - the manager had started to implement his ideas and we'd put in a good performance and should have won there rather than drawn 0-0. That gave us some confidence going into the Plymouth game, which felt like a must-win. They were just above us, but they'd started to pull away a bit and, on the day, it felt the game meant more to us than it did to them. I had been out injured for a while and was expecting to feel it after playing two games in the space of four days, but it turned out to be quite an easy game. The crowd were tense but got right behind us, because they knew every point was massive from then on."

But the club suffered a big blow in their next match when Accrington's Peter Murphy grabbed a 93rd-minute equaliser at Bootham Crescent to cancel out Adam Reed's strike, leaving the club in the relegation zone with three games to play. McGurk confessed that he feared the worst after that demoralising loss, saying: "If I'm honest, I felt that was it. I had come off at half-time and I went back to Middlesbrough and told my friends I thought that goal could send us down, because nobody expected us to get a result at Northampton in our next game. We saw the Accrington game as a must-win. It would have kept them in the relegation battle, so for them to get that point was a massive, massive blow and they didn't deserve it. I remember all their staff running on the pitch and they were banging on our dressing room door afterwards and it did feel like we could be relegated that day. Everyone was down. There were people in the dressing room trying to rally everyone like the manager's assistant and senior players. They were saying we had to take the positives from getting a point and now go and win the next two games which, at the time, didn't seem realistic, because they were tough fixtures."

Cresswell revealed, though, that the battling squad had got that defeat out of their system by the time they travelled to an in-form Northampton team for their next game seven days later. "That Accrington game was a pure fight from start to finish and, sometimes, fans want to see that fight, determination and hunger," he pointed out. "I think I was still fighting going down the tunnel after that game. I'm not condoning fighting and all that, but sometimes you need players to show passion and that it all means something by doing their best. You need to put everything on the line and, if you last 80 minutes but then you're gone, you come off. That's all fans want to see. It was a big blow in the 93rd minute and everyone was really disappointed, because we had done enough to win the game, but we bounced back again and knew, by the time we got to the changing room at Northampton, we could do it. I got injured in that game, but it had been nice to make that little bit of an impact to help keep the team up."

An unlikely first away win in 12 games at a Northampton side who had won 10 consecutive home matches subsequently saw City move three places outside of the relegation zone they had occupied for four fretful weeks and the importance of the club's final home fixture of the season was then ramped up. Opponents Southend still had an outside chance of reaching the play-offs and, at the time, communications director Sophie McGill reasoned: "This game is just as important to the club as last season's play-off final at Wembley. We would like to encourage everyone with an interest in York City to come down to Bootham Crescent to show support for the team. Please give our players that extra boost to help them achieve another vital three points."

The people of York answered the rallying call with 5,975 - the biggest Bootham Crescent crowd of the season - cramming in and many more locked out. Goals from Adam Reed in the first minute and Blair secured a 2-1 win, but not before a couple of late scares. The visitors had an 87th-minute effort ruled out for offside and captain Chris Smith cleared two chances off the line in stoppage time. McGurk was in no doubt that the supporters played their part in securing the required result at Bootham Crescent that afternoon, adding: "The atmosphere definitely helped us get that first goal and you could sense the importance of the game to the fans. I remember clearing the ball off one of their centre forwards early on and it went out for a throw in and even that got applauded. All the fans were behind everything we did and, as players, we definitely responded to that. I felt the fans almost responded better to being in a relegation battle than they did when we were going for promotion the following season. It was more important to stay in the Football League, than to be promoted to League One. We knew the club would lose so much money going back into the Conference and it would have been so demoralising and a massive blow to go straight down after just one season. There was so much at stake in terms of the youth structure and the new stadium. Southend still had a chance of promotion and I don't think you can over-state

Adam Reed celebrates his first-minute goal against Southend as York battle to stay in the Football League in 2013

the importance of that result and that run at the end of the season, considering the position we'd been in with six games to go. I thought one would be enough when we went in front, but the ball deflected off Jack (O'Connell) to one of their players for an equaliser. After we got the second goal, it felt like we would never lose the game, although the last ten minutes were scary and a bit frantic. We were being bombarded, but I looked around me and thought I could rely on Lanre (Oyebanjo) to my right. I also knew Chris Smith would put his body on the line to my left and Jack was a good defender as well. Nigel Worthington had created a strong spine to the team. That also included Pars (Dan Parslow) in midfield and Richard Cresswell up top before he got injured. He always put a shift in and, with Inghy in goal, there were four or five senior players right through the middle of the team. In a relegation battle, younger players look to people like that and think, if I copy what they are doing, we will be OK. There were bodies on the line and lots of emergency defending from everyone in that Southend game, but we hung on for a good result." Requiring a point to secure safety from their last match, the Minstermen then took all three in a 1-0 triumph at Dagenham.

The first season back in the Football League, meanwhile, had seen Harrogate and Gateshead stage "home" matches at Bootham Crescent after their pitches were deemed unplayable. In May, the ground also hosted the FA Women's Premier League Cup final with Aston Villa beating Leeds 5-4 on penalties after a 0-0 draw following extra time.

The returning Richard Cresswell poses outside the home dressing room

Manager Nigel Worthington and captain Chris Smith with their Manager of the Month and Player of the Month awards for April 2013

Two former European Cup winners - Edgar Davids and Gary Mills - were pitted against one another when the former Holland legend's Barnet team played at Bootham Crescent

The ground was packed as City fought for their League Two status during the final home game of the 2012-13 season against Southend

CHAPTER 35

Matty Blair back to deliver play-off pain

"I've probably had a thousand shots from outside the box in my career and three or four have flown in, so I will definitely be keeping that one on the Sky Planner".

The club started their second season back in the Football League - Nigel Worthington's only full campaign in charge - by enjoying an opening day victory at Bootham Crescent for the first time since 1999 with new signing Ryan Jarvis' goal seeing off Northampton 1-0. But, other than exciting anomalies such as a 4-2 victory over fallen giants Portsmouth, who brought 1,357 fans to Bootham Crescent, as well as a 4-1 success over Scunthorpe when all the hosts' goals were scored before the break, there was little else to cheer until the turn of the year, as City bobbed along in the lower reaches of the division.

In September, meanwhile, Bootham Crescent's family room received a makeover thanks to South Yorkshire-based organisation Flying Futures, as part of the National Citizen Service - a Government-backed programme for 15 to 17-year-olds. A 37-strong team of NCS recruits - the first to be signed up from York - followed a social action programme which required them to design, plan and execute a plan to improve a community facility or project and more than half of the group chose to revamp the former Smarties room at Bootham Crescent. The work took four days to complete with the family room continuing to be used for children's birthday parties and small school group visits right until the stadium's final years. It also hosted the match-day tuck shop, where young fans and any accompanying adults could buy hot and cold refreshments before games and during the half-time interval, with all profits generated invested into York City in the Community initiatives.

Back on the pitch, a 1-0 New Year's Day home victory over Morecambe, courtesy of another Jarvis goal, ended a run of 11 games without a win. The 1,500th fixture to be staged at Bootham Crescent, meanwhile, saw City fail to beat a team managed by ex-boss John Ward for a 13th consecutive game following a 0-0 draw with Bristol Rovers. Another 0-0 home draw in February against Southend equalled the club record of four consecutive home games without a goal but, after that match, a run of six successive victories, the club's longest winning sequence in the Football League for 30 years (since Denis Smith's 1983/84 record breakers) was bookended by Bootham Crescent triumphs over Exeter (2-1) and Torquay (1-0) and propelled the team into the play-off positions during March.

On-loan Charlton goalkeeper and future England international Nick Pope, who was instrumental during the team's upsurge in fortune, missed out on a club record, meanwhile, when Shay McCartan's 91st-minute equaliser for visitors Accrington Stanley denied him a sixth successive clean sheet in all competitions. It cancelled out Michael Coulson's penalty and represented the first goal City had conceded in 13 hours of football, meaning the team dropped one place out of the play-off zone with four games left to play. A 21st league clean sheet of the season during a 1-0 home win over Bury, following the same scoreline at top-seven rivals Oxford, set another club record though and put the club back on track for promotion. Inspirational centre-back Keith Lowe, brought to Bootham Crescent in November from Cheltenham, scored his first goal for the club in the win. Coulson's 77th-minute free kick in another

Future England goalkeeper Nick Pope was instrumental in the 2014 charge up the League Two table into the play-offs during a loan spell from Charlton. He is pictured catching a cross against Southend and went on to successfully bid for one set of goalposts when the club left Bootham Crescent

1-0 home victory against Newport then secured a play-off spot in the team's penultimate match of the regular season. The same player had earlier rattled the crossbar and a run of 16 games unbeaten also represented the second-best in the club's history behind the 1973/74 side that clinched promotion to the old second division.

Play-off fever in North Yorkshire was then doused as heavy afternoon and pre-match rain before the Friday night, first-leg tie against Fleetwood left the Bootham Crescent pitch waterlogged and unplayable. The 7.30pm kick-off was delayed for half-an-hour to give the game a chance of going ahead, but another downpour meant referee Carl Boyeson had no choice but to postpone the game 20 minutes later.

It went ahead three days later and ex-City hero Matty Blair got the only goal of the night when he bundled in a left-wing cross to the far post on 50 minutes. Despite half-chances for Coulson, Ryan Bowman and Adam Reed, Fleetwood might have taken a greater advantage into the second leg, as

Former hero Matty Blair bundles the ball over the line to give Fleetwood a first-leg lead in the 2014 League Two play-off semi-final

David Ball and Iain Hume both missed the target with only Pope to beat. Blair, meanwhile, kept his goal celebration low-key due to a fondness for his old team. "It was a muted one," he explained at the time. "I've got huge respect and feelings for this football club, but I am a Fleetwood Town player and I am desperate to get them all the way. I kept it as respectful as I could, but I did want to go mad, which is understandable. It is business. I want to score as many goals as I can, that's my job." Blair also confessed that City right-back Lanre Oyebanjo was unlucky not to have prevented his scrappy goalbound effort from crossing the line. "I was at the back post and I thought Lanre made a brilliant first block," Blair said. "He was very unlucky that it just bounced straight back to me and I just tapped it around him, but I am not going to grump over that too much. It all happened very quickly. The ball came over and I hit it well enough and Banj just threw himself in front of it, but it popped up for me. It happened too quickly for me even to think, but it was fortunate for us." The Minstermen were the better side in the return leg but could not put the ball in the net and a goal-less draw on the Lancashire coast booked Fleetwood's place at Wembley, where they were subsequently promoted.

City's next season at Bootham Crescent saw the team go a record 12 home games at the start of a campaign before winning in front of their own fans on Boxing Day. Lowe's 35th-minute header proved enough to see off Accrington 1-0 despite on-loan Middlesbrough teenager Brad Halliday's red card just past the hour mark, meaning the club also avoided equalling their longest sequence of games without a home win - set in 1981/82. The first Bootham Crescent match of the season had seen City unlucky to lose 1-0 to Doncaster, newly-relegated from the Championship, following a 90th-minute Harry Forrester goal. His strike left the Minstermen nursing a ninth successive first-round defeat in the League Cup - a miserable run stretching back to 1997. Another last-minute goal, scored by Northampton's Marc Richards, denied the club victory in their first league game at home following summer signing Jake Hyde's opening goal. Having also conceded an equaliser in stoppage time at Tranmere in their opening fixture, the goals represented a demoralising start to the campaign for Worthington's team. A 0-0 draw with Portsmouth, when on-loan striker Ryan Brunt squandered a simple late chance, proved to be Worthington's last home game in charge, as he resigned following a 3-1 defeat at Newport seven days later.

A 1-0 home loss to Shrewsbury - a team without a victory on their league travels in 14 fixtures - marked the start of new boss Russ Wilcox's reign with Jarvis sent off after 63 minutes. City then went on to become the only side in English football's fourth tier to ever reach Christmas without a home win before seeing off Stanley a day later. Despite a grass disease resulting in the top three inches of the pitch coming away from the soil, the Minstermen would end up relying on an upturn in fortunes at Bootham Crescent to stave off the threat of relegation following three consecutive home triumphs over Cheltenham (1-0), Hartlepool (1-0) and Morecambe (2-1). A long-range thunderbolt from skipper Russell Penn in the Morecambe match preserved the club's Football League status with three fixtures remaining. It was only Penn's second goal in 69 appearances, but he admitted afterwards that it was a great relief to see his shot fly into the net on a tense night and confessed that calls from the David Longhurst Stand encouraged him to take fire. He said: "I've not scored as many goals as I wanted this season and, because of the magnitude of the game and the fact that we were on top, I felt a great relief when it went in. It took away some of the pressure around the ground and a lot of the weight off my shoulders because the last couple of months have been intense around the place. The gaffer has always pushed me to shoot going back to our Scunthorpe days ten years ago and, since he came here, he has given me a lot of confidence in terms of positional play and other things. I've probably had a thousand shots from outside the box in my career and three or four have flown in, so I will definitely be keeping that one on the Sky planner. I was feeling confident at the time because we had started the second half well and, whilst I would usually just play a simple ball from that position, I had that much space and the crowd were pressuring me to shoot. Michael Coulson was calling for a pass, which he does all the time, even when they're not on, so that didn't surprise me, but I just decided to hit it and was pleased to see it go in." With social media just beginning to mushroom in popularity, Penn's Bootham Crescent strike was soon witnessed by a much larger audience too with 44,000 Facebook views quickly racked up. "It's all gone a bit mad on social media," he admitted at the time. "A lot of people come out of the woodwork when you score, but I understand that."

Sad news was to follow, though, the next day when former chairman Steve Beck - a talismanic figure in the battle to save the ground from the clutches of Douglas Craig - passed away at the age of 58 after a long battle with heart problems. He was in York Hospital on the night of the game and could probably hear the roar from his beloved Bootham Crescent when Penn's rocket hit the back of the net.

The football club and rugby league clubs, meanwhile, could not reach an agreement for York City Knights to play their home fixtures at Bootham Crescent after their stadium had been bulldozed to prepare the site for the new community stadium. Instead, the Knights played "home games" at a number of different venues, including Doncaster and Featherstone Rovers, as well as at local amateur outfits York RUFC and Heworth rugby league club.

Sunset Over Bootham Crescent

The club's first-ever performance analyst Luke Foulkes carries out his duties on the Popular Stand's rooftop gantry

A shot taken from above the David Longhurst Stand in 2014

CHAPTER 36

A deathly hush signals back-to-back relegations

"I'm devastated. The game meant everything and was comfortably one of the biggest in my career."

There were high hopes for the 2015/16 campaign after on-trial Frickley Athletic striker Reece Thompson's spectacular goal helped secure a 2-1 pre-season friendly victory at Bootham Crescent over Newcastle, whose York-born manager Steve McClaren unveiled £13million Serbian international forward Aleksandar Mitrovic to the visiting fans. Thompson netted in front of the away end that had been renamed The Prostate Cancer UK Stand that season in support of the men's health charity. He went on to sign professional terms and won his new club a penalty and converted another in a thrilling League Cup shoot-out victory over higher-division visitors Bradford. The score had ended 2-2 after extra-time during an incident-packed encounter. Bradford's League One rivals Doncaster were also seen off 2-0 during another upset at Bootham Crescent with summer signing Vadaine Oliver scoring both goals in a Johnstone's Paint Trophy triumph.

The Doncaster game would prove Russ Wilcox's last win in charge, though, as the board acted on the growing calls for him to be dismissed following a 3-1 home defeat to AFC Wimbledon. Wilcox delivered a withering verdict on his team at the final whistle of that game, before learning his fate, saying: "It was shambolic. We are fighting for our lives at the bottom of the league, but the first half was a non-event. We never turned up, didn't make a tackle and failed to get close to people or pass the ball well. I've protected players all season, but they were not good enough and have got to take responsibility for that. I will do, but the players have got to look at themselves as well. We had a go in the second half and got back into the game but, then, we did what we usually do - shot ourselves in the foot by conceding cheap goals. Their second goal was in slow motion and that's unacceptable."

Former Dundee United boss Jackie McNamara was brought in as Wilcox's replacement after backroom coaches Richard Cresswell and Jonathan Greening had one match in temporary charge at Crawley, which ended in a narrow 1-0 defeat. Cresswell had been promoted to first-team coach by Wilcox, but both him and Greening would part company with the club early in McNamara's reign. Nevertheless, the former Bootham Crescent trainee enjoyed his week-long caretaker reign, even though he would have loved to have been given the job on a permanent basis. "Everybody knows I applied for the job when Russ left, but the chairman said it was not the right time for me and I can understand why he said that," Cresswell reasoned. "For me, if I had been asked, even for one game, to stand on that Bootham Crescent touchline and manage the club, it would have been something else. It would have been a full circle and I think I could have made an impact, because I've always had confidence in my own ability. In the week building up to the Crawley game, I remember being in the office for hours trying to break things down and looking at everything to try and get a result. I enjoyed that week immensely. Likewise, when Russ brought me in for the end of the 2014/15 season as a first-team coach, I felt it was just as much an achievement when we stayed up, as it had been in 2013, because the team were being written off again."

Cresswell had originally been brought back to the club in a head of football operations role and loved sharing a cramped office, at the bottom of the rickety steel stairs leading up to the boardroom, with former team-mates and youth coaches Andy McMillan and Greening. "We didn't have the greatest of facilities, but we worked especially hard during a tough year to ensure the club fulfilled its EPPP obligations and had some great days in that office," he smiled. "It's not about the size of a stadium either, but the history of what's happened there and the blood, sweat and tears that have been shed there. It was a sad day when the doors were closed, but every club has to move on."

McNamara went on to endure an unwanted, record-breaking start to his tenure by suffering seven successive defeats, including a humiliating 5-1 Bootham Crescent reverse at the hands of Accrington Stanley. Following a frenzied raid on the loan market, six players (Mark Kitching, Stefan O'Connor, Jordan Lussey, Bradley Fewster, Kenny McEvoy and Danny Galbraith) were given their City debuts in the game, with all but one (Galbraith) of the new arrivals untried under-21 players from Premier League or Championship clubs. The next home match saw McNamara get off the mark with a 2-1 victory over Morecambe, but the club could not build the necessary momentum to claw themselves clear of the relegation zone.

York City Knights, meanwhile, were welcomed back to Bootham Crescent and, after a false start on January 3 when a friendly with Hull was postponed due to a waterlogged pitch, the rugby league club narrowly lost 20-16 to Castleford in a warm-up match. The following month, Knights beat amateur city rivals York Acorn 66-0 in the third round of the Ladbrokes Challenge Cup in front of a bumper crowd of 2,293. Tries were scored by Ryan Mallinder (two), Jonny

Tyler Craig scores a try for York City Knights during their 66-0 win over local amateurs York Acorn in the third round of the Challenge Cup. The game was watched by 2,293 fans

Presley, Ed Smith, James Morland (two), Harry Carter, Richard Wilkinson, Tyler Craig, Connor Bower, Danny Nicklas, Brett Turner and Kriss Brining. Nicklas (two) and Wilkinson (five) added conversions.

A surprise 3-1 victory for the football club over promotion-contenders Portsmouth in the penultimate home match of the season only delayed the inevitable, though, with relegation confirmed at Accrington four days later, before the final Bootham Crescent contest of another Football League era ended in a dismal 4-1 drubbing at the hands of Bristol Rovers. Billy Bodin's brace and a Jermaine Easter goal put the Pirates in the ascendancy, before York sub McEvoy replied on 81 minutes, only for the visitors to have the final say with a late Lee Mansell strike. Chants of "Jackie Out", accompanied those of "You're not Fit to Wear the Shirt" at an angry Bootham Crescent, but McNamara insisted he would fight on, having been told his job was not under threat by chairman Jason McGill. "I understand the frustration, but there's nobody more frustrated than me," McNamara argued. "I feel my hands are tied a little bit, because I'm waiting for the season to finish, so we can change and freshen things up. Since coming here, I've tried to improve things and get over the line, so we could change things that needed changing in the summer. It would be a sore

Tom Hill leads local amateurs York Acorn out for their third round Challenge Cup clash against York City Knights in 2016

Gary Mills is welcomed "home" by the David Longhurst Stand following his return as manager in October 2016

one for myself, therefore, if there was to be a change and somebody else was brought in after what we've been through. I want to instil my own things, show what I've done in my career and get the backing to prove people wrong by making changes for the good of the club and, hopefully, that's what I will be judged on."

Further problems over the Knights' hosting of home games at Bootham Crescent arose in July, meanwhile, when a Super 8 game against Doncaster was postponed, as the club were unable to come to an agreement with York City Council over the use of Bootham Crescent. Overuse of the ground was cited as a reason for the disagreement.

Despite a couple of big home wins over Woking (4-1) and Solihull (4-0), McNamara was then replaced by former boss Gary Mills two months into the new season with the team struggling in the lower reaches of the National League table. Unusually, McNamara stayed in charge on a caretaker basis for the 1-1 FA Cup fourth qualifying round draw with Manchester part-timers Curzon Ashton at Bootham Crescent before taking up a chief executive role at the club following Mills' re-appointment. Mills could not save City from a replay defeat at Curzon, before his homecoming at Bootham Crescent saw him pitched against a Chester team, managed by another former Bootham Crescent favourite Jon McCarthy.

One of the "We Are York" supporters' group's finest flag and banner displays greeted Mills with a colourful reception from the David Longhurst End and the returning manager, clearly emotional, said: "The welcome I got coming back was incredible. It told me the fans wanted me at the club and it was probably the best welcome I've ever had at a football club and that spurred me on to put things right for those supporters. It was emotional for me and my family and friends who were there. They shed the odd tear as well and there's nothing wrong with that, because it shows what it means." A stoppage-time Kane Richards equaliser denied Mills a victory and the team a first win in 10 matches, following Matt Fry's 70th-minute opener. Chester were the better side, though, deserving their share of the spoils on what was also a special afternoon for McCarthy, who added: "People know how much I enjoyed playing at Bootham Crescent and it was really nice to see the ground again. It hadn't changed much and I'm glad it hadn't. I did have a little walk across to the Popular Stand before the game, as I always used to as a player, because I tended to be on that wing in the first half and, then, it was always nice to play with the Main Stand fans behind you in the second half. It was very nice to come back, but I was at work. I was fortunate to play in a good York City team and I didn't want to go there with a side that didn't put on a good performance, so I was really pleased with how we played, and a point made it a nice day for me."

In November, meanwhile, Bootham Crescent hosted then Premier League outfit Middlesbrough under-23s against their Charlton counterparts with the club receiving a £3,000 hosting fee from the north-east outfit, whose training ground was out of action due to improvement work. City's February home match with Maidstone was also designated as the club's fourth annual Football v Homophobia match. The game was used to promote the message that football at Bootham Crescent was for everyone regardless of sexuality and that discrimination of any form was not welcome in the game. As part of the club's efforts to tackle homophobia and to show support for the local LGBT (Lesbian, Gay, Bisexual and Transgender) community, City donated 50 tickets for the match to York Pride.

More community stadium delays were announced in March, though, with the start of work again pushed back to September 2017, meaning the anticipated completion date was moved to early 2019. The problem was caused after the building contractors ISG pulled out of the project due to rising costs and the most-recent legal delay, which had seen Vue Cinemas unsuccessfully challenge the plan to build a new IMAX venue on the site.

Back at Bootham Crescent, Mills began to reverse the club's fortunes after making several astute signings and, from the end of February to the beginning of April, oversaw a run of five straight home wins - the best sequence for six years, stretching back to the early days of his first spell in charge of the club. Included in that sequence were FA Trophy home triumphs at the quarter-final and semi-final stage over Brackley and Lincoln respectively. In the first round of the competition, Worcester City had been seen off 3-1 in December with veteran striker Jon Parkin, who had returned to the club after a 12-and-a-half year absence, marking his second home debut with the opening goal. Fellow new signing Rhys Murphy also scored from the spot. Away victories over Harlow (2-1) and Nuneaton (3-0) followed, before Brackley were beaten in North Yorkshire, as Parkin, after seeing a penalty saved, grabbed the only goal of the game.

A two-legged tussle with National League table-toppers Lincoln represented by far the toughest challenge of the Trophy run, though, with the first leg staged at Bootham Crescent. The buoyant Imps had become the first non-League side to reach the FA Cup quarter-finals for more than a century, meaning the tie was played on a Tuesday night as the visitors were occupied with a trip to Arsenal on the weekend originally scheduled for the contest. Despite their league and cup heroics under the highly-rated Cowley management team of Danny and Nicky, Lincoln were desperate to earn the chance to play at Wembley for a first time in their 133-year history and 1,358 of the 3,294 crowd were away supporters. The visitors went on to dominate the first half and should have had a greater advantage at the interval than Lee Angol's 14th-minute penalty after Hamza Bencherif had hauled him down. But the Minstermen came out fighting in the second period and Oliver levelled the tie on 53 minutes when he headed in a left-wing cross from fellow striker Amari Morgan-Smith. On 69 minutes, substitute Adriano Moke, also brought back to City for a second spell by Mills, then sprinted three-quarters of the length of the pitch before trying his luck with an edge-of-the-box effort that deflected off fellow replacement Aidan Connolly to nudge the Minstermen in front.

Mills hailed his players' work-rate afterwards and expressed his confidence that the home win laid the foundations for the team to finish the job off at Sincil Bank. He said: "We didn't want to go there 1-0 down or whatever, but we're quite confident of winning all the games we play in and, if not, then drawing them. We don't even think about losing and, as long as they don't score more goals than us on Saturday, we'll be going to Wembley, but we also know you've always got to work hard to get there. Our philosophy was a bit different when we were in this situation before and we don't quite play the same good football, but the game is also about heart, desire and work-rate." The team went on to draw 1-1 at Lincoln with another sub - Scott Fenwick - converting an extra-time penalty to secure a 2-1 aggregate win.

There was a Bootham Crescent blow, though, for Mills and his team when, in their third-last home contest of the campaign, the club squandered an opportunity to climb out of the relegation zone for the first time since November. A Bromley team that had lost seven of their previous nine matches clinched a 2-0 victory over the Minstermen to end the hosts' run of five straight victories in front of their own fans. Louis Dennis opened the scoring for the visitors after just 69 seconds and Toby Sho-Silva made the points safe in the second half. A crowd of 3,000 - the second-highest league gate of the season - had turned up for the match, but the result meant Mills' men were still two points adrift of a position of safety with five fixtures left to play.

Back-to-back away wins at Chester and Solihull subsequently lifted the club out of the relegation zone, but another home setback against Mills' previous club Wrexham saw a 3-1 defeat leave City just one place above the National League North trapdoor on goal difference with two games to play.

Parkin had got the team off to a flying start on two minutes against Wrexham, but an own goal by Dan Parslow levelled the scores and second-half efforts by Jordan White and Leo Smith gave the Welshman a comfortable win, even though they had been enduring their worst win-less run since 2010 having failed to take maximum points from seven matches. A reflective Mills admitted that the tension of the situation might have been starting to get to his players on their own soil, following the first back-to-back home defeats since his return as manager in October. He said: "You can feel the atmosphere around our ground at the moment and it's different away from home but, sometimes, you can't help that. Even though I don't like using the word, we're all desperate to get the number of points we need to be safe and I think, when we concede a goal at home, the fans are only human, and they react to the situation. Ideally, when the opposition score, that's the time we need them to be vocal and behind the team, but I know it's difficult, because it's an accumulation of what's happened here over the last couple of years."

A 1-1 draw at Woking then saw City drop into the relegation zone ahead of a fraught final-day climax at Bootham Crescent when Forest Green, already assured of a play-off place, were the visitors.

Just under 4,000 fans watched the drama unfold, with the match also televised live on BT Sports. The Minstermen knew a home win would mean three results would have to go against them - namely wins for Torquay and Guiseley and at least a draw for Woking - for the club to go down. Torquay were at home to already-relegated North Ferriby, Guiseley hosted a Solihull Moors side who had secured survival the previous weekend, while Woking travelled to manager Garry Hill's old team Dagenham - another club whose play-off spot had already been confirmed. A draw for City, meanwhile, would only suffice if Guiseley lost and Braintree failed to win at Aldershot, who needed a result to secure their top-five position.

After a poignant minute's applause in the memory of former *Yorkshire Evening Press* reporter Malcolm Huntington, who had passed away three days before the game, York made a positive start. Long-throw specialist Sam Muggleton, who was handed his first start for the club following a March switch from Eastleigh, hurled the ball against the crossbar twice during the opening exchanges before the visitors forged in front on six minutes when Omar Bugiel sidefooted past on-loan keeper Scott Loach from 10 yards. Mills' team levelled just past the half-hour mark when Parkin swept home a first-time, left-footed finish from 15 yards following Simon Heslop's through ball. But parity was only short-lived as Bugiel strode through a parting home defence to prod past an exposed Loach from eight yards. At half-time, with Guiseley losing 1-0 to Solihull and Braintree drawing 0-0 at Aldershot, Mills instructed his team that just one goal, as it stood, would be sufficient to keep the club up and added that he would relay a message onto the pitch if that situation changed. Within three minutes of the restart, the Minstermen had climbed back out of the drop zone when Muggleton threw the ball in from the left and Parkin used his heel to steer an on-target Morgan-Smith effort past Forest Green keeper Sam Russell. Great chances then saw Asa Hall's close-range downward header kept out by Russell's legs and Oliver curl weakly at the away keeper after charging clear through the left channel. As the clock ticked down, though, news filtered through that Guiseley had levelled against Solihull with a stoppage-time own goal, which was greeted by a deathly hush initially, before desperate pleas of "Attack, Attack, Attack" rang around the ground. Keeper Loach was even thrown forward for a couple of late set-pieces, but the only chance to win the match and snatch a relegation reprieve fell to Sean Newton on his weaker right foot and his 93rd-minute effort flashed wide from 10 yards.

Moments later, the final whistle was met by another stunned silence, before a 40-strong band of protestors aimed their vitriol in the direction of the boardroom from the car park. An upset Mills said afterwards: "It's an emotional

Relegation to National League North sinks in following the 2-2 draw with Forest Green

and tough game and, personally, I want to say sorry that I couldn't do it for the fans, because they have been incredible with their support home and away. All I can say is I'm absolutely devastated for everybody connected with the club, because I take pride in what I do, and I haven't been able to do what I came back to the club to achieve. We came within a whisker of doing it and that's how close football can be at times. It hurts, and it will do for a while, but we have to face reality, be big and strong and stay proud of our football club." Mills also refused to criticise his squad's efforts during the second half of the campaign, declaring: "The fans need to know that I couldn't have got anything more out of this group of players since the turn of the year. They have been incredible for me, which we saw again as they came back from behind twice to draw against Forest Green."

Having scored 15 goals and claimed nine assists following his December arrival from Newport, Parkin took no solace from his own individual achievements after suffering a first career relegation at the age of 35.

Loyal fan Carol Deighton is consoled by husband Phil after relegation to National League North is greeted with a deathly hush around the stadium

559

The final whistle goes against Forest Green and York City are relegated to National League North

Summing up his thoughts after the game, Parkin admitted: "I'm devastated. The game meant everything and was comfortably one of the biggest in my career. At 90 minutes, a draw was enough, but it's the small margins that cost us and we ultimately fell short. We had three or four really good chances and their keeper pulled off three incredible saves so, on another day, we would have won the game 3-2 or 4-2."

After a 3-2 FA Trophy final victory over Macclesfield at Wembley, life in National League North started with a disappointing 1-0 home defeat to Telford, in which Parkin hit the crossbar. A little bizarrely, Bootham Crescent also went on to become the setting for a Bollywood film crew, who wanted the then 85-year-old ground to pose as the 1936 Berlin Olympic arena - perhaps as good a sign as any that the stadium had passed its use-by date - even though the German site could accommodate more than

Jon Parkin gets a consoling hug from his son at the end of the 2-2 draw with Forest Green that saw the club relegated to National League North

The unusual sight of swastikas in the Main Stand during the filming in 2017 of a scene, depicting the 1936 Olympics, for the Bollywood movie Gold

The unusual sight of Nazis in the car park during the filming in 2017 of a scene, depicting the 1936 Olympics, for the Bollywood movie Gold

100,000 spectators. The unusual sight of Swastika flags in the Main Stand was witnessed while filming took place for two weeks for a film called *Gold,* which depicted India's first Olympic gold medal in 1948. That honour went to the country's hockey team and the Bootham Crescent scenes were part of a segment looking back 12 years to the controversial Games when Adolf Hitler's attempt to prove his racial superiority ideology were defeated as black US sprinter Jesse Owens won four gold medals.

City's first season of sixth-tier football, meanwhile, would end in a disappointing 11th-placed finish - exactly halfway up the table - with Mills replaced by Martin Gray at the beginning of October after the latter left his post at Darlington. One record at the old ground tumbled, though, when veteran Parkin managed to net in eight consecutive home matches during a three-month period from October 7 to January 13. The final fixture of that sequence saw him score during a 2-1 triumph against Bradford Park Avenue that lifted the team back into the play-off positions, which extended down to seventh spot after the change to a six-team format in non-League football. But an injury to Parkin would see the side lose momentum during the final weeks of the season and only three more home fixtures were won from the final eight.

One, against eventual title-winners Salford City, watched by flat-capped visiting director and former England defender Gary Neville in the away end, saw Connolly secure a 1-0 triumph in February. But a 2-0 defeat in the first-ever Bootham Crescent league meeting with North Yorkshire neighbours Harrogate Town, who would also go up as play-off winners, kickstarted a nightmare April in which four straight defeats were suffered without scoring a goal. Former City striker Jake Wright, who returned to the club the following season, scored Harrogate's first goal and was joined on the scoresheet by future on-loan Minstermen forward Mark Beck. Along with Telford and Harrogate, others to take three points away from Bootham Crescent during a highly-disappointing campaign were FC United of Manchester, Tamworth and Blyth Spartans.

Amelia Perkins reads out the team line-ups on Junior Volunteer Day in 2018

CHAPTER 37

Relocation takes longer than anticipated

"It's the best I've heard the York fans and it was a magnificent feeling. To hear them roar like that was the best I've felt since coming here."

In what was billed as the final season at Bootham Crescent, Stockport County - the first ever visitors to the ground for a competitive fixture in 1932 - provided the opposition for the first home match of the season. During a greeting that was to be repeated throughout the campaign, flagbearers welcomed the players out onto the pitch with a big home shirt unveiled in the centre circle.cThe matchday programme also had a retro-style cover from different eras for each fixture while the team's chosen walk-out music was The White Stripes' *Seven Nation Army.*

When the action started against Stockport, City went on to produce a rousing second-half performance to defeat the pre-season title favourites 1-0, courtesy of Wes York's 77th-minute goal. A crowd of 3,218 turned up for the match and, echoing so many midweek evening contests from the past, the atmosphere was electric, as City supporters appeared determined to enjoy what was, at the time, scheduled to be the last night match at the ground. Afterwards, a buoyant Martin Gray enthused: "It's the best I've heard the York fans and it was a magnificent feeling. To hear them roar like that was the best I've felt since coming here and I'm delighted they went home happy."

Gray would only oversee two more home matches, though, with a 1-1 home draw against Curzon Ashton, in which Jon Parkin cancelled out Joe Guest's opening goal for the visitors, leading to his dismissal five games into the new campaign with the team already eight points adrift of league leaders Chorley. After a 0-0 draw at Brackley, youth-team manager Sam Collins, who had been promoted to caretaker boss, guided the side into the play-off positions with a 2-0 bank-holiday home triumph over Blyth Spartans courtesy of goals from subs Parkin and Adriano Moke. That game also saw a group of youngsters help out with many of the matchday responsibilities at Bootham Crescent as the club staged a Junior Volunteer Day. Six children, aged between seven and 12, performed a series of tasks on the afternoon, including acting as PA announcers and reading out the team line-ups before the game and announcing the goalscorers' names during it. They also interviewed Collins for the club website, helped take photographs, assisted the groundsman and conducted the 50-50 draw. Oliver Clarkson, Arthur Kay, Amelia Perkins, Aaron Fogg, Josh Crosby and Oscar Martin were chosen from a group of junior season-ticket holders, who had applied to take part after naming their favourite York City player, the best thing about supporting the club and what they wanted to be when they grew up.

Despite his last home game in charge witnessing a 4-0 thrashing of Darlington on New Year's Day, courtesy of goals from Hamza Bencherif (two), Jordan Burrow and Jake Wright, Collins was dismissed as manager, however, after a 1-0 loss at Curzon Ashton in the following fixture. Former Newcastle and Everton defender Steve Watson was lured from his job at then higher-league Gateshead to take over the reins, but the size of his task was underlined when his first contest at Bootham Crescent ended in a 4-1 defeat to eventual play-off winners Chorley with Burrow getting the consolation from the penalty spot. A 1-0 home triumph over Telford, which denied the visitors a play-off place following a 50th-minute Burrow goal, drew an underwhelming campaign to a close as the club finished in 12th position. The game also heralded the restoration of the old five-minute flag tradition. A replica of the missing old flag was reproduced by studying archive film footage and lowered as the 85th minute of the Telford match was completed. The intention was to fly and lower the flag as a sentimental gesture during the final fixture at Bootham Crescent. Further delays to the completion of the Community Stadium project, however, meant the game, or season, would not be the last to be played at the ground, as had been anticipated at the start of the campaign. A series of fans' games, giving supporters a final chance to tread the hallowed turf, still went ahead once the season was over until the end of June, with the belief that the club would now be relocating at some point during the next season. The full-pitch hire cost £500 plus VAT with a £350 plus VAT charge for half of the pitch. As well as a 90-minute game, the players got full access to the changing rooms and showers, with an additional package available for those that wanted post-match food and drink.

In April, meanwhile, a group of 50 businessmen and women, including the club's Foundation manager Paula Stainton, had participated in Bootham Crescent's first CEO Sleepout event, which saw them sleep overnight in the

David Longhurst Stand to raise £25,000 for the charity in its fight against poverty and homelessness.

In mid-July, more delays to the Community Stadium were then attributed to changes made to the design of the NHS outpatient clinics located at the complex. There were also issues relating to electrical supply connections that had further slowed down progress.

CHAPTER 38

A Covid-restricted final farewell

"We urge supporters to take this time to focus on their health and that of their family and friends. From everyone at the club, thank you for your continued support and we look forward to seeing you again soon."

As the club prepared for the latest "final" campaign at Bootham Crescent in the summer of 2019, a bumper pre-season crowd of 5,180 turned up for the visit of Leeds United, who had missed out on promotion to the Premier League in the Championship play-offs just a couple of months earlier. Jack Harrison (2), Kemar Roofe, Pablo Hernandez and Adam Forshaw were all on target for Marcelo Bielsa's full-strength line-up during a 5-0 away win for a Leeds team that would go on end their 17-year stint without top-flight football following a title-winning campaign. The heavy loss did not dent City's confidence going into the new season, however, with a goal from summer signing Andy Bond securing a 1-0 win over Brackley at Bootham Crescent that took the club to the top of a league table for the first time since 2006, following a return of seven points from the opening three games.

Tenants York City Knights were also doing their bit to bid a fond farewell to Bootham Crescent. An enthralled crowd of 4,007 watched the rugby club defeat the once-mighty Bradford Bulls 25-24 thanks to a dramatic 79th-minute drop goal by Liam Harris. The decisive kick clipped a post on its way over, just moments after Jordan Lilley's long-range effort had hit an upright and bounced out at the other end. The Knights went on to secure a play-off place with two fixtures of the regular season still to go by beating Featherstone 22-18 in another Bootham Crescent humdinger. The same opponents ended a brave bid for promotion to the Super League, however, by clinching a 30-4 play-off victory in front of 3,222 at the same venue.

At the end of August, meanwhile, the Main Stand was closed for the Minstermen's 1-1 draw against Steve Watson's former club Gateshead with traffic problems meaning many stewards could not get to the game and the club were left with a shortage of people to safely stage the match if all four sides of the ground were opened. Kick-off was delayed by 15 minutes as the home supporters in a 3,157 crowd were all accommodated in the David Longhurst or Popular stands. The club also asked supporters in the David Longhurst Stand to stop bringing flares and smoke bombs to games after two such devices were let off during the match.

In early October, meanwhile, Bootham Crescent was broken into, with items stolen from the medical room and kit room, both of which were also left damaged by the intruders. On the pitch, though, the club were still enjoying happier times and a benefit game was staged at the ground to honour Dan Parslow, whose 383rd appearance for the club - a 2-1 home defeat by Hereford in February - had proven to be his last after he suffered severe concussion during the first half of the game. The serious injury led to the retirement of the former Wales under-21 international, whose career placed him 10th on the club's all-time appearances list and saw him become the first player to win the Billy Fenton Memorial Trophy Clubman of the Year award three times. A match was played between a Parslow All-Stars XI and a Wembley Twice XI - the latter made up of fellow members of the 2012 Conference play-off final and FA Trophy-winning squads. Richard Pacquette scored a hat-trick, former manager Gary Mills came on as a right back and Jon Parkin had a spell in goal as the All Stars prevailed 7-4. A guard of honour welcomed Parslow onto the pitch, although he was only able to play for the first six minutes due to continued concerns over his head injury. Forty-one of his past City team-mates either played in or watched the game, with the sides managed by Mills and Andy Porter. Money raised from the match went towards funds for Parslow's benefit year and to the Headway charity, with 1,022 fans watching the contest.

Alex Kempster and Sean Newton, meanwhile, scored the goals that saw off National League visitors Stockport 2-0 to secure a place in the first-round proper of the FA Cup. The tie was televised by BT Sport in a 5.15pm Saturday evening kick-off slot and the win would represent the final time the Minstermen defeated a higher-division opponent at Bootham Crescent. At the end of October, Watson's men then set a new club record when goals from Kempster and Jordan Burrow sealed a 2-1 home triumph over Boston to register a 20th consecutive game without defeat. That surpassed the previous best sequence, set by the cherished 1973/74 side that secured second-tier football for the only time in the club's existence.

That figure became 21 following a 1-1 draw with Kidderminster but, disappointingly, the run ended after a 1-0 loss against Altrincham at Bootham

Crescent, denying the Minstermen a place in the FA Cup's second round for the first time since 2010. Tom Peers grabbed the only goal of the game on 82 minutes for a side that had not won away all season up to that point, with Bond having a penalty saved and Newton also hitting the crossbar, as City suffered their first defeat since Good Friday.

Storm clouds literally began to gather over Bootham Crescent after the turn of the year, however, as Storm Ciara, with its strong winds and heavy rainfall, wreaked havoc across the country. The iconic Popular Stand clock, donated by the Dearlove family in 1990 in memory of their son Phil, was one notable casualty. Having become dislodged, a decision was made to remove the clock and give it a spruce up ahead of the move to the Community Stadium, where it would be placed in the FanZone area.

The top-of-the-table team, meanwhile, fell apart somewhat during a disappointing 4-1 home reverse against Hereford at the start of March in the latest of many matches to be billed as "potentially" the final night fixture at Bootham Crescent. Kelsey Mooney and Lenell John-Lewis goals saw the Bulls lead 2-0 before the quarter-hour mark.

A Kempster reply reduced the deficit on 28 minutes, but second-half efforts from Jevan Anderson and John-Lewis completed a resounding defeat that was followed by two home players being threatened with physical violence outside the car park afterwards. Police investigated the matter with appeals sent out for witnesses as a disappointed Watson commented: "These lads go out and do their best every day in training and in every match. Do they really deserve to be confronted outside the car park and threatened? Absolutely not."

Ten days later, despite the National League not following the same protocol as the Premier League and Football League in suspending all fixtures to try and combat the global spread of the coronavirus Covid-19, City and Altrincham - the scheduled visitors to Bootham Crescent - took the joint decision to postpone their match the following day due to employees from both teams showing symptoms of the life-threatening, infectious disease and being required to self-isolate. The Knights' Challenge Cup match against Rochdale Hornets, scheduled for the following day, was also switched to the Millennium Stadium in Featherstone at little more than 24 hours' notice.

It was then announced on the next day - seven before the whole country were instructed to stay a home by the Government for a period of national lockdown - that Bootham Crescent would be "closed until further notice" as the ground underwent a deep clean. On April 2, with the National League North season having been postponed indefinitely, Bootham Crescent was subsequently "closed for the foreseeable future" with players and staff placed on furlough - the Coronavirus Job Retention Scheme, open to businesses across the country, that saw the Government pay 80 per cent of an employee's wages. In a club statement, chairman Jason McGill said: "The virus and the current crisis that surrounds us all is bigger than the club and bigger than football. So, for now, we urge supporters to take this time to focus on their health and that of their family and friends. From everyone at the club, thank you for your continued support and we look forward to seeing you again soon."

City were top of the table before the campaign was curtailed - two points ahead of King's Lynn, who had 10 games still to play compared to the leaders' eight. With Covid-19 responsible for the deaths of tens of thousands of people in the UK by mid-June and no prospect of the season being restarted and completed in front of supporters, National League clubs then voted in favour of ending the season. Final standings were subsequently decided on a points-per-games (PPG) basis, meaning King's Lynn leapfrogged the Minstermen in the table to claim the single automatic promotion spot. The National League then mistakenly suggested that play-off matches at sixth-tier level would not be allowed under the Government's coronavirus guidelines. In response, City led a proposal to promote the teams who had been placed second in the National League North and South tables, but that was rejected by the league's board. Following days of uncertainty and social media pressure from City and other clubs who objected to being denied the chance of promotion that would have normally been open to them by finishing between second and seventh in the table, the National League announced that, after seeking clarification from the Government, the play-off matches could be staged after all behind closed doors in late July, with sixth-tier football having been deemed to merit elite status.

Host clubs were required to develop a Covid-19 risk assessment and stadium management plan in order to stage ties. Social-distancing regulations and a National League edict, meanwhile, meant that City's players had to get changed in the Social Club, now known as the 1922 Bar, while their opponents were given use of both dressing rooms and sets of showers at Bootham Crescent. All the play-off games were streamed live by Sportradar with support from BT Sport, which meant supporters could watch from home for a charge of £5.99 per game. Following a trend set by Premier League and Championship clubs, who were completing their 2019/20 campaigns after a three-month break, City also announced that, courtesy of The Football Company's Fans At The Game initiative, supporters could pay £25 to ensure a cardboard cut-out image of themselves did get to watch the action from the Main Stand at Bootham Crescent.

With the clubs that placed from fourth to seventh in the PPG table competing in play-off quarter-finals for the right to travel to the sides that came second and third, City entertained fifth-placed Altrincham in the last four after the north-west outfit had overcome Chester 3-2.

In the build-up to the match, in a desperate bid to raise some revenue, Altrincham attempted to raffle off two places in the directors' box for the game at a charge of £10 a ticket, but were quickly informed that was not permitted by the terms of which club officials and board members could be in attendance at the matches.

It was a strangely eerie Bootham Crescent, therefore, that hosted another vital game in the club's history. Prior to kick-off, both teams knelt in support of the Black Lives Matter movement, which had gained followers worldwide following the death from asphyxiation in May of George Floyd in the United States after a white police officer Derek Chauvin had knelt on his neck for more than eight minutes. The gesture would continue to be repeated at football grounds across the country during the 2020/21 and 2021/22 seasons. When the action got underway, Kempster blazed wastefully over from close range with a gilt-edged chance and the visitors went on to forge ahead in the eighth minute when Josh Hancock squirmed a low shot in between keeper Pete Jameson's legs. Newton rattled the bar in response, but City's fate was sealed 15 minutes from time when Jordan Hulme headed against the bar and substitute Peers was alert to net from the rebound, meaning he had scored at Bootham Crescent in three separate competitions - the FA Cup, FA Trophy and play-offs - during an elongated 2019/20 season. A late Kallum Griffiths goal-line clearance prevented the deflated home side from suffering a heavier defeat with Watson admitting: "We weren't good enough in front of goal and that's the simple reason why we didn't win, but that kind of sums up the reason why we didn't win the league before points per game came into play." Altrincham then won promotion following a 1-0 win at Boston in the final.

In August, meanwhile, plans for 93 homes to be built on Bootham Crescent were officially approved with Persimmon Homes' application proposing that the pitch's centre circle would be recreated in the new site's central park and that the five-minute flagpole would be recreated displaying the club's crest and erected to mark the location of the ground's entrance. The old cricket pitch boundary wall was to be retained too, while six places within the new development, encompassing roads, walks and apartments, were to be named after past legends of the football club, including a David Longhurst Way and Keith Walwyn Walk. Supporters were invited to contact the club with suggestions, meanwhile, for the other four places. The planning report also stated that: "A laser scan of the football ground from the centre spot is required to enable future digital projects to recreate the ground virtually using an app." Furthermore, it was proposed that a section of the Popular Stand's terrace and tunnel, along with an original wall featuring artwork, would be retained as part of a memorial garden project to honour people commemorated at the ground, including those who had their ashes scattered there and those who had plaques there remembering their lives, such as the former players who had died in service during the War. As a consequence, all families with urns and caskets buried at the ground were asked to get in touch with the club, with the intention to reinter the ashes in the memorial garden. Groundstaff member Malcolm Ibbetson also made new urns for the ashes from leftover wooden seats located in the Main Stand. The legacy plan was conceived by the football club, Persimmon Homes and Historic England, who intended to use the project as a benchmark for how other sports, clubs and leisure venues might approach ground relocations.

Details were also revealed for supporters who wanted to buy seats when the ground was demolished, with prices ranging from £25 to £55. Season-ticket holders' seats were reserved to give them priority to purchase their seat. The club had previously asked fans to register their interest in any items at the ground and it was subsequently announced that expensive and antique items would be auctioned off, including boardroom furniture, turnstiles, floodlights, stands and metal fencing. Less expensive items such as signage, picket fencing, sections of crush barriers, pieces of terracing and bricks would also be made available by auction.

Such projects were once more put on the backburner, however, when it became clear that City would be kicking off yet another new league season, starting on Tuesday, October 6 with a home contest against Chorley, at Bootham Crescent due to a further delay to the Monks Cross project. The community stadium's building contractor the Buckingham Group had identified a drainage issue at the site, with Christmas 2020 given as the latest target for relocation.

Following on from the £125 million Premier League donation shared between Football League and National League clubs to help compensate for lost gate revenue, the Government also pledged a £10 million lifeline fund in October to be split between the 66 National League, National League North and South sides to give the 2020/21 campaign the best possible chance of being completed without revenue from supporters, who could still not attend fixtures due to the Covid-19 pandemic. An additional £11 million was promised to the same clubs the following month as part of the Government's Sport Winter Survival Package.

With the cardboard cut-outs moved to the Popular Stand as filming on a free "test" live stream was switched to the Main Stand, City got off to a positive start as Chorley were seen off 3-1 thanks to goals from Paddy McLaughlin and new signings Scott Barrow and Michael Woods. Following another free test stream for the 0-0 draw with Brackley, it was then announced that future home matches would be available at a cost of £7.99 per game, via the insight4 platform. But positive Covid-19 tests within the squad forced the players and management staff to self-isolate at home for two separate 14-day spells early in the season, meaning only two Bootham Crescent contests - and four league fixtures in total - were played during the opening two months of the season.

At the end of November, a surprise announcement by the Government paved the way for fans to watch games at Bootham Crescent again for the first time since March. A new three-tier system (later extended to four) had been introduced by Prime Minister Boris Johnson across the country to reflect the rate of coronavirus infection in different regions of the country. Tier 1 areas were subject to the fewest restrictions with up to 4,000 home supporters (or in smaller grounds 50 per cent of the capacity) allowed to attend matches. North Yorkshire was placed in Tier 2, where 2,000 home supporters or 50 per cent of the capacity were permitted. Despite the voluntary efforts of a team of supporters to carry out necessary work to the ground to satisfy safety certificate requirements, external providers were unable to certify parts of the stadium in time to admit fans again for the December 5 clash against Chester that the hosts went on to win 2-1. After another home triumph over Kettering (2-0) at an empty ground three days later, 400 fans were then let through the turnstiles for the Saturday, December 12 match against Spennymoor, as a pilot fixture, after all the tickets had been sold online from tickettailor.com to season-ticket holders living in Tier 1 or Tier 2 areas only. The Minstermen were denied a fourth straight win in the eagerly-anticipated contest as Glen Taylor's 84th-minute equaliser cancelled out Woods' early strike.

With people still nervous about attending large gatherings, a second game was then staged on Monday, December 28 in front of a crowd of 627, who saw

Josh King's 28th-minute goal secure a 1-0 victory over a Guiseley side reduced to 10 men following Isaac Currie's red card early in the second half. Nobody knew it at the time, but the game would prove to be the last competitive first-team fixture to be staged at Bootham Crescent with the subsequent January 2 contest against Bradford Park Avenue postponed due to a frozen pitch and the January 12 meeting with Fylde called off after a third Covid-19 outbreak in the squad. Manager Watson was among those from the playing and coaching staff who tested positive on this latest occasion.

Sunderland-born King's goal, therefore, claimed the distinction of being the last to be scored on the ground in a professional contest.

Ghosting in front of his marker, the 20-year-old centre back, who had previously played for Chester-le-Street Town and been part of the Carlisle United Park View Academy, met Newton's inswinging free kick from the right with a perfectly-timed, sidefooted volley on the edge of the six-yard box that beat visiting keeper Brad Wade at his near post. His effort was scored in front of an empty David Longhurst stand the scene of many a vigorously-celebrated goal over the previous 88 years but at least some supporters were there to witness and applaud it in the opened Main and Popular stands.

Had the fixtures against Park Avenue and Fylde gone ahead, City supporters would not have been able to attend in any case. With Covid rates rising alarmingly in York and across the country following the discovery of a new, more contagious variant of the coronavirus, fans were once again forbidden from attending live sporting events by the start of 2021. The Fylde match had also initially been pencilled in as the first match to be hosted at the community stadium, before a disagreement over a change to the lease and match day arrangement with the City of York Council delayed the move until the Gateshead match seven days later. That fixture was subsequently postponed too, as it fell within the required 10-day self-isolation period for Watson and his players. On the night of the scheduled Fylde game, the club streamed a showreel of the best games to be staged at Bootham Crescent on *YouTube* instead as an alternative means of bidding farewell. People that contributed a donation to a "virtual turnstile" to watch it were also given a digital commemorative edition of the matchday programme for the ground's final match against Guiseley.

Farewell to Bootham Crescent memorabilia could also be ordered online, including tea towels, oven gloves, BBQ aprons and coasters with designs based on photographs provided by fans from the club's history.

It had not been the goodbye the club had intended with fireworks and a local band pencilled in to celebrate the ground's final fixture. Further proposed first games at the Community Stadium then had to be postponed with Curzon Ashton's trip on Saturday, January 30 called off when the National League North and South seasons were halted for a two-week period as clubs expressed their unwillingness to accept Government loans and, therefore, incur debt to complete the season with revenue streams still decimated by the absence of supporters at fixtures. City had expressed a willingness to carry on playing but, even after the fortnight break, many clubs were still refusing to fulfil fixtures at the risk of incurring sanctions from the league with Farsley then declining the chance to christen the Community Stadium on February 13. Bootham Crescent was still being used, meanwhile, for training sessions but a proposed under-23 game between Hull City and Nottingham Forest had to be postponed due to a frozen pitch.

City did eventually get the opportunity to play at the Community Stadium on Tuesday, February 16 with a side featuring chairman Jason McGill's son Gabby, who had been signed on loan from Dunfermline, losing 3-1 to Fylde. Two days later, the National League North and South seasons were declared null and void, a decision based on a 24-19 majority vote among the member clubs. City, who had still only completed 13 fixtures by mid-February, were one of the clubs that voted in favour of carrying on the season. On that same day, Hull U23s did get to play at Bootham Crescent, losing 2-0 to their Wigan Athletic counterparts following goals from Adam Long and Alex Perry, but objections from City supporters over another team hosting the final fixtures to be staged at the ground meant an agreement with the Tigers was reconsidered. Instead, Hull's second string played their March fixtures at the Community Stadium instead.

City, meanwhile, beat Gateshead 3-1 in a behind-closed-doors training match at Bootham Crescent on February 25 with Jason Gilchrist, Harry Bunn and Barrow on target for the Minstermen. The game was played as a means of keeping players match fit in the hope that proposals put forward by those clubs that wanted to complete the season might be accepted by the FA. Ideas included both divisions continuing as mini leagues for those clubs that still wanted to play on - 12 National League South teams had voted in favour of completing the season, but only seven had from National League North - or an end to the regional split with all 19 teams competing in one national division. In mid-March, the FA decided against a continuation of fixtures in any format.

Subsequently, the demolition of the stadium began in earnest after it had been revealed that more than 1,350 bids had been received for the 132 items listed in a Bootham Crescent Blind Auction. Among the winning bidders was

England keeper Nick Pope, who bought one set of the goal posts as a permanent reminder of his successful loan spell at the club. Such was the clamour for a slice of Bootham Crescent memorabilia that the club also reported two break-ins with seats and patches of the hallowed turf among the items stolen.

The last-ever match to be staged at the ground then saw 32 City fans pay to play in a Red v Blues contest, which raised £4,000 with the proceeds split between the York Teaching Hospital Charity and the club's academy department. Chris Brooksbank (three), Curtis Roberts, Chris Tune, James Keller, Toby Joynson and a Peter Nowak own goal made the Blues' scoresheet in an 8-6 triumph, with Tom Haugh (two), Joe Scargill, James Brown, George Allen and a Xav Edmonds own goal responsible for the Reds' replies. The video of the match, played on Saturday, April 24, was also broadcast on *YouTube,* while a raffle was held for the honour of turning off the floodlights at Bootham Crescent for the very last time. Ann Laing a season ticket holder for more than 50 years was the winner, but asked that the privilege went to somebody "more deserving". It was subsequently proposed that James Abraham would perform the task and, at 8.52pm, on Tuesday, April 27, the loyal supporter, who had also performed voluntary tasks at the club for many years, primarily working alongside a succession of groundsmen, ensured that the lights went out at the cherished venue for one last time. Fans gathered outside the ground to witness the moment and, a month later, Bootham Crescent's club shop also closed for business on Thursday, May 27.

Six months later, more than 2,500 supporters then took the opportunity to visit Bootham Crescent for one final time and reflect on their memories as the club invited members of the public to walk around the old ground on November 28 or December 1 before the gates were closed for good and the demolition work was completed.

As well as bidding their final farewells, visitors could also buy assorted signage, old merchandise and memorabilia that had not been included in the earlier auctions. The keys to Bootham Crescent were then handed over to Persimmon Homes on April 4, 2022 after a final purchase price of £7 million was agreed. It was a deal that enabled the club to pay off money that was due to the Football Stadia Improvement Fund and the City of York Council, as well as the £285,000 still owed to disgraced Bootham Crescent Holdings directors Douglas Craig, Barry Swallow and Colin Webb.

Chairman Jason McGill, meanwhile, only received a capped amount of the capital his company JM Packaging had invested to cover losses during his stewardship. He had loaned the club some of that money as part of the 2006 takeover agreement but also waived the interest he was due according to the terms of that deal, which he had always maintained he would do.

Before the demolition trucks moved in, the lack of any significant improvements to the ground since the late 1990s showed, with the Grosvenor Road away end in a state of disrepair due to years of neglect. The capacity, meanwhile, in the ground's final season was 7,192, including seating for 3,371. The Main Stand could house 1,683 fans with 1,688 seats in the Popular Stand, 332 of which were set aside for away supporters, whose toilet facilities in the Grosvenor Road End included open-air urinals for men and Portakabins for women. A total of 1,785 spectators could be fitted into the away end, while there was room for 2,036 in the home end opposite - the inimitable David Longhurst Stand. The pitch dimensions, meanwhile, were 113.7 x 72.7 yards. Parking on matchdays had remained a problem until the very end following the advent of resident permits in neighbouring roads, although York Hospital had made their car park available to supporters for a charge from January 2014 onwards.

As fans prepared to leave the club's cherished home, meanwhile, even Fred Hemenway, who had watched the club at Bootham Crescent during all but the final three years following his death in 2017, recognised the need for a move. "I won't be very happy leaving Bootham Crescent, but the facilities aren't there now, and car parking has always been a problem," he pointed out.

Fellow City fanatic Guy Mowbray was also in agreement ahead of relocation to Monks Cross, but probably summed up the thoughts of most when he admitted: "Bootham Crescent was just home. That's how it felt, and it was a sad day when we left it behind. But moving was also obviously the right thing to do and was long overdue. I was at Sunderland when they moved from Roker Park, which was also steeped in history, but, as long as you get the new ground right, which Sunderland did, it soon becomes home because, ultimately, clubs are about the people that go there, more than the structures."

Josh King celebrates his goal against Guiseley during a 1-0 win on December 28, 2020. Due to the postponement of subsequent fixtures because of the Covid-19 pandemic, it was the last goal to be scored at Bootham Crescent in a competitive game. Picture: Adam Davy

The cardboard cut-outs get ready to watch a game during the 2020/21 season when fixtures had to be played behind closed doors due to restrictions in place to help stop the spread of the Covid-19 virus. Picture: Adam Davy

SOURCES

York City: The Complete Record by Dave Batters; *Citizens and Minstermen: A Who's Who of York City FC 1922-1997* by Dave Windross and Martin Jarred; *The Tale of Two Great Cities* by Chris Jones; York City South website; York City Supporters' Club 50th Anniversary 1922-1972 Souvenir Handbook; *The Yorkshire Evening Press* archives; York City & District FA 1908-09 Official List of Fixtures and Souvenir; *Football Grounds of Britain (3rd Edition)* by Simon Inglis; *Lincolnshire Echo*, ITV

ACKNOWLEDGEMENTS

Dave Batters, Norman Wilkinson, Graham Bradbury, Madalane Davey, Tommy Forgan, Alf Patrick, Fred Hemenway, Steph Davey, John McGhee, Mick Granger, Colin Addison, Malcolm Huntington, John Ledgeway, Andy Briggs, Chris Jones, Barry Tait, Graham Munday, Glyn Munday, Peter Lorimer, Paul Rawnsley, Chris Brass, Neil Warnock, Wilf McGuinness, Greg Dyke, Terry Fowler, Bobby Saxton, David Winterburn, Ted MacDougall, Denis Smith, Andy Warrington, John Bird, George Patterson, John Byrne, Jon McCarthy, David Ward, Brian Pollard, David McGurk, Paul Barnes, David Dunmore, Clayton Donaldson, Alan Woods, Ricky Sbragia, Keith Houchen, John Schofield, Andy McMillan, Guy Mowbray, Wayne Hall, Geoff Doyle, Manny Panther, Mark Simpson, Jeff Stelling, Billy McEwan, Gordon Staniforth, Martyn Woolford, Gary Swann, Andy Leaning, Paul Bowser, John MacPhail, Dean Kiely, Mark Lawrenson, Chris Topping, Richard Brodie, Christian Fox, David Stockdale, Jimmy Seal, John Chaplin, Philomena Starrs, Ian Savage, Billy Rudd, Charlie Twissell, Scott Jordan, Gary Ford, Richard Cresswell, Brian Little, Ian Seddon, Alan Little, Barry Lyons, Paul Keenan, Charlie Nicholas, Nigel Pepper, Graeme Crawford, Andy Dawson, David Meek, Tommy Heron, John Uttley, Marco Gabbiadini, Sue Jackson, Barry Jackson, Dave Thomas, Lyn Laffin, Andy Provan, Sir Alex Ferguson, Matty Blair, Russell Penn, Russ Wilcox, Jackie McNamara, Peter Turpin, Gary Mills, Sophie McGill, Rob McGill, Carole McGill, Chris Forth, Jon Parkin, Paul Thorpe, Nigel Burton, Odele Ayres, Liam Wright, Richard Adams, Steve Kilmartin, Irene Hagyard, Patricia Mason, Alan Stevenson, Julie Skelton - Appletree Design Solutions Ltd.

GRAPHIC DESIGN

ARTWORK

WEB DESIGN

appletree
design solutions

Julie Skelton
M 07954 359429

create@appletreedesigns.co.uk
www.appletreedesigns.co.uk